A MANUAL OF
THE LAW OF REAL PROPERTY

A Manual of
THE LAW OF
REAL PROPERTY

BY

THE HONOURABLE
SIR ROBERT MEGARRY,
LL.D.(Cantab.), Hon.LL.D.(Hull)

*One of Her Majesty's Judges of the Chancery Division
of the High Court of Justice*

FOURTH EDITION

BY

P. V. BAKER, B.C.L., M.A.

*of Lincoln's Inn, Barrister-at-Law,
Lecturer in the Law of Land in the Inns of Court,
Assistant Editor of the Law Quarterly Review*

LONDON
STEVENS & SONS LIMITED
1969

First edition	...	...	...	1946
Second impression, revised	...	1947
Third impression, revised	...	1949
Fourth impression	...	...	1951
Second edition	...	...	...	1955
Second impression	...	...	1960
Third edition	...	...	...	1962
Second impression	...	...	1967
Fourth edition	...	...	...	1969

Published by
Stevens & Sons Limited of
11 New Fetter Lane, London
— Law Publishers, and
printed in Great Britain by
The Eastern Press Limited
of London and Reading

SBN Hardback 420 42570 5
Paperback 420 42580 2

PREFACE

THE seven years which have elapsed since the last edition was published have seen important changes in the law, and the elevation of the author to be a judge of the Chancery Division. Mr. Justice Megarry's new responsibilities were assumed at the time when there were insistent calls for a new edition, and perforce he had to delegate its preparation to me. I have had the benefit of many discussions with him over the planning of this edition, but that is the sum of his direct contribution. Although the merits which the work retains must continue to be ascribed to him, I alone must be held responsible for the errors which have doubtless crept in.

The text has naturally been revised to take account of changes in the law down to the date of this preface. By far the most significant have been those made by the Perpetuities and Accumulations Act 1964, and these necessitated considerable rewriting of the chapter on future interests. I have also expanded the section on registration of title to reflect its growing importance. In this I have had welcome and expert assistance from Mr. R. B. Roper of H.M. Land Registry and from Miss Lindsay Megarry, barrister-at-law. Miss Megarry has also read the proofs of the whole book and saved me from many errors. I am most grateful to them.

It was with some trepidation that I suggested curtailing the earlier historical part of the book. Emboldened by the author's mild and encouraging reaction to this sacrilegious suggestion I have considerably reduced the sections on tenures, on the rule in *Shelley's Case*, on the effects of the Statute of Uses, and on legal remainders and executory interests. It is now nearly 45 years since the 1925 legislation abolished these survivals, and the proper course seemed to be to retain enough of the principles and spirit to make the development of the law intelligible, but to excise the detail, particularly as there are now better books on the history of the land law than when this book first appeared. No doubt something has been lost, for he who knows the expedients of yesterday may be better able to forge the devices of today. But I am conscious that the present generation of students have no more time than their predecessors to master the subject, and so the old complexities must make way for the new.

Most of the new complexities will be found in the penultimate chapter of the book. Formerly entitled " The Social Control of

Land," this has now been enlarged in scope to collect together all the restrictions on the right of land owners to use and dispose of it as they wish. Those who would have been fascinated by the incidents of the tenure of knight service may find consolation in crownhold, and as an attempt to secure some of the benefits to be derived from land for the State, the Land Commission Act 1967 can hold its own with the Statute of Uses any day.

The net effect of all these changes is to reduce the length of the text by some 24 pages, thus giving comfort to readers and publishers alike. To the former I offer my sympathy, to the latter my thanks for preparing the Tables of Cases and Statutes and the Index.

Finally, it seems appropriate to repeat words from the author's preface to the second edition. " In other respects the book is little changed. As with the first edition, it is ' primarily intended for the examination candidate whose main anxiety is not whether he will head the list but whether he will appear in it at all.' Friendly reviewers asserted that this was too modest an estimate. Yet throughout I have had in mind not those meteoric beings for whom the first class was ordained, but those who were as puzzled and confused as I was when introduced to a subject that seemed almost wholly unrelated to any other body of law in undergraduate life. To me, the order of topics has always seemed to be of prime importance. In this imperfect world, no arrangement is without its problems; yet on the whole, that which is here adopted does no great violence to theory, and (what matters more) seems to be the most approachable and convenient for the beginner." My hope is that I have succeeded in my attempts to pursue an objective which for over twenty years has brought comfort to generations of students.

P. V. B.

LINCOLN'S INN,
April 21, 1969

CONTENTS

CHAPTER 4

FUTURE INTERESTS

CHAPTER 5

SETTLED LAND AND TRUSTS FOR SALE

Contents

CHAPTER 6

CO-OWNERSHIP

CHAPTER 7

TRUSTS AND POWERS

CHAPTER 8

WILLS AND INTESTACY

CHAPTER 9

CONTRACTS AND CONVEYANCING

CHAPTER 10

LEASES AND TENANCIES

CHAPTER 11

COVENANTS AFFECTING LAND

CHAPTER 12

INCORPOREAL HEREDITAMENTS

CHAPTER 13

MORTGAGES

CHAPTER 14

DISABILITIES

CHAPTER 15

LIMITATION

TABLE OF CASES

xv

TABLE OF STATUTES

TABLE OF STATUTORY
INSTRUMENTS

ABBREVIATIONS

STATUTES

A.E.A.: Administration of Estates Act.
A.H.A.: Agricultural Holdings Act.
C.A.: Conveyancing Act.
I.E.A.: Intestates' Estates Act.
J.A.: Supreme Court of Judicature (Consolidation) Act.
L.C.A.: Land Charges Act.
L.P.A.: Law of Property Act.
L.P.Am.A.: Law of Property Amendment Act.
L.R.A.: Land Registration Act.
R.P.A.: Real Property Act.
S.L.A.: Settled Land Act.
T.A.: Trustee Act.

CASES

I.R.C.: Commissioners of Inland Revenue.
In b.: (In bonis) In the Goods of, In the Estate of.
S.E.: Settled Estate(s).
S.T.: Settlement Trust(s).
W.T.: Will Trust(s).

BOOKS AND PERIODICALS

Bl.Com.: Blackstone's Commentaries on the Laws of England, 15th ed., 1809.
Camb.L.J.: Cambridge Law Journal.
Challis R.P.: Challis's Law of Real Property, 3rd ed., 1911.
Co.Litt.: Coke's Commentary upon Littleton, 19th ed., 1832.
Conv.(N.S.): The Conveyancer, New Series, 1936–
Conv.(O.S.): The Conveyancer, Old Series, 1916–36.
Conv.Y.B.: Conveyancers' Year Book.
Col.L.R.: Columbia Law Review.
Cru.Dig.: Cruise's Digest of the Laws of England respecting Real Property, 4th ed., 1835.
Digby: Digby's Introduction to the History of the Law of Real Property, 5th ed., 1897.
Fearne C.R.: Fearne's Essay on the Learning of Contingent Remainders and Executory Devises, 10th ed., 1844.
Fry S.P.: Fry's Treatise on the Specific Performance of Contracts, 6th ed., 1921.
Gilbert, *Uses*: Gilbert's Law of Uses and Trusts, 3rd ed., 1811.
Gray, *Perpetuities*: Gray's Rule against Perpetuities, 4th ed., 1942.

Halsbury: Halsbury's Laws of England.

Harv.L.R.: Harvard Law Review.

Hayes, *Introduction*: Hayes' Introduction to Conveyancing, 5th ed., 1840.

H.E.L.: Holdsworth's History of English Law, 1922–66 (see (1945) 61 L.Q.R. 346).

Lewis: Lewis's Practical Treatise on the Law of Perpetuity, 1843.

Litt.: Littleton's Tenures: see Co.Litt.

L.J.News.: Law Journal Newspaper.

L.Q.R.: Law Quarterly Review.

Maitland, *Equity*: Maitland's Equity, 2nd ed., 1936.
  Forms of Action: Maitland's Forms of Action at Common Law, 1936.

Mod.L.R.: Modern Law Review.

M. & W.: Megarry and Wade's Law of Real Property, 3rd ed., 1966.

P. & M.: Pollock & Maitland's History of English Law, 2nd ed., 1898 (reprinted with new introduction 1968).

Perk.: Perkins' Profitable Book, 15th ed., 1827.

Preston, *Estates*: Preston's Elementary Treatise on Estates, 1820–27.

Prideaux: Prideaux's Forms and Precedents on Conveyancing.

Rob.Gav.: Robinson's Common-Law of Kent, or the Customs of Gavelkind, 3rd ed., 1822.

Sanders, *Uses*: Sanders' Essay on Uses and Trusts, 5th ed., 1844.

Scriven: Scriven's Treatise on the Law of Copyholds, 7th ed., 1896.

Shep.: Sheppard's Touchstone of Common Assurances, 7th ed., 1820.

S.J.: Solicitors' Journal.

Snell: Snell's Principles of Equity, 26th ed., 1966.

Theobald, *Land*: Theobald's Law of Land, 2nd ed., 1929.

Tudor L.C.R.P.: Tudor's Selection of Leading Cases on Real Property, Conveyancing, and the Construction of Wills and Deeds, 4th ed., 1898.

Williams R.P.: Williams' Principles of the Law of Real Property, 23rd ed., 1920.

  V. & P.: Williams' Treatise on the Law of Vendor & Purchaser, 4th ed., 1936.

GLOSSARY

[The object of this glossary is to provide a ready source of reference to the meanings of some of the more troublesome technical expressions used in the text. For the most part, brief but not necessarily exhaustive definitions have been given, with references by means of numerals in brackets to the pages of the text where further information can be obtained and the terms may be seen in their context; references which are essential to a proper understanding of the terms are in heavy type. Where the text contains a convenient collection and explanation of a number of contrasting terms, a simple reference to the appropriate pages is given instead of setting out the definitions.]

Abstract of title: an epitome of documents and facts showing ownership (**330**).
Ademption: the failure of a gift by will, *e.g.*, because the property ceases to exist or to belong to the testator (283).
Ad hoc settlement or trust for sale: one with special overreaching powers (**197**).
Administrators: persons authorised to administer the estate of an intestate (311); compare Executors.
Advowson: a right of presenting a clergyman to a vacant benefice (414).
Alienation: the act of disposing of or transferring.
Ante-nuptial: before marriage.
Appendant: attached to land by operation of law (428); compare Appurtenant.
Approvement: appropriation of portion of manorial waste free from rights of common (450).
Appurtenant: attached to land by act of parties (427); compare Appendant.
Assent: an assurance by personal representatives vesting property in the person entitled (314).
Assignment: a disposition or transfer, usually of a lease.
Assurance: the documentary or other evidence of a disposition or transfer.

Beneficial owner: a person entitled for his own benefit and not, *e.g.*, as trustee.
Beneficiaries: those entitled to benefit under a trust or will.
Betterment levy: a charge payable to the State on realising the development value of land (579); see also Development charge.
Bona vacantia: goods without an owner.

Cestui que trust: a beneficiary under a trust.
  „   „   *use*: a person to whose use property was conveyed (66).
  „   „   *vie*: a person for whose life an estate *pur autre vie* lasted (46).
Charge: an incumbrance securing the payment of money.
Collaterals: blood relations who are neither ancestors nor descendants.
Consolidation: a requirement that a mortgagor shall not redeem one mortgage without another (482).
Contingent: operative only upon an uncertain event (**84**); compare Vested.
Contractual tenancy: tenancy under a lease or agreement which is still in force; contrast Statutory tenancy.
Conversion: a change in the nature of property either actually or notionally (**146**).
Conveyance: an instrument (other than a will) transferring property.
Co-parceners: persons together constituting the heir (**229**).
Corporeal: accompanied by physical possession (68).

Covenant: a promise contained in a deed.
Coverture: the continuance of a marriage.
Curtesy: a widower's life estate in his wife's realty (294).
Customary heir: the heir according to a local custom.

Deed: a document signed, sealed and delivered.
Deed poll: a deed with only one party (333); compare Indenture.
Defeasance: the determination of an interest on a specified event.
Demise: a transfer, usually by the grant of a lease.
Determine: terminate, come to an end.
Development charge: payment to the State for the right to develop land (575); see also Betterment levy.
Devise: a gift of real property by will.
Distrain, distress: the lawful extra-judicial seizure of chattels to enforce a right, *e.g.*, to the payment of rent (371).
Dominant tenement: land to which the benefit of a right is attached (418); compare Servient tenement.
Dower: a widow's life estate in one-third of her husband's realty (296).
Durante viduitate: during widowhood.

Emblements: growing crops which an outgoing tenant may take (53).
Enceinte: pregnant.
Engross: prepare a fair copy (331).
En ventre sa mère: conceived but not born.
Equities: equitable rights.
Equity of redemption: the sum of a mortgagor's rights in the mortgaged property (**463**).
Escheat: a lord's right to ownerless realty (293, 524).
Escrow: a document which upon delivery will become a deed (333).
Estate: 1. the *quantum* of an interest in land (10).
   2. an area of land (10).
   3. the whole of the property owned by a deceased person (10, 310).
Estovers: wood which a tenant may take for domestic and other purposes (50).
Execute: 1. to perform or complete, *e.g.*, a deed.
   2. to convert, *e.g.*, to transform the equitable interest under a use into a legal estate (67).
Executors: persons appointed by a testator to administer his estate (311); compare Administrators.
Executory: not yet completed (contrasted with " executed ") (95, 215).
Executory interest: a valid future interest not complying with the legal remainder rules (**94**).
Executory limitation: a limitation creating an executory interest (**94**).
Executory trust: a trust the details of which remain to be set out in some further document (215).

Fee: base (34), conditional (36), determinable (30), simple (15), tail (15).
Feoffee to uses: a person holding property to the use of another (66).
Feoffment: a conveyance by livery [delivery] of seisin (19).
Fine: 1. a collusive action partially barring an entail (37); compare Recovery.
   2. a premium or a lump sum payment, *e.g.*, for the grant of a lease.
Foreclosure: proceedings by a mortgagee which free mortgaged property from the equity of redemption (472).
Freehold: 1. socage tenure (12).
   2. an estate of fixed but uncertain duration (**14**).

Gavelkind: a special custom of descent whereby land descended on intestacy to all children and not to eldest son alone (229).

General equitable charge: an equitable charge of a legal estate not protected by a deposit of title deeds (544).

Good consideration: natural love and affection for near relatives (60).

Hereditaments: inheritable rights in property (68).

Heritable issue: descendants capable of inheriting (295).

Hold over: remain in possession after the termination of a tenancy (347).

Hotchpot: the bringing into account of benefits already received before sharing in property (306).

Improved value: the value of land together with improvements to it (341).

In capite: in chief, immediately holding of the Crown (9).

Incorporeal: not accompanied by physical possession (68).

Incumbrance: a liability burdening property.

Indenture: a deed between two or more parties (333); compare Deed poll.

Infant: a person under 21 years of age.

In gross: existing independently of a dominant tenement (418, 428).

Instrument: a legal document.

Interesse termini: the rights of a lessee before entry (**346**).

Intestacy: the failure to dispose of property by will.

Issue: descendants of any generation (26).

Jointure: provision by a husband for his widow, usually under a settlement (204).

Jus accrescendi: right of survivorship (208).

Lapse: the failure of a gift, especially by the beneficiary predeceasing the testator (275).

Letters of administration: the authorisation to persons to administer the estate of a deceased person (311).

Licence: a permission, *e.g.*, to enter on land (378).

Limitation, words of: words delimiting the estate granted to some person previously mentioned (**20**, **27**); compare Purchase, words of.

Marriage articles: the preliminary agreement for a marriage settlement (215).

Merger: the fusion of two or more estates or interests (362).

Mesne: intermediate, middle (9).

Minority: the state of being an infant.

Next-of-kin: the nearest blood relations (299).

Nuncupative: oral (of wills) (267).

Overreach: to transfer rights from land to the purchase money therefor (81).

Override: to render rights void, *e.g.*, against a purchaser (81).

Parol: by word of mouth.

Particular estate: an estate less than a fee simple (87).

Per capita: by heads; one share for each person (301); compare *Per stirpes*.

Personal representatives: executors or administrators (311).

Per stirpes: by stocks of descent; one share for each line of descendants (300); compare *Per capita*.

Portions: provisions for children, especially lump sums for the younger children under a settlement (204).

Possibility of reverter: the grantor's right to the land if a determinable fee determines (31).

Post-nuptial: after marriage.

Powers: appendant (254), appurtenant (254), collateral (254), in gross (254), general (124), special (124).

Prescription: the acquisition of easements or profits by long user (436).

Privity of contract: the relation between parties to a contract (383).

Privity of estate: the relation of landlord and tenant (383).

Probate: the formal confirmation of a will, granted by the court to an executor (311).

Procreation, words of: words confining the persons mentioned to issue of a particular person (24).

Puisne mortgage: a legal mortgage not protected by a deposit of title deeds (544).

Pur autre vie: for the life of another person (15).

Purchase, words of: words conferring an interest on the person they mention (27); compare Limitation, words of.

Purchaser: a person who takes land by act of parties and not by operation of law (289).

Que estate: dominant tenement (438).

Recovery: a collusive action completely barring an entail (37); compare Fine, 1.

Remainder: the interest of a grantee subject to a prior particular estate (89).

Rent: chief rent (414), fee farm rent (414), ground rent (328), quit rent (414), rack rent (328), rent of assize (414), rentcharge (413), rent seck (414), rent service (413).

Restraint on anticipation: a restriction on a married woman disposing of capital or future income (520).

Restrictive covenant: a covenant restricting the use of land (403).

Reversion: the interest remaining in a grantor after granting a particular estate (87).

Riparian owner: the owner of land adjoining a watercourse (572).

Root of title: a document from which ownership is traced (62).

Satisfied term: a term of years created for a purpose since fulfilled (206).

Seisin: the feudal possession of land by a freeholder (**18**).

Servient tenement: land burdened by a right such as an easement (418); compare Dominant tenement.

Settlement: provisions for persons in succession (or the instruments making such provisions) (142, 160).

Severance: the conversion of a joint tenancy into a tenancy in common (226).

Severance, words of: words showing that property is to be held in distinct shares (213).

Spes successionis: a possibility of succeeding to property (22).

Squatter: a person occupying land without any title to it (536).

Statutory owner: persons with the powers of a tenant for life (153).

Statutory tenant: a person holding over under the Rent Restriction Acts (603); compare Contractual tenancy.

Statutory trusts: certain trusts imposed by statute, especially—
1. the trust for sale under co-ownership (**216**).
2. the trusts for issue on intestacy (**306**).

Sub-mortgage: a mortgage of a mortgage (498).

Sui juris: " of his own right," *i.e.*, subject to no disability.

Tenement: anything which may be held by a tenant.

Tenure: the set of conditions upon which a tenant holds land (**10**); compare Estate, 1.

Term of years: a period with a defined minimum for which a tenant holds land (75).

Terre tenant: a freehold tenant in possession (411).

Title: the evidence of a person's right to property.

Trust: bare (236), completely constituted (239), constructive (241), executed (215), executory (215), express (238), implied (240), incompletely constituted (239), precatory (238), resulting (241), secret (245).

Trust corporation: one of certain companies with a large paid-up capital, or one of certain officials (194).

Undivided share: the interest of a tenant in common or co-parcener (211, 230).

Use: benefit (65), resulting (242), shifting (95), springing (95).

User: use, enjoyment (Note: *not* the person who uses).

Vested: unconditionally owned (**84**); compare Contingent.

Vesting assent (156), declaration (251), deeds (156), instrument (156).

Voluntary conveyance: a conveyance not made for valuable consideration.

Volunteer: a person taking under a disposition without having given valuable consideration.

Waste: ameliorating (49), equitable (50), permissive (49), voluntary (49).

CHAPTER 1

INTRODUCTION

Sect. 1. Prefatory

THE English law of real property, traditionally described by Oliver Cromwell as " an ungodly jumble," is justly recognised as being a subject of great difficulty for the beginner, partly because of the intricate interlocking of its component parts and partly because of the complexity of the language, which involves the use of many technical terms. For these reasons, those coming new to the subject must not expect to understand everything at a first reading. In this subject more than any other it is economical of time and effort to read fast and often. Much that is incomprehensible at first will become clear on a second reading and perhaps obvious on a third. In order to understand complex ideas expressed in unfamiliar language it is necessary to master the language as soon as possible, and for this purpose a generous use should be made of the glossary which immediately precedes this page.

1. Scope of the subject. There are many possible ways of arranging a book on real property, each with its merits. In this book, the first consideration throughout has been to assist the reader by adopting an order which minimises the amount of repetition and preliminary explanation which is so often necessary.

The book falls into four divisions. The first deals with a man's rights over his own land, the second with his rights over his neighbour's land, the third with provisions ancillary to these rights, such as the registration of rights in land, and the fourth with some general matters. A brief survey of these divisions follows, partly to give an idea of the stuff real property is made of and partly to introduce some of the most important technical terms.

After some introductory passages, the first division, comprising Chapters 1 to 11, gives an account of tenures and estates. A tenure is a set of conditions upon which an estate or interest in land may be held. An estate or interest prescribes the length of time for which a person is entitled to land; thus X may hold land in fee simple (virtually for ever), in tail (for as long as he or any of his descendants live), for life, or for a period of years. Consideration

1

is then given to Law and Equity, the two systems of justice which for many centuries have operated side by side, together with the difference between legal estates (the estates recognised by Law) and the corresponding equitable interests. Future interests are discussed next. If land is given to A for life and after his death to B in fee simple, B is said to have a future interest. The two main aspects of future interests are first, the rules governing what future interests can be created (Chap. 4), and second, the provisions for selling or otherwise dealing with land when future interests in it have been created (Chap. 5). The next chapter deals with co-ownership, which arises when two or more persons are simultaneously entitled to land, as where X and Y are jointly entitled. These first chapters are the most difficult, and although the remainder of the book is not easy, the worst is over by the end of Chapter 6.

Trusts and powers are dealt with next. The general nature of a trust will be familiar to most readers; a power may be described as a right given to a man to dispose of property which is not his, as where a testator provides in his will that after the death of X certain property shall pass to such of X's children as X may appoint. This is followed by a chapter dealing with wills and intestacy. When a man dies, his property passes to those named in his will; any property not passing under his will (and all his property, if he left no will) passes under his intestacy, which means that it goes to those entitled under the rules laid down by statute. In either case, however, the property normally does not go direct to the beneficiaries (the persons entitled to benefit), but passes through the hands of the personal representatives of the deceased, namely, his executors if the will appointed any, and, if not, the administrators appointed by the court. After dealing with contracts and, very briefly, with conveyancing (the art of transferring interests in land), leases and tenancies are discussed. The division ends with a chapter on covenants affecting land; a covenant is a promise contained in a deed.

The second division, comprising Chapters 12 and 13, discusses incorporeal hereditaments. These are inheritable rights in land not accompanied by physical possession of the land. The most important are rentcharges, easements and profits *à prendre* (pronounced either " ay prender," or as in French). A rentcharge is a right over land ensuring the payment of a periodical sum, such as £100 a year. An easement is some right over a neighbour's land such as a right of way or a right of light, and a profit is similar, save that it confers the right to take something from the land, such as timber or gravel. Mortgages also fall within this division. A mortgage is an arrangement whereby the mortgagee lends money to the mortgagor and in return, in order to secure payment of the interest and repayment of the loan, receives certain rights over the land, such as the right to sell it.

The third division, comprising Chapters 14 to 16, deals with disabilities, such as the restrictions imposed on infants and lunatics in the exercise of their rights over land, and the statutes of limitation, which prevent the enforcement of rights over land when too long a period has elapsed; thus a landowner who fails for twelve years to evict a person who is wrongfully in possession of his land may lose his right to it. Registration is also dealt with; this includes registration of title and registration of charges. Registration of title, which is fully effective only in certain parts of England, extends to both ownership and incumbrances; the land register shows not only who is the owner of the registered land, but also what rights over that land belong to other persons. Registration of charges, on the other hand, extends only to certain incumbrances; it applies to all unregistered land.

The fourth division deals with two general matters. Chapter 17 discusses the changes in English land law in the last half century which Parliament has made in the interests of social justice, and the last chapter summarises the changes made by the 1925 property legislation.

2. Objects of learning the subject. The objects of learning the law of real property are—

(a) to acquire a knowledge of the rights and liabilities attached to interests in land; and

(b) to lay a foundation for the study of conveyancing.

It is not easy to distinguish accurately between real property and conveyancing. In general, it can be said that the former is static, the latter dynamic; real property deals with the rights and liabilities of landowners, conveyancing with the art of creating and transferring rights in land. Yet inevitably the two overlap, and often the exact place at which to draw the line is ultimately a matter of taste. But although this is a book on the law of real property, it is built upon a conveyancing foundation. In deciding what to include and what to exclude, conveyancing has played a large part. The reader's knowledge of land law has to be carried to the point when it will be possible for him to embark with profit on a study of conveyancing; the joints must be true and the overlapping restrained within due limits. It is, indeed, best to regard real property and conveyancing not as two separate though closely related subjects, but as two parts of the one subject of land law; it is convenience of teaching rather than any essential difference of nature that dictates the division.

Conveyancing necessarily influences any book on real property in another way, namely, by making it essential to include a substantial historical element. A conveyancer must deal both with ownership and incumbrances; in other words he must see not only that his client gets what he has agreed to buy but also that he gets it free from any burdens such as mortgages or rights of way which would make it less valuable. (In parenthesis, it must be noted that this division between ownership and incumbrances is not rigid; what in one transaction appears as an incumbrance, appears in another as the subject-matter of ownership. If A owns a mortgage on X's land, the mortgage is regarded as an incumbrance if X sells his land, but as the subject-matter of ownership if A sells his mortgage. Nevertheless, in any particular transaction the distinction is clear.) A conveyancer acting for a client who is purchasing property must investigate the title to the land, both as to ownership and as to incumbrances, for a period which is usually thirty years or more; those who are engaged in this work must consequently know the law not only as it is but also as it was.

3. The common law basis of the subject. The law of real property is part of the common law of England. The phrase " common law " or " at law," which will be frequently encountered, is employed in three senses :

    (i) in contrast with local custom;
    (ii) in contrast with statute law; and
    (iii) in contrast with equity.

The third is the most usual sense, the second less usual, the first comparatively rare; the context will normally make it plain which is meant. A word must be said on the third meaning. As will be seen later [1] certain rights could be enforced in the common law courts (*i.e.,* the King's ordinary courts), and these were known as legal rights. Other rights were not protected by the common law courts, but came to be protected by the Chancellor if he deemed this equitable. It was the Chancellor who first compelled trustees to carry out their trusts, and remedied wrongs which, because of non-compli-

---

[1] *Post,* pp. 54 *et seq.*

ance with some formality, the common law courts would not redress. Rights enforced by the Chancellor were known as equitable rights, for the Chancellor's Court, the Court of Chancery, was known as the Court of Equity. Equitable rights were (and still are) inferior to legal rights, in that a legal right would be enforced against everyone, whereas an equitable right would be enforced only against a person who the Chancellor considered was unable in good conscience to deny liability. Thus not only would a trustee be compelled to carry out his trust, but also if he gave or sold the trust property to a third person who knew that the trustee was committing a breach of trust, the equitable rights of the beneficiaries under the trust would be enforced against that third person, who would thus be compelled to carry out the trust. Ultimately, equitable rights became enforceable against the whole world except a bona fide purchaser for value of a legal estate without notice of the equitable right, or someone claiming title under such person.[2] Legal rights, on the other hand, were enforceable against everyone, without this exception.

The common law affecting real property has in the course of time been profoundly affected by equity, and today most questions on real property law fall for decision in the Chancery Division of the High Court; yet this is merely a procedural arrangement which must not be allowed to obscure the common law basis of the law of real property.

Sect. 2. Historical Outline

The history of the law of property in land can be divided into six periods.

1. Formulation of principles. This was the early period during which the common law courts formulated many of the fundamental rules of land law. A number of important statutes were passed during this period, which extended from the Norman Conquest to the end of the fourteenth century.

2. Growth of Equity. This was the period from about 1400 to 1535, when the jurisdiction of the Chancellor to give relief in cases not covered by the common law rules was firmly established and developed.

[2] See *post*, pp. 59 *et seq.*, where this is more fully discussed.

3. The Statute of Uses. This was the period from 1535 to the middle of the seventeenth century, when the great changes made by the Statute of Uses 1535 were being worked out.

4. Development of the modern law. This encompassed the end of the seventeenth century and the eighteenth century, when trusts, which had been considerably restricted by the Statute of Uses 1535, were once more enforced. The modern form of a strict settlement of land, by which land was "kept in the family," from one generation to another, was fully developed during this period.

5. Statutory reforms. This period consists of the nineteenth and twentieth centuries, when far-reaching reforms were made by Parliament. Many reforms were made during the nineteenth century, particularly between 1832 and 1845 and again between 1881 and 1890; but important though these were, they could not rival the 1925 property legislation in complexity and comprehensiveness. The Law of Property Act 1922 laid the foundation for the Acts of 1925, but most of it, together with extensive amendments of the law made by the Law of Property (Amendment) Act 1924, was repealed and replaced before it came into force. The provisions of these two Acts and of much of the earlier reforms were consolidated and divided up into six Acts; and these Acts and the unrepealed portions of the Act of 1922 all came into force on January 1, 1926. The "1925 property legislation" thus consists of:

The unrepealed portions of the Law of Property Act 1922.
The Settled Land Act 1925.
The Trustee Act 1925.
The Law of Property Act 1925.
The Land Registration Act 1925.
The Land Charges Act 1925.
The Administration of Estates Act 1925.

In addition, some amending statutes were subsequently passed, altering details in the principal Acts.

The genesis of the 1925 property legislation is important when construing it. The Acts of 1925 are all consolidating Acts, and a consolidating Act is presumed to change the law no more than the language necessarily requires. However, the Acts of 1922 and 1924 are professedly amending Acts, so that the presumption is not that the Acts of 1925 have not changed the old law, but that they have not changed the changes in that law made by the Acts of 1922 and 1924. Accordingly, in case of difficulty it is the precise language of the Acts of 1922 and 1924, though repealed, that must first be construed.[3]

6. Social control of land. This period overlaps the last; it consists of the last fifty years, during which, in the public interest, Parliament has enacted increasingly drastic provisions curtailing and restricting the rights of landowners.

Sect. 3. Meaning of " Real Property "

1. Land. The natural division of physical property is into land (or " immovables " as it is sometimes called) and other objects known as chattels or " movables." This simple distinction is inadequate. In the first place, chattels may become attached to land so as to lose their character of chattels and become part of the land itself.[4] Secondly, a sophisticated legal system of property has to provide not simply for the ownership of physical property, but also for the ownership of a wide variety of *interests* in such physical property, and also for the ownership of interests in non-physical or intangible property such as " advowsons "[5] or copyright.[6] Thirdly, for historical reasons English law has developed a distinction between " real property " and " personal property " which only approximately corresponds to that between " land " and other types of property.

2. History. In early law, property was deemed " real " if the courts would restore to a dispossessed owner the thing itself, the " *res*," and not merely give compensation for the loss.[7] Thus if X forcibly evicted Y from his freehold land, Y could bring a " real " action whereby he could obtain an order from the court that X should return the land to him. But if X took Y's sword or glove from him, he could bring only a personal action which gave X the choice of either returning the article or paying the value thereof. Consequently, a distinction was made between real property (or " realty "), which could be specifically recovered, and personal property (or " personalty "), which was not thus recoverable. In general, all interests in land are real property,

---

[3] *Re Turner's W.T.* [1937] Ch. 15; *Grey* v. *Inland Revenue Commissioners* [1960] A.C. 1; 74 L.Q.R. 487; 75 L.Q.R. 307.
[4] For " fixtures," see *post*, p. 375.
[5] For " advowsons," see *post*, p. 414.
[6] For interests in land, see *post*, p. 11.
[7] 3 H.E.L. 3, 4; and see T. C. Williams (1888) 4 L.Q.R. 394.

with the exception of leaseholds (or "terms of years"), which are classified as personalty. At first, a dispossessed leaseholder had no right to recover his land from anyone except the lessor who had granted him the lease. Against third parties, he remained without remedy until late in the thirteenth century, when he was enabled to recover damages but not possession. Not until 1468 was this rule seriously questioned, and when in 1499 it was finally decided that he might recover the land itself,[8] leaseholds had become too firmly established as personalty for this change to make any difference to their status. Thus, if a testator dies today, leaving a will giving all his realty to R and all his personalty to P, the reason for the leaseholds being included in the property passing to P lies in a rule which ceased to exist over 400 years ago.

3. Reasons for distinction. In early times there were no opportunities for investing in stocks and shares such as there are today. Money was therefore often employed in buying land and letting it out on lease in order to obtain an income from the capital. Further, the relationship between landlord and tenant was regarded as being mainly contractual, the tenant on his part agreeing to pay rent, and the landlord on his side agreeing to allow the tenant to occupy the land.[9] These conceptions were so far removed from the feudal system of landholding that leaseholds remained outside that system[10] and for a long time were hardly regarded as being rights in the land at all.

4. Classification. Although leaseholds are still classified as personalty, they differ from most of the other kinds of personalty in that they fall under the heading of "land," or "immovables" as opposed to "pure personalty," or "movables," such as furniture or stocks and shares. They are accordingly classified as "chattels real," the first word indicating their personal nature (cattle were the most important chattels in early days, hence the name), the second showing their connection with land.[11] The three types of interests may therefore be classified thus:

$$
\left.
\begin{array}{l}
Land \\
\\
Personalty
\end{array}
\right\}
\left\{
\begin{array}{l}
\text{(i) Realty.} \\
\left\{
\begin{array}{l}
\text{(ii) Chattels real.}^{12} \\
\text{(iii) Pure personalty.}
\end{array}
\right.
\end{array}
\right.
$$

8 See 3 H.E.L. 213–216.
9 2 P. & M. 106.
10 Challis R.P. 63.
11 See *Ridout* v. *Pain* (1747) 3 Atk. 486 at 492.
12 For other chattels real, of no importance today, see Co.Litt. 118b and M. & W. 17.

Although strictly a book on real property should exclude leaseholds, it has long been both customary and convenient to include them, and this course is adopted here.

5. Modern distinction. The legislation of 1925 has abolished many of the remaining differences between the law governing realty and that governing personalty.[13] For example, before 1926, if a person died intestate (*i.e.,* without a will), all his realty passed to his heir, while his personalty was divided between certain of his relatives; again, realty could be entailed and personalty could not. After 1925, however, realty and personalty both pass on intestacy to certain relatives, and both kinds of property can be entailed. Thus the modern emphasis is on the distinction between land and other property, though the term " real property " still has some significance and is still widely used.

Sect. 4. Tenures and Estates

The basis of English land law is that all land in England is owned by the Crown. A small part is in the Crown's actual occupation; the rest is occupied by tenants holding either directly or indirectly from the Crown.[14] " *Nulle terre sans seigneur* " (no land without a lord): there is no allodial land in England,[15] *i.e.,* no land owned by a subject and not held of some lord.

1. Lord and tenant. This position can be traced from the Norman Conquest. William I regarded the whole of England as his by conquest. To reward his followers and those of the English who submitted to him, he granted and confirmed certain lands to be held of him as overlord.[16] These lands were granted not by way of an out-and-out transfer, but to be held from the Crown upon certain conditions. Thus, Blackacre might have been granted to X on the terms that he did homage and swore fealty, that he provided five armed horsemen to fight for the Crown for forty days in each year, and the like. Whiteacre might have been granted to Y on condition that he supported the King's train in his coronation. X and Y (who were known as tenants *in capite* or in chief) might each in turn grant land to others (known as *mesne* tenants) to hold of them in return for

---

[13] See *post,* p. 616.
[14] 1 P. & M. 232, 233.
[15] Co.Litt. 1b.
[16] Williams R.P. 12.

services. In days when land and its rents and profits constituted nearly the whole tangible wealth of a country,[17] it was more usual to secure the performance of services by the grant of land in return for those services than it was to secure them by payment; the whole social organisation was based on landholding in return for service.[18]

2. Services. These services became to a certain extent standardised. Thus there was one set of services (which included the provision of armed horsemen for battle) which became known as knight service, and there was another set (which included the performance of some honourable service for the king in person) which was known as grand sergeanty. Each of these sets of services was known as a *tenure*, for it showed how the land was held (*tenere*, to hold).

3. Time. A further essential is the length of time for which the land was held. Land might be granted for life (for as long as the tenant lived), in tail (for as long as the tenant or any of his descendants lived), or in fee simple (for as long as the tenant or any of his heirs, whether descendants or not, were alive). Each of these lengths of tenancy was known as an *estate*, a word derived from *status*.[19] Thus the Crown might grant land to A for an estate in fee simple, and A in turn might grant it to B for life. But the ownership of the land remained in the Crown. A man might own one or more estates in land, yet he never owned any of the land itself. Ownership of the largest estate in land, the fee simple, has come more and more to resemble ownership of the land itself, but even today it is technically true to say that the whole of the land in England is owned by the Crown; a subject can own only an estate. Both in popular speech and in legal parlance, however, the word " estate " is often used in other senses. Thus it may describe an area of land (" the Blank Estate is for sale ") or assets generally (" the testator left a net estate of £50,000 "). The context will usually leave little doubt about which sense is intended.

4. Basic doctrines. There are thus two basic doctrines in the law of real property. These are known as—

    (i) the doctrine of tenures: all land is held of the Crown, either directly or indirectly, on one or other of the various tenures; and

---

[17] Challis R.P. 1.
[18] Williams R.P. 10.
[19] 2 H.E.L. 351, 352.

(ii) the doctrine of estates: a subject cannot own land, but can merely own an estate in it, authorising him to hold it for some period of time.

In short, the tenure answers the question " How is it held?," the estate the question " For how long? "

5. Effects of doctrines. It is this doctrine of estates, coupled with the permanence of land as opposed to mere destructible chattels, which makes the law relating to land so much more complex than the law governing chattels. At common law, it can in general be said that only two distinct legal rights can exist at the same time in chattels, namely, possession and ownership. If A lends his watch to B, the ownership of the watch remains vested in A, while B has possession of it. But in the case of land, a large number of legal rights could and still can exist at the same time. Thus the position of Blackacre in 1920 might have been that A was entitled to the land for life, B to a life estate in remainder (*i.e.*, after A's death), and C to the fee simple remainder. At the same time, D might own a lease for 99 years, subject to a sub-lease in favour of E for 21 years, and the land might be subject to a mortgage in favour of F, a rentcharge in favour of G, easements such as rights of way in favour of H, J, and K, and so on almost *ad infinitum*. Before 1926, all these estates and interests could exist as legal rights, and most, but not all, can exist as legal rights today.

It may thus be said that in the case of pure personalty, the unit of ownership is the chattel or other thing itself; it is either owned by one person (or several persons jointly or in common with each other), or it is not owned at all. In the case of land, however, the unit of ownership is not the land itself (which is necessarily owned by the Crown), but the estates and interests which have been artificially created in the land. In popular speech, one may refer to X's ownership of Blackacre; but technically, one should speak of X owning a lease of Blackacre, or a fee simple in Blackacre. This conception of the subject-matter of ownership being an abstract estate rather than the corporeal land was a remarkable and distinctive achievement of early English legal thought; it contributed greatly both to the triumphant flexibility of the English system and to its undoubted complexity.

The doctrine of tenure, now greatly attenuated, is briefly described in the following section, while the doctrine of estates, still of great significance, is considered in greater detail in the next chapter.

Sect. 5. Tenures

The disappearance of the social organisation based on landholding
in return for services has led over the centuries to extensive changes
in the rules of tenure, so that many tenures, formerly important, have
now vanished.

1. Extinct tenures. The tenancies which existed at common law
were divided into two main classes, free and unfree.

(a) *Free tenures.* There were three classes of free tenures :

A. Tenures in chivalry (or military tenures).
B. Tenures in socage.
C. Spiritual tenures.

Each of these categories was subdivided, but it is unnecessary to
consider in detail the different incidents and services to which each
gave rise.[20]   The statute *Quia Emptores* 1290 which prohibited the
creation of new tenures by anyone except the Crown, the Tenures
Abolition Act 1660 which converted tenures in chivalry into common
socage, and the Law of Property Act 1922, which abolished almost
all [21] the remaining incidents of the free tenures have contrived to
reduce all free tenures to one class, namely socage, now usually called
" freehold."   The process of attrition of tenures has also brought
about the disappearance of all intermediate tenures so that all freehold
land is now held directly of the Crown.

(b) *Unfree tenures.*[22]   The two unfree tenures were villein tenure
and, somewhat confusingly, " customary freeholds."   Their main distinguishing features were the uncertain varying nature of the services
to be rendered to the lord, and the absence of protection by the
King's Courts.   The tenant had to look for his protection to the court
of his lord.   Both these features disappeared in later centuries, but not
before it had been established that land held on an unfree tenure could
be transferred only by a surrender and admittance made in the lord's
court.   The transaction was recorded on the court rolls and the transferee given a copy of the entry to prove his title; he thus held " by
copy of the court roll," and the tenure became known as " copyhold."

(c) *Enfranchisement of copyholds.* Before 1926, provision had
been made by statute for the enfranchisement of copyholds, *i.e.*, the

---

[20] See M. & W., Chap. 2.
[21] A survival is escheat where a trustee in bankruptcy of a landowner disclaims, or
a corporation holding land is dissolved : see M. & W. 36, 37.
[22] See M. & W. 23–29.

conversion of land of copyhold tenure into socage. The Copyhold Acts of 1841, 1843 and 1844 provided for voluntary enfranchisement, *i.e.*, enfranchisement where both lord and tenant agreed. The Copyhold Acts of 1852, 1858 and 1887 (consolidated in the Copyhold Act 1894) enabled either lord or tenant to secure compulsory enfranchisement. But apart from any proceedings taken under these Acts, the various tenures remained substantially unaltered until the legislation of 1925 came into force. Finally, by the Law of Property Act 1922,[23] all remaining copyhold land was converted into land of freehold tenure. However, the incidents of copyhold land, unlike those of freehold land remained important and effective in 1925 and, therefore, could not be simply abolished without causing injustice to the lord. Some were abolished forthwith subject to the payment of compensation.[24] Others were preserved temporarily, but this class disappeared on or before December 31, 1935.[25] Lastly, there are a few which continue indefinitely unless abolished by written agreement between lord and tenant. These are:

   (i) Any rights of the lord or tenant to mines and minerals;

   (ii) Any rights of the lord in respect of fairs, markets and sporting;

   (iii) Any tenant's rights of common (*e.g.*, to pasture beasts on the waste land of the manor);

   (iv) Any liability of lord or tenant for the upkeep of dykes, ditches, sea walls, bridges and the like.

2. Modern tenures. As a consequence of the developments outlined above there is only one feudal tenure left today, namely socage, now called freehold. On the other hand, leasehold land has increased in importance.[26] Finally a new tenure has recently been invented to denote land which has been compulsorily acquired by the Land Commission and regranted by the Crown subject to statutory restrictions.[27] Thus modern tenures may be classified as:

   (1) Freehold;

   (2) Leasehold; and

   (3) Crownhold.

[23] s. 128 and 12th Sched., para. (1).
[24] L.P.A. 1922, 12th Sched., para. 1 ; 13th Sched., Pt. II, para. 13, as amended.
[25] *Ibid.*, ss. 128, 138, 13th Sched., Pt. II.
[26] See *post*, pp. 16, 19 and Chap. 10.
[27] See *post*, p. 587.

CHAPTER 2

ESTATES

Part 1

CLASSIFICATION

THE nature of an estate has already been discussed [1]; it is essentially an interest in land of defined duration. It is now necessary to consider the different kinds of estate. In doing this, much of the discussion will be in the past tense, for as will be seen [2] some of the estates can no longer exist as such, although corresponding rights can exist as interests (instead of estates) in land.

Estates were divided into two classes:

1. Estates of freehold;
2. Estates less than freehold. [3]

It should be noted that " freehold " here has nothing to do with freehold (or socage) tenure; it is merely that the same word is used to express sometimes the quality of the tenure, and sometimes the quantity of the estate. " Freehold," as normally used by the man in the street, unconsciously combines these senses; thus when a house agent advertises " a desirable freehold residence," he refers to a fee simple estate in land of freehold tenure.

Sect. 1. Estates of Freehold

There were three estates of freehold:

(a) fee simple;
(b) fee tail; and
(c) life estate. [4]

The fee simple and the life estate have always existed in English law; the fee tail was introduced by statute in 1285. Before considering the estates in any detail a brief account of each must be given.

---

[1] *Ante*, p. 9.
[2] *Post*, pp. 71 *et seq.*
[3] 1 Preston, *Estates*, 22.
[4] Co.Litt. 43b.

1. Fee simple. Originally this was an estate which endured for as long as the original tenant or any of his heirs survived. " Heirs " comprised any blood relations, although originally ancestors were excluded; not until the Inheritance Act 1833 could a person be the heir of one of his descendants. Thus at first a fee simple would terminate if the original tenant died without leaving any descendants or collateral blood relations (*e.g.*, brothers or cousins), even if before his death the land had been conveyed to another tenant who was still alive. But by 1306 it was settled that where a tenant in fee simple alienated the land, the fee simple would continue as long as there were heirs of the new tenant and so on, irrespective of any failure of the original tenant's heirs.[5] Thenceforward a fee simple was virtually eternal.[6]

2. Fee tail. This was an estate which continued for as long as the original tenant or any of his descendants survived. Thus if the original tenant died leaving no relatives except a brother, a fee simple would continue, but a fee tail would come to an end. The terms " fee tail," " estate tail," " entail " and " entailed interest " are often used interchangeably, although " fee tail " is the correct expression for a legal entail [7] and " entailed interest " is usually reserved for an equitable entail.[8]

3. Life estate. As its name indicates, this lasted for life only. The name " life estate " usually denoted that the measuring life was that of the tenant himself, *e.g.*, when the grant was to A for life. The form of life estate where the measuring life was that of some other person was known as an estate " *pur autre vie* " (pronounced " per *oh*ter vee," and meaning " for the life of another "), *e.g.*, to A so long as B lives.

A common feature of all estates of freehold was that the duration of the estate was fixed but uncertain.[9] Nobody could say when the death would occur of a man and all his heirs, or a man and all his descendants, or a man alone. But the duration was not wholly indefinite; the estate was bound to determine if some preordained event occurred. In the case of the fee simple and the fee tail, the word

---

[5] *Post*, p. 29.
[6] 1 Preston, *Estates*, 429; but see T. Cyprian Williams (1930) 69 L.J.News. 369, 385; 70 *ibid.* 4, 20; (1931) 75 S.J. 843 at 847.
[7] Litt. 13; 1 Preston, *Estates*, 420; Challis R.P. 60.
[8] See *post*, p. 41.
[9] Williams R.P. 65.

" fee " denoted (a) that the estate was an estate of inheritance, *i.e.*, an estate which, on the death of the tenant, was capable of descending to his heir [10]; and (b) that the estate was one which might continue for ever.[11] A life estate, on the other hand, was not a fee. It was not an estate of inheritance and it could not continue for ever. On the death of the tenant, an ordinary life estate determined, and an estate *pur autre vie* did not descend to the tenant's heir, but passed under the special rules of occupancy.[12] Life estates were sometimes called " mere freeholds " or " freeholds," as opposed to " freeholds of inheritance." *i.e. An equitable estate.*

Each estate of freehold could exist in a number of varied forms which will be considered in due course.

Sect. 2. Estates Less Than Freehold

At first, the three estates of freehold were the sole estates recognised by law; the only other lawful right to the possession of land was known as a tenancy at will,[13] under which the tenant could be ejected at any time, and which therefore hardly ranked as an estate at all. Terms of years grew up outside this system of estates; the lack of protection given to them by the courts, and early doubts whether terms for longer than 40 years were valid,[14] placed leaseholders in a position of inferiority from which they never recovered. Although by the six-teenth century terms of years had become recognised as legal estates [15] and were fully protected, yet they ranked below the three estates of freehold.[16] Leaseholders were regarded as holding their land in the name of their lords, the possession of the leasehold tenant being regarded as the possession of the lord.[17]

Today, the various forms of leasehold estates are of the first importance. Nevertheless, it is still not easy to find any satisfactory common element in them; perhaps it is not possible to evolve a more precise definition than " any estate not a freehold." The principal categories are as follows; they are dealt with more fully later.[18]

---

[10] 1 Preston, *Estates*, 262, 419; Challis R.P. 218.
[11] 1 Preston, *Estates*, 419, 480.
[12] *Post*, pp. 47 *et seq.*
[13] Challis R.P. 63.
[14] See Co.Litt. 45b, 46a.
[15] Challis R.P. 64.
[16] Co.Litt. 43b; and see *Re Russell Road Purchase Money* (1871) L.R. 12 Eq. 78 at 84.
[17] 1 Preston, *Estates*, 205, 206.
[18] *Post*, pp. 345–350.

1. Fixed term of certain duration. The tenant may hold the land for a fixed term of certain duration,[19] as under a lease for 99 years. The possibility of the term being extended or curtailed under some provision to this effect in the lease does not affect the basic conception, which is one of certainty of duration in the absence of steps being taken for extension or curtailment. A lease for " 99 years if X so long lives " also fell under this head; it was not an estate of freehold,[20] for although X might well die before the 99 years had run, the maximum duration of the lease was fixed. For all practical purposes, there was no chance of X outliving the 99 years, so that the duration of the lease would be the same as an estate granted " to X for life "; yet in law the former was less than freehold and the latter freehold. Partly as a result of the intervention of statute, such leases are comparatively rare today.[21]

2. Fixed term with duration capable of being rendered certain. A lease of land " to A from year to year," with no other provision as to its duration, will continue indefinitely unless either landlord or tenant takes some step to determine it. But either party can give half a year's notice to determine it at the end of a year of the tenancy, and thus ensure its determination on a fixed date. This, coupled with the fact that originally the lease was for an uncertain term of uncertain duration, classifies the estate as less than freehold. The same applies to quarterly, monthly, weekly and other periodical tenancies.[22]

3. Uncertain period of uncertain duration. A tenancy at will is a tenancy which may continue indefinitely or may be determined by either party at any time; it is thus less than freehold. In the same way, a tenancy at sufferance, which is similar in nature, is less than freehold.[23] Indeed, such tenancies are perhaps not estates at all.[24]

Sect. 3. Seisin

1. Meaning. One distinction between freeholders and owners of estates less than freehold was that only a freehold could carry seisin with it. It is difficult to define seisin satisfactorily.[25] It has nothing

---

[19] 1 Preston, *Estates*, 203.
[20] 1 Cru.Dig. 47.
[21] See *post*, p. 350.
[22] For these tenancies see *post*, p. 348.
[23] For these tenancies see *post*, p. 349.
[24] Consider *Wheeler* v. *Mercer* [1957] A.C. 416 at 427, 428.
[25] See, generally, Maitland's *Collected Papers*, Vol. I, pp. 329, 358, 407.

to do with the word " seizing," with its implication of violence. To medieval lawyers it suggested the very opposite: peace and quiet. A man who was put in seisin of land was " set " there and continued to " sit " there.[26] Seisin thus denotes quiet possession of land, but quiet possession of a particular kind.

2. Freeholder. Although at first the term was applied to the possession of a leaseholder as well as that of a freeholder, during the fifteenth century it became confined to those who held an estate of freehold.[27] A leaseholder merely had possession; only a freeholder could be seised.[28] And since the possession of a leaseholder was regarded as the possession of the freeholder from whom he held, a freeholder remained seised even after he had granted a term of years and gave up physical possession of the land; receipt of the rent was evidence of seisin. Further, only land of freehold tenure carried seisin with it. A copyholder could not be seised, even if he held a fee simple.

From this it will be seen that a person was seised if—

   (i) he held an estate of freehold,
   (ii) in land of freehold tenure, and
   (iii) either he had taken physical possession of the land, or a lease-holder or copyholder held the land from him.

3. Definition. Although it seems impossible to frame a satisfactory definition of seisin, to call it " that feudal possession of land which only the owner of a freehold estate in freehold land could have " is to express the most important elements. A man might be seised of many plots of land at the same time, even if none of them was under lease, for the requirement of physical possession did not mean that the person seised had to be in continuous occupation; seisin was not lost merely because he went away on a visit. Once seisin was acquired, it continued until another person acquired it.

4. Importance. The importance of seisin, which has greatly diminished in modern times, is shown in many ways. For example—

   (i) Feudal services could be claimed only from the tenant seised of the land.[29]

[26] 2 P. & M. 30.
[27] Challis R.P. 99.
[28] Litt. 324; Co.Litt. 17a, 200b.
[29] Challis R.P. 100.

(ii) A real action (one in which the land itself could be recovered and not merely damages) could be brought only against the tenant seised.[30]

(iii) Curtesy and dower could be claimed only out of property of which the deceased had been seised.[31]

(iv) Conveyances of freehold land could originally be made only by a feoffment with livery of seisin. This was a solemn ceremony carried out by the parties entering on the land, and the feoffor, in the presence of witnesses, delivering the seisin to the feoffee either by some symbolic act, such as handing him a twig or sod of earth, or by uttering some words such as "Enter into this land and God give you joy" and leaving him in possession of the land.

For these and other reasons, the common law abhorred an abeyance of seisin. Any transaction whereby one person lost seisin without transferring it to another was void.

Sect. 4. Position of Leaseholds Today

As has been seen, leaseholds were at first regarded as mere contractual rights to occupy land.[32] Despite their subsequent recognition as legal estates, they always remained outside the feudal system of landholding. Today, it is possible to regard leasehold as a tenure. Only in the case of leaseholds does there now arise a relationship of lord and tenant which has any practical importance. The one remaining feudal tenure, socage, has been shorn of all the incidents of any consequence, whereas in the case of leaseholds a valuable rent is nearly always payable, and the lord usually has power to forfeit the lease if the tenant does not fulfil his obligations. Further, the position as regards creating successive interests in leaseholds is substantially the same as for land held in socage. Thus just as socage land may be given "to A for life, remainder to B in tail, remainder to C in fee simple," so leasehold land may be given "to A for life, remainder to B in tail, remainder to C absolutely." Nevertheless, leaseholds also retain the principal characteristic of an estate, for they mark out the length of time for which the land is held. Consequently, although it may be true that for all practical purposes leaseholds have

---

[30] *Freeman* d. *Vernon* v. *West* (1763) 2 Wils.K.B. 165 at 166.
[31] *Post*, pp. 294, 296.
[32] *Ante*, pp. 7, 8.

completed the transition from contract via estate to tenure, it is better to regard them as being in a class by themselves, having features of both estates and tenures.

The details of leaseholds will be considered later.[33]

Part 2

ESTATES OF FREEHOLD

The two main points to be considered concerning estates of freehold are—

(1) the words required to create each of the estates, and
(2) the characteristics of each estate.

Sect. 1. Words of Limitation

1. " Limitation." " Words of limitation " is the phrase used to describe the words which limit (*i.e.*, delimit, or mark out) the estate to be taken. Thus in a conveyance today " to A in fee simple," the words " in fee simple " are words of limitation, for they show what estate A is to have.

2. Inter vivos. The rule at common law was that a freehold estate of inheritance could be created in a conveyance *inter vivos* (*i.e.*, a transfer of land between living persons) only by a phrase which included the word " heirs." A life estate could be created without using this word, but a fee simple or fee tail could not.[34] It is important to note that no other word would do: " relatives," " issue," " descendants," " assigns," " for ever," " in fee simple," " in tail," and so on, were all ineffective. " Heirs " was the sacred word of limitation, and had a magic which no other word possessed.

3. Wills. In the case of gifts by will, the attitude of the courts was different. A conveyance *inter vivos* was originally a solemn ceremony in which considerable importance attached to the proper procedure being followed. Later, the nature of a conveyance changed and became more complex, so that professional assistance was usually sought. Further, if there was any flaw in the transaction, the grantor

---

[33] *Post*, Chap. 10, p. 337.
[34] Co.Litt. 20a, 20b.

would usually still be alive to put things right. Consequently, conveyances *inter vivos* were construed strictly by the courts. Most wills of land, however, were first enforced by Chancery, which looked to the intent of any transaction rather than the form. When the Statute of Wills 1540 compelled common law courts to give effect to wills, both the words of the statute, which authorised any person to dispose of land " at his free will and pleasure," [35] and the former practice of Chancery, encouraged the courts to interpret wills liberally. Further, wills were often home-made, and, since they were inoperative until the testator's death, mistakes would usually lie hidden until it was impossible to put them right.[36] The result was that strict words of limitation were not required in wills. Provided the intention of the testator was clear, it would be effectuated.[37]

The detailed rules will now be considered, taking the fee simple, fee tail and life estate in turn and dealing separately under each head with conveyances *inter vivos* and wills.

A. *Words of Limitation for a Fee Simple*

I. CONVEYANCES INTER VIVOS

1. At common law.

(a) *Natural persons.* At common law, the proper expression to employ was " and his heirs " following the grantee's name, *e.g.,* " to A and his heirs." [38] " Heir " in the singular would not suffice, and the word " and " could not be replaced by " or " [39] : " to A or his heirs " gave A a mere life estate, and so did expressions not containing the word " heirs," *e.g.,* " to A for ever," or " to A in fee simple." [40]

It is important to note that the words " and his heirs " gave no estate in the land to the heirs. The words were mere words of limitation, delimiting or making out the estate which A was to take; they were not words of purchase, that is to say, they were not words which conferred any estate on the heirs themselves. (" Purchase " is here used in the technical sense as referring to any transaction, whether for value or not, whereby property is acquired by act of parties, as by

---

[35] ss. 1, 2.
[36] See *Newis* v. *Lark* (1571) 2 Plowd. 403 at 413.
[37] *Throckmerton* v. *Tracy* (1555) 1 Plowd. 145 at 162, 163.
[38] 2 Preston, *Estates*, 1.
[39] Co.Litt. 8b; Challis R.P. 221, 222.
[40] Litt. 1.

gift, and not merely by operation of law, as on intestacy.[41])   Thus if
A had a son at the time of the conveyance, the son acquired no estate
by it, but had merely a *spes successionis, i.e.,* a hope of succeeding to
the fee simple if A died without having disposed of it.[42]   Although
A's eldest son is his " heir " in the popular sense, the legal maxim is
" *nemo est heres viventis* " (a living person has no heir).[43]   A living
person may have an heir apparent, *i.e.,* a person who, if he survives
A, will be A's heir, such as his eldest son; or he may have an heir
presumptive, *i.e.,* a person who, if he outlives A and no person with a
better claim comes into existence, will be A's heir, such as his
daughter: but not until his death can A's heir be ascertained.[44]

Two special rules should be noticed.   First, a fee simple could not
be restricted to heirs of any particular sex; a conveyance " to A and
his heirs male " gave A the fee simple, the word " male " being
rejected for repugnancy.[45]

Secondly, a conveyance " to the heirs of A," A being dead at the
time of the conveyance, gave a fee simple to the person who was A's
heir.   Strictly, perhaps, the phrase should have been " to A's heir and
his heirs," but it was held that " to the heirs of A " had the same
effect.[46]   If A was alive at the time of conveyance, it failed utterly, for
as mentioned above, neither A's heir apparent nor heir presumptive
was A's " heir," and since the conveyance sought forthwith to divest
the grantor of the seisin and there was nobody in whom it could vest,
the conveyance was void.[47]   But if the gift was preceded by some
other estate of freehold, *e.g.,* if the conveyance was " to X for life,
remainder to the heirs of A," it could be valid, for there was a person, namely X, in whom the seisin could vest forthwith.   Provided A
died before X, so that A's heir was ascertained and ready to take the
seisin on X's death, the gift took effect as intended [48]; otherwise the
land reverted to the grantor on X's death.

(b) *Corporations.*   In the case of conveyances to corporations,
different rules applied.   A corporation aggregate consists of two or
more persons united together under some name to form a new legal
person having perpetual existence, *e.g.,* a Dean and Chapter, or a
limited company.   No words of limitation were needed in such a case;

---

[41] See *post,* p. 289.
[42] *Re Parsons* (1890) 45 Ch.D. 51 at 55.
[43] 2 Preston, *Estates,* 35.
[44] See 3 Cru.Dig. 328.
[45] *Idle* v. *Cook* (1705) 1 P.Wms. 70 at 77 ; contrast *post,* p. 26.
[46] *Marshall* v. *Peascod* (1861) 2 J. & H. 73.
[47] See *Else* v. *Osborn* (1717) 1 P.Wms. 387.
[48] Co.Litt. 378a.

a conveyance to the corporation *simpliciter, e.g.,* " to the Alpha Co. Ltd.," sufficed to pass the fee simple, for there was no reason to give it any other estate.[49] A corporation sole, on the other hand, comprises only one natural person. Thus the King, a bishop or a parson are all corporations sole in their official capacities. In such cases, a life estate to the individual holder of the office was a conceivable alternative to a fee simple, and so to create a fee simple a formula had to be used which indicated that the corporation rather than the individual should benefit.[50] This formula was " and his successors," *e.g.,* " to the Vicar of Bray and his successors." [51] Failure to use this phrase resulted in a mere life estate passing to the individual, though the use of " heirs " perhaps gave a fee simple to the individual.[52]

2. By statute.

(a) *After* 1881. It has been seen that at common law a conveyance " to A in fee simple " would create not a fee simple, but only a life estate.[53] This was remedied by the Conveyancing Act 1881 [54] enacting that in deeds executed after 1881 the words " in fee simple " would suffice to pass the fee simple. The expressions available at common law still remained effective; the Act merely supplied an alternative, and this alternative had to be employed as strictly as the older expression. Thus a conveyance " to A in fee " passed only a life estate, although if it could be shown that the omission of " simple " was an accident, the court had jurisdiction to carry out the common intention of the parties, and rectify the conveyance by inserting the missing word.[55]

(b) *After* 1925. By the Law of Property Act 1925, the necessity for words of limitation in creating a fee simple was abolished in the case of all deeds executed after 1925, for the grantee takes " the fee simple or other the whole interest which the grantor had power to convey in such land, unless a contrary intention appears in the conveyance." [56] This effect will be produced even if the conveyance is to a corporation sole.[57] In practice, the words " in fee simple " are always inserted to make it clear that there is no contrary intention.

[49] 2 Preston, *Estates,* 43–47.
[50] See *Ex p. Vicar of Castle Bytham* [1895] 1 Ch. 348 at 354.
[51] Co.Litt. 8b, 94b; and see *Bankes* v. *Salisbury Diocesan Council of Education Incorporated* [1960] Ch. 631.
[52] 2 Preston, *Estates,* 48; Co.Litt. 94b, n. (5).
[53] Shep. 106.
[54] s. 51.
[55] *Re Ethel and Mitchells and Butlers' Contract* [1901] 1 Ch. 945.
[56] s. 60 (1).
[57] s. 60 (2).

II. GIFTS BY WILL

1. Before 1838. Before 1838, no formal words of limitation were required in a will, but it was necessary for the will to show an intent to pass the fee simple.[58] Thus " to A for ever," or " to A and his heir," or " to A to dispose at will and pleasure " all sufficed to pass the fee simple.[59] But it was for the devisee to show that a fee simple was intended to pass; a devise " to A " prima facie passed merely a life estate.[60]

2. After 1837. By the Wills Act 1837,[61] the fee simple or other the whole interest of which the testator has power to dispose passes in a gift by any will made or confirmed after 1837 [62] unless a contrary intention is shown. This reverses the onus of proof; a devise " to A " now passes the fee simple unless a contrary intention is shown. But the old rule still applies where the will, instead of disposing of an existing interest, is creating a new interest, *e.g.*, a new rentcharge.[63]

B. *Words of Limitation for a Fee Tail*

I. CONVEYANCES INTER VIVOS

1. At common law. The expression required to create a fee tail was the word " heirs " followed by some words of procreation,[64] *i.e.*, words which confined " heirs " to descendants of the original grantee; an example is " to X and the heirs of his body." The word " heirs " was essential, but any words of procreation sufficed. Thus " to A and the heirs of his flesh " or " to A and the heirs from him proceeding " sufficed to create entails. But expressions such as " to A and his issue " or " to A and his seed " would not create a fee tail in a deed, for the vital word " heirs " was missing.

The reason why words of procreation were required was that " heirs " included relatives other than descendants of the grantee, such as his brothers and uncles. An entail, however, is an interest

---

[58] 2 Preston, *Estates*, 68.
[59] See, generally, 6 Cru.Dig., Chap. XI.
[60] 2 Preston, *Estates*, 78.
[61] s. 28.
[62] s. 34.
[63] *Post*, p. 410.
[64] 2 Preston, *Estates*, 477, 478.

which can pass only to descendants of the original grantee (though children adopted before the entail was created are now included [65]), and so "heirs" had to be restricted by the addition of words of procreation.

By the addition of suitable words, an entail could be further restricted so that it descended only to a particular class of descendants. There were thus the following types of entail [66]:

(i) a tail general, *e.g.*, "to A and the heirs of his body," where any descendants of A, male or female, could inherit;

(ii) a tail male, *e.g.*, "to A and the heirs male of his body," in which case only male descendants of A who could trace an unbroken descent from him through males could inherit, and not, *e.g.*, a son of A's daughter; and

(iii) a tail female, *e.g.*, "to A and the heirs female of his body," where corresponding rules applied.

In addition, a "special tail" could be created, confining the heirs entitled to those descended from a specified spouse, such as "to A and the heirs of his body begotten upon Mary," when only issue of A and Mary could inherit; Mary, of course, took nothing. A special tail could exist in any of the three above forms.

As in the case of a fee simple, the words following A's name were mere words of limitation. "To A and the heirs of his body" gave A a fee tail; it gave his heir apparent or heir presumptive no estate but only a *spes successionis*. But a conveyance "to the heirs of the body of A," A being dead, gave a fee tail to the heir of A's body,[67] although a conveyance "to the heir of the body of A" passed a mere life estate to the heir [68]; the former phrase could be expanded into "to the heir of the body of A and the heirs of the body of A," while the latter could not.

2. By statute. In the case of deeds executed after 1881, the Conveyancing Act 1881 [69] made provisions for entails similar to those made for a fee simple. In addition to the expressions which sufficed to create an entail at common law, the words "in tail" (not "in fee tail," it will be noted) following the name of the grantee (*e.g.*, "to X

---

[65] Adoption Act 1958, s. 16.
[66] See Litt. 21–29.
[67] *Mandeville's Case* (1328) Y.B. 2 Edw. 3, Hil., pl. 1, 2.
[68] *Chambers* v. *Taylor* (1837) 2 My. & Cr. 376.
[69] s. 51.

in tail ") would create a fee tail. If it was desired to restrict the entail to a particular class of descendants, apt words could be added, *e.g.*, " to A in tail male."

These rules still apply after 1925, the provisions of the Conveyancing Act 1881 being now replaced by the Law of Property Act 1925.[70] The effect of using informal words such as " to A and his issue " is to pass the fee simple either to A, or to A jointly with such of his issue as are alive at the time of the gift; the former seems the better view.[71]

II. GIFTS BY WILL

1. Before 1926. The rule before 1926 was that any words showing an intent to create an entail sufficed in a will, even if no technical expressions were used. Thus " to A and his seed," " to A and his heirs male," [72] " to A and his descendants," and " to A and his issue," [73] all usually sufficed to create entails. A devise " to A and his children " sometimes gave A an entail and sometimes gave the property to A and his children jointly; this is considered later.[74] " Children " prima facie meant descendants of the first generation only, and so was less apt to create an entail than words such as " issue," which prima facie included descendants of any generation and were thus the informal equivalent of " heirs of his body." [75]

2. After 1925. The above rule remained unaffected until the Law of Property Act 1925 [76] laid down that informal expressions should no longer suffice to create an entail in a will, but that expressions which would have been effective to create an entail in a deed before 1926 must be employed. Thus in deeds and wills alike either " heirs " followed by words of procreation, or " in tail," must now be used. As in the case of conveyances *inter vivos*, it seems that the effect of using informal expressions such as " to A and his issue " is to pass the fee simple either to A, or to A jointly with such of his issue as are alive when the testator dies.[77]

---

[70] ss. 60, 130.
[71] See (1936) 6 Camb.L.J. 67 ; (1945) 9 Camb.L.J. 46 ; *ibid.* (1946) p. 185.
[72] *Cf. ante*, p. 22.
[73] *Slater* v. *Dangerfield* (1846) 15 M. & W. 263 at 272.
[74] *Post*, p. 287.
[75] *Re Lord Lawrence* [1915] 1 Ch. 129 at 146.
[76] s. 130.
[77] *Supra.*

C. The Rule in Shelley's Case

1. The Rule. The Rule in *Shelley's Case* [78] applied before 1926 to both deeds and wills. The Rule may be stated thus:

> It is a rule of law that when an estate of freehold is given to a person, and by the same disposition an estate is limited either mediately or immediately to his heirs or to the heirs of his body, then if both limitations are legal or both equitable, the words " heirs " or " heirs of his body " are words of limitation and not words of purchase.

2. Operation of the Rule. If land was limited before 1926—

" to A for life, remainder to his heirs," or—
" to B for life and to the heirs of his body,"

the natural meaning of the words was that A and B should each take life estates, and that A's heir should take a fee simple and B's heir a fee tail. A and B would thus have been unable to defeat the claims of their heirs; notwithstanding any disposition which A and B might make by deed or will, on their deaths the land would have passed to their respective heirs. The Rule in *Shelley's Case*, however, required an unnatural effect to be given to such limitations. Under the Rule, the fee simple remainder did not pass to A's heir, but passed to A in addition to the life estate, with the result that A's life estate in possession and his fee simple in remainder merged together and gave him the fee simple in possession. Similarly B took a fee tail in possession. In each case the Rule prescribed that the words " remainder to his heirs " or " remainder to the heirs of his body " should be treated as words of limitation, marking out the estates taken by A and B; they were not permitted to operate as words of purchase conferring an interest on the persons they mentioned, namely, the heirs of A and B. The effect of the Rule was therefore to make a limitation " to A for life remainder to his heirs " the equivalent of a limitation " to A and his heirs." In each case A took the fee simple.

The Rule also applied where there was some estate or interest between the estate of freehold and the remainder, *i.e.*, where the remainder was limited " mediately," as " to C for life, remainder to X for life, remainder to the heirs of C." The result was that C took a life estate, X took a life estate in remainder, and C took the fee simple remainder, which he could dispose of in his lifetime or by will.

[78] (1581) 1 Co.Rep. 88b ; and see Challis R.P. 152–167.

3. Abolition of the Rule.   The rule was the product of feudal doctrines which had become obsolete.[79]   Hence by the Law of Property Act 1925,[80] the Rule was abolished for all instruments coming into operation after 1925.   Accordingly in a limitation " to A for life, remainder to his heirs " the word " heirs " is now a word of purchase and not a word of limitation.   The statute provides that the " same person or persons shall take as would in the case of freehold land have answered that description " [*i.e.,* " heirs," " heirs of the body," etc.] " under the general law in force before the commencement of this Act."   The heir or heir of the body, as the case may be, ascertained according to the general law in force before 1926 (and not under special customs such as gavelkind), now takes the remainder.   Thus in the above example A will take a mere life interest, while his heir takes the remainder in fee simple.   Had the remainder been " to the heirs of his body," probably the heir of A's body would have taken an entail.[81]

D.   Words of Limitation for a Life Estate

I.   CONVEYANCES INTER VIVOS

A life estate was created before 1926 either by words showing an intention to create a life estate, such as " to A for life," or by the use of expressions insufficient to create a fee simple or fee tail, such as " to A," or " to A for ever." [82]

After 1925, a fee simple (or the whole of the interest the grantor has power to convey, if it is less than a fee simple) passes unless the contrary intention is shown.[83]   Thus to create a life interest, words showing an intention to do so must normally be used, *e.g.,* " to A for life."

II.   IN WILLS

Before the Wills Act 1837, a devise passed only a life estate unless an intention to create a fee simple or fee tail was shown.   That Act provided that the fee simple passes unless a contrary intention is shown,[84] so that in this case also, words showing an intent to pass only a life interest are now essential.

---

[79] For the reasons for the rule, see *Van Grutten* v. *Foxwell* [1897] A.C. 658 at 668 ; Fearne C.R. 83 *et seq.* ; A. D. Hargreaves (1938) 54 L.Q.R. 70.
[80] s. 131.
[81] See *ante,* p. 26.
[82] *Re Irwin* [1904] 2 Ch. 752.
[83] *Ante,* p. 23.
[84] s. 28 ; see *ante,* p. 24.

Sect. 2. Nature of the Estates of Freehold

A. The Fee Simple

The fee simple is the most ample estate which can exist in land. Although in theory it still falls short of absolute ownership, in practice it amounts to this, for nearly all traces of the old feudal burdens have disappeared.

The tenant in fee simple has the important right of alienation, that is the right to transfer to another the whole or any part of his interest in the land. A consideration of this will be followed by a discussion of the various types of fee simple.

I. RIGHT OF ALIENATION

Today, a tenant in fee simple may dispose of his estate in whatever way he thinks fit either by will or *inter vivos*. This has not always been so. Before the Norman Conquest, much land seems to have been freely alienable by the tenants, but under the feudal system imposed after the Conquest the tendency was to restrict alienation. Two people might suffer if a tenant was able to dispose of his land: his heir and his lord.

1. Rights of the heir. In early law, the heir apparent or heir presumptive was regarded as having a definite interest in the land, so that the tenant could not dispose of the land without the heir's consent; and as subsequent events might show that the heir apparent or heir presumptive was not the person who would have succeeded to the land had it not been alienated, it was not unusual to get the consent of as many near relatives as possible.[85]

However, by about 1200 this doctrine had disappeared, and a tenant in fee simple was able to alienate his land *inter vivos* so as to defeat all claims of his heirs.[86] Thereafter the heir apparent or heir presumptive was regarded as having no estate or interest in the land but only a *spes successionis*. Further, by the beginning of the fourteenth century the existence of a fee simple had ceased to be in any way dependent upon the existence of heirs of the original grantee. Strictly, if land were given " to A and his heirs," the fee simple should

---

[85] 2 P. & M. 309, 310.
[86] *Ibid.*, 311, 313.

have determined as soon as A and all his heirs were dead, even if A had alienated the land. But a fee simple became virtually eternal when the courts decided that if a fee simple was alienated it continued to exist as long as the new tenant or any of his heirs lived.[87]

Although after the twelfth century a tenant in fee simple could alienate his land *inter vivos* and so defeat the expectations of his relatives, he could not dispose of it by will. In some cases devises were permitted as late as the latter half of the thirteenth century, but from the end of that century the rule was settled that land was not devisable, except by special custom, *e.g.*, gavelkind or burgage.[88] This remained law until wills of land were made possible by uses and later by the Statute of Wills 1540.

2. Rights of the lord. In the days when services were rendered in return for land, the personality of the tenant was important to the lord who might suffer if the tenant was able to alienate freely. But these objections lost much of their force during the thirteenth century when the services either ceased to be enforced or became commuted into money. After the statute of *Quia Emptores* 1290, all land held in fee simple was freely alienable.

II. TYPES OF FEE SIMPLE

A fee (or fee simple) may be absolute or modified; a modified fee is any fee except a fee simple absolute. There are four types of fee.

1. Fee simple absolute. This is the type most frequently encountered in practice, and is an estate which continues for ever. " Fee " denotes inheritability,[89] " simple " excludes entails, and " absolute " distinguishes modified fees.

2. Determinable fee. A determinable fee is a fee simple which will automatically determine on the occurrence of some specified event which may never occur. If the event is bound to happen at some time, the estate created is not a determinable fee. Thus before 1926 a grant " to A and his heirs until B dies " gave A an estate *pur autre vie*, and a grant " to C and his heirs " for a fixed term of years gave C a mere tenancy for a term of years. A grant to X and his heirs

---

[87] Y.B. 33–35 Edw. 1 (R.S.) 362 (1306).
[88] 3 H.E.L. 75, 76.
[89] See *ante*, p. 15.

until a specified lease was made, or to Y and his heirs " as long as such a tree stands," however, created determinable fees.[90] The estates of X and Y might continue for ever, but if the specified state of affairs came about, the fee determined and the land reverted to the original grantor. The grantor thus had a possibility of reverter, *i.e.*, a possibility of having an estate at a future time. If the occurrence of the determining event became impossible, the possibility of reverter was destroyed and the fee simple became absolute,[91] as where land was given " to A and his heirs until B marries " and B died a bachelor.

Determinable fees are rarely encountered in practice except under marriage settlements, where the settlor grants land to himself until the solemnisation of the marriage.[92] A fee simple limited to a corporation does not determine merely because the corporation is dissolved.[93]

3. A fee simple upon condition. In making a grant of a fee simple, a clause may be added providing that the fee simple is not to commence until some event occurs, or that it is to determine on the occurrence of some event. Conditions of the first type are conditions precedent [94]; a gift " to X and his heirs when X is 21 " is a gift of a fee simple with a condition precedent that X must attain his majority before he can take the land. These limitations are dealt with under future interests.[95] A condition subsequent is one which operates to defeat an existing interest, *e.g.*, a devise of land to X " on the condition that he never sells it out of the family " [96]; here the land passes to X, but it is liable to be forfeited if the condition is broken: X has a vested interest, liable to be divested.

The difference between a determinable fee and a fee simple defeasible by condition subsequent is not always easy to discern. The essential distinction is that the determining event in a determinable fee is included in the words marking out the limits of the estate, whereas a condition subsequent is a clause added to a limitation of a complete fee simple absolute which seeks to defeat it. Thus a devise to a school in fee simple " until it ceases to publish its accounts " would create a determinable fee, whereas a devise to the school in fee simple " on condition that the accounts are published annually "

---

[90] *Idle* v. *Cook* (1705) 1 P.Wms. 70 at 78.
[91] Challis R.P. 83, 254.
[92] See *post*, p. 243.
[93] *Re Strathblaine Estates Ltd.* [1948] Ch. 228.
[94] Pronounced " preeseedent," with the accent on the second syllable.
[95] *Post*, pp. 84 *et seq.*
[96] *Re Macleay* (1875) L.R. 20 Eq. 186.

creates a fee simple defeasible by condition subsequent.[97] Words
such as " while," " during," " as long as," " until " and so on are apt
for the creation of a determinable fee, whereas words which form a
separate clause of defeasance, such as " provided that," " on condition
that," " but if," " if it happen that," operate as a condition subsequent.[98]

It will be seen that the difference is primarily one of wording; the
determining event may be worked into the limitation in such a way
as to create either a determinable fee, or a fee simple defeasible by
condition subsequent, whichever the grantor wishes. The question is
whether the words limit the utmost time of continuance of the estate,
or whether they mark an event which, if it takes place in the course of
that time, will defeat the estate; in the first case the words form a
limitation, in the second a condition. In short, a limitation marks the
bounds or compass of the estate, a condition defeats the estate before
it attains its boundary.

There are practical differences between the two forms of fee:

(a) *Determination*: a determinable fee automatically determines
when the specified event occurs, for the natural limits of its existence
have been reached.[99] A fee simple upon condition merely gives the
grantor (or whoever is entitled to his realty, if the grantor is dead) a
right to enter and determine the estate when the event occurs; until
entry is made, the fee simple continues.[1]

(b) *Remoteness*: if a condition subsequent may possibly become
operative at too distant a date, it is void, and the fee simple is absolute,
whereas a determinable limitation is probably valid no matter how
far in the future the estate may determine.[2] These rules have been
modified and assimilated for interests created after July 15, 1964.[2a]

(c) *Existence at law*: a determinable fee cannot, it seems, exist
as a legal estate after 1925; but a fee simple subject to a condition
subsequent apparently can.[3]

(d) *Flexibility*: a determinable fee is more flexible than a fee
simple upon condition. There are certain restrictions upon the conditions on which a fee simple may be made liable to be defeated. A

---

[97] See *Re Da Costa* [1912] 1 Ch. 337.
[98] See 1 Sanders, *Uses* 156 ; Shep. 121.
[99] *Newis* v. *Lark* (1571) 2 Plowd. 403.
[1] *Matthew Manning's Case* (1609) 8 Co.Rep. 94b at 95b.
[2] *Post*, p. 120.   [2a] See *post*, p. 121.
[3] *Post*, pp. 74, 75.

condition subsequent is void, and the fee simple is absolute, if the condition infringes any of the following rules:

(i) It must not take away the power of alienation. One of the incidents of ownership is the right to sell or otherwise dispose of the property. A condition against alienation is said to be repugnant to this right, and contrary to public policy, if it substantially takes away the tenant's power of alienation; such conditions are thus void.[4] For example, conditions prohibiting all alienation, or all alienation during the life of some person, or alienation to anyone except X, have all been held void.[5] But certain partial restraints have been held valid; thus where land was devised to A " on the condition that he never sells it out of the family," the condition was held valid on the grounds that it did not prohibit any form of alienation except sale, it did not prohibit sales to members of the family, and it bound only A and not subsequent owners of the land.[6]

(ii) It must not be directed against a course of devolution prescribed by law. A condition rendering a fee simple liable to be defeated if the tenant dies intestate, becomes bankrupt, or has the estate seized in execution, is void, for on each of these events the law prescribes that a fee simple shall devolve in a particular way, and this course of devolution cannot be altered by condition.[7]

(iii) It must not be illegal, immoral or otherwise contrary to public policy. The condition under this head most frequently encountered is a condition in restraint of marriage. Partial restraints, prohibiting marriage with a Papist, or a Scotsman, or a person who had been a domestic servant, have been held good.[8] But total restraints (or restraints which are virtually total, *e.g.*, against marrying a person who has not freehold property worth £500 per annum) are void unless the intent is not merely to restrain marriage but simply to provide for the tenant until marriage,[9] or unless the tenant has already been married once.[10]

---

[4] *Bradley* v. *Peixoto* (1797) 3 Ves. 324.
[5] See *Re Cockerill* [1929] 2 Ch. 131.
[6] *Re Macleay* (1875) L.R. 20 Eq. 186; contrast *Re Brown* [1954] Ch. 39; and see (1954) 70 L.Q.R. 15.
[7] *Re Machu* (1882) 21 Ch.D. 838 (bankruptcy).
[8] *Jenner* v. *Turner* (1880) 16 Ch.D. 188 (domestic servant).
[9] See *Jones* v. *Jones* (1876) 1 Q.B.D. 279.
[10] *Newton* v. *Marsden* (1862) 2 J. & H. 356.

A determinable fee, on the other hand, is not so strictly confined. A devise of freeholds on trust for **X** " until he shall assign charge or otherwise dispose of the same or some part thereof or become bankrupt . . . or do something whereby the said annual income or some part thereof would become payable to or vested in some other person " has been held to give **X** a determinable fee.[11] On any of the events occurring X's estate would determine; if he died before any of them occurred, the fee simple would become absolute, for it ceases to be possible for any of them to occur. But although a fee may thus be made determinable on alienation or on bankruptcy or on similar events, a limitation would probably be void if it were contrary to public policy for the fee to be determinable on the stated event, *e.g.,* if the event is the return to her husband of a wife who is separated from him.

(e) *Effect of condition or limitation becoming void or impossible.* If a condition subsequent is void or becomes impossible, the donee takes a fee simple absolute, free from any condition[12]; but if a fee is made determinable upon an event contrary to law, the whole gift fails.[13]

4. A base fee. A base fee is a particular kind of determinable fee. The two essentials of a base fee are (a) it continues only so long as the original grantor or any heirs of his body are alive; and (b) there is a remainder or reversion after it.[14] Such estates are more fully dealt with below.[15]

Nature of modified fees. In general, the owner of a modified fee has the same rights over the land as the owner of a fee simple absolute: thus the common law refused to restrain him from committing acts of waste,[16] such as opening and working mines. Equity, on the other hand, intervened to prevent the commission of equitable waste, *i.e.,* acts of wanton destruction,[17] whereas the owner of a fee simple absolute is under no such restraint.

At common law the owner of a modified fee could not convey a fee simple absolute but merely a fee liable to determination, for a man cannot convey more than he has. Statute has qualified this

---

11 *Re Leach* [1912] 2 Ch. 422.
12 *Re Greenwood* [1903] 1 Ch. 749.
13 Consider *Re Moore* (1888) 39 Ch.D. 116 (personalty).
14 See *post*, pp. 38, 91.
15 *Post*, pp. 38, 43.
16 For waste, see *post*, p. 49.
17 *Re Hanbury's S.E.* [1913] 2 Ch. 357 at 365.

position.[18] Further, such a fee may become enlarged into a fee simple absolute, *e.g.,* by the determining event becoming impossible [19]; and there are special rules for the enlargement of base fees.[20]

B. The Fee Tail *or Entailed*

I. HISTORY

1. Before the Statute De Donis 1285: fees conditional on the birth of issue. The fee tail is a creature of statute. Before the Statute *De Donis Conditionalibus* 1285, no such estate existed; the common law recognised only two estates of freehold, the fee simple and the life estate, each existing in varying forms. It is the variants of the fee simple which must be dealt with here. One important form which became common not long after the Conquest was the *maritagium*. This was a gift of land, usually made by a father on the marriage of his daughter, whereby the land was conveyed to the daughter and her husband or one of them, and the heirs of their bodies. The *maritagium* might either be ordinary, or might be *liberum maritagium* (frank marriage), the latter form freeing the land from feudal services until the third heir entered, so enabling the new family to establish itself firmly before becoming liable for feudal services.[21]

Once the *maritagium* was generally recognised, donors began to evolve variations upon it, some of these being unconnected with any marriage. By the thirteenth century a number of variations were recognised, the most important being—

    (i) a gift to X and his heirs provided he had heirs of his body; this gave X a life estate until such an heir was born, whereupon his estate became a fee simple; and

    (ii) a gift to X and the heirs of his body; this gave X an estate of inheritance forthwith which reverted to the donor when X and all his issue were dead.

These must be contrasted with—

    (iii) a gift to X and the heirs of his body by a particular wife, which was an example of a *maritagium*; this gave X a mere life estate which swelled to a fee simple on birth of issue and sank into a life estate if all the issue predeceased X.[22]

---

[18] *Post,* pp. 160 *et seq.*
[19] *Ante,* p. 31.
[20] *Post,* pp. 43, 44.
[21] See 2 P. & M. 15, 16; 3 H.E.L. 111.
[22] See 3 H.E.L. 112, 113.

Before the end of the reign of Henry III in 1272, the courts had adopted a fixed construction of all gifts to a man and the heirs of his body, derived from a combination of the rules governing the above three cases. In all cases the words " heirs of the body " seem to have been read as if they imposed a condition that issue should be born, as in (i) above, the donee taking a fee conditional upon birth of issue, or, more shortly, a conditional fee. On the birth of issue, the donee was taken to have performed the condition for the purposes of alienation (*e.g.,* sale), forfeiture or escheat, and charging (as by charging it with the payment of £10 per annum): for these three purposes his position was the same as if he had a fee simple; this was borrowed from (i). Issue of the donee who succeeded to the land were in this respect in the same position as the donee. But subject to any of these events having occurred, the estate reverted to the donor when the donee and all his issue were dead; this was borrowed from (ii) and (iii).[23]

Such a construction had at least the merit of making land more easily alienable, but it was unpopular on account of the power of the donee on birth of issue to defeat both the expectations of his issue and the reversion of the grantor by alienating the land. The intentions of settlors were constantly being frustrated, and to remedy this the Statute *De Donis* was passed in 1285.

2. 1285–1834 : fee tail barrable by recovery or fine.

(a) *The new estate.* Strictly speaking, the Statute *De Donis* 1285 did not create any new estate but merely modified the rules relating to conditional fees.[24] Nevertheless this modification was so important that the estate was thenceforward renamed " fee tail," and for all practical purposes it may be regarded as a new estate.[25] The statute provided that in the case of these conditional gifts, the will of the donor should be observed *secundum formam in carta doni expressam* (according to the form expressed in the deed of gift) and that notwithstanding any alienation by the donee, the land should descend to his issue on his death and revert to the donor when the donee and all his issue were dead. Thus if the donee died leaving several sons, the eldest would inherit, except that if the customs of gavelkind or borough English applied, the land would pass to the heir of the donee's body according to the custom.[26]

23 *Ibid.*
24 Challis R.P. 60, 287, 288.
25 See *Willion* v. *Berkeley* (1561) 1 Plowd. 223 at 248.
26 Rob.Gav. 119, 120.

The name " fee tail " was given to the estate thus created, since the word " tail " showed that the fee was *talliatum* or *taillé, i.e.* cut down; unlike the fee simple, which could descend to any class of heirs, a fee tail could descend to only one class, namely, issue of the donee. Notwithstanding any act of the original tenant or his issue the land was bound to descend to the issue in tail in the proper way. The statute did not prevent a tenant in tail from alienating the land, but the estate so created could be defeated by his issue after his death. Nor could the rights of the issue be prejudiced by the tenant levying a fine (a fine being a collusive action in which the tenant agreed to judgment being entered against him [27]) or by any act of escheat or forfeiture. The statute " established a general perpetuity by Act of Parliament." [28] For nearly two centuries landowners were thus able to secure the unbroken descent of their land. However, freedom of alienation was ultimately secured by the ingenuity of practitioners and the courts. Two methods of " barring the entail " were evolved: the common recovery and the fine.

(b) *The common recovery. Taltarum's Case*,[29] decided in 1472, shows that there was then in full working order a process whereby a tenant in tail could bar the entail by means of a recently invented collusive action known as a " common recovery." The process employed was that an action claiming the land was brought against the tenant in tail with his consent; the court was prepared to allow this claim, provided judgment was entered against some third party for land of equal value to compensate the disappointed heirs. Consequently some " man of straw " was found against whom the second judgment could be given, and the matter could then proceed. The result of the action was that the tenant in tail was able to dispose of the whole fee simple, thus defeating the claims not only of the heirs of his body, but also those of any person entitled to any subsequent remainder, reversion or other estate. However, the action could be brought only by, or with the concurrence of, the person seised of the land; if land was given " to A for life, remainder to B and the heirs of his body," B could not suffer a recovery without the co-operation of A.

(c) *The fine.* A fine was a solemn form of conveyance whereby an agreement to convey the land was entered in the court records in the form of a compromise to an action. It was of earlier origin

[27] See *infra.*
[28] *Mildmay's Case* (1605) 6 Co.Rep. 40a.
[29] Y.B. 12 Edw. 4, Mich., pl. 25, f. 19a.

than the common recovery, but it did not become available for
barring entails until some time later. The judges' dislike of
unbarrable entails gave rise to judicial decisions which made it
possible for entails to be barred by common recoveries, but as the
Statute *De Donis* 1285 expressly prohibited the barring of entails
by fines, legislation was necessary to make fines effective. The Statute
of Fines 1489 was thought to have made a fine effective to bar the
issue in tail unless they asserted their rights within five years of the
fine, and the Statute of Fines 1540 confirmed this construction and
made the fine immediately effective to bar the issue.

A fine could be levied without the concurrence of the person
seised, but it was not so effective as a common recovery, for
although it barred the rights of the issue in tail, it did not bar the
owner of any subsequent remainder, reversion or other estate.[30]
The estate produced by a fine was known as a " base fee." In
effect a base fee was a fee simple which endured for as long as the
entail would have continued if it had not been barred, and determined when the entail would have ended.[31] Thus, if land was
limited to A for life, remainder to B in tail, remainder to C in fee
simple, and B barred his entail by a fine in favour of X, X took a
base fee. X remained entitled to the land for as long as B or any
of his issue lived, but when they were all dead, C became entitled
to the land.

A fine could be levied by one who had no entail but merely a
spes successionis, or only a contingent or executory interest in tail,[32]
i.e., an entail to which he would be entitled only if some specified
event occurred.[33] For example, a fine could be levied in B's lifetime
by one of his children and this would be effective to bar the entail
if it descended to that child or his issue in tail; and B could bar
his entail even if it was given to him conditionally upon his outliving
X, and X was still alive. But a person with only a *spes successionis*
could not suffer a recovery. It should also be noticed that not even
a recovery barred estates *prior* to the entail. Thus in the above
example a recovery suffered by B would not affect A's life estate.

(d) *Differences between fines and recoveries.* The main differences between fines and recoveries may be summarised as follows:

[30] *Margaret Podger's Case* (1613) 9 Co.Rep. 104a.
[31] *Ante*, p. 34.
[32] See *post*, pp. 84, 94.
[33] *The Case of Fines* (1602) 3 Co.Rep. 84a at 90a, b.

FINE	RECOVERY
(i) Action compromised.	(i) Action proceeded to judgment.
(ii) Consent of freehold tenant in possession not required.	(ii) Consent of freehold tenant in possession essential.
(iii) Not confined to owners of entails in possession.	(iii) Available only to owners of entails in possession.
(iv) Produced a base fee.	(iv) Produced a fee simple absolute.

Both these methods of barring entails became purely formal; all that a tenant had to do was to instruct his lawyers to take the necessary steps. It may seem strange that by means of a recovery the rights of any remainderman or reversioner could be completely defeated, but the courts were prepared to sacrifice him upon the altar of free alienability of land. Thus in the above example, during A's lifetime C's fee simple was safe if A refused to co-operate with B in barring the entail; but if A consented to this, or died, C was completely at B's mercy. However, although there was no legal obstacle to the barring of an entail, fines and recoveries were dilatory, complicated and expensive. By the Fines and Recoveries Act 1833, fines and recoveries were abolished and replaced by a simple method of barring entails.

3. After the Fines and Recoveries Act 1833. This masterpiece of parliamentary draftmanship substantially preserved the distinction between fines and recoveries, although the actions themselves were abolished. The Act provided that an entail could be barred by any assurance (*i.e.,* any conveyance or other transfer) by which a fee simple could be disposed of, except a will. It was essential, however, that the assurance should be either made or evidenced by a deed; and a mere declaration by deed that the entail was barred was not enough, for an assurance was what the Act required.[34] If the tenant barring the entail wished to retain the land himself, he conveyed it to some trustee for him; if he wished to dispose of it, he made the disentailing assurance in favour of the grantee. It was necessary for every disentailing assurance to be enrolled within six calendar months of execution, formerly in the Court of Chancery, and later in the Central Office of the Supreme Court.[35] A conveyance

---

[34] Fines and Recoveries Act 1833, ss. 15, 40; see *Carter* v. *Carter* [1896] 1 Ch. 62 (declaration of trust sufficient).
[35] Fines and Recoveries Act 1833, s. 41.

which did not comply with the provisions of the Act did not bar
the issue or the reversioner or remainderman.

The effect of a disentailing assurance varied according to whether
or not a protectorship of the settlement existed. If the tenant in
tail was entitled in possession to the land, there was no protectorship.[36]
But if he was not entitled in possession under the instrument creating
the entail and some other person was (as where land was held by
A for life, with remainder to B in tail), then there was a protectorship.
The protector of a settlement was—

> (i) not more than three persons appointed by the settlor to act
> as protector; such persons together constituted what was
> known as the "special protector." In default of a special
> protector, the protector was—
>
> (ii) the beneficial [37] owner of the first subsisting estate under the
> settlement which was not a mere lease for years.[38]

It was unusual to appoint a special protector. The usual form
of settlement gave the land to one person for life with remainder to
other persons in tail, with an ultimate remainder in fee simple, *e.g.,*
to A for life, remainder to B in tail, remainder to C in fee simple. In
such a case, there was a protectorship for as long as A lived. If no
special protector had been appointed, A was the natural protector.
But as soon as B's entail ceased to be in remainder and vested in
possession (as on A's death) the protectorship, whether special or
natural ceased.

The importance of the protectorship was that while it existed, a
disentailing assurance executed without the protector's consent
produced only a base fee. But if there was no protectorship, or if
there was a protector but he concurred in the disposition, a disentailing assurance conveyed a fee simple absolute.[39] This in effect
preserved the distinction between fines and recoveries. The protector was absolutely unfettered in exercising his discretion whether
or not to concur in the disentailment and accordingly could refuse
to concur unless he was given a bribe.[40]

Under the Act there was still power to bar a contingent or executory interest in tail, but not a mere hope of becoming entitled.
Thus if an entail is limited to whoever becomes entitled to a peerage

---

[36] *Ibid.* s. 22.
[37] See *Re Blandy Jenkins' Estate* [1917] 1 Ch. 46.
[38] Fines and Recoveries Act 1833, ss. 22, 32.
[39] *Ibid.* ss. 15, 22, 32, 34.
[40] *Bankes* v. *Baroness Le Despencer* (1843) 11 Sim. 508 at 527.

and the bar is effected by a possible future peer, the interest is contingent, and the bar is effective.[41] But issue in tail, *e.g.*, the eldest son of a tenant in tail, cannot now bar his possibility of succeeding to the entail.[42]

II. RIGHTS OF A TENANT IN TAIL

In general, a tenant in tail has the same rights of enjoyment of the land as a tenant in fee simple. He may thus commit all kinds of waste, including equitable waste, even if he is restrained from barring the entail by statute.[43] His position as regards alienation has been considered above although it may be noted that not until the sixteenth century was he able to grant leases binding after his death. A statute of 1540 [44] authorised him to grant leases for not more than twenty-one years or a period of three lives, and laid down that such leases should bind the tenant's issue but not any remainderman or reversioner. This was so until the middle of the nineteenth century, when considerable alterations were made in the law.[45]

III. TYPES OF ENTAIL

The various types of entail, such as special tail and tail male, have already been considered.[46]

IV. PRESENT LAW

The Law of Property Act 1925 has made some important amendments to the law of entails, but the general principles remain as before 1926. The following are the chief points to note.

1. Existence only in equity. It is no longer possible for a legal fee tail to exist.[47] After 1925, all entails must exist behind a trust; this means that the legal estate in fee simple must be vested in some trustees or trustee (who may be the tenant in tail himself) on trust for the person entitled in tail and everyone else interested in the land. This does not impair the benefits accruing from the

---

[41] Fines and Recoveries Act 1833, s. 15; *Re St. Albans' W.T.* [1963] Ch. 365.
[42] Fines and Recoveries Act 1833, s. 20.
[43] *Lord Glenorchy* v. *Bosville* (1733) Ca.t.Talb. 3 at 16; *Att.-Gen.* v. *Duke of Marlborough* (1818) 3 Madd. 498.
[44] 32 Hen. 8, c. 28.
[45] *Post*, pp. 144 *et seq.*
[46] *Ante*, p. 25.
[47] L.P.A. 1925, s. 1; *post*, p. 73.

land; only the bare legal ownership is affected. Since an entail is no longer an estate in the land itself, but only an interest under a trust, the proper title for an entail is no longer " estate tail " or " fee tail," but " entailed interest." Similarly a " base fee " can no longer be a legal estate but exists only as an equitable interest in the nature of a base fee. The Fines and Recoveries Act 1833 applies to these equitable interests in the same way as it applied to the legal estates before 1926.[48]

2. Personalty entailable. Any property, real or personal, may be entailed after 1925.[49] This was not so before 1926 for the Statute *De Donis* 1285 applied only to " tenements." [50] Thus the land itself, and inheritable rights in realty such as perpetual rentcharges (*e.g.,* £100 per annum charged on Blackacre) could be entailed, but life estates (which were not inheritable) and leaseholds and other personalty could not be entailed.[51] Before 1926, a gift of personalty " to A and the heirs of his body " or " to A in tail " gave A the absolute ownership of the personalty, whether the gift was by deed or will.[52] Informal words such as " to A and his issue " or " to A and his descendants " usually gave the property to A and such of his issue or descendants as were alive at the relevant date.[53]

Since 1925, entails can be created in personalty, and all the rules applying to entails of realty, including the words of limitation required, barring the entail, interests equivalent to a base fee, and the like, apply to entails of personalty. However, it is expressly provided that if after 1925 personalty is directed " to be enjoyed or held with, or upon trusts corresponding to trusts affecting," land which is already held in tail, this will be sufficient to entail the personalty.[54]

3. No new special protectors. Although any special protector appointed before 1926 continues in office, no special protector can be appointed after 1925.[55]

---

[48] L.P.(Am.)A. 1924, 9th Sched.
[49] L.P.A. 1925, s. 130.
[50] Challis R.P. 43, 47, 61.
[51] But see *post,* p. 48, as to life estates.
[52] *Dawson* v. *Small* (1874) 9 Ch.App. 651 ; and see *Portman* v. *Viscount Portman* [1922] 2 A.C. 473.
[53] *Re Hammond* [1924] 2 Ch. 276.
[54] L.P.A. 1925, s. 130 (4).
[55] L.P.A. 1925, 7th Sched.

4. No enrolment. A disentailing assurance made after 1925 need not be enrolled.[56]

5. Barring by will. Under the Law of Property Act 1925, s. 176, a tenant in tail can now bar his entail by will, and thus dispose of the fee simple. However, this power is subject to a number of limitations:

(a) It applies only to entails in possession: there is no power to bar an entail in remainder by will, even if the protector consents.

(b) The tenant in tail must be of full age.

(c) The will must be either executed after 1925 or confirmed by a codicil executed after 1925.

(d) The will must refer specifically either to—

(i) the property (*e.g.*, " Blackacre "),[57] or

(ii) the instrument under which it was acquired (*e.g.*, " all the property to which I succeeded under X's will "), or

(iii) entails generally (*e.g.*, " all property to which I am entitled in tail ").

This power extends to all entailed property, whether real or personal, whenever the entail was created. Further, it allows the owner of a base fee in possession to enlarge it by a disposition by will, provided he complies with the above conditions, and provided he is capable of enlarging it into a fee simple absolute without the consent of anyone else. But the section does not apply to a tenant in tail after possibility or to a tenant in tail restrained by statute from barring his entail.[58] Except so far as is necessary to give effect to the will, the entail or base fee is unaffected; thus if instead of disposing of the fee simple in the entailed land the testator merely devises a life interest, the entail will resume its natural devolution when the life interest ceases.

V. BASE FEES

The nature and mode of creation of base fees have already been considered.[59] The uncertainty of the duration of a base fee makes it an unsatisfactory interest in land, but it can be enlarged into a

---

[56] L.P.A. 1925, s. 133.

[57] See *Acheson* v. *Russell* [1951] Ch. 67.

[58] For these, see *post*, pp. 44, 45.

[59] *Ante*, pp. 34, 38, 40.

fee simple absolute in a number of ways. If land is given to A for life, remainder to B in tail, remainder to C in fee simple, a base fee created by B can be enlarged as follows:

(1) By the former tenant in tail (*i.e.,* B) executing a fresh disentailing assurance with the consent of the protector or after the protectorship has ceased (*e.g.,* after A's death). This can be done even after the base fee has been conveyed to a purchaser.[60]

(2) By the owner of the base fee acquiring the whole of the remainder or reversion in fee simple (*i.e.,* by B, or any person to whom he has conveyed the base fee, acquiring C's fee simple). This does not merge the base fee in the remainder or reversion and so subject the owner of the base fee to any burdens attached to the remainder or reversion, such as a mortgage, but enlarges the base fee into a fee simple absolute free from any incumbrances on the remainder or reversion.[61]

(3) By the owner of the base fee (*i.e.,* B or anyone to whom he has conveyed it) remaining in possession of the land for twelve years after the protectorship has ceased.[62]

(4) By a gift by will complying with section 176 of the Law of Property Act 1925.[63] This power is exercisable only by a person who is entitled to a base fee in possession and who could enlarge it without the concurrence of any person. Thus B can enlarge the base fee by will if the protectorship has ceased before he dies; but if B has conveyed the base fee to some third person, that person cannot enlarge it by will under any circumstances.

VI. INTERESTS IN TAIL AFTER POSSIBILITY

On the death of the specified spouse of a tenant in special tail without leaving any issue capable of inheriting the entail, the tenant becomes "a tenant in tail after possibility of issue extinct," the last three words usually being omitted for brevity. For example, if land is given "to A and the heirs of his body begotten on Mary," on the death of Mary without leaving issue, A is a tenant in tail after possibility. Such a tenant is in a peculiar position.

(a) He cannot bar the entail.[64]

---

[60] Fines and Recoveries Act 1833, ss. 19, 35; *Bankes* v. *Small* (1887) 36 Ch.D. 716.
[61] Fines and Recoveries Act 1833, s. 39.
[62] Limitation Act 1939, s. 11.
[63] *Ante*, p. 43.
[64] Fines and Recoveries Act 1833, s. 18.

(b) Yet although virtually in the position of a tenant for life, he is still technically a tenant in tail. Thus like all tenants in tail he is not liable for voluntary waste (damage to the land), although a tenant for life is: but he will be restrained from committing equitable waste (wanton destruction).[65]

An interest in tail after possibility can arise only on the death of the spouse specified in the limitation; it cannot arise out of a tail general, for even if the tenant in tail is unmarried and of a great age, it is always deemed possible that he or she will marry and have issue.[66]

VII. UNBARRABLE ENTAILS

1. No unbarrable entails. The common law rule which developed at the end of the sixteenth century was that it was impossible to create an unbarrable entail. By means of fines and recoveries, all entails could be barred, and any attempt to restrain the tenant from doing this was ineffective. Thus a condition that the tenant should not suffer a common recovery was repugnant to the entail and so void.[67] This rule was not affected by the Fines and Recoveries Act 1833.

2. Exceptions. Despite this general rule, there are certain entails which cannot be barred. These are:

(i) An interest in tail after possibility.

(ii) Entails created by the Crown for services rendered to the Crown, the reversion being in the Crown.[68]

(iii) Entails made unbarrable by special Acts of Parliament, such as the entails given to reward the first Duke of Marlborough and the first Duke of Wellington.[69]

3. Persons. Certain persons are unable to bar an entail, even if the entail is one which can be barred.

(i) An infant is generally regarded as being unable effectively to bar an entail. This disability is exploited to keep settled property tied up for as long as possible.[70]

---

[65] *Williams* v. *Williams* (1810) 12 East 209; *Cooke* v. *Whaley* (1701) 1 Eq.Ca.Abr. 400. For waste, see *post*, p. 49.   [66] Co.Litt. 28a.

[67] *Sir Anthony Mildmay's Case* (1605) 6 Co.Rep. 40a.

[68] Fines and Recoveries Act 1833, s. 18.

[69] 6 Anne, cc. 6, 7, 1706; 54 Geo. 3, c. 161, 1814.

[70] *Post*, p. 202; but see p. 517.

(ii) A person of unsound mind (under the Mental Health Act 1959 called a "patient") cannot bar his entails; but his receiver [71] can do so, under an order of the Court of Protection.[72]

(iii) A bankrupt cannot bar his entails; this can be done only by the trustee in bankruptcy.[73]

C. The Life Estate

After 1925 an interest in land for life can no longer exist as a legal estate but only as an equitable interest.[74] In general, the law of life estates set out below applies equally to the corresponding life interests after 1925.

I. TYPES OF LIFE ESTATE

The two types of life estate were the ordinary life estate and the estate *pur autre vie.*

1. Estate for the life of the tenant. The normal type of life estate was one for the life of the tenant. This arose either—

(i) by express limitation, as by a grant "to A for life" [75]; or

(ii) by operation of law, as in the case of curtesy and dower.[76]

2. Estate pur autre vie.

(a) *Nature of the estate.* An estate *pur autre vie* was an estate for the life of someone other than the tenant,[77] the person whose life measured the duration of the estate being called the "*cestui que vie*" (pronounced "setty ker vee"). An estate *pur autre vie* could arise either—

(i) by the owner of a life estate assigning it to another: *nemo dat quod non habet* (nobody can give what he has not got), so that the assignor could create no interest which would last for longer than his own life; or

(ii) by express grant, *e.g.,* "to A for the life of X."

---

[71] See *post*, p. 523.
[72] Mental Health Act 1959, s. 103 (1).
[73] Bankruptcy Act 1914, s. 55. The former disability of married women is obsolete.
[74] *Post*, p. 72.
[75] *Ante*, p. 28.
[76] See *post*, pp. 294 *et seq.*
[77] See, generally, *Doe* d. *Jeff* v. *Robinson* (1828) 2 Man. & Ry. 249.

Both types of life estate were estates of freehold, but neither was a freehold of inheritance, for they were not capable of descending to the tenant's heir on his death. A life estate ceased automatically when the tenant died, and although an estate *pur autre vie* continued during the life of the *cestui que vie* despite the tenant's death, it did not descend to the tenant's heir as such but passed according to the special rules of occupancy set out below.

Both types of life estate could be made determinable or subject to conditions subsequent [78] and were in general subject to similar rights and burdens.

(b) *Occupancy.* At common law, a tenant *pur autre vie* could not devise his estate, for it always devolved on his death according to the rules of occupancy.

(1) SPECIAL OCCUPANCY. If an estate *pur autre vie* was granted " to A and his heirs," on A's death the land passed to the special occupant for the rest of the life of the *cestui que vie.* The special occupant was always A's heir, who had a special right of occupation by reason of the mention of " heirs " in the grant: the heir did not take by descent from A, and was not liable for A's debts.[79]

(2) GENERAL OCCUPANCY. If an estate *pur autre vie* was merely granted " to A " without any mention of his heirs, A's heirs had no claim to the land [80] and there would be no freehold tenant. To avoid this, it was settled that the first person to enter the land after A's death should become entitled to it by general occupancy for the rest of the life of the *cestui que vie,* free from liability for A's debts.[81]

This somewhat odd position was changed by the Statute of Frauds 1677.[82] By this—

(i) a tenant *pur autre vie* was enabled to dispose of his interest by will;

(ii) if he failed to do so and there was no special occupant, the estate devolved on the tenant's personal representatives;

(iii) whether it passed to the heir or personal representatives, it was made available for the payment of the debts of the deceased.

---

[78] *Brandon* v. *Robinson* (1811) 18 Ves. 429 ; and see *Re Evans's Contract* [1920] 2 Ch. 469 ; see also *ante,* pp. 30, 31.

[79] See *Doe* d. *Blake* v. *Luxton* (1795) 6 T.R. 289 at 291.

[80] *Re Sheppard* [1897] 2 Ch. 67.

[81] Challis R.P. 359.

[82] s. 12.

Although the statute prevented any new general occupancy from arising, it failed to state whether the personal representatives could keep the estate for themselves or whether they held it for those entitled under the intestacy. The Common Recoveries Act 1740 [83] resolved the doubt by providing that the personal representatives should hold on trust for the next-of-kin of the tenant, *i.e.*, for those entitled on intestacy to the tenant's personal property. These statutory provisions had no application to special occupancy.

In the case of copyholds, the seisin was in the lord and so there was no need of a general occupant to prevent it from falling into abeyance. The rules of general occupancy thus did not apply unless there was a custom to the contrary, and on the death of the tenant the lord was entitled to the land.[84] But the rules of special occupancy applied to copyholds.[85]

No special occupancy can arise if a tenant *pur autre vie* dies after 1925; in every case the tenant's interests passes to his personal representatives who hold it on trust for the persons entitled under his will or intestacy.[86]

(c) *Quasi-entails.* An estate *pur autre vie,* not being an estate of inheritance, could not be entailed under *De Donis* 1285.[87] But if an estate for the life of X was granted " to Z and the heirs of his body " an estate known as a quasi-entail was created. Until terminated by X's death, this estate devolved on the heirs of Z's body successively in the same way as an entail, but it was not a true entail because the heirs took not by descent but as special occupants.[88] Subject to this theoretical distinction, the rules applicable to entails, *e.g.,* as to the barring of entails governed quasi-entails; the analogy between estates created out of a fee simple and those created out of a life estate was developed as far as possible.[89]

II. POSITION OF A TENANT FOR LIFE AT COMMON LAW

In considering the position of a tenant for life at common law, an important part is played by the law of waste (particularly as to timber and minerals), and the rules governing emblements and fixtures.

---

[83] s. 9.
[84] *Smartle* v. *Penhallow* (1703) 2 Ld.Raym. 994 at 1000.
[85] *Doe* d. *Lempriere* v. *Martin* (1777) 2 Wm.Bl. 1148.
[86] *Post,* p. 314.
[87] *Grey* v. *Mannock* (1765) 2 Eden 339 at 340.
[88] *Ex p. Sterne* (1801) 6 Ves. 156 at 158.
[89] *Re Barber's S.E.* (1881) 18 Ch.D. 624 at 629.

Waste

Although the law of waste is of importance in other connections, notably in the law of landlord and tenant, it is most suitably considered in relation to life interests, where it is applicable both to ordinary life interests and to interests *pur autre vie*. Technically, waste consists of any act which alters the nature of the land, whether for the better or for the worse, *e.g.*, the conversion of arable land into a wood or vice versa. Four types of waste must be considered, namely, ameliorating, permissive, voluntary and equitable waste.

1. Ameliorating waste. Alterations which improve the land, such as converting dilapidated store buildings into dwellings or a farm into a market garden, constitute ameliorating waste. Since the decision of the House of Lords in *Doherty* v. *Allman* [90] in 1878 the court is unlikely to grant an injunction to restrain such waste.

2. Permissive waste. This consists of the failure to do that which ought to be done, as by the non-repair of buildings or the failure to clean out a ditch or moat so as to prevent the foundations becoming rotten.[91] But mere non-cultivation of land is not permissive waste.[92] A tenant for life is not liable for permissive waste unless an obligation to repair is imposed upon him by the terms of the limitation under which he holds.[93]

3. Voluntary waste. Voluntary waste is " the committing of any spoil or destruction in houses, lands, etc., by tenants, to the damage of the heir, or of him in reversion or remainder." [94] Literally, this would include equitable waste, but the term voluntary waste is usually reserved for such voluntary waste as does not amount to equitable waste. Such acts as opening and working a mine in the land (but not merely working a mine already open),[95] or cutting timber,[96] are examples of voluntary waste. Timber consists of oak, ash and elm trees which are at least twenty years old and not too old to have a reasonably quantity of usable wood in them. Other trees may rank

---

[90] 3 App.Cas. 709 (conversion of dilapidated barracks into dwelling-houses by tenant for years).
[91] See, *e.g.*, *Powys* v. *Blagrave* (1854) 4 De G.M. & G. 448.
[92] *Hutton* v. *Warren* (1836) 1 M. & W. 466 at 472.
[93] *Re Cartwright* (1889) 41 Ch.D. 532.
[94] Bacon's *Abridgement*, 7th ed., Vol. 8, p. 379, definition of waste.
[95] See *Dashwood* v. *Magniac* [1891] 3 Ch. 306 at 360.
[96] *Honywood* v. *Honywood* (1874) L.R. 18 Eq. 306.

as timber by local custom, *e.g.*, beech in Buckinghamshire, willow in Hampshire and birch in Yorkshire and Cumberland; and custom may also prescribe some qualification other than an age of twenty years for the trees to be considered timber, *e.g.*, an age of twenty-four years, or a specified girth.[97]

A tenant for life is liable for voluntary waste unless his interest was granted to him by an instrument exempting him from liability for voluntary waste, *e.g.*, a grant " without impeachment of waste." [98] Where there is such an exception the tenant is said to be " unimpeachable of waste ": otherwise he is said to be " impeachable of waste." Thus if nothing is said about waste, the tenant is impeachable; in practice, however, he is usually made unimpeachable.

4. Equitable waste. " Equitable waste is that which a prudent man would not do in the management of his own property." [99] Acts of wanton destruction, such as stripping a house of all its lead, iron, glass, doors, boards, etc., to the value of £3,000,[1] or pulling down houses, or cutting timber planted for ornament or shelter (unless this is necessary for the preservation of part of the timber), fall under the head of equitable waste. A tenant for life is liable for equitable waste unless the document conferring his interest upon him shows an intention to allow him to commit equitable waste. It is not enough that his interest has been given to him without impeachment of waste; he must show that it is intended that he should be allowed to commit equitable as well as voluntary waste.[2]

Timber and minerals

Although largely governed by the general law of waste, the rights of a tenant for life with regard to timber and minerals are so important as to merit separate treatment.

1. Timber.

(a) *Estovers.* Whether impeachable of waste or not, a tenant for life can take reasonable estovers (or botes) from the land. These consist of wood and timber taken as—

(i) house-bote, for repairing the house or burning in it;

---

[97] *Ibid.* at p. 309 ; *Countess of Cumberland's Case* (1610) Moo.K.B. 812.
[98] *Re Ridge* (1885) 31 Ch.D. 504 at 507.
[99] *Turner* v. *Wright* (1860) 2 De G.F. & J. 234 at 243.
[1] *Vane* v. *Lord Barnard* (1716) 2 Vern. 738.
[2] L.P.A. 1925, s. 135.

(ii) plough-bote, for making and repairing agricultural implements; and

(iii) hay-bote, for repairing fences.

The tenant's right to house-bote does not entitle him to cut down timber in excess of his present needs in order to use it for any repairs which become necessary in the future, nor does it authorise him to sell the timber, even if he employs the proceeds in repairing, or the timber proves unfit for repairs.[3]

(b) *Timber estate.* On a timber estate (an estate cultivated mainly for the produce of saleable timber which is cut periodically), the tenant can cut and sell timber according to the rules of proper estate management even if he is impeachable of waste. The reason for this rule is that the timber properly cut on such an estate is part of the annual fruits of the land rather than part of the inheritance.[4]

(c) *Timber planted for ornament or shelter.* As has been seen,[5] it is equitable waste to cut timber planted for ornament or shelter, and only a tenant unimpeachable of equitable waste is permitted to do this.

(d) *Trees.* In general, a tenant for life, even if he is impeachable of waste, may cut dotards (dead trees not fit for use as timber) and all trees which are not timber, *e.g.*, in most cases willows or larches.[6] But there are a number of exceptions to this. It is voluntary waste to cut trees which would be timber but for their immaturity (unless the cutting is necessary to thin them out and so allow proper development) or to cut fruit trees in a garden or orchard.[7] Further, it is voluntary waste to cut wood which a prudent man would not cut, such as willows which help to hold a river bank together; and it is equitable waste to cut trees planted for ornament or shelter, or to grub up an entire wood. Where by reason of abnormal circumstances, such as extraordinary gales or war-time conditions, trees are severed before they are ripe for cutting, the court will direct that the tenant for life shall receive only part of the proceeds, the balance being held in trust for those entitled after his death.[8]

---

[3] Co.Litt. 41b, 53b.

[4] *Honywood* v. *Honywood* (1874) L.R. 18 Eq. 306 at 309, 310; *Dashwood* v. *Magniac* [1891] 3 Ch. 306.

[5] *Ante,* p. 50.

[6] *Re Harker's W.T.* [1938] Ch. 323.

[7] *Kaye* v. *Banks* (1770) Dick. 431.

[8] *Re Terry* (1918) 87 L.J.Ch. 577.

(e) *Normal rules.* Subject to the above special rules, the position is that a tenant for life who is unimpeachable of waste may cut and sell timber and keep all the proceeds.[9] But if the tenant is impeachable of waste, his only right to cut timber is that given to him by statute.[10] This authorises him to cut and sell timber ripe and fit for cutting, provided—

(i) the consent of the trustees of the settlement under which he holds his life interest, or an order of the court, is obtained; and

(ii) three-quarters of the proceeds are set aside as capital money: this means that the trustees hold this portion of the price on trust for all persons having any interest in the land, paying only the interest to the tenant for life. The remaining quarter of the proceeds is paid to the tenant for life.

(f) *Ownership of severed timber.* Until timber is severed, a tenant for life has no claim to it, so that if land is sold with the uncut timber on it, the life tenant cannot claim any share of the price even though he could lawfully have cut the timber.[11] Once the timber is severed it belongs to the life tenant if he was entitled to cut it, whether the severance was effected by the tenant, a stranger or an act of God, such as a storm: but if he was not entitled to sever it, it belongs not to him but to the owner of the next vested estate or interest of inheritance.[12]

2. Minerals. The mineral rights of a tenant for life depend on two factors, namely, whether the mine was already open when his tenancy began, and whether he is impeachable of waste.

(a) *Right to work mines.* A tenant for life may work a mine and take all the proceeds unless—

(i) he is impeachable of waste, and

(ii) the mine was not open when his tenancy began.

Where both these conditions are satisfied, he cannot work the mine at all, for to open and work an unopened mine is voluntary waste. But it is not waste to continue working a mine already open[13]

[9] *Lewis Bowles's Case* (1615) 11 Co.Rep. 79b.
[10] S.L.A. 1925, s. 66, replacing S.L.A. 1882, s. 35.
[11] *Re Llewellin* (1887) 37 Ch.D. 317.
[12] *Bewick* v. *Whitfield* (1734) 3 P.Wms. 267.
[13] See *Re Hall* [1916] 2 Ch. 488 at 493.

even if new pits are made on different parts of the same plot of land to pursue the same or a new vein, for the grantor, by opening or allowing the opening of the mines, has shown an intent that the minerals should be treated as part of the profits of the land.

(b) *Right to lease mines.* The Settled Land Act 1925 [14] authorises a tenant for life to grant mining leases for one hundred years or less, whether the mine is open or not and whether or not the tenant is impeachable of waste. In each case, subject to any contrary intention in the settlement, the tenant for life is entitled to three-quarters of the rent, except that if he is impeachable of waste and the mine is unopened, he is entitled to only one-quarter. The balance of rent is capital money and is held for the benefit of all those interested under the settlement.[15]

Emblements and fixtures

A tenant cannot foresee the date on which an estate *pur autre vie* or for his own life will determine, and so to encourage him to cultivate his land by assuring him of the fruits of his labour, the law gives him a right to emblements (pronounced *em*-blem-ents). This means that the tenant's personal representatives, or in the case of an estate *pur autre vie* the tenant himself, may enter the land after the life estate has determined and reap the crops which the tenant himself has sown.[16] This applies only to annual crops artificially produced, such as corn, hemp and flax, and not to things such as fruit trees and timber; further, it extends only to the crops actually growing at the determination of the tenancy.[17] Where the end of the tenancy is brought about by the tenant's own act (*e.g.*, where a life estate is granted to a widow until remarriage and she remarries) there is no right to emblements.[18]

Prima facie any fixtures attached to the land by a tenant for life must be left after his death for the person next entitled to the land; but trade fixtures and ornamental and domestic fixtures are excepted.[19]

[14] ss. 41, 42, 45–47, replacing earlier Acts: see *post*, pp. 171 *et seq*.
[15] S.L.A. 1925, s. 47; *Re Fitzwalter* [1943] Ch. 285.
[16] Co.Litt. 55b; *Grantham* v. *Hawley* (1615) Hob. 132.
[17] *Graves* v. *Weld* (1833) 5 B. & Ad. 105 at 119.
[18] *Oland's Case* (1602) 5 Co.Rep. 116a.
[19] See *post*, p. 378.

CHAPTER 3

LAW AND EQUITY

Part 1

GENERAL PRINCIPLES

THE difference between Law and Equity, which has already been mentioned in brief outline,[1] must now be considered in greater detail.

Sect. 1. The Historical Basis of Equity

1. The Common Law courts. The existence of Equity can best be explained historically. At the end of the thirteenth century the principal courts were (a) many local courts, held by feudal lords and others; and (b) the Royal courts, known as the Courts of Common Law, consisting of the courts of King's Bench, of Common Pleas, and of Exchequer. Each of the Royal courts at first had its own proper sphere, but by the end of the Middle Ages their jurisdictions overlapped so much that a plaintiff often had a choice between the three courts. By this time also they had attracted much of the litigation of the country, and although many of the local courts survived into the eighteenth century, most of them were in decline, or moribund.

2. The writ system. In general, no action could be started in any of the common law courts until a writ had been issued by the Chancellor. The Chancellor, who was usually an ecclesiastic, was the head of the King's Secretarial Department and occupied the position of Secretary of State for all departments. As keeper of the Great Seal with which writs were sealed, he was at the head of the English legal system.

The writs issued by the Chancellor differed for each different kind of action. Today, anyone claiming to be entitled to some remedy, such as the recovery of possession of land of which he has been dispossessed, or the payment of money owed to him, can issue a writ claiming the appropriate relief. The writ is in a form which leaves it to the plaintiff to state his claim in his own words. The same form can equally well be filled up with a claim for the possession of land as for payment of a debt, or damages for trespass: there is no special

[1] *Ante*, p. 4.

writ of ejectment, or debt, or trespass or any other matter. But in medieval days this was not so. Each different kind of action had its own writ, often with its own special procedure. " A writ of debt was very unlike a writ of trespass, and both were very unlike a writ of *mort d'ancestor* or a writ of right." [2] Often causes of action which seemed very similar in principle had separate writs. For example, if a tenant of land died and before his heir could enter the land a stranger took it, the heir could bring an action against the stranger for possession of the land. If the deceased tenant was the father of the heir, the action had to be started by a writ of *mort d'ancestor*; if he was the grandfather of the heir, *mort d'ancestor* was of no avail and a writ of *aiel* had to be used, while if he was the great-grandfather, a writ of *besaiel* was necessary. No action could succeed unless the correct writ was chosen. If a plaintiff who had inherited land from his grandfather began his action with a writ of *mort d'ancestor*, the action would fail even if he could prove conclusively that the land was his. He had to start again with a writ of *aiel* and pay the costs of his abortive action.

The selection of the correct writ was thus of great importance. Not until the Common Law Procedure Act 1852 were the old writs replaced by a single form of writ for all actions, and even then, until the Judicature Acts 1873–75 came into force, it was necessary to observe the form of action based on the old writs which was appropriate to the case. Sometimes there were two or more writs appropriate to the plaintiff's claim. Where this was so, one writ usually had procedural advantages over the other or others. For example, a plaintiff rarely chose a writ of right if it was possible to start his action by any other writ, for a writ of right was liable to be delayed by essoins, or excuses for non-appearance by the defendant, on the ground of illness or the like. A writ which had already been settled was known as a writ *de cursu*, a writ " of course," and could be obtained on paying the prescribed fee. But sometimes there was no known writ to fit the case, and the plaintiff would have to ask for the invention of a new writ.

At first new writs were invented with comparative freedom. But it did not follow that the courts would accept each new writ as being valid. Even if a suitor had surmounted the first obstacle by obtaining a writ, he might still fall at the second fence by failing to obtain the court's recognition of its validity. Nevertheless, the Register of Writs rapidly increased during the latter half of the twelfth century

[2] Maitland, *Forms of Action*, 5.

and the first half of the thirteenth: many new writs became writs *de cursu*, duly recognised by the courts.

This power to invent new writs was assailed by the barons. Recognising that the power to invent new remedies was a power to create new rights and duties, they procured the making of the Provisions of Oxford 1258, in which the Chancellor swore that he would seal no writ, except a writ *de cursu*, without the command of the King and his Council. Had this remained fully effective, it would have stifled the growth of the common law. But the Statute of Westminster II 1285 provided in the famous Chapter 24, *In Consimili Casu*, that the clerks in Chancery should have a limited power to invent new writs. If there already existed one writ and in a like case (*in consimili casu*), falling under like law and requiring like remedy, there was none, the clerks in Chancery were authorised to agree in making a writ, or else they were to refer the matter to the next Parliament. In effect, the statute authorised variations of existing writs *de cursu*, but it did not permit the invention of a totally new writ. Consequently a suitor whose grievance was not covered by a writ *de cursu*, or one *in consimili casu*, was still left without a remedy unless he could persuade Parliament to intervene.

3. Petitions to the King referred to the Chancellor. The result of this was that there were a number of cases where suitors could obtain no remedy from the courts. The only way of obtaining relief was to petition the King and his Council, for the King, as the Fountain of Justice, was regarded as having a residue of judicial power left in his hands. A petitioner might plead that he was entitled to a remedy although he could not obtain one from the common law courts. Perhaps his complaint was that his adversary had been guilty of some trick or breach of confidence; or that his adversary was rich and powerful and would bribe or intimidate jurors, and he himself was poor, old and sick; or that there had been some accident, such as the loss of a document, giving his adversary an advantage of which the common law courts, with their formal procedure, would not deprive him: and so the King was asked to find a remedy, " for the love of God and in the way of charity." Such petitions were heard by the King's Council, of which the Chancellor was an important member. The Chancellor, as keeper of the King's Conscience, was particularly well fitted to deal with such petitions, and during the reigns of Edward II and III many were referred to him. Ordinances in 1280 and 1293 and a Proclamation of 1349 provided that certain petitions should be directed to the Chancellor in the first place. After the reign of Edward III petitions were often addressed to the Chancellor alone. But although the Chancery became recognised as a court during the fourteenth and fifteenth centuries, the decisions upon the petitions were made either in the name of the King's Council or else with advice of the serjeants and judges. Not until 1474, it seems, did the Chancellor make a decree on his own authority, but after that date such decrees became frequent.[3]

4. The Court of Chancery. In this way there gradually came into existence a Court of Chancery in which the Chancellor, acting independently of the King's Council, sat as a judge administering a system of justice called Equity. After the end of the seventeenth century only lawyers were appointed to the office. Equity, which had varied with each Chancellor, began with Lord Ellesmere (1596–1617) to develop into a code of principles, and the work of Lord Nottingham (1673–82) in systematising the rules earned him the title of the Father of Equity. When Lord Eldon retired in 1827 the rules of equity were as fixed as those of the common law.

In the course of time various subsidiary officials were appointed to assist the Chancellor, a system of appeals grew up, and finally in 1875 the Chancery system was merged with the common law courts to form the present Supreme Court of Judicature. In short, what was once a method of petitioning the King for justice in exceptional cases gradually become a way of starting an action before a regular court of justice. But there were important differences between Chancery and the common law courts. The latter decided cases according to strict common law rules, and technicalities often played an important part. Chancery, on the other hand, mitigated the rigour of the common law, deciding cases in the light of what had seemed just and equitable to generations of Chancellors, and technical pleas were usually unsuccessful. Further, the common law courts were mainly concerned with enforcing the strict rights of the plaintiff regardless of his conduct, whereas Chancery was a court of conscience in which the court was technically more concerned with cleansing the conscience of the defendant, compelling him to disgorge any ill-gotten gains by acting *in personam* (on his person), *e.g.*, by imprisoning him. Consequently there was a marked difference between legal rights, the name for rights enforced by the courts of law, and equitable rights, enforced only by equity; this must now be examined in some detail.

[3] 1 H.E.L. 400–404.

Sect. 2. The Nature of Equitable Rights

A. *Distinction Between Legal and Equitable Rights*

At first sight it might seem that as long as a person had a right which
would be enforced by some court, it mattered little which court it was.
But there is a great difference between legal and equitable rights. This
is sometimes expressed by saying that " legal rights are rights *in rem,*
equitable rights are rights *in personam.*" A legal interest in land is
a right in the land itself, so that whoever acquires the land is bound
by that right, whether he knew of it or not. Equity, on the other
hand, would enforce equitable rights only against certain persons.
For example, if land was conveyed to T in fee simple on trust for A
in fee simple, there was at first no court which would compel T to
carry out his trust. Equity, however, began to intervene on behalf
of A if T was guilty of a breach of trust, and so A's interest, being
enforceable in equity but not at law, was merely equitable. It was a
right *in personam* enforceable against T alone, so that if he died or
conveyed the land to another, the trust would not be enforced against
the new tenant.

Then successive extensions were made. In 1465 it was laid down
that a trust would be enforced against anyone who took a conveyance
of the land with notice of the trust,[4] in 1483 the Chancellor said that
he would enforce a trust against the trustee's heir,[5] and in 1522 it was
said that a trust would be enforced against anyone to whom the land
had been given.[6] After it had been decided that others such as the
executors and creditors of the trustees would be bound by the trust,
it finally became established as one of the most important rules of
equity that trusts and other equitable rights would be enforced against
everyone except a bona fide purchaser of a legal estate for value without notice of these rights, or somebody claiming through such a
person. Equitable rights thus gradually came to look less and less
like mere rights *in personam* and more and more like rights *in rem.*
Although it is possible still to regard them as rights *in personam,* it is
perhaps best to treat them as hybrids, being neither entirely one nor
entirely the other. They have never reached the status of rights
in rem, yet the class of persons against whom they will be enforced is
too large for mere rights *in personam.*

4 Y.B. 5 Edw. 4, Mich., pl. 16.
5 Y.B. 22 Edw. 4, Pasch., pl. 18.
6 Y.B. 14 Hen. 8, Mich., pl. 5 at p. 7.

The difference between legal and equitable rights as regards a purchaser without notice may be illustrated as follows. In 1920 X bought the fee simple in Blackacre. In 1921 he granted a legal easement of way across one corner to L, and an equitable easement of way across the other corner to E. As long as X still owned Blackacre, no substantial difference appeared between the rights of L and E: both were enforceable against X. But as soon as the land was conveyed to a third party, Y, the distinction between the rights of L and E became apparent. Even if Y purchased the land without notice of L's easement, it bound him, for it was a right *in rem.* But if Y could prove that he was a bona fide purchaser for value of a legal estate without notice of E's easement, he took free from it.

This doctrine of purchaser without notice must now be considered more fully.

B. The Purchaser Without Notice

The plea of purchaser of a legal estate for value without notice is " an absolute, unqualified, unanswerable defence." [7] The onus of proof lies on the person setting it up: it is a single plea, and cannot be regarded as a plea of a purchaser for value, to be met by a reply of notice. [8] The principal points to note are as follows.

1. Bona fide. The purchaser must act in good faith.

2. Purchaser for value. The words " for value " are included to show that value must have been given, because " purchaser " in its technical sense does not necessarily imply this. [9] " Value " includes money, money's worth (*e.g.,* other land, or stocks and shares) and marriage. [10] The value need not be full value, [11] but it must all have been actually paid or given before the purchaser receives notice of the equity. [12] " Money or money's worth " usually consists of some present consideration in the sense used in the law of contract, but it also includes the satisfaction of an existing debt. [13] " Marriage," however, extends only to a future marriage; an ante-nuptial agreement (*i.e.,* a promise made in consideration of future marriage) is

---

[7] *Pilcher* v. *Rawlins* (1872) 7 Ch.App. 259 at 269.
[8] *Wilkes* v. *Spooner* [1911] 2 K.B. 473 at 486.
[9] See *post,* p. 289.
[10] *Wormald* v. *Maitland* (1866) 35 L.J.Ch. 69 at 73.
[11] *Basset* v. *Nosworthy* (1673) Rep.t.Finch. 102.
[12] *Tourville* v. *Naish* (1734) 3 P.Wms. 307.
[13] See *Thorndike* v. *Hunt* (1859) 3 De G. & J. 563.

deemed to have been made for value, but a promise made in respect of a past marriage (a post-nuptial agreement) is not. When an ante-nuptial marriage settlement is made, valuable consideration is deemed to have been given both by the spouse and by the unborn issue of the marriage.[14] " Good consideration " (the natural love and affection which a person has for his near relatives) is of small importance and does not amount to value.[15] " Purchaser " is not confined to a person who acquires a fee simple; it includes, for example, mortgagees and lessees, who are purchasers *pro tanto* (to the extent of their interests).[16]

3. Of a legal estate. The purchaser normally must show that he has acquired some legal estate in the land and not a mere equitable interest.[17] If the purchaser acquires merely an equitable interest, his equity is later in time than the prior equitable interest, and as between competing equities the first in time normally prevails; where part of the equitable interest is already vested in the owner of the prior equity, the subsequent purchaser can take only what remains.[18]

There are three qualifications to this rule.

(a) *Better right to legal estate.* A purchaser without notice who acquires only an equitable interest will nevertheless take free from equities if his purchase gives him the better right to a legal estate. Thus if a legal estate is conveyed not to the purchaser but to a trustee for him, and the trustee is also without notice, the purchaser takes free from equities.[19]

(b) *Subsequent acquisition of legal estate.* A purchaser without notice who at the time of his purchase fails to obtain either a legal estate or the better right to one will nevertheless prevail over a prior equity if he subsequently gets in a legal estate, even if he then has notice of the equity. As between himself and the owner of the prior equity, there is equal equity, and the legal estate will prevail.[20] But if the purchaser knowingly acquires the legal estate in breach of trust, he will not take free from the interests of the beneficiaries under that trust.[21]

---

[14] *Macdonald* v. *Scott* [1893] A.C. 642 at 650.
[15] *Cf. post*, p. 242.
[16] See *Goodright* d. *Humphreys* v. *Moses* (1774) 2 Wm.Bl. 1019.
[17] See *Pilcher* v. *Rawlins* (1872) 7 Ch.App. 259 at 268, 269.
[18] *Phillips* v. *Phillips* (1862) 4 De G.F. & J. 208 at 216 ; *Cave* v. *Cave* (1880) 15 Ch.D. 639.
[19] See *Assaf* v. *Fuwa* [1955] A.C. 215.
[20] *Bailey* v. *Barnes* [1894] 1 Ch. 25 ; and see *post*, p. 511.
[21] *Harpham* v. *Shacklock* (1881) 19 Ch.D. 207.

(c) *Mere equities.* Although a purchaser of an equitable interest without notice of prior equitable interests does not take free from them, he takes free from any " mere equities " of which he has no notice.[22] Mere equities fall short of being actual interests in the land, and in the main are rights to equitable relief in respect of property. They include the right to have a transaction set aside for fraud [23] or to have an instrument rectified for mistake, as where by mistake a lease stated the rent to be £130 a year instead of £230 a year.[24]

4. Without notice. There are three kinds of notice.

(a) *Actual notice.* A person has actual notice of all facts of which he has actual knowledge, however that knowledge was acquired; but he is not regarded as having actual notice of facts which have come to his ears only in the form of vague rumours.[25] By statute, a number of rights have become registrable in the registers of land charges, and it has been provided that registration of such rights constitutes actual notice; this subject is dealt with below.[26]

(b) *Constructive notice.* A person has constructive notice of all facts of which he would have acquired actual notice had he made those inquiries and inspections which he ought reasonably to have made, the standard of prudence being that of men of business under similar circumstances.[27] Thus a purchaser has constructive notice of a fact if he—

(i) had actual notice that there was some incumbrance and a proper inquiry would have revealed what it was, or

(ii) has, whether deliberately or carelessly, abstained from making those inquiries that a prudent purchaser would have made.[28]

The occupation of land by a tenant is notice to a purchaser of the rights of the tenant in the land, though not of any " mere equity," such as his right to apply to the court to have his tenancy agreement rectified,[29] nor of the rights of the landlord [30]; and notice that property

---

[22] *Phillips* v. *Phillips* (1862) 4 De G.F. & J. 208; *Cave* v. *Cave* (1880) 15 Ch.D. 639.
[23] *Ernest* v. *Vivian* (1863) 33 L.J.Ch. 513.
[24] *Garrard* v. *Frankel* (1862) 30 Beav. 445.
[25] *Lloyd* v. *Banks* (1868) 3 Ch.App. 488; *Barnhart* v. *Greenshields* (1853) 9 Moo.P.C. 18 at 36.
[26] *Post,* pp. 79 *et seq.,* 547 *et seq.*
[27] L.P.A. 1925, s. 199; *Bailey* v. *Barnes* [1894] 1 Ch. 25 at 35.
[28] *Jones* v. *Smith* (1841) 1 Hare 43 at 55; *Oliver* v. *Hinton* [1899] 2 Ch. 264.
[29] *Smith* v. *Jones* [1954] 1 W.L.R. 1089; but see *Green* v. *Rheinberg* (1911) 104 L.T. 149.
[30] *Hunt* v. *Luck* [1902] 1 Ch. 428; and see *Caunce* v. *Caunce* [1969] 1 W.L.R. 286.

is subject to certain trusts is notice of all the trusts to which it is
subject in the hands of the trustees.

Again, a purchaser has constructive notice of all rights which he
would have discovered had he investigated the title to the land for the
period allowed by law in the case of an open contract, *i.e.*, one which
(*inter alia*) prescribes no special length of title. This period was
originally at least sixty years, but by the Vendor and Purchaser Act
1874,[31] it was reduced to at least forty years, and by the Law of
Property Act 1925,[32] it is now at least thirty years. The period is
" at least " thirty years, for the purchaser can call for a good root of
title which is at least thirty years old, and see all documents subsequent thereto which trace the dealings with the property. A good
root of title is a document which deals with the whole legal and equitable interest in the land, describes the property adequately, and
contains nothing to throw any doubt on the title. Thus if the title
consists of a series of conveyances respectively twelve, seventeen,
twenty-nine and forty-eight years old, as well as older deeds, a purchaser under an open contract can require the production of the
conveyance forty-eight years old and all subsequent conveyances. If
in fact he fails to investigate the title at all, or else investigates it for
only part of this period (*e.g.*, because he has agreed to accept a shorter
title), he is fixed with constructive notice of everything that he would
have discovered had he investigated the title for the full statutory
period.[33]

(c) *Imputed notice.* If a purchaser employs an agent, such as a
solicitor, any actual or constructive notice which the agent receives
may be imputed to the purchaser.[34] Before the Conveyancing Act
1882, notice received by an agent in a previous transaction was occasionally imputed to a purchaser, but this discouraged the employment
of local solicitors with knowledge of local affairs[35] and was modified
by the Act. Only actual or constructive notice which the agent
acquires as such in the particular transaction in question is now
imputed to a purchaser.[36] Where the same solicitor acts for both
parties, any notice he acquires may be imputed to both parties, except
where he enters into a conspiracy with one to conceal something from
the other.[37]

---

[31] s. 1.   [32] s. 44.
[33] See *Re Cox and Neve's Contract* [1891] 2 Ch. 109 at 117, 118.
[34] *Re The Alms Corn Charity* [1901] 2 Ch. 750.
[35] See *Re Cousins* (1886) 31 Ch.D. 671.
[36] L.P.A. 1925, s. 199, replacing C.A. 1882, s. 3.
[37] *Sharpe* v. *Foy* (1868) 4 Ch.App. 35 ; but see *Re Cousins, supra.*

5. Successors in title. The protection given to a purchaser without notice extends also to his successors in title, even if they take with notice[38]; for otherwise the owner of the equity could, by widely advertising his right, make it difficult for the purchaser without notice to dispose of the land for as much as he had paid for it. To this rule there is one exception, which prevents it being abused. If a person bound by the equity sells to a purchaser without notice and later acquires the property again, he cannot shelter behind the immunity of that purchaser.[39]

Sect. 3. Equitable Remedies

1. Remedies discretionary. A further distinction between law and equity lay in the matter of remedies. In general, if a legal right was infringed, the person injured was entitled as of right to a legal remedy, usually damages. Thus if A trespassed on X's land, X had a legal right to sue him for damages and, on proving his case, he was entitled to damages as of right. If the trespass was trivial the damages might be nominal (*e.g.*, forty shillings) or contemptuous (*e.g.*, one farthing) and X might be ordered to pay the costs: but he had a right to judgment. A plaintiff seeking an equitable remedy, on the other hand, had no *right* to anything at all: equitable remedies were discretionary, and even if the plaintiff proved his case, equity might refuse to give him any assistance, *e.g.*, on the ground that the case was trivial or that it would be inconvenient to grant an equitable remedy. However, the discretion was exercised not arbitrarily according to the whim of the judge but according to settled principles, and thus in effect a plaintiff could succeed in equity only if, in addition to a right having been infringed, there was no equitable principle which prevented him from being granted a remedy.[40]

2. The remedies. The principal remedies given by equity were specific performance (an order to a person to carry out his obligations) and injunction (an order to a person to refrain from doing some act in the future or, more rarely, to put right something already done). Not until the Chancery Amendment Act 1858 could equity award damages. This Act provided that in any case where the Chancery had power to entertain an application for an injunction or specific performance, it could award damages either in addition to or in

---

[38] *Harrison* v. *Forth* (1695) Prec.Ch. 51 ; *Wilkes* v. *Spooner* [1911] 2 K.B. 473.
[39] *Gordon* v. *Holland* (1913) 82 L.J.P.C. 81.
[40] See *Haywood* v. *Cope* (1858) 25 Beav. 140 at 151–153.

substitution for such injunction or specific performance. This did not alter the rule that equitable remedies were discretionary, neither did it enable courts of equity to award damages in all cases; if the case was one where the Chancery was not in a position to grant specific performance or an injunction, it could award no damages under the Act.[41]

In the same way that the Chancery was originally unable to give the legal remedy of damages, the common law courts were unable to give the equitable remedies of specific performance and injunction. Consequently a plaintiff who wanted, say, damages for past trespasses and an injunction to restrain future trespasses, originally had to commence proceedings both in one of the common law courts and in Chancery.

Sect. 4. Fusion of the Courts of Law and Equity

By the Judicature Act 1873,[42] the superior courts of law and equity were fused into one Supreme Court, divided into a High Court and Court of Appeal. For convenience, the High Court was divided into five divisions, each of which had certain matters assigned to it. Since 1880, when the Common Pleas Division and Exchequer Division were merged into the Queen's Bench Division, there have been three divisions :

> the Chancery Division,
> the Queen's Bench Division, and
> the Probate, Divorce and Admiralty Division.

The Queen's Bench Division hears common law cases, the Chancery Division hears equity cases, and the title of the other Division sufficiently indicates the matters with which it deals. But it is important to notice that these are only divisions of one court, the High Court, and not separate courts; each division of the High Court has jurisdiction to enforce both legal and equitable rights and give both legal and equitable remedies. This means that it is no longer necessary to go to two separate courts to enforce legal and equitable rights or to obtain legal and equitable remedies. If a point of equity arises in an action in the Queen's Bench Division, for example, the court can deal with it; and it will not be fatal to an action if it is started in the wrong division, for the case will be transferred to the proper division.

---

41 See *Lavery* v. *Pursell* (1888) 39 Ch.D. 508.
42 Which, by the Supreme Court of Judicature (Commencement) Act 1874, s. 2, came into force on November 1, 1875.

Law and equity nevertheless remain distinct: the systems have not been fused, although they are now both administered by the same court.[43] A legal right is still enforceable against a purchaser without notice, while an equitable right is not. Equitable rights are still enforceable only by equitable remedies, subject to the jurisdiction conferred by the Chancery Amendment Act 1858. Indeed, the distinction between the two systems is emphasised by the provision that where there is any conflict between the rules of law and those of equity, the rules of equity shall prevail. Conflicts rarely occur, but there have been cases where this provision has been operative and the most important will be considered later.[44] The Court of Chancery is a ghost, but like many other English legal ghosts, its influence can be seen on every side.

Part 2

SPECIES OF EQUITABLE RIGHTS BEFORE 1926

Sect. 1. Trusts

1. Origin. Everyone today is familiar with the nature of trusts, whereby the ownership of property is vested in one or more persons (the trustees) who hold it for the benefit of others (the beneficiaries). The ancestor of the trust is the use, which had substantially the same nature. The word " use " was derived not from the Latin " *usus* " but from the Latin " *opus* " in the phrase " *ad opus* " (on his behalf) *via* the Old French " *al oes* " or " *al ues* " and hence " to the use of " : thus land was conveyed " to A and his heirs to the use of B and his heirs." [45]

Although there are records of uses having been created even before the Norman Conquest, the only uses found for some time after the Conquest appear to have been merely temporary uses, *e.g.,* while a man was on a crusade. In about 1225 the Franciscan friars came to England. The rules of their Order prevented their owning property, and so land was conveyed, for example, to some town to the use of the friars.[46] After this, uses of a permanent nature became more common, and by the middle of the fourteenth century they were frequent.

---

[43] *Salt* v. *Cooper* (1880) 16 Ch.D. 544 at 549.
[44] *Post*, pp. 342 *et seq.*
[45] Maitland, *Equity*, 24.
[46] 2 P. & M. 231–238.

2. Enforced by equity. After early hesitations, the common law courts refused to recognise uses. If land was conveyed by A " to B and his heirs to the use of C and his heirs " the common law courts refused to compel the feoffee to uses, B, to hold the land for the benefit of C, the *cestui que use* (pronounced " setty ker use "). B was the person seised, and the common law would take notice of his rights alone; C had no interest which the law would recognise, for " uses were but imaginations." [47] Nevertheless, many uses were created in reliance on the honour and good faith of the feoffees to uses, and consequent breaches of trust occurred. Towards the end of the fourteenth century the Chancellor's aid was sought, and although there is no record of a decree in favour of a *cestui que use* until 1446, probably relief was given in the first quarter of the fifteenth century.[48]

3. Duties. The duties of the feoffees to uses towards their *cestui que use* were threefold : they were bound—

  (i) to permit him to take the profits of the land (" pernancy of profits ");

 (ii) to dispose of the land in accordance with his instructions; and

(iii) to take all necessary proceedings to protect or recover the land.[49]

Although at first the *cestui que use* was regarded as merely having a right to compel the feoffees to uses to carry out their duties, the rights of the *cestui que use* were so extensive that it was soon recognised that he had an estate in the land.[50] The legal estate was in the feoffees to uses, the equitable estate in the *cestui que use* : the former had the husk, the latter the kernel. With some qualifications, it could be said in Chancery that " the equity is the land."

4. Legal and equitable interests. Frequently the legal and equitable interests in property go together; a person who has had the legal fee simple in Blackacre conveyed to him normally receives the equitable fee simple as well. But although there is often no need to consider separately the legal and equitable estate in land, in some cases this is the only way to arrive at a proper understanding of the subject.[51] The ability of the beneficial owner of a legal estate (*i.e.,*

---

[47] *Chudleigh's Case* (1595) 1 Co.Rep. 113b at 140a ; and see Maitland, *Equity*, 28.

[48] Ames, *Lectures on Legal History*, 237.

[49] 4 H.E.L. 431.

[50] *Brent's Case* (1583) 2 Leon. 14 at 18.

[51] Consider, *e.g.,* joint tenancies and tenancies in common ; *post*, pp. 212 *et seq.*

one who has the equitable interest as well as the legal estate for his own benefit) to separate the legal from the equitable interest is one of the fundamentals of English law.

5. The Statute of Uses. It was possible by conveying lands to use to evade most feudal liabilities, as they fell only upon the person or persons who were seised of land. All that was needed was the selection of suitable and sufficient feoffees so that the land was never seised by a single feoffee whose death would give rise to the feudal incidents which became due upon the death of the tenant. The evasion seriously affected the King who was always lord and never tenant. After various manoeuvres, in 1535 " the Statute of Uses was forced upon an extremely unwilling parliament by an extremely strong-willed king." [52] The effect of this was to " execute " all uses to which it applied, taking the legal estate out of the feoffees to uses and converting the equitable interests of the *cestuis que use* into corresponding legal estates.

6. The use upon a use. Soon after the statute was passed it was held that a use upon a use was void,[53] so that a conveyance " to A and his heirs to the use of B and his heirs to the use of C and his heirs " gave the whole legal and equitable interests to B and nothing to A or C. After the Restoration the feudal incidents were mainly abolished,[54] and the Chancellor by 1676 was enforcing the use in C's favour as a trust.[55] The statute survived until its repeal by the Law of Property Act 1925 [56] with the consequence that legal uses and equitable trusts existed and developed side by side resulting in a system of great flexibility and unrivalled complexity. As will be seen,[57] the number of legal estates and interests was severely curtailed by the 1925 legislation, and all other interests must be equitable.

Sect. 2.   Other Equitable Rights

The Chancellor did not confine his intervention to the enforcement of uses or trusts, though that always remained the most important part of his jurisdiction. There were three other important areas of real property in which he intervened.

---

[52] Maitland, *Equity*, 34; the King was Henry VIII.
[53] *Tyrrel's Case* (1557) 2 Dy. 155a.
[54] Above, p. 12.
[55] *Grubb* v. *Gwillim* (1676) 73 S.S. 347; and see *Symson* v. *Turner* (1700) 1 Eq.Ca. Abr. 383.
[56] 7th Sched.   [57] *Post*, p. 72.

1. Mortgages. If A conveyed his land to B as security for a loan, equity would allow A at any time after repayment of the loan fell due, and despite any contrary provisions in the mortgage, to recover his land by paying B what was due to him under the loan. The development of this equitable right is described later.[58]

2. Restrictive covenants. Normally a contract is binding upon and enforceable by the parties alone. But during the nineteenth century it was held that if a landowner covenants not to use his land in a certain way for the benefit of neighbouring land, the covenant could be enforced in equity against successors in title of the covenantor thus imposing an equitable burden on his land.[59]

3. Estate contracts. Where a person contracts to purchase an interest in land, he is at once considered to have an equitable interest in that land even before he has paid the price and has had the legal estate of the vendor conveyed to him.[60]

Sect. 3. Creation of Equitable Rights

Equitable rights in land arose under three heads:—

  (i) Informality: where the proper formalities for the creation or conveyance of a legal estate were not observed.
 (ii) Inability: where the grantor had power only to create or convey an equitable interest.
(iii) Intention: where the grantor provided that only an equitable interest should arise.

1. Informality. At law, in order to create or transfer a legal estate, certain formalities had to be observed. The rule was that " Corporeal hereditaments lie in livery, incorporeal hereditaments lie in grant." A corporeal hereditament was an inheritable right in realty which was accompanied by physical possession of the land, *e.g.*, a fee simple in possession; for such estates, a feoffment with livery of seisin[61] was essential. An incorporeal hereditament was an inheritable right in land not accompanied by physical possession, such as a fee simple in remainder or a rentcharge; for such interests, a feoffment was inappropriate but a deed of grant was essential. Leases for a term of years

[58] *Post*, p. 462.
[59] *Post*, p. 402.
[60] *Lysaght* v. *Edwards* (1876) 2 Ch.D. 499.
[61] *Ante*, p. 19.

were not hereditaments and at first could be created orally, but the Statute of Frauds 1677 [62] made writing necessary in nearly all cases. The Real Property Act 1845 [63] made a deed essential for most leases; it also made a deed an alternative to a feoffment of corporeal hereditaments, and provided that if a feoffment was employed it would be void unless evidenced by a deed. Thus after the Act it became substantially true to say that without a deed no legal estate could be created or transferred.

Equity, on the other hand, was not so strict. In accordance with the maxim " Equity treats that as done which ought to be done," equity regarded an enforceable contract to create or convey an interest in land as being as effective as if the transaction had been properly carried out. Further, equity would regard an attempt to create or convey an interest in land which failed through lack of a deed as being a contract to carry out the transaction and thus as effective in equity. These rules, however, were subject to the transaction being for value and being sufficiently evidenced in writing or by a sufficient act of part performance [64] ; in general, a mere oral transaction relating to land and supported by no act of part performance would not be enforced even in equity. In short, a transaction by deed was normally essential to the creation or transfer of a legal estate; writing or part performance sufficed in equity.

2. Inability. If X owned only an equitable interest, *e.g.*, a right under a trust, he had no power to create a legal estate out of it. So far as the common law was concerned, he had no interest in land at all, and thus could create nothing that the common law would recognise. But he could create or transfer interests valid in equity.

3. Intention. Even if a deed was employed, and the grantor had power to create or convey a legal estate, if the grantor provided that only an equitable interest should be created or transferred, no legal estate would pass.

Sect. 4. Equity Follows the Law

There could exist a whole range of equitable estates or interests corresponding to the legal estates and interests in land. A fee

[62] s. 1.
[63] ss. 2, 3.
[64] This is intended to summarise very briefly what is dealt with more fully at pp. 341 *et seq.*, *post.*

simple, fee tail, life estate, mortgage, easement and nearly every
other interest might be either legal or equitable. Thus if A granted
a lease to B to hold on trust for C, B had a legal term of years and C
an equitable term. If the fee simple owner of Blackacre granted Y a
lease for 99 years, Y's lease would be legal if it was granted by deed,
equitable if merely in writing. If a person held an equitable interest
it would usually be found either that his interest arose under a trust
or else that it was created without employing the formalities necessary
at law.

Certain interests could exist only in equity: if Blackacre was bound
by a restrictive covenant, this could never cast a legal burden on anyone who subsequently acquired the land, although it might well bind
him in equity. But apart from these cases, there was a strict parallel
in law and in equity. In most cases the maxim " Equity follows the
law " applied: " the Chancery moulded equitable estates and interests
after the fashion of the common law estates and interests." [65] The
court tended to treat an interest in the land in the same way whether it
was legal or equitable.[66] Thus equitable entails had to be barred in the
same way as legal entails [67]: equitable interests passed on intestacy
to the same persons as legal estates: there was curtesy out of equitable
interests in the same way as out of legal estates: an equitable tenant
for life was in the same position as regards equitable waste as a legal
tenant for life, and so on. But in certain matters, equity considered
that there was good reason for refusing to follow the law. For
example—

  (i) there was no dower out of equitable interests until the Dower
      Act 1833;
 (ii) certain future interests (known as executory interests) which
      could not at first exist at law were permitted in equity;
(iii) equitable remainders were not liable to destruction in the
      same way as legal remainders;
 (iv) equity allowed a mortgagor to recover the property mort-
      gaged if he paid all that was due, even though he no longer
      had any legal right to redeem the property;
  (v) until the Intestates' Estates Act 1884, equitable interests were
      not liable to escheat.[68]

---

[65] Maitland, *Equity*, 108.
[66] See *Re Somerville and Turner's Contract* [1903] 2 Ch. 583 at 588.
[67] *Kirkham* v. *Smith* (1749) Amb. 518.
[68] These matters are all dealt with elsewhere under their appropriate heads.

The reason for the first of these rules was that dower was a nuisance to conveyancers, the second rested on technical grounds and the third and fourth avoided hardship: the reason for the last rule was that escheat was a feudal incident and equity's attitude towards feudal incidents was that they applied to legal estates alone.

With regard to words of limitation, equity followed the law in part only. If the grantor used informal words showing a clear intention to create a fee simple or fee tail, *e.g.,* a limitation on trust for A " absolutely," [69] these were as effective as formal words. But if strict conveyancing language was employed, the limitation was construed in the same way as a legal limitation and in the absence of proper words of limitation only a life estate passed. This was so even if a general intention to pass some other interest could be gathered from the instrument,[70] although in this case if the court was asked to rectify the instrument and not merely construe it, words of limitation necessary to carry out the grantor's intention would be inserted.[71]

It will thus be seen that in some important points equity refused to follow the law. Nevertheless it has been said with some justice that " the cases, where the analogy fails, are not numerous; and there is scarcely a rule of law or equity, of a more ancient origin, or which admits of fewer exceptions, than the rule, that equity followeth the law." [72]

Part 3

THE 1925 LEGISLATION

It has been seen that a purchaser who buys without notice of some adverse right is bound by that right if it is legal and takes free from it if it is equitable. Consequently, the fewer the legal estates and interests that can exist in land the less precarious the position of a purchaser. The complexities of the doctrine of the purchaser without notice have also been seen. In this field the property legislation of 1925 reformed the law in three major respects, namely—

    (i) by reducing the number of legal estates and interests that can exist in land;

---

[69] *Re Arden* [1935] Ch. 326.
[70] *Re Bostock's Settlement* [1921] 2 Ch. 469.
[71] *Banks* v. *Ripley* [1940] Ch. 719.
[72] Co.Litt. 290b, n. 1, xvi.

    (ii) by increasing the number of cases in which registration in the land charges register takes the place of the doctrine of notice; and

    (iii) by increasing the number of rights which will be " overreached " on a conveyance, *i.e.,* transferred from the land to the purchase money that represents it.

These three heads will be considered in turn.

Sect. 1. Reduction in the Number of Legal Estates

Section 1 of the Law of Property Act 1925 has reduced the number of legal estates that can exist in land to two, and the number of classes of legal interests to five. The distinction, broadly, is that a legal interest is a right over the land of another. The terms of the first three subsections of section 1 are as follows:

" 1.—(1) The only estates in land which are capable of subsisting or of being conveyed or created at law are—

    (*a*) An estate in fee simple absolute in possession;

    (*b*) A term of years absolute.

(2) The only interests or charges in or over land which are capable of subsisting or of being conveyed or created at law are—

    (*a*) An easement, right, or privilege in or over land for an interest equivalent to an estate in fee simple absolute in possession or a term of years absolute;

    (*b*) A rentcharge in possession issuing out of or charged on land being either perpetual or for a term of years absolute;

    (*c*) A charge by way of legal mortgage;

    (*d*) . . . and any other similar charge on land which is not created by an instrument;

    (*e*) Rights of entry exercisable over or in respect of a legal term of years absolute, or annexed, for any purpose, to a legal rentcharge.

(3) All other estates, interests, and charges in or over land take effect as equitable interests."

It should be noted that the section does not provide that the estates and interests mentioned in subsections (1) and (2) are *necessarily* legal, but merely that they alone *can* be legal. Before 1926, as has been seen,[73] no legal estate could be created unless the proper formalities were employed and the grantor both had the power and manifested the intention to create or convey a legal estate. The effect of section 1 of the Law of Property Act 1925 is to add a fourth requirement, namely, that the right must be mentioned in subsections (1) or (2) of that section. For example, a life interest or an entail cannot be legal estates after 1925, for they are not included in section 1. Such rights usually arise under wills or family settlements, as distinct from the fee simple absolute or term of years, which are the subject of commercial transactions and so are made capable of being legal estates, if they comply with the conditions of section 1.

Probably the incidents of equitable interests are similar to those attaching to corresponding legal estates before 1936. Thus the position of a tenant for life as regards waste seems to have remained unchanged despite the conversion of his legal life estate into an equitable life interest at the beginning of 1926. There is no express provision on this point but " equity follows the law." [74]

The general scheme of the section is to deal with the legal rights of ownership in the land itself in subsection (1) and with legal rights over the land of another in subsection (2). However, this is complicated by the definition of " land " given by the Act. " Land " is defined as including, unless the context otherwise requires, any corporeal or incorporeal hereditament and among the latter is mentioned an advowson.[75] An advowson is the right of presenting a clergyman to a living [76] and is a species of real property. By reading subsection (1) in the light of the definition of " land," it seems clear that a fee simple in possession in an advowson is a legal estate and so is a term of years absolute in an advowson. On this basis, a rentcharge for a term of years, for example, may be classed as a legal estate either by virtue of being included in subsection (1) under " land," or by virtue of being expressly mentioned in subsection (2) (*b*). However, this is of small practical importance except with regard to advowsons, which could not otherwise be held for a legal estate.

It will be noted that the rights mentioned in subsection (1) are called legal estates and those mentioned in subsection (2) are called legal interests or charges. This is a convenient distinction between rights over a person's own land and rights over the land of another,

---

[73] *Ante*, p. 68.
[74] *Ante*, p. 69.
[75] L.P.A. 1925, s. 205 (1) (ix).
[76] *Post*, p. 414.

but both types of right are referred to in the Act as "legal estates," and have the same incidents attached to them as attached to legal estates before 1926.[77] The title of "estate owner" is given to the owner of a legal estate.[78] Before 1926, equitable rights in land were frequently and properly called equitable estates, but they should now be called equitable interests and the name "estate" reserved for legal rights.

The various legal estates and interests must now be examined more closely.

1. (a) "Fee simple absolute in possession." The meaning of "*fee simple*" has already been considered.[79]

"*Absolute*" is used to distinguish a fee simple which will continue for ever from a modified fee,[80] such as a determinable fee or a fee simple subject to a gift over in favour of another, *e.g.,* a devise " to A and his heirs, but if B marries Jane, to B and his heirs." A fee simple defeasible by condition subsequent [81] would also be excluded from this category but for the Law of Property (Amendment) Act 1926. A fee simple defeasible by condition subsequent arises most frequently in connection with rentcharges. In some parts of the country, particularly Manchester and the north, it is a common practice to sell a fee simple for a comparatively small sum in cash and a perpetual rentcharge (an annual sum charged on the land). The remedies for non-payment of a rentcharge include a right to enter on the land temporarily to collect the rents and profits; further, in a number of cases an express right of re-entry is reserved by the conveyance, entitling the grantor to enter and determine the fee simple and thus regain his old estate if the rent is a specified number of days in arrear. The reservation of a right of re-entry clearly made the fee simple less than absolute, and it was thought by some that even a temporary right of entry might have this effect. This meant that those who had purchased land in this way before 1926 and had obtained legal estates suddenly found that their estates might no longer be legal and that it was doubtful who had the legal estate. Further, the complicated provisions of the Settled Land Act 1925 probably applied.[82]

[77] L.P.A. 1925, s. 1 (4).
[78] *Ibid.*
[79] *Ante*, pp. 15, 30.
[80] See *ante*, p. 30.
[81] *Ante*, p. 31.
[82] *Post*, pp. 162 *et seq.*

To remedy this state of affairs the Law of Property (Amendment) Act 1926 [83] provided that " a fee simple subject to a legal or equitable right of entry or re-entry is for the purposes of this Act a fee simple absolute." While this undoubtedly meets the difficulty it was meant to deal with, the wide terms in which it was drawn appear to have done more than was intended. The effect of a condition subsequent annexed to a fee simple is to give rise to a right of re-entry exercisable on breach of the condition and until this right of re-entry is exercised the fee simple continues.[84] Consequently, by virtue of the Amendment Act, every fee simple defeasible by condition subsequent appears to rank as a legal estate, even though it is far from being " absolute " in the ordinary sense of the word. Further, by statute, certain land held for special purposes, such as schools or highways, will be divested and, *e.g.*, revert to the grantor when the special purpose is at an end; nevertheless, such a fee simple is expressly declared to be absolute.[85]

" *In possession* " means that the estate is a present estate and not in remainder or in reversion.[86] It includes not only physical possession of the land but also the receipt of rents and profits or the right to receive them, if any. Thus a fee simple is still " in possession " even though the tenant has granted a lease, for he is entitled to the rent reserved by the lease. But if land has been granted " to A for life, remainder to B in fee simple," the interests of both A and B are necessarily equitable, for a life interest cannot now be legal and B's fee simple is not in possession.[87]

1. (b) " Term of years absolute." " *Term of years* " is defined as including a term of less than a year, or for a year or years and a fraction of a year, or from year to year.[88] In effect, " term of years " seems to mean a term for any period having fixed and certain duration as a minimum. Thus, in addition to a tenancy for a specified number of years (*e.g.*, " to X for ninety-nine years "), such tenancies as a yearly tenancy or a weekly tenancy are " terms of years " within the definition, for there is a minimum duration of a year or a week respectively. But a lease " for the life of X " cannot exist as a legal

---

[83] Sched., adding a clause to L.P.A. 1925, s. 7 (1).
[84] *Ante*, p. 32.
[85] L.P.A. 1925, s. 7 (1); *Tithe Redemption Commission* v. *Runcorn U.D.C.* [1954] Ch. 383.
[86] See *District Bank Ltd.* v. *Webb* [1958] 1 W.L.R. 148.
[87] See, however, the Welsh Church (Burial Grounds) Act 1945, s. 1, for a curious qualification of L.P.A. 1925, s. 1.
[88] L.P.A. 1925, s. 205 (1) (xxvii).

estate and the same, perhaps, applies to tenancies at will or at sufferance (if they are estates at all [89]) for their duration is wholly uncertain.

"*Absolute.*" A term of years is not prevented from being absolute merely by being liable to determination by notice, re-entry, operation of law or by a provision for cesser on redemption or in any other event (other than the dropping of a life, or the determination of a determinable life interest).[90] This means that a term of years may be absolute even if it contains a clause enabling the parties to determine it at certain specified periods, such as at the end of the first five or ten years, or if it provides (as is almost always the case) that the landlord may determine it if the rent is not paid or a covenant is broken. "Operation of law" is illustrated by the doctrine of satisfied terms,[91] and a proviso for cesser on redemption by the law of mortgages.[92]

It will be seen from this that by the express provisions of statute, a term of years absolute may consist of a tenancy which is neither a "term of years" nor "absolute" according to the natural meaning of the words, *e.g.*, a monthly tenancy liable to be forfeited for non-payment of rent. "Absolute" really has very little meaning here.

It should be noted that, unlike a fee simple absolute, a term of years absolute may be a legal estate even though not "in possession." A lease to commence in five years' time may thus be legal, although there is now a limit to the length of time which may elapse between the grant of a lease and the commencement of the term.[93] There is no limit to the length of a term of years absolute: thus terms of three thousand years are common in the case of mortgages. But there is no such thing as a lease in perpetuity.[94]

2. (a) "An easement, right, or privilege in or over land for an interest equivalent to an estate in fee simple absolute in possession or a term of years absolute." This head includes both easements and, it seems, profits *à prendre*.[95] An easement confers the right to use the land of another in some way, or to prevent it from being used for certain purposes. Thus rights of way, rights of water and rights of

---

[89] See *ante*, p. 17.
[90] L.P.A. 1925, s. 205 (1) (xxvii).
[91] *Post*, p. 206.
[92] *Post*, p. 464.
[93] *Post*, pp. 345, 346.
[94] See *Sevenoaks, Maidstone and Tunbridge Ry.* v. *London, Chatham and Dover Ry.* (1879) 11 Ch.D. 625 at 635.
[95] For easements and profits see *post*, pp. 417 *et seq.*

light may exist as easements. A profit *à prendre* gives the right to take something from the land of another, *e.g.*, peat, fish or wood. These rights can be legal only if they are held for interests equivalent to one of the two legal estates: thus a right of way for twenty-one years may be legal but a right of way for life must be equitable.

2. (b) " A rentcharge in possession issuing out of or charged on land being either perpetual or for a term of years absolute." " *A rentcharge* " is a right which, independently of any lease or mortgage, gives the owner the right to a periodical sum of money, with the payment of which some land is burdened,[96] as where the fee simple owner of Blackacre charges the land with a payment of £50 per annum to X.

" *In possession.*" Under the subsection a rentcharge to start at a date subsequent to that on which it is granted cannot be legal, whether it is perpetual or for a term of years absolute. But the Law of Property (Entailed Interests) Act 1932 [97] provides that a rentcharge is " in possession " notwithstanding that the payments are limited to commence or accrue at a date subsequent to its creation, unless the rentcharge is limited to take effect in remainder after or expectant on the failure or determination of some other interest.[98] Thus if X conveys land to Y in consideration of a perpetual rentcharge becoming payable one year after the conveyance, the rentcharge may nevertheless be legal; but if a perpetual rentcharge is granted " to A for life, remainder to B absolutely," B's interest cannot be legal until A's death.

" *Issuing out of or charged on land.*" " Land " includes another rentcharge.[99] Thus if P charges his fee simple estate in Blackacre with the payment to Q of £100 per annum in perpetuity, Q can create a legal rentcharge of £50 per annum in favour of R, charged on his rentcharge of £100.

" *Being either perpetual or for a term of years absolute.*" " Perpetual " is used here in place of " fee simple absolute " used in 2 (a) above. This verbal difference seems to be of no practical importance.

2. (c) " A charge by way of legal mortgage." This needs no comment here save to point out that this is one of the ways of creating

---

[96] For rentcharges see *post*, p. 408.
[97] s. 2.
[98] See (1932) 73 L.J.News. 321.
[99] L.P.A. 1925, ss. 122, 205 (1) (ix); see *post*, p. 410.

a legal mortgage today, the other being by the grant of a term of years absolute on certain conditions. Both forms are dealt with later.[1]

2. (d) ". . . and any other similar charge on land which is not created by an instrument." This group comprises periodical payments with which land is burdened by operation of law and not by some conveyance or other voluntary act of parties. Formerly land tax and tithe rentcharge were expressly mentioned in this category, but those expressions have been repealed.[1a]

Land tax was a small annual tax on land first imposed in 1692, continued by annual statutes up to and including 1797, and made perpetual by the Land Tax Perpetuation Act 1798, which was for the most part replaced by the Land Tax Redemption Act 1802.[2] It was abolished in 1963.[3]

Tithe rentcharge was abolished by the Tithe Act 1936. It was a type of rentcharge imposed by statute in lieu of the former right of parsons and others to one-tenth of the produce of land. Land formerly burdened with tithe rentcharge is now subject to a tithe redemption annuity,[4] and although this is not expressly stated to be a legal interest, it clearly falls within that category as being a " similar charge on land which is not created by an instrument."

2. (e) " Rights of entry exercisable over or in respect of a legal term of years absolute, or annexed, for any purpose, to a legal rentcharge." As already mentioned,[5] a legal term of years absolute is usually subject to the right of the landlord to re-enter if the tenant fails to pay rent or comply with the covenants. Such a right may be a legal right, and the same applies to any right of entry or re-entry attached to a legal rentcharge, *e.g.*, if the rent is not paid.

Concurrent legal estates. Any number of legal estates may exist concurrently in the same piece of land.[6] Thus A may have the legal fee simple in Blackacre, subject to a legal mortgage in favour of B. a legal rentcharge in favour of C, a legal lease in favour of D and so on.

---

[1] *Post*, pp. 464 *et seq.*
[1a] Tithe Act 1936, 9th Sched.; Finance Act 1963, 14th Sched., Part VI.
[2] See, generally, *R.* v. *Commissioners of Land Tax for the Tower Division, Middlesex* (1853) 2 E. & B. 694.
[3] Finance Act 1963, Part V, 14th Sched.
[4] Tithe Act 1936, s. 3 ; see *post*, pp. 415 *et seq.*
[5] *Ante*, p. 76.
[6] L.P.A. 1925, s. 1 (5).

Sect. 2. Extension of System of Registration of Charges

Before 1926, provision had been made for the registration of certain rights affecting land, such as pending actions. Such rights were unenforceable against a subsequent purchaser of the land if they were not registered before the purchase was made. The rights thus registrable were comparatively few and unimportant. The Land Charges Act 1925 has greatly extended this system, and many important rights are now void against a purchaser unless duly registered. Wherever a right is void against a person for non-registration, that person is not prejudicially affected by notice of the right: but once the right is registered, the registration is deemed to constitute actual notice to all persons and for all purposes connected with the land affected.[7] Thus, in connection with registrable rights, the old rules about notice have no application. If a right is void against a purchaser for non-registration then even if he actually knows of the right, he is deemed to have no notice of it: on the other hand, if it is duly registered, he cannot plead that he has no notice of it. The test is now the state of the register, not of the purchaser's mind.

However, it is best not to try to translate this system of registration into terms of the old scheme founded on the position of a purchaser without notice,[8] but to treat it as a separate system. The reasons for this are—

(1) Certain legal rights are registrable, and if not registered, are void against a purchaser. Even though the absence of registration is treated as an absence of notice, the old system did not enable a purchaser without notice to take free from *legal* rights. The new system thus deprives these legal rights of some of the security against purchasers which they formerly enjoyed.

(2) Under the old system, a purchaser without notice took free from equities if he gave *value* and acquired a *legal estate.* An unregistered right is sometimes void against a purchaser if he gave *value* and acquired *any estate, legal or equitable,* and sometimes void against a purchaser only if he gave *money or money's worth* and acquired a *legal estate.*

Consequently the position created by the extension of registration is best described as follows:

(i) Most legal rights are not registrable; these continue to be good against the whole world.

[7] L.P.A. 1925, ss. 198, 199.
[8] *Ante,* p. 59.

    (ii) Some equitable rights are not registrable; these continue to be good against the whole world except a bona fide purchaser for value of a legal estate without notice or someone claiming through such a person.

    (iii) A few legal rights and many equitable rights are registrable. If these are not registered, they will be void for non-registration against certain purchasers, irrespective of any question of notice. If they are registered, they bind every purchaser, again irrespective of notice.

The following is a summary of the most important rights which are registrable after 1925. They are dealt with in detail later.[9]

1. Legal interests.

(a) A charge on land imposed under certain statutes such as the Agricultural Holdings Act 1948.

(b) A puisne (pronounced " puny ") mortgage, *i.e.,* a legal mortgage not protected by a deposit of title deeds relating to the legal estate affected.

(c) A charge for death duties, if arising after 1925.

2. Equitable interests.

(a) A limited owner's charge. This includes a charge on land acquired by some limited owner, such as a tenant for life, who pays out of his own pocket estate duty (which is a death duty payable on the death of the previous owner) which should have been borne by the estate.

(b) A general equitable charge, *i.e.,* an equitable charge which affects a legal estate in land but is not secured by a deposit of title deeds relating to the legal estate affected.

(c) An estate contract, *i.e.,* a contract to convey or create a legal estate.

(d) A restrictive covenant, *i.e.,* a covenant restricting the use of land; this is registrable only if it is made after 1925 and is not made between lessor and lessee.

(e) An equitable easement, right or privilege: this is registrable only if created after 1925.

---

[9] *Post,* pp. 541 *et seq.*

Sect. 3. Extension of Overreaching Provisions

1. Settlements. Where it is desired to give land to persons in succession, *e.g.,* to A for life, and then to B for life and then to C in fee simple, two methods are available, namely, the strict settlement and the trust for sale. Under the strict settlement (often called merely a " settlement " and the land " settled land ") the control over the land is normally vested in the tenant for life, A: under the trust for sale trustees control the land. In each case, if the land is sold, the rights of the beneficiaries are " overreached," *i.e.,* they are transferred from the land to the purchase-money, which is paid to trustees. This is independent of any question of notice; provided the purchaser pays the money to the trustees (who must be either not less than two in number or a trust corporation [10]) he takes the land free from the claims of the beneficiaries. Although the beneficiaries lose any prospect of enjoying the land itself, they are not defrauded in any way, for they have corresponding interests in the purchase-money. This distinguishes overreaching from an interest being overridden, *i.e.,* being void against a purchaser without notice, or for want of registration: if an interest is overreached, it is transferred from the land to money in the hands of trustees; if an interest is overridden, it ceases to be enforceable.

2. Equitable rights. After 1925, the rights of beneficiaries under a settlement or trust for sale are always equitable. Before 1926, the rights of the beneficiaries under a settlement might be either legal or equitable, according to whether the legal estate had been conveyed to the beneficiaries or had been given to trustees on trust for them. But whether their rights were legal or equitable, they could nevertheless be overreached: the common law validity of a legal estate against all the world could not prevail against an express provision in the settlement or a statute. To this extent, the 1925 legislation may be said to have curtailed the power of overreaching. However, the extensions of the overreaching powers are much more significant than this somewhat theoretical curtailment. The chief extensions are the following:

(i) Trusts for sale are imposed by statute in certain cases where they did not exist before, *e.g.,* under an intestacy, or in the case of a beneficial joint tenancy or tenancy in common.[11]

---

[10] *Post,* pp. 194.
[11] *Post,* pp. 216, 302.

(ii) A conveyance under certain special trusts for sale or settlements (usually called "*ad hoc*" trusts for sale or settlements) will overreach several equitable rights which could not be thus overreached before 1926.[12]

The first of these provisions means that there are now more cases in which a conveyance will overreach equitable rights, the second means that some conveyances now have a wider overreaching effect than before.

3. Other overreaching conveyances. Although settlements and trusts for sale are the most important sources of overreaching conveyances, they are not the only sources. Thus if X has mortgaged his land to M, and then fails to pay the interest, M has a statutory power to sell the estate which X mortgaged to him (even though it is not vested in M), free from X's equitable right to redeem it. X's rights will then be transferred to the purchase-money in M's hands, for M is a trustee for X of any surplus after discharging the mortgage.[13] Again, a conveyance by personal representatives will overreach the claims of the beneficiaries under the will or intestacy.[14] A further example of an overreaching conveyance is one made under an order of the court where any capital money arising from the transaction is paid into, or in accordance with the order of, the court.[15]

In general, only equitable rights can now be overreached; with few exceptions, such as a mortgagee's power to overreach subsequent mortgages on exercising his power of sale, there is no power to overreach legal rights.[16]

SUMMARY SHOWING EFFECT OF A SALE OF LAND ON LEGAL AND EQUITABLE RIGHTS OVER IT

1. The purchaser takes subject to all legal rights.

Exceptions: He takes free from—

(a) the few legal rights which are void against him for want of registration; and

(b) the few legal rights which are overreached.

[12] *Post,* p. 197.
[13] *Post,* p. 476.
[14] *Post,* pp. 195, 315.
[15] L.P.A. 1925, ss. 2, 50.
[16] See *post,* pp. 192 *et seq.*

2. The purchaser takes subject to all equitable rights.

Exceptions: He takes free from—

(a) equitable rights which are void against him for want of registration: notice is irrelevant;

(b) the many equitable rights which are overreached, *e.g.*, under a settlement or trust for sale: again, notice is irrelevant; and

(c) unregistrable equitable rights in respect of which he can show either that he is a bona fide purchaser of a legal estate for value without notice, or else that he claims through such a person. Although this third class is of considerable importance, both historically and as forming a residuary category for rights outside the previous heads, it is of relatively small practical significance today, for registration and overreaching between them account for most of the important rights encountered in practice.

Chapter 4

FUTURE INTERESTS

Part 1

INTRODUCTION: VESTED AND CONTINGENT INTERESTS

1. Vested interests. A future interest in land is an interest which confers a right to the enjoyment of the land at a future time, such as a right to the land after the death of a living person. A future interest may be either vested or contingent. " Vested " when used by itself (as here) means " vested in interest," *i.e.,* that there is a present fixed right of future enjoyment; this contrasts with a right " vested in possession," which carries with it a right of present enjoyment. Thus if land is devised on trust for X for life with remainder to his first and other sons successively for life, each son obtains a vested interest at birth, and it is immaterial that the interests of the younger sons may not vest in possession until long after X's death.[1]

2. Conditions for vesting. A future interest is vested if two conditions are satisfied:

(i) that the person or persons entitled to the interest are ascertained; and

(ii) that the interest is ready to take effect forthwith upon the determination of all the preceding estates and interests.[2]

(a) *Conditions satisfied.* Thus if land is given—
" to A for life, remainder to B for life, remainder to C in fee simple,"

the interests of B and C are both vested. Neither is vested in possession, for A has the only interest which is vested both in interest and in possession. But if A's life interest were to terminate forthwith, an ascertained person, B, is ready to take the land, and so B's interest is vested. Even if A is aged twenty-three and B ninety-seven, so that it is most improbable that B's interest will ever vest in possession, B nevertheless has a vested interest; an interest may be vested

---

[1] See *Evans* v. *Walker* (1876) 3 Ch.D. 211.

[2] Fearne C.R. 9, 216; *Re Legh's S.T.* [1938] Ch. 39 at 52. For the purposes of the rule against perpetuities, there is an additional condition: see *post,* p. 86.

even if there is no certainty of its taking effect in possession at any time, for otherwise no future life interest or entail would be vested. If land is given to X in tail, remainder to Y in fee simple, Y's remainder is vested, not because X's entail is bound to determine at some time (for this is not the case), but because the whole fee simple has been split up between X and Y, and Y has been *invested* with a portion of it.

(b) *Person not ascertained.* If the person to take is not ascertained, his interest is contingent, even though it is bound to take effect at some time. For example, if property is given—

"to A and B for their joint lives, with remainder to the survivor,"

the death of one before the other is bound to occur at some time, yet since it is uncertain who will be the survivor, the remainder is contingent.[3] Similarly, a gift to the heir of a living person is contingent, for until that person dies his heir cannot be ascertained.

(c) *Interest not ready.* Although the gift is in favour of a specified person, it will not be vested if it is made to depend upon some event occurring, *e.g.*—

"to A upon attaining 25 or marrying," or—
"to B if he returns to England."

In such cases, the interests of A and B are contingent until the event occurs, when they become vested.

3. Size of interest.

(a) *General.* For most purposes[4] an interest will be vested even if the size of the beneficiary's interest has not been finally ascertained. For example, where land is devised in trust for—

"A for life, remainder to all his children who shall attain the age of 21 years,"

each child obtains a vested interest on attaining his majority; but these vested interests are liable to open to let in each child who subsequently attains full age.[5] Thus if X and Y are the only children who have attained their majority, they each have a vested interest in one-half of the property, subject to that interest being partially divested in favour of subsequent children. When Z becomes 21, the

---

[3] See *Re Legh's S.T.* [1938] Ch. 39.
[4] For an exception, see *post*, p. 86.
[5] See *Re Lechmere and Lloyd* (1881) 18 Ch.D. 524.

shares of X and Y each fall to one-third and Z has the other third; and so on for the other children. X and Y, having vested interests, can dispose of their shares either *inter vivos* or by will, although even in the hands of the transferee the shares will be liable to be diminished by other children attaining full age. But any child of A who dies before he is 21 never has any interest in the property.[6]

(b) *Rule against perpetuities.* A long line of cases has established that the size of a beneficiary's interest must be ascertained before the interest is vested for the purposes of the rule.[7] Thus a gift before 1926 to trustees for such of the children of X as attained the age of 25 (X being alive at the date of the gift and having no child aged 25 or more) was totally void because, as will be seen, a child might attain the age of 25 outside the period allowed by the rule.[8] It mattered not that one or more children attained the age within the period because until it was known how many children would ultimately reach the given age, the size of the share to be taken by each beneficiary was uncertain. This aspect of vesting is considered more fully later.[9]

4. Vesting subject to divesting. A remainder may be vested and yet subject to some provision which may operate to defeat the remainder completely. For example, if before 1926 land was held on trust for A for life, remainder on trust for A's issue as A should appoint, and in default of appointment on trust for all A's children equally, the remainder to the children was vested, subject to being divested to the extent of any appointment made by A[10]; similar principles apply to corresponding trusts after 1925. In cases of doubt, the law favours early vesting, and every interest is construed as being vested forthwith if that is possible; if not, it is treated as becoming vested as soon as possible.

5. Assignability. In the sense that all vested interests give a present right to future enjoyment, the name " future interests " is hardly appropriate. If land is given—

" to X for life, remainder to Y in fee simple,"

Y has a present interest in fee simple which is future only as to the possession of the land. Y can sell, give away, devise or otherwise

---

6 See *Rhodes* v. *Whitehead* (1865) 2 Dr. & Sm. 532.
7 See, *e.g.*, *Pearks* v. *Moseley* (1880) 5 App.Cas. 714.
8 *Boreham* v. *Bignall* (1850) 8 Hare 131.
9 *Post*, pp. 105, 118.
10 *Re Master's Settlement* [1911] 1 Ch. 321.

dispose of his fee simple at any time he wishes. Nevertheless, for convenience, vested interests which are not coupled with a right of present enjoyment are usually dealt with under the head of future interests. Contingent interests are more clearly entitled to be described as future interests, for until the contingency occurs, the person entitled has no estate but merely a possibility of acquiring one. For this reason, contingent remainders and executory interests [11] could not be alienated at common law,[12] though they could be devised, or assigned in equity, and they passed to the heir on intestacy. The Real Property Act 1845 [13] made such interests alienable at law.

Part 2

THE DEVELOPMENT OF FUTURE INTERESTS

Sect. 1. Classification

The two main categories into which future interests fall are reversions, and future interests other than reversions; these will be considered in turn.

A. Reversions

1. Nature of reversions. A " particular estate " in land may be defined as some estate or interest less than a fee simple, *i.e.,* either a fee tail, a life interest or a term of years: it is a mere part (*particula*) of the fee simple. If the owner of an estate in land creates one or more particular estates out of his own estate, the residue of his original estate which he retains is known as a reversion. Thus if a tenant in fee simple grants a life interest or a lease for a term of years, the fee simple which he retains is a reversion. If, on the other hand, the tenant creates a particular estate and by the same instrument disposes of some or all of the residue of his estate to one or more other persons, the interests of those other persons are not reversions but remainders. In the case of a reversion, the land reverts to the grantor when the particular estate determines; in the case of a remainder, it remains away from him for the benefit of some third party. It follows that while there may be many remainders

[11] See *post*, pp. 89, 94.
[12] Challis R.P. 76.
[13] s. 6, now L.P.A. 1925, s. 4 (2).

created out of one estate, there can be but one reversion. Thus if X a tenant in fee simple, grants land—

" to A for life, remainder to B for life, remainder to C in tail,' he retains the reversion in fee simple, and yet has created two remainders, namely, those of B and C. Further, a reversion arises by operation of law, a remainder by act of parties.

2. All reversions are vested. From its very nature, it follows that a reversion is a vested interest [14]; the grantor, or, if he is dead, his representatives, stand ready to receive the land as soon as the particular estate determines. From a feudal point of view, a free holder reversioner on a term of years has an estate which is vested both in interest and in possession, for the grant of a lease does not deprive a grantor of seisin and he therefore has what is properly called a freehold in possession subject to the term. From this point of view, a reversion on a lease is not a reversion or, indeed, a future interest at all; but from a more practical point of view such interests are generally treated as reversions today.

3. Reversions after 1925. Before 1926 a reversion might be legal or equitable, according to whether the estate out of which it was created was legal or equitable. After 1925, a reversion upon an entail or life estate is necessarily equitable; the land will be settled land and the legal estate will be vested in the tenant for life or statutory owner.[15] A reversion upon a term of years, however, can still exist as a legal estate, because—

(a) if the owner of a legal fee simple absolute in possession grants a lease, his estate remains a legal estate, for " possession " includes the right to receive the rents and profits, if any; and

(b) if the owner of a legal term of years absolute grants a sub-lease, there is nothing in this to render his estate any the less legal; any number of legal estates can exist concurrently in the same land.[16]

B. Remainders

In addition to reversions, there were three principal types of future interests before 1926, namely—

[14] Challis R.P. 67.
[15] *Post*, pp. 160 *et seq.*
[16] *Ante*, p. 78.

(1) Legal remainders;
(2) Future trusts; and
(3) Legal executory interests.

These will be considered in turn.

I. LEGAL REMAINDERS

1. Definition. A remainder is the estate created when a grantor who, having granted away a particular estate, by the same instrument grants to another person an estate in the same land limited to commence after the particular estate,[17] *e.g.,* " to A for life, remainder to B in fee simple." In general, the particular estate and any remainders or reversion expectant thereon are all parts of the same estate, together constituting the whole estate in the land.[18]

2. History. Even before 1066, it had become recognised that vested remainders could be created.[19] Early lawyers saw little difficulty in the owner of a fee simple splitting it up into a number of successive vested interests, for the whole interest in the land was immediately transferred to ascertained persons. Each owner had a present estate in the land, even though for most of them enjoyment of the land was not present but deferred. But contingent remainders presented far more difficulty. Thus if land was conveyed to A for life, remainder to the heirs of B (a living person), it was difficult to say where the fee simple was. The grantor appears to have tried to convey the whole of his estate, yet until B's death it could not be said who was the heir to whom the remainder was given. As late as 1410 it was said that such a remainder was void,[20] but in 1431 it was said to be good [21] and in 1453 this was confirmed by the whole court.[22] After this, the courts no longer required that all the estates should be vested forthwith, but were satisfied if there was an immediate transfer of the seisin; nevertheless it was not finally admitted until the middle of the sixteenth century that contingent remainders which depended on some contingency other than the ascertainment of the remainderman (such as a remainder to X " when he marries ") were valid.[23]

---

[17] And see *post*, p. 91.
[18] Challis R.P. 77–79.
[19] 2 P. & M. 21.
[20] Y.B. 11 Hen. 4, fo. 74, pl. 14.
[21] Y.B. 9 Hen. 6, fo. 23, pl. 19.
[22] Fitzherbert's Abridgment, Feffments et Faits, p. 99.
[23] 7 H.E.L. 88.

3. Legal and equitable remainders. Remainders could be legal only if the grantor had power to dispose of a legal estate. Naturally no legal estate could be created by anyone who had a mere equitable interest vested in him, although he could create equitable remainders. Unlike equitable remainders (which are dealt with under the head of future trusts), legal remainders were subject to certain strict rules largely based on the sanctity of seisin, and these must now be examined.

4. Rules governing legal remainders. There were four main rules governing legal remainders.

(a) *A remainder was void unless when it was created it was supported by a particular estate of freehold created by the same instrument.*[24]

It was impossible at common law to create a freehold estate which would spring up in the future by itself. Thus if a grant of land was made—

" to A's first son and the heirs of his body,"

and A had no son at the time of the grant, the grant was void. The reason was that the common law required that the seisin should pass out of the grantor into the grantee at the moment when the estate of freehold was created.[25] Had the conveyance been—

" to X for life, remainder to A's first son and the heirs of his body,"

the gift to A's son would not have infringed this rule, for X would take an estate of freehold and thus could receive the seisin forthwith. Put technically, X's particular estate supported the contingent remainder to A's son.

(b) *A remainder after a fee simple was void.*

Clearly if land was given—

" to A and his heirs, remainder to B and his heirs,"

the limitation to B was void, for A's fee simple absolute exhausted the whole interest in the land and left nothing for B. But the rule was not confined to a fee simple absolute; it applied equally to a fee simple defeasible by condition subsequent or to a determinable fee.[26] Thus where land was given—

" to the Dean and Chapter of A and their successors, on condition that they pay £14 per annum to the Dean and Chapter of

---

[24] Fearne C.R. 281, 301.
[25] *Goodtitle* d. *Dodwell* v. *Gibbs* (1826) 5 B. & C. 709 at 716.
[26] *Earl of Stafford* v. *Buckley* (1750) 2 Ves.Sen. 170; Challis R.P. 83.

> B; but when they cease to do this, their estate shall cease and the
> Dean and Chapter of B and their successors shall have it,"

or—

> "to A and his heirs for as long as X has heirs of his body, and
> then to B and his heirs,"

in each case the second limitation infringed this rule and was void.[27]
In the first case, the grantor had the right to re-enter when the condition was broken; in the second, the land automatically reverted to the grantor when X's issue died out. In other words, a fee could not be mounted on a fee.

To this rule there was one exception. Although a base fee was a species of fee simple, a remainder could exist after a base fee.[28] This could arise only where land had been given in tail with remainders over; in such a case, the subsequent conversion of the fee tail into a base fee did not affect the remainders. But although a determinable fee could be created with the same duration as a base fee (*e.g.*, A's fee in the last example, which would endure for the same period as a base fee created by X, had X owned a tail general), such a fee was not a base fee and there could be no remainder upon it.[29]

(c) *A remainder was void if it was limited so that it could take effect in defeasance of the particular estate.*

Since a remainder is defined as "a limitation so framed as to be immediately expectant on the *natural* determination of a particular estate of freehold," it followed that a future limitation which might cut short the particular estate could not be a valid remainder. Thus if a conveyance was made—

> "to A for life, but if he becomes bankrupt, to his children immediately,"

or—

> "to A for life, but if B has a son five years old, A's estate shall cease and the land pass to that son,"

the last gift in each limitation was void and the condition was ineffective: A took a full life estate in each case, and the grantor the reversion.[30] This is a consequence both of the definition of a remainder and of the rule that if a condition was broken, only the grantor or his heirs could take advantage of it and enter the land.

[27] *Anon.* (1538) 1 Dy. 33a; *Colthirst* v. *Bejushin* (1551) 1 Plowd. 21 at 29.
[28] *Ante*, pp. 34, 38.
[29] Challis R.P. 325.
[30] See *Cogan* v. *Cogan* (1596) Cro.Eliz. 360; *Blackman* v. *Fysh* [1892] 3 Ch. 209.

It will be noticed that in the above examples, the provision cutting short the remainder was part of the subsequent limitation; a complete life estate was given to A, and the subsequent limitation then sought to cut it short. In other words, the grantor was attempting to create a life estate defeasible by condition subsequent. Had the limitation been worded differently and a determinable life estate created, the desired result could have been achieved. For example, land might have been limited—

" to X until he becomes bankrupt,"
or—
" to Y for as long as she remains a widow,"

and in such cases the life estate would have come to a natural end upon the bankruptcy or remarriage respectively. Consequently a remainder limited after such an estate was perfectly valid: a conveyance—

" to P *durante viduitate* [*i.e.*, during widowhood], remainder to Q and his heirs "

gave Q a valid remainder, for there was nothing in the remainder which cut short P's limited life estate.[31]

(d) *A remainder was void*—

    (i) *unless it was so limited that it* **could** *take effect during the continuance of the particular estate or at the moment of its determination; and*

    (ii) *unless it* **did** *in fact take effect in this way.*

Each branch of this rule was founded on the common law abhorrence for an abeyance of seisin; when the particular estate determined, it must be possible for the seisin to pass forthwith to the next remainderman. In the case of a contingent remainder, the first branch of the rule meant that the remainder was bad from the start if it was incapable of vesting while the particular estate continued.[32] For example, a conveyance—

" to A for life, remainder to such child or children of his as shall attain the age of 21 after his death "

gave A a life estate, but gave nothing to his children, for the limitation expressly provided that only those children attaining their majority *after* A's death could take and so attempted to create an abeyance of

---

[31] See *Dean* v. *Dean* [1891] 3 Ch. 150 at 155.
[32] Fearne C.R. 307, 398.

seisin. In the case of a remainder purporting to be vested, the rule meant that the remainder was void *ab initio* if it was limited to start at some stated time after the particular estate determined. Thus a conveyance—

> " to A for life and one day after his death to B and his heirs "

gave B no estate or interest.

The second branch of the rule meant that even if the remainder complied with the first part of the rule and so escaped being void *ab initio*, it nevertheless failed unless it in fact vested during the continuance of the particular estate or at the moment it determined.[33] For example, a limitation—

> " to A for life, remainder for life to the first son of B to attain the age of 21, remainder to C and his heirs "

clearly complied with the first branch of the rule; but if in fact A died before any son of B had reached his majority, the remainder to B's son failed under the second branch.[34] If A's life estate came to an end in some way other than by his death, the remainder similarly failed unless it had already vested.

5. The " timely vesting " rule. It will be noticed that with one exception all the legal remainder rules could be applied as soon as the limitation was made. It could be determined forthwith whether a remainder was supported by a particular estate of freehold, whether it was so worded that it could cut short the particular estate and so on. But whether or not a limitation complied with rule (d) (ii) could be determined only by waiting to see what the future brought. In short, there was no " wait and see " about rules (a), (b), (c) and (d) (i); rule (d) (ii) alone was a " wait and see " rule. The importance of this will be seen when the rule in *Purefoy* v. *Rogers* [35] is considered.[36]

II. FUTURE TRUSTS

The strict common law rules relating to remainders did not apply to equitable interests. If the whole legal estate was vested in trustees, the common law was satisfied, for it took no cognisance of equitable

---

[33] *Cunliffe* v. *Brancker* (1876) 3 Ch.D. 393.
[34] *White* v. *Summers* [1908] 2 Ch. 256.
[35] (1671) 2 Wms.Saund. 380.
[36] *Post*, p. 96.
[37] *Corbet's Case* (1600) 2 And. 134 at 147 (a use is " solement imaginacion ").

interests at all.[37]   Nor did equity see any reason for applying to equitable interests the rigid common law rules founded largely on a strict view of the sanctity of seisin; in this respect, equity refused to follow the law.[38]   For example, if before 1535 it was desired to give land—

" to A and his heirs until B marries and then to B and his heirs,"

it has been seen that the common law refused to permit this.   But if A and B were given only equitable interests, the desired result could be achieved, *e.g.*, by a limitation—

" to X and his heirs to the use of A and his heirs until B marries and then to the use of B and his heirs."

Again, it was impossible at common law to convey land to the heir of B, a living person.   But a conveyance before 1535—

" to Y and his heirs to the use of B's heir and his heirs "

vested the legal fee simple in Y, who held it at first on a resulting use for the grantor.   When B died, an equitable fee simple sprang up in B's heir.

After the Statute of Uses 1535, the limitations to uses in such cases were executed, and they became legal executory interests as explained below.   Yet when the use upon a use became enforceable,[39] the future trust again came into vogue.   Thus a conveyance in 1800—

" unto and to the use of A and his heirs in trust for B's first son to marry "

had the same result as a conveyance in 1500—

" to A and his heirs to the use of B's first son to marry."

The advantage of being able to create limitations free from the legal remainder rules was to a certain extent offset by the fact that the beneficiaries took only equitable interests and so were dependent upon the honesty of the trustees; but this was usually not a very serious drawback.

III. LEGAL EXECUTORY INTERESTS

1. New legal interests.   Before the Statute of Uses 1535, apart from reversions, the only future interests which could be created were legal remainders, which were subject to the strict legal remainder rules but gave the security of a legal estate, and future trusts (then called uses).

[37] For footnote, see p. 93.
[38] See *Re Finch* (1881) 17 Ch.D. 211 at 229.   [39] *Ante*, p. 67.

which were free from the legal remainder rules but gave the beneficiaries mere equitable interests. The effect of the Statute of Uses 1535
was to make it possible to create future interests which had the best
of both worlds, giving the owners legal estates and yet being free from
the legal remainder rules.

Before 1535, the effect of a conveyance—

> " to T and his heirs to the use of A and his heirs, but to the use
> of B and his heirs as soon as B is called to the Bar "

was to give T the legal fee simple on trust for A and B, A taking an
equitable fee simple subject in equity to a gift over to B in fee simple.
After 1535, the effect of T being seised to the use of A and B was that
the use was executed, T dropped out, and the equitable interests of A
and B became exactly corresponding legal estates. Thus notwithstanding the rule that there could be no fee upon a fee, A took a legal
fee simple and upon B being called to the Bar, B obtained a vested
legal fee simple in his stead. The legal remainder rules could not
prevail against the express provision of the statute that the *cestuis
que use* should be seised and possessed of the like estates as they had
in the use.

2. Legal executory interests. These new legal estates were known
as " legal executory interests." " Executory " was used in the sense
of " yet to be executed or carried out." There were two main
divisions.

(a) *Springing uses.* A springing use was one which sprang up in
the future without being supported by any particular estate. Thus a
conveyance—

> " to X and his heirs to the use of Y and his heirs after my death "

or—

> " to X and his heirs to the use of Y and his heirs in four years
> time "

created springing uses.[40] Until the grantor died in the first example,
and until four years had elapsed in the second, the grantor had a legal
fee simple by way of resulting use.

(b) *Shifting uses.* A shifting use was one where the estate shifted
over from one person to another on some event occurring. Thus a
conveyance—

---

[40] *Davies* v. *Speed* (1691) 2 Salk. 675; *Roe* d. *Wilkinson* v. *Tranmer* (1757) 2 Wils.
K.B. 75.

" to X and his heirs to the use of A and his heirs on condition
that if A does not pay £2,000 to the grantor within 15 days it
should be to the use of B and his heirs "

or—

" to X and his heirs to the use of A and his heirs until B is
evicted from his house by A and then to the use of B and his
heirs "

gave a legal estate in fee simple to A and on the specified event
occurring gave B a legal estate in fee simple by way of shifting use.[41]

(c) *Mode of creation.* The result of these rules was that all that
was required to validate a limitation *inter vivos* which infringed the
legal remainder rules was the insertion of the formula—

" to X and his heirs to the use of . . ."

before the desired limitations; the Statute of Uses 1535 did the rest.
But in assurances *inter vivos* the insertion of some phrase such as this
was essential; the court would not supply it if it was omitted.

3. Wills. However, in wills a more lenient rule was adopted.
Even if no use was inserted, the court gave the same treatment to a
devise as if a use had been inserted. In other words, in transactions
inter vivos, springing and shifting limitations could be created at law
only by a conveyance to uses; in wills, such limitations were given
effect to even though no use was declared.[42] This was probably due
to the wording of the Statute of Wills 1540, which gave a testator
power to dispose of land " at his free will and pleasure." Consequently a shifting devise—

" to A and his heirs, but if A fails to convey Blackacre to my
executors, to B and his heirs,"

or a springing devise—

" to the child of which my wife is now enceinte " [43]

was fully effective, although if contained in a deed the first would
have given no interest to B and the second would have been totally
void. Any interest of which the will did not dispose descended to the
testator's heir.

4. Rule in Purefoy v. Rogers. It might be thought from the foregoing passages that if a limitation was contained in a grant to uses or

---

[41] See *Brent's Case* (1583) 2 Leon. 14 at 16; *Earl of Kent* v. *Steward* (1634) Cro.Car.
358.
[42] *Pells* v. *Brown* (1620) Cro.Jac. 590.
[43] *Gulliver* v. *Wickett* (1745) 1 Wils.K.B. 105.

n a will, the legal remainder rules were completely ousted. This was
not so. " Now, if there be one rule of law more sacred than another,
it is this, that no limitation shall be construed to be an executory or
shifting use, which can by possibility take effect by way of remainder." [44] This was known as the rule in *Purefoy* v. *Rogers*,[45] a case
which extended to wills a doctrine laid down in *Chudleigh's Case* [46]
for dispositions *inter vivos*. The effect of the rule was that if a legal
limitation, when made, was capable of conforming with the legal
remainder rules, it must be treated as a legal remainder, even though
it was contained in a conveyance to uses or a will; consequently,
if as events subsequently turned out a legal remainder rule was
infringed, the limitation failed. In other words, a legal limitation in a
will or conveyance to uses could be treated as an executory interest
only if, on the face of it, it was incapable of complying with the legal
remainder rules. There was no exception to this rule,[47] and it was a
rule of law which applied notwithstanding any contrary intention.[48]

IV. SUMMARY OF FUTURE INTERESTS (OTHER THAN REVERSIONS)
AT THE BEGINNING OF THE NINETEENTH CENTURY

1. Legal remainders. These arose either—

(a) where a future interest was created *inter vivos* without the
intervention of a use; or

(b) where a future interest was created by a conveyance to uses or
a devise, and the rule in *Purefoy* v. *Rogers* was complied with.

2. Future trusts. These arose either—

(a) *inter vivos*, by means of a use not executed by the Statute of
Uses 1535; or

(b) by means of a devise showing an intent that the legal estate
should be vested in trustees.

3. Legal executory interests. These arose either—

(a) *inter vivos*, by means of an executed use; or

(b) by devise,

provided that, in either case, the rule in *Purefoy* v. *Rogers* was ousted
by patent failure to comply with the rules governing legal remainders.

44 *Cole* v. *Sewell* (1843) 4 Dr. & War. 1 at 27.
45 (1671) 2 Wms.Saund. 380.
46 (1595) 1 Co.Rep. 113b at 137b, 138a.
47 *Doe.* d. *Mussell* v. *Morgan* (1790) 3 T.R. 763 at 765.
48 *White* v. *Summers* [1908] 2 Ch. 256 at 267.

Sect. 2. Statutory Reforms

A. Destruction of Contingent Remainders

1. Natural destruction. The combined effect of the " timely vesting " rule and the rule in *Purefoy* v. *Rogers* was frequently fatal to the validity of a remainder. If it did not vest in time, it suffered natural destruction owing to operation of these rules.

2. Artificial destruction. Natural destruction was not the only danger: a remainder might suffer artificial destruction. By certain devices derived from medieval law it was possible to bring about the premature determination of the particular estate. Thus if the tenant for life was disseised, or if the particular estate was forfeited, surrendered, enlarged or disclaimed, the contingent remainders were liable to be destroyed. The devices were favoured by the courts because they countered the tendency to perpetuities which settlements involved.[49]

3. Trustees to preserve contingent remainders. By a conveyancing device invented in the seventeenth century it became possible to protect contingent remainders against artificial destruction.[50] This was done by interposing a vested remainder to trustees to take the place of the particular estate if it were prematurely destroyed. The device was successful in the settlements in which it was employed, but not all settlors or testators were prudent enough to insert it, and in any event it did not preserve contingent remainders from natural destruction.

4. Statutory reforms. The various methods of destroying contingent remainders were abolished by a succession of nineteenth century statutes.

(a) *The Real Property Limitation Act* 1833 effectively ended the destruction of the remainder following the dispossession of the tenant for life.[51]

(b) *The Real Property Act* 1845 abolished the destruction of the remainder by forfeiture, surrender or merger (enlargement).[52]

---

[49] See 7 H.E.L. 217, 218.
[50] See 7 H.E.L. 112.
[51] ss. 4, 5, 39.
[52] s. 8.

(c) *The Contingent Remainders Act* 1877 substantially abolished the destruction of the remainder by disclaimer. Of far greater importance, it abolished the " timely vesting " rule and thereby put an end to the natural destruction of contingent remainders.

5. Land Transfer Act 1897. This Act was concerned with the general law, but although it was not specifically concerned with contingent remainders, it had an important effect on them. It provided that when a person died after 1897, all his realty should vest in his personal representatives in the same way as his personalty.[53] As the legal estate was thus vested in the testator's personal representatives, the rights of the beneficiaries were necessarily equitable. It was accordingly impossible for a legal remainder or legal executory interest to be created by the will of a testator dying after 1897; the only future interests which could arise under such a will were future trusts. This position was not affected by the personal representatives conveying the legal estate to the beneficiaries after completing the administration of the testator's property. The rights of the beneficiaries clearly ought not to depend upon the exact moment at which the personal representatives carried out their ministerial duty of clothing the beneficiaries with the legal estate, and consequently the rule was that interests which were equitable in their inception retained their immunity from destruction when they became legal.[54]

B. *Legislation of* 1925

The two main statutory changes are—

(1) the Statute of Uses 1535 has been repealed [55]; and
(2) no future estate in real property can be legal, for the only legal estate in realty now possible is the fee simple absolute in possession.[56]

The result is therefore that—

(i) legal remainders can no longer exist, for the second reason above, and
(ii) legal executory interests can no longer exist, for both reasons; but
(iii) future trusts can still exist.

[53] *Post*, p. 313.
[54] *Re Freme* [1891] 3 Ch. 167.
[55] *Ante*, p. 67.
[56] *Ante*, p. 72.

After 1925, therefore, all future interests in realty must necessarily be equitable, the legal estate being vested in some trustee or trustees. Neither the legal remainder rules nor *Purefoy* v. *Rogers* can apply; the Real Property Act 1845, s. 8, and the Contingent Remainders Act 1877, are repealed.[57] Legal remainders and legal executory interests existing before 1926 were automatically converted into equitable interests. Thus the comparatively simple law of future trusts, free from feudal rules and statutory modifications, now applies to all future interests. In all cases, the land will either be settled land and subject to the code laid down by the Settled Land Act 1925, or else be subject to a trust for sale. This means that there is full freedom to dispose of the land itself, notwithstanding the rights of the beneficiaries, for their rights will be transferred from the land to the purchase-money which represents it.[58]

Part 3

RULES AGAINST REMOTENESS

For many years, future interests have been subject to a number of rules limiting the period for which a settlor could exercise control over property. Thus a settlor could not render the capital of property for ever inalienable, nor could he settle property so that it might vest an inordinate number of years in the future. The following are the rules:

(1) The rule in *Whitby* v. *Mitchell*,[59] sometimes called the old rule against perpetuities, or the rule against double possibilities.

(2) The rule against perpetuities. This is sometimes referred to as the modern rule against perpetuities to distinguish it from *Whitby* v. *Mitchell*.

(3) The rule against inalienability or perpetual trusts.

(4) The rule against accumulations.

Whitby v. *Mitchell* was a rule dating from the sixteenth century. It applied only to legal (and, later, equitable) remainders, and so when executory interests became more and more popular, some restraint had to be devised to keep them within bounds. This restraint became known as the modern rule against perpetuities, being first dealt with

[57] By the L.P.A.(Am.)A. 1924, 10th Sched.
[58] *Post*, pp. 160, 184.
[59] (1890) 44 Ch.D. 85.

at length in 1685 by the House of Lords in the *Duke of Norfolk's
Case*.[60] The rule gradually crystallised, and reached its final form in
1833.[61] It is far wider than *Whitby* v. *Mitchell*, for it extends to all
interests in all property. The rule against inalienability is also based
on decided cases of respectable antiquity. The rule against accumulations, on the other hand, is of comparatively modern statutory origin,
starting with the Accumulations Act 1800. All the rules except the
rule in *Whitby* v. *Mitchell* are still in force.

Sect. 1. The Rule in Whitby v. Mitchell [62]

1. The Rule. Although this rule is now known by the name of a
case decided in 1890 in which it was thoroughly discussed, it seems
to be of considerable but uncertain age. Stated in its simplest form,
the rule was as follows:

> If an interest in realty is given to an unborn person, any remain-
> der to his issue is void, together with all subsequent limitations.

Thus if land was limited—

> " to A for life, remainder to his daughter for life, remainder to
> her children and their heirs " (A having no daughter at the time
> of the gift),

the life estates of A and his daughter were valid, but the remainder to
the daughter's children was void. Further, if the children had instead
been given mere life estates, followed by a fee simple in favour of B,
the gift to B was also void.[63]

2. Rival rules. The rule is sometimes referred to as " the rule
against double possibilities " or " the rule that a possibility upon a
possibility is void," but these descriptions are unsuitable. At one
time there were no less than three supposed rules which tended to
become confused with each other. Two of these so-called rules never
became accepted as law. The third was the rule in *Whitby* v.
Mitchell. The two abortive rules were:

(a) *The rule against remote possibilities*, which postulated that a
limitation to take effect upon a remote or unlikely contingency was

60 3 Ch.Ca. 1. The leading modern work is Morris and Leach, *The Rule Against
   Perpetuities*, 2nd edition.
61 *Cadell* v. *Palmer* (1833) 1 Cl. & F. 372.
62 (1890) 44 Ch.D. 85.
63 *Re Mortimer* [1905] 2 Ch. 502.

void and that the law permitted only common or likely possibilities
The rule seems to have started with *Cholmley's Case* in 1597,[64] bu
the difficulty of drawing any line between common and remote con
tingencies made its application a matter of great uncertainty. The
supposed rule never had any real vitality and soon became discredited

(b) *The rule against double possibilities*, which appears to have
been first suggested in the *Rector of Chedington's Case* in 1598.[65]
The principle seems to have been that a limitation which depended
upon more than one possibility was void. However, a gift to A for
life with remainder to the eldest grandson of B (a bachelor) involved
at least two possibilities, namely, that B might have no child, and that
even if he had a child, the child might have no son; yet the remainder
was valid, and the same applied to a remainder to the first son of Z to
be 21. In the face of cases such as these it was difficult to maintain
that there was any real rule against double possibilities and it has been
said that the rule " never had any real existence; it perished almost a
soon as it drew breath." [66]

3. " Perpetual freeholds." The rule in *Whitby* v. *Mitchell* met
the ingenuity of settlors who wished to keep land in their families
indefinitely. Ever since *Taltarum's Case* in 1472 [67] it has been pos
sible to bar an entail, and so a limitation—

" to **X** and the heirs of his body "

gave no assurance that the land would descend from father to son for
any length of time. A settlor might consequently create what was
known as a " perpetual freehold " by giving the land—

" to **X** for life, remainder to his son for life, remainder to the
son's son for life "

and so on *ad infinitum*, thus creating a series of life estates closely
resembling an unbarrable entail. The modern rule against perpe
tuities, which would have invalidated such a device, did not begin to
emerge until the seventeenth century,[68] and so the rule in *Whitby* v
Mitchell was evolved to meet the danger.[69]

---

[64] 2 Co.Rep. 50a.
[65] 1 Co.Rep. 148b at 156b.
[66] Charles Sweet (1912) 12 Col.L.R. 199 at 216.
[67] *Ante*, p. 37.
[68] See *post*, p. 103.
[69] See *Perrot's Case* (1594) Moo.K.B. 368 at 371, 372.

4. The Rule after 1925. In modern times, the rule in *Whitby* v. *Mitchell* was at best a useless survival. The perpetuity rule formed a uniform and satisfactory guard against any real mischief of remoteness, and the somewhat narrow and technical rule in *Whitby* v. *Mitchell*, by sometimes invalidating gifts despite their compliance with the perpetuity rule, was a purposeless trap for unwary draftsmen. Accordingly, the rule in *Whitby* v. *Mitchell* was abolished for all instruments coming into operation after 1925,[70] including an appointment made after 1925 under a power conferred before 1926.[71]

Sect. 2. The Rule against Perpetuities

A. History

1. Need for rule. The requirement that a legal remainder must vest during the continuance of the particular estate or at its end normally made it impossible for such a remainder to vest at a very remote date[72]; a remainder after a life estate had to vest during that estate, a remainder after an entail could be barred, and there could be no remainder after a fee simple. But by means of springing and shifting uses, estates could be made to spring up or shift at remote future dates, thus leaving the ultimate ownership and right of alienation uncertain for a long time. A rule was finally settled which kept such interests within due limits; this allowed settlors to leave the ultimate ownership uncertain for a maximum period of a lifetime plus a further 21 years. This corresponds to the practice under a strict settlement; if land is settled on H for life with remainder to his son in tail, the maximum period which can elapse before the entail can be barred is H's lifetime plus the son's minority, *i.e.*, 21 years.[73]

2. Development. It was many years before the rule was finally settled. As early as 1662 the limitation of a term of years to several living persons in succession had been held good,[74] and in 1679 an executory devise which might not have vested until the expiration of a lifetime plus 21 years was held valid.[75] But the rule became firmly

---

[70] L.P.A. 1925, s. 161.
[71] *Re Leigh's Marriage Settlement* [1952] 2 All E.R. 57. For powers of appointment, see *post*, p. 124.
[72] See *ante*, p. 91, and *post*, p. 122.
[73] See *post*, pp. 143, 203.
[74] *Goring* v. *Bickerstaffe* (1662) Pollex. 31.
[75] *Taylor* d. *Smith* v. *Biddall*, 2 Mod. 287.

established only by stages. The *Duke of Norfolk's Case*[76] in 1685
settled beyond doubt that a shifting use bound to take effect, if at all
during a life in being was valid. In 1797 it was settled that a child
en ventre sa mère (conceived but not born) might be treated as a life
in being,[77] thus extending the period by a possible further 9 months
or so, and by then it had become accepted that the effect of a statute
of 1698 [78] was that the period of 21 years after the life in being also
might be extended to cover a further period of gestation if it existed.
In 1805 it was finally settled that the lives in being might be chosen at
random and be unconnected with the property,[79] and by 1833 the
rule was completed by the decision of the House of Lords in *Cadell*
v. *Palmer* [80] that the period of 21 years was an absolute period without reference to any minority, but that the periods of gestation could
be added only if in fact gestation existed.

   3. Statutory reform. The rule was invented and developed by the
judges without the intervention of Parliament. In the main it
achieved a sound solution to the problem of perpetuity, but its undue
rigidity produced anomalies requiring reform. Minor amendments
were made by the Law of Property Act 1925, followed by major
alterations under the Perpetuities and Accumulations Act 1964. As
is customary, these statutes did not sweep away the old law, but built
upon it. Thus an understanding of the old law is still essential in
order to appreciate the changes. Moreover, the former law still
governs future interests taking effect under past dispositions, for the
Act of 1964 applies only to instruments taking effect after its commencement, *i.e.*, instruments made after July 15, 1964.[81]

B. Statement of the Rule

The rule may be stated thus:

   (1) A limitation of any interest in any property, real or personal,
       is void if it is capable of vesting after the perpetuity period has
       expired.

   (2) The perpetuity period consists of a life or lives in being at the

---

[76] 3 Ch.Ca. 1.
[77] *Long* v. *Blackall*, 7 T.R. 100.
[78] Statute of Posthumous Children 1698.
[79] *Thellusson* v. *Woodford* (1805) 11 Ves. 112.
[80] 1 Cl. & F. 372.
[81] s. 15 (5).

time of the gift, together with a further period of 21 years; and where gestation actually exists, the period of gestation may be added.

The principal points must now be considered in some detail.

1. Meaning of " vest." The meaning of " vest " has already been considered.[82] The rule does not require that an interest should be incapable of vesting *in possession* after the period has run, but only that it should be incapable of becoming vested *in interest* outside the period.[83] Thus if land is devised on trust for X for life with remainder to his first and other sons successively for life, the limitations are valid even if X was a bachelor at the time of the gift. Each of X's sons obtains a vested interest at birth, and these interests are not invalidated by the fact that some of the sons may not be entitled to possession of the property until after the period has run[84]; it is thus immaterial that if X was a bachelor at the time of the gift and his eldest son outlives him by 50 years, the interest of the second son will not vest in possession until 29 years after the perpetuity period has run.

2. No " wait and see " at common law. In general,[85] the unreformed rule deals with possibilities, not probabilities or actual events. Every limitation must be considered at the time when the instrument creating it takes effect. Thus a deed must be considered at the time when it is executed, while a will must be considered at the moment of the testator's death.[86] If at the relevant moment there is the slightest possibility that the perpetuity period may be exceeded, the limitation is void, even if it is most improbable that this in fact will happen and even if, as events turn out, it does not.[87] For example, if property is given—

> " to A [a bachelor] for life, remainder to his widow for life, remainder to the eldest of his brothers living at the widow's death,"

the remainder to the brother is bad if A's parents are alive. It is just possible that A will marry someone who was not alive at the time of

[82] *Ante*, p. 84.
[83] *Evans* v. *Walker* (1876) 3 Ch.D. 211.
[84] *Re Hargreaves* (1889) 43 Ch.D. 401.
[85] See *post*, pp. 117, 118, 126, for qualifications of this rule.
[86] *Vanderplank* v. *King* (1843) 3 Hare 1 at 17.
[87] These words were approved in *Re Watson's S.T.* [1959] 1 W.L.R. 732 at 739.

the gift, and if A's wife survived him for more than 21 years, the property might become vested outside the period in a brother born after the date of the gift. This possibility renders the gift to the brother void, even if A is very old and unlikely to marry or in fact marries someone alive at the time of the gift, and even if A's parents are so old that they are most unlikely to have any more children. For the purposes of the perpetuity rule, no person is ever deemed too old to have children,[88] though for other purposes the courts take a more realistic view of preternatural fertility[89]; but statute prevents the lawful marriage (and so lawful issue) of a person under the age of 16 years.[90] Again, a gift of property to certain persons " if the minerals under the said farm should be worked " offends the perpetuity rule and is void because of the possibility that the minerals will be worked after the perpetuity period has run.[91]

It is immaterial that the gift may never vest at all; the question is whether, if it does vest, it is capable of vesting *outside* the period. A gift to the first son of X, a bachelor, may never vest at all, for X may never have a son. But this possibility does not render the gift void for perpetuity; the gift is incapable of vesting outside the perpetuity period, for if X does have a son, the son must be born or conceived during X's lifetime, and X is the life in being. In short, the gift is bound to vest, *if it vests at all*, within the perpetuity period. Again, a gift by will—

" to the first of my daughters to marry after my death "

is valid, even though no daughter may marry; for if any daughter does marry, she must do so in her own lifetime, and since the testator is dead when the gift takes effect, no further daughters can be born and all those who are alive or *en ventre sa mère* rank as lives in being. Had the gift been made by deed, it would have been void, for the donor might have had further daughters after the date of the gift (who would not have been lives in being) and one of these might have been the first to qualify for the gift by marrying more than 21 years after the death of the donor and all his other daughters.

A gift which would otherwise be too remote may be validated by the insertion of an express clause confining its vesting to the proper period. Thus a gift by a testator to such of his issue as should be living

[88] See *Ward* v. *Van der Loeff* [1924] A.C. 653 (persons aged 66).
[89] See, *e.g., Re White* [1901] 1 Ch. 570.
[90] *Re Gaite's W.T.* [1949] 1 All E.R. 459 (Age of Marriage Act 1929); but see J. H. C. Morris (1949) 13 Conv.(N.S.) 289.
[91] *Thomas* v. *Thomas* (1902) 87 L.T. 58.

when some gravel pits should become exhausted is void as it stands, even if it is highly probable that the pits will be worked out in five or six years.[92] The gift would have been valid, however, if worded ' to such of my issue living 21 years after my death or when the gravel pits are exhausted, whichever first happens "; and a gift to bodies existing " when the residue of my estate is realised " has been construed as being confined to the " executor's year," [93] *i.e.*, one year from death.[94] But a clause seeking to confine the vesting within the period must do so explicitly; a void gift is not validated merely by the addition of words providing that the vesting shall be postponed only " so far as the rules of law and equity will permit." [95]

3. Future parenthood. The Act of 1964 has replaced the rigid rule that no person is too old to have children with a statutory presumption

(a) that a male can have a child at the age of 14 or over, but not under that age, and

(b) that a female can have a child at the age of 12 or over, but not under that age or over the age of 55.[96]

This presumption may be rebutted by showing that in a particular case a living person will or will not be able to have a child at the time in question.[97]

" Having a child " extends to having a child " by adoption, legitimation or other means." [98] This extension is not of great practical significance as, in the absence of a contrary indication, references to children or issue or the like in a will or settlement do not include children legitimated or adopted after the date of the gift.[99]

If events falsify the presumptions, the High Court has a general discretion to make such order as it thinks fit for placing the persons interested in the property in the position they would have been if the presumptions had not been [1] applied.

4. " Wait and see " under the Act of 1964.

(a) *The new rule.* The common law rule has one great advantage, one can see at the outset whether the gift is good or bad. But it

---

[92] *Re Wood* [1894] 3 Ch. 381.
[93] See *post*, p. 310.
[94] *Re Petrie* [1962] Ch. 355.
[95] *Portman* v. *Viscount Portman* [1922] 2 A.C. 473; contrast *Re Vaux* [1939] Ch. 465. [96] s. 2 (1).
[97] *Ibid.* [98] s. 2 (4).
[99] See Legitimacy Act 1926, s. 3; Adoption Act 1958, s. 16.
[1] s. 2 (2).

frequently frustrates the intentions of settlors and testators by striking down limitations which almost certainly would vest within the period. To meet these cases the Act of 1964 has introduced the rule of " wait and see " to limitations in instruments taking effect after July 15, 1964,[2] which would be void at common law. For such a gift the Act provides that it is not to be treated as if it were subject to the rule against perpetuities until " it becomes established that the vesting must occur, if at all, after the end of the perpetuity period." [3] It is now permissible to look at actual rather than possible events, so that the disposition does not become void until it is clear that it is going to vest, if it vests at all, outside the period.

(b) *Examples.* We may take the example previously given [4]—

> " to A [a bachelor] for life, remainder to his widow for life, remainder to the eldest of his brothers living at the widow's death."

The remainder to the brother was bad at common law if A's parents were alive. But under the Act one can wait and see whether one or other of the following probable events occurs: either A dies unmarried, or he marries someone who is alive at the date of the gift, or his parents die without having any more children. If any of these events occurs, the remainder must vest, if at all, within the period, and the gift will be valid. But if A marries someone who is not born at the date of the gift who survives him by more than 21 years, and A's parents do not have another son until after the date of the gift, it will " become established " that the vesting must occur if at all after the end of the period and hence the remainder to the eldest brother will fail.

Similarly, a gift by a testator to such of his issue as should be living when some gravel pits should become exhausted, which is void at common law, will be valid if the pits become exhausted within 21 years of the death of the survivor of those of his issue who are living at his death.

(c) *Consequences.* The practical consequences of the new rule will not be as great as one might suppose from so radical an amendment of the rule. In the first place, the great majority of limitations in fact comply with the old rule, and it is not to be expected that the Act will bring about a relaxation of the standards of drafting. Secondly, the new rule does not extend the period: it does not enable

---

[2] See *ante*, p. 104.   [3] s. 3 (1).   [4] *Ante*, p. 105.

a donor to do anything which he cannot achieve within the framework of the common law rule by the use of an express clause confining the vesting to the proper period.[5]

5. The perpetuity period.

(a) *At common law.*

(1) LIVES IN BEING. For a person to be a life in being for the purposes of the rule, it is unnecessary that he should receive any benefit from the gift or that he should be in any way connected with the beneficiaries.[6] Nor is there any restriction upon the number of lives selected, provided it is reasonably possible to ascertain who they are, " for let the lives be never so many, there must be a survivor, and so it is but the length of that life "[7]: " If a term be limited to one for life, with twenty several remainders for lives to other persons successively, who are all alive and in being, so that all the candles are lighted together, this is good enough."[8] For example, gifts by a testator to such of his descendants as are living 21 years after the death of the last survivor of the members of a given school at the testator's death,[9] or 20 years after the death of the last survivor of all the lineal descendants of Queen Victoria living at the testator's death,[10] have been held valid. In the latter case, the testator died in 1926 when there were some 120 lives in being and it was reasonably possible to follow the duration of their lives; a similar limitation today might well be void for uncertainty,[11] though the living descendants of King George V may safely be selected.[12]

From one point of view, everyone alive at the time of the gift is a life in being in the literal sense. Nevertheless, the only lives in being which have to be considered in relation to the perpetuity rule are those which are mentioned in the gift either expressly or by implication. In the above examples, lives in being have been expressly mentioned, but this is not always the case. If a testator gives property to such of his grandchildren as attain the age of 21, his children can be taken as lives in being. They are all bound to have been born by the time of the testator's death, and a gift to

---

5 See *ante*, pp. 106, 107.
6 *Cadell* v. *Palmer* (1833) 1 Cl. & F. 372.
7 *Scatterwood* v. *Edge* (1697) 1 Salk. 229.
8 *Howard* v. *Duke of Norfolk* (1681) 2 Swans. 454 at 458.
9 *Pownall* v *Graham* (1863) 33 Beav. 242 at 245, 247.
10 *Re Villar* [1929] 1 Ch. 243.
11 Consider *Re Moore* [1901] 1 Ch. 936.
12 See *Re Leverhulme* [1943] 2 All E.R. 274.

grandchildren presupposes the existence of children. The gift is therefore good, for no grandchild can take longer than 21 years from its parents' death to reach the age of 21. But a gift to the grandchildren of a living person is bad, unless the class is restricted in some way, *e.g.*, to those living at the death of a life in being [13]; the living person might have another child after the date of the gift and then, after all those alive at the date of the gift had died, that child might have a child.

Consequently, it can be said that everyone who is—

(i) alive at the time of the gift, and
(ii) mentioned in it either expressly or by implication,

should be considered as a life in being; but other persons, the length or shortness of whose lives have no bearing on the gift, may be ignored. In the case of limitations made *inter vivos*, the date of the instrument and, in the case of wills, the date of the testator's death, is the time when the period starts running and the facts must be ascertained; to be a life in being, a person must be alive at that moment.

The lives must be human lives, and not the lives of animals. [14]

(2) IF THE LIMITATION IS MADE WITHOUT REFERENCE TO LIVES IN BEING, THE PERIOD IS 21 YEARS. A gift by a testator to all his issue living 50 years after his death, or to all the children of X (who is alive) living 28 years after the testator's death, is void. [15] It is true that in the first case the testator's children and in the second X could be taken as lives in being, but in neither case has the period selected any relation to their lives; it is a period in gross, and neither the immediate death nor the prolonged life of the testator's children or of X will alter the date of vesting. Consequently the gifts must be treated as if there were no lives in being, with the result that the period is 21 years.

(3) A CHILD EN VENTRE SA MÈRE IS TREATED AS HAVING BEEN BORN. For the purposes of the perpetuity rule, a child *en ventre sa mère* is treated as if it had been born. Two cases can arise:

(i) A child may be *en ventre sa mère* at the beginning of the period, *i.e.*, at the time of the gift; in this case, the child is treated as a life in being. [16] Thus if a testator gives property

---

[13] *Wetherell* v. *Wetherell* (1863) 1 De G.J. & S. 134 at 139, 140.
[14] See *Re Kelly* [1932] I.R. 255 at 260, 261.
[15] *Speakman* v. *Speakman* (1850) 8 Hare 180; *Palmer* v. *Holford* (1828) 4 Russ. 403.
[16] *Re Wilmer's Trusts* [1903] 2 Ch. 411 at 421.

for life to the child with which his wife is enceinte, with a remainder contingent upon certain circumstances existing at that child's death, the remainder is good, for the contingency must be resolved at the child's death and the child is treated as the life in being.[17]

(ii) A child may be *en ventre sa mère* during the period; in this case, the period is extended as far as is necessary to include the period of gestation. Thus if property is given to the first of A's sons to reach his majority, the gift is valid even if A's only son was unborn at A's death; the perpetuity period in such a case is A's lifetime plus the period of gestation and 21 years.

It will be seen from this that two periods of gestation may arise in the same case; both are allowed. If property is given to Jane's eldest child for life, with remainder to the first son of that child to be 21 and Jane is pregnant with her first child at the time of the gift, the remainder does not infringe the perpetuity rule even though Jane's child may be a son who dies leaving his wife enceinte of an only son. Jane's child is treated as a life in being, and the perpetuity period will be extended to cover the period of gestation of the child's son.[18]

These rules do not allow the addition of any period or periods of nine months or so in all cases; they apply only where gestation actually exists.[19]

(b) *Reform by Law of Property Act 1925, s. 163.* A frequent cause of gifts failing was that they were made contingent upon the beneficiary attaining an age greater than 21. Thus property might be given—

" to the first of A's children to attain the age of 25."

In certain circumstances, the gift would be good; if A was dead at the time of the gift, he could have no further children and since every possible claimant was a life in being, the gift would be valid.[20] Further, even if A was alive, if one of his children had attained the age of 25 at the date of the gift, the limitation was valid as being an immediate gift to an ascertained person.[21] But if A was alive and no child had attained the age of 25, the gift was bad. This was so

---

17 *Long* v. *Blackall* (1797) 7 T.R. 100.
18 See *Thellusson* v. *Woodford* (1805) 11 Ves. 112 at 143, 149, 150.
19 *Cadell* v. *Palmer* (1833) 1 Cl. & F. 372 at 421, 422.
20 *Southern* v. *Wollaston* (1852) 16 Beav. 276.
21 *Picken* v. *Matthews* (1878) 10 Ch.D. 264.

even if a child had attained the age of 24, for there was no certainty
that he would not die before his twenty-fifth birthday and a child born
after the date of the gift be the first child to reach the age of 25.[22]

To deal with cases such as this, section 163 of the Law of Property
Act 1925 lays down that in certain circumstances the age of 21 may
be substituted for the offending age. This may be done only if—

(i) the limitation is contained in an instrument executed after
1925, or in the will of a testator dying after 1925 but in either
case before the commencement of the Act of 1964; and

(ii) the limitation would otherwise be void; and

(iii) the excess is in the age of the beneficiary or class of beneficiaries.

The first point needs no illustration; the second may be illustrated
by considering the limitation mentioned above, namely, " to the first
of A's children to attain the age of 25." Before 1926, if A was alive
and no child had reached the age of 25, the gift failed; if made after
1925, section 163 substitutes " 21 " for " 25 " and the gift is good, the
first child to attain the age of 21 taking the property at that age. But
if A had been dead, the gift would have been valid without the aid of
section 163 and so " 25 " remains undisturbed. In the result, if A's
eldest child is aged 19 at the time of the gift, whether he must wait
two years or six before becoming entitled depends upon whether A is
alive or dead.

The third point may be illustrated by cases where vesting is postponed for a fixed period of years. A gift to the testator's issue living
50 years after his death was void before 1926 [23] and was not validated
by section 163, for the " 50 " is not the age of a beneficiary.

(c) *Act of 1964.*

(1) LIVES IN BEING. It is controversial whether the introduction of
the " wait and see " principle requires any alteration in the rules for
ascertaining the lives in being. Some contend that no alteration is
necessary. They argue that the lives in being at common law are not
confined to those which necessarily limit the vesting of the gift within
the perpetuity period, but are those which are so connected with the
gift as to restrict the period of vesting, and they may or may not
restrict it sufficiently to save it at common law.[24] Others say that the

---

[22] See, *e.g.*, *Re Finch* (1881) 17 Ch.D. 211.
[23] See *ante*, p. 110.
[24] Morris and Wade (1964) 80 L.Q.R. 486 at 495 to 501.

new rule would achieve nothing if it were tied to the lives in being at common law, as gifts whose vesting is restricted by those lives are valid anyway without having to wait and see. Therefore, it is said, unless some definition of the lives in being for the purposes of the new rule is provided, there would be only two possible periods in which to wait and see: either a mere 21 years from the date of the gift, or, at the other extreme, 21 years beyond the life of any person in the world living at the date of the gift.[25]

The framers of the Act of 1964 have adopted the latter view and have provided four categories of lives, all of whom must be both in being and ascertainable at the date of the gift. Further, lives in the second and third categories which are defined by description are to be disregarded if they are so numerous as to render it impracticable to ascertain the death of the survivor.[26] If there are no lives in the four categories which satisfy the preceding conditions, the " wait and see " period is 21 years from the date of the gift.[27]

The four categories are as follows.[28]

(a) The donor: " the person by whom the disposition was made."

(b) A donee: " a person to whom or in whose favour the disposition was made, that is to say—

    (i) in the case of a disposition to a class of persons, any member or potential member of the class;

   (ii) in the case of an individual disposition to a person taking only on certain conditions being satisfied, any person as to whom some of the conditions are satisfied and the remainder may in time be satisfied;

 (iii) and (iv) [these concern special powers of appointment discussed below [29]];

   (v) in the case of any power, option or other right, the person on whom the right is conferred."

(c) A donee's parent or grandparent.

(d) The owner of a prior interest.

In many cases these complicated provisions produce the same lives in being as the common law rule, but there are divergences. Sometimes more lives are available under the Act. Thus a gift " to A's

[25] Allan (1965) 81 L.Q.R. 106.
[26] s. 3 (4) (*a*).
[27] s. 3 (4) (*b*).
[28] s. 3 (5).
[29] *Post*, p. 125.

first grandson to attain 21 " where A is alive and without an adult
grandson at the date of the gift is void at common law as A is the only
life in being and his first grandson to attain 21 might do so more than
21 years after A's death. Under the " wait and see " rule, which
applies as the gift is void at common law, the lives in being are the
donor, A, any existing children of A (under (c) above), and any
existing infant grandchildren (under (b) (ii) above), so that one waits
and sees whether a grandchild reaches 21 within 21 years of the death
of the survivor of those lives. Occasionally fewer lives are available
under the new rule than under the old. Thus " royal lives " cannot
be specified for the purposes of the " wait and see " rule.[30]

(2) REDUCTION OF FIXED AGES. For instruments taking effect after
July 15, 1964, the Act of 1964 has replaced the Law of Property Act
1925, s. 163, with a more flexible provision. It operates where a
disposition satisfies the following conditions—

(a) It is limited by reference to the attainment by any person or
persons of a specified age exceeding 21 years.[31] The corresponding
provision of section 163 applied only to the excessive age of a beneficiary, but this will apply to such a limitation as one to an as yet
unborn person " living when A's eldest son attains 25."

(b) It is apparent when the disposition is made or becomes
apparent later—

(i) that it would otherwise be void for remoteness, but
(ii) that it would not be so void if the specified age had been 21
years.

(c) It is not saved by the " wait and see " rule.

If these conditions are satisfied, the disposition is treated as if it
had been limited by reference to the nearest age which would have
prevented it from being void.[31] Here again the new provision diverges
from section 163 under which the reduction was to 21 years in every
case.

Thus if there is a gift by will to A's children at 25, where A is
alive at the date of the testator's death, one first " waits and sees "
whether the gift is valid without alteration. This will be so if all A's
children were alive at the testator's death, or were all over four at A's
death. If, however, A's youngest child was not alive at the testator's

---

[30] For royal lives see *ante*, p. 109. But note the alternative fixed period provision:
post, p. 115.
[31] s. 4 (1).

death but was a year old at A's death, the vesting age will be reduced
to 22 years.

The new provision, unlike section 163, also caters for gifts which
specify two or more specified ages. If there is a gift by will to A's
sons who attain 30 and his daughters who attain 25, and on A's
death after the testator his youngest son is 8 and his youngest
daughter is 3, the vesting dates will be cut down to 29 for sons and 24
for daughters.[32]

(3) SURVIVING SPOUSES. A gift to such of the children of A as
should be living at the death of the survivor of A and his widow frequently failed at common law because of the possibility that A might
marry a person not born at the date of the gift. This notorious trap
of the " unborn widow " has been eliminated by the Act of 1964. If a
gift which refers to the death of the survivor of a person in being and
his or her spouse is not saved by the " wait and see " rule, it is to be
treated as " if it had instead been limited by reference to the time
immediately before the end of " the perpetuity period.[33] Thus in the
example above, if A is survived by his widow, the gift will vest 21
years after the death of A if the widow is then still living, so that the
children then living will take even if one or more of them subsequently die before the widow.

(4) ALTERNATIVE FIXED PERIOD. The Act of 1964 contains one
completely new concept. As an alternative to the perpetuity period
based on lives in being, it is permissible to specify a fixed period of
years not exceeding 80 as the perpetuity period.[34] The period must be
expressly specified; it cannot be left to be implied as in a gift by
will to such of the testator's descendants living 80 years after his
death. He must add some such expression as " which I specify as
the perpetuity period for this gift." It will be noted that this period
can be used with much the same effect as the " royal lives " clauses
at common law.

**6. Where a deed or will contains several limitations, the rule must
be applied to each limitation separately.** Thus if there is a gift—

" to A for life, remainder to his eldest son for life, remainder to
B's eldest grandson in fee simple,"

the perpetuity rule must be applied to each of the three limitations

[32] See s. 4 (2).
[33] s. 5.
[34] s. 1.

separately. If all are valid, no difficulty arises; but if one or more are bad, the following rules must be applied.

(a) *No limitation is void merely because it is followed by a void limitation.*[35] A gift " to A for life " standing by itself is clearly good, and it is not invalidated merely because a limitation which infringes the rule is added, *e.g.,* " to A for life, remainder to the first of his descendants to marry a Latvian." In such a case, A takes a life interest and after his death the property reverts to the grantor or passes under his will or intestacy.

(b) *A limitation which is subsequent to and dependent upon a void limitation is itself void.*[36] It will be noticed that a limitation is not void merely because it follows a void limitation; it is invalidated by the rule only if in addition to following the void limitation it is also dependent upon it.[37] Thus if a testator devises property in fee simple—

" to the first of X's sons to become a clergyman, but if X has no such son, to Y in fee simple,"

and when the testator dies X is alive, the first part of the gift is void since the required event might occur more than 21 years after the death of lives in being. The gift to Y is subsequent to and dependent upon this void limitation; not until X and all his sons have died without any son having become a clergyman can it be said that Y is entitled. Thus even though the gift to Y is in favour of a living person, it fails as being dependent upon a void limitation.[38]

On the other hand, if property is given—

" to A for life, remainder for life to any wife he may marry, remainder for life to any husband whom such wife may marry, remainder to such of A's children as attain the age of 21,"

the gifts to A and his wife are both valid, for A is a life in being and his wife must be ascertained in his lifetime. But the limitation to the wife's husband is void for perpetuity, since A's wife may not be alive at the time of the gift and may marry more than 21 years after A's death. Nevertheless, the gift to A's children is valid, for

---

[35] *Garland* v. *Brown* (1864) 10 L.T. 292.
[36] *Re Abbott* [1893] 1 Ch. 54; *Re Hubbard's W.T.* [1963] Ch. 275.
[37] See *Re Coleman* [1936] Ch. 528.
[38] *Proctor* v. *Bishop of Bath and Wells* (1794) 2 Hy.Bl. 358.

although it follows a void limitation, it has its own independent date of vesting which cannot exceed the perpetuity period.[39]

The precise meaning of " dependent " in this context is obscure. Sometimes it seems to mean no more than " contingent," so that there is no special rule as to " dependence." But sometimes a remainder which seems plainly vested is struck down as being " dependent " upon a prior void limitation.[40] Such cases can be explained on the principle that if a testator intends the remainder not to take effect until the prior limitation ends, it would be contrary to that intention to allow the remainder to take immediate effect merely because the prior limitation is void for perpetuity. The remainder accordingly falls with the prior limitation. Thus if a testator gives property for life to the first son of A (a bachelor) to marry, and then to B, he may well have intended no immediate gift to B. Further, where a void limitation stands between two or more valid limitations, the limitation following the void limitation will be held dependent on it, and so invalid, unless it will " dovetail in and accord with " the prior valid limitations.[41]

(c) *Act of* 1964. The whole doctrine of " dependence " was so unsatisfactory and obscure that the Act of 1964 has abolished it for gifts made after July 15, 1964. Such a gift is not void merely because it is " ulterior to and dependent upon " a void gift. Further, the existence of the prior void gift will no longer prevent the acceleration of the vesting of the subsequent gift.[42]

7. Alternative contingencies. Where a gift expresses two alternative contingencies upon which the property may vest, and one contingency is too remote and one is not, the gift is good if in fact the valid contingency occurs.[43] Thus in one case,[44] a testator gave property to his grandchildren and issue of his grandchildren living—

> " on the decease of my last surviving child or on the death of the last surviving widow or widower of my children as the case may be whichever shall last happen."

It was held that this gift did not infringe the perpetuity rule as it stood, and that if in fact one of the testator's children outlived all

---

[39] See *Re Coleman* [1936] Ch. 528.
[40] *Re Backhouse* [1921] 2 Ch. 51.
[41] *Monypenny* v. *Dering* (1852) 2 De G.M. & G. 145 at 182.
[42] s. 6.
[43] *Hodgson* v. *Halford* (1879) 11 Ch.D. 959.
[44] *Re Curryer's W.T.* [1938] Ch. 952.

the other children and their spouses, the gift would be valid. There were two alternatives:

(i) that one of the testator's children (a life in being) would be the last survivor, or

(ii) that the spouse of one of the testator's children (not necessarily a life in being) would be the last survivor;

if the former actually occurred, the gift did not infringe the rule. To this extent, there is a " wait and see " in the perpetuity rule.

The foregoing applies only if the two alternative contingencies are expressed in the gift.[45] If only one contingency is expressed in the gift and that may be too remote, the gift fails even if there are in fact two contingencies. Thus in *Proctor* v. *Bishop of Bath and Wells*,[46] only one contingency was expressed, namely, that if no son of X became a clergyman, Y should be entitled. In fact, two contingencies were implicit in the gift, namely,

(i) X might leave no son; this must be known at X's death, which would be within the period:

(ii) X might leave one or more sons, who might become clergymen more than 21 years after X's death, which would be outside the period.

Nevertheless, the gift to Y was void *ab initio,* for the only contingency expressed was a void one. Had the gift over been worded—

" but if no son of X shall become a clergyman, or if X shall leave no son, to Y in fee simple,"

the gift to Y would have been valid if X had died leaving no son, *i.e.,* if the valid contingency had occurred.[47]

The Act of 1964 has not specifically altered these rules, but its general " wait and see " provisions will apply if the unduly remote contingency occurs, or if there is only one composite contingent gift.

8. Application to class gifts.

(a) *At common law.* A class gift is a gift of property to all who come within some description, the property being divisible in shares varying according to the number of persons in the class.[48]

---

[45] *Re Bence* [1891] 3 Ch. 242.
[46] *Ante*, p. 116.
[47] *Miles* v. *Harford* (1879) 12 Ch.D. 691 at 703.
[48] *Pearks* v. *Moseley* (1880) 5 App.Cas. 714 at 723 ; *Kingsbury* v. *Walter* [1901] A.C. 187 at 192.

Thus gifts of property—

"to my children who shall live to be 25," or—
"to all the nephews and nieces of my late husband who were living at his death, except A and B"

are class gifts. But gifts of property to be equally divided between—

"the five daughters of X," or—
"my nine children,"

or a gift of £2,000—

"to each of my daughters,"

are not class gifts, for a distinct one-fifth or one-ninth share or the sum of £2,000 is given to each child exactly as if he or she had been named.

The perpetuity rule applies to class gifts in the following way. If a single member of the class might possibly take a vested interest outside the period, the whole gift fails, even as regards those members of the class who have already satisfied any required contingency.[49] A class gift cannot be good as to part and void as to the rest: "the vice of remoteness affects the class as a whole, if it may affect an unascertained number of its members."[50] Until the total number of members of the class has been ascertained, it cannot be said what share any member of the class will take, and this state of affairs will continue as long as it is possible for any alteration in the number to be made.

Thus if before 1926 personalty was given—

"to A for life and after his death to be equally divided between all his children who shall attain the age of 25,"

an intent being shown to include every child of A, the remainder was void even as regards children alive at the time of the gift, who were thus lives in being.[51] This is so even if A is in fact many years past the age of child-bearing, for in theory other children might be born, and since one of these might not be 25 until more than 21 years after the death of all lives in being at the time of the gift, the period might be exceeded.[52]

(b) *Act of* 1964. The Act has abolished the rule that class gifts

---

[49] *Leake* v. *Robinson* (1817) 2 Mer. 363.
[50] *Pearks* v. *Moseley* (1880) 5 App.Cas. 714 at 723.
[51] *Leake* v. *Robinson, supra.*
[52] And see *post,* p. 284, for rules of construction which sometimes save class gifts; M. & W. 237–239.

cannot be good as to part and void as to the remainder. It eliminates those members of the class who fail to take vested interests within the period.[53] Thus we may take a gift by will

" to all the children of A who marry."

If A had predeceased the testator the gift would be good at common law. But if A survives the testator the gift would be bad at common law even though A already had children who were married because he might have had a further child who married more than 21 years after A's death. Under the Act one first waits to see how many children marry during the period (21 years after the death of A and of any children living at A's death). Any children then unmarried will be eliminated and the property divided between the married children.

9. Application to determinable and conditional interests.[54]

(a) *Determinable interests.* " The rule against perpetuities is not dealing with the duration of interests but with their commencement, and so long as the interest vests within lives in being and 21 years it does not matter how long that interest lasts." [55] Thus it can be said that the perpetuity rule does not invalidate a limitation merely because it provides that an interest shall cease at some future date outside the perpetuity period. Accordingly where property is given to an unborn person—

" for life or until she becomes a member of the Roman Catholic Church "

or—

" for life or until marriage,"

the specified event may occur outside the perpetuity period but the limitation is nevertheless valid.[56] The better view is that it is immaterial that the determinable interest is a fee simple and the event on which it will determine may not happen for centuries, *e.g.,* where property is conveyed to the X Co. Ltd. in fee simple until the premises are used otherwise than as a biscuit factory. When the event occurs, no new estate arises; the X Co. Ltd.'s fee simple terminates, and the grantor's possibility of reverter, which from the start has been vested in interest, takes effect.[57]

---

[53] s. 4 (4).
[54] See also *ante*, p. 32.
[55] *Re Chardon* [1928] Ch. 464 at 468.
[56] *Wainwright* v. *Miller* [1897] 2 Ch. 255; *Re Gage* [1898] 1 Ch. 498.
[57] But see *Hopper* v. *Corporation of Liverpool* (1944) 88 S.J. 213; contrast 1945 Conv.Y.B. pp. 203–206. And see further M. & W. 250, 251.

A similar rule applies to resulting trusts.[58] Where land is conveyed to trustees in trust for an orphans' home, and on failure of
that trust, in trust for the then owner of other land, the gift over is
plainly void for perpetuity; instead, there will be a resulting trust
for the grantor's estate, and this will not be held void for perpetuity.[59]

(b) *Conditional interests.* A condition may be either precedent
or subsequent.[60] A condition precedent is one which must be fulfilled before the beneficiary is entitled to a vested interest, *e.g.*—
   " to X and his heirs when he marries."
In such a case the perpetuity rule applies, for a new interest is
limited to arise when the event occurs; consequently, if the condition
might be fulfilled outside the perpetuity period the whole gift fails.[61]

A condition subsequent is one which authorises the grantor or
his representatives to determine an existing interest. Thus a gift of
land to X in fee simple—
   " on condition that he never sells it out of the family,"
gives the grantor a right of re-entry if the condition is broken. If
such a condition infringes the perpetuity rule it is void, but the
interest which it was to defeat is not invalidated. Thus if there is a
valid gift by a testator to his grandchildren followed by a clause
providing for the forfeiture of the interest of any grandchild who
should forsake the Jewish faith or marry outside that faith, all the
beneficiaries take absolute interests; the forfeiture clause is void
since it might not take effect until the perpetuity period had expired,
but there is nothing to invalidate the gift to the grandchildren.[62]

It will be noticed that a breach of a condition subsequent gives
rise to a right of re-entry, so that some active step must be taken to
determine the estate; a determinable limitation, on the other hand,
requires no future activity, for the estate automatically determines by
force of the original limitation.

(c) *Act of* 1964. Under the Act of 1964 the rules for determinable
and conditional interests have been assimilated. The rule against perpetuities is to apply to possibilities of reverter and resulting trusts
created by dispositions made after the Act as if they were in the
form of conditions subsequent.[63]

---

[58] For these, see *post*, p. 241.
[59] *Re Cooper's Conveyance Trusts* [1956] 1 W.L.R. 1096.
[60] *Ante*, p. 31.
[61] See, *e.g.*, *Pickford* v. *Brown* (1856) 2 K. & J. 426.
[62] *Re Spitzel's W.T.* [1939] 2 All E.R. 266.
[63] s. 12.

10. Application to legal contingent remainders. After much con-
troversy, it was finally settled that the perpetuity rule applied to legal
contingent remainders in the same way as to other future interests.[64]
However, the rule rarely destroyed such remainders, for they were
usually saved by the " timely vesting " rule, which provided that a
remainder failed altogether unless it vested during the continuance,
or at the determination, of the preceding particular estate.[65] Thus
if land was given—
       " to A for life, remainder to the first male heir of B,"
it might be many centuries before B had a male heir, for all his
heirs might be females. But it could be said from the first that one
of two events was bound to occur: either—

  (i) there would be a male heir of B at the time of A's death,
   or
  (ii) there would not.

If the first alternative occurred, the remainder would be valid and
would have vested during a life in being, *i.e.*, A's life; if the second
occurred, the remainder became void under the legal remainder rule
requiring it to vest during the continuance of the particular estate.
Consequently, whichever event in fact occurred, it could be said from
the start that the remainder could never become vested outside the
perpetuity period.[66] That very dependence upon the particular estate
which was the cause of their fragility saved such remainders from
the perpetuity rule and gave them a chance of being valid instead of
being declared void forthwith. The rule in *Purefoy* v. *Rogers*,[67] by
treating all legal limitations as remainders if they could be valid as
such, saved many limitations made by will or by a single use from
being destroyed by the perpetuity rule. On the other hand, the
effect of the Land Transfer Act 1897 was that no limitation under
the will of a testator dying after 1897 could create a legal remainder,
for the legal estate vested in his personal representatives.[68] The rights
of the beneficiaries were accordingly merely equitable, and so, not
being dependent on a particular estate, were exposed to the full force
of the perpetuity rule.

  However, although a single legal contingent remainder was never
void for perpetuity, if there were two or more of such interests in

[64] *Re Frost* (1889) 43 Ch.D. 246 ; *Re Ashforth* [1905] 1 Ch. 535.
[65] *Ante*, p. 92.
[66] See *Doe* d. *Winter* v. *Perratt* (1843) 9 Cl. & F. 606.
[67] *Ante*, p. 96.
[68] See *ante*, p. 99.

succession, the second and subsequent remainders might be destroyed by the perpetuity rule. For example, if land was given—

> " to A for life, remainder for life to any husband she may marry, remainder to all A's children living at the death of the survivor of A and her husband," or—
>
> " to B for life, remainder to all B's children for life, remainder to the surviving child in tail,"

the second remainder in each case was void for perpetuity.[69] In the first example, the legal remainder rules merely required that the ultimate remainder should vest during the lifetime of the survivor, who might be a husband not born at the date of the gift. In the second example, the survivor might not be ascertained until more than 21 years after the death of B and all his children living at the time of the gift.

Legal remainders which were saved from the perpetuity rule before 1926 by the rule requiring them to vest during the continuance of the particular estate were not destroyed by the perpetuity rule when they were converted into equitable interests at the beginning of 1925.[70]

11. Application to powers. Settlements often authorise trustees, tenants for life and others to do things which they would not otherwise be entitled to do. One class of such powers may authorise acts of administration, such as the sale or leasing of the settled land.[71] Other powers, known as powers of appointment, may authorise an alteration of the beneficial interests. The application of the rule against perpetuities to powers is somewhat complicated.

(a) *Administrative powers.*

(1) AT COMMON LAW. In general, an administrative power which was exercisable outside the perpetuity period was void, *e.g.,* a power to lease or sell during the lifetime of an unborn person.[72]

(2) ACT OF 1964. It was generally thought that the extension of the rule to administrative powers was unwarranted, and that it ought to be confined to the invalidation of the remote vesting of beneficial interests. Accordingly the Act provides that the rule is not to operate to invalidate a power conferred on trustees and other persons " to sell lease exchange or otherwise dispose of any property for

---

[69] *Re Frost* (1889) 43 Ch.D. 246; *Re Ashforth* [1905] 1 Ch. 535.
[70] L.P.A. 1925, 1st. Sched., Pt. I.
[71] See *post,* p. 169.
[72] *Re Allott* [1924] 2 Ch. 498.

full consideration, or to do any other act in the administration (as opposed to the distribution) of any property " [73] Exceptionally, this provision is retrospective to the extent that it applies to the exercise after the commencement of the Act of a power in a settlement or will taking effect before the commencement.[74]

(b) *Powers of appointment*.[74] A power of appointment is a power for the person to whom it is given (" the donee of the power ") to appoint property to such persons (" the objects of the power ") as he may select.

(1) GENERAL AND SPECIAL POWERS. A power is a " special power " if the donee's choice is restricted to a limited class of objects, such as X's children, and a " general power " if his choice is unrestricted.

(i) *At common law.* For the purposes of the perpetuity rule, the general test is whether or not the donee of the power is as free to dispose of the property as an absolute owner. Thus for this purpose a joint power of appointment has been held special,[75] and so has a power to appoint with the consent of X,[76] unless, perhaps, X's consent is a requisite merely to the exercise of the power and he has no control over the amounts appointed or the persons to benefit, in which case the power may be general. Whether a power to appoint " to anyone except Z " is general or special for this purpose is doubtful; but it is settled that a power may be general even if it is made exercisable by will only and not *inter vivos*.[77]

(ii) *Act of* 1964. The Act of 1964 has codified the distinction between general and special powers. It adopts the formulation worked out in the cases and resolves the doubts which have been mentioned. In dispositions taking effect after the Act a power is treated as a special power unless

(a) it is expressed to be exercisable by one person only, and

(b) it could be exercised by him so as to transfer the property to himself without the consent of any other person or compliance with any condition other than a formal condition relating only to the mode of exercise of the power.[78]

The provision also confirms that a power may be general even

---

[73] s. 8 (1).
[74] s. 8 (2). For the general rule, see *ante*, p. 104.
[75] *Re Churston S.E.* [1954] Ch. 334.
[76] *Re Watts* [1931] 2 Ch. 302.
[77] *Rous* v. *Jackson* (1885) 29 Ch.D. 521.
[78] s. 7.

if it is made exercisable by will only. It will be noted that a power to appoint " to anyone except Z " is general.

(2) VALIDITY OF THE POWER. In connection with the application of the perpetuity rule to powers of appointment, two separate points have to be considered:

(a) Does the power itself infringe the rule?

(b) If it does not, does the appointment made under the power infringe the rule?

(i) *A special power.* A special power of appointment is subject to the ordinary rule relating to powers and is thus void if it could be exercised outside the period; time runs from the date when the instrument creating the power took effect.[79] Thus if the donee of the power will not necessarily be ascertained within the period (if at all) or is capable of exercising the power when the period has expired, it is bad.[80] But a power exercisable only by a person living when it was created can never be void for remoteness.

If a power complies with these conditions, it is not void merely because an appointment which offends the rule might be made under it[81]; thus where a living person is given the power to appoint to his issue, he might make an appointment to his great-great-grandchildren, but this possibility does not invalidate the power itself or an appointment which in fact complies with the rule.

The Act of 1964 applies the new " wait and see " principle to powers created by instruments taking effect after July 15, 1964. The power is to be treated as void only if, and so far as it is, not fully exercised within the perpetuity period.[82]

If a power is void for remoteness, a gift in default of appointment (*e.g.,* " but if no appointment shall be made, to X and Y equally ") is not thereby invalidated; provided it does not itself infringe the rule, it is valid.[83]

(ii) *A general power.* For the purposes of the perpetuity rule, a general power to appoint by deed or will is so nearly akin to absolute ownership that principles similar to those appropriate to absolute ownership are applied: the perpetuity rule is satisfied if the power must be acquired within the period, if at all, even if the

[79] *Re De Sommery* [1912] 2 Ch. 662.
[80] *Re Abbott* [1893] 1 Ch. 54.
[81] *Slark* v. *Dakyns* (1874) 10 Ch.App. 35.
[82] s. 3 (3).
[83] *Re Abbott, supra.*

power might be exercised outside the period.[84] But if the power is exercisable by will only, it will be bad if it might be exercised outside the period; in this case the general rule applies.[85]

Here too the Act of 1964 applies the new " wait and see " principle. A general power created by an instrument taking effect after July 15, 1964, will not be void on the ground that it might be acquired at too remote a time, but will be valid unless and until it becomes established that it will not be exercisable within the period.[86]

(3) VALIDITY OF APPOINTMENTS. If the power itself is void, clearly no valid appointment can be made under it. But even if the power itself is valid, an appointment made under it may nevertheless be too remote.

(i) *A special power.* In the case of a special power of appointment, the property is fettered from the moment the power is created. It can be said at once that either an appointment will be made in favour of one or more of the designated class of persons or else it will pass to those nominated to take in default of appointment, or, if none, to the grantor. Consequently the perpetuity period starts to run from the creation of the power.[87] However, as has been seen,[88] the mere fact that the power authorises the making of an appointment which may be too remote does not invalidate it, and until the appointment has been made, it cannot be seen if in fact it is too remote. Consequently, contrary to the general rule in matters of perpetuity, even at common law " the principle seems to be to wait and see." [89] When the appointment is ultimately made, it must be examined to see whether the interests appointed are bound to vest (if at all) within 21 years of the dropping of the lives of persons who were living or *en ventre sa mère* [90] at the time of the creation of the power and not at the time of the appointment. Further, the facts existing at the time of the appointment must be taken into account when deciding this point. In short, in ascertaining the *lives in being* the relevant time is that of the *creation of the power*; in ascertaining the *facts* of the case, the relevant time is that of the *making of the appointment*.

---

[84] See *Re Fane* [1913] 1 Ch. 404.
[85] *Wollaston* v. *King* (1868) L.R. 8 Eq. 165.
[86] s. 3 (2).
[87] *Re Thompson* [1906] 2 Ch. 199.
[88] *Supra.*
[89] *Re Witty* [1913] 2 Ch. 666 at 673.
[90] *Re Stern* [1962] Ch. 732.

Some examples may make this clearer.

(i) Devise to A for life with power to appoint to his children: A appoints to his son B " when he is 23 ": B was unborn at the testator's death but aged 3 at the time of the appointment. A is the only life in being, but since the property is bound to vest (if at all) within 20 years of his death, the appointment is good. Had B been under the age of 2 at the time of the appointment, then if it had been made before 1926 it would have been void; if it was made after 1925, B would have taken when he was 21.[91]

(ii) Marriage settlement upon C for life, remainder as he should appoint among his issue: C appoints in favour of his daughter D, postponing the vesting of her interest until her marriage: D is unmarried at the date of the appointment. The appointment is void. A few years later, D marries and C then executes a document confirming the void appointment. D is entitled to the property, since the confirmation operates as a fresh appointment, and taking the facts existing at the time of the appointment the property has vested during the lifetime of a person alive at the date of the settlement, namely, C.[92]

(iii) Deed giving property to F for life with power to appoint to his issue: F appoints by his will in favour of his grandchildren G and H (neither of whom was alive at the date of the gift) for their joint lives as tenants in common, with remainder to the survivor. The interest for their joint lives is valid but the remainder is void.[93]

The Act of 1964 has enlarged the scope of the " wait and see " relation to the exercise of special powers. If the powers in the examples given above are created after July 15, 1964,[94] the result will be as follows:

(i) Even if B is under 2 at the time of the appointment, he will take at 23 if he attains that age within the period, *e.g.*, within 21 years of the death of A, and if he will not do so, he will take at 21 (or if he is one year old) at 22.[95]

---

[1] L.P.A. 1925, s. 163; *ante*, p. 111.
[2] This is based on *Morgan* v. *Gronow* (1873) L.R. 16 Eq. 1.
[3] *Re Legh's S.T.* [1938] Ch. 39.
[4] The Act does not apply to appointments made after July 15, 1964, under special powers taking effect before that date: s. 15 (5).
[5] See *ante*, pp. 114, 115.

(ii) The first appointment will be valid unless and until it appears that D will not marry within the perpetuity period commencing from the date of the settlement.

(iii) The remainder is valid if it in fact vests within the period, *i.e.,* 21 years after the death of the survivor of the donor, F and any of F's children living at the date of the deed.

(ii) *A general power.* Since the property is unfettered until the appointment has been made, the donee of the power being able to deal with it as he wishes, the perpetuity period does not begin to run until the date of the appointment. Thus for the purposes of the perpetuity rule there is no difference between the exercise of a general power and a conveyance by an absolute owner.

The difference between appointments under general and special powers may be summarised thus. In both cases, the relevant facts are those existing at the time of the appointment; but the time at which the lives in being must be ascertained is the creation of the power in the case of a special power, and the exercise of the power in the case of a general power.

12. Contracts, covenants and options.

(a) *At common law.*

(1) PERSONAL OBLIGATIONS. The rule against perpetuities does not apply to contracts in so far as they create mere personal obligations, *e.g.,* to pay mining royalties.[96] The rule is directed against the vesting of interests in some specific property at too remote a date, and personal contracts do not do this. Further, even if a contract confers a right to an interest in some specific property exercisable at too remote a date, the rule did not prevent damages [97] or specific performance [98] being awarded against a party to the contract; for the court is merely enforcing his personal obligations, and not any rights of property.

(2) PROPRIETARY INTERESTS. Where, however, the plaintiff's case depends not on a personal obligation but on the existence of an interest in specific property, the rule applies. Thus if a lease for 99 years confers on the lessee and his assigns an option to purchase the freehold at any time during the lease [99] (an option appurtenant to the

---

[96] *Witham* v. *Vane* (1883) Challis R.P. 440; and see M. & W. 264–268.
[97] *Worthing Corporation* v. *Heather* [1906] 2 Ch. 532.
[98] *Hutton* v. *Watling* [1948] Ch. 26, 398.
[99] *Woodall* v. *Clifton* [1905] 2 Ch. 257.

lease), or a corporation is given an option to purchase or take a lease of land [1] (an option in gross), an action to enforce the option against a successor in title of the person who granted the option cannot be based on any personal obligation, and must depend on the burden of the option running with the land. The rule accordingly makes the option unenforceable against the successor unless its exercise is confined within the period.

(3) COVENANTS TO RENEW LEASE. Exceptionally, a covenant in a lease giving the tenant the right to an extension of the term is not void merely because it can be exercised outside the perpetuity period.[2]

(b) *Statutory modifications.* The Act of 1964 has made three changes in relation to dispositions in instruments taking effect after July 15, 1964.

(1) PERSONAL OBLIGATIONS. The Act reverses the rule that damages may be obtained against an original contracting party, even though the interest conferred by the contract is void for perpetuity. A disposition *inter vivos* which creates an interest in property is void between the original contracting parties wherever it would be void for perpetuity against a third party.[3]

(2) OPTIONS APPURTENANT TO LEASES. The rule against perpetuities is not to apply to an option for a lessee to purchase the freehold or superior leasehold title which is exercisable only by the lessee or his successors in title and which ceases to be exercisable not later than a year after the end of the lease.[4]

(3) OPTIONS IN GROSS. An option to acquire for value any interest in land is subject to a specially short perpetuity period of 21 years only.[5] The " wait and see " principle applies, so that even if no time limit is specified in the instrument conferring the option, it will remain exercisable for 21 years.

C. Cases in which the Perpetuity Rule Does Not Apply

The preceding section has indicated some cases to which the Rule does not apply, namely—

---

[1] *London and South Western Ry.* v. *Gomm* (1882) 20 Ch.D. 562.
[2] *Woodall* v. *Clifton, supra,* at pp. 265, 268 ; *Weg Motors Ltd.* v. *Hales* [1962] Ch. 49 ; but see *post,* p. 345.
[3] s. 10.
[4] s. 9 (1).
[5] s. 9 (2).

(a) Personal obligations
(b) Covenants for renewal of a lease,
(c) Covenants in a lease for the purchase of the landlords' reversion.

There are a few other exceptions.

1. Certain limitations after entails. A limitation which is bound to take effect, if at all, during the continuance, or at the moment of the determination, of an entail is not rendered void by the rule, even though the entail may continue for longer than the perpetuity period.[6] Thus a gift to X in tail, with remainder to such of Y's issue as are alive when the entail determines, is valid, even though the persons entitled to take the remainder may not be ascertained for several hundred years.[7]

This exception, however, does not protect limitations which can or must vest when an interval has elapsed after the determination of the entail.[8] If property is given to trustees in trust for A in tail, remainder to the first of the great-grandchildren of B to attain the age of 30, A's entail is valid but the remainder is void, for it might very well vest many years after the period has run and the entail has determined.

2. Certain gifts to charities. The general rule is that a gift to a charity is subject to the rule in the same way as any other gift.[9] However, if there is a gift to one charity followed by a gift over to another charity on a certain event, the gift over is not void merely because the event may occur outside the perpetuity period. Thus if property is given to Charity A with a proviso that it shall go to Charity B if Charity A fails to keep the testator's tomb in repair, the gift over is valid.[10] To this extent alone are charities exempted from the rule against perpetuities.[11]

3. Certain rights of entry and re-entry. The right to re-enter and determine a lease if a covenant is broken, which most leases give to the landlord, is excepted from the perpetuity rule.[12] Again, the

---

[6] *Nicolls* v. *Sheffield* (1787) 2 Bro.C.C. 215.
[7] See *Heaseman* v. *Pearse* (1871) 7 Ch.App. 275 at 282, 283.
[8] See *Bristow* v. *Boothby* (1826) 2 Sim. & St. 465.
[9] *Chamberlayne* v. *Brockett* (1872) 8 Ch.App. 206.
[10] *Re Tyler* [1891] 3 Ch. 252.
[11] See also the exemption from the rule against inalienability, *post*, p. 133.
[12] *Re Tyrrell's Estate* [1907] 1 I.R. 292 at 298.

statutory remedies for enforcing payment of a rentcharge [13] or any like powers or remedies conferred by any instrument were expressly excepted from the rule in 1925 [14]; for rentcharges created after July 15, 1964, the Act of 1964 [15] extends the exemption to all powers and remedies for enforcing rentcharges.[15] Further, the Law of Property Act 1925 [16] sets out a list of certain rights retrospectively excepted from the rule, such as a right of entry created in order to enable minerals to be worked or to enable repairs to be executed.

A right of re-entry in respect of a fee simple is not within this exception and will accordingly be void if exercisable outside the perpetuity period.[17]

4. Mortgages. " The rule has never been applied to mortgages," and thus a clause postponing the mortgagor's right to redeem the property is not invalid merely because the right is postponed for longer than the perpetuity period.[18]

Sect. 3. The Rule against Inalienability

1. The rule. It is a fundamental principle of English law that property must not be rendered inalienable. Thus a devise of land to be retained in perpetuity for use as a family burial ground is void.[19] The question in every case is whether there is some provision preventing the property in question from being disposed of; a gift is bad if effect can be given to it only by holding the property for ever and applying the income for the purposes specified.[20] Either the terms of the gift, or, in the case of trusts for an association or club, the rules of the society, may make the property inalienable. But if a gift is made without any such restriction, prima facie it will be valid. Thus gifts—

> on trust for an old boys' club to be used as a committee thought best; or—
>
> to the trustees of the London Library for general purposes; or—
>
> to a convent to be paid to the superior

[13] *Post*, p. 410.
[14] L.P.A. 1925, s. 121 ; see *post*, p. 412.
[15] s. 11 (1).
[16] s. 162.
[17] *Re Trustees of Hollis' Hospital and Hague's Contract* [1899] 2 Ch. 540; L.P.A. 1925, s. 4; and see *ante*, p. 32.
[18] *Knightsbridge Estates Trust Ltd.* v. *Byrne* [1939] Ch. 441 at 463 ; on appeal, [1940] A.C. 613.
[19] *Yeap Cheah Neo* v. *Ong Cheng Neo* (1875) L.R. 6 P.C. 381.
[20] See *Cocks* v. *Manners* (1871) L.R. 12 Eq. 574 at 585, 586.

have been held valid, for there is nothing to prevent the capital being alienated.[21]　A gift to the chairman of the Athenæum Club for the Club may be so worded that the capital is intended to be inalienable and the income earmarked in perpetuity for the general benefit of the Club, or it may be so worded that the capital is intended to be divided immediately between all the then members of the Club; the former gift will be void and the latter valid.[22]

The principle is sometimes called " the rule against trusts of perpetual duration." It is also sometimes called the rule that gifts which " tend to a perpetuity " are void. The Act of 1964 expressly refrains from making any alteration in the law relating to dispositions under which property is to be applied for purposes other than the benefit of any person or class of persons.[23]

2. The period.　Although property cannot be rendered inalienable for ever, or for a period to which no clear and definite limit is set,[24] it seems that a limitation rendering property inalienable for a maximum period of a life or lives in being at the time of the gift, with a further 21 years, may be valid.[25]　This period of a life in being and 21 years is borrowed from the rule against perpetuities discussed above.[26]　An example was formerly provided by the restraint upon anticipation, which was a provision restraining a married woman from disposing of property or anticipating the future income in any way; it is dealt with more fully later.[27]　A restraint upon anticipation imposed upon a living woman did not infringe the rule against inalienability, for alienation was restrained only during her lifetime. But a restraint imposed upon property given to an unborn female was prima facie void, for she might have married, and so brought the restraint into operation, more than 21 years after the death of all persons alive at the date of the gift[28]; in such a case, the donee took the property free from the restraint, although if the restraint had been worded so as to be operative only during the proper period, it would have been valid.

---

21 See, *e.g., Re Prevost* [1930] 2 Ch. 383.
22 See *Re Ray's W.T.* [1936] 2 All E.R. 93 at 97, 98 ; and see *Leahy* v. *Att.-Gen. for New South Wales* [1959] A.C. 457 at 477.
23 s. 15 (4).
24 *Re Wightwick's W.T.* [1950] Ch. 260.
25 See *Re Dean* (1889) 41 Ch.D. 552 at 557.
26 *Ante,* p. 109.
27 *Post,* p. 520. Restraints upon anticipation can no longer exist.
28 *Fry* v. *Capper* (1853) Kay 163.

3. Assignability. If some legal *persona* has an assignable right to the income, it seems that the rule against inalienability is not infringed. The beneficiary can dispose of his interest by assigning the right to the future income, and this is so even if the payment of the income is dependent upon some act being performed (*e.g.*, the maintenance of a tomb) and so may cease at a future date; such a condition would make it less easy to find a purchaser but not impossible.[29] It is different where there is a trust for the upkeep of a tomb or animals, so that there is nobody who can consent to the alienation, or where the beneficiary is an unincorporated society and the gift shows an intention to benefit future as well as present members, so that it will never become possible for all those who are intended to benefit to concur in putting an end to the trust.[30]

4. Charities. Charities are exempt from the rule against inalienability; no gift for charitable purposes is void merely because it renders property inalienable in perpetuity.[31]

Sect. 4. The Rule against Accumulations

This rule resembles the rule against inalienability in that it is directed against remoteness of control over a vested interest rather than against interests which may vest at too distant a date. The rule was first laid down by the ill-drafted Accumulations Act 1800, which was passed as a result of *Thellusson* v. *Woodford*.[32] In that case, Mr. Thellusson by his will directed that the income of his property should be accumulated during the lives of his sons, grandsons and their issue who were living at his death, and that on the death of the survivor, the accumulated fund should be divided among certain of his descendants. This direction, being confined to lives in being, was held valid, but as it was calculated that the accumulated fund would amount to many millions of pounds, Parliament intervened to prevent further directions of this nature.

At common law, the rule was that a direction to accumulate was valid if it was confined to the perpetuity period,[33] so that Mr.

---

[29] *Re Chardon* [1928] Ch. 464; Tudor, *Charities* (5th ed., 1929), p. 701; and see *Re Wightwick's W.T., supra.*
[30] *Carne* v. *Long* (1860) 2 De G.F. & J. 75.
[31] *Chamberlayne* v. *Brockett* (1872) 8 Ch.App. 206 at 211; contrast the perpetuity rule, *ante*, p. 130.
[32] (1799) 4 Ves. 227; (1805) 11 Ves. 112; hence the Act is often called " the Thellusson Act."
[33] *Wilson* v. *Wilson* (1851) 1 Sim.(N.S.) 288 at 298.

Thellusson might have effectively directed accumulation for a further 21 years; probably he did not do so because the permissibility of the extra period of 21 years after lives in being was not firmly established when he made his will.

A. The Statutory Periods

1. The periods. The present law is contained in the Law of Property Act 1925,[34] and the Perpetuities and Accumulations Act 1964.[35] If the disposition took effect before July 16, 1964, a direction or power[36] to accumulate may be validly given for any one (but not more) of the following periods:

(1) The life of the grantor or settlor.

(2) 21 years from the death of the grantor, settlor or testator.

(3) The minority or respective minorities of any person or persons living or *en ventre sa mère* at the death of the grantor, settlor or testator.

(4) The minority or respective minorities only of any person or persons who under the limitations of the instrument directing accumulation would for the time being, if of full age, be entitled to the income directed to be accumulated.

For dispositions taking effect after July 15, 1964, two further periods have been added.[37]

(5) 21 years from the making of the disposition.

(6) The minority or respective minorities of any person or persons in being at that date.

2. Choice of periods. The question which period has been chosen in each particular case is one of construction.[38] The first two and the fifth periods cause little difficulty. Of the first, it should be noted that it is the only period of a life available for accumulation, and that it must be the life of the grantor or settlor himself and not of some third person. The second period is a fixed term of years which starts to run at the beginning of the day after the testator's death and

---

[34] ss. 164–166.
[35] ss. 13, 14.
[36] *Re Robb* [1953] Ch. 459; Act of 1964, s. 13 (2). *Re Robb* was disapproved in *Re Earl of Berkeley* [1968] Ch. 744, but not so as to affect this point.
[37] Act of 1964, s. 13 (1).
[38] *Jagger* v. *Jagger* (1883) 25 Ch.D. 729.

expires at the end of the twenty-first anniversary of his death.[39]
Thus if a testator directs accumulations to start at the end of an
interval after his death and continue for 21 years, he has exceeded
the second period. The second period was of little use save in wills.
Now, the fifth period allows the period of 21 years to run from the
date of the settlement.

The third, fourth and sixth periods are all minorities. They differ
in the following respects:

(i) The third and sixth periods are confined to the minorities of
persons alive or *en ventre sa mère* at the death of the grantor,
settlor or testator, or at the date of the settlement, as the case
may be. The fourth period is not.

(ii) The third and sixth periods are not restricted to the minorities of those who are prospectively entitled to any benefit
under the gift, whereas the fourth period is confined to the
minorities of those who can say " but for my infancy I should
be absolutely entitled to the income being accumulated." [40]

(iii) The third and sixth periods can never exceed a single
minority; for even if accumulation is directed during a large
number of minorities, the period is in effect merely the
longest of these minorites. Under the fourth period, on the
other hand, accumulation during successive minorities is
possible.

An example may make this clear.[41] A testator devises
the residue of his property between all the children of his
sons, whether born before or after his death, the income of
their shares to be accumulated during their respective
minorities. At the testator's death, there is only one child
of his sons alive, and she is an infant named D. The whole
of the income must be accumulated during this minority,
the direction to accumulate falling within the fourth period;
for if she was of full age she would for the time being be
entitled to the whole of the income. After D attains her
majority, a child C is born to one of the testator's sons.
C becomes entitled to one half of the estate, subject to the
same liability, *i.e.*, that his share may be partially divested
by the birth of other children. During the minority of C,
the income from his share must be accumulated, even though

[39] *Gorst* v. *Lowndes* (1841) 11 Sim. 434.
[40] *Jagger* v. *Jagger, supra,* at p. 733, as corrected in *Re Cattell, infra,* at p. 189.
[41] See *Re Cattell* [1914] 1 Ch. 177.

the income from the whole of the residuary estate has already been accumulated once.

If D had not been born until after the testator's death, there could have been no accumulation under the fourth period until her birth, for not until then would her minority have commenced.

3. Purchase of land. Where after June 27, 1892, accumulation is directed for the sole purpose of purchasing land, only the fourth period may be selected. But this restriction does not apply to accumulations to be held as capital money under the Settled Land Act 1925 or any of the Acts which it replaces.[42]

4. Ambit of rules. These rules apply whether the limitations are contained in a deed or a will, whether the accumulation is at compound or, it seems, merely simple interest,[43] and whether the whole or any part of the income of a fund is to be accumulated.[44] Yet there is no accumulation if the income is merely saved up as security for the payment of annuities, and is not added to capital.[45]

B. Excessive Accumulation

1. Exceeding perpetuity period. If the period for which accumulation is directed may exceed the perpetuity period, the direction to accumulate is totally void, *e.g.*, where accumulation was directed until a lease with over 60 years to run had " nearly expired." [46]

2. Exceeding accumulation period. If the period for which accumulation is directed cannot exceed the perpetuity period but exceeds the relevant accumulation period, the direction to accumulate is good *pro tanto* and only the excess over the appropriate accumulation period is void; the statutory provisions are merely restrictive of the wider powers formerly enjoyed.[47]

Which is the appropriate period depends on the circumstances.[48] Thus where accumulation is directed for the lifetime of any person

[42] L.P.A. 1925, s. 166; see *post*, p. 194.
[43] See *Re Garside* [1919] 1 Ch. 132.
[44] *Re Travis* [1900] 2 Ch. 541.
[45] *Re Earl of Berkeley* [1968] Ch. 744.
[46] *Curtis* v. *Lukin* (1842) 5 Beav. 147.
[47] *Leake* v. *Robinson* (1817) 2 Mer. 363 at 389.
[48] See *Re Ransome* [1957] Ch. 348 at 361.

(other than the settlor in the case of an *inter vivos* settlement), accumulation will take place for 21 years from the date of the settlement or, as the case may be, from the testator's death if the named person so long lives.[49] This uses the second or fifth periods, and these periods are also the most appropriate whenever accumulation is directed for a period of years, and the same applies where accumulation is directed until X is 25,[50] or from the time Y remarries until her death,[51] or from the death of either A or B until the death of the survivor. In each of these cases, if accumulation is still continuing 21 years after the date of the settlement or the death of the testator, it must cease forthwith even if it has been proceeding for only a short period, *e.g.*, 2 years.[52]

Again, if property is given by will to all the children of X (a living person) who attain their majority, and accumulation of the whole fund is directed while any child of X is an infant, the first two periods are clearly not intended and the fourth is not appropriate, for the accumulation is directed to continue for as long as *any* child is an infant even if some of the children are 21; even though the latter children are of full age, they are not entitled to the income to be accumulated within the wording of the fourth period. Consequently the third period is the most appropriate, and so far as it is exceeded the direction is void; accumulation will therefore cease as soon as all children living at the testator's death are 21.[53]

C. Surplus Income

The income for any period during which accumulation is invalidly directed passes to the persons who would have been entitled had no excessive accumulation been directed.[54] Thus if there is an absolute gift subject only to an excessive trust for accumulation, the original donee is entitled to any income not validly accumulated. For example, where property is given by will to X, subject to a direction that the income exceeding a certain figure is to be accumulated during X's life for the benefit of Y, the accumulation must cease 21 years

---

[49] *Griffiths* v. *Vere* (1803) 9 Ves. 127. In the case of a settlement *inter vivos* made before July 16, 1964, the first period was the most appropriate, and accumulations continued during the period common to the lives of the settlor and the named person : *Re Lady Rosslyn's Trust* (1848) 16 Sim. 391.

[50] *Crawley* v. *Crawley* (1835) 7 Sim. 427.

[51] *Weatherall* v. *Thornburgh* (1878) 8 Ch.D. 261.

[52] *Shaw* v. *Rhodes* (1836) 1 My. & Cr. 135.

[53] *Re Watt's W.T.* [1936] 2 All E.R. 1555.

[54] L.P.A. 1925, s. 164.

after the testator's death and the surplus income will go to X.[55] But otherwise, the income reverts to the settlor or his estate, or in the case of a gift by will, passes under any residuary gift, or, in default, to the persons entitled on intestacy.[56]

D. The Rule in Saunders v. Vautier

Under the rule in *Saunders* v. *Vautier*,[57] a beneficiary of full age who has an absolute indefeasible interest in property may at any time, notwithstanding any direction to accumulate, require the transfer of the property to him and terminate any accumulation; a man may do as he likes with his own, and the same applies to a charity.[58] Thus if property is given to A with a direction to accumulate the income for his benefit until he is 24, A can demand payment of both the original property and the accumulations as soon as he is 21.[59] The rule applies, however, only if the beneficiary or beneficiaries seeking to put an end to the accumulation together comprise every person who has any vested or contingent interest in the property.[60] Thus it will not apply if there is a gift to a class of persons or charities not yet determined, or to beneficiaries whose interests are contingent or liable to be defeated by some event occurring.

E. Exceptions to the Rule against Accumulations

The rule against accumulations does not apply in the following cases.[61]

1. Payment of debts: a provision for accumulation for the payment of the debts of any person.[62] This includes an accumulation directed for the payment of any debts, whether of the settlor or testator, or any other person.[63] Indeed, an accumulation for the payment of the debts of the settlor or testator is valid even if it may exceed the perpetuity period[64]; such a direction can cause little mischief, for the creditors may terminate the accumulation at any

---

55 *Trickey* v. *Trickey* (1832) 3 My. & Cr. 560.
56 *Mathews* v. *Keble* (1867) L.R. 4 Eq. 467 at 473, 474 (affd. 3 Ch.App. 691).
57 (1841) 4 Beav. 115; affd. Cr. & Ph. 240.
58 *Wharton* v. *Masterman* [1895] A.C. 186; contrast *Re Levy* [1960] Ch. 346.
59 *Josselyn* v. *Josselyn* (1837) 9 Sim. 63.
60 *Berry* v. *Geen* [1938] A.C. 575.
61 See L.P.A. 1925, ss. 164, 165.
62 L.P.A. 1925, s. 164.
63 *Viscount Barrington* v. *Liddell* (1852) 2 De G.M. & G. 480.
64 *Bateman* v. *Hotchkin* (1847) 10 Beav. 426.

time by demanding payment. But an accumulation to pay the debts of any other person must be confined within the perpetuity period.

The exception includes any debts, whether existing or contingent, provided the accumulation is directed bona fide for their payment; thus it extends to accumulations to discharge a mortgage or to provide for liability under a leasehold covenant not yet broken.[65] It does not extend to debts not in existence when the instrument directing accumulation took effect, *e.g.*, estate duty payable on the death of a tenant for life.[66]

2. Portions: a provision for accumulation for raising portions for any legitimate issue of the grantor, settlor or testator or any person to whom an interest is limited under the settlement.[67] This is an exception from the rule against accumulations only; such accumulations must be confined to the perpetuity period. The meaning of " portions " here is not clear. It is not confined to sums raised out of real estate, nor to provisions for the benefit of the younger children of a marriage.[68] It does not, however, apply where there is no existing obligation to use the fund for portions but a mere future discretionary power,[69] nor where the direction is to accumulate the income from the whole of a testator's estate, for " it is not raising a portion at all, it is giving everything." [70]

3. Timber or wood: a provision for accumulation of the produce of timber or wood.[71] Although excepted from the accumulation rules, such a direction will be void if it exceeds the perpetuity period.[72]

4. Maintenance of property: a provision for maintaining property at its present value. Directions to devote surplus income to maintaining buildings in a proper state of repair, or to apply a fixed annual sum to keep up an insurance policy to replace the capital lost by not selling leaseholds, are outside the rule against accumulations;

---

[65] *Re Hurlbatt* [1910] 2 Ch. 553.
[66] *Re Rochford's S.T.* [1965] Ch. 111.
[67] L.P.A. 1925, s. 164; see also *post*, p. 204.
[68] *Re Stephens* [1904] 1 Ch. 322.
[69] *Re Bourne's S.T.* [1946] 1 All E.R. 411.
[70] *Edwards* v. *Tuck* (1853) 3 De G.M. & G. 40 at 58.
[71] L.P.A. 1925, s. 164.
[72] *Ferrand* v. *Wilson* (1845) 4 Hare 344.

though they add income to capital, they merely keep up the property and do not add to it, so that there is no true accumulation.[73] But they must be confined to the perpetuity period.[74]

5. Minority: accumulations made during a minority under the general law or any statutory power. While the person entitled to any trust property is an infant, a statutory power is given to the trustees to apply the income for his maintenance; subject thereto, they are bound to accumulate the residue of the income.[75] It is expressly provided that the period of such accumulation is to be disregarded when determining the period for which accumulations are permitted.[76] Thus if a testator directs accumulation for 21 years after his death and the beneficiary at the end of this period is an infant, the accumulations both for the 21 years and during the minority are valid.[77]

6. Certain commercial contracts: transactions which cannot fairly be described as settlements or dispositions. Many commercial transactions involve a measure of accumulation, such as partnership agreements which provide for the accumulation of certain profits, and investment trusts which capitalise part of their income. Such transactions are outside the Act,[78] which merely provides that no person may " settle or dispose " of property in breach of the Act [79]; and many of them are also outside the perpetuity rule as creating merely personal obligations.

Part 4

SUMMARY OF THE INTERESTS TO WHICH THE RULES RELATING TO FUTURE INTERESTS APPLY

First, it may be convenient to summarise the interests to which the various rules relating to future interests apply. The position is as follows.

(1) **The legal remainder rules.** These applied only to legal remainders of realty.

---

[73] *Vine* v. *Raleigh* [1891] 2 Ch. 13 ; *Re Gardiner* [1901] 1 Ch. 697.
[74] *Curtis* v. *Lukin* (1842) 5 Beav. 147.
[75] T.A. 1925, s. 31.
[76] L.P.A. 1925, s. 165.
[77] *Re Maber* [1928] Ch. 88.
[78] See *Bassil* v. *Lister* (1851) 9 Hare 177 at 184 ; *Re A.E.G. Unit Trust (Managers) Ltd.'s Deed* [1957] Ch. 415.
[79] L.P.A. 1925, s. 164 (1).

(2) The rule in *Purefoy* v. *Rogers*. This applied only to legal limitations of realty in a will or by way of use.

(3) The rule in *Whitby* v. *Mitchell*. This applied only to legal and equitable remainders in realty.

(4) (a) The rule against inalienability.

    (b) The rule against perpetuities.

    (c) The rule against accumulations.

These applied, and still apply, to all interests in any property.

Secondly, a short illustration of the interaction of some of the rules may be found useful. A devise to X (a bachelor) for life and then to the first of his sons to attain the age of 25 years may be taken as an example. If the testator died in 1870, the devise to the son was treated as a legal remainder,[80] so that it took effect if a son was 25 before X died, but otherwise it failed under rule (d) (ii) of the legal remainder rules.[81]

If the testator died in 1910, the gift to the son took effect as a future trust [82] and so was void for perpetuity. If the testator died in 1930, the son's interest was saved from the perpetuity rule by reading " 25 " as " 21," [83] and so was valid. Finally, if the testator died in 1965, the son's interest would vest in him at 25 if he attained that age during X's lifetime or within 21 years of his death,[84] or if the son was not then 25, it would vest in him at the age he had then attained, *i.e.*, some age between 21 and 25.[85]

---

[80] *Purefoy* v. *Rogers*; *ante*, p. 96.
[81] *Ante*, p. 92.
[82] Land Transfer Act 1897, *ante*, p. 111.
[83] L.P.A. 1925, s. 163 ; *ante*, p. 99.
[84] Perpetuities and Accumulations Act 1964, s. 3, *ante*, p. 108.
[85] *Ibid.* s. 4, *ante*, p. 114.

CHAPTER 5

SETTLED LAND AND TRUSTS FOR SALE

Part 1

BEFORE 1883

IT is now necessary to turn from matters of substance to matters of machinery. The last chapter discussed the rules regulating the various future interests in land which can be created, and this chapter will examine how land which is the subject of future interests is managed and disposed of. The starting point is to consider settlements.

The basic idea of a settlement is to make provision out of property for two or more persons in succession. Settlements were frequently made on marriage, providing for the spouses and issue by giving the property to the husband for life, with remainder to the children in tail subject to paying the wife an annual sum. But not all settlements are marriage settlements, and for most purposes it can be taken that a settlement exists whenever future interests in property have been created otherwise than for money or money's worth.

By the middle of the nineteenth century two methods of settling land were firmly established; these were the strict settlement and the trust for sale.

Sect. 1. The Strict Settlement

1. Principal provisions. A strict settlement was the type of settlement employed " to keep land in the family." Provided the various rules of law and equity were observed, the settlor might create such limitations as he thought fit, but since the Commonwealth, the type of settlement most frequently encountered has been the marriage settlement giving a life interest to the husband and entails to the children. Provision was also made for the wife by giving her a jointure (an annual income during widowhood), and for the children who did not obtain the land under the entails by giving them portions (lump sums of money to assist them in their

careers and in matrimony).[1] This form of settlement was adopted
because it made provision for all members of the family and yet
preserved the land as a unit. The device of giving the husband a
mere life estate with remainder to his son in tail (the son, of course,
being unborn at the time of the settlement, which was made shortly
before the marriage) was adopted as being the best way of keeping
the land in the family. If an entail had been given to the husband,
he could at once have barred it; and under the rule in *Whitby* v.
Mitchell,[2] a succession of life estates to the husband, his son, the
son's son and so on was invalid after the first gift to an unborn
person.

2. Alienation.

(a) *Settlement and resettlement.* The effect of such a settlement
was to render land substantially inalienable until the eldest
son became able to bar the entail on attaining his majority.
Shortly after the son's twenty-first birthday he was usually persuaded
(often by some financial inducement) to bar the entail with his
father's consent; the land was then resettled on the husband for life,
remainder to the son for life, remainder to the son's son in tail. The
land was thus tied up for another generation. This process of settlement and resettlement prevented any person of full age from having
more than a life estate; and the tenant in possession of the land
was always a tenant for life. The tenant for life could alienate his
life estate, but that was all; no matter how desirable or necessary it
was, he had no power to sell the fee simple in any part of the land,
or to grant leases which would be binding after his death. If
improvements to the property were required, he could effect them
only if he paid for them out of his own pocket. Unless he was
unimpeachable of waste, the discovery of valuable minerals beneath
the land was of little importance to him, for he could not open mines,
and even if he was unimpeachable of waste, he could not grant
mining leases with an adequate security of tenure for the lessee. In
short, for many purposes the land was sterilised.

(b) *Powers in settlement.* These defects were frequently met by
a series of provisions in the settlement. Many powers were given to
the tenant for life, such as powers to grant specified leases which
would be binding on his successors. He was also empowered to sell

---

[1] For details, see *post*, pp. 203–206.
[2] *Ante*, p. 101.

the fee simple provided the purchase money was paid to trustees to hold on the trusts of the settlement; his own rights and the rights of his son and the other beneficiaries were thus overreached.[3] Usually the bulk of the land would be retained and not sold, but a power of sale was useful for emergencies.

(c) *Legal estate.* The legal estate in settled land might be either split up between the beneficiaries or vested in trustees, according to the way in which the settlement was made. For example, a conveyance—

" to T and his heirs to the use of A for life, remainder to B and the heirs of his body, remainder to C and his heirs "

gave A a legal life estate, B a legal fee tail and C a legal fee simple. If the conveyance had been worded—

" unto and to the use of T and his heirs in trust for . . ."

the legal fee simple would have been in T, and A, B and C would have had merely equitable interests. In the first case, the settlement conferred the desired powers upon A by means of legal powers operating under the Statute of Uses 1535; the settlement took effect as if the land had been given to A for life and then, subject to such sales, leases and other authorised dealings as A made, to B in tail with remainder to C in fee simple. In the second case, the powers conferred upon A would be merely equitable, but T was bound to give effect to any authorised disposition made by A, and the court would compel him to create or transfer the necessary legal estate.[4]

(d) *Absence of powers.* Although it was thus possible for a settlement to provide the necessary powers, in many cases this was not done, especially where the settlement was made by will. In such cases the land could not be dealt with unless the expense of obtaining a private Act of Parliament was incurred. Further, even if the powers were inserted, difficulties sometimes arose over the construction to be put upon them, and in any case the settlement became of formidable length.

3. Intervention of statute. This position was dealt with by a series of statutes passed in the nineteenth century. Starting with Acts such as the Settled Estates Drainage Acts 1840 and 1845 concerning certain limited improvements, the legislature proceeded to enact the Settled Estates Acts 1856 and 1877, which enabled

[3] *Ante,* p. 81.
[4] See *Re Brown* (1886) 32 Ch.D. 597 at 601.

the court to authorise a number of dealings and even enabled the tenant for life to grant certain leases without application to the court. These comparatively timid measures remained the law until the Settled Land Act 1882, drafted by Mr. Wolstenholme, was piloted through Parliament by Lord Cairns.

Sect. 2. Trusts for Sale

1. Origin. Compared with strict settlements, settlements by way of trust for sale are of comparatively recent orgin.[5] It is true that trusts for sale created by will can be traced back for some 500 years, but most of the earliest of these trusts seem to have been designed to raise sums of money, *e.g.,* for the payment of debts, rather than to provide for persons by way of succession. Trusts for sale created *inter vivos* are more recent in origin; not until about a century ago do marriage settlements by way of trust for sale appear to have become at all common. The purpose of such trusts for sale usually differed greatly from that of a strict settlement. Where the property to be settled was a family estate on which the beneficiaries would reside and over which the tenant for life would wish to exercise direct control, the settlor usually employed a strict settlement which would keep the land in the family. Where, however, the property was in the nature of an investment, such as a row of suburban villas, there would be no desire to keep it in the family in any particular form, nor would the tenant for life wish to live on it or manage it: in such cases, a trust for sale would be employed, the primary object of such a settlement being to produce a regular income for the beneficiaries.

2. Retention unsold. For these reasons, in a trust for sale the legal estate was vested in the trustees upon trust to sell the land and hold the income until sale and the proceeds thereafter upon specified trusts for the beneficiaries. The trustees were usually given power to postpone sale in their discretion, and to manage the land until sale. Thus as long as the land produced a satisfactory income, it could be retained, and the trustee need not sell until market conditions made an advantageous sale possible. Often the consent of the beneficiaries entitled in possession was made requisite to a sale. The purchase-money arising on a sale was usually directed to be invested in stocks, shares and other securities.

[5] See, generally, J. M. Lightwood (1927) 3 Camb.L.J. 59.

3. Conversion. The effect of creating a trust for sale was that even before sale, the rights of the beneficiaries were deemed to be rights in personalty. Equity treated that as done which ought to be done, and since there was a binding obligation to sell the land sooner or later, the beneficiaries were treated as having forthwith interests in the purchase-money into which the land was to be converted: this is known as the equitable doctrine of conversion. For this reason, trusts for sale are often referred to as " personalty settlements," in common with settlements of stocks and shares and other personal property. They are also sometimes called " traders' settlements," since they are more appropriate to the urban property of business men than the rural estates of the landed gentry.

Part 2

THE SETTLED LAND ACT 1882

The Settled Land Act 1882, which was passed as the result of a period of agricultural depression, had as its paramount object the well-being of settled land. " The leading purpose of the Legislature was to prevent the decay of agricultural and other interests occasioned by the deterioration of lands and buildings in the possession of impecunious life-tenants." [6] The general scheme of the Act was to give the tenant for life under the settlement wide powers of dealing with the land free from the trusts of the settlement without making any application to the court, and to protect the rights of the beneficiaries in the case of a sale by shifting the settlement from the land to the purchase-money, which had to be paid into court or into the hands of the trustees. A purchaser was not concerned with the rights of the beneficiaries, even if he had full knowledge of them; those rights were not destroyed, but, being overreached, were transformed from rights in the land to rights in the money paid for it.

In this legislation, the term " settlement " sometimes means the documents by which the land was settled, but more usually means the state of affairs resulting from them [7]; the context usually indicates which. The Act also applied in a somewhat unsatisfactory way to trusts for sale. [8] The following is a brief statement of the principal provisions of the Act.

---

[6] *Bruce* v. *Marquess of Ailesbury* [1892] A.C. 356 at 363.
[7] See *Re Spencer's S.E.* [1903] 1 Ch. 75 at 79; *Re Ogle's S.E.* [1927] 1 Ch. 229 at 233.
[8] *Post,* p. 150.

Sect. 1. Settled Land

A. Definition of Settled Land

Any land, or any estate or interest therein, which was the subject of any document or documents whereby it stood for the time being limited to, or in trust for, any persons by way of succession, was deemed to be settled land and so subject to the Act, whether the settlement was made before or after the Act.[9] Thus if freehold land was conveyed or given by will—

" unto and to the use of A and his heirs in trust for X for life, remainder in trust for Y and his heirs,"

or freehold land was conveyed—

" to A for life remainder to B and his heirs," or

" to X and his heirs to the use of Y and the heirs of his body," in each case the land was settled land; and leasehold land might similarly be settled. In the third case the requirement that there should be an element of succession was satisfied by the resulting use to the grantor in fee simple subject to Y's entail.

In one case, land was deemed settled land even if no element of succession was involved: this was where an infant was entitled in possession to land.[10]

B. Powers of the Tenant for Life

1. The powers. The object of the Act was to give to one person wide and unfettered powers of sale, exchange, leasing, mortgaging and otherwise dealing with the land.[11] That person was the tenant for life or other limited owner in possession, such as a tenant in tail, tenant in fee simple subject to a gift over, or person entitled to a base fee.[12] For convenience, the phrase " tenant for life " is used to include not only those who had an actual life estate, but any other person who had the powers of a tenant for life. If the tenant for life was an infant, the trustees of the settlement could exercise the statutory powers on the infant's behalf.[13]

2. Tenant for life a trustee. In relation to the exercise of his statutory powers, the tenant for life was deemed to be a trustee for

[9] S.L.A. 1882, s. 2.
[10] S.L.A. 1882, s. 59; and see M. & W. 296.
[11] S.L.A. 1882, ss. 3, 6, 18.
[12] *Ibid*. ss. 2, 58.
[13] *Ibid*. s. 60.

the other beneficiaries, and was bound to consider their interests.[14]
This provision did not affect the exercise by the tenant for life of
any powers exercisable by virtue of his estate and not by virtue of
the Act: thus if a tenant for life had a common law right to keep
money paid for accepting the surrender of a lease and did not have
to rely upon his statutory powers, he could retain the money.[15] But
where the tenant for life sought to exercise his statutory powers, the
provision that he was deemed a trustee in that respect enabled the
court to intervene if he sought to sell at a price infinitely below
the value of the property [16] or to make an investment which, although
not outside his powers, was undesirable. Nevertheless, provided the
transaction was a proper one, it would not be invalidated merely
because the motive of the tenant for life was not very commendable,
e.g., that " he is selling out of ill will or caprice, or because he does
not like the remainderman, because he desires to be relieved from
the trouble of attending to the management of land, or from any
other such object, or with any such motive." [17]

3. Powers unfettered.   Subject to this restriction, the tenant for
life was in general unfettered in the exercise of his powers. They
could not be taken away or cut down either directly or indirectly,
nor could he curtail or divest himself of them or effectively contract
not to exercise them.[18] Additional or larger powers could be
conferred by the settlor on the tenant for life or the trustees, and
the Act in no way restricted such powers.[19] However, so far as the
settlement conferred on the trustees powers to do things which the
Act already authorised the tenant for life to do, the terms of the Act
prevailed and the trustees were unable to exercise such powers without the consent of the tenant for life.[20] The tenant for life was thus
normally in complete control of the land, even if he was " a spend-
thrift, who has ruined himself by his own extravagance and folly,
who has brought disgrace on the family name, and who has exposed
the family estate to destruction for the rest of his life." [21]

---

[14] *Ibid.* s. 53 ; *Re Lord Stamford's S.E.* (1889) 43 Ch.D. 84 at 95.
[15] *Re Penrhyn's Settlement* [1922] 1 Ch. 500.
[16] *Wheelwright* v. *Walker (No.* 1) (1883) 23 Ch.D. 752 at 762.
[17] *Cardigan* v. *Curzon-Howe* (1885) 30 Ch.D. 531 at 540.
[18] S.L.A. 1882, ss. 50–52.
[19] *Ibid.* ss. 56, 57.
[20] S.L.A. 1882, s. 56.
[21] *Re Marquis of Ailesbury's S.E.* [1892] 1 Ch. 506 at 535.

C. *The Trustees of the Settlement*

The Act contained an elaborate definition of the persons who were the trustees of the settlement, but in any settlement made after 1882 they normally consisted of those persons expressly appointed as trustees of the settlement for the purposes of the Act.[22] It is important to note that whether or not the legal estate was vested in the trustees, they had no real control over the land. The more important of their functions were as follows—

(i) Capital money arising on any transaction, such as the sale of the land, had to be paid either to the trustees or into court, and unless the settlement otherwise provided,[23] the trustees had to be two or more in number to give an effective receipt.[24]

(ii) Before entering into certain transactions, such as selling or leasing, the tenant for life had to give one month's written notice by registered letter to the trustees and, if known, to their solicitor.[25]

(iii) In a few specified cases, the tenant for life had to obtain the consent of the trustees or an order of the court, *e.g.,* if he wished to sell the principal mansion house.[26]

In short, the full control of the land was in the hands of the tenant for life, and the trustees merely had certain supervisory functions designed to protect the interests of the beneficiaries.

D. *Effect of a Sale or Other Dealing*

The effect of a dealing with the settled land such as a sale was that the rights of the beneficiaries under the settlement were overreached, provided that the money was paid to the trustees, being not less than two in number, or into court.[27] This was so whether the legal estate was vested in trustees or split up between the beneficiaries. A tenant for life had a statutory power to convey something not vested in him, namely, the whole legal estate. The capital money in the hands of the trustees, which had to be invested in accordance with the Act, was

[22] S.L.A. 1882, s. 2; S.L.A. 1890, s. 16.
[23] Contrast *post*, p. 194.
[24] S.L.A. 1882, ss. 22, 39.
[25] *Ibid.* s. 45.
[26] *Ibid.* s. 15; S.L.A. 1890, s. 10.
[27] S.L.A. 1882, ss. 20, 22, 39.

treated as being land.[28] " The effect of a sale under the Settled Land Act is merely to substitute money for land, and whatever rights persons had in the land are preserved to them in the money produced in its sale." [29] For example, if land was settled on " A for life, remainder to B for life, remainder to C and his heirs," the effect of a sale by A was to vest the legal fee simple in the purchaser, free from the legal rights of A, B and C, who took corresponding rights in the capital money. Thus C had a fee simple in remainder in the capital money, which, on his death would pass with the rest of his realty under his will or, if he was intestate, to his heir. If the land had been conveyed " unto and to the use of " trustees on trust for the beneficiaries, the position was exactly the same : A's statutory power of sale enabled him to transfer to the purchaser the legal estate vested in the trustees.

This power of the tenant for life to defeat the expectations of those in remainder who wished to enjoy the settled land itself might seem to be unjust, but " what the statute intended to do was to release the land from the fetters of the settlement—to render it a marketable article notwithstanding the settlement." [30] It was more important in the public interest that land should be freely alienable despite any settlement than that " sentimental considerations " [31] should be allowed to sterilise it.

Sect. 2. Trusts for Sale

1. Application of the Act. The original draft of the Act did not apply to land held on trust for sale, but " the unprompted wisdom of Parliament " added a section, section 63, " drafted in a fine style of perplexed verbiage," [32] which provided that such land was to be deemed settled land, and thus within the Act, if the proceeds of sale or income were to be applied or disposed of for any person or persons for life or any other limited period. The effect of this was to defeat the main purpose of a trust for sale (namely, that the land should be sold as and when the trustees thought best); the hands of the trustees were tied by the prohibition in the Act against their exercising any power to sell given to them by the settlement unless

[28] *Ibid.* s. 22.
[29] *Hampden* v. *Earl of Buckinghamshire* [1893] 2 Ch. 531 at 544.
[30] *Bruce* v. *Marquess of Ailesbury* [1892] A.C. 356 at 361.
[31] *Ibid.* at p. 362.
[32] 27 S.J. 113 ; 28 S.J. 322.

the tenant for life gave his consent.[33] Under a trust for sale, the trustees were normally intended to have control. Yet in consequence of section 63, the wide powers given by the Act were all vested in the tenant for life.

2. Order of court. One solution of the difficulty would have been to repeal the section added by Parliament. Instead, the Settled Land Act 1884, s. 7, provided that in the case of trusts for sale within the Settled Land Act 1882 the tenant for life should be unable to exercise his statutory powers unless he obtained an order of the court. Until such an order was made, the trustees were empowered to sell without the consent of the tenant for life.[34] A purchaser could safely deal with the trustees for sale unless such an order had been registered as a *lis pendens* (pending action).[35]

The result of this was substantially to restore the position as it was before 1883. Land subject to a trust for sale was nominally settled land, but unless the tenant for life had obtained an order from the court, he had none of the statutory powers and the trustees had the sole unfettered power of sale. However, they had no powers of leasing, mortgaging or otherwise dealing with the land except by way of sale unless the trust for sale conferred these powers on them expressly or by implication.[36]

3. Trust or power. Whether in any given case a trust for sale existed was often a matter of some complexity. A mere *power* of sale given to trustees was not a *trust* for sale: there had to be some obligation upon the trustees to sell, although the fact that they were empowered to postpone sale indefinitely or that a sale could be made only at the request or with the consent of a tenant for life did not prevent a trust for sale from falling within this category.[37] But there was no trust for sale within the Act if there was merely a trust to sell at the request of a tenant for life who had power to revoke the trust, or if the trust for sale was exercisable not immediately but only at some future date or only in certain very limited cases.[38] A trust " to retain or sell the land " might or might not be construed as a

---

[33] *Ante*, p. 148.
[34] S.L.A. 1884, s. 6.
[35] See *post*, p. 541.
[36] *Walker* v. *Southall* (1887) 56 L.T. 882 ; *Re Bellinger* [1898] 2 Ch. 534.
[37] *Re Wagstaff's S.E.* [1909] 2 Ch. 201.
[38] *Re Goodall's Settlement* [1909] 1 Ch. 440.

trust for sale, depending on whether the general intention of the settlement was that the land should be sold or that it should be retained as land.[39]

4. Bare trusts. It should be noted that the Settled Land Acts never applied to a trust where one or more persons of full age were entitled in possession absolutely and there was no element of succession, whether there was a trust for sale or a mere trust. Thus a conveyance " unto and to the use of A and his heirs in trust for B and C and their heirs " created a bare trust which was not within the Acts.

Part 3

THE SETTLED LAND ACT 1925

The Settled Land Act 1925 continued the policy of the Act of 1882, but with a number of important alterations. These alterations will be considered first, before dealing with the other provisions of the Act.

Sect. 1. Basic Alterations Made by the Act of 1925

A. Trusts for Sale are Excluded from the Act

Land subject to " an immediate binding trust for sale " is expressly excluded from the definition of settled land.[40] Trusts for sale are now governed by the Law of Property Act 1925 and are considered later under a separate head.[41]

B. The Legal Estate is Normally in the Tenant for Life

Before 1926, the legal estate in settled land was either vested in trustees or split up between the beneficiaries, depending upon how the settlement was made.[42] After 1925, the settlor has no choice, and with the exceptions stated below, the legal estate is always vested in the tenant for life. Where a settlement is made after 1925, the

[39] *Re Johnson* [1915] 1 Ch. 435 (trust for sale); *Re White's Settlement* [1930] 1 Ch. 179 (no trust for sale).
[40] S.L.A. 1925, s. 1 (7), added by L.P.(Am.)A. 1926, Sched.
[41] *Post,* p. 184.
[42] *Ante,* p. 144.

legal estate must be conveyed to the tenant for life, unless, of course, it is already vested in him,[43] as is the case where the owner of property settles it upon himself as tenant for life, with remainders over ("with remainders over" is a concise way of referring to the remainders following the life interest without setting them out in detail). In the case of a settlement made before 1926, the legal estate was automatically vested in the tenant for life at the first moment of 1926.[44]

Thus today the tenant for life has the legal estate as well as the statutory powers vested in him, and he holds both the estate and the powers on trust for himself and the other beneficiaries under the settlement.[45] This emphasises the dual capacity of a tenant for life: he holds two interests in the land, the legal estate as trustee and his own interest beneficially.[46] Owing to section 1 of the Law of Property Act 1925, his beneficial interest will now normally, but not necessarily, be equitable.[47]

In two cases, however, the legal estate and statutory powers are vested, not in a tenant for life, but in the statutory owner.[48] These two cases are as follows.

1. Tenant for life an infant. A legal estate cannot be vested in an infant after 1925 and it would be undesirable to give him the statutory powers. Consequently, where the tenant for life is an infant the legal estate and the statutory powers are vested in the statutory owner, consisting of—

    (i) a personal representative if the land is vested in him and no vesting instrument [49] has been executed, *e.g.*, where the settlement has been made by the will of a testator who has just died; but otherwise,

    (ii) the trustees of the settlement.

2. No tenant for life. Where under a settlement there is no tenant for life, the legal estate and statutory powers are vested in the statutory owner, consisting of—

---

[43] S.L.A. 1925, s. 4.
[44] L.P.A. 1925, 1st Sched., Pt. II, para. 6.
[45] S.L.A. 1925, ss. 16, 107.
[46] See, generally, *Re Liberty's W.T.* [1937] Ch. 176.
[47] *Ante,* p. 72 and *post,* pp. 160–164.
[48] S.L.A. 1925, ss. 4, 23, 26, 117; L.P.A. 1925, 1st Sched., Pt. II, paras. 3, 5, 6.
And on the death of a tenant for life the legal estate normally vests temporarily in personal representatives: see *post,* p. 181.
[49] For vesting instruments, see *post,* p. 156.

(i) any person of full age upon whom the settlement expressly confers the powers; if none,

(ii) the trustees of the settlement.

The question who is a tenant for life and the cases where there is no tenant for life are dealt with below.[50] For the present, it is sufficient to say that there usually is a tenant for life, but that in those cases where there is not the Act of 1925 has effected a considerable improvement, for in such cases before 1926 the land could not be dealt with at all.

It will be seen from this that whereas before 1926 the legal estate and statutory powers might be vested in different persons (*e.g.,* where land was conveyed " unto and to the use of T1 and T2 and their heirs in trust for A for life, remainder to B and his heirs "), the scheme of the Act of 1925 is to ensure that they shall not be separated. It should be noted, however, that the legal estate is never vested in the trustees of the settlement as such, although they may hold it in some other capacity, such as statutory owner or special personal representatives.[51]

C. All Settlements Must be Made by Two Documents

Before 1926, a settlement was usually made by one document. If the settlement was made by will, the will constituted the settlement, whereas a settlement *inter vivos* was made by deed. The result was that if the land was sold, the purchaser had to examine the lengthy and, for this purpose, mainly irrelevant provisions of the settlement to discover the principal facts essential to his obtaining a good title; these were normally—

(i) that the land he had agreed to buy was included in the settlement;

(ii) that the person who had agreed to sell to him was the duly constituted tenant for life; and

(iii) that the persons to whom he was proposing to pay the purchase-money were the duly appointed trustees of the settlement.

To discover these facts was often a tedious task, for the settlement was a long document setting out the trusts in full and a purchaser often had to waste time in reading clauses which were of no interest

[50] *Post,* pp. 164, 165.
[51] *Post,* p. 181.

to him in order to ascertain the few simple facts he required. In addition, all the details of the family's arrangements were laid bare to a stranger's gaze. There was, of course, no question of the purchaser being prejudiced by the notice he had of the beneficiaries' interests, for whether they were legal or equitable and whether or not he knew what they were, statute had laid down that he took free from them provided he paid his money to the trustees or into court.

The Settled Land Act 1925 avoids these disadvantages by providing that every settlement made after 1925 must be made by two documents, a vesting instrument and a trust instrument. The vesting instrument contains all the information to which a purchaser is entitled; it gives him, in effect, a short certificate of the few matters with which he is concerned. The trust instrument sets out the details of the settlement and the purchaser is normally not concerned with them. The trusts are said to be " behind the curtain " formed by the vesting instrument, and the curtain is one behind which the purchaser is not entitled to peep. Settlements made before 1926 are brought into line by the provision that the document creating the settlement is to be treated as the trust instrument, and that before the land can be dealt with a vesting instrument must be executed. These provisions must now be examined in greater detail.

1. Settlements made after 1925.

(a) *Settlements made inter vivos.* Every settlement of a legal estate in land made *inter vivos* after 1925 must be made by two deeds, a principal vesting deed and a trust instrument.[52] The contents of these deeds are as follows:

TRUST INSTRUMENT

This—

   (i) Declares the trusts affecting the settled land.

  (ii) Bears any *ad valorem* stamp duty payable in respect of the settlement.

 (iii) Appoints trustees of the settlement.

 (iv) Contains the power, if any, to appoint new trustees of the settlement.

  (v) Sets out, either expressly or by reference, any powers intended to be conferred by the settlement in extension of those conferred by the Act.

---

[52] S.L.A. 1925, ss. 4, 5.

This—

    (i) Describes the settled land, either specifically or generally.

    (ii) Declares that the settled land is vested in the person or persons to whom it is conveyed, or in whom it is declared to be vested, upon the trusts from time to time affecting the settled land.

    (iii) States the names of the trustees of the settlement.

    (iv) States the names of any persons empowered to appoint new trustees of the settlement.

    (v) States any additional or larger powers conferred by the trust instrument.

It will be noticed that the last three particulars in each document are similar, the only difference being that whereas the trust instrument actually makes the appointment and confers the powers, the vesting deed merely recites what has been done by the trust instrument. The first two particulars in each of the deeds are, of course, completely dissimilar. The second requirement of a vesting deed is worded so as to cover two cases: (a) where the vesting deed acts as a conveyance from the settlor to the tenant for life or statutory owner, as where X settles property on A for life with remainders over; and (b) where the same person is both settlor and tenant for life, so that there is no transfer of the legal estate, as where Z on his marriage settles property on himself for life with remainders over.

    (b) *Settlements made by will.* Where land is settled by the will of a testator dying after 1925, the will is treated as the trust instrument and the testator's personal representatives, after providing for debts and death duties, hold the land on trust to execute a vesting instrument in favour of the tenant for life or statutory owner on being required to do so.[53] The vesting instrument may be either a vesting deed or a vesting assent. A vesting assent is a document merely in writing containing the same particulars as a vesting deed [54]; it attracts no stamp duty, whereas a vesting deed, being a deed, must carry a ten shillings stamp.

2. Settlements made before 1926. A deed creating a settlement existing at the beginning of 1926 is treated as a trust instrument. The Act provided that as soon as was practicable the trustees of the settlement might, and at the request of the tenant for life or statutory

---

[53] S.L.A. 1925, ss. 6, 8.
[54] *Ibid.* s. 8.

owner must, execute a vesting deed.[55] Normally this conveys no
estate but merely declares that the legal estate in the settled land is
vested in the tenant for life or statutory owner, for in nearly all cases
the Law of Property Act 1925 automatically vested the legal estate
in him at the beginning of 1926[56]; but if in fact the legal estate was
outstanding, the vesting deed operates to convey it.

This provision is of little assistance to a purchaser, however, for
this is one of the two important cases where the trust instrument is
not kept behind the curtain.[57] Despite the existence of a vesting
deed, a purchaser must verify from the settlement that the vesting
deed includes the land in question and that the proper persons are
tenant for life and trustees of the settlement.[58]

3. Section 13. Some provision had to be made to prevent
evasions of the requirement that there should be a vesting instrument.
While a vesting deed is not invalidated merely by some error in the
statements required to be contained in it,[59] the absence of any vesting
instrument at all usually makes it impossible to deal with the land.
First, a settlement of a legal estate in land made by a single document
cannot transfer or create a legal estate; the tenant for life or statutory owner, however, can require the trustees of the settlement to
execute a vesting deed.[60] Secondly, section 13 of the Settled Land
Act 1925 (sometimes called the " paralysing section ") in effect
provides that where a tenant for life or statutory owner has become
entitled to have a vesting instrument executed in his favour, no disposition of a legal estate can be made until a vesting instrument has
been executed in accordance with the Act; until this has been done,
any purported disposition of the land *inter vivos* by any person
operates only as a contract for valuable consideration to carry out the
transaction after the requisite vesting instrument has been executed.

To this rule there are four exceptions.

(a) *Disposition by personal representative.* The section does not
apply where the disposition is made by a personal representative.[61]
Thus if a settlement was made before 1926 and the tenant for life

---

[55] *Ibid.* 2nd Sched., para. 1.
[56] L.P.A. 1925, 1st Sched., Pt. II, paras. 3, 5, 6.
[57] For the other case, see *post,* p. 159.
[58] S.L.A. 1925, s. 110.
[59] S.L.A. 1925, s. 5.
[60] *Ibid.* ss. 4, 9.
[61] *Ibid.* s. 13.

has just died without a vesting deed having been executed, the legal
estate (which was nevertheless automatically vested in the tenant for
life at the beginning of 1926) duly passes to his personal representatives, who can dispose of the land without a vesting instrument being
executed, *e.g.,* if part of the land is sold to raise money for death
duties.

(b) *Purchaser without notice.* The section does not apply where
the disposition is made to a purchaser of a legal estate without notice
of the tenant for life or statutory owner having become entitled to a
vesting instrument.[62] For example, if by a deed A settles land on
himself for life with remainders over, and then, suppressing the deed,
sells the land to a purchaser who is ignorant of the settlement, the
purchaser gets a good title even though no vesting deed has been
executed.

(c) *Settlement at an end.* The section does not apply where the
settlement has come to an end before a vesting instrument has been
executed. Thus where at the end of 1925 X was a tenant in tail in
possession free from any trusts or incumbrances, it has been held that
if before any vesting instrument is executed he bars the entail and so
terminates the settlement, it is unnecessary for a vesting instrument
to be executed before he conveys the land to a purchaser.[63] When
the land ceases to be settled, the fetters of section 13 drop off.

(d) *Section 1 of the Amendment Act.* Section 13 does not apply
where advantage is taken of section 1 of the Law of Property
(Amendment) Act 1926. In a limited class of cases, this allows
settled land to be dealt with as if it were not settled; the section is
dealt with below.[64]

An illustration of the operation of these provisions is given by
the case of a settlor who attempts to make a settlement *inter vivos*
after 1925 in favour of his son and family by a single document. In
such a case—

    (i) The document is ineffective to transfer or create any legal
        estate, which thus remains vested in the settlor.

    (ii) The document is treated as a trust instrument.

    (iii) As soon as it is practicable the trustees of the settlement
        may, and at the request of the tenant for life or statutory

---

[62] *Ibid.,* as amended by L.P.(Am.)A. 1926, Sched.
[63] *Re Alefounder's W.T.* [1927] 1 Ch. 360.
[64] *Post,* p. 163.

owner must, execute a principal vesting deed, which will operate to take the legal estate out of the settlor and vest it in the tenant for life or statutory owner.

(iv) Until the trustees have duly executed the vesting deed, section 13 operates to prevent any disposition of the land being made. It will be noticed that the section prevents the settlor from rectifying his mistake by executing a vesting deed himself; it is the trustees of the settlement, and they alone, who can execute the vesting deed. If there are no trustees and no persons able and willing to appoint trustees, an application must be made to the court for the appointment of trustees.

(v) Even after a vesting deed has been executed the settlement is not as satisfactory as one made in the proper manner, for the document creating the settlement, although treated as the trust instrument, is not behind the curtain. This is the other of the two important exceptions to the rule that a purchaser is not concerned with the trust instrument.[65] A purchaser must examine the document creating the settlement to see that it includes the land in question and that the proper persons are tenant for life and trustees of the settlement.

4. Subsidiary vesting deed. Where a settlement of land is already in existence and other land is brought into the settlement, a subsidiary vesting deed is required to convey the land to the tenant for life or statutory owner. The contents of a subsidiary vesting deed are as follows—

(i) particulars of the last or only principal vesting deed affecting land subject to the settlement;

(ii) a statement that the land conveyed is to be held upon and subject to the same trusts and powers as the land comprised in the principal vesting deed;

(iii) the names of the trustees of the settlement;

(iv) the name of any person entitled to appoint new trustees of the settlement.[66]

It is unnecessary to refer to the trust instrument or to any additional powers conferred thereby.

---

[65] For the first exception, see *ante*, p. 157.
[66] S.L.A. 1925, s. 10.

Sect. 2. Other Provisions Relating to Settled Land

The other provisions relating to settled land in the main correspond
to similar provisions in the Act of 1882, although in a number of
cases important extensions and additions have been made.

A. Essentials of Settled Land

The three essential points to consider are—

> (1) whether the land is settled land;
> (2) who is the tenant for life; and
> (3) who are the trustees.

I. DEFINITION OF SETTLED LAND

1. " Settlement." Land is settled land if " it is or is deemed
to be the subject of a settlement." [67] By section 1 of the Settled Land
Act 1925, a settlement is created by any document or documents
(including an Act of Parliament [68]) whereby one of the following
conditions is satisfied.

(a) *Succession*: the land stands limited in trust for any persons
by way of succession.

In addition to cases such as limitations " to A for life, remainder
to B in fee simple," this definition seems to be wide enough to cover
the following cases which are somewhat superfluously set out in the
section as independent heads, namely, where land is limited in trust
for any person in possession—

> (i) for an entailed interest, whether or not capable of being
> barred or defeated;
> (ii) for an estate in fee simple or for a term of years absolute
> subject to an executory gift over (*e.g.,* a devise to trustees
> in trust for " A in fee simple but for B in fee simple when B
> marries ");
> (iii) for a base or determinable fee, including a fee determinable
> by condition, or any corresponding interest in leasehold
> land;

or where—

> (iv) land is limited in trust for any person for an estate in fee
> simple or for a term of years absolute contingently on the

---

[67] *Ibid.* s. 2.
[68] See, *e.g., Re Lord Hereford's S.E.* [1932] W.N. 34.

happening of any event (*e.g.,* a devise to trustees in trust for X in fee simple if his brothers die under the age of 21 years). In all these cases there is an element of succession sufficient to satisfy the definition in (a). Thus if S settles land upon trust for X in tail, the land stands limited in trust for persons by way of succession and the limitations arise under the settlement; for any estate or interest not disposed of under the settlement and remaining in or reverting to the settlor or anyone deriving title under him is deemed to arise under the settlement, with the consequence that S's fee simple reversion upon X's entail is deemed to arise under the settlement.[69]

(b) *Infants*: the land stands limited in trust for an infant in possession for an estate in fee simple or for a term of years absolute.

(c) *Family charges*: the land stands charged, whether voluntarily or in consideration of marriage or by way of family arrangement, with the payment of any sums for the benefit of any persons.

Before the abolition of restraints upon anticipation,[70] the existence of such a restraint also made land settled land. This had not been the case under the Settled Land Act 1882.

2. " Limited in trust." It will be noted that under heads (a) (succession) and (b) (infants), but not (c) (family charges), it is necessary for the land to be " limited in trust " if it is to fall within the definition; if there is no trust, the land is not settled land. In all cases where property is given by will, there is necessarily a trust for the beneficiaries by reason of the legal estate first vesting in the testator's personal representatives, so that the interests of the beneficiaries operate only in equity until the personal representatives clothe them with the legal estate. Where the disposition is made *inter vivos* it will be made either—

(i) by a proper vesting deed and trust instrument, whereupon the legal estate vests in the tenant for life as trustee, or

(ii) by a single instrument, in which case the legal estate will remain in the settlor and only an equitable interest will be transferred; for none of the interests mentioned in (a) is capable of existing at law (except, it seems, a fee determinable by condition [71]), and in (b) by reason of an infant's inability after 1925 to hold a legal estate in land, no legal estate passes.

---

[69] See *Re Hunter and Hewlett's Contract* [1907] 1 Ch. 46.

[70] See *ante*, p. 132 and *post*, p. 520.

[71] See *ante*, p. 75. *Quaere*, whether the land is settled land in this case.

Consequently, on the principle that there is a trust if the legal estate is in one person and the equitable interest in another, the grantor will hold the land in trust.

Under head (c), no limitation by way of trust is required. Whether the estate which is subject to the family charges is conveyed direct to the beneficiary or whether it is held in trust for the beneficiary, the land is nevertheless settled land.

3. New provisions. Although heads (a) and (b) substantially repeat the provisions of the Settled Land Act 1882, there are two cases in which land which was not settled land before 1926 becomes settled land after 1925; and until restraints upon anticipation were abolished, there were three. The two cases are—

(a) *Head* (c): *family charges.* Before 1926 even if settled land had become vested in one person in fee simple, it continued to be settled land if there still existed a jointure or provisions for portions or annuities under a settlement, provided in each case that they were not merely sums presently payable but were limited to arise in the future, thus satisfying the requirement that the land should be limited to persons by way of succession.[72] The provision in the Act of 1925 is wider than this, and contains no requirement of futurity. It is essential that the sum of money should have been charged on the land either voluntarily, or in consideration of marriage, or by way of family arrangement; the Act does not apply if the charge was created for money or money's worth, as where a tenant in fee simple sells his land and takes a charge on it as part of the price. But subject to this requirement, it is immaterial whether the provision is present or future, whether it is for capital or annual sums, or whether it is for a limited period (*e.g.,* for life) or in perpetuity. Thus if a testator devises land to trustees on trust to pay a perpetual annuity to X, and subject thereto on trust for A in fee simple, the land becomes settled land.[73]

The effect of this provision was that at the beginning of 1926 much land which had previously not been settled land was forthwith converted into settled land. In a number of cases this caused hardship to those who had purchased such land before 1926. The practice in such cases was that unless the land could be freed from the charges, as by the owners of the charges all releasing them in return for a

---

[72] *Re Mundy and Roper's Contract* [1899] 1 Ch. 275.
[73] *Re Austen* [1929] 2 Ch. 155.

share of the purchase-money, the vendor conveyed the land to the
purchaser subject to the charges but with an indemnity against them,
i.e., the vendor agreed to pay the charges himself and so ensure that
they would not be enforced against the land. In cases where this had
been done, the astonished purchaser found (if, indeed, he could understand the matter at all) that at the beginning of 1926 his land had
become settled land and that it could be sold only after compliance
with the troublesome Settled Land Act procedure, *e.g.,* as to the
appointing of trustees and the execution of a vesting deed.

To meet this situation, the Law of Property (Amendment) Act
1926, s. 1, provides that where a person of full age is beneficially
entitled in possession to land in fee simple or for a term of years
absolute subject to charges of this kind, he can nevertheless create or
convey a legal estate subject to the charges in the same way as if the
land were not settled land. This applies whether the charges arose
before 1926 or after 1925, and whether the person entitled to the
land is the tenant under the settlement or a purchaser from him; but
it applies only if the sole reason for the land being deemed settled
land is that it is subject to the charges and not, for example, when it
is also entailed. Where the Amendment Act applies, a vendor may
thus sell the land either (i) free from the charges, by making use of
the Settled Land Act procedure, or (ii) subject to the charges, by
virtue of the Amendment Act.

(b) *Dower assigned by metes and bounds.* The position of dower
must be distinguished from that of curtesy, though both are rare
today. Before 1926, where a married woman died and her husband
took curtesy, the element of succession required to make the land
settled land was satisfied by the fact that he took a mere life estate
and that subject thereto the land passed to his wife's heir. Nevertheless, until the Settled Land Act 1884 [74] expressly declared that in
such a case the husband was deemed to take under a settlement made
by his wife, the land was not settled land within the meaning of the
Settled Land Act 1882, since the husband's interest arose by operation of law and not under any document.[75] This provision of the
Act of 1884 is repeated in the Act of 1925 [76] and so the existence of
curtesy makes the land settled land under head (a) above.

Yet although the position of curtesy is unchanged, the position of
dower assigned by metes and bounds has been altered. The mode in

[74] s. 8.
[75] *Re Pocock and Prankerd's Contract* [1896] 1 Ch. 302 at 306; *ante,* p. 147.
[76] S.L.A. 1925, s. 20.

which dower is enjoyed is either that the widow receives one-third of
the income of the land or else that she has her dower "assigned by
metes and bounds," *i.e.,* has a distinct one-third part of the land
marked out for her exclusive occupation for the rest of her life.[77]
The former method did not create a settlement before 1926 and still
does not do so. The latter method did not create a settlement
before 1926, for although the requisite element of succession
was present, the wife claimed her third under the general law and
not under any document, and there was no provision that dower
should be deemed to arise under a settlement as there was in the case
of curtesy. But after 1925 (when new rights of dower can rarely
arise[78]), it is provided that the letters of administration or probate
of the husband's estate shall be deemed to be a settlement made by
the husband,[79] so that the widow's one-third is settled land.

II. DEFINITION OF TENANT FOR LIFE

1. Tenant for life. An elaborate definition of "tenant for life"
is given by the Settled Land Act 1925.[80] The definition includes not
only a person entitled to a life interest but a tenant in tail, a tenant in
fee simple subject to a gift over or to family charges, a tenant for
years terminable on life, a tenant *pur autre vie,* a person entitled to
the income of land for his own or any other life and (formerly) a
married woman entitled to a fee simple subject to a restraint on
anticipation.

In addition to falling within the above category a person must also
be of full age and beneficially entitled in possession[81]; thus a trustee
for another person, or somebody who is entitled only to a future
interest in the land, cannot be a tenant for life under the Act. The
practical effect of the definition is that where there is some person of
full age beneficially entitled to either the possession of settled land or
the whole of the income from it, that person will be the tenant for
life. The position where two or more persons are thus entitled
jointly or in common is dealt with later.[82]

---

[77] *Post*, p. 298.
[78] See *post*, p. 309.
[79] S.L.A. 1925, s. 1 (3).
[80] ss. 19, 20; and see M. & W. 328–331.
[81] *Re Morgan* (1883) 24 Ch.D. 114 at 116; *Re Jemmett and Guest's Contract* [1907]
     1 Ch. 629.
[82] *Post*, p. 222.

2. Cases where there is no tenant for life. Although there will normally be a tenant for life under the above provisions, there are some cases where there is no tenant for life, as where land is given to trustees on trust to pay X a fixed annuity [83] or a definite fraction of the income,[84] with a direction to accumulate the balance, or where there is an immediate discretionary trust, such as a direction to trustees to pay the income to such one or more members of a class of persons as they think fit, no member being entitled as of right to any of the income.[85] In these cases the legal estate and statutory powers are in the statutory owner.[86]

The position where the tenant for life is an infant has already been dealt with.[87]

III. DEFINITION OF TRUSTEES OF THE SETTLEMENT

The trustees of the settlement are defined by section 30 of the Settled Land Act 1925. There are five heads, which must be applied in turn; thus if there are any trustees under one head, they exclude any under a subsequent head. The definition is as follows:

(i) The persons who, under the settlement, are trustees with power to sell the land (even if this power is subject to the consent of anyone) or with power of consenting to or approving the exercise of a power of sale.

For example, if in a settlement on A for life, with remainders over, there is a trust giving X and Y a general [88] power to sell the land, this will make them trustees of the settlement, in preference even to any other persons expressly appointed Settled Land Act trustees. X and Y will in fact have no power to sell the land for, as will be seen,[89] this power is taken away from them and given to the tenant for life; nevertheless, the attempt to give them the power suffices to make them trustees of the settlement.

(ii) The persons declared by the settlement to be trustees thereof for the purposes of the Settled Land Acts 1882 to 1890, or 1925, or any of them.

---

[3] *Re Jefferys (No. 2)* [1939] Ch. 205.
[4] *Re Frewen* [1926] Ch. 580.
[5] *Re Gallenga W.T.* [1938] 1 All E.R. 106.
[6] *Ante*, p. 153.
[7] *Ante*, p. 153.
[8] See *Re Carne's S.E.* [1899] 1 Ch. 324.
[9] *Post*, p. 178.

This is the head under which the trustees of the settlement will usually be found, for cases under head (i) are rare. It should be noted that it is not sufficient to appoint X and Y " trustees of the settlement " [90]: the appointment will be ineffective unless words such as " for the purposes of the Settled Land Act 1925 " are added.

> (iii) Persons who, under the settlement, are trustees with power of sale or of consenting to or approving a sale, or upon trust for sale, of *other* land held under the same settlement and upon the same trusts.

> (iv) Persons who, under the settlement, are trustees with a *future* power of sale, or under a *future* trust for sale, or with a power of consenting to or approving the exercise of such a future power of sale, even if the power or trust does not take effect in all events.

Thus if there is a settlement of Blackacre and Whiteacre which gives trustees a power of sale over Blackacre alone, clause (iii) makes those trustees Settled Land Act trustees of both properties.[91] Again, if Greenacre is settled on A for life with remainder to X and Y on trust for sale, clause (iv) makes X and Y Settled Land Act trustees.[92]

> (v) The persons appointed by deed by those able to dispose of the whole equitable interest in the settled land.

For example if land is settled on A for life, remainder to B in tail, remainder to C in fee simple, A and B between them can dispose of the whole equitable interest in the land and thus can appoint trustees of the settlement.[93]

Where a settlement arises under a will or intestacy and there are no trustees under any other provisions, the personal representatives of the deceased are trustees of the settlement until other trustees are appointed.[94] This useful provision deals with the most frequent cause of a lack of trustees, namely, a will made without proper legal advice. Where even this provision fails (*e.g.*, where there is a home-made settlement created *inter vivos*) the court has power to appoint trustees on the application of any person interested under the settlement.[95]

---

[90] Consider *Re Bentley* (1885) 54 L.J.Ch. 782.
[91] *Re Moore* [1906] 1 Ch. 789.
[92] *Re Johnson's S.E.* [1913] W.N. 222.
[93] *Re Spearman S.E.* [1906] 2 Ch. 502.
[94] S.L.A. 1925, s. 30.
[95] For the appointment, replacement, and removal of trustees, see *post*, pp. 246–253.

B. *Compound Settlement*

1. Definition. Before 1926, difficulties sometimes arose in the case of compound settlements. " Compound settlement " is the term used to describe the state of affairs when the trusts affecting the land in question are created by two or more instruments. The most usual example of a compound settlement arises where land has been settled on A for life with remainder (subject to provisions for others of the family) to his son in tail; on the son attaining his majority, A and the son bar the entail and resettle the property on A for life, remainder to the son for life, with remainders over.[96] Where such a process takes place there are three distinct settlements to consider—

(1) the original settlement;

(2) the resettlement; and

(3) the compound settlement, which is a separate entity.[97]

2. Position of tenant for life. Formerly the position of a tenant for life under a compound settlement was as follows.

(i) He could exercise his powers as tenant for life under the original settlement, and provided there were trustees under that settlement, he could, on disposing of the land, overreach the rights of the beneficiaries under both the settlement and the resettlement[98]; but while acting under the settlement he could not avail himself of any additional powers conferred by the resettlement.

(ii) He could act as tenant for life under the resettlement, availing himself of any additional powers conferred by it, but in this case he could not, on disposing of the land, overreach the rights of beneficiaries under the original settlement.[99]

(iii) He could act as tenant for life under the compound settlement, exercising any additional powers conferred by either settlement; and provided there were trustees of the compound settlement, he could overreach the rights of the beneficiaries under both the settlement and the resettlement.[1]

3. Tenant for life and trustees of compound settlement. As the third method combined the advantages of the first two methods, it was

6 See *post*, p. 202.
7 See *Re Coull's S.E.* [1905] 1 Ch. 712 at 720.
8 *Re Lord Wimborne and Browne's Contract* [1904] 1 Ch. 537.
9 See *Re Mundy and Roper's Contract* [1899] 1 Ch. 275 at 295.
1 *Re Phillimore's Estate* [1904] 2 Ch. 460.

important to know in any given case whether there were any trustee of the compound settlement and whether the tenant for life could ac under the compound settlement. Except where trustees of the com pound settlement were appointed by the persons together able t dispose of the whole equitable interest, they could be appointed onl by the court; for on making a settlement, the settlor probably had n power to declare who should be the trustees of any resettlement, an on a resettlement being made, an appointment of trustees thereo could not bind beneficiaries under the original settlement.[2] As regard the tenant for life, it was settled law that where one person was tenan for life under both settlements, or under the resettlement alone, h could act as tenant for life under the compound settlement.[3] In th example given above, A could exercise the powers of a tenant fo life under either settlement or under the compound settlement; it wa immaterial whether or not the life estate conferred on him by th resettlement was expressed to be " in restoration and confirmation " of his life estate under the settlement.[4]

4. Need for trustees of compound settlement. In most cases th comparative rarity of trustees of the compound settlement caused n difficulty, as, for example, where the tenant for life wished to sell fre from the rights of the beneficiaries under both settlements, and h held under the original settlement of which there were properl appointed trustees, or where he held under the resettlement an merely wished to exercise additional powers conferred thereby. Bu in one case, trustees of the compound settlement were needed in orde to achieve the desired object; this was where there was no tenant fo life under the original settlement and the tenant for life under the re settlement wished to overreach the rights of beneficiaries under th original settlement. In this case it was impossible to avoid th expense of an application to the court if no such trustees existed.[5]

5. After 1925. After 1925, this difficulty no longer exists. Wher before 1926 the court had appointed trustees of the compound settle ment, they continue in office. In other cases, it has been provided ir

[2] *Re Spencer's S.E.* [1903] 1 Ch. 75.
[3] *Re Phillimore's Estate* [1904] 2 Ch. 460.
[4] See *Re Constable's S.E.* [1919] 1 Ch. 178, overruled on another point by *Parr* v *Att.-Gen.* [1926] A.C. 239.
[5] *Re Trafford's S.E.* [1915] 1 Ch. 9.

ffect that even in the case of settlements made before 1926, the
rustees of the original settlement, or in default, the trustees of the
esettlement, shall be trustees of the compound settlement.[6]

C. Powers of the Tenant for Life

The powers and position of a tenant for life remain substantially the
ame as under the Act of 1882, although a number of important
details have been modified. Such changes as have been made mainly
give the tenant for life wider powers. In general, what follows applies
o statutory owners as well as to tenants for life. As was the case
under the Act of 1882, a tenant for life is normally subject to no
ontrol in the exercise of his powers. The chief safeguards against the
abuse of his powers are—

(1) his position as a trustee for the beneficiaries;

(2) the provision that in the case of the most important powers, he
must give notice to the trustees of his intention to exercise
them; and

(3) the provision that in a few exceptional cases he must not
exercise his powers without the leave of the trustees or an
order of the court.

The position of the tenant for life as trustee has already been men-
ioned, and will be further considered later.[7] His powers are
onsidered below.

I. POWERS EXERCISABLE UPON GIVING NOTICE [8]

f the tenant for life intends to make a sale, exchange, lease, mortgage or charge, or to grant an option, he must give written notice to
he trustees of the settlement, and, if known, to the solicitor for the
rustees. The notice must be given by registered letter posted at least
one month before the transaction or the contract therefor, and is
nvalid unless when it is given the trustees consist of two or more
persons or a trust corporation; thus if there are no trustees, a tenant
or life is not entitled to exercise these powers. The object of this
provision for giving notice seems to be to enable the trustees to pre-

[6] S.L.A. 1925, s. 31.
[7] See *ante*, pp. 147, 153, *post*, p. 177.
[8] S.L.A. 1925, ss. 38–48, 51, 71, 101.

vent any fraudulent dealing by applying to the court for an in
junction.[9] In fact, however, it affords comparatively little protection
for—

   (i) the trustees are apparently under no obligation to interfer
with an improper transaction [10];

  (ii) except in the case of a mortgage or charge, a general notic
suffices, *e.g.*, " take notice that I intend from time to time t
exercise any or all of my powers under the Settled Land Ac
1925." In such cases, however, the tenant for life must, a
the request of a trustee of the settlement, give reasonable in
formation as to any sales, exchanges or leases effected, i
progress or immediately intended [11];

 (iii) any trustee may by writing accept less than one month'
notice, or waive it altogether [12]; and

 (iv) a person dealing in good faith with the tenant for life is no
concerned to inquire whether notice has been given.[13] Ever
if there are no trustees, a bona fide purchaser for value of
legal estate gets a good title if the transaction is one on whic
no capital money is payable, *e.g.*, the grant of a lease fo
which no premium is payable.[14]

Each of the powers in respect of which notice is normally require
must now be examined.

1. Power to sell. A tenant for life may sell the settled land o
any part thereof, or any easement, right or privilege of any kind ove
the land.[15] He may, for example, sell to a railway company the righ
to tunnel under the land. With certain qualifications, he must obtai
the best consideration in money that can reasonably be obtained. I
one case [16] a tenant for life was made an offer by another beneficiary
but being unwilling to sell to him, proposed to sell to a third part
for a lower price; the court restrained the tenant for life from sellin
for less than the price offered by the beneficiary, or from selling a
all without informing the beneficiary of the proposed price and givin
him two days in which to increase his offer. But there is no need fo

   [9] *Wheelwright* v. *Walker (No. 1)* (1883) 23 Ch.D. 752.
  [10] S.L.A. 1925, s. 97.
  [11] *Ibid.* s. 101.
  [12] *Ibid.*
  [13] *Ibid.*
  [14] *Mogridge* v. *Clapp* [1892] 3 Ch. 382.
  [15] S.L.A. 1925, ss. 38, 39.
  [16] *Wheelwright* v. *Walker (No. 2)* (1883) 31 W.R. 912.

the sale to be by auction. Further, a purchaser is protected by the provision that if he deals in good faith with the tenant for life, he is to be conclusively taken, as against all the beneficiaries, to have given the best consideration reasonably obtainable and to have complied with all the requirements of the Act; this applies both to sales and other dealings such as leases.[17] Thus a purchaser who made a good bargain and bought for £2,000 property which he forthwith resold for £3,000 was held to be protected.[18]

2. Power to exchange. Settled land, or any part of it, or any easement, right or privilege over it, may be exchanged for other land or any easement, right or privilege.[19] For " equality of exchange " (*i.e.*, to adjust any difference in value) capital money may be paid or received.

3. Power to lease

(a) *The power.* The settled land, or any part of it, or any easement, right or privilege over it, may be leased for any period not exceeding—

   (i) 999 years for building or forestry;

   (ii) 100 years for mining;

   (iii) 50 years for any other purpose.[20]

Before 1926 the periods were 99, 60 and 21 years respectively, and there was no special provision for forestry leases. After 1925, however, the new periods apply even if the settlement was made before 1926. A building lease is one made partly in consideration of erecting, improving, adding to or repairing buildings or an agreement to do this[21]; the advantage to the settled land is that in return for a reduced rent the lessee must leave on the land at the end of his lease the new or improved buildings. By the Forestry Act 1967, a forestry lease means a lease to the Minister of Agriculture, Fisheries and Food for purposes authorised by the Act.

(b) *Conditions of lease.* Every lease of settled land must comply with the following conditions.[22]

   (i) It must be made by deed.

[17] S.L.A. 1925, s. 110.
[18] *Hurrell* v. *Littlejohn* [1904] 1 Ch. 689.
[19] S.L.A. 1925, ss. 38, 40.
[20] *Ibid*. s. 41.
[21] *Ibid*. s. 44.
[22] S.L.A. 1925, s. 42. For defective leases, see M. & W. 345, 346.

(ii) It must be made to take effect in possession not more than one year after its date, or in reversion after an existing lease with not more than 7 years to run at the date of the new lease. Thus if a tenant for life grants a lease to commence in 14 months' time, it is invalid unless it is to commence after the determination of an existing lease.

(iii) It must reserve the best rent reasonably obtainable in the circumstances, regard being had to any fine (*i.e.*, a premium or lump sum) taken, and to any money laid out or to be laid out for the benefit of the land. Any fine is capital money. A lease granted by a tenant for life in return for a bribe or the release from a claim for damages against him personally has accordingly been held not to comply with the statutory requirements.[23] A nominal or reduced rent may be reserved for not longer than the first 5 years of a building lease or the first 10 years of a forestry lease, and in the case of mining or forestry leases, there are wide powers to vary the rent, *e.g.*, according to the value of the minerals or trees taken.[24]

(iv) It must contain a covenant by the lessee for payment of rent and a condition of re-entry (*i.e.*, a provision for forfeiture of the lease) on rent not being paid within a specified time not exceeding 30 days.

(v) A counterpart (*i.e.*, copy) of the lease must be executed by the lessee and delivered to the tenant for life; it is sufficient evidence that this has been done if the tenant for life duly executes the lease.

It will be seen that normally a lease must be by deed and notice must be given to the trustees. In certain cases, however, these requirements are relaxed. A lease at the best rent reasonably obtainable without a fine and not exempting the lessee from liability for waste has two privileges:

(i) if it is for not more than 21 years, it may be made without giving notice to the trustees; and

(ii) if it is for not more than 3 years, it may also be made merely in writing and not by deed.[25]

As a corollary to his power to grant leases, a tenant for life has wide powers of accepting surrenders of leases and of varying or

---

[23] *Re Handman and Wilcox's Contract* [1902] 1 Ch. 599.
[24] S.L.A. 1925, ss. 44, 45, 48.
[25] S.L.A. 1925, s. 42.

waiving the terms of any lease.[26]   These powers are exercisable without notice to the trustees.

(c) *Rent from leases.*   The normal rule is that the tenant for life is entitled to the whole of the rent from leases of the settled land.[27] But as seen above,[28] this does not apply to mining leases, where the capital value of the land is being diminished.   The general rule as to rent from mining leases granted under the Act is that, subject to any contrary intention in the settlement, the tenant for life is entitled to three-quarters of the rent unless he is impeachable of waste and the mine is an unopened one, when he is entitled to only one-quarter of the rent; the balance in each case is capital.[29]   These provisions, however, apply only to rent from leases granted under the Act, so that if the lease is granted under an express power in the settlement,[30] or if the lease or a contract therefor [31] was made before the land was settled or resettled,[32] the tenant for life is entitled to the whole of the income.   It must also be remembered that the rules as to the tenant for life working the minerals himself are different from the rules as to leases,[33] and that where the tenant for life has not a life interest but some interest such as a fee simple subject to a gift over, he may be unimpeachable of waste even if the settlement is silent on the subject; the owner of a mere life interest, on the other hand, is impeachable unless the settlement exempts him from liability for waste.[34]

4. Power to mortgage or charge.   In the absence of a contrary provision in the settlement, a tenant for life has no power to mortgage or charge the legal estate for his own benefit.   If he wishes to raise money for his own use, he can of course do so by mortgaging his beneficial interest, consisting of his life interest, entail or whatever interest he has.   The legal estate, on the other hand, can be mortgaged only for certain specified purposes for the benefit of the settled

---

[26] *Ibid.* ss. 52, 59.
[27] See, *e.g., Re Wix* [1916] 1 Ch. 279.
[28] *Ante,* p. 53.
[29] S.L.A. 1925, s. 47.
[30] *Earl of Lonsdale* v. *Lowther* [1900] 2 Ch. 687.
[31] *Re Kemys-Tynte* [1892] 2 Ch. 211.
[32] *Re Arkwright's Settlement* [1945] Ch. 195.
[33] He can keep the whole of the profits unless he is impeachable of waste and the mine is unopened, when he cannot work it at all: *ante,* p. 52.
[34] *Ante,* pp. 34, 41, 50.

land or those entitled under the settlement, *e.g.*, to pay for improvements, discharge incumbrances or provide money which is required to be raised under the provisions of the settlement, such as portions.[35]

5. Power to grant options. A tenant for life may grant an option in writing to purchase or take a lease of all or any part of the settled land or of any easement, right or privilege over it. But—

(i) the price or rent must be the best reasonably obtainable and must be fixed at the time of granting the option; a tenant for life thus has no power to agree to sell at a price to be fixed by arbitration;

(ii) the option must be made exercisable within an agreed number of years not exceeding 10; and

(iii) the option may be granted with or without any consideration being paid, but if any is paid, it is capital money.[36]

II. POWERS EXERCISABLE WITH CONSENT OF THE TRUSTEES
OR UNDER AN ORDER OF THE COURT

In the following cases, the tenant for life can exercise his powers only with the consent of the trustees of the settlement or under an order of the court.

1. Power to dispose of the principal mansion house. If the tenant for life wishes to make a disposition (whether by sale, lease, exchange or otherwise[37]) of the principal mansion house, if any, and the pleasure-grounds and park,[38] and the lands, if any, usually occupied therewith, the consent of the trustees or an order of the court is required—

(i) if the settlement was made before 1926 and does not expressly provide to the contrary; or

(ii) if the settlement was made after 1925 and expressly requires such consent or order to be obtained.[39]

In other cases, no consent is required, but the usual notice must be given.

---

[35] S.L.A. 1925, ss. 16, 71; and see M. & W. 347, 348. For portions, see *ante*, pp. 139, 142, and *post*, p. 204.

[36] S.L.A. 1925, s. 51.

[37] *Ibid.* s. 117.

[38] See *Pease* v. *Courtney* [1904] 2 Ch. 503.

[39] S.L.A. 1925, s. 65.

If a house is usually occupied as a farmhouse, or if the site of a house and the pleasure-grounds and park and lands, if any, usually occupied therewith do not together exceed 25 acres, the house is not deemed a principal mansion house.[40] In other cases, it is a question of fact whether at any given moment a house is a principal mansion house. Where two separate establishments are comprised in the same settlement, there may be two principal mansion houses, or one may be subsidiary to the other, as where one is used as the main residence and the other as a shooting-box.[41] Again, a house may cease to be a principal mansion house, as where it is let as a school; and if the tenant for life then uses a smaller house on the estate as his home, that may become a principal mansion house.[42]

2. Power to cut and sell timber. This has already been dealt with.[43] It is only if the tenant for life is impeachable of waste that he requires the consent of the trustees or an order of the court and three-quarters of the proceeds are capital money; if he is unimpeachable, he needs no consent or order and may keep all the proceeds.

3. Power to compromise claims. Subject to the consent in writing of the trustees, the tenant for life has a wide power to compromise and settle disputes relating to the settled land or any part thereof.[44]

4. Power to sell settled chattels. With the leave of the court the tenant for life may sell any chattels settled to devolve with the land,[45] as furniture, pictures and the like sometimes are.

5. Power to effect any proper transaction. The court has a statutory jurisdiction to authorise the tenant for life to effect any transaction not otherwise authorised by the Act or the settlement if it is for the benefit of the land or the beneficiaries and is a transaction which an absolute owner could validly effect.[46] This power even permits the court to sanction alterations in the beneficial interests under the settlement.[47]

---

[40] S.L.A. 1925, s. 65.
[41] *Gilbey* v. *Rush* [1906] 1 Ch. 11 at 21.
[42] *Re Feversham S.E.* [1938] 2 All E.R. 210.
[43] *Ante*, pp. 50 *et seq.*
[44] S.L.A. 1925, s. 58.
[45] S.L.A. 1925, s. 67; and see M. & W. 350–352.
[46] S.L.A. 1925, s. 64; Settled Land and Trustee Acts (Court's General Powers) Act 1943, s. 2.
[47] *Re Simmons* [1956] Ch. 125.

1. Power to effect improvements.[48]

(a) *Making the improvements.* A tenant for life may of course effect improvements to the land at his own expense, but if he wishes the cost to be borne either temporarily or permanently by capital money, or to be raised by a mortgage or charge of the settled land, he must comply with the Act. Under the Act of 1882, before the improvements were effected, the tenant for life had to submit to the trustees or the court a scheme for their execution.[49]

This is no longer necessary. The tenant for life must first ascertain that the proposed improvements are within the list of those authorised by the Act. He must then obtain the appointment of a surveyor or engineer, for capital money cannot be applied in paying for improvements unless—

(1) if the money is in the hands of the trustees,

    (a) a certificate is furnished by a competent engineer or able practical surveyor employed independently of the tenant for life, certifying—

        (i) that the work or some specific part thereof has been properly executed; and

        (ii) the amount properly payable in respect thereof; or

    (b) an order of the court directs or authorises payment:

(2) if the money is in court,

    (a) a report or certificate of the Minister of Agriculture, Fisheries and Food is given; or

    (b) a report of a competent engineer or able practical surveyor approved by the court is given; or

    (c) such other evidence as the court thinks fit is given.

(b) *Repayment.* When the improvements are paid for out of capital, the question arises whether or not the tenant for life must repay the money. This depends on the nature of the improvements. A long list is set out in the Third Schedule to the Act, which is divided into three parts:

    (i) If the improvement falls within Part I (*e.g.,* drainage or erection of bridges) or is authorised by the settlement, repayment cannot be ordered. In the case of agricultural

---

[48] S.L.A. 1925, ss. 83–87; and see M. & W. 353–358.
[49] S.L.A. 1882, s. 26.

land, ordinary repairs reasonably required for proper farming are somewhat surprisingly included under this head if effected after April, 1948.[50]

(ii) If the improvement falls within Part II (*e.g.*, the restoration or reconstruction of buildings damaged or destroyed by dry rot), the trustees or the court have a discretion to order repayment by instalments.

(iii) If the improvement falls within Part III (*e.g.*, the installation of artificial light in a building), the trustees or the court must order repayment by instalments.

The number of the instalments is within the discretion of the court or the trustees, except that the trustees may not order more than 50 half-yearly instalments.

2. Power to select investments for capital money. Capital money must be applied in one or more of the 21 methods specified in the Act.[51] These include investment in trustee securities, paying for improvements, and the purchase of land held in fee simple or on a lease with 60 or more years unexpired.[52] The tenant for life may select which of these methods of application shall be employed, in default of which the trustees make the choice.

D. Position of the Tenant for Life

1. The tenant for life is trustee both of the land and of his powers. This has been considered above.[53] One further point which must be mentioned concerns the right of the tenant for life to acquire any or all of the settled land for himself. It is a settled rule of equity that no trustee may acquire the trust property for himself either directly or indirectly, no matter how fair the transaction may be, for otherwise the trustee might be in a position where his interest conflicts with his duty.[54] To avoid this difficulty, the Settled Land Act 1925 [55] authorises the trustees of the settlement to exercise all the powers of a tenant for life in carrying out any transaction whereby the tenant for life acquires any interest in the settled land.

---

[50] See the cases cited in *Re Lord Brougham and Vaux's S.E.* [1954] Ch. 24; H. W. R. Wade [1954] Camb.L.J. 63.

[51] S.L.A. 1925, s. 73.

[52] See *Re Wellsted's W.T.* [1949] Ch. 296.

[53] *Ante*, pp. 147, 153.

[54] *Fox* v. *Mackreth* (1791) 2 Cox Eq. 320.

[55] s. 68.

2. No powers can be given to anyone except the tenant for life.
Any power, other than a power of revocation or appointment, which
the settlement purports to give to anyone except the tenant for life,
is exercisable not by that person but by the tenant for life as if it
were an additional power conferred by the settlement.[56] Thus if
land is devised " to X and Y in fee simple with power to sell, on
trust for A for life and then for B absolutely " the power of sale
purported to be given to X and Y is divested from them and given
to A; this is the case even despite the statutory power of sale which
A already has. But the abortive attempt to give a power of sale to
X and Y may not be wholly ineffective, for it may make them
Settled Land Act trustees.[57]

3. The statutory powers cannot be ousted, curtailed or hampered.
The settlor may confer additional powers on the tenant for life and
such powers are exercisable in the same way is if they were conferred by the Act.[58] Further, nothing in the Act in any way restricts
powers which the settlement gives to the tenant for life or purports
to give to the trustees to be exercised with the approval of the tenant
for life; the powers given by the Act and the settlement are
cumulative. But in other respects, so far as the settlement and the
Act conflict in relation to powers exercisable under the Act, the Act
prevails.[59] Thus if the settlement provides that no sale shall be
made without the consent of some specified person, this provision
is inconsistent with the unfettered power of sale given by the Act and
the latter prevails.[60]

In particular, it is enacted that any provision in any document
is void to the extent to which it purports or tends to prevent or
discourage the tenant for life from exercising his statutory powers
or from requiring the land to be vested in him.[61] This applies even
when the attempt to restrain the exercise of the powers is made by
way of determinable limitation; a settlement on " Y for life until
he attempts to alienate the land " gives Y a life interest which
continues despite any alienation by him. Notwithstanding anything
in a settlement, the exercise of a statutory power can never cause
a forfeiture.

[56] S.L.A. 1925, s. 108.
[57] *Ante*, p. 166.
[58] S.L.A. 1925, s. 109.
[59] *Ibid.* s. 108.
[60] *Re Jefferys (No. 2)* [1939] Ch. 205.
[61] S.L.A. 1925, s. 106; see *Re Aberconway's S.T.* [1953] Ch. 647.

The operation of these provisions is most frequently invoked by conditions of residence, *e.g.,* a proviso in the settlement that the tenant for life shall forfeit his interest on ceasing to reside on the settled land. In such cases, if the tenant for life ceases to reside for some reason other than the exercise of his statutory powers (as where he prefers to live elsewhere) the proviso for forfeiture is operative and he loses his interest.[62] But if the reason for his ceasing to reside is that he has exercised his statutory powers, as by leasing or selling the land, there is no forfeiture and he continues to be entitled as tenant for life, receiving the rent from the lease or the income from the purchase-money.[63]

4. The tenant for life cannot assign, release or contract not to exercise his powers.[64]

(a) *Exercise of powers.* Once a person has become a tenant for life, he is incapable of divesting himself of his powers, even if he parts with his entire beneficial interest, as he is entitled to do; it is he, and not the assignee of his beneficial interest, who alone can exercise the statutory powers.[65] However, in three cases the statutory powers may become exercisable by someone other than the tenant for life.

(1) EXTINGUISHMENT OF INTEREST. Where the interest of the tenant for life has been assured, with intent to extinguish it, to the person next entitled under the settlement, the statutory powers cease to be exercisable by the tenant for life and become exercisable as if he were dead.[66] Thus if land is settled on A for life, remainder to B for life, remainder to C in fee simple, the effect of A surrendering his life interest to B is to make the statutory powers exercisable by B instead of A, and A must forthwith convey the legal estate to B by a vesting deed. If B then surrenders his life interest to C, he must convey the legal estate to C, but by an ordinary conveyance, for the land ceases to be settled land.[67]

(2) ORDER OF COURT. If the tenant for life—

    (i) has ceased to have a substantial interest in the land, whether by bankruptcy, assignment or otherwise, and

---

[62] *Re Trenchard* [1902] 1 Ch. 378.

[63] *Re Orlebar* [1936] Ch. 147.

[64] S.L.A. 1925, s. 104.

[65] *Re Earl of Carnarvon's Chesterfield S.E.* [1927] 1 Ch. 138 at 145, 146.

[66] S.L.A. 1925, s. 105.

[67] See *post*, p. 183.

(ii) either consents to an order being made or else has unreasonably refused to exercise his statutory powers,

any person interested in the land may apply to the court for an
order authorising the trustees to exercise any or all of the statutory
powers in the name and on behalf of the tenant for life.[68] Such an
order prevents the tenant for life from exercising any of the powers
affected by the order, but until it has been registered[69] the order
does not affect those dealing with the tenant for life. Such an order
vests neither the legal estate nor the statutory powers in the trustees,
who do not become the statutory owner; the order merely authorises
the trustees to exercise the powers on behalf of the tenant for life
and in his name.

(3) MENTAL PATIENT. Where the tenant for life is a mental
patient, his receiver may, in his name and on his behalf under an
order of the Court of Protection, exercise his statutory powers.[70]

(b) *Position of assignees.* The position of an assignee of the
beneficial interest of a tenant for life depends upon whether the
assignment was made before 1926 or after 1925. The reason for
this difference is that although it was desirable to relax the control
formerly exercised by an assignee over the tenant for life, it would
not have been just to have altered the law to the detriment of
assignees who had parted with their money before 1926 on the
strength of the law as it then was.

(1) WHERE THE ASSIGNMENT WAS MADE BEFORE 1926. If the
assignment was made for money or money's worth, the tenant for
life can exercise his powers to the prejudice of the assignee only if
the assignee consents.[71] However, a purchaser is not concerned to
see that the consent has been obtained, and no consent is required—

(i) for the grant of leases authorised by the Act at the best rent
without a fine, unless the assignee is actually in possession
of the land, or

(ii) for the investment of capital money in trustee securities.

(2) WHERE THE ASSIGNMENT WAS MADE AFTER 1925. Even if the
assignment was made for money or money's worth, the consent of

---

[68] S.L.A. 1925, s. 24.
[69] As " an order affecting land ": *post*, p. 542.
[70] Mental Health Act 1959, s. 103 (1). For mental patients, see *post*, p. 522.
[71] S.L.A. 1925, s. 104.

the assignee is not required for the exercise of the statutory powers.[72] But for the application of capital money affected by the assignment for any purpose other than for investment in trustee securities, the consent of the assignee is necessary if the assignment so provides or takes effect by operation of the law of bankruptcy, and the trustees have notice of this. Further, unless the assignment otherwise provides, notice of any intended transaction must be given to the assignee.

In both cases, if the land is sold the rights of the assignee are transferred to the capital money which represents the land; and provision is made for obtaining consents in any cases of difficulty.

5. Death of tenant for life. When a tenant for life dies, the question what happens to the settled land at once arises. The beneficial interest of the tenant for life may cease (as where he held a life interest) or it may pass to the person next entitled to it, either directly (as in the case of an entail) or through his personal representatives (as in the case of a determinable fee simple).[73] The legal estate, on the other hand, is bound to devolve on someone, and the method of devolution depends upon whether the land continues to be settled land or whether the settlement comes to an end with the death of the tenant for life. For example, if land is settled on A for life, remainder to B for life, remainder to C in fee simple, the land remains settled land if B is alive when A dies. If B is dead or if he subsequently dies, the land thereupon ceases to be settled land unless rights such as voluntary rentcharges still exist under the settlement, or before B's death C had settled his fee simple.[74] If on B's death the land had forthwith become subject to a trust for sale, it would similarly have ceased to be settled land.[75]

(a) *If the land remains settled land,* the proper course to be adopted is for the special personal representatives (who will be the trustees of the settlement[76]) to take a grant of probate or letters of administration of the estate of the deceased tenant for life, limited to the settled land. They hold the land on trust to convey it to the next tenant for life on being required to do so, the conveyance being made by a vesting deed or a vesting assent.[77]

---

[72] *Ibid.*
[73] See *post*, Chap. 8 (p. 263), for the devolution of beneficial interests on death.
[74] *Re Norton* [1929] 1 Ch. 84; *In b. Taylor* [1929] P. 260.
[75] *Re Bridgett and Hayes' Contract* [1928] Ch. 163.
[76] A.E.A. 1925, s. 22.
[77] S.L.A. 1925, ss. 7, 8.

(b) *If the land ceases to be settled land,* the above provisions do not apply.[78] The legal estate will vest in the general personal representatives, and the person entitled, whether as beneficial owner, trustee for sale or otherwise,[79] is entitled to call upon them to convey the land to him by an ordinary conveyance or simple assent, *i.e.,* one which does not contain the particulars required in a vesting deed or vesting assent.[80]

E. Determination of Settlements

1. Duration of settlements. Land once settled remains settled so long as—

    (i) any limitation, charge or power of charging under the settlement still exists or is capable of being exercised, or

    (ii) the person beneficially entitled in possession is an infant,

unless in either case the land is held on trust for sale.[81] Once land is either held on trust for sale or else vested in a person of full age free from all actual or possible rights under the settlement, the settlement is at an end.

2. Deed of discharge. When a settlement comes to an end, it is necessary that there should be some document on the title to the legal estate which will show that the land has ceased to be settled land; for a purchaser is not concerned with the trusts of the settlement. This need is supplied by a " Deed of Discharge," [82] which is a deed executed by the trustees, declaring that they are discharged from the trusts as regards the land concerned; in cases of difficulty, the court may instead make an order discharging the trustees. Unless the deed of discharge otherwise provides, a purchaser is entitled to assume that the land is no longer settled land and is not subject to a trust for sale. The need for a deed of discharge is emphasised by the provision that once land is the subject of a vesting instrument, the tenant for life cannot dispose of anything but his beneficial interest except in accordance with his Settled Land Act or other statutory powers.[83] Even if he is an absolute owner at law and in equity, until a deed of discharge is executed he cannot dispose of the legal estate in a way not authorised by statute.

[78] *Re Bridgett and Hayes' Contract, supra.*
[79] See *Re Thomas* [1939] Ch. 513.
[80] S.L.A. 1925, ss. 7, 8 ; but see *In b. Mortifee* [1948] P. 274.
[81] S.L.A. 1925, s. 3 ; L.P.(Am.)A. 1926, Sched.
[82] S.L.A. 1925, s. 17.
[83] S.L.A. 1925, s. 18.

3. No deed of discharge. There are two cases where no deed of discharge is required.

(a) *No vesting instrument executed.* If the settlement comes to an end before a vesting instrument has been executed,[84] no deed of discharge is required.[85]

(b) *Ordinary conveyance or assent on the title.* If a vesting instrument has been executed, but there is a subsequent conveyance or assent on the title which does not contain a statement of the names of the Settled Land Act trustees, a bona fide purchaser for value of a legal estate is both entitled and bound to assume that every statement in the assent or conveyance is correct and that the person in whom the land was thereby vested holds it free from all rights under the settlement.[86] One consequence of this provision is that whenever a settlement comes to an end on the death of a tenant for life, the land can be disposed of without a deed of discharge being executed. Thus if land is settled on X for life, remainder to Y in fee simple, on X's death the settlement is at an end. X's general personal representatives will therefore execute a simple assent vesting the land in Y, and as this assent will contain no mention of Settled Land Act trustees, a purchaser cannot object to Y's title merely because no deed of discharge has been executed.

F. Functions of Settled Land Act Trustees

It may perhaps be useful to collect together the principal functions of Settled Land Act trustees. They are—

   (i) to receive and hold capital money[87];

  (ii) to receive notice from the tenant for life of his intention to effect certain transactions[88];

 (iii) to give consent to certain transactions[89];

 (iv) to act as special personal representatives on the death of a tenant for life[90];

  (v) to act as statutory owner if the tenant for life is an infant or there is no tenant for life[91];

---

[84] As in *Re Alefounder's W.T* [1927] 1 Ch. 360; *ante*, p. 158.
[85] See S.L.A. 1925, s. 17.
[86] S.L.A. 1925, s. 110.
[87] *Ante*, p. 149, and *post*, p. 194.
[88] *Ante*, p. 169.
[89] *Ante*, p. 174.
[90] *Ante*, p. 181.
[91] *Ante*, p. 153.

(vi) to exercise the powers of the tenant for life if he wishes to acquire the settled land for his own benefit [92];

(vii) to exercise the powers of the tenant for life where he has no substantial beneficial interest and either consents to such exercise or unreasonably refuses to exercise his powers [93]; and

(viii) to exercise a general supervision over the well-being of the settled land. [94]

Part 4

TRUSTS FOR SALE AFTER 1925

1. What is a trust for sale. It has been seen [95] that after 1925 land cannot be settled land if it is subject to an " immediate binding trust for sale." Whenever land is limited in trust for persons by way of succession or for some other reason falls within the definition of settled land, it will be governed by the Settled Land Act 1925 unless it can be shown that it is subject to a trust for sale of this nature. The meaning of the phrase is thus of great importance and must be examined carefully.

(a) *There must be a* **trust** *for sale.* As before 1926, there must be a true trust to sell and not a mere power of sale. [96] Thus a conveyance to trustees on trust for persons in succession, giving the trustees a power of sale, makes the land settled land; the conveyance operates as an imperfect settlement and the trustees cannot sell. [97] Some of the difficulties which arose from trusts " to retain or sell the land " [98] are solved by the provision that in a disposition or settlement coming into operation after 1925, such a trust shall be construed as a trust for sale with power to postpone sale [99]; it will be noticed that this solution is only partial, since it does not alter the position if the disposition or settlement took effect before 1926. [1]

---

[92] *Ante,* p. 177.
[93] *Ante,* pp. 179, 180.
[94] See *ante,* p. 149; *Re Boston's W.T.* [1956] Ch. 395 at 405.
[95] *Ante,* p. 152.
[96] *Ante,* p. 151.
[97] *Ante,* pp. 158, 178.
[98] *Ante,* p. 151.
[99] L.P.A. 1925, s. 25.
[1] *Re White's Settlement* [1930] 1 Ch. 179.

(b) *The trust for sale must be " immediate."* Here again, the position is substantially the same as before 1926 [2]; a trust to sell at some future date, *e.g.,* when X attains the age of 25, does not prevent land from being settled land.[3] But if there is a trust for sale which is immediately operative, this takes the land out of the Settled Land Act 1925, even if the trustees have power to postpone the sale and even if a sale cannot be made without the request or consent of some person.[4]

(c) *The trust for sale must be " binding."* The interpretation of the word " binding " has given rise to considerable difficulty. Three views have been put forward.

(i) That it means a trust for sale capable of binding, in the sense of overreaching, as many interests as possible. As will be seen shortly,[5] a special type of trust for sale (usually known as an *" ad hoc* trust for sale ")* comes into existence if the trustees consist of either two or more trustees appointed or approved by the court, or a trust corporation, the advantage of such a trust for sale being that a greater number of equitable interests can be overreached on a sale of the land than is possible under an ordinary trust for sale. In *Re Leigh's Settled Estates (No.* 1),[6] Tomlin J. held that where there was an equitable interest which could be overreached only under these wider overreaching powers, an ordinary trust for sale was not " binding "; and in subsequent cases he adhered to this view. If this is correct, it has the disadvantage that a great number of trusts for sale in the ordinary sense of the word are not trusts for sale within the meaning of the 1925 legislation. The decision met with much criticism suggesting either that it was wrong or else that it must be strictly confined to the enactment on which it was decided [7] and not be extended to the other references to trusts for sale in the 1925 legislation.

(ii) That the word " binding " was inserted to emphasise that a revocable trust for sale is excluded or else that the word is mere surplusage. This was the view taken by Romer J. in *Re Parker's Settled Estates,*[8] and his dissent from the decision of Tomlin J. was greeted with relief by those who felt that this view was preferable

---

[2] *Ante*, p. 151.
[3] *Re Hanson* [1928] Ch. 96.
[4] L.P.A. 1925, s. 205 (1) (xxix).
[5] *Post*, pp. 196 *et seq.*
[6] [1926] Ch. 852.
[7] S.L.A. 1925, s. 20 (1) (viii).
[8] [1928] Ch. 247 at 261.

to one which excluded from the status of trust for sale innumerable trusts which were indubitably trusts for sale as that phrase has always been understood by lawyers. But as Tomlin J. said in *Re Leigh*,[9] " There must be, it seems to me, some significance in the word ' binding ' here. It is incredible that the word should have no meaning." Consequently, the best view seems to be the third, which is—

(iii) That a " binding " trust for sale is one which is capable of binding the whole legal estate which has been settled and not merely part of it.[10] If the whole legal estate is vested in the trustees for sale as such, the trust for sale is " binding," even if equitable interests such as charges under a former settlement are still outstanding. But if part of the legal estate is outstanding, such as a legal term of years to secure portions,[11] or if the settlor had not vested any legal estate in the trustees, *e.g.*, because he had none, or because the conveyance purported only to convey an equitable interest,[12] there is no binding trust for sale. For example, if land is settled on A for life, subject to an equitable rentcharge, with remainder to B in fee simple, and B conveys his fee simple on trust for sale for the benefit of various persons, the land does not become subject to a binding trust for sale on A's death : B could not give the trustees anything more than he had, namely, an equitable fee simple, and they cannot call for a conveyance to themselves of the legal estate, for they could do this only if the land was free from all rights under the settlement [13] and this is not the case as long as the rentcharge exists. If, on the other hand, A had died and the legal estate had been duly vested in B before he had created the trust for sale, the conveyance on trust for sale would have effectively vested the whole legal estate in the trustees for sale and the land would have become subject to a " binding trust for sale " even though the equitable rentcharge was still outstanding.

It seems safe to say that the first alternative is now generally recognised as being wrong, and that although the second view is innocuous, the third is almost certainly correct. It is clearly desirable that there should be an end to " what is in fact perfectly useless litigation. . . . In all these cases there is clearly a power of

---

[9] [1926] Ch. 852 at 859.
[10] *Re Parker's S.E.* [1928] Ch. 247 at 262 ; *Re Norton* [1929] 1 Ch. 84 at 88.
[11] See *post*, pp. 205, 206.
[12] *Re Beaumont S.E.* [1937] 2 All E.R. 353 ; *Re Sharpe's Deed of Release* [1939] Ch. 51.
[13] S.L.A. 1925, s. 7.

sale. The only question is, who is to exercise it? This may be of importance to the solicitors of the parties. To the parties themselves it is [usually] a matter of entire indifference." [14]

2. How a trust for sale comes into existence. A trust for sale may arise—

(a) expressly, by land being deliberately limited on trust for sale, or

(b) by operation of statute.

(a) *Express trusts for sale.* With a view to keeping the trusts off the title, the general practice for many years has been to employ two documents, namely, a conveyance on trust for sale and a trust instrument; it was this practice which suggested the vesting deed and trust instrument of the Settled Land Act 1925. Although today two documents are almost invariably employed to create a trust for sale *inter vivos*, there is nothing in the 1925 legislation to make this essential. In the case of testamentary trusts for sale, the usual position before 1926 was that the will was the sole document concerned. After 1925, a written assent is required to vest the legal estate in the trustees for sale, so that now there will usually be two documents in such cases. But even if a trust for sale is created by a single document, it is now provided that a purchaser of the legal estate from the trustees for sale is not concerned with the trusts affecting the rents and profits of the land until sale and the proceeds of sale thereafter, whether or not the trusts are declared by the same instrument as that by which the trust for sale is created.[15]

Where a trust for sale was created before 1926, the legal estate remains vested in the trustees for sale if it was already vested in them; if not, it automatically vested in them at the beginning of 1926.[16]

(b) *Statutory trusts for sale.* A trust for sale is imposed by statute in a number of cases. For example—

(i) if two or more persons are entitled to land as joint tenants or tenants in common, a trust for sale is normally imposed by the Law of Property Act 1925 [17];

(ii) the Administration of Estates Act 1925 imposes a trust for sale on the property of a person dying intestate [18]; and

[14] J.M.L. (1929) 67 L.J.News. 24.
[15] L.P.A. 1925, s. 27.
[16] L.P.A. 1925, 1st Sched., Pt. II, paras. 3, 6.
[17] *Post*, p. 216.
[18] *Post*, p. 302.

(iii) if trustees lend money on mortgage and the property becomes vested in them free from the right of repayment (*e.g.*, by foreclosure), they hold it upon trust for sale.[19] This preserves the character of the trust property: the money was pure personalty, and under the doctrine of conversion, the rights of the beneficiaries under a trust for sale are treated as interests in pure personalty, even if the subject-matter of the trust is land.

3. Position of trustees for sale.

(a) *Power of postponement.*   Unless a contrary intention appears, a power to postpone sale is implied after 1925 in every trust for sale of land, even if it was created before 1926.[20]   In the absence of an express provision to the contrary, the trustees are not liable in any way if they postpone sale indefinitely in the exercise of their discretion, nor is a purchaser of the legal estate concerned with directions respecting the postponement of sale.[21]   If the trustees cannot agree whether or not to postpone sale, the land must be sold, for the majority cannot override the minority; if a power is given to trustees, all must concur before it can be exercised, and thus the power of postponement is exercisable only if all trustees concur.[22]   Nevertheless, many trusts for sale are created with the intention that the land shall be retained for a long time before being sold, an intention which is effectuated by the trustees duly concurring in exercising their power to postpone the sale.   As a means of making a settlement, the trust for sale has become a recognised alternative to settled land.[23]

(b) *Continuance of trust.*   Once a trust for sale has been created, the trust is, for the protection of any purchaser thereunder, deemed to be subsisting until the land has been conveyed either to the beneficiaries themselves or to some other person under their direction.[24] This meets the difficulty that if all the possible beneficiaries were of full age and subject to no disability, they could put an end to the trust for sale by electing to have the land retained as land.   For this reason, purchasers who knew that all the possible beneficiaries were *sui juris* sometimes raised objections to a sale without the concurrence of the

---

[19] L.P.A. 1925, s. 31.

[20] L.P.A. 1925 s. 25.

[21] *Ibid.*

[22] *Re Mayo* [1943] Ch. 302.

[23] For a comparison of the two methods, see *post*, pp. 199 *et seq.* For the application of income, see M. & W. 375.

[24] L.P.A. 1925, s. 23.

beneficiaries; formerly this difficulty was overcome by requiring one of the beneficiaries to concur in the conveyance, thus showing that there had not been a unanimous election to terminate the trust for sale.[25]

(c) *Powers of trustees.* The powers of trustees for sale have been considerably extended by the Law of Property Act 1925. Before 1926, they had no powers of leasing, mortgaging or otherwise dealing with the land except by way of sale [26]; after 1925 they have all the powers both of a tenant for life of settled land and of Settled Land Act trustees.[27] Thus trustees for sale can exercise even those powers which are exercisable by a tenant for life only with the consent of the trustees of the settlement. Further, where settled land becomes vested in the Settled Land Act trustees in the form of trust for sale known as the " statutory trusts," [28] the trustees have all the additional powers (if any) conferred by the settlement on the tenant for life, statutory owner or trustees of the settlement.[29]

(d) *Curtailment of powers.* The extent to which the powers of trustees for sale can be curtailed by the settlement is uncertain. It is clear that the Law of Property Act 1925 contemplates the exercise of their power of sale or any other of their powers being made subject to the requirement that the consent of specified persons should be first obtained; for if the consent of more than two persons is required, the Act provides that a bona fide purchaser for value is protected if the consent of any two of such persons is obtained, and further, that he need not concern himself with the consents of any persons under disability.[30] But this provision applies only to a purchaser: the trustees will be guilty of a breach of trust if they do not obtain the full number of consents stipulated. Any consent required from an infant, however, may be given by his parent or guardian, and that of a mental patient by his receiver; and the court has power to dispense with consents which cannot be obtained.[31] But although it is clear that consents may be made requisite to the trustees exercising their powers, it is by no means clear whether the powers can be taken away or curtailed in any other way. It is

[25] See *Re Jenkins and H. E. Randall & Co.'s Contract* [1903] 2 Ch. 362.
[26] *Ante*, p. 151.
[27] L.P.A. 1925, s. 28; see *Re Wellsted's W.T.* [1949] Ch. 296.
[28] See *post*, p. 223.
[29] L.P.A. 1925, s. 28; L.P.(Am.)A. 1926, Sched.
[30] L.P.A. 1925, s. 26.
[31] L.P.A. 1925, ss. 26, 30; Mental Health Act 1959, ss. 103 (1), 149 (1).

arguable that as the trustees have all the powers of a tenant for life and as the powers of a tenant for life cannot be restricted in any way,[32] so the powers of trustees for sale cannot be hampered except so far as is provided by statute: and perhaps this argument [33] will ultimately be accepted by the courts.

4. Rights of the beneficiaries. After 1925, the person for the time being entitled to the income from a trust for sale has none of the powers of a tenant for life of settled land, for all the powers are vested in the trustees for sale. However, this rule is subject to three qualifications.

(a) *Delegation.* The trustees may revocably and in writing delegate certain powers to the person of full age (not being merely an annuitant) who for the time being is beneficially entitled in possession to the net rents and profits of the land for his life or any less period.[34] The powers which may be so delegated are the powers of, and incidental to, leasing, accepting surrenders of leases and management. The powers thus delegated must be exercised in the names and on behalf of the trustees; but if they are misused, the liability rests not on the trustees but on the person exercising the powers, who is deemed to be in the position of a trustee. If the trustees refuse to delegate these powers, an application to the court may be made to compel them to do so.[35]

(b) *Order of court.* Where at the end of 1925 an order under section 7 of the Settled Land Act 1884 was in force, authorising the person entitled to the income to exercise any of the powers under the Settled Land Act 1882,[36] such powers are exercisable by that person in the same way as if they had been delegated to him by the trustees under the foregoing provisions,[37] even if they are powers which in fact could not be thus delegated, *e.g.*, a power of sale.[38]

(c) *Consultation.* In some cases the trustees are under an obligation, so far as is practicable, to consult the persons of full age for the time being beneficially interested in possession in the rents and profits of the land until sale, and must, so far as is consistent with

---

[32] *Ante*, p. 178.
[33] Urged but not decided in *Re Davies' W.T.* [1932] 1 Ch. 530; see at pp. 532, 533.
[34] L.P.A. 1925, s. 29.
[35] L.P.A. 1925, s. 30.
[36] See *ante*, p. 151, for this provision.
[37] L.P.A. 1925, s. 29.
[38] *Re Leigh's S.E. (No. 1)* [1926] Ch. 852 at 862.

the general interests of the trust, give effect to their wishes, or to the wishes of the majority in value. However, there are many express trusts for sale to which this provision does not apply, for it is confined to trusts for sale which either are created by statute or show an intention that this provision is to apply. Further, the trustees are not bound to follow the wishes of the beneficiaries, nor is a purchaser concerned to see that the trustees have complied with this requirement.[39]

5. The doctrine of conversion. Equity looks upon that as done which ought to be done, and it has long been settled that as soon as land is held upon trust for sale, the rights of the beneficiaries must be regarded as interests in the money into which the trustees are bound sooner or later to convert the land.[40] This doctrine has its roots in the simple principle that when property has been given to a trustee, it must not lie in his power to alter the devolution of beneficial interests by committing a breach of duty; if land is given to trustees on trust for sale, it must not be possible for them by delaying sale to prevent the interests of the beneficiaries from being treated as the settlor intended them to be treated, *i.e.*, as interests in personalty. Thus even before the land is sold the beneficiaries are regarded as owning personal property. For example, a testator made a will before 1926 leaving all his realty to R and all his personalty to P. He owned a share in freehold land, and the effect of the 1925 legislation was to impose a trust for sale on this land.[41] The doctrine of conversion consequently applied, so that on his death after 1925 his interest in the property passed under his will to P and not to R.[42]

The imposition of trusts for sale by the 1925 legislation had further consequences which had scarcely been foreseen. If at the end of 1925 two or more persons were entitled to land as tenants in common in tail, the land became subject to a trust for sale at the beginning of 1926. The effect of this was to convert the entails into absolute interests, for the rights of the beneficiaries became personalty and, although after 1925 personalty can be entailed,[43] there was no provision by which this could be done by an instrument executed

---

[39] L.P.A. 1925, s. 26; L.P.(Am.)A. 1926, Sched.
[40] *Fletcher* v. *Ashburner* (1779) 1 Bro.C.C. 497.
[41] *Post*, p. 216.
[42] *Re Kempthorne* [1930] 1 Ch. 268.
[43] *Ante*, p. 42.

before 1926.[44]   The Law of Property (Entailed Interests) Act 1932 [45] retrospectively amended the law, providing that in such cases an entail should be deemed to exist in the proceeds of sale.

Part 5

OVERREACHING EFFECT OF DISPOSITIONS

Sect. 1.   Under the Settled Land Act 1925

As already explained,[46] an interest in land is said to be overreached if it is transferred from land to the purchase money on a sale or other disposition being made.   The Settled Land Act 1925, after first authorising a tenant for life to effect a sale or other transaction by deed, goes on to state the overreaching effect of such a deed.

1. Rights under the settlement.[47]   The deed is effectual to pass the land or other interest concerned " discharged from all the limitations, powers, and provisions of the settlement, and from all estates, interests, and charges subsisting or to arise thereunder "; it is immaterial whether or not a purchaser has notice of these rights. In short, the purchaser takes the land free from all the rights under the settlement.   The Act then makes certain qualifications to this rule : the land is to pass to the purchaser discharged from the above rights, " but subject to and with the exception of " [48]—

   (a) All legal estates and charges by way of legal mortgage having priority to the settlement.

In nearly every case this provision is mere surplusage, for no power is given to overreach rights prior to the settlement and so the qualification is unnecessary.   If X makes a legal mortgage of land and later settles the land, the tenant for life has no power to overreach the mortgage, which continues to bind the land.

   (b) All legal estates and charges by way of legal mortgage which have been conveyed or created for securing money actually raised at the date of the deed.

This is a true exception, for it excludes something which otherwise would have been included in the overreaching provision.   Thus if a

---

[44] *Re Price* [1928] Ch. 579.
[45] s. 1.
[46] *Ante*, p. 81.
[47] S.L.A. 1925, s. 72.
[48] See *Re Dickin and Kelsall's Contract* [1908] 1 Ch. 213 at 221.

tenant for life creates a legal mortgage to pay for improvements or raise portions, and the mortgagee has actually paid the money, the mortgage cannot be overreached even though it is an interest arising under the settlement. " Mortgagees who have actually lent their money on the security of the land are regarded as strangers to the settlement, and are not to have the security which they bargained for on the land itself transferred to the purchase-money at the will of the tenant for life." [49] If the money has not in fact been paid (*e.g.*, where a legal term of years has been created to secure portions which have not been raised [50]) the right is overreached.[51]

    (c) All leases and grants of other rights (except annuities, limited owner's charges and general equitable charges [52]) which at the date of the deed are—

        (i) binding on the successors in title of the tenant for life, and

        (ii) duly registered if capable of registration.

This is also a true exception, but unlike the previous provisions it is not confined to legal rights. It thus apparently applies to a restrictive covenant creating a mere equitable burden on the land.

    2. Rights prior to the settlement. Having dealt with the exceptions to the rule that all rights arising under the settlement can be overreached, the Act proceeds to the converse case, namely, the exceptions to the rule that rights prior to the settlement cannot be overreached. The Act [53] provides that—

    (1) an annuity,

    (2) a limited owner's charge, and

    (3) a general equitable charge

shall be overreached on a disposition under the Act even if they have been duly protected by registration; these rights are treated as if they had been created by the settlement even if in fact they arose before it came into existence. They are all rights which can be represented in terms of money and so will not suffer from being transferred to the purchase-money.

    It cannot be said that the overreaching provisions, which in the main reproduce corresponding provisions in the Settled Land Act

[49] *Re Mundy and Roper's Contract* [1899] 1 Ch. 275 at 289, *per* Chitty L.J.
[50] See *post*, pp. 205, 206.
[51] See *Re Du Cane and Nettlefold's Contract* [1898] 2 Ch. 96 at 108.
[52] For these rights, see *ante*, p. 80, and *post*, pp. 542, 544.
[53] S.L.A. 1925, s. 72.

1882, are very happily drawn. For those who wish to have a bird's
eye view of their effect (necessarily at the expense of some accuracy)
the position may be represented as follows:

    (i) There is in general no power to overreach legal rights.

    (ii) Subject to the three exceptions set out above, there is no
power to overreach equitable rights already existing when the
settlement was made.

    (iii) There is power to overreach all the equitable rights of the
beneficiaries under the settlement, including derivative rights
e.g., the rights of a mortgagee of the beneficial interest of a
tenant for life.

3. Payment of capital money.   There is one important condition
which must be observed if a deed is to take effect under the Act and so
have an overreaching effect.   This is the rule that notwithstanding
anything to the contrary in the settlement,[54] any capital money
payable in respect of the transaction must be paid either—

    (i) to, or by the direction of, all the trustees of the settlement
who must be either two or more in number or a trust corporation (the definition of " trust corporation " includes certain
officials such as the Public Trustee and certain companies
with a large paid-up capital[55]), or

    (ii) into court.[56]

It lies with the tenant for life to decide which of the two methods of
payment shall be adopted, although if there are no trustees he cannot
direct payment into court.[57]   If a purchaser fails to pay his money in
accordance with these provisions and pays it, for example, to the
tenant for life, he will not get a good discharge and will be unable to
make a good title to a subsequent purchaser.[58]   Where no capital
money arises on a transaction (as where a lease is granted without
taking a fine) in favour of a bona fide purchaser for value of a legal
estate, it takes effect under the Act and thus has an overreaching effect
even though there are no trustees.[59]

4. Capital money as land.   The capital money and any investments representing it are for all purposes of disposition, transmission

---

[54] Contrast *ante*, p. 149.
[55] See *Snell*, p. 206.
[56] S.L.A. 1925, s. 18.
[57] S.L.A. 1925, s. 75 ; *Hatten* v. *Russell* (1888) 38 Ch.D. 334 at 345.
[58] *Re Norton and Las Casas' Contract* [1909] 2 Ch. 59.
[59] S.L.A. 1925, s. 110.

and devolution (but not otherwise, *e.g.*, for purposes of death duties [60]) treated as land, and are held for and go to the same persons, in the same manner and for the same estates, interests and trusts, as the land wherefrom they arise would have been held and have gone under the settlement.[61] Thus where settled freeholds were sold and X became solely entitled under the settlement, a will left by X which was effective only to dispose of personalty would not dispose of the capital money [62]; and if X had died before 1926, his heir and not his next-of-kin would have been entitled to it.[63] In short, the state in which the settled property happens to be at any given moment, whether it is land, investments or money, cannot affect the rights of the beneficiaries or those claiming under them.

Sect. 2. Under a Trust for Sale

Strictly speaking, a trust for sale has no overreaching effect, for by the equitable doctrine of conversion so long as the land remains unsold the rights of the beneficiaries are already deemed to be rights in the purchase-money into which it will ultimately be converted. Consequently it cannot be said that a sale or other transaction transfers the rights of the beneficiaries from the land to the purchase-money, for strictly they never were attached to the land. Nevertheless, it is convenient to use the term " overreaching " as including the process by which the beneficiaries have their rights in what is money in theory but land in fact transferred to what is money both in theory and in fact.

A disposition under a trust for sale is effective to overreach the equitable rights of the beneficiaries thereunder; there is no power to overreach legal estates, nor, apparently, to overreach rights already existing when the trust for sale was created. As already seen, a purchaser of a legal estate from the trustees for sale is not concerned with the trusts affecting the rents and profits of the land until sale and the proceeds of sale thereafter even if the trusts are declared by the instrument which created the trust for sale.[64] However, to have an overreaching effect, the proceeds of sale or other capital money, notwithstanding anything to the contrary in the trust for sale, must not be paid to or applied by the direction of fewer than two persons

---

[60] *Earl of Midleton* v. *Baron Cottesloe* [1949] A.C. 418.
[61] S.L.A. 1925, s. 75.
[62] *Re Cartwright* [1939] Ch. 90.
[63] *Re Cutcliffe's W.T.* [1940] Ch. 565.
[64] L.P.A. 1925, s. 27; *ante*, p. 187.

as trustees for sale except where the trustee is a trust corporation.[65] There is no provision for payment into court. Where no capital money arises, it is unnecessary to have more than one trustee.

Proceeds of sale or other capital money arising under a trust for sale may be applied in the same way as capital money arising from settled land.[66] This does not, however, effect a conversion into realty, and the rights of the beneficiaries remain rights in personalty.[67] Any land acquired under this provision must be conveyed to the trustees for sale on trust for sale.[68]

Sect. 3. Under *Ad Hoc* Settlements and Trusts for Sale

The original intention of the 1925 legislation was that a conveyance under a settlement or trust for sale should overreach not only the interests of the beneficiaries but also prior equities as well. This provision was attacked in Parliament, and ultimately a workable scheme was produced and duly embodied in the 1925 legislation. Clearly some equities cannot be overreached; thus a restrictive covenant (*e.g.*, against building) and an equitable easement (*e.g.*, an equitable right of way) cannot become corresponding rights in the purchase-money. The present scheme is that dispositions under ordinary settlements and trusts for sale have the overreaching effect considered above, and that those under certain special settlements and trusts for sale have a special wider overreaching effect. To obtain this wider effect the settlement or trust for sale must have " guaranteed " trustees, *i.e.*, either trustees appointed or approved by the court, or a trust corporation. The idea is that such trustees are likely to be particularly trustworthy and that this will console those whose rights are overreached but would not have been overreached under an ordinary settlement or trust for sale. That is the theory; in practice, little use is made of such settlements and trusts for sale, for the additional overreaching powers conferred are meagre. The details of such settlements and trusts for sale are as follows.

1. Creation.

(a) *Ad hoc settlements*. If a person of full age is beneficially entitled in possession to a legal estate subject to any equitable interests or powers, then for the purpose of overreaching these rights

---

[65] L.P.A. 1925, ss. 2, 27; L.P.(Am.)A. 1926, Sched.
[66] L.P.A. 1925, s. 28; *Re Wellsted's W.T.* [1949] Ch. 296; *ante*, pp. 176, 177.
[67] *Re Kempthorne* [1930] 1 Ch. 268.
[68] L.P.A. 1925, s. 28.

he may by deed declare that the legal estate is vested in him on trust to give effect to all equitable interests and powers affecting the legal estate.[69] Such a deed is treated as a vesting deed and must be executed either by two or more individuals approved or appointed by the court, or by a trust corporation, who must be stated to be Settled Land Act trustees. Thereupon the land is deemed to be settled land and the estate owner becomes a tenant for life; the instruments creating his estate and the equitable interests or powers are deemed to be the trust instrument, in default of which a trust instrument must be executed contemporaneously with the vesting deed. It will be noticed that these provisions are inappropriate to land which is already settled, for normally there will be no person *beneficially* entitled in possession to a *legal* estate : the provisions contemplate only settlements set up *ad hoc* (expressly for the purpose).

(b) *Ad hoc trusts for sale.* If a legal estate is subject to a trust for sale and the trustees thereof are either—

    (i) two or more individuals approved or appointed by the court, or their successors in office, or

    (ii) a trust corporation,

then the effect of a conveyance is to overreach equities having priority to the trust for sale, with the exceptions set out below.[70] It will be noticed that this provision is not confined to trusts for sale created *ad hoc*, but extends to any trusts for sale, whether already in existence or set up expressly for the purpose of overreaching equities : provided the conditions as to trustees are satisfied, the wider overreaching powers exist.[71] Nevertheless, " *ad hoc* trusts for sale " is a convenient name for such trusts even if they have not in fact been set up *ad hoc.*

2. Overreaching effect of dispositions. As regards the overreaching effect of a conveyance or other disposition, the provisions as to *ad hoc* settlements and *ad hoc* trusts for sale are in similar terms.[72] Equitable rights having priority to the settlement or trust for sale are overreached with the exception of—

    (a) equitable interests protected by a deposit of documents relating to the legal estate affected;

---

[69] S.L.A. 1925, s. 21.
[70] L.P.A. 1925, s. 2.
[71] *Re Leigh's S.E. (No. 2)* [1927] 2 Ch. 13.
[72] S.L.A. 1925, s. 21 ; L.P.A. 1925, s. 2.

    (b) restrictive covenants;

    (c) equitable easements;

    (d) estate contracts;

    (e) equitable interests protected by registration under the Land Charges Act 1925 other than—

        (i) annuities,

        (ii) limited owner's charges, and

        (iii) general equitable charges.

It will be observed that the last three rights can be overreached under an *ad hoc* settlement or an *ad hoc* trust for sale. Such rights can, indeed, be overreached under an ordinary settlement, so that no wider powers are given in this case; but probably they cannot be overreached under an ordinary trust for sale, so that in this respect an *ad hoc* trust for sale has marked advantages over an ordinary trust for sale. Apart from these three rights, however, the list of exceptions given above covers all the important equitable rights likely to be encountered in practice. The first exception is designed to cover temporary equitable mortgages and charges where the lender has secured himself by obtaining the title deeds. Heads (b), (c) and (d) could not, from their very nature, be overreached. Head (e) adds little to the previous provisions, for apart from the spouse's right to occupy a house owned by the other,[72a] the only rights it includes are included under (b), (c) and (d). These rights are, in general, capable of registration only if created after 1925,[73] so that, for example, a restrictive covenant is protected by head (b) if created in 1920 and by heads (b) and (e) if created in 1930.

    Although in general *ad hoc* settlements and trusts for sale may be said to be both complicated and ineffective, there are certain equitable rights which will be overreached by an *ad hoc*, but not by an ordinary, settlement or trust for sale. One example is a widow's right of dower not assigned by metes and bounds.[74] Again, a rentcharge for life created before 1926 by a marriage settlement is neither an annuity nor a general equitable charge,[75] and if the land is vested in trustees for sale subject only to the rentcharge, the approval of the trustees by the court will confer *ad hoc* powers and make it possible to overreach the rentcharge.

[72a] See *post*, p. 546.
[73] *Post*, pp. 545, 546.
[74] *Ante*, p. 163.
[75] See *ante*, p. 80, and *post*, pp. 542, 544.

Sect. 4. Summary of Overreaching Provisions

In broad outline, the position may be said to be as follows:

- (a) A conveyance under an ordinary trust for sale overreaches the rights of the beneficiaries thereunder.
- (b) A conveyance under an ordinary settlement overreaches—
  - (i) the rights of the beneficiaries thereunder, and
  - (ii) annuities, limited owner's charges and general equitable charges.
- (c) A conveyance under an *ad hoc* settlement or trust for sale overreaches—
  - (i) the rights of the beneficiaries thereunder;
  - (ii) annuities, limited owner's charges and general equitable charges; and
  - (iii) certain other equities, such as a widow's right of dower not assigned by metes and bounds.

Part 6

METHODS OF SETTLING LAND

Sect. 1. Comparison of Settled Land with Trusts for Sale

A person proposing to settle land today can do so either by making the land settled land or by creating a trust for sale. The changes made by the 1925 legislation have endowed trusts for sale with all the technical advantages of settled land; for example, entails can now be created under trusts for sale, and trustees for sale have all the powers of a tenant for life. A question which sometimes arises is which method to employ in any given case. The following are some of the points which should be considered.

1. Control of the land is in the hands of the trustees under a trust for sale, but in the hands of the tenant for life in the case of settled land. Thus if the land is a family estate on which the tenant for life will reside, the land should be made settled land, but if it consists of a row of suburban villas, a trust for sale should be created to free the beneficiaries from the burden of managing the property. Again, if the proposed tenant for life is a bad business man it may be better to create a trust for sale.

2. Restrictions on dealings. Although it is now impossible to create a settlement which will effectively prevent the land from being sold or otherwise dealt with, some measure of restraint can be imposed under a trust for sale, where the trustees may be obliged to obtain the consent of specified persons before dealing with the land. Settlements and trusts for sale have thus changed places since the middle of the last century. In those days, a settlement was a method of keeping a particular piece of land in the family, and a trust for sale was used where the nature of the land was immaterial; today the trust for sale can to some extent achieve what the settlement cannot.

3. Economy. The trust for sale is usually less complicated and expensive than settled land, and so is the more suitable alternative for small estates. The difficulty of discovering in whom the legal estate and statutory powers are vested occurs not infrequently in the case of settled land, but rarely in the case of trusts for sale. A testator who makes his own will leaving his house to his widow during widowhood, then to his daughter until she marries, and then to his children equally, is unwittingly invoking most of the provisions designed by the legislature for large family estates. The whole creaking structure of Settled Land Act trustees, special personal representatives, vesting assents, deeds of discharge and so on may be involved for a house or cottage worth a few hundred pounds. If instead of this the testator had devised his land to trustees on trust for sale, all these difficulties would have been avoided. The trouble is that the words " on trust for sale " or their equivalent are required to take land out of the Settled Land Act, and these words have not reached the consciousness of the average testator who makes his own will.

4. Preservation of a unit. A trust for sale is more convenient than a strict settlement where a settlor wishes to provide for his children equally. A strict settlement, on the other hand, is normally used " to make an eldest son," *i.e.*, to give the principal benefit to the eldest son and make provision for the younger children a subsidiary matter.[76] Before 1926, the doctrine of conversion and the impossibility of creating entails in personalty combined to make trusts for sale unsuitable for this purpose. As already seen,[77] this difficulty no

---

[76] See *post*, pp. 203 *et seq.*
[77] *Ante*, p. 42.

longer exists, although the doctrine of conversion must still be considered, *e.g.*, when drafting a will for a beneficiary under a trust for sale.

Sect. 2. Land Companies

A modern alternative to settled land and trusts for sale is the land company. A landowner who wants to settle his property conveys his land to a private company (which he forms for the purpose) in return for shares in the company; he then proceeds to settle or distribute the shares as he wishes. Similar arrangements can be made if the land is already settled. Freedom from the complexities of settled land is thus purchased at the price of complying with the comparatively simple regulations governing private companies. Formerly, however, the most important feature was that these arrangements made it possible to effect substantial savings of death duties and surtax, and to a lesser extent income tax.[78] Successive statutes [79] have now eroded the financial attractions of land companies, so that they have lost their popularity. The details of these companies lie outside the scope of this book.

Part 7

USUAL TRUSTS OF MARRIAGE SETTLEMENTS

Settlements and trusts for sale often arise under wills, in which case the trusts depend entirely upon the testator's wishes. The trusts of settlement and trusts for sale created *inter vivos* may also be in any form, but where they are made on marriage conveyancing practice has settled standard forms of the trusts which are usually employed, either with or without variation.

Sect. 1. A Strict Settlement Made upon Marriage

A. *Historical Sketch*

The history of the present form of marriage settlement shows a continuous interplay between the ingenuity of settlors and their advisers, judicial decisions, and statutes.

(i) One of the earliest forms of settlement was the *maritagium*.

---

[78] See also *post*, p. 615.
[79] See, *e.g.*, Finance Act 1930, ss. 34–38; Finance Act 1938, s. 49; Finance Act 1940, ss. 43–59; Finance Act 1944, ss. 35–40; Finance Act 1965, Part IV.

The construction which the courts put upon this and other conditional gifts, however, soon enabled the donee to defeat the claims of his issue.[80]

(ii) This new-found freedom of disposition was met by the Statute *De Donis* 1285 enabling a settlor to give the donee a fee tail which was bound to descend to his issue. About two centuries later, judicial decisions made it possible for entails to be barred.[81]

(iii) Settlors then tried inserting conditions against the barring of entails. The courts countered this by inventing the doctrine that it was impossible to create an unbarrable entail.[82]

(iv) Some settlors tried to create the virtual equivalent of an unbarrable entail by limiting a succession of life estates from father to son *ad infinitum*. This was met by the invention of the rule against such limitations which later became known as the Rule in *Whitby* v. *Mitchell*, making void every limitation subsequent to the limitation to the first unborn generation.[83]

(v) In the sixteenth century the basis of the modern form of strict settlement was evolved.[84] Land was limited to the husband (H) for life with remainder to his son in tail. H had no entail which he could bar, so that until H had a son who attained the age of 21, the settlement could not be upset. By the time H had a son of full age, H would probably have acquired a desire to see his family established, so that he would persuade his son (usually by offering him a substantial income) to join with him in barring the entail and resettling the resultant fee simple on H for life, remainder to the son for life, remainder to the son's son in tail. Thus until the son had a son who was of full age, the land was again securely tied up. The essential feature of the resettlement was that H's son cut down his entail to a mere life interest.

It will be noticed that the settlor could prescribe the person who should be entitled to the land only until H's son was 21. After this, the continuance of the land in the family was dependent upon a resettlement being made. If H died before his son was 21, the son could bar his entail and obtain a fee simple absolute as soon as he was of full age, and the scheme broke down. But while H lived, a protectorship of the settlement existed and the son by himself could

[80] *Ante*, p. 35.
[81] *Ante*, p. 36.
[82] *Ante*, p. 45.
[83] *Ante*, p. 101.
[84] See, *e.g.*, *Holcroft's Case* (1596) Moo.K.B. 486.

create only a base fee upon which little money could be raised; it was therefore not unlikely that he would fall in with H's suggestion of a resettlement. By this method of settlement and resettlement, land could be kept in the family from generation to generation, for centuries on end. Apart from express provisions in the settlement, it was impossible to dispose of the fee simple except at the moment of the resettlement, and the land became virtually inalienable.

(vi) As has been seen, Parliament met these difficulties by enacting the Settled Land Act 1882, making all settled land alienable. There is now no method of ensuring that land shall remain in the family for any period, for it can always be sold, and although the beneficiaries will have corresponding rights in the purchase-money, the land itself will be gone.

B. Present Position

The old method of settlement and resettlement may still be employed, though for fiscal reasons its popularity is waning.[85] Although the land itself cannot be rendered inalienable, this method ensures that either the land itself or the capital money representing it will remain in the family for generations. The core of the process of settlement and resettlement has already been examined; it is—

SETTLEMENT	RESETTLEMENT
(1) H for life	(1) H for life
(2) Son in tail	(2) Son for life
	(3) Son's son in tail

Round this core has been built a complex structure which makes provision for H's wife and the younger children of the marriage; for although it is true that the effect of a strict settlement is to " make an eldest son," this does not mean that the other children have nothing. The present form of strict settlement dates from the time of the Commonwealth and has remained substantially unchanged since the end of the seventeenth century.[86] The trusts are best explained by taking as an illustration the provisions usually made where H, a tenant in fee simple, is settling his land on the occasion of his marriage with W. Such a settlement is normally made a few days before the marriage, and the trusts are as follows.

[85] See *post*, p. 615.
[86] See 7 H.E.L., 376–380; Scrutton, *Land in Fetters*, 118–120.

1. Determinable fee: For H in fee simple until the celebration of the marriage. This is to guard against the marriage not taking place. H takes a determinable fee which becomes a fee simple absolute if either party dies before the marriage is solemnised. If the marriage duly takes place but later is annulled, H remains absolutely entitled [87]; and to cover the possibility that the parties may not marry and may thus leave the determinable fee to continue until either H or W dies, a proviso is sometimes inserted that if the marriage is not solemnised within 12 months, the trusts of the settlement shall become void and the land revert to the settlor, H.[88]

2. Pin money: Thereafter, a rentcharge of £x per annum to W during the joint lives of H and W, by way of pin money. This provides W with an income for her personal expenses.

3. Life interest: Subject thereto, to H for life. This is usually granted without impeachment of waste.

4. Jointure: Subject thereto, a rentcharge of £y per annum to W for life if she survives H, by way of jointure. This will be for a larger amount than the pin money, since it is intended to support W completely after H's death. Today, the word "jointure" merely means a provision made for a wife after the death of her husband.[89]

5. Portions: Subject thereto, a trust for portions for the younger children of the marriage. Portions for children are sums of money secured for them out of property springing from or settled upon their parents.[90] The object of the provision for portions is to give a capital sum to each child of the marriage other than the child who takes the land, so that all of them will be provided for.

6. Entails:

   (i) Subject thereto, for the first and other sons successively in tail male.

   (ii) Subject thereto, for the first and other sons successively in tail general.

   (iii) Subject thereto, for all the daughters in equal shares as tenants in common in tail general with cross remainders.

---

[87] *Re Wombwell's Settlement* [1922] 2 Ch. 298.
[88] Challis R.P. 257.
[89] *Re De Hoghton* [1896] 2 Ch. 385; for an older use, see *post*, p. 297.
[90] *Jones* v. *Maggs* (1852) 9 Hare 605 at 607; see also *ante*, pp. 139, 142.

The effect of these provisions is best shown by an example. Suppose that H and W have had two sons and two daughters, and that each son has had a son and a daughter, thus:

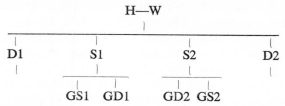

S1 takes under (i) and on his death GS1 becomes entitled under the same provision. On the death of GS1 without issue, the tail male given to S1 determines and S2 becomes entitled under (i). On his death, GS2 succeeds to the land and on his death without issue the provisions of (i) are exhausted. GD1 is therefore entitled under the tail general given to S1 by (ii), and on her death without issue, GD2 is similarly entitled under S2's tail general. On her death without issue, (ii) is exhausted and D1 and D2 become entitled under (iii). Each has a distinct half share which will be inherited by her issue, but if, say, D2 dies without issue, the cross remainder will carry her half share to D1.

7. Reversion: Subject thereto, for H in fee simple. Thus on failure of the entails, the land reverts to H and will pass under his will or intestacy.

8. Miscellaneous provisions. The details of the portions are usually included here, and provision is made for the wife and issue of any future marriage of H, *e.g.*, if W dies and H remarries. The provisions which the Settled Land Act 1925 requires to be inserted in a trust instrument [91] (*e.g.*, the appointment of trustees of the settlement) are also inserted.

A word should be added about the pin money, jointure and portions. As an annual income is required for pin money and the jointure, these can be secured by a rentcharge. Adequate remedies are given by statute for enforcing payment of rentcharges,[92] so that W is properly protected. Portions, on the other hand, cannot be secured by rentcharges because capital and not annual sums are required. The traditional device employed to secure payment of

[91] *Ante*, p. 155.
[92] *Post*, pp. 410 *et seq.*

portions is for the settlement to create a long term of years (*e.g.*, a thousand years) in favour of trustees on trust to raise the sums specified.   As the provision for portions precedes the entails, the eldest son takes the land subject to a burden which he cannot shake off by barring his entail.   The trustees can raise the money by sale or mortgage of the term of years,[93] which, being granted to them without impeachment of waste and without any rent being reserved, is of great value.   Often, however, the money is paid either out of capital or by the eldest son out of his own pocket so as to clear the estate.[94]   On payment of the money, the term of years becomes a " satisfied term " and automatically ceases.[95]   This has not always been the position, but the complicated situation which formerly existed need not be examined here.   The modern tendency is to avoid the cumbersome device of creating portions terms by inserting in the settlement a trust to raise portions which can be effectuated by the creation of a legal mortgage if necessary.

Sect. 2.   A Trust for Sale Made upon Marriage

If H is marrying W and settling land upon trust for sale, the usual trusts are as follows:

  (a) for H until the marriage; thereafter

  (b) for H for life; then

  (c) for W for life; then

  (d) for the children or remoter issue of the marriage in such
        shares—
        (i) as H and W jointly by deed appoint; in default,
        (ii) as the survivor may by deed or will appoint; in default,

  (e) for such of the children of the marriage as attain the age of 21
        years or being females marry under that age; in default,

  (f) for H absolutely.

It will be noted—
        (i) that no pin money is provided for W;
        (ii) that if W survives H, she is entitled to the whole income from
              the property and not merely a jointure;
        (iii) that subject to the life interests of H and W, the issue are
              entitled absolutely and not in tail;

---

[93] *Kelly* v. *Lord Bellew* (1707) 4 Bro.P.C. 495.
[94] See *Burrell* v. *Earl of Egremont* (1844) 7 Beav. 205.
[95] L.P.A. 1925, s. 5.

(iv) that H and W are able to choose which of their issue shall
benefit; they are not confined to their children, but can, for
example, appoint to their grandchildren and exclude their
children. If they fail to make an appointment, however, it is
the children who share equally to the exclusion of the remoter
issue.

CHAPTER 6

CO-OWNERSHIP

HITHERTO no consideration has been given to cases where two or more persons have been entitled to the simultaneous enjoyment of land. Four types of such ownership must be considered:

(1) Joint tenancy.
(2) Tenancy in common.
(3) Co-parcenary.
(4) Tenancy by entireties.

The terms " co-ownership," " concurrent interests " and " estates and interests in community " may each be used to include all four forms of co-ownership. Of the four, the first two are far more important than the others and they will be considered together.

Part 1

JOINT TENANCY AND TENANCY IN COMMON

Sect. 1. Nature of the Tenancies

A. Joint Tenancy

" A gift of lands to two or more persons in joint tenancy is such a gift as imparts to them, with respect to all other persons than themselves, the properties of one single owner." [1] Although as between themselves joint tenants have separate rights, as against everyone else they are in a position of a single tenant. The intimate nature of joint tenancy is shown by the two principal features, the right of survivorship and the " four unities."

1. The right of survivorship.

(a) *The right.* This is the distinguishing feature of a joint tenancy. On the death of one joint tenant, his interest in the land passes to the other joint tenants by the *jus accrescendi* (right of survivorship), and this process continues until there is but one survivor, who then holds the land as sole tenant.[2] This *jus accrescendi* takes precedence over

[1] Williams R.P. 143.
[2] Litt. 280.

208

any disposition made by a joint tenant's will, and the same principle applies if a joint tenant dies intestate; a joint tenancy cannot pass under a will or intestacy.[3] For this reason, among others, joint tenants were said to be seised " *per mie et per tout*," " *mie* " meaning " not in the least " [4]; each joint tenant holds nothing and yet holds the whole. In other words, a joint tenant may become entitled to nothing or to all, according to whether or not he survives his fellows.

(b) *Corporations*. The common law held that although a corporation could be a tenant in common, no joint tenancy could exist between a corporation and a natural person. A corporation never died and the natural person could thus have no effective right of survivorship. The rule was extended so as to prevent any joint tenancy existing between two or more corporations. A conveyance to the X Co. Ltd. and the Y Co. Ltd., jointly, made the companies tenants in common.[5] After a tentative half-measure of reform,[6] Parliament provided in 1899 that a corporation should be able to acquire and hold any property in joint tenancy in the same manner as if it were an individual.[7] This provision became necessary as banks and other corporations were taking up the work of acting as trustees.

(c) *Trustees*. Trustees are always made joint tenants because of the convenience of the trust property passing automatically by the *jus accrescendi* to the surviving trustees when one trustee dies; if trustees were made tenants in common, a conveyance of the trust property to the surviving trustees by the personal representatives of the deceased trustee would be necessary. The *jus accrescendi* of a joint tenancy is often unsuitable for beneficial owners because it introduces an element of chance, but it is ideal for trustees.

2. The four unities must be present. The four unities of a joint tenancy are the unities of possession, interest, title and time.[8]

(a) *Unity of possession*. Each joint tenant is as much entitled to possession of any part of the land as the others.[9] No tenant can point to any part of the land as his own to the exclusion of the others; if he could, there would be separate ownership and not joint tenancy. In this respect, the position is similar to that of partners; no partner

---

3 Litt. 287.
4 *Murray* v. *Hall* (1849) 7 C.B. 441 at 455n.; contrast *post*, p. 232.
5 Litt. 296, 297.
6 National Debt (Stockholders Relief) Act 1892, s. 6.
7 Bodies Corporate (Joint Tenancy) Act 1899.
8 Their initial letters form the convenient mnemonic P.I.T.T.
9 Litt. 288; *Bull* v. *Bull* [1955] 1 Q.B. 234.

can point to any particular asset of the business as being his, for each is entitled to possession of all the assets.

Unity of possession is common to all forms of co-ownership.

(b) *Unity of interest.* The interest of each joint tenant is the same in extent, nature and duration, for in theory of law they hold but one estate. This means [10]—

  (i) that although in theory of law each tenant has the whole of the property, the rents and profits of the land are divided equally between the tenants;

 (ii) that there can be no joint tenancy between those with interests of a different nature, *e.g.*, a freeholder and a tenant for years; and

(iii) that there can be no joint tenancy between those whose interests are similar but of different duration. Thus before 1926, a tenant in fee simple and a tenant in tail both owned freeholds, but the differing durations of the estates prevented them from being held in joint tenancy.

(c) *Unity of title.* Each joint tenant must claim his title to the land under the same act or document.[11] This requirement is satisfied if all the tenants acquired their rights by the same conveyance or if they simultaneously took possession of land and acquired title to it under the Statutes of Limitation.[12]

(d) *Unity of time.* The interest of each tenant must vest at the same time. This does not necessarily follow from the existence of unity of title. For example, if land was conveyed " to A for life, remainder to the heirs of B and C," and B and C died at different times in A's lifetime, B's heir and C's heir took the fee simple remainder as tenants in common; the heirs could not take as joint tenants for although there was unity of title, there was no unity of time.[13]

Two exceptions to the necessity for unity of time grew up: neither in a conveyance to uses nor in a gift by will was the rule applied. Thus if a bachelor conveyed land to the use of himself and any wife he might marry, when he married he held as a joint tenant with his wife. Again, if land was devised or conveyed to the use of A

---

[10] See Co.Litt. 188a ; 2 Bl.Com. 181.
[11] Co.Litt. 189a, 299b.
[12] *Post*, Chap. 15, p. 527.
[13] Co.Litt. 188a ; 2 Bl.Com. 181.

for life with remainder to the use of the children of B, each child of B born in A's lifetime acquired a vested interest at birth, yet the disparity of time did not prevent them from taking as joint tenants.[14]

B. Tenancy in Common

A tenancy in common differs greatly from a joint tenancy.

1. The tenants hold in undivided shares. Unlike joint tenants, tenants in common hold in undivided shares: each tenant in common has a distinct fixed share in property which has not yet been divided among the co-tenants.[15] There is no *jus accrescendi*; the share of each tenant is fixed once and for all and is not affected by the death of one of his companions. When a tenant in common dies, his interest passes under his will or intestacy, for his undivided share is his to dispose of as he wishes.[16]

2. Only the unity of possession is essential. Although the four unities of a joint tenancy may be present in a tenancy in common, the only unity which is essential is the unity of possession. In particular, it should be noted that the unity of interest may be absent and the tenants may hold unequal interests, so that one tenant in common may be entitled to a one-fifth share and the other to four-fifths, or one may be entitled for life and the other in fee simple.[17]

Sect. 2.   Estates in which the Tenancies Could Exist

In general, before 1926 joint tenancies and tenancies in common could exist at law or in equity (*i.e.*, as legal estates or as equitable interests), and in possession or in remainder, in any of the estates of freehold or in leaseholds.[18] Thus if land was given to A and B as joint tenants for their lives, they enjoyed it jointly for their joint life, and the survivor enjoyed the whole for the rest of his life.[19] If A and B had converted their joint tenancy into a tenancy in common, the survivor would have been entitled only to half for the

---

[14] *Ruck* v. *Barwise* (1865) 2 Dr. & Sm. 510; *Doe* d. *Hallen* v. *Ironmonger* (1803) 3 East 533.

[15] *Fisher* v. *Wiggs* (1700) 12 Mod. 296 at 302.

[16] Challis R.P. 368.

[17] Co.Litt. 189a; Williams R.P. 148; 2 Bl.Com. 191.

[18] Williams R.P. 143.

[19] *Moffat* v. *Burnie* (1853) 18 Beav. 211.

rest of his life. Again, if X and Y were joint tenants for the life of
X, if X survived he became sole tenant of the whole for the rest of
his life, whereas if Y were the survivor he took nothing, for the
estate which he acquired by survivorship was one which determined
at the moment he received it.

After 1925, the position is substantially the same except that a
tenancy in common can no longer exist at law; this is dealt with
below.[20]   Further, since life estates and entails can exist only in
equity,[21] even a joint tenancy in these interests must also be equitable.

Sect. 3.   Mode of Creating the Tenancies

The key to a proper understanding of joint tenancies and tenancies
in common is always to consider the legal estate separately from
the equitable interest.[22] Thus it may be found that at law A and B
are joint tenants, while in equity they are tenants in common. The
effect of A's death on the legal joint tenancy is that B is solely
entitled; in equity, on the other hand, A's share passes under his
will or intestacy. In the result, B holds the legal estate on trust for
himself as to his share, and for A's personal representatives as to
A's share.

The mode of creating joint tenancies and tenancies in common
must now be considered.

A. Before 1926

I. AT LAW

At law, the presumption was in favour of a joint tenancy.[23] There
were three main reasons for this. First, to a feudal lord, a joint
tenancy was preferable to a tenancy in common because the operation
of the doctrine of survivorship made it more likely that the land
would ultimately vest in a single tenant from whom the feudal services could more conveniently be exacted than from a number
sharing the burden. Secondly, tenants had the same preference;
for a tenancy in common rendered certain feudal services due
separately from each tenant, thus increasing the burden on the land,
whereas a joint tenancy avoided this. " The law loves not fractions

---

[20] *Post*, p. 216.
[21] *Ante*, p. 72.
[22] Despite *Re Selous* [1901] 1 Ch. 921, criticised in Williams V. & P. 501, 502.
[23] *Morley* v. *Bird* (1798) 3 Ves. 628.

of estates, nor to divide and multiply tenures." [24] Thirdly, conveyancers had a similar preference. Joint tenants held by a single title, whereas the title of every tenant in common had to be separately examined. If a joint tenant died, there was merely one tenant the less, and still but one title, whereas if a tenant in common died, it might be found that his share had been left equally between his twelve children, thus increasing by eleven the titles to be investigated. The rule at law was thus that if land was conveyed to two or more persons a joint tenancy of the legal estate was created unless either—

(i) one of the unities was absent; or

(ii) words of severance were employed.

1. Absence of unities. The four unities have already been considered. If there was unity of possession but one or more of the other unities were missing, the parties took as tenants in common; if there was no unity of possession, the parties took as separate owners.

2. Words of severance. Any words in the grant showing that the tenants were each to take a distinct share in the property amounted to words of severance and thus created a tenancy in common. Words which have been held to have this effect include—

" share and share alike "

" to be divided amongst "

" equally "

" between."

Further, words showing that the tenants were to take unequal interests (such as " two-thirds to A and one-third to B ") sufficed to create a tenancy in common; and even if there were no clear words of severance, the gift taken as a whole might show that a tenancy in common was intended.[25] Thus provisions for the use of capital or income, or both, for the maintenance and advancement of those concerned created a tenancy in common.[26] For example, if under a settlement on children containing such provisions an advance was made to one child, it would have to be debited against that child's share and this could not be done unless the child was a tenant in common and so had a distinct share.[27]

[24] *Fisher* v. *Wigg* (1700) 1 Salk. 391 at 392, *per* Holt C.J.

[25] See, *e.g.*, *Surtees* v. *Surtees* (1871) L.R. 12 Eq. 400.

[26] *Re Dunn* [1916] 1 Ch. 97.

[27] See *L'Estrange* v. *L'Estrange* [1902] 1 I.R. 467 at 468, 469; and see M. & W. 411–413.

II. IN EQUITY

Despite the feudal and conveyancing advantages of a joint tenancy, equity did not favour it. Equity looked to the beneficial interests of the co-tenants and preferred the certainty and equality of a tenancy in common to the element of chance which the *jus accrescendi* of a joint tenancy introduced. " Survivorship is looked upon as odious in equity," [28] and nonetheless because few laymen contemplate that a gift to two or more persons gives rise to such a right.[29] This preference for a tenancy in common was manifested by equity holding that a tenancy in common would exist in equity not only in those cases where it existed at law, but also in certain other cases where an intention to create a tenancy in common could be discerned. In short, there was a tenancy in common in equity in the following five cases:

1. Tenancy in common at law. There was a tenancy in common in equity whenever there was a tenancy in common at law.[30]

2. Purchase-money provided in unequal shares. If two or more persons together purchased property and provided the money in unequal shares, the purchasers were presumed to take as tenants in common in shares proportionate to the sums advanced [31]; thus if A found one-third and B two-thirds of the price, they were presumed tenants in common as to one-third and two-thirds respectively. If, on the other hand, the purchasers provided the money in equal shares, they were presumed joint tenants. These presumptions could be rebutted by evidence of circumstances showing that those providing the purchase-money equally intended to take as tenants in common or *vice versa*.

3. Loan on mortgage. Where two or more persons advanced money on mortgage, whether in equal or unequal shares, equity presumed a tenancy in common in the land between the mortagees. " If two people join in lending money upon a mortgage, equity says, it could not be the intention, that the interest in that should survive. Though they take a joint security, each means to lend his own and take back his own." [32] " It is obvious, however, that this proposition

[28] *R.* v. *Williams* (1735) Bunb. 342 at 343.
[29] See *Re Woolley* [1903] 2 Ch. 206 at 211.
[30] *Ante*, p. 213.
[31] *Lake* v. *Gibson* (1729) 1 Eq.Ca.Abr. 290 at 291.
[32] *Morley* v. *Bird* (1798) 3 Ves. 628 at 631, *per* Arden M.R.

cannot be put higher than a presumption capable of being rebutted." [33] Yet it should be noted that the " joint account clause " which is normally inserted in mortgages to make the mortgagees figure as joint tenants to the outside world and so simplify the mechanism of discharging the mortgage [34] does not affect this presumption of a tenancy in common in the relationship of the mortgagees *inter se*.[35]

4. Partnership assets. Where partners acquired land as part of their partnership assets, they were presumed to hold it as tenants in common.[36] " *Jus accrescendi inter mercatores locum non habet* " : the right of survivorship has no place between merchants. The rule extended to any joint undertaking with a view to a profit, even if there was no formal partnership between the parties; the legal estate might be held on a joint tenancy, but in equity the partners were presumed to be entitled in undivided shares, so that the surviving partners (or whoever held the legal estate) would be compelled to hold the legal estate on trust for those entitled to the property of a deceased partner as far as his share was concerned.[37]

5. Executory trusts. These are trusts where the details have not been set out but a further document is to be drawn up to give effect to the settlor's intention; thus " marriage articles," which are the preliminary agreement for a marriage settlement, create executory trusts and the marriage settlement itself creates executed trusts. In such cases there was a tenancy in common where any intention to create such a tenancy could be found or presumed. " Joint tenancy as a provision for the children of a marriage, is an inconvenient mode of settlement," [38] for no child could rely upon having a distinct share for his family until he had severed his joint tenancy (*i.e.,* converted it into a tenancy in common) nor could any advance to a child be set against his share until this had been done.[39] Accordingly the court would readily infer that a provision in marriage articles or other executory trusts for the benefit of a class of children was intended to be a provision for them as tenants in common, despite the absence of words of severance.[40]

[33] *Steeds* v. *Steeds* (1889) 22 Q.B.D. 537 at 541, *per* Wills J.
[34] *Post*, p. 497.
[35] *Re Jackson* (1887) 34 Ch.D. 732.
[36] *Lake* v. *Craddock* (1732) 3 P.Wms. 158.
[37] See *Re Fuller's Contract* [1933] Ch. 652.
[38] *Taggart* v. *Taggart* (1803) 1 Sch. & Lef. 84 at 88.
[39] *Ante*, p. 213.
[40] See *Mayn* v. *Mayn* (1867) L.R. 5 Eq. 150.

B. *After* 1925

For reasons which will appear shortly,[41] substantial changes in the law have been made by the Law of Property Act 1925.

1. A legal tenancy in common cannot exist after 1925. Even if there are clear words of severance, after 1925 the legal estate cannot be held on a tenancy in common.[42] As is explained below, a tenancy in common can still exist in equity, but at law the only form of co-ownership possible after 1925 is a joint tenancy. Thus a conveyance today " to A, B and C in fee simple as tenants in common " (all being of full age) will vest the legal estate in A, B and C as joint tenants, although in equity they will be tenants in common.[43] If A had been an infant, his rights in equity would not have been affected, but no legal estate would have vested in him.[44] If A, B and C had all been infants, the legal estate would have remained in the grantor, though it is not clear whether the grantor would be deemed to have made an agreement for value to execute a settlement in their favour and in the meantime to hold the land in trust for them, or whether the transaction would be void.[45]

2. The legal estate is held upon trust for sale.[46]

(a) *The statutory trusts.* After 1925, subject to the special provisions relating to settled land,[47] land is held upon the " statutory trusts " whenever it is conveyed to or held by two or more persons beneficially, whether as tenants in common[48] or joint tenants.[49] The " statutory trusts " may be summarised thus:

> upon trust to sell the land, and stand possessed of the net proceeds of sale and of the net rents and profits until sale upon such trusts and subject to such powers and provisions as may be requisite for giving effect to the rights of those interested in the land,[50] whether beneficially or as trustees.[51]

---

[41] *Post*, p. 220.
[42] L.P.A. 1925, ss. 1 (6), 34 (1), 36 (2).
[43] *Ibid.* s. 34 (2).
[44] *Ibid.* s. 19 (2).
[45] See M. & W. 420.
[46] See M. & W. 422–429.
[47] *Post*, p. 222.
[48] L.P.A. 1925, s. 34 (2), 1st Sched., Pt. IV.
[49] *Ibid.* s. 36 (1).
[50] *Ibid.* s. 35.
[51] *Re Hayward* [1928] Ch. 367.

(b) *Overreaching*. Apart from a somewhat debatable special overriding effect,[52] the trusts for sale created by the statutory trusts take effect in the same way as the trusts for sale considered above.[53] In particular, the land must be sold unless either all trustees concur in postponing sale (as they often do) or a sale would defeat the object of the trust or be a breach of the contractual obligations of the trustee who seeks to sell.[54] Further, the overreaching provisions apply. Consequently a purchaser is concerned not with the beneficial interests in the land but only with the legal estate vested in the trustees for sale. Provided he pays his purchase-money to trustees for sale who are either two or more in number or a trust corporation, he takes free from the rights of the beneficiaries. To a purchaser who does this, it is immaterial whether in equity there are three or thirty people entitled, or whether they are joint tenants or tenants in common. In practice, on a conveyance to joint tenants or tenants in common, it is usual for the conveyance to be made on an express trust for sale.

(c) *Union in sole tenant*. If the whole legal estate and equitable interest become vested in one person, the trust for sale is at an end,[55] as where A and B were joint tenants at law and in equity, and A dies. Further, by the Schedule to the Law of Property (Amendment) Act 1926, it was provided that nothing in the Law of Property Act 1925 was to affect the right of a survivor of joint tenants who is solely and beneficially interested to deal with his legal estate as if it were not held on trust for sale. Thus B can make title by himself despite the fact that a sole trustee for sale is unable to give a proper receipt for purchase-money. There was formerly a practical difficulty of satisfying a purchaser in such circumstances that B was in truth solely entitled in equity. An act of severance might have occurred in A's lifetime causing A and B to become tenants in common.[56] This situation has been remedied by the Law of Property (Joint Tenants) Act 1964, which is retrospective to January 1, 1926.[57] It provides that in favour of a purchaser of a legal estate, a survivor of one or more joint tenants is " deemed to be solely and beneficially interested if he conveys as beneficial owner[58] or the conveyance includes a

---

2 See J.M.L., 73 L.J.News. 41, 57, 75, 93, 111.
3 *Ante*, pp. 184 *et seq*.
4 *Re Buchanan-Wollaston's Conveyance* [1939] Ch. 738 ; *Jones* v. *Challenger* [1961] 1 Q.B. 176.
5 *Re Cook* [1948] Ch. 212.
6 See *post*, p. 226.
7 s. 2.
8 See *post*, p. 334.

statement that he is so interested." [59] Where the survivor has himself died, his personal representatives have similar powers. The Act does not apply if before the conveyance by the survivor, a memorandum recording the severance is indorsed on or annexed to the conveyance which vested the land in the joint tenants.[60] Nor does it apply where a bankruptcy petition or receiving order has been registered,[61] or where the title to the land is registered.[62]

3. The legal estate usually cannot be vested in more than four persons. The position here is clear in the case of tenancies in common and rather less clear in the case of joint tenancies; each will be dealt with separately—

(a) in respect of tenancies created after 1925; and

(b) in respect of tenancies created before 1926.

(a) *Tenancies created after* 1925.

(1) TENANCIES IN COMMON. If land is conveyed to trustees for sale on trust for tenants in common, the general prohibition against the number of trustees of land exceeding four applies.[63] If the conveyance is expressed to be made to the tenants in common themselves, and they are of full age, statute provides for it to operate as a conveyance " to the grantees, or, if there are more than four grantees, to the first four named in the conveyance, as joint tenants upon the statutory trusts." [64] Further, a gift of land by will to tenants in common operates as a gift to the Settled Land Act trustees of the will, or, if none, to the testator's personal representatives, upon the statutory trusts [65]; and the number of Settled Land Act trustees or personal representatives cannot exceed four.

(2) JOINT TENANCIES. There are no provisions dealing expressly with the number of persons in whom the legal estate can be vested when two or more persons are beneficially entitled as joint tenants. But the trust for sale arising in such cases involves the general provision that in a trust for sale of land made or coming into operation after 1925, the number of trustees shall not exceed four,[66] and

---

[59] s. 1.
[60] *Ibid.*
[61] See *post*, pp. 542, 543.
[62] s. 3. See *post*, p. 554.
[63] *Post*, p. 247.
[64] L.P.A. 1925, s. 34 (2); for infants, see *post*, p. 515.
[65] L.P.A. 1925, s. 34 (3).
[66] *Post*, p. 247.

" where more than four persons are named as such trustees, the first four named (who are able and willing to act) shall alone be the trustees." [67] In the case of a devise to joint tenants, the general prohibition against more than four trustees of land coupled with the fact that there is a trust for sale prevents the personal representatives from vesting the legal estate in more than four persons.

(b) *Tenancies created before* 1926.

(1) TENANCIES IN COMMON. Elaborate transitional provisions [68] were enacted with the object of ensuring that the legal estate should vest in suitable persons at the first moment of 1926. In the transition from the old system to the new, it was necessary to provide machinery for finding a safe home for the legal estate which could no longer remain in tenants in common as such. There are four separate heads which must be taken in order; if a case falls under both Head 1 and Head 3, for example, the operative provisions are those of Head 1.[69] The provisions are extremely complicated and can only be given in bare outline.

Head 1. *Trustees or personal representatives.* If the entirety of the land was vested in trustees or personal representatives, it remained vested in them.

Head 2. *Beneficial owners.* If the entirety of the land (not being settled land) was vested absolutely and beneficially in not more than four persons of full age entitled thereto in undivided shares free from incumbrances affecting undivided shares, it vested in them as joint tenants upon the statutory trusts.

Head 3. *Settled land.* If the entirety of the land was settled and under the law in force before 1926,[70] it vested in the trustees of the settlement as joint tenants upon the statutory trusts. If there were no such trustees it vested in the Public Trustee upon the statutory trusts, although he cannot act in the trust until requested in writing by persons interested in more than one half of the land.

Head 4. *Any other case.* In any case not covered by the above heads, the land vested in the Public Trustee, subject to the provisions set out under Head 3 against his acting in the trust until requested.

(2) JOINT TENANCIES. The complex transitional provisions applying to tenancies in common do not apply to joint tenancies. Unless

the land was settled land, it remained vested in the persons in whom
it was vested before 1926,[71] even if they exceeded four in number
There is no restriction upon the numbers except the general provision
that until the number of trustees is reduced below four no new
trustees can be appointed.[72]

Where under the Settled Land Act 1925 the land is settled land,
the above provisions do not apply and the legal estate automatically
vested in the two or more persons of full age (without limit as to
number) who were the joint tenants for life [73]; there is no trust for sale

It will be noticed that the three main changes introduced by the
1925 legislation all assist the purchaser. The prohibition of a legal
tenancy in common and the limitation of the number of tenants of
the legal estate to four means that purchasers are no longer exposed
to the burden of having to investigate the titles of each of, say, thirty
legal tenants in common, some of whom might own a sixty-eighth
share worth just over £10, and who might be so scattered about the
world that it took six months to get all their signatures to the conveyance.[74] Further, the overreaching effect of a trust for sale enables
a purchaser to ignore the equitable rights of the beneficiaries. These
benefits may be thought to have been dearly purchased when the
complexity of the transitional provisions is considered, but it canno
be denied that they are very considerable improvements in the law

II. IN EQUITY

On the position in equity after 1925, there is little to be added to
the foregoing. Strictly there can be no " tenancy " in common after
1925 because those interested hold no estate or interest in the land
but are entitled merely as beneficiaries under a trust for sale; the
1925 legislation throughout refers not to " tenancies in common '
but to " undivided shares." In general, however, the rights of these
beneficiaries correspond to the rights of tenants in common before
1926, and the same applies to those entitled in equity as joint tenants

Sect. 4. Special Rules for Husband and Wife

A. Before 1926

1. One share between them. For many purposes, the common
law treated husband and wife as one person. As will be seen

---

[71] See L.P.A. 1925, 1st Sched., Pt. II, para. 6 (*b*).
[72] T.A. 1925, s. 34 (1); *post*, p. 247.
[73] L.P.A. 1925, 1st Sched., Pt. II, para. 6 (*c*); S.L.A. 1925, s. 19 (2).
[74] See A. H. Cosway (1929) 15 Conv.(o.s.) 83.

shortly,[75] a conveyance to a husband and wife without words of severance formerly created a tenancy by entireties, which was virtually an unseverable joint tenancy. The Married Women's Property Act 1882 prevented the creation of such tenancies after 1882, but it did not affect the other principal manifestation of the unity of husband and wife, namely, the rule of construction [76] that in the absence of a contrary intention, a conveyance to a husband and wife and third parties, whether as joint tenants or tenants in common, gave the husband and wife only one actual or potential share between them.[77] For example, a limitation before 1926 to

"H and W and X in equal shares"

created a tenancy in common under which X took one half and H and W (the husband and wife) the other.

2. Exclusion of rule. This rule of construction yielded to any contrary indication, however slight. Mere words of severance, such as "in equal shares" were not enough, for they merely showed that the interest taken by the unit consisting of husband-and-wife was to be held under a tenancy in common and not a joint tenancy. But the rule might be excluded by the way in which copulatives were used. For example, the form of the limitations in the first column below has been held sufficient to exclude the rule and give H and W one share each, whereas the form of the limitations in the second column did not oust the rule, and H and W took one share between them.

RULE EXCLUDED	RULE APPLIED
to "H W and X"	to "H and W, and X"
to "A, B, H and W"	to "A B and H and W"
to "H1, W1, X, Y, Z, H2 and W2"	to "A, and H, and W"

The distinction between these turns upon the use of the copulative "and." It is perhaps best explained by saying that if "H and W" were enclosed in a bracket, or replaced by a single symbol such as "Q," the limitations in the second column would still read smoothly

---

[5] *Post,* p. 232.

[6] *Re Jeffery* [1914] 1 Ch. 375.

[7] See *Re Wylde's Estate* (1852) 2 De G.M. & G. 724; *Re March* (1884) 27 Ch.D. 166.

and naturally, whereas those in the first column would not. Thus—

"A, B, (H-and-W)," or

"A, B, Q"

from column 1 should be contrasted with

"A B and (H-and-W)," or

"A B and Q"

from column 2. "Though a man may devise to ten persons, and add an (*and*) betwixt every person's name, yet it is not natural or usual to add an (*and*) till you come to the last person."[78] If the donor "couples the husband and the wife together in such a way as to refer to them jointly as husband and wife, then the ordinary rule applies."[79]

The rule had no application to persons who were unmarried when the limitation took effect but who intermarried afterwards, nor did it apply to class gifts,[80] *e.g.*, a gift to the grantor's nephews and nieces, two of whom were married to each other.[81]

B. After 1925

By the Law of Property Act 1925,[82] a husband and wife are to be treated as two persons for the purpose of the acquisition of any interest in property under a disposition made or coming into operation after 1925, so that the rule has disappeared except in respect of limitations which took effect before 1926.

Sect. 5. Position of Settled Land

Before 1926, where land fell within the definition of settled land but two or more persons were together entitled in possession, they together formed a composite tenant for life, whether they held as joint tenants, tenants in common or otherwise.[83] After 1925, their position depends upon whether in equity they are entitled as joint tenants or in undivided shares (which includes co-parcenary[84]).

---

[78] *Bricker* v. *Whatley* (1684) 1 Vern. 233.

[79] *Re Jeffery* [1914] 1 Ch. 375 at 380.

[80] For which see *ante*, p. 118, and *post*, p. 283.

[81] *Re Gue* (1892) 61 L.J.Ch. 510.

[82] s. 37.

[83] S.L.A. 1882, s. 2 (6).

[84] *Post*, pp. 230, 231.

A. Joint Tenants

If two or more persons of full age are entitled as joint tenants, they together constitute the tenant for life.[85] If any of them are infants, such one or more of them as for the time being is or are of full age constitute the tenant for life [86]; if they are all infants, the legal estate and statutory powers are vested in the statutory owner [87] until one of them is of full age.[88] The land thus remains settled land and there is no trust for sale.

B. Undivided Shares [89]

1. Trust for sale. If after 1925 two or more tenants in common or co-parceners become entitled in possession to settled land, the land forthwith ceases to be settled land and becomes subject to a trust for sale. The Settled Land Act trustees can require the legal estate to be conveyed to them if it is not already vested in them [90]; they will hold it on the statutory trusts, namely, on trust for sale, with power to postpone sale, holding the income until sale and the proceeds thereafter upon such trusts and subject to such provisions as are requisite for giving effect to the rights of the persons interested in the land.[91] Thus if land is settled on A for life, remainder to B and C in equal shares as tenants in common for life, remainder to the children of B and C in fee simple, when A dies the land will be held upon trust for sale and must be vested in the Settled Land Act trustees.

2. Land ceasing to be settled. This provision that the legal estate shall be vested in the Settled Land Act trustees and not in the persons beneficially entitled applies even if the land ceases to be settled at the moment when the tenants in common or co-parceners become entitled in possession. Thus if land is settled on A for life, remainder to his children in fee simple in equal shares as tenants in common, the land ceases to be settled land on the death of A, for it becomes subject to an immediate binding trust for sale. Nevertheless, A's personal representatives must convey the legal estate to the Settled

---

[85] S.L.A. 1925, s. 19 (2).
[86] *Ibid.* s. 19 (3).
[87] *Ante*, p. 153.
[88] L.P.A. 1925, s. 26 (4), (5).
[89] See M. & W. 435–438.
[90] S.L.A. 1925, s. 36 (1); L.P.A. 1925, 1st Sched., Pt. IV, para. 2.
[91] S.L.A. 1925, s. 36 (2), (6).

Land Act trustees as joint tenants upon trust for sale, and not to the children [92]; to this extent the land retains traces of its former status as settled land.

3. Land devolving as a whole. There is one exception to the above provision, and that is where at the end of 1925 there were two or more tenants for life of full age entitled under some settlement in undivided shares and the whole of the land was limited to devolve together (not in undivided shares) after the cesser of all their interests in the income. In such a case, there is no trust for sale; the persons entitled hold the legal estate as joint tenants and form a composite tenant for life, without, of course, affecting their rights in equity.[93] For example, if land was settled on A and B as tenants in common for life with remainder to C for life, remainder to D in fee simple, this provision would apply, for after the cesser of the interests of A and B the land is limited to devolve as an undivided whole; thus A and B will form a composite tenant for life and there will be no trust for sale. Had the land been limited after the death of A and B to their respective children, the ordinary rule would have applied and the Settled Land Act trustees would have held the land on trust for sale.[94]

4. Overreaching powers. Where the normal rule applies, the Settled Land Act trustees hold on a special form of trust for sale which enables them to overreach not only the rights under the trust for sale but also any other rights existing under a former settlement and not protected by a legal mortgage, even if these rights are prior to the trust for sale.[95] For example, if land is settled on A for life subject to an equitable rentcharge for B, with remainder to C and D as tenants in common, on the death of A the Settled Land Act trustees hold on trust for sale with power to overreach B's rentcharge even though it has priority to the trust for sale.

Sect. 6. Determination of Joint Tenancies and Tenancies in Common

Joint tenancies and tenancies in common may be determined by partition or by union in a sole tenant; joint tenancies may also be

---

[92] *Re Thomas* [1939] Ch. 513.

[93] L.P.A. 1925, 1st Sched., Pt. IV, para. 4.

[94] And see *Re Barrat* [1929] 1 Ch. 336.

[95] S.L.A. 1925, s. 36 (2); L.P.A. 1925, 1st Sched., Pt. IV, para. 1 (3), as amended by L.P.(Am.)A. 1926, Sched.

etermined by severance, which converts them into tenancies in
ommon.

A. *Partition*

1. No power at common law. Joint tenants and tenants in
ommon have always been able to make a voluntary partition of the
and concerned if all agreed; their co-ownership thus came to an end
y each of them becoming sole tenant of the piece of land allotted to
im. But at common law, there was no right to compel a partition.
Co-parceners, who took their land by descent from the former
wner,[96] were allowed to insist upon partition, for as their co-
wnership was " cast on them by the act of the law, and not by their
wn agreement, it was thought right that the perverseness of one
hould not prevent the others from obtaining a more beneficial
nethod of enjoying the property." [97] This argument, however, did
ot apply to joint tenancy or tenancy in common, for these forms of
o-ownership necessarily arose by act of parties.

2. Partition Acts. By the Partition Acts 1539 and 1540, a
tatutory right to compel partition was conferred upon joint tenants
nd tenants in common, one tenant being entitled to insist upon a
artition, however inconvenient it might be. It was not until the
Partition Act 1868 that the court was empowered to decree a sale
nstead of partition, an order which might be highly desirable where,
or example, the cost of partition proceedings would exceed the
alue of the property, or where a single house had to be partitioned
nto thirds, and the owner of two-thirds was given all the chimneys
nd fireplaces and the only stairs.[98]

3. Sale. The Partition Acts have now be repealed. Instead,
ubject to certain qualifications, a power is given to the trustees for
ale in whom the legal estate is vested to effect a partition with the
onsent of the beneficiaries.[99] If the trustees or any of the bene-
iciaries refuse to agree to a partition, any person interested may
pply to the court, which may make such order as it thinks fit,[1]
uch as an order for sale.[2]

---

6 *Post*, pp. 229–231
7 Williams R.P. 243, 244.
8 See *Turner* v. *Morgan* (1803) 8 Ves. 143, 11 Ves. 157n.; but if there had been
  three houses, each share would have consisted of one house and not one-third
  of each house: *Earl of Clarendon* v. *Hornby* (1718) 1 P.Wms. 446.
9 L.P.A. 1925, s. 28 (3).
1 L.P.A. 1925, s. 30.
2 See *Re Solomon, a bankrupt* [1967] Ch. 573.

B. Union in a Sole Tenant

Joint tenancies and tenancies in common may be determined by the entirety of the land becoming vested in a sole tenant. Thus where one of two surviving joint tenants dies, the other becomes sole tenant and the joint tenancy is at an end. Similarly if one joint tenant or tenant in common acquires the interests of all his fellows, as by purchase, the co-ownership is at an end.

Because in theory each joint tenant is seised of the whole of the land, the appropriate way for one joint tenant to transfer his rights to another before 1926 was by a release operating to extinguish rather than to convey any rights, and so requiring no words of limitation; but any sort of conveyance would be construed as a release,[3] and it has now been retrospectively provided that the transaction could also be effected by grant.[4] A tenant in common, on the other hand, could not release his share to his fellows, but had to convey it by some assurance by which a sole tenant could have conveyed his land, for " a release supposes the party to have the thing in demand." [5]

Co-ownership in land is also extinguished if the land is sold to a purchaser, for the co-ownership is transferred from the land to the proceeds of sale.

C. Severance

The common law mitigated the uncertainty of the *jus accrescendi* by enabling a joint tenant to destroy the joint tenancy by severance. " The duration of all lives being uncertain, if either party has an ill opinion of his own life, he may sever the jointenancy by a deed granting over a moiety [*i.e.*, conveying one half] in trust for himself; so that survivorship can be no hardship, where either side may at pleasure prevent it." [6] " Severance " strictly includes partition, but the word is normally used to describe the process whereby a joint tenancy is converted into a tenancy in common, and it is used in this sense here. Although no joint tenant owned any distinct share in the land, yet each had a potential share equal in size to that of his companions, and so depending upon the number of joint tenants at the time in question. Thus if there were five joint tenants, each had

[3] See *Re Schär* [1951] Ch. 280.
[4] L.P.A. 1925, s. 72 (4).
[5] Litt. s. 304, n. 1.
[6] *Cray* v. *Willis* (1729) 2 P.Wms. 529, *per* Verney M.R.

he right to sever his joint tenancy and become tenant in common of one undivided fifth share; if one joint tenant died before the severance, each of the survivors had a potential quarter share, and so on.

I. BEFORE 1926

Before 1926, a joint tenancy could be severed both at law and in equity. Severance was effected by destroying one of the unities. Unity of time could not be severed, and severance of the unity of possession meant partition, but severance of the unity either of title or of interest converted a joint tenancy into a tenancy in common. A joint tenancy could be severed in the following ways.

1. By acquisition of another estate in the land. Although it was not fatal to a joint tenancy that one of the tenants was initially given some further estate in the land than his joint tenancy, the subsequent acquisition of an additional estate in the land destroyed the unity of interest and severed the joint tenancy.[7] Thus if land was limited to A, B and C as joint tenants for life, with remainder to C in fee simple, the mere existence of C's fee simple remainder did not destroy his tenancy for life; however, if A acquired C's fee simple, A's life estate merged in the fee simple and severed his joint tenancy for life. It should be noted, however, that this method of severance required that some estate different from the estate held in joint tenancy should be acquired. Thus in the above example if A released his interest to B, B took A's one-third share as tenant in common, but his joint tenancy with C in the remaining two-thirds was not affected.

2. By alienation. If a joint tenant alienated his interest *inter vivos*, his joint tenancy was severed and the person to whom the interest was conveyed took it as a tenant in common with the other joint tenants, for he had no unity of title with them.[8] Such a severance did not affect the other joint tenants, who remained joint tenants *inter se*. Thus if A, B and C were joint tenants, and A sold his interest to X, X became tenant in common of one-third and B and C joint tenants of two-thirds. If B then died, C alone profited by the *jus accrescendi*, X and C being left as tenants in common as to one-third and two-thirds respectively. If one of the tenants mortgaged his interest, this also severed the joint tenancy as to his share, and the same applied if a joint tenant became bankrupt. The better

---

[7] *Wiscot's Case* (1599) 2 Co.Rep. 60b.
[8] See *Partriche* v. *Powlet* (1740) 2 Atk. 54.

opinion was that if a joint tenant of freehold land granted a lease of his interest, this also effected a severance; but this was not clearly settled.

3. In equity, by contract. Equity treats that as done which ought to be done, and so far as the equitable interest was concerned, an enforceable contract by a joint tenant to alienate his interest was as effective to sever a joint tenancy as an actual alienation.[9]

II. AFTER 1925

After 1925, a legal joint tenancy can never be severed so as to create a legal tenancy in common; but this does not prevent one joint tenant from releasing his interest to the others, nor does it affect the right to sever a joint tenancy in equity.[10]

In equity, a severance can be effected—

1. By the methods available before 1926. These are dealt with above.

2. By notice in writing. It is provided [11] that " where a legal estate (not being settled land) is vested in joint tenants beneficially, and any tenant desires to sever the joint tenancy in equity, he shall give to the other joint tenants a notice in writing of such desire," whereupon the parties concerned are to be treated in equity as if there had been an actual severance. The effect of a severance is now limited to the tenants' interests in equity in the proceeds of sale.

An example illustrating the present position may be useful. In 1930, X purported to convey land to A, B, C, D and E in fee simple; all were of full age. The legal estate vested in A, B, C and D on the statutory trusts; in equity, A, B, C, D and E were tenants in common if there were words of severance or if it was one of equity's special cases, but otherwise joint tenants. If they were joint tenants and A died, B, C and D would then hold the legal estate on the statutory trusts for B, C, D and E as joint tenants; E would not automatically fill the vacancy at law, but could, of course, be appointed a new trustee in place of A. If B afterwards sold his interest to P, then B, C and D would hold the legal estate on the statutory trusts for P as tenant in common of a quarter and C, D and

---

[9] *Brown* v. *Raindle* (1796) 3 Ves. 256.
[10] L.P.A. 1925, s. 36 (2).
[11] *Ibid.*

E as joint tenants of three-quarters. If C then severed his joint tenancy (*e.g.*, by agreement with D and E), the legal estate would remain in B, C and D as before, on the statutory trusts for P and C as tenants in common of one-quarter each, and D and E as joint tenants of half. On D's death, B and C would hold on the statutory trusts for P, C and E as tenants in common as to one-quarter, one-quarter and one-half respectively.

Part 2

CO-PARCENARY

Sect. 1. Before 1926

A. Origin of Co-Parcenary

When a person died intestate before 1926, his real property descended to his heir, who in most cases was a single person; thus if the intestate died leaving sons, normally the eldest was the heir. But sometimes two or more persons together constituted the heir, and in this case they took the land as " parceners " or " co-parceners," the latter expression being the more common. This occurred—

(i) At common law, where the intestate's nearest relatives were two or more females; thus where a man died leaving three daughters and no sons, the three daughters took as co-parceners; and

(ii) By the custom of gavelkind, where the intestate's nearest relatives were two or more males: thus where a man died leaving several sons, they took as co-parceners.[11a]

In theory of law, co-parceners together constituted a single heir[12]: " they be but one heire, and yet severall persons." [13] They were called parceners because, as already seen, every co-parcener had a common law right to have a partition made.[14]

B. Nature of Co-Parcenary

Co-parcenary bore resemblances both to joint tenancy and tenancy in common. It resembled joint tenancy in that—

[11a] For gavelkind, see Rob.Gav. 3 *et seq.*, 112, 113.
[12] *Evans* v. *Evans* [1892] 2 Ch. 173 at 185.
[13] Co.Litt. 164a.
[14] *Ante*, p. 225.

1. The four unities were normally present. Co-parcenary could arise only by operation of law; a devise or conveyance to the heirs of a person who had, say, two daughters and no sons made those daughters joint tenants and not co-parceners.[15] As co-parcenary could thus arise only by descent on intestacy, the four unities were usually present. But this was not always the case. Thus if X died intestate leaving two daughters, and one of these subsequently died intestate leaving three granddaughters, the three granddaughters and the surviving daughter would be co-parceners (for co-parcenary could continue as long as the land continued to descend on intestacy), yet the daughter would have a half share and each granddaughter a one-sixth share, the half and the sixths having been acquired at different times and being held by different titles.

2. Co-parceners were jointly seised for some purposes. Thus a statute which applied to persons who were " seised . . . jointly " has been held to apply to co-parceners [16]; again, each co-parcener was sufficiently seised of the whole land for him to be able to transfer his interest to his fellows by release.[17]

On the other hand, co-parcenary resembled tenancy in common in that—

3. There was no jus accrescendi. The estate of a deceased co-parcener passed under his will or intestacy in the same way as the estate of a tenant in common [18]; thus it was subject to curtesy or dower.

4. Co-parceners held in undivided shares. Each co-parcener held a distinct but undivided share which might be equal or unequal in size to the shares of the others. Thus the shares might be initially equal and subsequently become unequal, as in the example above, or they might be initially unequal, *e.g.*, where a man had two daughters and one predeceased him leaving two daughters, in which case the surviving daughter would take a half and the granddaughters a quarter each. For the purpose of alienation *inter vivos* or on death, each co-parcener was solely seised of his or her share.

It will be seen that although it is possible to say that co-parcenary was intermediate in its nature between joint tenancy and tenancy in

---

[15] *Owen* v. *Gibbons* [1902] 1 Ch. 636.

[16] See *Re Greenwood's Trust* (1884) 27 Ch.D. 359 (Trustee Act 1850, s. 10).

[17] See *ante*, p. 226.

[18] *Re Matson* [1897] 2 Ch. 509.

common, the rights of the co-parceners *inter se* resembled in general those of tenants in common. Co-parcenary is best regarded as " not a joint tenancy, but a tenancy in common of a peculiar nature, having some of the incidents of a joint tenancy." [19]

C. *Determination of Co-Parcenary*

Co-parcenary might come to an end—

  (i) by partition;
  (ii) by union in a sole tenant; or
  (iii) by alienation; if a co-parcener alienated his share, it was forthwith held under a tenancy in common, the other tenants remaining co-parceners *inter se*.

Sect. 2. After 1925

A. *Transitional Provisions*

Any co-parcenaries existing at the end of 1925 were dealt with by the transitional provisions in the same way as tenancies in common,[20] for these provisions applied to all cases of undivided shares. The land thus became subject to a trust for sale and the co-parcenary existed only as an equitable interest in the proceeds of sale.

B. *Deaths after* 1925

Descent to the heir has, in general, been abolished in the case of deaths after 1925, so that co-parcenary normally cannot arise after 1925. But in two cases, real property still descends to the heir according to the general law in force before 1926:

  (i) Where the deceased was a lunatic of full age at the end of 1925 and dies intestate in respect of the land without having recovered his testamentary capacity; and
  (ii) Where the owner of an entail dies without having barred it.[21]

In neither of these cases can co-parcenary arise under the custom of gavelkind, for descent is to the heir according to the *general* law. However, in the second case and perhaps also in the first, co-parcenary in equity can still arise if two or more females or their issue are

[19] *McMurray* v. *Spicer* (1868) L.R. 5 Eq. 527 at 538, *per* Malins V.-C.
[20] *Ante,* p. 219.
[21] *Post,* p. 310.

entitled. In both cases, the land will be held on trust for sale, so that the co-parcenary, like a tenancy in common, would exist in the proceeds of sale and not in the land itself.

If co-parceners become entitled in possession to settled land, they are apparently in the same position as tenants in common, *i.e.*, the land ceases to be settled land and is thenceforward held on the statutory trusts.[22]

Part 3

TENANCY BY ENTIRETIES

Sect. 1. At Common Law

1. Creation. Before 1883, when land was limited to a husband and wife in such a way that they would have taken as joint tenants if they had not been married, they took as tenants by entireties and not as joint tenants, even if the land was expressly conveyed to them " as joint tenants." [23] Thus before 1883 a conveyance to—

" H and W "

made them tenants by entireties; and a conveyance to—

" H and W and X "

made H and W tenants by entireties *inter se* and joint tenants with X.[24] If at the time of the devise or conveyance the parties were not married, their subsequent marriage did not convert their joint tenancy into a tenancy by entireties; and if tenants by entireties were divorced, they became ordinary joint tenants.[25]

2. Nature. A tenancy by entireties could exist in any estate, whether in fee, for life, for years or otherwise. The nature of the tenancy was virtually that of an unseverable joint tenancy; neither husband nor wife could dispose of any interest in the land without the concurrence of the other, nor could one of them cause a forfeiture of the land. The unity of the husband and wife was regarded as so complete that they were said to be seised " *per tout et non per mie*," [26] the survivor being entitled to the whole of the land by force of the

---

[22] *Ante*, p. 222.
[23] *Pollok* v. *Kelly* (1856) 6 Ir.C.L.R. 367.
[24] *Back* v. *Andrew* (1690) 2 Vern. 120.
[25] *Thornley* v. *Thornley* [1893] 2 Ch. 229.
[26] Contrast *ante*, p. 209.

original limitation, discharged of the other's right to participate, and not, as in the case of joint tenancy, by virtue of survivorship on the death of the other tenant. Unlike joint tenants, neither tenant was regarded as having any potential share in the land; " between husband and wife there are no moieties." [27] Not even the rents and profits were divided; the husband was entitled to the whole of the income accruing during their joint lives.[28] " The husband and wife have not either a joint estate, a sole or several estate, nor even an estate in common. From the unity of their persons by marriage, they have the estate entirely as one individual " [29]; and, it may be added, that individual was the husband.

Sect. 2. The Married Women's Property Act 1882

This Act did not affect existing tenancies by entireties, but it prevented the creation of such tenancies after 1882; a limitation to a husband and wife after 1882 without words of severance made them ordinary joint tenants.[30]

Sect. 3. The Law of Property Act 1925

Few tenancies by entireties still existed at the end of 1925. Those that remained were, without prejudice to any beneficial interest (*e.g.,* the husband's right to the whole of the income during the joint lives), forthwith converted into joint tenancies.[31]

Part 4

PARTY WALLS

Sect. 1. Before 1926

1. Categories. Where a wall separates land owned by A from land owned by B, the wall may be either in the sole ownership of one party free from any rights of the other, or a party wall. There appears to be no precise legal definition of the term " party wall." Four possible meanings are as follows [32]:

[27] *Marquis of Winchester's Case* (1583) 3 Co.Rep. 1a at 5a.
[28] *Chamier* v. *Tyrell* [1894] 1 I.R. 267.
[29] 1 Preston, *Estates*, 131.
[30] *Thornley* v. *Thornley* [1893] 2 Ch. 229.
[31] L.P.A. 1925, 1st Sched., Pt. VI.
[32] See *Watson* v. *Gray* (1880) 14 Ch.D. 192 at 194, 195.

(a) *Tenancy in common*: the two adjoining owners are tenants in common of the wall.

(b) *Divided*: the wall is divided longitudinally into two strips, one belonging to each of the neighbouring owners.

(c) *Divided with easements*: the wall is divided as in (b), but each half is subject to an easement of support in favour of the owner of the other half.

(d) *Ownership subject to easement*: the wall belongs entirely to one of the adjoining owners, but is subject to an easement or right in the other to have it maintained as a dividing wall.

2. Presumption. The presumption was in favour of a party wall falling within the first category, at all events if evidence was given that each owner had exercised dominion over the entire wall.[33] The first category had the disadvantage that either owner could insist upon a partition, but it was less unsatisfactory than the second category, where either owner, acting with reasonable care, could remove his half of the wall and leave a structure which was perhaps incapable of standing alone.[34] Neither owner could pull down a wall of the first kind except for the purpose of rebuilding it with all reasonable dispatch,[35] nor could either prevent the other from enjoying any part of the wall, as by covering the top with broken glass or replacing it with part of a shed.[36] There was no presumption in favour of the third or fourth categories because these could be established only on proof that the appropriate easements existed.

3. Ownership of soil. The presumption in favour of the first category applied only where the exact situation of the boundary could not be shown, or where the site of the wall could be shown to have been owned in common.[37] Where the wall was built entirely on A's land, the presumption was that the wall was A's; and where the wall was built on the boundary, so that substantially half the soil on which it stood was A's and half B's, the case usually fell into the second or third category, the wall being regarded as divided into two walls each of half the thickness.[38] The principle in these cases was that " as a

[33] *Ibid.*
[34] See *Cubitt* v. *Porter* (1828) 8 B. & C. 257 at 264.
[35] *Cubitt* v. *Porter* (1828) 8 B. & C. 257.
[36] *Stedman* v. *Smith* (1857) 8 E. & B. 1 at 6, 7.
[37] See *Wiltshire* v. *Sidford* (1827) 1 Man. & Ry. 404 at 407, 409.
[38] *Murly* v. *M'Dermott* (1838) 8 A. & E. 138 at 142.

matter of law, the property in the wall followed the property in the land upon which it stood." [39] Subject to this, the ownership of the wall was a question of fact for the jury. A wall might even be in sole ownership for part of its height and a party wall for the rest.[40]

In some parts of the country, particularly London, these rules have been modified to some extent by statute.[41]

Sect. 2. After 1925

Unless special provision had been made, all party walls in the first category would have become subject to a trust for sale after 1925. It was consequently provided that after 1925 all party walls in this category should be deemed to be severed vertically, and that the owner of each part should have such rights of support and user over the rest of the wall as were requisite for giving the parties rights similar to those which they would have enjoyed had they been tenants in common of the wall.[42] The practical effect of this provision is to translate all party walls in the first category into the third. Apart from this, the law of party walls remains unchanged.

---

[39] *Jones* v. *Read* (1876) 10 Ir.R.C.L. 315 at 320, *per* Palles C.B.
[40] *Weston* v. *Arnold* (1873) 8 Ch.App. 1084.
[41] *e.g.*, the London Building Acts (Amendment) Act 1939, Pt. VI, replacing earlier statutes.
[42] L.P.A. 1925, s. 38 (2), 1st Sched., Pt. V.

CHAPTER 7

TRUSTS AND POWERS

THE nature of trusts and powers has already been briefly considered [1]; the basic distinction between them is that whereas a trust is normally imperative, binding the trustee to carry out his duty, a power is discretionary, enabling the donee of the power to exercise it if he wishes but not binding him to do so. Much of the law of trusts and powers is more appropriate to textbooks on equity than to a book on real property, but some account must be given here of the points which most concern the law of land. They will be dealt with under the heads of—

(1) Trusts.
(2) Trustees.
(3) Powers.

Part 1

TRUSTS

Sect. 1. Classification

A. Conveyancing Classification

From the point of view of a conveyancer, a trust of land may fall under one of three heads:

(1) Settled land.
(2) Trust for sale.
(3) Bare trust.

The first two have already been dealt with.[2] A bare, or simple, trust arises when a trustee or trustees hold property (whether legal or equitable) on trust for a person who is of full age and absolutely beneficially entitled, the nature of the trust not being prescribed by the settlor but being left to the construction of the law, as where **X** conveys land—

"to T in fee simple on trust for A in fee simple."

[1] *Ante*, p. 2.
[2] *Ante*, Chap. 5, p. 142.

In such a case, the position of the parties is similar to that under a simple use before 1535 [3]; T is bound to permit A to occupy the land or receive the rents and profits and must obey A's instructions about the disposition of the land. A bare trust may also arise where on a purchase of land the money is provided by one person but the conveyance is made to another; thus where P, wishing to keep his name out of the transaction, provides N with the money to buy the land, N holds on a bare trust for P.[4]

Bare trusts of land existing at the end of 1925 have ceased to exist, for by the Law of Property Act 1925, where at the end of 1925 a person was entitled to require a legal estate (not vested in trustees for sale) to be vested in him, the legal estate automatically vested in him at the beginning of 1926.[5] But there is nothing to prevent bare trusts from being created after 1925.

B. Equity's Classification

In equity, trusts may be classified as trusts imposed by statute, express, implied, resulting or constructive trusts.

1. Trusts imposed by statute. Various trusts are imposed by statute. Thus—

(i) A statutory trust for sale is imposed in the case of joint tenancies and tenancies in common.[6]

(ii) Where a person dies intestate, in certain cases his personal representatives hold his property on statutory trusts for his relatives.[7]

(iii) By virtue of the Settled Land Act 1925, an attempted conveyance of a legal estate in land to an infant operates as a contract to make a settlement upon the infant and in the meantime to hold the land on trust for him.[8]

(iv) A statutory trust for sale is created when property on the security of which trustees have lent money becomes vested in them by foreclosure, or where trustees of a personalty settlement exercise a power conferred thereby to invest money in the purchase of land.[9]

---

[3] *Ante*, p. 66.
[4] See *Dyer* v. *Dyer* (1788) 2 Cox Eq. 92 at 93 ; and *post*, p. 243.
[5] First Sched., Pt. II, paras. 3, 6 (*d*).
[6] *Ante*, p. 216.
[7] *Post*, pp. 306, 307.
[8] *Post*, p. 515.
[9] L.P.A. 1925, ss. 31, 32 ; *ante*, p. 188 ; for foreclosure, see *post*, pp. 472 *et seq.*

Both (i) and (ii) are referred to in the 1925 legislation as " the
statutory trusts." Although other trusts imposed by statute are in a
sense " statutory " trusts, they are not thus referred to, and to avoid
confusion they are perhaps better called " trusts imposed by statute."

2. Express trusts. These are trusts declared by a settlor. To
create an express trust, the " three certainties " of a trust must be
present, *i.e.,* imperative words, certainty of subject-matter, and
certainty of objects.[10]

(a) *The three certainties.*

(1) IMPERATIVE WORDS. The settlor must indicate that a trust is
intended. The old rule was that words such as " in the full confidence " or " recommending " or " my dying request " would prima
facie be construed as creating a trust; these were called precatory
words. The present law, however, is that precatory words create no
trust unless the instrument as a whole shows an intention that they
should.

Where the words are not imperative, the donee holds the property
beneficially free from any trust.

(2) CERTAINTY OF SUBJECT-MATTER. Both the property to be
vested in the trustee and the beneficial interest to be taken by each
beneficiary must be defined with sufficient certainty. If there is no
certainty as to what is conveyed to the trustee, the entire transaction
is ineffective, *e.g.,* if a testator purports to leave " some of my
property " to trustees. Examples of uncertainty of beneficial interest
occur where defined property is given to X on trust that he should
leave to A and B " the bulk " of it or " such parts of my estate as he
shall not have sold or disposed of." In such cases the donee holds
the property beneficially free from any trust, unless it is clear that the
whole of the property was intended to be held on trust and the only
uncertainty is which part was intended for each beneficiary, when the
donee will hold on a resulting trust for the settlor.

(3) CERTAINTY OF OBJECTS. The objects (*i.e.,* the persons or
purposes intended to benefit by the trust) must be defined with sufficient certainty. Trusts for " encouraging undertakings of general
utility " or " acts of hospitality or charity " are void for uncertainty
of object. If, however, the objects selected are exclusively charitable,
the trusts will not fail merely because the particular mode in which

[10] See, generally, *Snell*, 122 *et seq.*

the trusts are to be carried out is left uncertain; the Crown in some cases and the court in others will direct a suitable mode of application.

If there is uncertainty of objects, there is a resulting trust for the settlor.

(b) *Completely and incompletely constituted trusts.* Express trusts may be either executed or executory; this classification has already been considered [11] and must not be confused with the division of trusts into completely constituted trusts and incompletely constituted trusts. A trust is completely constituted as soon as the trust property is vested in the trustee; until this has been done, it is incompletely constituted. All trusts created by will are completely constituted, but they may be either executed or executory; a bequest of £10,000 to A and B on trust to buy land with it, and settle the land on C and his children, is executory but nevertheless completely constituted.

A trust may be completely constituted in either of two ways [12]—

(1) VESTING IN TRUSTEES: by the trust property being effectually vested in the trustees upon the requisite trusts.[13]

(2) DECLARATION OF TRUST: by "a present irrevocable declaration of trust" being made by the settlor.[14] It is not essential that the settlor should use the words "I declare myself a trustee," but he must do something equivalent to this. Thus where a merchant in Canton wrote to his London agents directing them to set aside £1,000 to be employed for the benefit of his children, and by a later letter declared that he considered himself as having no further control over it, he was held to have declared himself a trustee.[15] But although words of direct gift have occasionally been construed as declarations of trust,[16] it is now generally regarded as settled that an imperfect attempt to transfer property to a volunteer (a person giving no valuable consideration) or to trustees for a volunteer will not be construed as a declaration of trust.[17] Nor will the court compel the settlor to perfect his attempted transfer at the suit of a volunteer, for "there is no equity in this court to perfect an imperfect gift."[18] Thus if A owns

---

[11] *Ante,* p. 215.

[12] *Milroy* v. *Lord* (1862) 4 De G.F. & J. 264 at 274.

[13] See *Richards* v. *Delbridge* (1874) L.R. 18 Eq. 11.

[14] See *Re Cozens* [1913] 2 Ch. 478 at 486.

[15] *Vandenberg* v. *Palmer* (1858) 4 K. & J. 204.

[16] See, *e.g., Morgan* v. *Malleson* (1870) L.R. 10 Eq. 475.

[17] *Jefferys* v. *Jefferys* (1841) Cr. & Ph. 138 : *Jones* v. *Lock* (1865) 1 Ch.App. 25 ; but for a statutory exception, see *post,* p. 515 ; see also *ante,* p. 157.

[18] *Milroy* v. *Lord* (1862) 4 De G.F. & J. 264 at 274, *per* Turner L.J.

leasehold property and, wishing to give it to E, indorses on the lease " This deed and all thereto belonging I give to E from this time forth," neither this indorsement nor the delivery of the lease to E's mother on his behalf (E being an infant) will give E any beneficial interest in the lease; the legal term of years has not been vested in E or his mother, for a deed is required to do this,[19] and A's words of gift will not be construed as a declaration of trust.[20]

It must not be thought that no trust will be enforced in favour of a volunteer. The importance of the distinction between a completely and incompletely constituted trust lies in the fact that if a trust is completely constituted, it can be enforced by the beneficiaries even if they are volunteers,[21] whereas if the trust is incompletely constituted, it will be enforced at the suit of beneficiaries who gave valuable consideration [22] but cannot be enforced by volunteers.[23]

(c) *Formalities.* The formalities required for the creation of a trust will be considered shortly [24]; for the present, it suffices to say that a trust of land must be evidenced by writing but that a trust of pure personalty is enforceable even if merely declared orally.

3. Implied trusts. An implied trust is said to arise where, without any conveyance of the property in question having been made, two people enter into such a relationship with each other that equity implies therefrom that one holds on trust for the other. Thus if one person agrees for value to make a settlement or conveyance of his estate, equity forthwith deems him to be a trustee of that estate for the beneficiaries or the purchaser. In the case of a contract of sale, the trust is of a peculiar nature, for the vendor has certain valuable rights against the purchaser, such as an equitable lien for the price.[25] Nevertheless, the trust relationship is established, for it will be a breach of trust for the vendor to convey the land to anyone except the purchaser or negligently to allow the land to be damaged.[26] Another case of an implied trust arises where two people agree to leave their property in the same way (*e.g.,* to the survivor for life, with remainder

[19] *Post,* p. 353.
[20] *Richards* v. *Delbridge* (1874) L.R. 18 Eq. 11.
[21] *Paul* v. *Paul* (1882) 20 Ch.D. 742.
[22] *Pullan* v. *Koe* [1913] 1 Ch. 9.
[23] *Re Plumptre's Marriage Settlement* [1910] 1 Ch. 609.
[24] *Post,* p. 244.
[25] *Mackreth* v. *Symmons* (1808) 15 Ves. 329.
[26] *Clarke* v. *Ramuz* [1891] 2 Q.B. 456.

to X) and make wills in pursuance thereof. In such a case, on the death of one of them, the property then owned by the survivor is forthwith impressed with an implied trust for X.[27]

4. Constructive trusts. These are trusts arising by operation of equity from a fiduciary relationship already in existence. Thus if by virtue of his position a person in a fiduciary position obtains any valuable interest in property for himself, the general rule is that he holds it on a constructive trust for the beneficiaries, as where a trustee of a lease obtains a renewal for his own benefit,[28] or a tenant for life accepts a bribe not to oppose the passage of an Act of Parliament authorising the construction of a railway over the settled land.[29] Again, anyone who receives or deals with trust property knowingly in breach of trust is liable as a constructive trustee.[30]

5. Resulting trusts. A resulting trust is said to exist where, on a conveyance of property, a trust arises by operation of equity. Three cases must be considered.

(a) *Trusts not exhaustive.* Where a disposition of property is made by the owner and all or part of the equitable interest is not effectively disposed of, there is a resulting trust for the owner. If the property is conveyed expressly on trust, *e.g.,*

" to X on trust,"

there is no difficulty; a trustee can take no benefit from the fact that the declared trusts do not exhaust the beneficial interest, and so much of the equitable interest as is not disposed of results to the grantor. Thus if G conveys property to X on trust for a beneficiary who is dead, there is a resulting trust of the entire beneficial interest in favour of G.[31] Again, where before 1926 G conveyed land to trustees on trust for herself for life and then on trust for her heir-at-law, without words of limitation, the heir took only a life estate and there was a resulting trust in fee simple in favour of G.[32] In every case, however, the rule that there is a resulting trust yields to a contrary intention showing that the trustee was intended to take beneficially.

---

[27] *Dufour* v. *Pereira* (1769) 1 Dick. 419.
[28] *Keech* v. *Sandford* (1726) Sel.Ca.t.King 61.
[29] *Pole* v. *Pole* (1865) 2 Dr. & Sm. 420.
[30] See *Snell*, 202–204.
[31] *Re Tilt* (1896) 74 L.T. 163.
[32] *Re Davison's Settlement* [1913] 2 Ch. 498.

(b) *Voluntary conveyance*. Where the property is not conveyed expressly on trust, the matter is more difficult. On this point, resulting trusts must be compared with resulting uses. Before 1926 a resulting use carried back a legal estate to the grantor, whereas a resulting trust carries back a mere equitable interest. It was settled law that if G conveyed land to X in fee simple without any consideration, good or valuable,[33] and without expressing any uses, there was a resulting use to G in fee simple which was executed by the Statute of Uses 1535.[34] Such a conveyance was thus totally ineffective and G was treated as if he held the same legal estate as before.[35] To prevent this result, an express use in X's favour (*e.g.*, " unto and to the use of X and his heirs ") or a nominal consideration was inserted.

Whether or not this doctrine applied to resulting trusts was never settled. By analogy, a voluntary conveyance before 1926 by G " unto and to the use of X and his heirs " should have given X a mere legal estate with a resulting trust of the fee simple to G, unless an intention to benefit X could be shown. The better opinion was that this was indeed the case, but some disputed this conclusion. However, any presumption of a resulting trust was rebutted if X was the wife or child of G, for the good consideration raised a presumption of advancement[36]; and in any case evidence could be given to show that X was intended to take beneficially unless this would contradict the provisions of the conveyance. A nominal consideration did not prevent a resulting trust, however,[37] and to avoid doubts as to the effectiveness of a voluntary conveyance to a stranger, not only had the conveyance to be made " unto and to the use of X and his heirs," but also words had to be added to show that X was intended to hold the land for his own benefit.

By the Law of Property Act 1925, in a voluntary conveyance executed after 1925 no resulting trust for the grantor is to be implied merely by reason that the property is not expressed to be conveyed for the use or benefit of the grantee.[38] In the absence of such a provision the failure to express a use would have meant that the doctrine of resulting uses would have carried back to the grantor an interest which, owing to the repeal of the Statute of Uses 1535, would have

[33] See *ante*, pp. 59, 60.
[34] See *ante*, p. 67.
[35] *Beckwith's Case* (1589) 2 Co.Rep. 56b at 58a.
[36] See *Lord Grey* v. *Lady Grey* (1677) 2 Swans. 594 at 598; *post*, p. 243.
[37] See *Sculthorp* v. *Burgess* (1790) 1 Ves.Jun. 91 at 92.
[38] s. 60 (3), (4).

been equitable instead of legal. But although the Act deals with the difficulty raised by the doctrine of resulting uses, it perhaps fails to meet the possibility that the grantor may obtain an equitable interest under the doctrine of resulting trusts. Thus, although a voluntary conveyance need no longer be worded " unto and to the use of X and his heirs " to avoid a resulting use, but may be worded " to X in fee simple," words should still be added to show that no resulting trust is intended, such as " free from any resulting trust in favour of the grantor."

No resulting trust is presumed where there is a presumption of advancement. If X is the wife or child of the grantor, or the grantor is *in loco parentis* to him (*e.g.*, by having adopted him), the grantor is presumed to have intended X to take beneficially, though this presumption is rebuttable by evidence of a contrary intention.[39] Other relationships, such as the grantor being the wife, mother, step-mother or aunt of X, raise no presumption of advancement.[40]

(c) *Purchase in the name of another.* Where a conveyance is made to one person, but the purchase-money is provided by another as purchaser, there is a resulting trust in favour of the person providing the purchase-money. If V conveys land to P, A being the real purchaser and as such providing the purchase-money, prima facie P holds on a resulting trust for A.[41] Nevertheless, this is only a presumption which can be rebutted either—

(i) by evidence that P was intended to benefit,[42] or

(ii) by the presumption of advancement.

CLASSIFICATION OF TRUSTS

The above equitable classification of trusts must not be taken as settled. Some authorities include statutory trusts under the head of express trusts, and treat " constructive trusts " as a term including all except express trusts. In practice, the category into which a trust falls is often of little importance; except for the distinction between express trusts and other trusts,[43] the division is primarily one of convenience for textbook writers.

---

[39] See, generally, *Snell*, 192.
[40] Contrast *post*, p. 307.
[41] See *Dyer* v. *Dyer* (1788) 2 Cox Eq. 92 at 93.
[42] *Fowkes* v. *Pascoe* (1875) 10 Ch.App. 343.
[43] See *post*, pp. 244, 245.

Sect. 2. Formalities Required for the Creation of a Trust

A. Pure Personalty

An enforceable trust of pure personalty can be validly created by word of mouth, whether the owner is declaring himself a trustee of the property or is transferring it to a third party on trust for the beneficiaries.[44]

B. Land

1. Evidenced by writing. Before 1677, a trust of land could be created by word of mouth, but thereafter the Statute of Frauds 1677 [45] and now the Law of Property Act 1925 [46] provided that a declaration of trust respecting any land or any interest therein must be evidenced either by writing signed by some person able to declare the trust, or else by his will. The chief points to note on this provision are as follows:

(a) " *Any land.*" This includes leaseholds, and included copyholds before they were abolished.

(b) " *Evidenced.*" The actual words in both statutes are " manifested and proved." It is settled that this does not require that the declaration should actually be made in writing, but that it suffices if an oral declaration is supported by some signed acknowledgment or declaration in existence when the action is begun, such as a letter,[47] or a recital in a deed, even if this is made some time after the trust is declared.[48] The writing must show not only that there is a trust but also what its terms are.[49]

(c) " *Some person able to declare the trust.*" This means the owner of the beneficial interest, so that if a trust is declared of an equitable interest held under an existing trust, the writing must be signed by the beneficiary, the signature of the trustees not being sufficient.[50]

2. Exceptions. To these requirements, there are two important exceptions:

---

[44] See *M'Fadden* v. *Jenkyns* (1842) 1 Ph. 153.
[45] ss. 7, 8.
[46] s. 53 (1) (*b*).
[47] *Childers* v. *Childers* (1857) 1 De G. & J. 482.
[48] *Rochefoucauld* v. *Boustead* [1897] 1 Ch. 196 at 206.
[49] *Smith* v. *Matthews* (1861) 3 De G.F. & J. 139; and see *post*, pp. 320, 321.
[50] *Kronheim* v. *Johnson* (1877) 7 Ch.D. 60.

(a) *Resulting, implied or constructive trusts.* They do not affect the creation or operation of resulting, implied or constructive trusts.[51]

(b) *Fraud.* The court will not permit them to be used as an engine of fraud. " It is a fraud on the part of a person to whom land is conveyed as a trustee, and who knows it was so conveyed, to deny the trust and claim the land himself. Consequently, notwithstanding the statute, it is competent for a person claiming land conveyed to another to prove by parol evidence that it was so conveyed upon trust for the claimant, and that the grantee, knowing the facts, is denying the trust and relying upon the form of conveyance and the statute, in order to keep the land himself." [52]

It is on this principle that secret trusts are enforced.[53] If a testator informs X of his intention to leave property to X to be held on trust for Y, and X acquiesces, whether expressly or by silence, this trust will be enforced even though it is not contained in the will or evidenced by writing. This applies whether the will discloses that the property is held upon trust without disclosing the beneficiary [54] (*e.g.,* " to X upon trusts which I have already communicated to him ") or whether the gift is apparently beneficial (*e.g.,* " to X absolutely " [55]). However, in the latter case it suffices if the trusts are communicated at any time before the testator's death,[56] whereas in the former case there is some rather unsatisfactory authority for saying that unless the trusts have been declared to and agreed by X before or at the time of making the will, and the will shows this to be the case, there will be a resulting trust to the settlor.[57]

Sect. 3. Formalities Required for the Transfer of an Interest Under a Trust

By the Law of Property Act 1925,[58] a disposition [59] of an existing equitable interest or trust must either be in writing signed by the person disposing of it or his agent authorised in writing, or else be made by will. On this, the following points should be noted.

[51] L.P.A. 1925, s. 53 (2), replacing Statute of Frauds 1677, s. 8.
[52] *Rochefoucauld* v. *Boustead* [1897] 1 Ch. 196 at 206, *per* Lindley L.J.
[53] See *McCormick* v. *Grogan* (1869) L.R. 4 H.L. 82 at 88.
[54] *Blackwell* v. *Blackwell* [1929] A.C. 318.
[55] *Re Boyes* (1884) 26 Ch.D. 531.
[56] *Moss* v. *Cooper* (1861) 1 J. & H. 352.
[57] *Re Keen* [1937] Ch. 236; see, generally, *Snell,* 117–122.
[58] s. 53 (1) (*c*), replacing Statute of Frauds 1677, s. 9.
[59] See *Grey* v. *I.R.C.* [1960] A.C. 1 (oral direction); *Oughtred* v. *I.R.C.* [1960] A.C. 206 (oral agreement).

(a) "*In writing.*" A parol assignment supported by evidence thereof in writing is not enough. Unlike the rule for the creation of trusts, the rule here requires the assignment itself to be written, and is thus not a mere rule of evidence.

(b) "*Signed by the person disposing of it or his agent authorised in writing.*" This should be contrasted with—

(i) the rule for the creation of a trust of land, where the signature of an agent is not enough [60]; and

(ii) the rule for contracts for the disposition of land, where the signature of an agent suffices even if his authority was given only by word of mouth.[61]

(c) *Pure personalty.* The rule applies to pure personalty as well as land. Although a trust of pure personalty is enforceable even if it is not evidenced in writing, once the trust has been created, a disposition of any interest under it is void unless it is in writing.

Part 2

TRUSTEES

Sect. 1. Appointment of Trustees

A. Original Appointment

1. Appointment. Trustees are usually appointed by the settlor when creating the trust. If he neither makes an appointment nor makes any provision for one, the court may appoint trustees; once the trust has been created, the settlor has no power of making an appointment unless he has reserved such a power. A person appointed trustee need not accept the trust even if he had agreed to do so before it was created, provided he disclaims the trust before he has accepted it either expressly or by acting as trustee.[62] A disclaimer should preferably be express but it may be inferred from conduct [63]; and although the presumption is in favour of acceptance, a person appointed a trustee who maintains a complete inactivity in relation

---

[60] *Ante,* p. 244.
[61] *Post,* p. 323.
[62] See *Noble* v. *Meymott* (1851) 14 Beav. 471.
[63] *Re Birchall* (1889) 40 Ch.D. 436.

to the trust for a long period may be held thereby to have disclaimed the trust.[64] Disclaimer retrospectively divests the person appointed both of his office and of the trust property.[65]

2. Maximum number. Not more than four trustees of settled land or land held on trust for sale can be appointed if the settlement or trust for sale is created after 1925. If more than four are named as trustees, the first four who are able and willing to act become trustees to the exclusion of the others.[66] Where, at the beginning of 1926, there were more than four trustees of settled land or land held on trust for sale, all the trustees continue to act but no new trustees can be appointed until the number has dropped below four.[67] These provisions apply only to land, and in general there is no limit to the number of trustees of pure personalty.

3. Minimum number. There is no minimum number of trustees even in the case of land. But in the case of settled land or land held on trust for sale, notwithstanding any contrary provision, a sole trustee cannot give a valid receipt for capital money unless that trustee is a trust corporation.[68] This restriction, however, does not affect the right of a sole personal representative acting as such to give valid receipts for purchase-money,[69] *e.g.*, where a sole administrator sells under the trust for sale which is imposed on all the property of an intestate.[70]

B. Replacement

1. The power. Even if there are properly appointed trustees when the trust is created, it may later become necessary to appoint new trustees, *e.g.*, owing to the death of trustees. The events upon which new trustees can be appointed may be specified in the trust instrument; this is not usual, however, and reliance is normally placed on the statutory provisions, which apply notwithstanding any such express provision [71] unless a contrary intention is shown.[72] By the

---

[64] *Re Clout and Frewer's Contract* [1924] 2 Ch. 230 (29 years' inactivity).
[65] *Re Martinez' Trusts* (1870) 22 L.T. 403.
[66] T.A. 1925, s. 34 (2).
[67] T.A. 1925, s. 34 (1).
[68] S.L.A. 1925, s. 18 (1); L.P.A. 1925, s. 27 (2); see *ante*, pp. 194, 195.
[69] L.P.A. 1925, s. 27 (2).
[70] *Post*, p. 302.
[71] See *Re Wheeler and De Rochow* [1896] 1 Ch. 315.
[72] T.A. 1925, s. 69 (2).

Trustee Act 1925,[73] a new trustee or trustees may be appointed if a trustee—

(1) is dead, or
(2) remains outside the United Kingdom for a continuous period exceeding twelve months, or
(3) desires to be discharged from all or any of his trusts or powers, or
(4) refuses to act, or
(5) is unfit to act, or
(6) is incapable of acting, or
(7) is an infant, or
(8) is removed under a power in the trust instrument.

2. Mode of appointment. The appointment must be in writing and must be made [74]—

(1) by the person or persons nominated by the trust instrument for the purpose of appointing new trustees; in default of there being any such person able and willing to act,
(2) by the remaining trustees; in default,
(3) by the personal representatives of the last remaining trustee; in default,
(4) by the court.

3. Who may be appointed. It is expressly provided that the person making the appointment may appoint himself.[75] Even if he appoints a person whom the court would not normally appoint, such as a beneficiary, or the husband of a beneficiary, or the solicitor to the trustees or beneficiaries, the appointment will not thereby be rendered invalid [76]; but an appointment of an infant as trustee, whether of realty or personalty, is void.[77] Where a single trustee was originally appointed, the appointment of a single trustee in his place is valid,[78] except that in the case of settled land or land held on trust for sale, a sole trustee (not being a trust corporation) cannot be appointed under the statutory power if, after his appointment, he would be

---

[73] s. 36 (1), replacing earlier provisions.
[74] T.A. 1925, s. 41, replacing earlier provisions.
[75] T.A. 1925, s. 36 (1).
[76] *Re Earl of Stamford* [1896] 1 Ch. 288.
[77] L.P.A. 1925, s. 20.
[78] T.A. 1925, s. 37 (1) (c), replacing earlier provisions.

unable to give receipts for capital money,[79] as would be the case if there were no other trustee. There is never any obligation to appoint more than two trustees even if originally more than two were appointed.[80] The appointment may increase the number of trustees, provided that in the case of settled land or land held on trust for sale, the number is not increased above four.[81]

C. *Additional Trustees*

Even though no occasion has arisen for the appointment of new trustees, if there are not more than three trustees and none of them is a trust corporation, one or more additional trustees may be appointed, provided the effect of the appointment is not to increase the number above four. The appointment must be made by the same persons and in the same way as an appointment of new trustees, except that there is no provision for an appointment by the personal representatives of the last remaining trustee, or for the appointor to appoint himself.[82]

Sect. 2. Retirement and Removal of Trustees

1. Retirement. A trustee may retire—

(i) If another trustee is appointed in his place; this has already been considered.[83]

(ii) If no new trustee is being appointed in his place, provided that after his discharge there will be left either two or more individuals or a trust corporation to act in the trust. The retirement is effected by a deed declaring the trustee's desire to retire; this is executed by the retiring trustee, the continuing trustees and the person entitled to appoint new trustees, all of whom must concur in the retirement.[84]

(iii) If authorised to do so by an express power in the trust instrument.

(iv) With the consent of all the beneficiaries if they are all *sui juris* and between them absolutely entitled to the trust property.

[79] *Ibid.* s. 37 (2).
[80] *Ibid.* s. 37 (1) (*c*), replacing earlier provisions.
[81] *Ibid.* s. 34 (2).
[82] *Ibid.* s. 36 (6); *Re Power's S.T.* [1951] Ch. 1074.
[83] *Ante*, p. 248.
[84] T.A. 1925, s. 39 (1), replacing earlier provisions.

   (v) With the leave of the court; this method should be employed only in cases of difficulty, for if the trustee applies to the court without good cause he may have to pay his own costs.[85]

2. Removal. A trustee may be removed—

  (i) Under the power to appoint new trustees considered above.[86]

 (ii) Under any express power to do so contained in the trust instrument.

(iii) Under the court's inherent jurisdiction to remove a trustee where it is necessary for the safety of the trust property or the welfare of the beneficiaries,[87] as where the trustee has been inactive for a long while, or his interests conflict with those of the beneficiaries, or there has been friction with the beneficiaries on the mode of administering the trust.[88]

Sect. 3. Vesting of Trust Property

Some trustees have no property vested in them, as is often the case with trustees of settled land; in such cases, no question of the devolution of trust property arises. But where property is vested in trustees, questions of the transfer of the trust property arise on their death, retirement or removal, or on the appointment of new trustees.

A. On Death

Trustees are always made joint tenants or joint owners of the trust property, whether it is real or personal. The advantage of this is that on the death of one trustee the estate or interest vested in him passes to the surviving trustees by the doctrine of survivorship.[89] Before 1882, however, if a sole surviving trustee died, any realty which he held on trust passed under his will or intestacy in the same way as the property which he owned beneficially, except that it was still subject to the trust. This inconvenience was removed by the Conveyancing Act 1881,[90] which provided that in the case of deaths after 1881, the estate or interest held on trust should vest in the personal representatives of the deceased trustee notwithstanding any

---

[85] *Porter* v. *Watts* (1852) 21 L.J.Ch. 211.
[86] *Ante*, p. 247.
[87] *Re Wrightson* [1908] 1 Ch. 789 at 803.
[88] *Letterstedt* v. *Broers* (1884) 9 App.Cas. 371.
[89] *Ante*, p. 208.
[90] s. 30, now replaced by A.E.A. 1925, s. 1.

provision in his will. Until new trustees are appointed, the personal representatives may exercise any power or trust exercisable by the former trustee, without being obliged to do so.[91]

B. *On Appointment of New Trustees*

1. Vesting declaration. On an appointment of new trustees, the trust property has to be vested in the new trustees jointly with any continuing trustees. Formerly, a formal conveyance of the trust property by the persons in whom it was vested was necessary; if A and B were trustees and C was appointed a new trustee on A's death, B had to convey the trust property to himself and C jointly.[92] But by section 40 of the Trustee Act 1925,[93] if an appointment of new trustees is made by deed, a declaration therein by the appointor that the property shall vest in the trustees (a " vesting declaration ") is sufficient to vest the property in them. This applies to all deeds executed after 1881 [94]; and if the deed is executed after 1925, a vesting declaration is implied in the absence of an express provision to the contrary.[95]

These provisions apply even if the trust property is not vested in the appointor. He has a statutory power to transfer what he has not got. Thus where A and B are the trustees and X has the power to appoint new trustees, if A dies and X appoints C a trustee in his place, the deed of appointment will vest the trust property in B and C jointly.

2. Exceptions. In certain cases the trust property cannot be transferred by a vesting declaration, either express or implied. These cases are when the property consists of—

(1) (before 1926) legal estates in copyholds [96];

(2) land which the trustees hold by way of mortgage for securing trust money;

(3) land held under a lease with a provision against assigning or disposing of the land without consent, unless—

    (i) the requisite consent has first been obtained, or

[91] T.A. 1925, s. 18 (2).
[92] See M. & W. 168.
[93] Replacing earlier provisions.
[94] T.A. 1925, s. 40 (6).
[95] *Ibid.* s. 40 (1).
[96] T.A. 1893, s. 12 (3), replacing C.A. 1881, s. 34 (3).

> (ii) the vesting declaration would not be a breach of cov-
> enant or give rise to a forfeiture;

(4) any share, stock or other property which is transferable only in
books kept by a company or other body, or in a way directed
by statute.[97]

In these excepted cases the trust property must be transferred by the
method appropriate to the subject-matter, *e.g.*, in the case of shares, by
a duly registered transfer. The reasons for (1) and (4) are apparent
when the normal mode of transfer of such property is considered;
(2) is included to avoid bringing the trusts on to the title, for otherwise
when the borrower sought to repay the loan, he would have to investigate the trust documents to see that he was paying the right persons;
and (3) is included to avoid accidental breaches of the terms of the
lease.

3. Vesting orders. The court has a wide jurisdiction to make
vesting orders where this is desirable.[98]

C. On Retirement or Removal

Where a trustee retires or is discharged from a trust without a new
trustee being appointed, and the transaction is effected by deed, the
trust property can be divested from the former trustee and vested
solely in the continuing trustees by means of a vesting declaration.
This applies only if the deed is executed by the retiring trustee, the
continuing trustees and any person with power to appoint new
trustees; if the deed is executed after 1925, a vesting declaration is
implied.[99] There are the same exceptions as in the case of vesting
declarations on the appointment of new trustees. This special provision is necessary since the *jus accrescendi* operates only on death
and not on retirement.

Sect. 4. Procedure in the Case of Settled Land and Trusts for Sale

1. One document. Although it is undesirable, a trust for sale may
be created by only one instrument. In this case, when a new trustee
is appointed, the appointment may be made by a single document.
This may be merely in writing, but it should be by deed so that the

---

[97] T.A. 1925, s. 40 (4), replacing earlier provisions.
[98] T.A. 1925, ss. 44–56.
[99] *Ibid.* s. 40 (2), replacing earlier provisions.

legal estate may be vested in the new and continuing trustees by virtue of section 40 of the Trustee Act 1925,[1] thus avoiding the necessity of a separate conveyance. In addition, a memorandum must be indorsed on or annexed to the instrument creating the trust for sale, stating the names of those who are the trustees after the appointment is made,[2] and not merely the names of the new trustees.

2. Two documents. Normally, however, a trust for sale is created by two documents. In this case, and in the case of settled land, the procedure is more complicated. There must be [3]—

    (i) An instrument to go with the conveyance on trust for sale or the vesting instrument.

    (ii) An appointment to go with the trust instrument.

    (iii) An indorsement on the conveyance on trust for sale or on the vesting instrument stating the names of those who are the trustees after the appointment.

In the case of settled land, the first document must be a deed; it merely states who are now the trustees. In the case of a trust for sale, it may be merely in writing, but, as above, should be by deed in order to take advantage of section 40 of the Trustee Act 1925; in either case it effects the actual appointment of the persons named in it as trustees for sale. A similar procedure applies if a trustee of settled land is discharged without a new trustee being appointed. The second document, both for settled land and trusts for sale, is an appointment which may be either in writing or by deed.[4]

Part 3

POWERS

The word " power " is normally used in the sense of an authority given to a person to dispose of property which is not his. The person giving the power is called the donor and the person to whom it is given the donee.

---

[1] *Ante*, p. 251.

[2] T.A. 1925, s. 35 (3).

[3] *Ibid.* s. 35 ; S.L.A. 1925, s. 35 (1).

[4] T.A. 1925, s. 35 ; S.L.A. 1925, s. 35 ; see *ante*, p. 251.

Sect. 1. Classification

One classification of powers is the following [5]:

(i) Powers simply collateral, *i.e.*, those where the donee has no interest in the property subject to the power.

(ii) Powers in gross, where the donee has some interest in the property but the exercise of the power cannot affect that interest, *e.g.*, where property is given to X for life with power to appoint after his death.

(iii) Powers appendant or appurtenant, where the donee has some interest in the property and the exercise of the power can affect that interest.

This classification has little significance today, and a more useful classification is the following.

1. Common law powers. Before power to devise legal estates in land was given by the Statute of Wills 1540, customs existed in some boroughs enabling land to be devised. In such cases it was possible for a testator to give his executors power to sell the land without devising it to them. Such a power was a common law power, for by virtue of the common law, a legal estate could be conveyed by a person in whom it was not vested.[6] Powers of attorney, under which one person authorises another to do certain acts on his behalf, such as to convey land, are much more important examples of common law powers.

2. Powers operating under the Statute of Uses 1535. If land was given—

" to A and his heirs to such uses as B shall appoint,"

upon B making an appointment in favour of X, the legal estate vested in X forthwith; until this happened, there was a resulting use to the grantor.[7] This applied only between 1535 and 1926.

3. Statutory powers. A number of statutes have given powers to convey legal estates. For example, the Settled Land Act 1882

---

[5] See *Re D'Angibau* (1880) 15 Ch.D. 228 at 232, 233.
[6] See 3 H.E.L. 136, 137, 153, 271.
[7] *Ante*, p. 242.

authorised a tenant for life to convey a legal estate not vested in him,[8] and the Law of Property Act 1925 gives a mortgagee a similar power.[9]

4. Equitable powers. Unlike the powers mentioned above, equitable powers enable the donee to transfer only an equitable interest. For example, a conveyance in 1920—

"unto and to the use of X and his heirs in trust for Y for life, with remainder on such trusts as Z shall appoint"

gave Z an equitable power.[10]

The 1925 legislation has increased the number of equitable powers. The Law of Property Act 1925[11] provides that "every power of appointment over, or power to convey or charge land or any interest therein, whether created by a statute or other instrument or implied by law, and whether created before or after the commencement of this Act, . . . operates only in equity." This, however, must be read subject to some qualification, for various legal powers still exist. Thus—

(i) a legal mortgagee, on exercising his power of sale, has power to convey a legal estate vested in the mortgagor[12];

(ii) a power of attorney may still enable one person to convey a legal estate vested in another[13]; and

(iii) Settled Land Act trustees may sometimes, in the name of the tenant for life and on his behalf, convey the legal estate vested in him.[14]

Apart from cases such as these, a legal estate can today be conveyed only by the person in whom it is vested. A conveyance of a legal estate by a tenant for life is no longer a conveyance under a statutory power enabling him to convey what was not vested in him, but a conveyance by the estate owner. This, and the abolition of legal powers operating under the Statute of Uses 1535, makes it possible to say that by the 1925 legislation "the basis of conveyancing was shifted from powers to estates."[15]

[8] *Ante*, p. 149.
[9] *Post*, pp. 474 *et seq.*
[10] See *ante*, pp. 67, 206.
[11] s. 1 (7).
[12] *Post*, pp. 474 *et seq.*
[13] See L.P.A. 1925, ss. 1 (7), 7 (4).
[14] *Ante*, pp. 177, 180; see also *ante*, p. 251.
[15] 1 Prideaux (24th ed. 1948) 5.

Sect. 2. Powers of appointment

A. Introductory

Statutory powers are more conveniently considered under their appropriate heads, but powers of appointment, which are powers given under some settlement or trust authorising the donee to make an appointment of some or all of the trust property, must be discussed here.

1. General or special. Powers of appointment are traditionally classified as either general or special. A general power imposes no restrictions upon the donee's choice, allowing him to appoint to anyone, including himself. Thus a gift—

" to X for life, remainder as he shall appoint "
gives X a life interest and a general power of appointment. A special power fetters the donee's choice by providing that he can appoint the property only among a limited class of persons, known as the " objects " of the power, as where A is given a power to appoint among his issue. Powers to appoint to anyone except a named person or group of persons are perhaps best regarded as forming a third category,[16] sometimes called " hybrid powers." [17] However, if the dichotomy of general and special powers is adopted, such a power may be classified as special for the purposes of section 27 of the Wills Act 1837,[18] and general for the rule against perpetuities [19]; but as soon as the excluded person or persons are all dead or cannot come into existence, the power becomes general.[20]

2. Default of appointment. Most powers are followed by a provision for some person or persons to take in default of appointment; if this is omitted, the grantor is entitled in default of appointment. The effect of an appointment is to divest the interest of those entitled in default of appointment to the extent of the appointment.

B. Defective Exercise of Powers

The general rule is that any condition prescribed for the execution of a power must be observed, otherwise the appointment will be void.

---

[16] See *Re Jones* [1945] Ch. 105.
[17] See *Re Triffitt's Settlement* [1958] Ch. 852 ; J. G. Fleming (1948) 13 Conv.(N.S.) 20.
[18] *Post*, pp. 285, 286.
[19] *Ante*, p. 124.
[20] *Re Harvey* [1950] 1 All E.R. 491.

It is immaterial how absurd or unreasonable the conditions are.[21] However, this position has been modified by statute and by equity.

1. Formalities.

(a) *Wills.* By the Wills Act 1837,[22] an appointment by will is valid, so far as concerns execution and attestation, if it is executed with the formalities required for wills (*i.e.*, signed by the testator in the presence of two witnesses who then sign their names [23]), even if the instrument creating the power requires other formalities, such as ten witnesses.

(b) *Deeds.* By the Law of Property Act 1925,[24] an appointment by deed is valid as regards execution and attestation if it is signed in the presence of, and attested by, two witnesses, even if the instrument creating the power requires other formalities.

Deeds and wills are thus on a similar footing in this respect. But it must be noticed that these provisions apply only to formalities concerning execution and attestation, such as a requirement that the document should be executed in a certain place in the presence of three witnesses.[25]

2. Relief in equity.

There is nothing in the statutory provisions to make it unnecessary to comply with other requirements (*e.g.*, as to obtaining the consent of specified persons), and an appointment not made in accordance with such requirements is void.[26] However, in a limited class of case, equity will intervene and treat the defective appointment as valid. This will be done only if both the following conditions are satified:

(a) *Defect formal.* The defect must be merely formal and not one of substance. Thus, if under a power to appoint by deed the donee appoints by will, equity will grant relief.[27] But if there is a power exercisable only by will, equity will not aid an appointment by deed,[28] for the power was not intended to be exercised until the donee's death,

---

[21] *Rutland* v. *Doe* d. *Wythe* (1843) 10 Cl. & F. 419 at 425.
[22] s. 10.
[23] *Post*, pp. 267 *et seq.*
[24] s. 159, replacing earlier provisions.
[25] See *Hawkins* v. *Kemp* (1803) 3 East 410.
[26] See, *e.g.*, *Cooper* v. *Martin* (1867) 3 Ch.App. 47.
[27] *Tollet* v. *Tollet* (1728) 2 P.Wms. 489 ; contrast *Re Hambro's Marriage Settlements* [1949] Ch. 484.
[28] *Reid* v. *Shergold* (1805) 10 Ves. 370.

and the donee was meant to be free to modify the appointment until then.

(b) *Deserving appointee.* The relief must be sought by a purchaser, creditor or charity, or the wife or legitimate child of the donee of the power.

It should be noted that although equity gives relief against the defective exercise of the power in these cases, it never gives relief against failure to exercise the power at all.[29]

C. *Excessive Execution*

An appointment which exceeds the limits set to the power, either expressly or by law, is said to be an excessive execution of the power. This may be illustrated by an appointment which infringes the rule against perpetuities or attaches an unauthorised condition to the interest appointed, or by an appointment to an illegitimate child made under a power to appoint to legitimate children.[30] In such cases, the rule is that the appointment is valid so far as it is proper and void as to the excess only; but if it is impossible to draw a clear boundary between what is proper and what is excessive, the whole appointment is bad. Thus if, under a power to appoint to children, an appointment is made to a child for life with remainder to a grandchild, the appointment is valid as to the life interest of the child only.[31] Again, a lease for 26 years granted under a power to lease for 21 years is valid for 21 years.[32] But if under a special power there is an appointment to a class of persons composed partly of persons who are not objects of the power, and the shares in which they are to take are not specified, the whole appointment fails, for it is impossible to sever the good from the bad.[33]

No appointment is bad merely because little or nothing is appointed to one or more of the objects, unless the power provides that each object shall receive some minimum amount at least and the donee does not comply with this requirement.[34] The law was once otherwise, hence the phrase "Cut off with a shilling."

---

[29] *Holmes* v. *Coghill* (1806) 12 Ves. 206.
[30] *Re Kerr's Trusts* (1877) 4 Ch.D. 600.
[31] *Doe* d. *Nicholson* v. *Walford* (1840) 12 A. & E. 61.
[32] *Campbell* v. *Leach* (1775) Amb. 740.
[33] *Re Brown's Trust* (1865) L.R. 1 Eq. 74.
[34] L.P.A. 1925, s. 158, replacing the Illusory Appointments Act 1830 and Powers of Appointment Act 1874.

D. Fraud on a Power

I. INVALIDITY OF APPOINTMENT

A special power of appointment must be exercised " bona fide for the end designed, otherwise it is corrupt and void." [35] The donee must, in making the appointment, act in relation to the power as a trustee would act; he must " act with good faith and sincerity and with an entire and single view to the real purpose and object of the power, and not for the purpose of accomplishing or carrying into effect any bye or sinister object (I mean sinister in the sense of it being beyond the purpose and intent of the power) which he may desire to effect in the exercise of the power." [36] An appointment which does not satisfy these conditions is void as a fraud on the power even if there is no " fraud " in the ordinary sense.[37]

An appointment may be deemed fraudulent and void on any of three grounds:

1. Corrupt purpose: the appointment was made with a corrupt purpose, as by the donee appointing to one of his children who is seriously ill, expecting that the child would die and that he would take the property appointed as the child's next-of-kin.[38] " If a father . . . charges a portion for his child, not because the child wants it, but because the child is delicate in health, and likely to die, this court has authority to defeat such an act." [39]

2. Foreign purpose: the appointment was made for purposes foreign to the power. Thus where a mother appoints property to a child with the intent that the child should use it for the benefit of the father, who was not an object of the power, the appointment will be set aside even though the child was ignorant of the mother's intention.[40]

3. Bargain to benefit non-objects: the appointment was made in pursuance of a previous agreement with the appointee whereby persons who were not objects of the power obtained some benefit, as

---

[35] *Aleyn* v. *Belchier* (1758) 1 Eden 132 at 138.
[36] *Duke of Portland* v. *Lady Topham* (1864) 11 H.L.C. 32 at 54, *per* Lord Westbury L.C.
[37] *Vatcher* v. *Paull* [1915] A.C. 372 at 378.
[38] *Wellesley* v. *Earl of Mornington* (1855) 2 K. & J. 143.
[39] *Keily* v. *Keily* (1843) 4 Dr. & War. 38 at 55, 56, *per* Sugden L.C.
[40] *Re Marsden's Trust* (1859) 4 Drew. 594 ; *cf. Re Burton's Settlements* [1955] Ch. 82.

where the donee bargained for some advantage for himself [41] or a stranger [42] as a condition of making the appointment. In the case of a power to appoint to one person only, an appointment may be fraudulent and void under this head but not under the previous head. [43]

An appointment which is a fraud on the power under the above rules is usually treated as a whole even if the fraud affects only part; the entire appointment is thus bad. [44] But if the fraudulent part is clearly separable from the rest, the court may hold only the fraudulent part void and the rest valid. [45] Further, a fraudulent appointment is merely void: the appointor may nevertheless subsequently make a fresh appointment, although if this appointment is in favour of the same person it must be shown that it is not tainted with the same fraud as the original appointment. [46] And the doctrine of fraud on a power does not apply to the exercise of a power to revoke a revocable appointment. [47]

II. POSITION OF A PURCHASER

1. Void or voidable. Before 1926, the position of a purchaser of an interest which had been fraudulently appointed depended upon whether that interest was legal or equitable. If the interest was legal, the appointment was not void but voidable, *i.e.*, it was good until set aside, so that if before the appointment was avoided the interest passed to a purchaser for value without notice of the fraud, he took a good title. But if the interest was equitable, the appointment was void *ab initio* and so even a purchaser without notice got no title. [48]

2. Statutory protection. Since after 1925 all powers of appointment are equitable, the position of a purchaser is now more precarious. However, the Law of Property Act 1925 [49] gives a very limited measure of protection to purchasers and those deriving title under them. The protection applies whenever the appointment was made, provided the purchase was made after 1925. The purchaser must show—

---

[41] *Cochrane* v. *Cochrane* [1922] 2 Ch. 230.
[42] *Re Dick* [1953] Ch. 343.
[43] *Re Nicholson's Settlement* [1939] Ch. 11.
[44] See, *e.g.*, *Agassiz* v. *Squire* (1854) 18 Beav. 431.
[45] *Harrison* v. *Randall* (1852) 9 Hare 397.
[46] *Re Chadwick's Trusts* [1939] 1 All E.R. 850.
[47] *Re Greaves* [1954] Ch. 434.
[48] *Cloutte* v. *Storey* [1911] 1 Ch. 18.
[49] s. 157.

(i) that he bought for money or money's worth without notice of the fraud or circumstances from which it might have been discovered upon making reasonable inquiries; and

(ii) that the appointee with whom he dealt was not less than 25 years of age.

Even if he proves this, he is protected only to the extent of the amount to which, at the time of the appointment, the appointee was presumptively entitled in default of appointment. For example, if A has power to appoint £5,000 among his children and in default of appointment the children share equally, a purchaser from one of the children is protected to the extent of only £1,000 if A had five children at the date of the appointment; if A had two children at that time, £2,500 is the limit of the protection. This is so even if the whole £5,000 has been appointed to one child. A purchaser would have no protection if in default of appointment some third party, such as the British Museum, was entitled to the property.

E. Determination of Powers

A power may be extinguished either expressly or impliedly.

1. Express determination. A power may be expressly determined by release or by contract not to exercise it.[50] This may either totally or partially extinguish the power. A partial release may exclude part of the property from the operation of the power, leaving the rest subject to it, or prevent the power being exercised in favour of one or more of the objects.[51] The rules relating to frauds on a power do not apply to the release of a power, so that a bargain to release the power may be made by the donee of the power with those entitled to take in default.[52]

The donee of a power may also disclaim it.[53] Disclaimer does not destroy the power but renders the donee who disclaims incapable of exercising it; it can still be exercised by any other donees.

2. Implied determination. A power may be impliedly determined by any dealing inconsistent with the further exercise of the power.[54] Thus if a husband appoints one-quarter of the income to his wife for

---

[0] L.P.A. 1925, s. 155, replacing earlier provisions.
[1] *Re Brown's Settlement* [1939] Ch. 944.
[2] *Re Somes* [1896] 1 Ch. 250.
[3] L.P.A. 1925, s. 156, replacing earlier provisions.
[4] *Foakes* v. *Jackson* [1900] 1 Ch. 807.

life, and subject thereto he appoints the property to his children, he cannot, after the death of his wife, appoint a life interest in one-fourth to his second wife, for he has exhausted the power.[55] There is also an implied release when all the purposes for which the power was created cease to exist.[56]

---

[55] *Re Hancock* [1896] 2 Ch. 173.
[56] See *Wolley* v. *Jenkins* (1856) 23 Beav. 53.

CHAPTER 8

WILLS AND INTESTACY

THIS chapter falls into three parts. The first two parts deal with wills and intestacy respectively, setting out the rules which determine who is beneficially entitled to property after the death of the owner. The third part deals with personal representatives, who, acting under a grant of probate or letters of administration, hold the property of the deceased not for their own benefit but for the purpose of administering it (including the payment of debts and the like) and then vesting what is left in the persons beneficially entitled.

Part 1

WILLS

Sect. 1. Freedom of Testation

1. **Historical development.** For some while after the Norman Conquest it was possible for a man to dispose of both his realty and his personalty by will. At first, his powers of disposition over personalty were confined to a fixed proportion, his widow and children being entitled to the rest; but during the 14th century the restrictions disappeared in nearly all parts of the country, although in some places the restrictions survived until the 17th and 18th centuries, the last to disappear being those in London, abolished in 1724.[1] Realty, on the other hand, could at first be freely devised but by the end of the 13th century all power of testamentary disposition had disappeared except in the case of certain local customs, such as gavelkind. But this restriction was soon evaded by means of uses,[2] and the general belief[3] that the Statute of Uses 1535 had abolished this indirect power of testamentary disposition provoked such an outcry that the Statute of Wills 1540 was passed, authorising the devise of all socage land and two-thirds of land held by knight service.[4] When the Tenures Abolition Act 1660 converted

---

[1] See 3 H.E.L. 552.
[2] See 4 H.E.L. 420–423.
[3] Probably unfounded; see (1941) 7 Camb.L.J. 354.
[4] For the details see (1941) 7 Camb.L.J. 357.

all land held by tenure in chivalry into land of socage tenure, all land became devisable. However, this power extended only to estates in fee simple: land held in tail could not be disposed of by will until the Law of Property Act 1925 made this possible.[5]

Copyhold land was not within the Statute of Wills 1540 and devises were effected by the testator in his lifetime making a surrender to the uses of his will. However, by Preston's Act 1815, a devise without a previous surrender was rendered effective and the Wills Act 1837 applied to copyholds as well as to lands of other tenures. It is this latter Act which applies to wills of all property, real or personal, today.

2. Inheritance (Family Provision) Act 1938.

(a) *Will or intestacy.* From the fourteenth century until 1939 there was in general no restriction upon a testator's power to dispose of property as he thought fit: for good reasons or bad, he might give all his property to a mistress or to charities, and leave his family penniless. The Inheritance (Family Provision) Act 1938 gives the court a limited power to modify the effect of a will in certain cases, and by the Intestates' Estates Act 1952, the rules of intestate succession are also subjected to this power.

(b) *Ambit of Act.* The Act of 1938 applies to any testator (or testatrix) dying domiciled in England after July 13, 1939,[6] and the Act of 1952 applies to such persons dying after 1952.[7] The scope of the Acts was extended by the Family Provision Act 1966 which made a number of detailed amendments. If the deceased leaves a spouse, infant son, unmarried daughter, or a son or daughter incapable of supporting himself or herself through some mental or physical disability, and reasonable provision is not made by the will or the rules of intestacy (or both in combination) for his or her maintenance,[7a] the court may order reasonable provision for maintenance to be made out of the estate.[8] Application must be made to the court not later than [9] six months after the grant of probate or letters of administration although the court may in its discretion extend the time, *e.g.*, if a new will or codicil substantially affecting the situation is discovered.[10]

---

[5] *Ante*, p. 43.
[6] s. 6 (2).
[7] s. 7.
[7a] See *Re Goodwin* [1969] Ch. 283.
[8] Act of 1938, s. 1 (1), as amended by Act of 1952 and Act of 1966, s. 2.
[9] *Re Searle* [1949] Ch. 73.
[10] Act of 1938, s. 2, as amended by Act of 1966, s. 5.

" Son " and " daughter " include a child adopted by the deceased
under the Adoption of Children Acts 1926–1958 [11] and a child *en
ventre sa mère*,[12] but not an illegitimate child.[13]

(c) *Extent of order.* Where the Act applies, the court may order
the payment of maintenance for the above relatives by periodical
payments of a specified amount, or by payments equal to the whole or
any part of the income of the estate, or by a lump sum payment [14];
the court may distribute the burden between those entitled to specific
gifts and those entitled to residue, as it thinks fit.[15] The maintenance
must cease at latest—

    (i) in the case of a spouse, on remarriage;

    (ii) in the case of a daughter who has not married or is under
disability, on marriage or the cesser of her disability, whichever is the later;

    (iii) in the case of an infant son, on his attaining his majority;

    (iv) in the case of a son under disability, on the cesser of his
disability;

and in any case, it ceases at death.[16]

(d) *Discretion of court.* The court's power is entirely discretionary
and all the relevant factors must be considered, including the conduct
of the dependant in question, and the reasons of the deceased for
not providing for the dependant, including those stated in any
statement in writing signed by the deceased and dated.[17] There is a
limited power for the court to vary any order [18] and to make an
interim order.[19]

(e) *Maintenance orders.* After 1958, somewhat similar provisions
enable the court to make a maintenance order in favour of a person
whose marriage to the deceased has been ended by a decree of divorce
or nullity.[20]

[11] Adoption Act 1958, s. 58 (2).
[12] Act of 1938, s. 5 (1).
[13] *Re Meakin* [1955] Ch. 194.
[14] *Ibid.* ss. 1 (4), 3 (1A), as amended by the Act of 1966.
[15] *Re Simson* [1950] Ch. 38; *Re Preston* [1969] 1 W.L.R. 317.
[16] Act of 1938, s. 1 (2).
[17] *Ibid.* s. 1 (6), (7).
[18] *Ibid.* s. 4.
[19] *Ibid.* s. 4A, added by Act of 1966, s. 6.
[20] Matrimonial Causes Act 1965, ss. 26–28A, replacing Matrimonial Causes (Property
and Maintenance) Act 1958, ss. 3–6.

Sect. 2. Nature of a Will

1. A will is ambulatory. Until the death of the testator, a will has no effect at all, but operates as a mere declaration of his intention, which may be changed from time to time. For this reason, a will is said to be "ambulatory." This distinguishes a will from a conveyance, settlement or other dealing *inter vivos*, which operates at once or at some fixed time.

A will is also ambulatory in that it "speaks from death," *i.e.*, it is capable of disposing of all property owned by the testator at his death, even if acquired after the date of the will. Before 1838, this was true only of personalty: a will could not dispose of realty acquired between the making of the will and death. By the Wills Act 1837, however, unless a contrary intention appears, a will now speaks from death with regard to both real and personal property.[21]

2. A will is revocable. Notwithstanding any declaration in the will itself or any other document, a will can be revoked at any time.[22] However, although a binding contract not to revoke a will does not prevent its revocation,[23] and will prima facie be construed as not extending to revocation by marriage,[24] such a contract binds the testator's assets, so that if the will is revoked, the beneficiaries thereunder can compel the person to whom the assets have passed to hold these on trust for them in accordance with the terms of the contract.[25]

3. Codicils. A codicil is similar to a will and is governed by the same rules. A testamentary document is usually called a codicil if it is supplementary to a will and adds to, varies or revokes provisions in the will: if it is an independent instrument, it is called a will. Although sometimes indorsed on a will, a codicil may be a separate document, and can stand by itself even after the revocation of the will to which it is supplementary.[26] Codicils are construed in such a way as to disturb the provisions of a will no more than is absolutely necessary to give effect to the codicil.[27]

---

[21] s. 24; see *post*, p. 283.
[22] *Vynior's Case* (1610) 8 Co.Rep. 81b.
[23] *In b. Heys* [1914] P. 192.
[24] *Re Marsland* [1939] Ch. 820.
[25] *Dufour* v. *Pereira* (1769) 1 Dick. 419; and see *ante*, p. 239. The authorities are reviewed in *Re Oldham* [1925] Ch. 75.
[26] *In b. Savage* (1870) L.R. 2 P. & D. 78.
[27] *Doe* d. *Hearle* v. *Hicks* (1832) 1 Cl. & F. 20.

Sect. 3. The Formalities of a Will

A. History

The Statute of Wills 1540 [28] required a will of realty to be in writing, although it was unnecessary for it to be signed by the testator, or witnessed. Wills of personalty could be made by word of mouth. The Statute of Frauds 1677 [29] required all wills of realty not only to be in writing, but also to be signed by the testator (or by some person in his presence and by his direction) and attested in his presence by at least three credible witnesses. The statute also laid down [30] such stringent requirements for nuncupative (*i.e.*, oral) wills of personalty over £30 that thereafter wills of personalty were usually made in writing. Written wills of personalty required no witnesses and did not need to be signed by the testator if written by him, or even by someone else, if acknowledged by the testator.[31]

The Wills Act 1837 repealed these provisions as regards all wills made after 1837 and substituted a uniform code for both realty and personalty.

B. Formal Wills

I. EXECUTION

The present rules governing the execution of a formal will are as follows.[32]

1. Writing: the will must be in writing. Any form of writing, printing, typewriting and the like may be employed. No special form of words need be used: all that is required is an intelligible document.

2. Signature by testator: the will must be signed by the testator, or by someone else in his presence and by his direction. The testator's signature may be made in any way, provided there is an intention to execute the will. Thus initials,[33] a stamped name, a mark,[34] a signature in a former or assumed name [35] or " your loving

---

[28] s. 1.
[29] s. 5.
[30] See ss. 19, 20.
[31] See 3 H.E.L. 538.
[32] Wills Act 1837, s. 9.
[33] *In b. Savory* (1851) 15 Jur. 1042.
[34] *In b. Finn* (1936) 53 T.L.R. 153 (thumb-mark).
[35] *In b. Redding* (1850) 2 Rob.Ecc. 339.

Mother " [36] all suffice. But a seal is not enough, for the will must
be signed and sealing is not signing.[37] Similar principles apply to
signature by someone on behalf of the testator. Thus signature of
his own name instead of that of the testator is sufficient.[38] But it is
essential that the signature should be made in the testator's presence
and authorised by him, either expressly or by implication.[39]

3. Position of signature: the signature must be at the foot or end
of the will. At first this requirement was interpreted liberally, but
later the courts insisted upon a strict compliance, and probate was
refused to a will which left no room for signature at the end of the
third side and was signed in the middle of a blank fourth side.[40]
Consequently the Wills Act Amendment Act 1852 was passed, containing elaborate provisions for most of the positions in which a
signature could possibly appear. The effect of the Act is that if it
is apparent from the face of the will that the testator intended to
give effect to the will by the signature which the witnesses attested,[41]
probate will be granted; but nothing which was inserted after the
will was signed, or which follows the signature in space, will be
effective. In short, probate will be granted to every part of the will
except that which comes after the signature either in time or in space.

For example, where a will ended in the middle of the third page
of a sheet of paper and was executed at the bottom of the fourth
page, the intervening space being left blank, probate was granted.[42]
In another case,[43] the will was written on one sheet of paper, one
side of which contained all the bequests and the other the usual
opening words " This is the last Will and Testament," the appointment of an executor and, beneath these, the signature of the testatrix.
It was held that the proper way to read the will was to start with the
bequests and then to turn over; the will was thus admitted to
probate. The court may even ignore the numbered order of the
pages in order to reduce the signature to the foot or end of the will,[44]
or be satisfied with a signature in a space ruled off half-way down
the only page of the will,[45] or on the envelope containing the will.[46]

---

[36] *In b. Cook* [1960] 1 W.L.R. 353.
[37] *Wright* v. *Wakeford* (1811) 17 Ves. 454.
[38] *In b. Clark* (1839) 2 Curt. 329.
[39] *In b. Marshall* (1866) 13 L.T. 643.   [40] *Smee* v. *Bryer* (1848) 1 Rob.Ecc. 616.
[41] *In b. Bercovitz* [1962] 1 W.L.R. 321 (two signatures, only one attested).
[42] *Hunt* v. *Hunt* (1866) L.R. 1 P. & D. 209.
[43] *In b. Long* [1936] P. 166.   [44] *In b. Smith* [1931] P. 225.
[45] *In b. Hornby* [1946] P. 171.
[46] *In b. Mann* [1942] P. 146 ; contrast *In b. Bean* [1944] P. 83.

But although the court will go to all lengths within the limit of reasonable construction to save a will from defeat by such formal defects it will not resort to physical interference with it, such as folding or bending the paper.[47]

Effect will be given to dispositions contained in a document which has not been executed as a will if the document is incorporated in a will. For this to be the case—

(i) the will must clearly identify the document to be incorporated;

(ii) the will must refer to the document as being already in existence and not as one subsequently to be made; and

(iii) the document must in fact be in existence when the will is executed.[48]

4. Presence of witnesses: the testator must either make or acknowledge the signature in the presence of two witnesses present at the same time. Whether the signature to the will is made by the testator or by someone in his presence and by his direction, there is no need for witnesses to be present at the time of the signature if they are present when the testator subsequently makes a proper acknowledgment of the signature. But either the signature or the acknowledgment must be made in the simultaneous presence of two witnesses. An express acknowledgment is desirable but not essential; a gesture by the testator may suffice,[49] and an acknowledgment by a third party is effective if it can be shown that it should be taken to be the acknowledgment of the testator.[50]

It is desirable but not essential that the witnesses should be of full age and sound intelligence; yet a blind person cannot be a witness, for the will cannot be signed in his " presence." [51]

5. Signature by witnesses. The witnesses must then sign in the presence of the testator. No form of attestation is necessary although a proper attestation clause showing that the will has been executed in accordance with the statutory requirements will facilitate the grant of probate. All that is necessary is that after the testator's signature has been made or acknowledged in the joint presence of two witnesses, they should sign their names in the testator's presence.

[47] See *Re Stalman* (1931) 145 L.T. 339.
[48] See *University College of North Wales* v. *Taylor* [1908] P. 140.
[49] See *In b. Davies* (1850) 2 Rob.Ecc. 337.
[50] *Inglesant* v. *Inglesant* (1874) L.R. 3 P. & D. 172.
[51] *In b. Gibson* [1949] P. 434.

There is no provision allowing a witness to acknowledge his signature. Thus if the testator signs in the presence of A, who signs his name, and then B is called in, and both the testator and A acknowledge their signatures to B, who then signs, probate will be refused. The testator did not sign or acknowledge his signature in the presence of two witnesses until B was called in, and A's subsequent acknowledgment of his signature is no substitute for signing after the testator as required by the Act.[52]

There is no need for the witnesses to sign in each other's presence,[53] although this is both usual and desirable.

II. ALTERATIONS

Every obliteration, interlineation or other alteration made after a will has been executed must itself be executed in the same way as a will; in default, it is ineffective unless it revokes any part of the will by rendering it illegible.[54] The signatures of the testator and the witnesses should be written either opposite the alteration (*e.g.*, in the margin) or else at the foot or end of, or opposite to, a memorandum referring to the alteration.[55] Signature by means of initials suffices.

An obliteration or erasure of part of a will, even though unattested, is effective to revoke that part, since it amounts to a destruction of that part,[56] and the same applies to the pasting of paper over part of a will,[57] provided the words are not decipherable by any natural means, such as by the use of magnifying glasses or by holding the will up to the light.[58] The court will not permit physical interference with the will, as by using chemicals or removing paper pasted over the words[59]; and an obliteration is not ineffective merely because the original words can be deciphered by making another document, *e.g.*, an infra-red photograph.[60]

III. REVOCATION

A will or codicil may be revoked by another will or codicil, by destruction, or by marriage.

---

[52] *Wyatt* v. *Berry* [1893] P. 5.
[53] *In b. Webb* (1855) Dea. & Sw. 1.
[54] Wills Act 1837, s. 21.
[55] *Ibid.*
[56] See *post*, pp. 271, 272.
[57] *In b. Horsford* (1874) L.R. 3 P. & D. 211.
[58] *Ffinch* v. *Combe* [1894] P. 191.
[59] *In b. Horsford, supra*; contrast *In b. Gilbert* [1893] P. 183.
[60] *In b. Itter* [1950] P. 130.

1. By another will or codicil. A revocation clause expressly revoking all former wills is effective provided it is contained in a document executed with the proper formalities.[61] This is so even if the testator had been misled as to the effect of the clause,[62] but not if the testator did not know of the presence of the clause.[63] A will is not revoked merely because a later will is entitled (as is usual) " This is the last will and testament of me " or some similar phrase.[64]

A will is revoked by implication if a later will is executed which merely repeats the former will or is inconsistent with it, although if the repetition or inconsistency is merely partial, those parts of the former will which are neither repeated in the later will nor inconsistent with it remain effective.[65] Any number of testamentary documents may be read together, each being effective except so far as subsequently varied or revoked; the sum total constitutes the testator's will.[66]

2. By destruction. A will is revoked if it is destroyed by the testator, or by some person in his presence and by his direction, with intent to revoke it.[67] There are thus two elements, an act of destruction and an *animus revocandi* (intention to revoke).

(a) *Destruction.* It is not necessary that the will should be completely destroyed; there must, however, be some burning, tearing or other destruction of the whole will or some essential part of it, as by cutting off the signature of the testator or the witnesses.[68] It is not enough for the testator to draw a line through part of the will, indorse it " all these are revoked " and kick it into the corner.[69] Destruction of part of a will normally revokes that part alone, unless the part destroyed is so important as to lead to the conclusion that the rest cannot be intended to stand alone.[70]

If a will has been destroyed without being revoked (*e.g.,* because an *animus revocandi* was lacking), it is proved by means of a draft or copy, or even by oral evidence.[71] A will in the testator's possession which cannot be found at the testator's death is presumed to

---

[61] Wills Act 1837, s. 20.
[62] *Collins* v. *Elstone* [1893] P. 1.
[63] *In b. Moore* [1892] P. 378.
[64] *Simpson* v. *Foxon* [1907] P. 54.
[65] *Lemage* v. *Goodban* (1865) L.R. 1 P. & D. 57.
[66] *In b. Fenwick* (1867) L.R. 1 P. & D. 319.
[67] Wills Act 1837, s. 20.
[68] *Williams* v. *Tyley* (1858) Johns. 530.
[69] *Cheese* v. *Lovejoy* (1877) 2 P.D. 251.
[70] *Leonard* v. *Leonard* [1902] P. 243.
[71] *Sugden* v. *Lord St. Leonards* (1876) 1 P.D. 154.

have been destroyed by him *animo revocandi* and cannot be proved unless the presumption is rebutted by evidence of non-revocation.[72]

(b) *Intent to revoke*. The testator must have an *animus revocandi* at the time of the destruction. If a will is intentionally torn up by a testator who is drunk [73] or believes the will to be ineffective, it is not revoked, for an intent to destroy the document is no substitute for the requisite intent to revoke the will. " All the destroying in the world without intention will not revoke a will, nor all the intention in the world without destroying: there must be the two." [74]

Revocation of a will may be conditional, in which case the will remains unrevoked until the condition has been fulfilled. One particular kind of conditional revocation is known as dependent relative revocation. If revocation is relative to another will and intended to be dependent upon the validity of that will, the revocation is ineffective unless that other will takes effect. Thus if a will is destroyed by a testator who is about to make a new will, and the evidence shows that he intended to revoke the old will only if he executed the new one, the old will remains valid if the new will is never executed.[75] Another example arises in the case of revival: if Will No. 1 is revoked by Will No. 2, the revocation of Will No. 2 is not sufficient to revive Will No. 1,[76] so that if the testator revokes Will No. 2 in the mistaken belief that he is thereby reviving Will No. 1, the doctrine of dependent relative revocation applies and the revocation of Will No. 2 is ineffective.[77] Again, if a testator obliterates a legacy and by unattested writing substitutes a new legacy, the old legacy remains effective if the court is satisfied that it was revoked only on the (erroneous) supposition that the new legacy would be effective.[78]

3. By marriage. Marriage automatically revokes all wills made by the parties to the marriage.[79] There are two exceptions to this.

(a) *Certain appointments*. An appointment by will under a power of appointment is not revoked by the marriage of the testator unless, in default of appointment, the property would pass to his heir,

---

[72] *Eckersley* v. *Platt* (1866) L.R. 1 P. & D. 281.
[73] *In b. Brassington* [1902] P. 1.
[74] *Cheese* v. *Lovejoy* (1877) 2 P.D. 251 at 253, *per* James L.J.
[75] *Dixon* v. *Treasury Solicitor* [1905] P. 42.
[76] *Post*, p. 273.
[77] *Powell* v. *Powell* (1866) L.R. 1 P. & D. 209; *In b. Bridgewater* [1965] 1 W.L.R. 416.
[78] *In b. Horsford* (1874) L.R. 3 P. & D. 211.
[79] Wills Act 1837, s. 18.

customary heir, executor, administrator or the person entitled as his statutory next-of-kin,[80] *i.e.*, in effect, to those who would take if he died intestate. The general intention of this provision is that if the testator's new " family " will get the property even if the will is revoked, there is no harm in allowing marriage to revoke it. But if the property would pass out of the " family " in default of appointment, the will is allowed to stand so far as it exercises the power of appointment, and no farther.[81]

(b) *Contemplation of marriage.* A will made after 1925 and expressed to be in contemplation of a marriage is not revoked by the solemnisation of the marriage contemplated.[82] This exception applies only if the will refers to the particular marriage in fact celebrated; it is not enough for the testator to declare in the will that it is " made in contemplation of marriage," [83] though an inferential reference to a particular marriage suffices, such as " to my fiancée," giving her name.[84]

IV. REVIVAL

A will revoked by destruction *animo revocandi* can never be revived.[85] Any other will can be revived, but only by re-execution with the proper formalities or by a codicil showing an intention to revive it.[86] If a will has been revoked by a subsequent will, the first will is thus not revived merely by the revocation of the later will.[87] If a will is first partially revoked, then wholly revoked, and then revived, the revival does not extend to the part partially revoked unless an intention to this effect is shown.[88]

C. *Informal Wills*

Certain persons are excepted from the rules that a testator must be of full age and must comply with the usual formalities.[89]

I. PRIVILEGED TESTATORS

1. A soldier in actual military service. The testator must not merely be in an army; when he makes the will he must be actually

---

[80] *Ibid.*; for those entitled as statutory next-of-kin, see *post*, pp. 299, 302.
[81] See *In b. Russell* (1890) 15 P.D. 111; *In b. Gilligan* [1950] P. 32.
[82] L.P.A. 1925, s. 177. [83] *Sallis* v. *Jones* [1936] P. 43.
[84] *In b. Langston* [1953] P. 100.
[85] *In b. Reade* [1902] P. 75.
[86] Wills Act 1837, s. 22.
[87] *In b. Hodgkinson* [1893] P. 339.
[88] Wills Act 1837, s. 22.
[89] *Ibid.* s. 11.

serving in connection with military operations which are or have been taking place or are believed to be imminent [90]; in one case service at a camp in England in August 1940 was held sufficient.[91] A soldier is deemed to be in actual military service from the moment he receives mobilisation orders until the full conclusion of the operations. "Soldier" includes both officers and other ranks, a female army nurse,[92] and a member of the Air Force,[93] or Women's Auxiliary Air Force.[94]

2. A mariner or seaman at sea. This includes both members of the Royal Navy and merchant seamen, and extends to a female typist employed on a liner.[95] It includes an admiral directing naval operations on a river,[96] a master mariner in his ship lying in the Thames before starting on her voyage,[97] and a seaman whose ship is permanently stationed in harbour.[98] It also extends to a seaman on shore leave from his ship, or under orders to join a new ship.[99]

3. A member of Her Majesty's Naval or Marine Forces so circumstanced that, had he been a soldier, he would have been in actual military service.[1] This enables a member of the navy or marines who has been called up to make an informal will even though he has not joined his ship.[2]

II. EXTENT OF THE PRIVILEGE

A will made by a testator who at the time of making the will comes within one of the above categories has the following privileges:

1. It is immaterial that the testator is an infant. This has always applied to wills of personalty, provided the infant is at least 14 years of age if a male and at least 12 if a female.[3] In the case of realty, this privilege seems to have been accidentally curtailed after 1925 in the case of infants who have never married.[4]

90 *Re Wingham* [1949] P. 187.   91 *In b. Spark* [1941] P. 115.
92 *In b. Stanley* [1916] P. 192.
93 Wills (Soldiers and Sailors) Act 1918, s. 5.
94 *In b. Rowson* [1944] 2 All E.R. 36.
95 *In b. Hale* [1915] 2 I.R. 362.
96 *In b. Austen* (1853) 2 Rob.Ecc. 611.
97 *In b. Patterson* (1898) 79 L.T. 123.
98 *In b. M'Murdo* (1867) L.R. 1 P. & D. 540.
99 *In b. Newland* [1952] P. 71 ; *In b. Wilson* [1952] P. 92.
1 Wills (Soldiers and Sailors) Act 1918, s. 2.
2 *In b. Yates* [1919] P. 93.
3 *Hyde* v. *Hyde* (1711) Prec.Ch. 316.
4 See A.E.A. 1925, s. 51 ; *post*, p. 518.

2. The will can be made or revoked informally. The will may be made in writing, with or without witnesses or signature, or it may be nuncupative; thus informal words of farewell spoken at a railway station may suffice.[5] The testator need not know that he is making a will, provided he gives deliberate expression to his wishes as to the destination of his property on his death,[6] *e.g.*, "If I stop a bullet everything of mine will be yours." [7] Those entitled to make an informal will may also revoke a will, even if it has been made formally, in an informal manner, *e.g.*, by an unattested letter to a relative asking that the will should be burned, "for I have already cancelled it." [8]

These privileges have always applied to wills of personalty, and extend to wills of realty if the testator dies after February 6, 1918.[9] A will properly made under the above conditions remains valid indefinitely unless revoked, even after the military or other service is over.[10]

Sect. 4. Operation of Wills

A. Lapse

I. GENERAL RULE

A legacy or bequest (*i.e.*, a testamentary gift of personalty) or a devise (*i.e.*, a testamentary gift of realty) is said to lapse if the beneficiary dies before the testator. In such a case, unless a contrary intention is shown, the gift fails and the property comprised in it falls into residue, which means that it passes under any general or residuary gift in the will,[11] such as "all the rest of my property I leave to X." If there is no residuary gift, or if the gift which lapses is itself a gift of all or part of the residue, there is a partial intestacy and the property passes to the persons entitled on intestacy.[12]

II. EXCLUSION OF THE GENERAL RULE

1. No lapse. The Wills Act 1837 excludes this general rule in two important cases:

---

[5] *In b. Yates* [1919] P. 93. [6] *In b. Spicer* [1949] P. 441.
[7] *Re Stable* [1919] P. 7; contrast *In b. Knibbs* [1962] 1 W.L.R. 852.
[8] *In b. Gossage* [1921] P. 194; but see *post*, p. 517.
[9] Wills (Soldiers and Sailors) Act 1918, s. 3.
[10] *Re Booth* [1926] P. 118.
[11] Wills Act 1837, s. 25.
[12] *Ackroyd* v. *Smithson* (1780) 1 Bro.C.C. 503; *post*, pp. 288 *et seq.*

(a) *Entails*: by section 32, subject to any contrary intention, there is no lapse if property is given to a person in tail and he predeceases the testator, leaving issue living at the testator's death capable of inheriting under the entail.

(b) *Gifts to issue*: by section 33, subject to any contrary intention, there is no lapse if property is given to a child or other issue of the testator who leaves issue living (and not merely *en ventre sa mère*, it seems [13]) at the testator's death.

In neither case does the Act give anything to the issue whose survival prevented the lapse; it merely provides that the gift shall take effect as if the legatee or devisee had died immediately after the testator. Accordingly if T leaves £2,000 by his will to his daughter D, who dies some years before him, the legacy lapses unless she left issue who survived both herself and T, in which case the £2,000 forms part of D's estate. If D died a bankrupt, it passes to her trustee in bankruptcy [14]; if she was solvent but bequeathed all her property to charities or strangers, it passes to them under her will.[15] Only if D's issue is entitled under her will or intestacy will they benefit.

Formerly, the fiction that D survived T resulted in estate duty being payable twice, once on T's death and once on D's [16]; and if the property concerned was realty, D's husband was entitled to curtesy out of it if the necessary conditions were fulfilled.[17] However, the fiction is applied only so far as is necessary to prevent a lapse. Thus where it saves from lapse a gift by a father who died in 1940 to a son who died intestate in 1920, the property carried to the son's estate passes under the rules of intestacy in force at the date of the son's real, and not his notional, death.[18]

2. Exceptions. In four cases section 33 does not apply to prevent a lapse.

(a) *Appointments under special powers*: section 33 does not apply to an appointment by will under a special power,[19] for it is confined to cases where property is "devised or bequeathed." It does, however, apply to appointments under general powers.[20]

---

[13] See *Elliott* v. *Lord Joicey* [1935] A.C. 209, disapproving *Re Griffiths' Settlement* [1911] 1 Ch. 246.

[14] *Re Pearson* [1920] 1 Ch. 217.   [15] *Re Hayter* [1937] 2 All E.R. 110.

[16] *Re Scott* [1901] 1 K.B. 228, in effect reversed by Finance Act 1958, s. 29 (2).

[17] *Eager* v. *Furnivall* (1881) 17 Ch.D. 115; *post*, p. 294.

[18] *Re Basioli* [1953] Ch. 367.

[19] *Holyland* v. *Lewin* (1883) 26 Ch.D. 266; *ante*, p. 256.

[20] *Eccles* v. *Cheyne* (1856) 2 K. & J. 676.

(b) *Class gifts*: section 33 does not apply to class gifts,[21] such as a gift to "all my children," even if in fact there is only one member of the class.[22] The reason for this is that membership of a class is normally ascertained at a testator's death and those dying before the testator fail to become members of the class. Strictly, there is no question of lapse; it is merely that nothing has ever been given to those who predecease the testator. But a gift of property "to be equally divided between my five daughters" is not a class gift, for there is a gift to each individual alive at the date of the will; section 33 will accordingly apply if one of the children predeceases the testator.[23]

(c) *Interests terminable on donee's death*: section 33 does not preserve gifts which would in any case terminate with the donee's death, *e.g.*, gifts of a life interest or joint tenancy.[24]

(d) *Certain contingent gifts*: section 33 does not preserve a contingent gift such as a bequest "to X as and when he is 25" if X dies aged 24, even if he would have attained the requisite age had he in fact outlived the testator.[25]

III. COMMORIENTES

Where a devisee or legatee dies at nearly the same time as the testator, it is necessary to determine which survived the other in order to know whether the gift lapsed. Similar questions between *commorientes* (those dying together) arise on intestacy and in respect of joint tenancies. Before 1926, there was no means of settling the question if there was no evidence of the order of deaths. Thus if two people perished in a shipwreck, in the absence of evidence of survivorship the estate of one could not benefit under the will or intestacy of the other, for it was impossible for the personal representatives to establish the survivorship essential to their case. In the case of deaths after 1925, however, where it is uncertain which survived the other, for all purposes affecting the title to property the younger is deemed to have survived the elder, subject to any order of the court.[26] This rule applies equally to cases of simple uncertainty, as where one of the parties is on a ship which founders with

---

[21] See *ante*, p. 118 and *post*, p. 283.
[22] *Re Harvey's Estate* [1893] 1 Ch. 567.
[23] *Re Smith's Trusts* (1878) 9 Ch.D. 117.
[24] See *Re Butler* [1918] 1 I.R. 394.
[25] *Re Wolson* [1939] Ch. 780.
[26] L.P.A. 1925, s. 184. For an exception, see *post*, p. 306 (intestate spouses).

all hands on an uncertain date and the other dies at home during that period, and to common disasters, such as virtually simultaneous deaths in an air-raid.[27] But for the purposes of death duties, the old rule has now been restored, and each is deemed to have died simultaneously, so that there can be no second liability for duty on the death of a notional survivor.[28]

B. Gifts to Witnesses

1. Former invalidation of will. In the case of wills of realty, the Statute of Frauds 1677 required that all wills should be attested by at least three *credible* witnesses. If a witness to such a will was given either a devise or a legacy by the will, he was deemed not to be credible, and if his disqualification left less than three credible witnesses, the will was void as to the realty comprised in it. The same applied to legacies or devises to the spouse of a witness. The Wills Act 1751 provided that a legacy or devise to a witness should be void but that his attestation should no longer be invalidated. The Act somewhat curiously made no provision for legacies or devises to the spouse of a witness, and these still invalidated the attestation of the witness.[29]

2. Invalidation of gift. The Wills Act 1837[30] put matters on a more rational basis by providing that the attestation of a beneficiary or his or her spouse should be valid, although the beneficiary can claim no benefit under the will, either as to realty or personalty.

3. Limits of the rule. This rule does not apply in the following cases.

(a) *Informal wills*: where no witnesses at all are necessary for the validity of the will, as where the testator is a soldier in actual military service.[31]

(b) *Sufficient other witnesses*: where the testator dies after May 29, 1968, the attestation by a beneficiary or his or her spouse is to be disregarded if the will is duly executed without that attestation.[32]

(c) *Signed not as witness*: where the person has signed the will

[27] *Hickman* v. *Peacey* [1945] A.C. 304.
[28] Finance Act 1958, s. 29 (1).
[29] *Hatfield* v. *Thorp* (1822) 5 B. & Ald. 589.
[30] s. 15.
[31] *Re Limond* [1915] 2 Ch. 240.
[32] Wills Act 1968, s. 1, reversing *Re Bravda* [1968] 1 W.L.R. 479.

not as a witness but merely, for example, to show that he agrees with the testator's leaving him less than his brothers and sisters.[33]

(d) *Subsequent marriage*: where the marriage of the beneficiary to the witness occurred after the date of the will.[34]

(e) *Fiduciary gifts*: where the gift to the witness is to him as a trustee and not beneficially.[35]

(f) *Confirmation*: where the gift is made or confirmed by any will or codicil not attested by the beneficiary. Thus if there is a gift by will confirmed by codicil, a beneficiary who witnesses only one document is entitled to the gift since he can claim under the other document.[36]

4. Acceleration. The effect of the rule in the case of a limited interest is to accelerate the subsequent interests. Thus if property is given to A for life, with remainder to B, the effect of A attesting the will is that B is entitled to the property as soon as the testator dies.[37] Similarly if property is given to X, Y and Z as joint tenants, and X attests the will, Y and Z are entitled to the whole of the property.[38]

C. Gifts to Persons Feloniously Causing the Testator's Death

A person guilty of murder or manslaughter can take no benefit under the will or intestacy of his victim,[39] so that a murderer's prospective interest under his victim's intestacy devolves as if the murderer did not exist.[40] This does not apply, however, if the slayer was insane at the time.[41]

Sect. 5. Construction of Wills

The construction of wills is a vast subject of which only a few of the more important rules can be mentioned here.

A. General Rule

The cardinal rule of construction is that effect must be given to the intention of the testator as expressed in the will, the words being

---

[33] *Kitcat* v. *King* [1930] P. 266.
[34] *Thorpe* v. *Bestwick* (1881) 6 Q.B.D. 311.
[35] *Cresswell* v. *Cresswell* (1868) L.R. 6 Eq. 69.
[36] *Re Marcus* (1887) 56 L.J.Ch. 830; *Re Trotter* [1899] 1 Ch. 764.
[37] *Jull* v. *Jacobs* (1876) 3 Ch.D. 703.
[38] *Young* v. *Davies* (1863) 2 Dr. & Sm. 167.
[39] *Re Sigsworth* [1935] Ch. 89.
[40] *Re Callaway* [1956] Ch. 559.
[41] *Re Pitts* [1931] 1 Ch. 546.

given their natural meaning except so far as that leads to absurdities or inconsistencies.[42] The will alone must be looked at, and, in general, no evidence can be received to contradict the meaning of the words used in the will. " The will must be in writing, and the only question is, what is the meaning of the words used in that writing." [43] If the rule were otherwise, the requirement that a will should be in writing might largely be set at naught.

However, although words will usually be given their natural meaning, or the most appropriate of their several natural meanings, there is nothing to prevent words from being construed in some special sense if the will clearly shows that they are used in that sense; and in recent years the courts have been rather more ready to perceive that the testator has used words otherwise than according to their " strict " meaning.[44] Thus " children " bears the natural meaning of " legitimate children," [45] but if the testator inserts a clause providing that by " children " he means to include illegitimate children, the word will bear the wider meaning. This is sometimes known as the " dictionary principle ": the testator, by showing in the will that he has used a word in a particular sense, has made his own dictionary for the purposes of the will. An express definition clause is not necessary. A gift " to all J's children except X," where X is illegitimate, operates to include all J's children, legitimate or illegitimate, except X.[46] If the will was made after 1949 or confirmed after April 1, 1959, children who were formally adopted before the will was made are included.[47]

B. Extrinsic Evidence

Since only the words of the will may be considered, extrinsic evidence (*i.e.*, evidence not gathered from the will itself) is normally inadmissible. However, this is subject to certain qualifications.

1. Surrounding circumstances. Evidence of facts and circumstances existing when the will was made is always admissible. " You may place yourself, so to speak, in [the testator's] arm-chair." [48] Thus extrinsic evidence is admissible to show that certain words had

---

[42] See *Abbott* v. *Middleton* (1858) 7 H.L.C. 68 at 114.
[43] *Grey* v. *Pearson* (1857) 6 H.L.C. 61 at 106, *per* Lord Wensleydale.
[44] See *Perrin* v. *Morgan* [1943] A.C. 399.
[45] *Re Pearce* [1914] 1 Ch. 254.
[46] *Re Lowe* (1895) 61 L.J.Ch. 415 ; and see *Re Davidson* [1949] Ch. 670.
[47] Adoption Act 1958, ss. 16 (2), 17 (2), 59, 5th Sched., para. 4.
[48] *Boyes* v. *Cook* (1880) 14 Ch.D. 53 at 56, *per* James L.J.

a peculiar meaning to the testator by the custom of the district or the usage of the class of persons to which he belonged. Again, nicknames, or symbols used by the testator in his trade, may be explained; thus it may be shown that a gift for "mother" was intended for the testator's wife, whom he always described thus,[49] or that a gift by a childless testator to "my children" was intended for his step-children.[50]

2. Equivocations.

(a) *Ambiguity.* Evidence of the testator's intention is admissible to explain an equivocation. There is said to be an equivocation or ambiguity in a will when there is a description of a person or thing which can apply equally well to two or more persons or things. Thus if a testator devises his close (enclosed land) " in the occupation of W " and he has two such closes, there is an equivocation.[51]

(b) *Latent or patent.* An ambiguity is said to be latent when the will is apparently perfect on the face of it, but on attempting to apply it an ambiguity appears. Extrinsic evidence of the testator's intention is always admissible to explain such an ambiguity. Thus if a testator makes a devise " to my son John " and leaves two sons of that name, extrinsic evidence is admissible to show that the testator believed the elder son to be dead and intended the land for the younger son.[52] An ambiguity is said to be patent when the will itself discloses that the description fits more than one person or thing. Extrinsic evidence of the testator's intention is often said to be inadmissible in the case of patent ambiguities, but this is not universally true and the position is far from clear. Thus evidence of the testator's intention was admitted in one case where there was a gift to " George Gord the son of Gord," and other parts of the will showed that there were two men called Gord with sons named George.[53]

(c) *Intention.* Once extrinsic evidence of the testator's intention is admitted, it will be given effect to even if it shows that someone apparently outside the scope of the gift was intended. Thus in one case [54] a testatrix gave part of her property " to my nephew Arthur

---

[49] Consider *Thorn* v. *Dickens* [1906] W.N. 54 (where the entire will consisted of the words " All for mother ").
[50] *Re Jeans* (1895) 72 L.T. 834.
[51] *Richardson* v. *Watson* (1833) 4 B. & Ad. 787.
[52] *Lord Cheyney's Case* (1591) 5 Co.Rep. 68a at 68b.
[53] *Doe* d. *Gord* v. *Needs* (1836) 2 M. & W. 129. The sidenote misses the point.
[54] *Re Jackson* [1933] Ch. 237.

Murphy." She had two legitimate nephews of that name, and extrinsic evidence was admitted to explain this ambiguity. The evidence admitted showed that the testatrix intended to benefit an illegitimate nephew called Arthur Murphy, and it was held that he took to the exclusion of the two legitimate nephews. Had there been only one legitimate and one illegitimate nephew, there would have been no ambiguity, for " nephew " prima facie means " legitimate nephew "; consequently no extrinsic evidence would have been admitted and the legitimate nephew would have taken.[55]

(d) *Uncertainty.* If extrinsic evidence fails to resolve an ambiguity, the gift is void for uncertainty.[56] The same applies where the description is on the face of it indefinite, *e.g.*, a gift by a testator " to one of the sons of X," X having at the time several sons.[57]

C. Contradictions

1. Rule of thumb. Extrinsic evidence is not admissible to explain a contradiction in a will, *e.g.*, a gift of " one hundred pounds (£500) to X." In such a case, the rule is that the second expression prevails over the first [58] since it is the latest in the testator's mind; this contrasts with a deed, where the former of two inconsistent expressions prevails, for what has once been done cannot be undone. Before resorting to such a rule of thumb, however, the court tries to reconcile the two provisions in some way.[59]

2. Engrafted gift. An important example of such a reconciliation is the rule in *Lassence* v. *Tierney*,[60] which applies to deeds as well as to wills.[61] This rule has been stated as follows : " If you find an absolute gift to a legatee in the first instance, and trusts are engrafted or imposed on that absolute interest which fail, either from lapse or invalidity or any other reason, then the absolute gift takes effect so far as the trusts have failed to the exclusion of the residuary legatee or next-of-kin as the case may be." [62] Thus if there is a gift to X of a fee simple or an absolute interest in personalty, and later in the will or in a codicil there is a direction that the property given to X

[55] *Re Fish* [1894] 2 Ch. 83.
[56] *Richardson* v. *Watson* (1833) 4 B. & Ad. 787.
[57] *Strode* v. *Russel* (1708) 2 Vern. 621 at 624, 625.
[58] *Re Hammond* [1938] 3 All E.R. 308.
[59] See, *e.g., Re Gare* [1952] Ch. 80.
[60] (1849) 1 Mac. & G. 551.
[61] See *Att.-Gen.* v. *Lloyds Bank Ltd.* [1935] A.C. 382.
[62] *Hancock* v. *Watson* [1902] A.C. 14 at 22, *per* Lord Davey.

shall be held for X for life with remainder to his children, if the gift
to the children wholly or partly fails (*e.g.*, through there being no
children or through the perpetuity rule being infringed), the gift of
the fee simple or absolute interest to X takes effect, instead of the
property passing under a residuary gift or as on intestacy.[63] For
the rule to apply, there must be an initial absolute gift which is
subsequently cut down; one continuous limitation containing both
gift and restrictions will normally not bring the doctrine into play,[64]
nor will a gift in which the names of the beneficiaries are immediately followed by the words " subject to the provisions hereinafter
contained." [65]

D. A Will Speaks From Death

I. AS TO PROPERTY

A will speaks from death as regards all property comprised in it,
unless it shows a contrary intention.[66] This means that a will is
capable of disposing of all property owned by the testator at his
death even if he only acquired it after making his will. Thus a
gift of " my shares in the XYZ Co., Ltd." includes not only those
owned when the will was made but also those acquired subsequently [67]; and a devise of land carries with it all fixtures attached
to the land, even if they were affixed after the will was made.[68]

However, while the rule applies to all generic descriptions (*i.e.*,
descriptions of a class of objects which may increase or decrease)
and is not confined to general or residual gifts, it has no application
to a gift of a specific object existing at the date of the will. Thus
if a testator makes a will giving " my piano " to X and subsequently
sells his piano and buys another, X has no claim to it.[69] The bequest
is said to have been adeemed, a term applied to the failure of a gift
by the property concerned ceasing to exist, or ceasing to belong to
the testator, between the date of his will and his death.

II. AS TO PERSONS

1. Class gifts.

(a) *Class fixed at death.* The rule of construction adopted by

---

63 See *Watkins* v. *Weston* (1863) 3 De G.J. & S. 434.
64 *Re Payne* [1927] 2 Ch. 1.
65 *Re Cohen's W.T.* [1936] 1 All E.R. 103.
66 Wills Act 1837, s. 24.
67 *Trinder* v. *Trinder* (1866) L.R. 1 Eq. 695 ; contrast *Re Tetsall* [1961] 1 W.L.R. 938
(" my 750 shares ").   68 For fixtures, see *post*, pp. 375 *et seq.*
69 *Re Sikes* [1927] 1 Ch. 364.

the courts in determining the effect of class gifts is the same as in other cases, namely, to carry out the intention of the testator as expressed in the will. In the absence of any such intention, the primary rule is that if any member of the class is in existence at the testator's death, membership of the class is fixed at that moment, so that persons dying before the testator [70] or born after his death are excluded.[71] Thus under a gift to " all of my sisters " the sisters alive at the testator's death take to the exclusion of any born afterwards. In short, the will speaks from death.

(b) *Rule excluded.* There are, however, a number of secondary rules which should be mentioned.[72]

(1) NO MEMBER LIVING. If no member of the class is alive at the testator's death, the gift prima facie includes all members born at any future date.[73] Thus if a testator gives property " equally among A's children," a child born after the testator's death can claim a share only if A had no children at the testator's death.

(2) LIFE INTEREST EXISTING. If a life interest precedes the class gift (*e.g.,* " to X for life remainder to Y's children "), all those alive when the life interest ceases are entitled to share in the gift.[74] Further, those who survive the testator but die before the life interest ceases are included and their shares will pass under their wills or intestacies.[75] Similarly, if a valid direction for accumulation is made, the class does not close until the accumulations cease.[76]

(3) REVERSIONARY INTEREST GIVEN. Again, if a reversionary interest [77] is given by will, the class remains open until the interest falls into possession. Thus if property is settled on S for life with remainder to T absolutely, and T dies in S's lifetime, leaving his interest to X's children, all of X's children born before S's death are entitled to share in the gift.[78]

(4) CONDITIONAL GIFT. If a gift is contingent upon the beneficiaries fulfilling some condition, such as attaining the age of 21 years, the Rule in *Andrews* v. *Partington* [79] applies, and the class remains

---

[70] *Fitzroy* v. *Duke of Richmond* (1858) 28 L.J.Ch. 750.
[71] *Viner* v. *Francis* (1789) 2 Cox Eq. 190.
[72] See the summary in *Re Chartres* [1927] 1 Ch. 466 at 471, 472.
[73] *Weld* v. *Bradbury* (1715) 2 Vern. 705.
[74] *Re Knapp's Settlement* [1895] 1 Ch. 91 at 96.
[75] *Greenwood* v. *Greenwood* [1939] 2 All E.R. 150.
[76] *Re Stephens* [1904] 1 Ch. 322.
[77] See *post*, p. 310.
[78] *Walker* v. *Shore* (1808) 15 Ves. 122.
[79] (1791) 3 Bro.C.C. 401.

pen until one member has fulfilled the condition; it then closes.[80] f one member has fulfilled the condition at the testator's death, the class is ascertained then.[81]

(c) *The principle.* The principle behind these rules (which apply o realty and personalty alike) has been said to be one of convenience ather than of construing the testator's intention,[82] though it yields o a contrary intention.[83] As soon as any member of a class is entitled to call for his share, the class must be closed, for otherwise he size of the share to be given to him cannot be ascertained. But subject to this requirement, the class is kept open for as long as possible. Thus if property is given to A for life, remainder to all he testator's grandchildren who attain the age of 21 years, the class remains open until A has died and a grandchild has attained his majority; neither event by itself suffices to close the class.[84]

2. Gifts to individuals. In the case of gifts to individuals, the date of the will, and not the date of the testator's death, is normally he relevant time. Thus a gift " to the eldest son of my sister " is a gift to the eldest at the date of the will; if he dies before the testator, he gift lapses and the eldest son at the testator's death has no claim. Similarly, a bequest " to Lord Sherborne " is a gift to the holder of he title at the date of the will.[85] But like all rules of construction, his yields to a contrary intention, and a legacy " to the Lord Mayor of London for the time being " operates as a gift to the person holding that office at the testator's death,[86] while a gift " to the Mayor of Lowestoft for the benefit of poor and needy fishermen of Lowestoft " takes effect as a gift to the Mayor of Lowestoft for the time being, and not as a gift to a particular person who is Mayor at a particular time.[87]

E. *Exercise of Powers of Appointment*

A general devise or bequest (*e.g.,* " I give all my property to X ") operates to exercise a general power of appointment unless a contrary

---

[0] *Re Bleckly* [1951] Ch. 740.
[1] *Picken* v. *Matthews* (1878) 10 Ch.D. 264.
[2] *Re Emmet's Estate* (1880) 13 Ch.D. 484 at 490. See, generally, J. H. C. Morris (1954) 70 L.Q.R. 61.
[3] See *Re Wernher's S.T.* [1961] 1 W.L.R. 136.
[4] *Re Paul's S.T.* [1920] 1 Ch. 99; and see, generally, M. & W. 508–511.
[5] *Re Whorwood* (1887) 34 Ch.D. 446.
[6] *Re Daniels* (1918) 87 L.J.Ch. 661.
[7] *Re Pipe* (1937) 106 L.J.Ch. 252.

intention is shown by the will.[88] On the other hand, a special power
(which for this purpose includes a power to appoint to " anyone
except X ") is not exercised by a general bequest or devise unless
the will shows a contrary intention, as by referring to the power or
to the property concerned.[89]

F. " To A, but if He Die Without Issue, to B "

1. Before 1838. The construction put on a gift " to A, but if he
die without issue, to B " before the Wills Act 1837, was that in the
case of realty A took an entail with remainder to B, while in the case
of personalty A took an absolute interest. This odd result was
achieved by construing " if he die without issue " as meaning " if he
dies and his issue dies out," so that B was only to take when the last
of A's descendants was dead. This displayed an intention to create
an entail which was given effect to in the case of realty.[90] The gift
to B not only followed an entail but also was vested and so did not
infringe the perpetuity rule; but A might bar the entail even if he
had no issue and so B's chance of taking the land was remote. In
the case of personalty, A took an absolute interest,[91] for personalty
could not be entailed,[92] and even if A had no issue the gift over
could not be effective because it infringed the perpetuity rule.[93]

2. The Wills Act 1837. The Wills Act 1837 [94] in effect provided
that the natural meaning should be given to such gifts and that A
should take the fee simple in realty and the absolute interest in
personalty, subject in each case to a gift over to B if at A's death no
issue of A was living. The inconvenience of this was that A could
never know during his lifetime whether or not the gift over to B
would take effect. Even if A had many children and grandchildren
alive, they might all perish in some calamity before his death and so
leave him to " die without issue."

3. After 1882. Accordingly, it has been enacted [95] that where by
deed or will any such gift was made after 1882 in the case of land
(whether given in fee simple or otherwise) or after 1925 in the case

---

[88] Wills Act 1837, s. 27.
[89] *Re Ackerley* [1913] 1 Ch. 510 at 515.
[90] *Counden* v. *Clerke* (1614) Hob. 29.
[91] *Chandless* v. *Price* (1796) 3 Ves. 99.
[92] *Ante,* p. 42.
[93] *Candy* v. *Campbell* (1834) 2 Cl. & F. 421.
[94] s. 29.
[95] L.P.A. 1925, s. 134, extending C.A. 1882, s. 10.

of any property, the gift over to B becomes void as soon as any issue of A attains the age of 21; but this does not apply to entails, which, being barrable, require no such provision. A's interest thus becomes absolute either if any issue attains the age of 21 (even if none survives A) or if A dies leaving any issue (even if none attains the age of 21). Further, even before A's interest has become absolute, land subject to such a gift over is alienable, for the gift over makes the land settled land and A is in the position of a tenant for life, although if he sells under his statutory powers the purchase-money will be subject to a corresponding gift over.[96]

G. The Rule in Wild's Case

1. Before 1926. Under the Rule in *Wild's Case*,[97] which yielded to any contrary intention, the effect of a devise " to A and his children " depended upon the facts existing when the will was made. The Rule was laid down in terms which included a devise " to A and his issue " as well as a devise " to A and his children," but in modern times it seems never to have been applied to the former expression.[98] The Rule operated as follows.

(a) *No children living.* If A had no children when the will was made, he took an estate tail, even if children had been born before the testator's death. " Children " was construed as a word of limitation, for the only way in which the testator could have intended to benefit A's children under an immediate gift was by their being entitled to succeed under A's entail. By barring the entail, A could of course prevent his children from taking anything.

(b) *Children living.* If A had children living (and not merely conceived but not born [99]) when the will was made, the word ' children " was treated as a word of purchase and A took jointly with all his children living at the testator's death in accordance with the usual rules for class gifts.

2. After 1925.

(a) *No children living.* If no children were living at the date of the will, A cannot take an entail, for an entail can no longer be created by informal words.[1] In such cases, a fee simple interest

---

6 *Ante,* pp. 160, 164, 192.
7 (1599) 6 Co.Rep. 16b at 17a b.
8 For which see *ante,* p. 26.
9 *Roper* v. *Roper* (1867) L.R. 3 C.P. 32.
1 *Ante,* p. 26.

passes, to which A, it seems, is solely entitled, even if children are born after the will is made but before the testator dies [2]; but some take the view that A takes it jointly with any of his children living at the testator's death.[3]

(b) *Children living.* The second branch of the Rule has not been affected. As before, A takes jointly with all his children living at the testator's death.

Part 2

INTESTACY

The rules relating to intestacy must now be considered. If the deceased died wholly intestate, leaving no effective will, these rules govern the devolution of all his property, while if he died partly testate and partly intestate, they apply to all the property which does not pass under his will.

Before 1926, realty and personalty descended differently. All the realty vested in the heir, whereas the personalty devolved on the next-of-kin. Thus if a widower died intestate leaving three sons and four daughters, the eldest son was the heir and took all the realty, but all seven children shared the personalty equally. In the case of deaths occurring after 1925, both realty and personalty devolve in the same way under the new code of intestacy; and for those dying after 1952, the Intestates' Estates Act 1952 made some important modifications to the new code, though leaving it basically unchanged.[3a] Three separate sets of rules must therefore be considered:

1. Realty before 1926.
2. Personalty before 1926.
3. All property after 1925, subject to modifications after 1952.

Sect. 1. Realty Before 1926

Upon an intestacy occurring before 1926, the general rule was that all realty which was vested in the deceased passed to his heir subject to the rights of the surviving spouse. The heir was ascertained at the moment of the death of the intestate and not before, for *nemo est haeres viventis.* The rules for ascertaining the heir were partly

---

[2] L.P.A. 1925, s. 130. [3] See *ante*, p. 26.
[3a] For details after 1966, further slight modifications were made by the Family Provision Act 1966.

common law rules and partly statutory; the Inheritance Act 1833 made a number of important changes in the old law. The rules for ascertaining the heir will be considered before setting out the rights of the surviving spouse.

A. Ascertainment of the Heir

The ten rules for ascertaining the heir fall under the four heads of the purchaser, the issue, ancestors and collaterals, and relatives of the half blood.

I. THE PURCHASER

1. <u>Descent was traced from the last purchaser.</u>[4]

The last purchaser was the person who last acquired the land otherwise than by descent on intestacy, escheat, partition or inclosure,[5] *i.e.*, otherwise than by operation of law. A person who acquired the land by buying it or having it given or devised to him was a purchaser for this purpose, and the descent was traced from the last purchaser. For example, if F bought land and died intestate, his eldest son S inherited it as heir to F. If S then died intestate, descent was traced from F; the land descended to the heir of F and not to the heir of S. But if F had devised the land to S, on the death of S intestate, descent had to be traced from S, for he was the last purchaser. Until the contrary was shown, the person last entitled was deemed to be the last purchaser.

There was one modification of this rule. By the Law of Property Amendment Act 1859,[6] if there was no heir of the purchaser, descent could be traced from the person last entitled to the land. For example, if B, a bastard, bought land and died intestate leaving a widow and one child, that child inherited the land. If the child then died intestate and without issue, descent had to be traced afresh from B. Since B's issue had died out and in the eyes of the law he had no ancestors (for a bastard is *filius nullius*, the child of no one), there was a failure of the heirs of B; B's widow was not entitled, for she was no blood relation of B. In these circumstances the Act of 1859 allowed descent to be traced from the person last entitled, namely, B's child, in which case B's widow could inherit the land; although no blood relation of B, she was a blood relation of her child.

---

[4] Inheritance Act 1833, ss. 1, 2. Previously, descent had been traced from the person last seised: 3 Cru.Dig. 328.

[5] For partition see *ante*, p. 225, and for inclosure see *post*, p. 450.

[6] s. 19.

II. THE ISSUE

2. The issue were preferred to the other relatives, the male issue being preferred to the female issue.

3. The elder male was preferred to the younger male, but females of the same degree all took equally as co-parceners.

4. Issue of a deceased person represented him, being preferred among themselves according to rules 2 and 3.

These three rules were common law rules.[7] They are perhaps best made clear by illustrations. In these, " P " stands for the purchaser and the other letters indicate the relationship to him of the others concerned. Thus " S " and " D " stand for " son " and " daughter " respectively, " GS " and " GD " for " grandson " and " granddaughter," " U " and " A " for " uncle " and " aunt," and the like. The numerals are used to distinguish two or more of the same relationship and, where relevant, show the order of birth; and the circles indicate death.

(a)

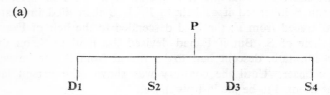

(i) S2 is the heir.

(ii) If S2 predeceased P leaving no issue, S4 is the heir.

(iii) If both S2 and S4 predeceased P leaving no issue, D1 and D3 took as co-parceners, together constituting the heir.

(b)

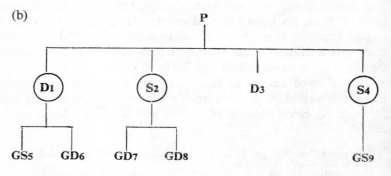

---

[7] 3 Cru.Dig. 331–333.

Here, D1, S2 and S4 have all predeceased P, leaving children.

  (i) GD7 and GD8 inherit as co-parceners.

 (ii) If they predeceased P leaving no issue, GS9 is the heir.

(iii) If GS9 also predeceased P leaving no issue, GS5 and D3 inherit as co-parceners.[8]

III. ANCESTORS AND COLLATERALS

5. If the purchaser left no issue, his nearest lineal ancestor was entitled, issue of a deceased ancestor representing the ancestor according to rule 4.[9]

This reversed the common law rule that an ancestor could not inherit; but even before 1834, collaterals (issue of an ancestor who are not themselves ancestors of the purchaser) could inherit.[10]

6. Paternal ancestors and their issue were preferred to maternal ancestors and their issue, and male paternal ancestors and their issue were preferred to female paternal ancestors and their issue.[11]

Rules 5 and 6 meant that the purchaser's mother and her relations could not inherit the land unless every single relation on the father's side was dead, ancestors as well as collaterals. A second cousin twice removed on the paternal side was preferred to the purchaser's mother herself. Thus the order of succession was—

  (i) The purchaser's father;

 (ii) The issue of the purchaser's father, such as brothers and sisters of the purchaser or his nephews and nieces;

(iii) The father of the purchaser's father;

(iv) Issue of the father of the purchaser's father;

and so on.

Where issue of an ancestor were entitled, they were preferred among themselves according to rules 2, 3, and 4. Further, each class had to be entirely exhausted before moving on to the next; a single member of class (ii) excluded the paternal grandfather.

Before 1834 the position was similar to the extent that collaterals on the father's side were preferred to those on the mother's side; but ancestors could not inherit.[12]

7. The mother of the more remote male paternal ancestor and her heirs were preferred to the mother of the less remote male paternal ancestor and her heirs.[13]

---

[8] *Cooper* v. *Frame* (1850) 19 L.J.Ch. 313.
[9] Inheritance Act 1833, s. 6.   [10] Williams R.P. 247.
[11] Inheritance Act 1833, s. 7.
[12] 3 Cru.Dig. 351.
[13] Inheritance Act 1833, ss. 7, 8.

When it became impossible to trace any further male paternal ancestors and their issue, the female paternal ancestors and their issue came next. Among these, the mother of the more remote male paternal ancestor came first. This may be illustrated thus:

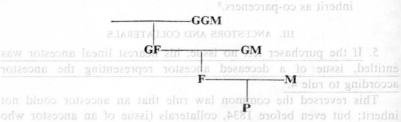

The father of GF cannot be traced, and so the order of succession is (i) F; (ii) F's issue; (iii) GF; (iv) GF's issue; (v) GGM; (vi) GGM's heirs (*i.e.*, her issue first, and upon failure of them, her ancestors and their issue); (vii) GM; (viii) GM's heirs; (ix) M. A descendant of a grandfather of GGM was thus preferred to M, whose chances of being P's heir were indeed remote. How far this rule was law before 1834 is not clear, but the Act confirmed the better opinion in support of the rule.[14]

8. On failure of paternal ancestors and their issue, similar rules applied to the maternal ancestors and their issue.[15]

IV. RELATIVES OF THE HALF BLOOD

Before 1834, no relative of the half blood could succeed as heir[16]; the Inheritance Act 1833 altered this rule. Two persons are said to be related by the half blood when they trace descent from different marriages of a common ancestor.

9. If the common ancestor was a male, relatives of the half blood took next after relatives of the whole blood of the same degree.[17]

For example,

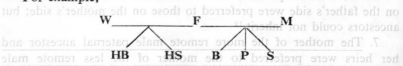

F has married first W and then M. If P dies without issue, the order of succession is (i) F; (ii) B, a brother of the whole blood.

---

14 Williams R.P. 249; 3 Cru.Dig. 354–387.
15 Inheritance Act, 1833, ss. 7, 8.
16 3 Cru.Dig 342.
17 Inheritance Act 1833, s. 9.

and his issue; (iii) S, a sister of the whole blood, and her issue; (iv) HB, a brother of the half blood, and his issue; (v) HS, a sister of the half blood, and her issue.

10. If the common ancestor was a female, relatives of the half blood took next after her.[18]

For example,

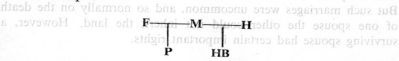

M married first F and then H. On the death of P without issue, M could not claim the land if F or any relation of his was alive. Only after all the paternal relatives had been exhausted was M entitled, and then next after her came HB, who could have no better right than her.

This example may be contrasted with the following:

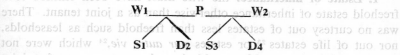

P married first W1 and then W2. On P's death intestate, S1 was the heir. If S1 later died intestate and without issue, S3 inherited the land. It is true that S3 was only a half-brother of S1 whereas D2 was his sister of the whole blood, but descent had to be traced from P, and all P's children are necessarily equally closely related to him; a man cannot have children of the half blood.

Variations by local custom. So far as the rules set out above were statutory, they overrode any local custom. The rules which were not statutory, however, applied only if there was no local custom to the contrary. Thus rule 3 was varied by the customs of gavelkind and borough English [19]; and frequently the heir to copyhold land was ascertained according to some local custom, so that the customary heir and the heir at common law were different persons.

Escheat. If no heir could be traced, the land escheated *propter defectum sanguinis* [20] to the feudal lord. If no mesne lord could prove that the land was held of him, it escheated to the Crown.

---

[18] *Ibid.*   [19] *Ante*, p. 229.
[20] Co.Litt. 13a; 3 Cru.Dig. 398; M. & W. 18.

Equitable interests did not escheat until the Intestates' Estates Act 1884 [21]; prior to that the trustees took the property beneficially. [22]

B. Rights of a Surviving Spouse

Occasionally there would be a marriage between two persons so related by blood that on the death of one, the other was the heir. But such marriages were uncommon, and so normally on the death of one spouse the other could not inherit the land. However, a surviving spouse had certain important rights.

I. A WIDOWER

A widower was entitled to a life estate in the whole of the real property of his deceased wife. This right was known as curtesy, or, more fully, an estate by the Curtesy of England. It could be claimed only if certain conditions had been fulfilled.

1. Estate of inheritance: the wife must have been entitled to a freehold estate of inheritance otherwise than as a joint tenant. There was no curtesy out of estates less than freehold such as leaseholds, nor out of life estates [23] or estates *pur autre vie*, [24] which were not estates of inheritance. Nor could there be curtesy out of a joint tenancy, for the right of survivorship of the other tenants excluded any such claim. [25] But if the wife was entitled either solely or as a tenant in common or co-parcener to a fee simple or fee tail, the husband might claim his curtesy. [26]

2. Seisin or possession: the wife must have been either seised " in deed," or else entitled in possession to an equitable interest. There was no curtesy out of estates either in remainder or reversion. The common law rule was that even an estate in possession gave rise to no curtesy unless the wife had actually taken possession of the land. [27] Seisin in law (*i.e.*, the right to seisin) was not enough: seisin in deed was required. [28] However, entry on the land by the husband on behalf of his wife sufficed, and in the case of incorporeal hereditaments,

---

[21] ss. 4, 7.
[22] *Burgess* v. *Wheate* (1759) 1 Wm.Bl. 123.
[23] *Boothby* v. *Vernon* (1725) 9 Mod. 147.
[24] *Stead* v. *Platt* (1853) 18 Beav. 50.
[25] *Palmer* v. *Rich* [1897] 1 Ch. 134 at 141.
[26] 2 Cru.Dig. 394, 408.
[27] Co.Litt. 29a.
[28] See *Parker* v. *Carter* (1845) 4 Hare 400 at 418.

some act of ownership (such as receiving the rent under a rentcharge or making a presentation in the case of an advowson) took the place of entry.[29] Further, if seisin in deed was impossible, as where the wife died an instant after becoming entitled to the property, seisin in law sufficed.[30]

Equity, which followed the law and allowed curtesy out of equitable interests,[31] required the equitable equivalent of seisin in deed, consisting of some act, such as receipt of the income of the land from the trustees, which showed that the wife had the present enjoyment of the equitable interest.[32]

3. Actual birth of heritable issue: the husband had no claim to curtesy unless issue of the marriage capable of inheriting the land had been born alive. Thus if the wife was seised of a tale male and only female issue had been born, the husband took no curtesy[33]; but if a son was born alive, the husband at once became prospectively entitled to curtesy even if the son died a few minutes later leaving nobody to inherit the entail after the wife's death.[34]

The issue must have been born alive. The old test was whether the child was heard to cry out, although this was not necessary if other proof of live birth could be given.[35]

4. No disposition of land: the land must not have been disposed of either *inter vivos* or by will. At common law a wife could not alienate realty *inter vivos* without her husband's concurrence and could not devise land even with his consent. The husband could thus prevent her from disposing of her land, but if it was alienated his claim to curtesy was defeated.

Both equity and statute modified this rule. If realty was conveyed to the " separate use " of the wife, equity allowed her to dispose of it by herself either *inter vivos* or by will; and by the Married Women's Property Act 1882, if a married woman had married or acquired property after 1882, she was able to dispose of it by herself as if she were unmarried.[36] In each case, the husband could claim curtesy only if his wife had disposed of the property neither *inter vivos* nor by will.[37]

[29] Tudor L.C.R.P. 109.
[30] See *Eager* v. *Furnivall* (1881) 17 Ch.D. 115; and see *ante*, p. 277.
[31] *Watts* v. *Ball* (1708) 1 P.Wms. 108.
[32] *Casborne* v. *Scarfe* (1738) 1 Atk. 603 at 606.   [33] Co.Litt. 29b.
[34] See, *e.g.*, *Jones* v. *Ricketts* (1862) 10 W.R. 576.
[35] *Paine's Case* (1587) 8 Co.Rep. 34a at 35a.   [36] See *post*, p. 520.
[37] *Cooper* v. *Macdonald* (1877) 7 Ch.D. 288 (equity); *Hope* v. *Hope* [1892] 2 Ch. 336 (statute).

Variations of curtesy. The existence of curtesy and the conditions under which it could be claimed were modified in the case of
land subject to customs such as gavelkind.[38] Further, there was no
curtesy out of copyholds unless the custom of the particular manor
allowed it.[39]

II. A WIDOW

A widow's rights fell under two heads, namely, dower, and the
Intestates' Estates Act 1890.

Dower

A widow was entitled to dower, which was a life interest in one
third of the realty of her deceased husband, provided the following
conditions were satisfied.

1. Estate of inheritance: the husband must have been entitled to
a freehold estate of inheritance otherwise than as a joint tenant. The
same rules applied here as in the case of curtesy.[40]

2. Seisin or possession: the husband must have been either seised
in law or else (after 1833) entitled in possession to an equitable interest.
Seisin in deed was not required,[41] for the wife had no means of compelling the husband to make an actual entry. But the estate had to
be in possession; there was no dower out of remainders or reversions.

Equity refused to follow the law, and gave no dower out of
equitable interests.[42] The reason for this was that dower was not
defeated by any disposition by the husband; a wife's prospective
right of dower attached to any land of her husband even if he disposed
of it. The inconvenience which this caused to conveyancers induced
equity to refuse to give dower out of equitable interests. However,
the Dower Act 1833 [43] made equitable interests in possession subject
to dower, provided the parties married after 1833.

3. Birth of heritable issue possible: it must have been possible for
heritable issue of the marriage to be born, although the actual birth

---

[38] See *Re Howlett* [1949] Ch. 767 ; *ante*, p. 229.
[39] Scriven 74.
[40] See Litt. s. 36.
[41] Litt. s. 448.
[42] *Chaplin* v. *Chaplin* (1733) 3 P.Wms. 229.
[43] ss. 2, 14.

of such issue was not required.[44] Thus if land was given " to A and the heirs male of his body," his widow could claim dower even if no issue, or only female issue, had been born. But if land was given " to A and the heirs of his body begotten on Mary," and A married Jane, Jane could not claim dower, for by no possibility could her issue inherit the land.

4. Dower not barred: after 1833, the land must not have been disposed of by deed or will, nor must a declaration in bar of dower have been made. As mentioned above, the husband could not at common law defeat his wife's prospective right of dower by alienating the land. Dower attached to all freehold estates of inheritance of which the husband was seised at any time, however short, during the marriage, even if this had occurred many years before his death.[45] This inconvenience could be avoided by the husband ensuring that he became entitled only in equity, as by having any land he acquired conveyed to trustees on trust for him; this, however, was unsatisfactory. Dower was also barred if the wife before marriage agreed to accept a jointure, *i.e.*, an estate in realty for her life at least, to take effect as soon as her husband died, made expressly in satisfaction of her dower.[46] But this meant making substantial provision for the wife in advance, and so a satisfactory alternative was sought. This was found in the somewhat complicated " uses to bar dower " invented by Fearne in the eighteenth century.[47] These uses were based on giving the husband a mere life interest coupled with a power of appointment and need not be considered here in detail.

Such devices were rendered unnecessary by the Dower Act 1833,[48] which provided that if the parties married after 1833, dower could not be claimed out of any land disposed of by the husband either in his lifetime or by his will, nor out of land in respect of which he had made a declaration by deed or will in bar of dower. The Act also made dower subject to the husband's debts [49]; formerly it took precedence over such claims.

Variations of dower. The widow's right to dower in gavelkind land was subject to special rules.[50] The extent of dower varied in

---

44 Litt. s. 53.
45 See 1 Cru.Dig. 157.
46 Statute of Uses 1535, s. 6. For the modern use of the term " jointure," see *ante*, p. 204.
47 Fearne C.R. 347.
48 ss. 4, 6, 7.
49 s. 5.
50 See Rob.Gav. (5th ed.) 141–144; *ante*, p. 229.

different parts of the country, so that dower might extend to the whole of the land, or to half or one-quarter of it.[51] There was no dower in copyholds, but in many manors there was a custom for widows to have free-bench, which corresponded to dower, and was normally a life estate in one-third of the land.[52] The Dower Act 1833 did not apply to copyholds.[53]

Mode of enjoyment of dower. A widow was entitled to have one-third of the land assigned to her for her life. This assignment was to be effected within the quarantine, namely, the period of 40 days after the husband's death during which *Magna Carta* 1215, c. 7, allowed the widow to remain in his house. The assignment was made by the person entitled to the land[54] and the widow was usually entitled to have it made " by metes and bounds," *i.e.*, by having the boundaries of her portion marked out. She might, however, accept dower in some other form, as by receiving one-third of the rents and profits of the land.[55] In default of agreement, she could apply to the court, which would order the sheriff to assign by metes and bounds land to the value of one-third of the whole at the date of assignment.[56] Where this was impossible, dower was assigned in the most convenient manner; thus dower out of an advowson entitled the widow to each third presentation,[57] and dower out of a villein entitled the widow to every third day's work.[58]

Intestates' Estates Act 1890

A widow, in addition to any right of dower, was sometimes entitled to £500. This right arose under the Intestates' Estates Act 1890, s. 1, if her husband—

(i) died after September 1, 1890,
(ii) leaving no will of any effect,[59] and
(iii) leaving no issue surviving him.

The £500 carried interest at 4 per cent. per annum from the death until payment and was charged rateably on the realty and personalty.[60]

---

[51] Litt. s. 37; Co.Litt. 33b.
[52] See Scriven 69.
[53] *Smith* v. *Adams* (1854) 5 De G.M. & G. 712.
[54] Tudor L.C.R.P. 124.
[55] *Williams* v. *Thomas* [1909] 1 Ch. 713 at 731, 732.
[56] *Williams* v. *Thomas* [1909] 1 Ch. 713.
[57] Co.Litt. 32a.
[58] Co.Litt. 32a.
[59] See *Re Cuffe* [1908] 2 Ch. 500.
[60] I.E.A. 1890, ss. 2, 3.

For example, if the realty was worth four times as much as the personalty, £400 was paid out of the realty and £100 out of the personalty. If the husband's total estate was £500 or less at his death,[61] his widow took it all, provided the above conditions were satisfied. The Act made no provision for surviving husbands.

Sect. 2. Personalty Before 1926

As has been seen, all realty descended on intestacy to one person, the heir, thus preserving the estate intact. Leaseholds and other personalty, on the other hand, passed to the next-of-kin as ascertained according to the rules laid down by the Statute of Distribution 1670, as explained and amended by the Statute of Frauds 1677 and the Statute of Distribution 1685.

Subject to certain special rules, the property devolved upon all next-of-kin of the same degree equally. The degrees of relationship were ascertained by counting the number of steps between the deceased and the relation in question, counting directly in the case of those related lineally and through the common ancestor in the case of collaterals. Thus if X died intestate leaving the following relatives (in which GF stands for grandfather, U for uncle, N for nephew or niece, and so on)—

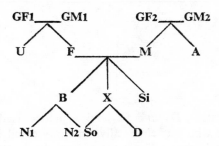

F, M, So and D are relatives of the first degree, GF1, GF2, GM1, GM2, B and Si are relatives of the second degree, and U, A, N1 and N2, relatives of the third degree.

The special rules were as follows:

---

[61] See *Re Heath* [1907] 2 Ch. 270.

I. SURVIVING SPOUSE

1. Widower: if the deceased left a husband, he took the whole of the personalty absolutely, to the exclusion of the other relatives.[62]

2. Widow and issue: if the deceased left a widow and issue, the widow took one-third absolutely[63]; this contrasts with dower, where the widow's third was hers for life only.

3. Widow and no issue: if the deceased left a widow and no issue, the widow took—

    (a) her £500 under the Intestates' Estates Act 1890 if the necessary conditions had been fulfilled[64];

    (b) one-half of the residue absolutely.[65]

II. OTHER RELATIVES

Subject to the above claims of the surviving spouse, if any, personalty devolved as follows:

4. Issue: the issue of the deceased took *per stirpes*, males taking equally with females and the younger equally with the elder.[66] "*Per stirpes*" means "through the stocks of descent." An example will make this clear.

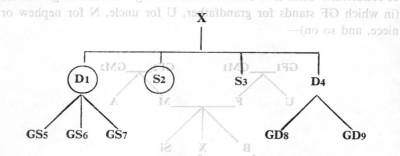

X dies intestate, D1 and S2 having predeceased him. Each of his children who was either alive or represented by issue formed a stock of descent. There were thus three stocks of descent, namely, those of D1, S3 and D4. X's personalty would therefore be divided into thirds. One-third would be divided among

---

[62] Statute of Frauds 1677, s. 25.
[63] Statute of Distribution 1670, s. 5.
[64] *Ante*, p. 298.
[65] Statute of Distribution 1670, s. 6.
[66] *Ibid.* s. 5.

the children of D1, who took her share and so got one-ninth each. One-third would pass to S3, and the remaining third to D4; GD8 and GD9 would get nothing, for their mother D4 was still alive. This rule of descent *per stirpes* applied even if all the children were dead.[67] Thus if all X's children had predeceased him, the grandchildren would not take *per capita* (one share for each head) but still *per stirpes*; in other words, instead of taking one-fifth each, each of the children of D1 would take one-sixth and each of the children of D4 one-quarter.

Where the intestate was a father, any advances made in his life-time to his child had to be brought into hotchpot (*i.e.*, into account) when distributing the estate[68]; but this rule did not apply if the intestate was the mother,[69] or died only partially intestate.[70]

5. Father: in default of surviving issue, the intestate's father was entitled absolutely.[71]

6. Mother, brothers and sisters: if the father also predeceased the intestate, the mother, brothers and sisters shared equally.[72] Children, but not remoter descendants, of a deceased brother or sister took their parents' share.[73] Thus the mother (first degree), a brother (second degree) and the child of a deceased sister, *i.e.*, a nephew or niece (third degree) might share the personalty equally. But if the mother, brothers and sisters had all predeceased the intestate, the children of the brothers and sisters did not take *per stirpes* under this rule, but *per capita* under the general rule.[74]

In default of mother, brothers and sisters, the general rule applied, and the next-of-kin of the same degree took *per capita*.[75] Any relative of one degree would exclude all relatives of remoter degrees.

It will be noted that there was no preference for the whole blood; relatives of the half blood took equally with those of the whole blood.[76] Nor were males preferred to females, or the elder to the younger. In these respects, the rules were perhaps more reasonable than those applying to realty; but there seems little to justify some of the complexities.

---

[67] *Re Natt* (1888) 37 Ch.D. 517. [68] Statute of Distribution 1670, s. 5.
[69] *Holt* v. *Frederick* (1726) 2 P.Wms. 356.
[70] *Re Roby* [1908] 1 Ch. 71.
[71] *Blackborough* v. *Davis* (1701) 1 P.Wms. 41 at 51.
[72] Statute of Distribution 1685, s. 7.
[73] Statute of Distribution 1670, s. 7.
[74] *Re Ross's Trusts* (1871) L.R. 13 Eq. 286.
[75] Statute of Distribution 1670, s. 6.
[76] *Watts* v. *Crooke* (1690) Show.P.C. 108.

Bona vacantia. If no next-of-kin could be found according to the above rules, the Crown was entitled to the personalty of the intestate as *bona vacantia* (goods without an owner). If the deceased had appointed an executor (*e.g.*, if he had made a will which, apart from the appointment of an executor, was totally or partially ineffective through the premature death of the beneficiaries or some other cause), the executor might be entitled for his own benefit. Before the Executors Act 1830, the appointment of an executor entitled him to undisposed-of personalty even in preference to the next-of-kin unless they could show from the will that they were intended to benefit.[77] The Act, however, obliged the executor to hold the property on trust for the next-of-kin unless a contrary intention could be shown. But the Act did not alter the position as between the executor and the Crown,[78] and unless a contrary intention was shown the executor was entitled.[79]

Sect. 3. All Property After 1925

A. The New Rules of Intestacy

Where a person dies intestate after 1925, no distinction is made between realty and personalty. By the Administration of Estates Act 1925, all property, whether real or personal, which does not already consist of money is held on trust for sale.[80] The personal representatives of the deceased have power to postpone sale for such period as they think proper. However, unless required for the purpose of administration for want of other assets, " personal chattels " (see below) are not to be sold without special reason, and reversionary interests (such as an interest in a trust fund which will not fall into the intestate's estate until the life interest of some third person has ceased) are similarly not to be sold without special reason.

Out of the fund thus produced, the personal representatives must pay all funeral, testamentary and administration expenses, debts and other liabilities, and set aside a fund to meet the pecuniary legacies (if any) bequeathed by any will of the deceased.[81] The residue must then be distributed to the persons beneficially entitled under rules which are on a much more reasonable basis than those obtaining before 1926, and were in the main laid down by the Administration

---

[77] *Bishop of Cloyne* v. *Young* (1750) 2 Ves.Sen. 91.
[78] *Re Jones* [1925] Ch. 340 at 344.
[79] *Att.-Gen.* v. *Jefferys* [1908] A.C. 411.
[80] s. 33 (1).
[81] A.E.A. 1925, s. 33 (2).

of Estates Act 1925. The Intestates' Estates Act 1952 made important modifications for persons dying intestate after 1952: the main changes were directed to improving the position of a surviving spouse. If the intestate died between the end of 1925 and the beginning of 1953, the surviving spouse took the " personal chattels " absolutely, £1,000 absolutely, and a life interest in only half the residue, if the intestate left issue, but otherwise in the whole of the residue. The surviving spouse had no claim to the residuary capital unless the deceased left no parent, no brother or sister or their issue, no grandparent, and no uncle or aunt or their issue; it did not matter whether the relationship to the intestate was of the whole blood or of the half blood. A single grandparent, niece or first cousin would take the residue to the exclusion of the widow; and where the intestate was of moderate means, a mere life interest in the residue might well be inadequate to support his widow.

The Intestates' Estates Act 1952 accordingly amended the rules laid down by the Administration of Estates Act 1925 so as to give the surviving spouse £5,000 (instead of £1,000), or, if the intestate left no issue, £20,000 and the *capital* of half the residue, and not a mere life interest. Further, the relations of the intestate were divided into two groups, and if the intestate died leaving no issue, and none of the group of nearer relations, then the surviving spouse took the whole estate to the exclusion of any of the more remote relations. A number of other changes were made by the Act of 1952, and for deaths after 1966 the sums of £5,000 and £20,000 have been increased to £8,750 and £30,000 respectively by the Family Provision Act 1966.[82] The present rules, for all deaths intestate after 1966, are set out below.

1. The surviving spouse. The rights of the surviving spouse, whether husband or wife, depend upon whether the intestate left issue or any " near relations," a convenient term to describe the parents, and the brothers and sisters of the whole blood and their issue (" issue " as usual meaning any descendant, however remote). There are three categories.[83]

(a) *Issue.* If the intestate leaves any issue (whether or not there are any " near relations "), the surviving spouse takes the following interests.

(1) THE PERSONAL CHATTELS ABSOLUTELY. " Personal chattels " are elaborately defined. They include horses, cars, domestic

---

[82] s. 1. The Lord Chancellor has power to make an order increasing these sums.
[83] A.E.A. 1925, s. 46.

animals, plate, linen, china, glass, books, pictures, prints, furniture, jewellery, " articles of household or personal use or ornament," and wines and consumable stores, but not chattels used for business purposes, money, or securities for money.[84] Roughly speaking, the phrase includes everything that goes to make a home, and rather more besides, but not the house itself; the phrase has a meaning quite distinct from " personalty " or " personal property."

(2) £8,750 ABSOLUTELY, free of death duties and costs, with 4 per cent. interest thereon from the date of death until it is paid or appropriated. Both the £8,750 and the interest thereon are charged on the residuary estate, though the interest is payable primarily out of income and not capital.[85]

(3) A LIFE INTEREST in half the residuary estate.

(b) *No issue but near relations.* If the intestate leaves no issue but one or more " near relations," the surviving spouse takes the following interests.

(1) THE PERSONAL CHATTELS ABSOLUTELY.

(2) £30,000 ABSOLUTELY.

(3) HALF THE RESIDUARY ESTATE ABSOLUTELY.

(c) *No issue and no near relations.* If the intestate left no issue and no " near relations," the surviving spouse is entitled to the entire residuary estate absolutely.

These provisions are subject to a number of subsidiary rules.

(1) PURCHASE OF LIFE INTEREST. Within twelve months of probate or letters of administration being first taken out (or within such extended period as the court may grant), a surviving spouse who takes a life interest may (even if an infant) by notice in writing to the personal representatives elect that his or her life interest shall be purchased for a capital sum reckoned in accordance with rules laid down in the Act. If the surviving spouse is the sole personal representative, written notice must be given to the principal probate registrar.[86] This right under the Act of 1952 to compel a purchase replaces a mere power under the Act of 1925 for the personal representative to purchase the life interest.

(2) PURCHASE OF MATRIMONIAL HOME. The surviving spouse may by writing require the personal representatives (even if he or she is

[84] *Ibid.* s. 55 (1) (x).
[85] I.E.A. 1952, s. 1 (4).
[86] A.E.A. 1925, s. 47A. (The Act of 1925 is cited as amended by I.E.A., 1952.)

one of them) to appropriate to him or her any dwelling-house forming part of the residuary estate in which he or she was resident at the death of the intestate: usually this will be the matrimonial home. This does not apply where the intestate's interest in the house is a mere tenancy which would determine (or could be determined by the landlord) within two years of his death, nor where the house is part of larger property held by the intestate unless the court is satisfied that the exercise of the surviving spouse's right is not likely to diminish the value of assets in the residuary estate or make them more difficult to dispose of. These provisions of the Act of 1952 in effect give the surviving spouse a power to compel the personal representatives to exercise for the house the general discretionary power of appropriation conferred by the Act of 1925 [87]; the property appropriated is taken, at a proper valuation, to have satisfied to that extent the property to which the surviving spouse is absolutely entitled. The personal representatives must not unnecessarily sell the house within twelve months after probate or letters of administration have first been taken out, and the surviving spouse's right to require an appropriation is exercisable only during that period or any extension granted by the court. [88]

(3) PARTIAL INTESTACY. As before 1926, these provisions apply to a partial intestacy. But under the Act of 1952, the sums of £8,750 or £30,000 mentioned above (unlike the former sum of £1,000) must be diminished by the value of any beneficial interest acquired by the surviving spouse under the will of the deceased. [89] However, it is sometimes advantageous to the surviving spouse to disclaim any interest under the will and rely solely on the rules governing intestacy. For example, the surviving spouse may be given a life interest by the will, and the remainder of the deceased's property may pass as on intestacy. In this case, the duty of the personal representatives to distribute the estate does not arise until the death of the surviving spouse, who accordingly is not entitled until then to be paid the £8,750 or £30,000 with interest. The surviving spouse may accordingly prefer to disclaim the testamentary life interest and take forthwith under the intestacy. [90]

(4) SEPARATION. If husband and wife are separated by a judicial separation or a separation order, on the wife's death intestate any

[87] By s. 41.
[88] I.E.A. 1952, 2nd Sched.
[89] A.E.A. 1925, s. 49 (1) (*aa*).
[90] See *Re McKee* [1931] 2 Ch. 145; *Re Thornber* [1937] Ch. 29.

property acquired by her after the separation devolves as if her husband were then dead [91]; but there is no corresponding rule for the husband's property.

(5) COMMORIENTES. Although the general rule laid down for commorientes [92] applies in general to intestacy, the Act of 1952 has modified its application as between husband and wife. When the intestate and his or her spouse die in circumstances rendering it uncertain which survived the other, the rules of intestacy apply as if the spouse had not survived the intestate.[93] Thus if the wife, W, is younger than the husband, H, and both perish in a common disaster, then for the purposes of H's intestacy W will be treated as not having survived him. This avoids W taking benefits under H's intestacy which would almost instantly pass under her will or intestacy; H's property accordingly passes as if no spouse had survived him. This exception to the general rule is confined to intestacy as between spouses; it does not affect wills, nor does it apply to other relations, *e.g.*, issue.

2. The issue. Subject to the rights of the surviving spouse, if any, the property is held on the statutory trusts for the issue.[94] Under these trusts, the property is held upon trust for all the children of the deceased living at his death in equal shares, subject to three qualifications.

(a) *Subject to representation*, *i.e.*, subject to the rule that issue of a deceased child stand in his shoes and take his share; descent is thus *per stirpes*.

(b) *Subject to the rule that no issue attains a vested interest until he is 21 years old or married.* This in effect means that if an infant dies without having married, the property must be dealt with from that moment as if the infant had never existed.[95] Thus if X dies leaving a widow and infant son, the widow takes a life interest in half the residue. If the son dies before either marrying or attaining his majority, the widow forthwith takes absolutely either half the residue, or all, depending on whether any " near relations " survived the intestate.

(c) *Subject to hotchpot.* There are two rules governing this.

[91] Matrimonial Causes Act 1965, s. 20 (2); Matrimonial Proceedings (Magistrates' Courts) Act 1960, s. 2 (1) (*a*), replacing earlier legislation.
[92] See *ante*, p. 277.
[93] A.E.A. 1925, s. 46 (3).
[94] A.E.A. 1925, s. 46 (1).
[95] See A.E.A. 1925, s. 47 (2).

(1) INTER VIVOS. If they wish to share in the distribution of the estate, children (but not remoter issue) must bring into account any money or property which the deceased has in his lifetime paid them or settled for their benefit by way of advancement or upon marriage.[96] For example, if the estate is worth £16,000 and there are three children, one of whom has received an advancement of £2,000 in the intestate's lifetime, that child can claim only £4,000 out of the £16,000; the other two children each receive £6,000. Had the first child received an advancement of £10,000, he could not be compelled to refund any part of it for distribution between the others. The obligation to bring property into hotchpot is subject to any contrary intention appearing from the circumstances of the case, but applies even if the deceased was the mother of the children.[97] In determining what advances must be brought into hotchpot, a distinction must be drawn between payments made to start a child in life, and casual or periodical sums paid in the ordinary course of events, or so as to relieve the child from temporary difficulties; the former alone need be brought into hotchpot.[98]

(2) PARTIAL INTESTACY. In the case of partial intestacy, issue of the deceased, whether children or remoter descendants, must, subject to any contrary intention shown by the deceased, bring into hotchpot any benefit received under his will.[99] Thus if a grandchild of the deceased has received £1,000 from him, he need not bring it into hotchpot if it was an advancement made *inter vivos* (for he is not a child of the deceased), but he must bring it into account if it is given him by will.

If no issue attains a vested interest, then, subject to the claim of the surviving spouse (if any) the relatives of the deceased are entitled in the following order [1]; any member of one class who takes a vested interest excludes all members of subsequent classes.

3. The parents of the deceased are entitled in equal shares absolutely; if one is dead the survivor is entitled absolutely.

4. The brothers and sisters of the whole blood, on the statutory trusts.

A division must be made here, for at this point the " near relations " end. Those included in the foregoing classes may take an

---

[96] A.E.A. 1925, s. 47 (1).
[97] Contrast *ante*, p. 243.
[98] See *Taylor* v. *Taylor* (1875) L.R. 20 Eq. 155 at 157; *Re Hayward* [1957] Ch. 528.
[99] A.E.A. 1925, s. 49.
[1] *Ibid*. s. 46 (1).

interest even though the intestate left a surviving spouse; those in the subsequent classes cannot.

5. The brothers and sisters of the half blood, on the statutory trusts.

6. The grandparents, if more than one in equal shares.

7. The uncles and aunts of the whole blood, on the statutory trusts.

8. The uncles and aunts of the half blood, on the statutory trusts.

9. The Crown (or the Duchy of Lancaster or Duke of Cornwall) as *bona vacantia* in lieu of any right to escheat.

A number of points arise on the foregoing list.

(1) STATUTORY TRUSTS. The statutory trusts for the brothers, sisters, uncles and aunts are the same as those for the issue of the deceased, save that the provisions relating to hotchpot do not apply.[2] Thus deceased brothers, sisters, uncles and aunts are represented by their descendants, their interests in every case being contingent upon their attaining full age or marrying. "Uncles" and "aunts" include only blood relations; an aunt's husband, although bearing the courtesy description of uncle, has no claim.

(2) ILLEGITIMATE CHILDREN. Only legitimate relations can claim under the foregoing provisions, including those legitimated under the Legitimacy Act 1926 by the subsequent marriage of their parents. However, although illegitimate relations normally have no claim, by the Legitimacy Act 1926,[3] an illegitimate child or his issue will, if there are no legitimate children, take the same interest on his mother's intestacy as if he had been legitimate; and the mother of an illegitimate child will take the same interest on the child's intestacy as if he had been legitimate and she the only surviving parent. These provisions do not extend to other illegitimate relationships and are confined to intestacy.

(3) ADOPTED CHILDREN. On deaths before 1950, even a formal adoption order made no change in the rights of the parties on intestacy: the child could claim under the intestacy of his true parents (and not his adoptive parents), and his true parents could claim under his intestacy. For deaths after 1949, this rule has been reversed. A formal adoption order (as distinct from a mere *de facto* adoption) puts both child and adoptive parents in the same position for all

---

[2] *Ibid.* s. 47 (3).
[3] s. 9.

subsequent intestacies as if the child were their child, born in lawful wedlock, and not the child of any other person; but this does not apply to property entailed before the adoption order was made.[4]

(4) CROWN DISCRETION. In practice, the Crown modifies its strict rights under head No. 9 by making provision for dependants of the deceased, whether related to him or not, and for others for whom he might reasonably have been expected to make provision. This purely discretionary power, which the Act of 1925 confirms,[5] is made all the more necessary by the Crown's increased prospects of succeeding to property of an intestate. Before 1926, any relation, however remote, could claim as heir or next-of-kin, and mesne lords could claim land by escheat. After 1925, no relation more remote than a grandparent or the descendant of a grandparent can claim, and there can be no escheat to a mesne lord on intestacy.[6]

(5) EXECUTOR'S CLAIMS. On a partial intestacy, the executor cannot take undisposed-of property beneficially unless an intention to this effect is shown by the will [7]; this rule now applies to an executor as against both the Crown and the statutory next-of-kin.[8]

B. Survivals of the Old Rules

I. REALTY

In the case of all persons dying after 1925, the foregoing rules supersede the old rules relating to intestacy, and no curtesy or dower can arise.[9] However, the old general law of descent of realty still has to be applied in three cases.

1. Lunatic: any realty (including an interest under a trust for sale of realty) [9a] which a lunatic of full age at the end of 1925 then owned, and as to which he subsequently dies intestate without having recovered testamentary capacity, descends according to the general law in force before 1926.[10] Since the *general* law in force before 1926 applies, customs such as gavelkind are ignored [11]; and a child legitimated under the Legitimacy Act 1926 has no claim.[12] Curtesy and dower still arise in such cases.

---

[4] Adoption Act 1958, ss. 16 (1), 17 (1), 59, 5th Sched.
[5] A.E.A. 1925, s. 46 (1).
[6] See *ante*, p. 293.
[7] A.E.A. 1925, s. 49.
[8] See *Re Skeats* [1936] Ch. 683; contrast the position before 1926 (*ante*, p. 302).
[9] A.E.A. 1925, s. 45 (1).
[9a] And including former copyholds: *Re Sirett* [1969] 1 W.L.R. 60.
[10] *Ibid.* s. 51 (2); see *Re Bradshaw* [1950] Ch. 582.
[11] *Re Higham* [1937] 2 All E.R. 17.   [12] *Re Berrey* [1936] Ch. 274.

2. Entail: an entail not disposed of by the will of the deceased descends in accordance with the general law in force before 1926.[13] It is curious that while curtesy can arise out of such an interest,[14] dower cannot.[15]

3. Limitation to heir: if property is limited after 1925, whether *inter vivos* or by will, to the heir of a deceased person, it passes to the heir according to the general law in force before 1926.[16] This is not a case of descent on intestacy, for the heir takes as purchaser.

II. PERSONALTY

In the case of personalty, the old rules never apply to deaths after 1925. These rules still retain some of their importance, however particularly in showing title to leaseholds, and in the practice of reversion conveyancing. Thus if in 1920 personalty was settled upon A for life with remainder to B absolutely, and B died intestate in 1924, B's reversion (which is called by this name, although technically a remainder) passed to his next-of-kin. If the person at present entitled to B's reversion (A still being alive) wishes to sell or mortgage it, he will have to prove that he is duly entitled to it, thus invoking the old rules of intestacy.

Part 3

PERSONAL REPRESENTATIVES

Sect. 1. Introductory

1. Vesting of property. The beneficial devolution of property on death has been considered above; it is now necessary to discuss the means by which the property becomes vested in those beneficially entitled. The general rule today is that all property first vests in the personal representatives of the deceased, who in due course (and normally within the " executor's year," *i.e.*, one year from the death) are required to transfer to the beneficiaries any of the property not required in the due administration of the estate, *e.g.*, for payment of debts. In this context " estate " is used not in the technical sense of an estate in land, but as a collective expression for the sum total of the assets and liabilities of the deceased.

---

[13] L.P.A. 1925, s. 130 (4); A.E.A. 1925, s. 51 (4).
[14] L.P.A. 1925, s. 130 (4).
[15] See A.E.A. 1925, s. 45 (1).
[16] L.P.A. 1925, s. 132; A.E.A. 1925, s. 51 (1).

2. Executors. " Personal representatives " is a phrase which includes both executors and administrators. If a person makes a will, he may (but need not) appoint one or more persons to be his executor or executors, with the duty of paying debts, death duties and funeral expenses, and ultimately of distributing the estate to those entitled. The executor derives his powers from the will,[17] although he must obtain confirmation of his position by " proving the will," *i.e.*, obtaining a grant of probate from the court. If a sole or only surviving executor who has obtained probate dies having himself appointed an executor, the latter, on proving the original executor's will, becomes executor of the original testator also. This " chain of representation " may be continued indefinitely until broken by failure to appoint an executor, or failure of an executor to obtain a grant of probate.[18]

3. Administrators. If a person dies without having appointed an executor, or if none of the executors he has appointed is able and willing to act, application must be made to the court by some person or persons interested in the estate for " letters of administration " appointing an administrator or administrators. The duties of an administrator are substantially the same as those of an executor. If the deceased left no will, simple administration is granted; if he left a will, the grant is of administration *cum testamento annexo* (" with the will annexed ").[19] Provision is also made for certain limited grants of administration, such as grants confined to settled land,[20] grants " save and except " settled land,[21] and grants *durante minore aetate* (" during the minority " of the sole executor).[22] There is no " chain of representation " for administrators. If a sole or last surviving administrator dies without completing the administration of the estate, application must be made for a grant of administration *de bonis non administratis* (more shortly, *de bonis non*), which is a grant " in respect of the goods left unadministered."

Sect. 2. Devolution of Property on Personal Representatives
The devolution of the property of the deceased upon his personal representatives can be divided into three stages :
1. Before 1898;
2. Between 1897 and 1926; and
3. After 1925.

---

[17] *Biles* v. *Caesar* [1957] 1 W.L.R. 156.
[18] See A.E.A. 1925, s. 7, replacing 25 Edw. 3, st. 5, c. 5, 1351.
[19] J.A. 1925, s. 166.   [20] *Ibid.* s. 162.
[21] See A.E.A. 1925, s. 23.   [22] J.A. 1925, s. 165.

A. Before 1898

I. REALTY

The common law rule was that the realty of the deceased did not vest in his personal representatives but passed immediately to the heir or devisee, as the case might be. If any dispute arose as to who was entitled under the will or intestacy, it was settled by the common law courts. There was never any need for the grant of probate or letters of administration. Even if executors had been appointed, they had no power over the realty of the deceased and were thus unable to sell it to pay debts. Instead, the creditors had to sue the heir or devisee, and their right to do this did not extend to all debts until the Administration of Estates Act 1833. The position was the same if, there being no executor, someone had obtained a grant of administration. The only case in which the personal representatives could exercise control over the realty was if the deceased gave them some express or implied power to deal with it, as by devising it to them for the purposes of administration or by charging it with the payment of debts.[23]

II. PERSONALTY

In the case of personality the position was very different. All personality (including, as usual, leaseholds) vested in the personal representatives. If an executor was appointed, the property vested in him from the moment of death, although it was necessary for him to confirm his position by obtaining probate of the will. If no executor was appointed, the property first vested in the Ordinary (*i.e.*, the appropriate bishop), and, after the Court of Probate Act 1858,[24] in the Probate judge. A grant of administration had to be obtained by some person interested in the estate; when made, the administrator's title related back to the moment of death. In either case the personal representatives had full control over the property and could use it for the payment of debts and other liabilities, handing over the surplus to those entitled under the will or intestacy. Probate and letters of administration were originally granted by the ecclesiastical courts, but the Court of Probate Act 1857 substituted a Court of Probate which was subsequently replaced by the High Court under the Judicature Acts 1873 and 1875.

---

[23] L.P.Am.A. 1859, ss. 14–18.
[24] s. 19.

B. *Between* 1897 *and* 1926

The ill-drafted Land Transfer Act 1897 was passed to "establish a Real Representative." Under the Act, in the case of deaths after 1897 all property, whether real or personal, vested in the personal representatives in the same way as leaseholds had vested before 1898,[25] save that in the case of an intestacy realty vested in the heir pending the appointment of an administrator.[26] The personal representatives thus became both real and personal representatives, although their old name is still used. They had full powers of administration [27] and could thus sell realty to raise money for the payment of debts. There were a few exceptions to the rule that all property vested in them,[28] including the unfortunate distinction that although equitable interests in copyholds vested in them,[29] legal estates in copyhold did not [30]; and in one case, property not owned by the deceased vested in them, namely, real estate over which he had a general power of appointment which he exercised by his will.[31]

Subject to the due administration of the estate, the personal representatives held the property on trust for those beneficially entitled, who could call for a transfer of it to themselves.[32] If the heir was entitled, the realty had to be transferred by a conveyance, but if a devisee was entitled, property might be vested in him by a conveyance or an assent.[33] An assent did not even need to be in writing; any conduct by the executors showing that they assented to the gift would suffice, as by letting the beneficiary take possession of the property.[34] A consequent difficulty was that an essential link in a title might consist of disputable facts instead of a clear transaction apparent on the face of the title deeds.

To make a valid transfer of realty, all the personal representatives who had taken out a grant had to concur [35]; but over personalty (including leaseholds) they had a joint and several power, so that one of several personal representatives could make a good title by himself.[36]

---

[25] s. 1 (1).
[26] *Re Griggs* [1914] 2 Ch. 547.
[27] Land Transfer Act 1897, s. 2.
[28] See *infra*.
[29] *Re Somerville and Turner's Contract* [1903] 2 Ch. 583.
[30] Land Transfer Act 1897, s. 1 (4).
[31] *Ibid*. s. 1 (2).
[32] *Ibid*. s. 2 (1).
[33] *Ibid*. s. 3 (1).
[34] *Wise* v. *Whitburn* [1924] 1 Ch. 460.
[35] Land Transfer Act 1897, s. 2 (2), as amended by C.A. 1911, s. 12.
[36] See *Williams on Executors* (14th ed., 1960), Chap. 37.

C. *After* 1925

1. Vesting. The Administration of Estates Act 1925 substantially repeats the provisions of the Land Transfer Act 1897. In the case of deaths after 1925, all land owned by the deceased, including leaseholds, vests in the personal representatives,[37] with the following exceptions:

- (i) Entails, unless disposed of by the deceased's will.[38] Probably entails did not vest in the personal representatives before 1926, but the position was somewhat uncertain.[39]
- (ii) Property to which the deceased was entitled as a joint tenant [40]; this was so before 1926.[41]
- (iii) Property to which the deceased was entitled as a corporation sole.[42] This repeats the rule before 1926.
- (iv) Interests which ceased on the death of the deceased,[43] such as an interest for his life. This was so before 1926.

As before 1926, property subject to a general power of appointment exercised by the will of the deceased passes to his personal representatives.[44] On an intestacy, both realty and personalty vest in the Probate judge (*i.e.*, the President of the Probate, Divorce and Admiralty Division) until administration is granted.[45]

2. Assents. After 1925, an assent is no longer a mere recognition by the personal representatives that the land is not needed by them, *e.g.*, for the payment of debts, but is a conveyance which vests the estate in the person named. Accordingly, it is provided that no assent made after 1925 (even if the deceased died before 1926) will pass a legal estate in land unless it is in writing and signed by the personal representative.[46] A bona fide purchaser for value is no longer concerned with the terms of the will; he can rely on the grant of probate or letters of administration, coupled with an assent or conveyance executed by the personal representatives, as constituting his title.[47]

[37] A.E.A. 1925, ss. 1 (1), 3 (1).
[38] *Ibid.* s. 3 (3).
[39] Williams R.P. 116.
[40] A.E.A. 1925, s. 3 (4).
[41] Land Transfer Act 1897, s. 1 (1).
[42] A.E.A. 1925, s. 3 (5).
[43] *Ibid.* s. 1 (1).
[44] *Ibid.* s. 3 (2).
[45] *Ibid.* ss. 9, 55 (1) (xv).
[46] *Ibid.* s. 36 (2), (4).
[47] *Ibid.* ss. 36 (4), (7), 39 (1).

3. Ownership of assets. While the administration is proceeding, the personal representatives are the legal and equitable owners of all assets not specifically devised and bequeathed. The beneficiaries entitled to residue have no interest, legal or equitable, in specific assets. They merely have the right to compel the personal representatives to administer the estate properly.[48]

4. Powers. Personal representatives now have all the powers of trustees for sale,[49] and thus all the powers of a tenant for life and trustees under the Settled Land Act 1925.[50] Although they should sell the property only if this is necessary for the purposes of administration, a conveyance to a purchaser for value in good faith is not invalidated merely because he knows that all the debts and other liabilities have been met.[51] Nor is a conveyance to a purchaser for value in good faith invalidated merely because the probate or letters of administration under which the personal representatives acted are subsequently revoked.[52]

Personal representatives no longer have a several power of disposition over leaseholds if the deceased died after 1925.[53] They still have joint and several powers over pure personalty or, if the deceased died before 1926, over leaseholds; but they have only joint authority over realty and, if the deceased died after 1925, over leaseholds.

Sect. 3. Number of Personal Representatives

A. Maximum

No grant of probate or letters of administration can be made to more than four personal representatives in respect of the same property.[54] If more than four executors are appointed by a testator, they must decide among themselves who shall apply for probate.

B. Minimum

Unlike trustees for sale, there is no provision that a sole personal

---

[48] *Commissioner of Estate Duty (Queensland)* v. *Livingston* [1965] A.C. 694; *Eastbourne Mutual B.S.* v. *Hastings Corporation* [1965] 1 W.L.R. 861.
[49] A.E.A. 1925, s. 39.
[50] *Ante*, pp. 169 *et seq. Quaere* whether they have " *ad hoc* " powers (see *ante*, pp. 196 *et seq.*) as being " approved or appointed by the court."
[51] A.E.A. 1925, ss. 36 (8), 55 (1) (xviii).
[52] *Ibid*. ss. 37, 55 (1) (xviii), retrospectively confirming *Hewson* v. *Shelley* [1914] 2 Ch. 13.
[53] A.E.A. 1925, s. 2 (2).
[54] J.A. 1925, s. 160 (1).

representative cannot give a valid receipt for purchase money; a sole personal representative, whether original or by survivorship, has full power to give valid receipts for capital money or any other payments.[55] However, if any person interested in the estate is an infant or has a life interest in it, a sole administrator (other than a trust corporation) must not be appointed by the court after 1925.[56] A sole executor can act under such circumstances, but the court has power to appoint additional personal representatives.[57]

Sect. 3. Number of Personal Representatives

A. Maximum

No grant of probate or letters of administration can be made to more than four personal representatives in respect of the same property. If more than four executors are appointed by a testator, they must decide among themselves who shall apply for probate.

B. Minimum

Unlike trustees for sale, there is no provision that a sole personal

---

55 L.P.A. 1925, s. 27 (2).
56 J.A. 1925, s. 160 (1).
57 *Ibid.* s. 160 (2).

CONTRACTS

A CONTRACT to sell or make any other disposition of land is made in the same way as any other contract. As soon as there is an agreement for valuable consideration between the parties on the essential terms, there is a contract between the parties; and this is so whether the agreement was reached orally or in writing.

However, although a valid contract relating to land may be made orally, it will be unenforceable by the most important method of enforcing contracts, namely, by action, unless either the statutory requirements as to written evidence of the contract, or the requirements of equity as to part performance, have been satisfied. Thus, when considering whether an agreement relating to land can be enforced by action, two separate points fall to be considered:

(1) whether there is a contract at all, and

(2) if so, whether that contract is enforceable by action.

In addition, some mention will be made of—

(3) the practice concerning contracts relating to land.

Sect. 1. The Existence of a Contract

There must be a final and complete agreement between the parties on at least the essential terms, namely—

(i) the parties;

(ii) the property;

(iii) the consideration;

(iv) (in the case of the grant of a lease) the commencement and the period of the lease.

If an offer is accepted " subject to contract " [1] or " subject to suitable arrangements being arranged between your solicitors and mine," [2] or " subject to surveyor's report," [3] or some similar provision,

---

[1] *Botley* v. *Vidal* (1905) 49 S.J. 634.

[2] *Lockett* v. *Norman-Wright* [1925] Ch. 56.

[3] *Marks* v. *Board* (1930) 46 T.L.R. 424.

the effect is that until the necessary contract or arrangements have been made there is no contract and either party can withdraw. An agreement " subject to contract " must be distinguished from an unconditional acceptance of an offer coupled with a statement that the terms should be embodied in some formal document, *e.g.*, " I accept your offer and have asked my solicitor to prepare a contract "; in this case, the parties are bound at once, even though no formal contract is ever prepared.[4]

There is no need for a contract to be made by any formal document or phrases. But where a formal agreement is drawn up, usually each party signs one copy, and there is no binding contract until these copies have been exchanged.[5]

Sect. 2. The Enforceability of the Contract

The contract will be unenforceable by action unless there is either a sufficient memorandum thereof in writing or a sufficient act of part performance.

A. *Memorandum in Writing*

By the Law of Property Act 1925, s. 40 (1),[6] it is provided that " no action may be brought upon any contract for the sale or other disposition of land or any interest in land, unless the agreement upon which such action is brought, or some memorandum or note thereof, is in writing, and signed by the party to be charged or by some other person thereunto by him lawfully authorised."

1. " No action may be brought." Since 1852 it has been settled that the effect of non-compliance with the statute is not to make the contract void but merely to make it unenforceable by action.[7] " The Statute of Frauds does not avoid parol contracts but only bars the legal remedies by which they might otherwise have been enforced." [8] It is true that to deprive a party to a contract of his right to bring an action upon it is to deprive him of one of his most important rights, but it does not render that contract useless; the Act is no bar to the contract being enforced in any way except by action. Thus, if a

---

[4] See *Rossiter* v. *Miller* (1878) 3 App.Cas. 1124 at 1139, 1151.
[5] *Eccles* v. *Bryant* [1948] Ch. 93.
[6] Replacing part of the Statute of Frauds 1677, s. 4.
[7] *Leroux* v. *Brown* (1852) 12 C.B. 801 ; and see *Delaney* v. *T. P. Smith, Ltd.* [1946] K.B. 393.
[8] *Maddison* v. *Alderson* (1883) 8 App.Cas. 467 at 474, *per* Lord Selborne L.C.

purchaser pays a cash deposit to the vendor under an oral contract, the vendor may forfeit (*i.e.*, keep) that deposit if the purchaser defaults.[9] If there were no contract at all, the deposit would have to be returned.[10] Again, if a cheque is given in part payment under an oral contract for the sale of land, an action will lie if the purchaser refuses to honour it, for the action is not on the contract for the sale of land but is on the cheque.[11]

2. " The sale or other disposition of land or any interest in land."

The section applies to a contract for any disposition of any interest in land, whether by sale, mortgage, lease or otherwise. It applies equally to a contract for the creation of a new interest in land as to the disposition of an existing interest. " Land " is very widely defined.[12] It includes an interest under a trust for sale of land,[13] but not annual crops such as corn or potatoes, which require the periodical application of labour for their production; these are known as *fructus industriales*.[14] *Fructus naturales*, on the other hand, are sometimes included. This term applies to the natural products of the soil, such as grass and timber, and also the products of those plants and trees which, although needing attention at first, do not require it each year to produce a crop,[15] such as fruit from fruit trees.[16] *Fructus naturales* are treated as land within the statute unless either they are to be severed by the vendor and not by the purchaser [17] or else the contract binds the purchaser to sever them as soon as possible.[18]

A contract for the sale of fixtures together with the land to which they are attached falls within section 40,[19] and the same applies to a sale of fixtures separately from the land to a stranger, either by the landlord or, it seems, the tenant.[20] But the sale by the tenant to his landlord of fixtures which the tenant is entitled to remove is neither a sale of land nor a sale of goods, for the substance of the

9 *Monnickendam* v. *Leanse* (1923) 39 T.L.R. 445.
10 *Chillingworth* v. *Esche* [1924] 1 Ch. 97.
11 *Low* v. *Fry* (1935) 152 L.T. 585.
12 L.P.A. 1925, s. 205 (1) (ix).
13 *Cooper* v. *Critchley* [1955] Ch. 431; but see *Stevens* v. *Hutchinson* [1953] Ch. 299.
14 See *Duppa* v. *Mayo* (1669) 1 Wms.Saund. 275.
15 *Marshall* v. *Green* (1875) 1 C.P.D. 35 at 40.
16 *Rodwell* v. *Phillips* (1842) 9 M. & W. 501.
17 *Smith* v. *Surman* (1829) 9 B. & C. 561.
18 *Marshall* v. *Green* (1875) 1 C.P.D. 35 (and see the summary of the decisions at p. 42).
19 See *Vaughan* v. *Hancock* (1846) 3 C.B. 766.
20 See *Underwood Ltd.* v. *Burgh Castle Brick and Cement Syndicate* [1922] 1 K.B. 123.

agreement is merely a waiver by the tenant of his right to remove the fixtures.[21]

3. "Some memorandum or note thereof, is in writing."

(a) *Existence of the document.* The contract itself may be made orally; all that is required is that before the action is begun [22] a written memorandum of the contract should have come into existence. For example, a memorandum made over 14 years after the contract may suffice [23]; and even if it has been lost or destroyed, it may be proved by oral or other secondary evidence, like any other missing document.[24] Even a document made before the contract came into existence may be sufficient, for it is settled that if a written offer is accepted orally, the written offer may be a sufficient memorandum to support an action against the person making it,[25] although the onus of proving such an acceptance is high.[26]

(b) *Form.* The memorandum need not be in any special form, nor is it necessary that it should have been intended to act as a memorandum: "the question is not one of intention of the party who signs the document, but simply one of evidence against him." [27] Nor need the memorandum consist of a single document. If the terms of the contract and the signature cannot be found in any one document, but can be gathered from two or more documents, then these documents can be taken together as the memorandum, provided the signed document refers to the others. Any reference in the signed document, whether express or implied, may be explained by evidence to show that it is another document which is being referred to and to identify that document.[28] Thus a telegram accepting "your offer" may refer sufficiently to a written offer received by the sender.[29] Again, it is not essential that the reference should be in words, for the nature of one document may refer to another; a signed carbon copy of a letter may thus refer sufficiently to the top copy upon which the defendant's signature appeared.[30] And if the signed document merely refers to another transaction, evidence is admissible to identify any document relating to that transaction which

---

[21] *Lee* v. *Gaskell* (1876) 1 Q.B.D. 700; and see *post*, pp. 376 *et seq.*
[22] *Lucas* v. *Dixon* (1889) 22 Q.B.D. 357.
[23] *Barkworth* v. *Young* (1856) 4 Drew. 1.
[24] *Barber* v. *Rowe* [1948] 2 All E.R. 1050.
[25] *Reuss* v. *Picksley* (1866) L.R. 1 Ex. 342.
[26] *Watson* v. *Davies* [1931] 1 Ch. 455 at 468.
[27] *Re Hoyle* [1893] 1 Ch. 84 at 99, *per* Bowen L.J.
[28] *Long* v. *Millar* (1879) 4 C.P.D. 450.
[29] *Godwin* v. *Francis* (1870) L.R. 5 C.P. 295.
[30] *Stokes* v. *Whicher* [1920] 1 Ch. 411.

will supply the missing terms.[31] But it is essential that there should be some reference in the signed document to the other document or documents or transaction, for evidence cannot be admitted to connect one document with another when, on being placed side by side, the signed document still does not appear to refer to the other.[32]

Where two documents are both signed, they may be read together even if neither refers to the other, provided it can be shown that they each refer to the same subject-matter.[33] Further, two documents which are separable without damage to either may constitute one document where they are in fact treated as one, as with a paper book and a leather cover which are connected only by the former being slipped into the latter and habitually used with it.[34]

(c) *Statement of all terms.* The memorandum must accurately state all the terms of the contract.[35] " If the memorandum is not in accordance with the true contract, it is a bad memorandum." [36] Thus a memorandum is defective if it records as a single contract to buy three houses what in fact consisted of three distinct contracts,[37] or if it describes the vendor as " solicitor for the vendor." [38] However, if the memorandum merely omits an unimportant stipulation which is for the benefit of one party alone (and not, *e.g.*, an important provision which is for the benefit of both parties, such as one relating to vacant possession [39]), that party can enforce the contract if he waives the stipulation [40]; similarly, if the omitted stipulation is to the detriment of one party alone, he can probably enforce the contract if he agrees to perform the stipulation.[41]

(d) *Certainty.* The terms of the contract are sufficiently stated if they fall within the rule *id certum est quod certum reddi potest* (that is certain which can be made certain). Thus, while it is essential that the memorandum should disclose each party to the contract, or his agent,[42] it suffices if, without being named, each party is so described that his identity cannot be fairly disputed,[43] *e.g.*, if the memorandum

---

[31] *Timmins* v. *Moreland Street Property Co. Ltd.* [1958] Ch. 110 at 130.
[32] See, *e.g.*, *Taylor* v. *Smith* [1893] 2 Q.B. 65.
[33] *Studds* v. *Watson* (1884) 28 Ch.D. 305.
[34] *Jones Brothers* v. *Joyner* (1900) 82 L.T. 768.
[35] *Beckett* v. *Nurse* [1948] 1 K.B. 535.
[36] *Crane* v. *Naughten* [1912] 2 I.R. 318 at 324, *per* Gibson J.
[37] *Smith* v. *MacGowan* [1938] 3 All E.R. 447.
[38] *Jarrett* v. *Hunter* (1886) 34 Ch.D. 182.
[39] *Hawkins* v. *Price* [1947] Ch. 645.
[40] *North* v. *Loomes* [1919] 1 Ch. 378 at 385, 386.
[41] *Martin* v. *Pycroft* (1852) 2 De G.M. & G. 785; as to *Burgess* v. *Cox* [1951] Ch. 383 to the contrary, see (1951) 67 L.Q.R. 299.
[42] *Davies* v. *Sweet* [1962] 2 Q.B. 300.   [43] *Carr* v. *Lynch* [1900] 1 Ch. 613 at 615.

refers to the "proprietor"[44] of the property, or states that "the vendor will convey as legal personal representative."[45] But references to the "vendor"[46] or "landlord"[47] or "my clients"[48] are not sufficient by themselves, for these descriptions may fit many persons; the proprietor of land is not the only person who can be the vendor, for many other persons such as mortgagees or even complete strangers may enter into a contract to sell the land. Similar principles apply to descriptions of the property concerned.[49]

4. "Signed by the party to be charged or by some other person thereunto by him lawfully authorised."

(a) "*Party to be charged.*" Signature by both parties to the contract or their agents is not required; the statute requires signature by or on behalf of the party to be charged, namely, the party against whom it is sought to enforce the contract. Thus where there is a contract between A and B, and A alone has signed a memorandum, the contract is enforceable by action by B against A but not by A against B.[50]

(b) "*Signed.*" The word "signed" has been given an extended meaning by the courts. Provided the name of the party to be charged appears in some part of the document in some form, whether in writing, typewriting, print or otherwise, there will be a sufficient signature if that party has shown in some way that he recognises the document as an expression of the contract.[51] Thus memoranda in the handwriting of A, the defendant, which began "I, A, agree"[52] or "A agrees"[53] or "sold A"[54] without any other signature, have all been held sufficiently signed on the ground that A has shown by his writing that he recognises the existence of the contract mentioned in the document. But the mere occurrence of the defendant's name in a memorandum written by him does not necessarily amount to a signature; thus if A writes out a document beginning "Articles of agreement made between A and B" and ending "As witness our

44 *Rossiter* v. *Miller* (1878) 3 App.Cas. 1124.
45 *Fay* v. *Miller, Wilkins & Co.* [1941] Ch. 360; but see (1941) 57 L.Q.R. 452.
46 *Potter* v. *Duffield* (1874) L.R. 18 Eq. 4.
47 *Coombs* v. *Wilkes* [1891] 3 Ch. 77.
48 *Lovesy* v. *Palmer* [1916] 2 Ch. 233.
49 See, *e.g., Auerbach* v. *Nelson* [1919] 2 Ch. 383.
50 See *Boys* v. *Ayerst* (1822) 6 Madd. 316.
51 See *Halley* v. *O'Brien* [1920] 1 I.R. 330 at 339; and see *Leeman* v. *Stocks* [1951] Ch. 941.
52 *Knight* v. *Crockford* (1794) 1 Esp. 190.
53 *Bleakley* v. *Smith* (1840) 11 Sim. 150.
54 *Johnson* v. *Dodgson* (1837) 2 M. & W. 653.

hands " without any signatures, the statute is not satisfied,[55] for A's name must be inserted in such a way as to "have the effect of authenticating the instrument," [56] or "to govern what follows." [57]

(c) *Agent's authority.* The statute makes no special provision about the mode in which an agent must receive his authority to sign a memorandum, so that it is not necessary that the authority should be given in writing.[58] However, it must be shown not only that the agent signing the document has authority to act as agent but also that he has authority to sign a memorandum of the same kind of contract as that upon which the plaintiff relies.[59] In the case of auction sales, the auctioneer is an express agent for the vendor and his authority to sell includes authority to sign a memorandum for him; further, when the purchaser makes the highest bid and the hammer falls, he is deemed to have given the auctioneer authority to sign a memorandum on his behalf.[60] The auctioneer thus has authority to sign for both parties,[61] and although the vendor may revoke his authority before the property is sold, it seems that neither vendor nor purchaser can revoke it after the fall of the hammer.[62] The auctioneer's authority to sign for the purchaser is confined to the time of the sale,[63] but his authority to sign for the vendor, by whom he was expressly constituted agent, is of a more permanent character.[64] A solicitor acting for both parties may similarly be authorised to sign for each.[65]

B. A Sufficient Act of Part Performance

Since 1686, equity has addressed itself to what may be described as "the task of decorously disregarding an Act of Parliament" [66] by means of the doctrine of part performance. The fundamental idea behind this doctrine, which was firmly established by a decision of the House of Lords in 1701,[67] is that if the plaintiff has done acts in performance of his part of the contract, it would be fraudulent

---

[55] *Hubert* v. *Treherne* (1842) 3 Man. & G. 743.
[56] *Ogilvie* v. *Foljambe* (1817) 3 Mer. 53 at 62, *per* Grant M.R.
[57] *Lobb* v. *Stanley* (1844) 5 Q.B. 574 at 582, *per* Coleridge J.
[58] *Heard* v. *Pilley* (1869) 4 Ch.App. 548; contrast *ante*, pp. 245, 246.
[59] *Thirkell* v. *Cambi* [1919] 2 K.B. 590 at 598.
[60] *Emmerson* v. *Heelis* (1809) 2 Taunt. 38 at 48.
[61] *Chaney* v. *Maclow* [1929] 1 Ch. 461.
[62] See Williams V. & P. 23.
[63] *Bell* v. *Balls* [1897] 1 Ch. 663.
[64] *M'Meekin* v. *Stevenson* [1917] 1 I.R. 348 at 354.
[65] *Gavaghan* v. *Edwards* [1961] 2 Q.B. 220.
[66] *Spencer* v. *Hemmerde* [1922] 2 A.C. 507 at 519, *per* Lord Sumner (spoken of another statute).
[67] *Lester* v. *Foxcroft* (1701) Colles P.C. 108.

of the defendant to plead the statute as a defence, and consequently equity will enforce the contract despite the absence of any sufficient memorandum. Equity took the view that it could not allow the statute to be made an instrument of fraud.[68] However, although based on fraud, the doctrine cannot be explained on that ground alone [69]; thus it would clearly be fraudulent for a defendant who has received payment from the plaintiff to set up the statute as a defence, yet it is settled that the mere payment of money is not by itself a sufficient act of part performance.[70] In such cases, equity has regard to the practical results of enforcing or refusing to enforce the contract; it is easy enough for the plaintiff to be reinstated to his former position by the return of his money.[71]

Statutory recognition has now been accorded to the doctrine of part performance, for section 40 (2) of the Law of Property Act 1925 provides that subsection (1), which requires writing, " does not affect the law relating to part performance."

I. REQUIREMENTS TO BE SATISFIED

For the doctrine of part performance to apply, certain conditions must be satisfied.

1. Evidence of the contract: the court requires clear evidence, whether parol or otherwise, that there was a contract certain and definite in its terms.[72] No amount of what would otherwise be part performance will render certain a contract which is void for uncertainty or make into an agreement that which is not an agreement at all.

2. Contract specifically enforceable: even if the terms of the contract are clear, it is essential that the contract should be one of which, had it been properly evidenced in writing, specific performance would have been granted by equity.[73] Equity would refuse this discretionary remedy on a number of grounds, such as misrepresentation, hardship or unreasonable delay [74]; and if the interest in land is a tenancy for a very short period, *e.g.*, a month or two, equity might well refuse specific performance.[75]

---

[68] See *Whitbread* v. *Brocklehurst* (1784) 1 Bro.C.C. 404 at 413.
[69] See *Maddison* v. *Alderson* (1883) 8 App.Cas. 467 at 474.
[70] See *Britain* v. *Rossiter* (1879) 11 Q.B.D. 123 at 130, 131.
[71] See *Chaproniere* v. *Lambert* [1917] 2 Ch. 356.
[72] *Cooth* v. *Jackson* (1801) 6 Ves. 12 at 38.
[73] *Elliott* v. *Roberts* (1912) 28 T.L.R. 436 at 437, 438.
[74] See Fry S.P., Part III.
[75] See *Lavery* v. *Pursell* (1888) 39 Ch.D. 508 at 519; *Glasse* v. *Woolgar* (1897) 41 S.J. 573.

3. Act by the plaintiff: the act of part performance must have been done by the plaintiff with the knowledge of the defendant that it was done on the faith of the contract.[76] It will be noticed that whereas in the case of a memorandum in writing it is the signature of the defendant that is necessary, what is required in the case of part performance is an act by the plaintiff who is seeking to enforce the contract [77]; for if the party refusing to perform the contract has done the only act of part performance, there is no fraud but merely a loss to himself.

4. Performance referable to the contract: the act of part performance must be " unequivocally referable to the contract." Yet although the fourth requirement is usually expressed in the above form,[78] this cannot be properly understood without further explanation.

(a) " *Unequivocally referable.*" The true meaning of the phrase appears to be that the act or acts of part performance must be such that by themselves they suggest that the only reasonable explanation of them is that the parties had entered into some contract of the kind alleged affecting the land in question.[79] The view has been held, it seems, that the part performance must not merely indicate that there is some contract affecting the land, but also show the terms of that contract. However, " in the nature of things no act of part performance could be so eloquent as to point unequivocally to one particular contract and no other." [80] And the true rule appears to be that the part performance must necessarily indicate that there is some contract of the kind alleged,[81] leaving the terms of the contract to be established by parol evidence.[82]

(b) " *Part performance.*" The act of part performance will thus rarely be sufficient unless it consists of some act physically affecting the land. Further, the acts must have been done in performance of the contract and not merely in preparation for its performance.[83] Thus, viewing the land or measuring it, or giving instructions for a lease or a conveyance to be prepared, are insufficient acts of part performance.

---

[76] *Dann* v. *Spurrier* (1802) 7 Ves. 231.
[77] See *Caton* v. *Caton* (1865) 1 Ch.App. 137.
[78] See, *e.g.*, *Morphett* v. *Jones* (1818) 1 Swans. 172 at 181.
[79] See *Maddison* v. *Alderson* (1883) 8 App.Cas. 467 at 491.
[80] Williams, *Statute of Frauds, Sect. IV* (1932), p. 253.
[81] See *Rawlinson* v. *Ames* [1925] Ch. 96 at 114.
[82] *Frame* v. *Dawson* (1807) 14 Ves. 386 at 388; *Kingswood Estate Co. Ltd.* v. *Anderson* [1963] 2 Q.B. 169.
[83] Fry S.P. 295.

The usual act of part performance is concerned with possession of the land. If a leasehold tenant agrees to take a new lease [84] or buy [85] the land, and remains in possession after his existing lease has expired, there is no sufficient act of part performance since the tenant's possession might well be due to his holding over as a tenant at sufferance [86] and not because of the alleged contract. But where the owner of land gives possession of it to a person to whom he has contracted to sell or lease or assign the land, there is a sufficient act of part performance on the part of the former party to the contract by his giving possession [87] and on the part of the latter party by his taking possession.[88] The former suffers the detriment of giving up possession of his land: the latter is liable to be treated as a trespasser and evicted unless he is allowed to rely upon the contract under which he claims.[89] It is the change of possession that is the important feature; the duration of the possession is immaterial, a single hour being sufficient. *A fortiori* there is sufficient part performance if the change of possession is followed by the plaintiff, on the faith of the agreement, expending money on improving the premises.[90]

Although the retention of possession by a leasehold tenant whose tenancy has expired is not by itself a sufficient act of part performance, there will be sufficient part performance by such a tenant if he spends money on effecting substantial improvements of the type which a mere yearly tenant would not make [91]; and if an increased rent is paid and accepted under a new contract of tenancy, there will be sufficient part performance both by the tenant [92] and, it seems, by the landlord.[93] It will be noticed that in this case two acts, neither of which would be sufficient by itself, together amount to sufficient part performance.

The mere fact that a landowner builds or repairs a house under an oral contract of sale is not a sufficient act of part performance to enable him to enforce the contract, for his act is equally referable to his ownership of the land.[94] But if a landowner submits to his workmen effecting alterations to a building under the personal supervision of the defendant, who frequently visits the premises and

84 *Re The National Savings Bank Association* (1867) 15 W.R. 753.
85 *Lincoln* v. *Wright* (1859) 4 De G. & J. 16 at 20.
86 See *post*, p. 349.
87 *Hohler* v. *Aston* [1920] 2 Ch. 420.
88 *Sharman* v. *Sharman* (1893) 67 L.T. 834.
89 *Clinan* v. *Cooke* (1802) 1 Sch. & Lef. 22 at 41.
90 *Reddin* v. *Jarman* (1867) 16 L.T. 449.
91 *Brennan* v. *Bolton* (1842) 2 Dr. & War. 349 at 355, 356.
92 *Miller & Aldworth Ltd.* v. *Sharp* [1899] 1 Ch. 622.
93 *Conner* v. *Fitzgerald* (1883) 11 L.R.Ir. 106.
94 *Rawlinson* v. *Ames* [1925] Ch. 96 at 114.

tells the workmen how she wants certain details carried out, this is sufficient part performance by the landowner of a contract to sell or lease the land, for his act in having the work done in the way suggested by the defendant clearly indicates that there is some contract between them which relates to the building.[95]

II. EFFECT OF PART PERFORMANCE

1. Evidence of all terms admissible. The effect of a sufficient act of part performance is to enable evidence to be given of all the terms of the contract, including terms to which the acts of part performance have no relation.[96] " The effect of the removal of the barrier set up by the statute . . . is to open the door to parol evidence of the whole agreement." [97] Thus if a landlord agrees to grant a tenant a lease with an option to purchase the freehold, part performance by the tenant which is unequivocally referable to the agreement to grant a lease entitles him to demand not merely the term of years but also the option.[98]

2. Enforceable only in equity. Nevertheless, a party seeking to enforce a contract merely supported by part performance is not in so good a position as if the contract were evidenced in writing, for part performance makes the contract enforceable only in equity and not at law.[99] A contract properly evidenced in writing is enforceable at law, and the plaintiff, on proving his case, is entitled as of right to an award of damages; equity may in addition grant him the discretionary remedy of specific performance. A contract merely supported by part performance, on the other hand, gives the plaintiff no right to any remedy at all. Equity may award him specific performance if it thinks the case a proper one, but that lies in the discretion of the court; and no damages can be awarded if the case is one where equity has no power to grant specific performance or an injunction.[1]

C. Cases in which neither Writing nor Part Performance is Required

Neither writing nor part performance is required—
    (i) where the sale is by the court [2];

[95] *Rawlinson* v. *Ames* [1925] Ch. 96.
[96] *Sutherland* v. *Briggs* (1841) 1 Hare 26 at 32.
[97] *Brough* v. *Nettleton* [1921] 2 Ch. 25 at 28, *per* P. O. Lawrence J.
[98] *Brough* v. *Nettleton, supra.*
[99] *O'Herlihy* v. *Hedges* (1803) 1 Sch. & Lef. 123 at 130.
[1] See *ante*, pp. 63, 64.   [2] L.P.A. 1925, s. 40 (2)

(ii) where the defendant does not plead the absence of writing as a defence; the defendant is not bound to take advantage of the section and if he fails to plead it he renounces the benefit of it [3]; or

(iii) where it was due to the fraud of the defendant that the contract was not put into writing [4]; the court will not allow the section to be used as an engine of fraud.

Sect. 3. Contracts in Practice

A. Cases where it is Usual to Have a Contract

Whenever a transaction involves payment of a capital sum, it is usual for it to be governed by a contract. Thus where land is being sold in fee simple, or a lease at a ground rent (a rent representing the value of the land without the buildings on it) is being assigned in consideration of a capital payment, a formal contract is normally made. If, on the other hand, no capital payment is involved, there is usually no contract, *e.g.*, on the grant or assignment of a lease at a rack rent (a rent representing the full value of the land and buildings). And a mortgage, although involving a capital payment, is rarely preceded by a contract.

B. Types of Contract

There are three main types of contract.

1. Open contracts. In these, only the essential terms [5] have been expressly agreed between the parties, the remaining terms being left to the general law.

2. Contracts by correspondence. In the case of contracts by correspondence, the Law of Property Act 1925 [6] provides that the Statutory Form of Conditions of Sale 1925, made by the Lord Chancellor, shall govern the contract, subject to any modification or contrary intention expressed in the correspondence.

3. Formal contracts. It is always open to the parties to make a contract in such terms as they think fit, subject to the rule that certain provisions contrary to the policy of the law are void, such as any provision that the conveyance should be prepared by a solicitor appointed by the vendor.[7] In practice, various standard forms of

---

[3] *James* v. *Smith* [1891] 1 Ch. 384.
[4] *Maxwell* v. *Montacute* (1719) Prec.Ch. 526.
[6] s. 46.

[5] See *ante*, p. 317.
[7] L.P.A. 1925, s. 48 (1).

conditions have been settled, and prints of them may be purchased, *e.g.*, The Law Society's Conditions of Sale, and the National Conditions of Sale. These conditions, with such emendations as are desirable to fit the particular case, are usually employed, since they avoid the labour of preparing a special set of conditions for each case.

The above division of the types of contracts is not rigid; thus the parties may agree a few special conditions and leave the rest to the ordinary rules of law, thus creating a contract which is in part formal and as to the remainder an open contract.

C. Terms of a Contract

The following are examples of the matters usually dealt with in a formal contract for the sale of land.

1. Provision for the payment of a deposit (usually 10 per cent. of the purchase-money) and for the payment of interest on the purchase-money if completion is delayed.

2. The length and nature of the title to be deduced by the vendor, and any special provisions, *e.g.*, as to making no objection to some specified defect in title or flaw in the evidence of title.

3. The time within which the abstract of title,[8] requisitions on title and other matters must be dealt with.

4. The date and place for completion of the sale.

5. Power for the vendor to rescind the contract or re-sell the property in certain circumstances, such as the purchaser's insistence on objections to the title or failure to perform the contract.

Part 2

CONVEYANCING

Conveyancing may be regarded as the application of the law of real property in practice. It is an immense subject and only a very brief outline of a few of the chief features can be given here.[9] Although conveyancing does not form part of the subject of real property, every student should have some idea of the relationship between the two subjects. Even before the contract is signed, and if time permits, the purchaser, or more normally his solicitor, will have sent to the vendor written " inquiries on draft contract " or " preliminary inquiries " so as to obtain information or confirmation as to the state

---

[8] *Infra.*
[9] See generally M. & W. 581–618.

of the property. The steps taken after the contract has been made will depend on whether the title is registered or unregistered. Registered titles are becoming increasingly widespread and are dealt with separately.[9a] The procedure where the title is unregistered is shortly considered here under two heads, first, the steps to be taken between making a contract and completion of the purchase, and secondly, the form of the conveyance.

Sect. 1. From Contract to Completion

The usual sequence of events on the sale of a freehold by V to P are as follows; most of the steps are normally taken by the solicitors for the parties rather than by the parties in person.

1. Signature of the contract. This has been dealt with above. Whenever time permits, the purchaser will usually first send the vendor written " inquiries on draft contract " so as to obtain information or confirmation as to the state of the property.

2. Delivery of abstract. Within the time mentioned in the contract, V must deliver to P the abstract of title. This document consists in part of an epitome of the various documents, and in part of a recital of the relevant events, such as the births, deaths and marriages which affect the title. The abstract starts with a good root of title [10] and traces the devolution of the property down to V. Thus a very simple abstract might consist of—

   (i) an epitome of a conveyance by A to B;
   (ii) a recital of B's death;
   (iii) a recital of probate of B's will being granted to X and Y;
   (iv) an epitome of the assent by X and Y in favour of V.

3. Consideration of abstract. P then peruses the abstract of title, considers the validity of the title shown, and checks the abstract against V's title deeds.

4. Requisitions on title. P's examination of the abstract usually discloses a number of points upon which he requires further information. This further explanation is obtained by means of " requisitions on title," a series of written questions which P delivers to V. Requisitions usually consist of a mixture of genuine objections or requests for information (*e.g.*, as to the date of some death, or as to the

---

[9a] *Post*, p. 554.
[10] *Ante*, p. 62.

existence of some incumbrance which the abstract does not disclose), and statements of the obvious, *e.g.*, that V, having agreed to sell free from incumbrances, must discharge a mortgage or obtain the concurrence of his mortgagee to the sale of the property free from the mortgage. Requisitions also usually seek confirmation of the answers to the inquiries on draft contract.

5. Replies to requisitions. V then answers the requisitions within the agreed time; if his answers are unsatisfactory on any point, P may make further requisitions.

6. Draft conveyance. P next prepares a draft conveyance in the form which he thinks it should take. He sends this draft to V for his approval; V makes in red ink any emendations he considers necessary, returns it to P, who makes any further amendments in green ink, and so on until the conveyance is agreed. P then engrosses the conveyance (*i.e.*, prepares a fair copy of it) and sends it to V for execution.

7. Searches. A few days before the date fixed for completion, P makes his searches. Normally, these will be limited to searches of the registers of land charges in London and the registers of local land charges.[11]

8. Completion. Completion then takes place, usually at the office of V's solicitor. This involves V delivering to P the engrossment of the conveyance duly executed by V; only if P is entering into some obligation towards V, as by binding himself to observe restrictive covenants, will the conveyance be executed by P as well. In addition to receiving the conveyance, P is entitled to receive the title deeds. However, V may retain any deed which—

   (i) relates to other land retained by him; or
   (ii) creates a trust which is still subsisting; or
   (iii) relates to the appointment or discharge of trustees of a
       subsisting trust.[12]

If V retains any deeds, he must give P an acknowledgment of P's right to production of the deeds and, unless V is a mortgagee or trustee of the land, an undertaking for their safe custody.[13]

In return, P pays V the purchase money either in cash or by bankers' draft. The exact amount due is settled by the " completion statement " which apportions the rates and other outgoings up to the exact day of completion.

[11] See *post*, pp. 541 *et seq.*, 552.   [12] L.P.A. 1925, s. 45 (9).
[13] For the effect, see L.P.A. 1925, s. 64.

Sect. 2. The Conveyance

A. Precedent of a Conveyance

Commencement
and date

THIS CONVEYANCE is made the 1st day of June, 1969,

Parties

BETWEEN John Bull of No. 1 Weelkes Street Farnaby in the County of Tye Composer (hereinafter called "the vendor") of the one part and Orlando Gibbons of No. 1 Morley Street Dowland in the County of Tallis Organist (hereinafter called "the purchaser") of the other part

Recitals

WHEREAS—

(1) The vendor is the estate owner in respect of the fee simple of the property hereby assured for his own use and benefit absolutely free from incumbrances
(2) The vendor has agreed with the purchaser to sell to him the said property free from incumbrances for the price of £10,000.

Testatum

Consideration

Receipt clause

Operative words

NOW THIS CONVEYANCE WITNESSETH that in consideration of the sum of £10,000 now paid by the purchaser to the vendor (the receipt whereof the vendor hereby acknowledges) the vendor As Beneficial Owner hereby conveys unto the purchaser

Parcels

ALL THAT messuage or dwellinghouse with the yard gardens offices and outbuildings thereto belonging known as No. 1 Byrd Street Purcell in the County of Norcome which premises are more particularly delineated and coloured pink on the plan annexed to these presents

Habendum

Testimonium

TO HOLD the same unto the purchaser in fee simple

IN WITNESS WHEREOF the parties to these presents have hereunto set their hands and seals the day and year first above written

Attestation clause

Signed sealed and delivered by the vendor in the presence of Edward Elgar clerk to Messrs. Delius Field and Stanford solicitors	JOHN BULL

Seal.

B. *Details of the Conveyance*

In considering the very simple form of conveyance set out above, the following points should be noticed.

1. Commencement. The old practice was for the initial words to be " This Indenture." An indenture was a deed with the top of the parchment indented, *i.e.*, having an irregular edge. The deed was written out twice on a single sheet of parchment, which was then severed by cutting it with an irregular edge; the two halves of the parchment thus formed two separate deeds which could be fitted together to show their genuineness. This contrasted with a " deed poll," a deed to which there was only one party, which at the top had been polled, or shaved even. The modern practice is for the commencement to describe the general nature of the document, *e.g.*, " This Conveyance," " This Mortgage " and the like.[14]

2. Date. Whatever date is in fact inserted in the conveyance, the document takes effect from the date upon which it was signed, sealed and delivered by the parties to it.[15] A deed which has been signed and sealed but not delivered is ineffective; delivery is effected formally by uttering words such as " I deliver this as my act and deed," or informally by doing some act showing that the deed is intended to be operative. A deed may be delivered in escrow, *i.e.*, delivered on the condition that it is not to become operative until some stated event occurs.[16] Usually a vendor of land will execute the conveyance some days before completion and deliver it to his solicitor in escrow, the condition being the completion of the purchase by the purchaser.

3. Parties. If any other person is an essential party to the transaction, such as a mortgagee who is releasing the property from his mortgage, he will be included as a party.

4. Recitals. These are of two types:

(a) *Narrative recitals*, which deal with matters such as how the vendor became entitled to the land; and

(b) *Introductory recitals*, which explain how and why the existing state of affairs is to be altered, *e.g.*, that the parties have agreed for the sale of the property.

5. Testatum. This is the beginning of the operative part of the conveyance.

---

[14] See L.P.A. 1925, s. 57.   [15] *Norton on Deeds* (2nd ed., 1928), p. 189.
[16] See *Beesly* v. *Hallwood Estates Ltd.* [1961] Ch. 105.

6. Consideration. The consideration is stated to show (*inter alia*) that the transaction is not a voluntary one.[17]

7. Receipt clause. This is inserted to save a separate receipt being given. Further, a solicitor who produces a conveyance containing such a clause which has been duly executed by the vendor thereby demonstrates that he has authority from the vendor to receive the purchase money.[18]

8. Operative words. These effect the actual conveyance of the property. A most important part of them is the phrase " As Beneficial Owner." These words involve some consideration of the subject of covenants for title.

(a) *The covenants.* In order to shorten conveyances and other documents, the Law of Property Act 1925 [19] provides that where for valuable consideration a person conveys and is expressed to convey land " as beneficial owner " the following covenants for title are implied:

(i) Good right to convey: the vendor has power to convey the land.

(ii) Quiet enjoyment: the purchaser shall have quiet enjoyment of the land.[20]

(iii) Freedom from incumbrances: the land is free from any incumbrances other than those subject to which the conveyance is expressly made.

(iv) Further assurance: the vendor will execute such assurances and do such things as are necessary to cure any defect in the conveyance.

In the case of a sale of leaseholds, the following additional covenants are implied:

(v) That the lease is valid.

(vi) That the rent has been paid and the covenants in the lease duly performed.[21]

Where a person conveys and is expressed to convey (whether or not for value) " as settlor " the only convenant implied is one for further assurance, binding that person and those claiming under him. Where a person conveys " as trustee," " as mortgagee," " as personal

---

[17] See *ante*, p. 242.
[18] L.P.A. 1925, s. 69.
[19] s. 76, 2nd Sched., replacing C.A. 1881, s. 7.
[20] See *post*, p. 364.
[21] L.P.A. 1925, s. 76, 2nd Sched.

representative," " as receiver," or " under an order of the court " the only covenant implied is that the grantor has not himself incumbered the land.[22]

(b) *Enforceability of the covenants.* The rules for enforcing covenants for title are as follows.

The benefit of the covenants runs with the land, so that each person in whom the land is for the time being vested is entitled to enforce the covenant.[23] Thus if V enters into the covenants with P, and later P sells the land to Q, Q is entitled to enforce the covenants for title against V, even though Q was not a party to the conveyance from V to P which created the obligations.

As regards the burden of the covenant, the person liable is the person entering into the covenant. He does not, however, always make himself responsible for the acts of everyone. If land is conveyed " as beneficial owner " the general rule is that the vendor makes himself responsible for the acts and omissions of—

(i) himself, and
(ii) those claiming through, under, or in trust for him, and
(iii) those through whom he claims otherwise than by purchase for money or money's worth, and those claiming under them.[24]

Thus if V conveys land to P for value " as beneficial owner," and P subsequently discovers undisclosed incumbrances, he can sue V on the covenants for title if those incumbrances were created by V, or those claiming through, under or in trust for V, or those through whom V claims otherwise than by purchase for money or money's worth, and those claiming under them. This last phrase means that V will not be responsible for the acts of someone from whom he *bought* the land, but that he will be responsible for the acts of somebody who made a voluntary conveyance of the land to him, or gave it to him under a marriage settlement.

Where a person creates a mortgage " as beneficial owner," the covenants for title implied are absolute[25]; the mortgagor thus makes himself responsible for the acts of everyone. As stated under (a) above, the liability on the covenants implied by using phrases other than " as beneficial owner " is limited to the grantor's own acts.

[22] *Ibid.* s. 76, 2nd Sched. Similarly " as committee," before the Mental Health Act 1959, 8th Sched.: see *post*, p. 523.
[23] L.P.A. 1925, s. 76 (6).
[24] *Ibid.* 2nd Sched.; *David* v. *Sabin* [1893] 1 Ch. 523 at 532, 533. And see M. & W. 612–617.
[25] L.P.A. s. 76, 2nd Sched.

9. Parcels. The parcels describe what is conveyed; often the conveyancer employs a plan for this purpose, but this is not essential, *e.g.*, if an accurate verbal description can be given, or the property can be described by reference to a plan on an earlier conveyance. The purchaser is entitled on completion to all fixtures attached to the land at the date of the contract,[26] for they are part of it; and the conveyance will transfer them with the land, without special mention.

10. Habendum. This shows that the purchaser is to hold the land for his own benefit and not upon trust for a third party. It also contains the usual words of limitation.[27] It is followed by the acknowledgment and undertaking [28] where these are to be included.

11. Testimonium, and

12. Attestation clause. These need no comment.

---

[26] For fixtures, see *post*, pp. 375 *et seq.*
[27] *Ante*, pp. 20 *et seq.*
[28] *Ante*, p. 331.

Chapter 10

LEASES AND TENANCIES

Part 1

INTRODUCTORY

BEFORE considering leases in detail, some mention will be made of their history and terminology.

Sect. 1. History

1. Leases. A lease, as generally understood today, is a document creating an interest in land for a fixed period of certain duration,[1] usually in consideration of the payment of rent. This has not always been so, and it is not always the case even today.

2. Leases for lives. The owner of a life estate in land was able to recover the land itself if he was dispossessed, whereas until the end of the fifteenth century a tenant for a term of years could not do so. One result of this was that in early times it was a common practice for a lessee to take a lease of land for the duration of a specified number of lives, instead of for a specified term of years. Thus, instead of a lease for 99 years, a tenant would take a lease for the life of the survivor of X, Y and Z. The tenant had an estate *pur autre vie*, which, being an estate of freehold and classified as real property,[2] entitled him to recover the land if he was dispossessed. The disadvantage of the uncertainty of the period was outweighed by the advantages it gave to the tenant and sometimes to the lord. The rent payable was usually fairly small, but a fine was paid when the lease was granted; a further fine was payable when, on the termination of the lives, the tenant exercised the right the lease gave him to replace them and so extend the lease. If the lessor was a corporation such as a monastery or college, the fines were treated as income by the then members of the corporation, to the disadvantage of their successors. Leases for life finally lost their popularity when legislation in the first half of the nineteenth century compelled corporations to add such fines to their capital.[3]

[1] See *ante*, p. 17.　　　　[2] *Weigall* v. *Brome* (1833) 6 Sim. 99; *ante,* pp. 7, 46.
[3] See Radcliffe, *Real Property* (2nd ed., 1928), p. 28.

3. Leases for fixed terms of years. Leases for fixed terms of years are used today for more purposes than one.

(1) The usual type of lease is the occupational lease, where the tenant holds at a rent or in consideration of a fine, or both, and himself occupies the property, or sub-lets it. This type is dealt with in this chapter.

(2) In many cases leases are granted as a mere conveyancing device. Such leases are granted without a fine and at no rent, in order to provide security for the payment of money. The two most important examples are:

    (i) The lease granted by a mortgagor to the mortgagee as security for the money lent.

    (ii) The lease granted under a marriage settlement to trustees to secure payment of the portions for the younger children.

In each case it is unusual for the lessee to take possession of the land. These leases are dealt with under mortgages and settlements respectively.[4]

Sect. 2. Terminology

It is important to be familiar with the terms used in the law of leases. A lease is sometimes referred to as a " demise " and the premises in question as the " premises demised." The term " tenancy " is normally used for interests lasting for a relatively short period only, while " lease " usually indicates a more enduring interest; there is no hard-and-fast division, and in this chapter " lease " normally includes " tenancy." " Lease " and " term of years " are virtually synonymous terms today; before 1926 a term of years could only be regarded as one kind of lease, since leases for lives were by no means unknown. Today, leases for lives have nearly all disappeared.[5] " Lease " is often used interchangeably for the document and the " term of years " or " leasehold interest " created by it, although strictly it merely means the document.

The grantor of a lease is known as the lessor, the person to whom it is granted as the lessee. On the grant of a lease, the lessor retains a reversion, which he may assign; similarly, the lessee may assign the lease. Instead of assigning the lease (*i.e.*, transferring the property for the whole of the period for which it is held), the owner of the lease may grant a sub-lease (or underlease) for some

---

[4] See *post*, p. 464, and *ante*, pp. 205, 206.
[5] *Post*, p. 350.

shorter period, the parties to this sub-lease being known as the sub-lessor and sub-lessee respectively. Where the original lessor and original lessee have both assigned their interests, the new owners of the reversion and the lease are sometimes called the lessor and lessee, although it is better to keep these expressions for the original parties to the lease, and refer to the owners for the time being, whether original or by assignment, as the landlord and the tenant.

These expressions may be illustrated as follows:

This diagram is the usual way of representing the following events. X grants a 99 years' lease to A and then assigns the reversion to Y. B takes an assignment of A's lease and grants a sub-lease to C for 21 years, C assigning his sub-lease to D. As to the 99 years' lease, X is the " lessor," Y is the " assignee of the reversion " or " landlord," and A the " lessee." B is in a dual position; as to the 99 years' lease, he is the " assignee " or " tenant " and as to the 21 years' lease he is " sub-lessor " or " landlord." C is the " sub-lessee," and D the " assignee " of the sub-lease, or the " sub-tenant."

Part 2

CREATION OF LEASES

Sect. 1. Essentials of a Lease

A. The Right to Exclusive Possession must be given [6]

The tenant must have the right to exclude all other persons from the premises demised. A right to occupy certain premises for a fixed period cannot be a tenancy if the person granting the right remains in general control of the property, as is normally the case with rooms in an inn or boarding-house [7]; a mere lodger has no tenancy. Thus in *Wells* v. *Kingston-upon-Hull Corporation* [8] a

---

[6] See M. & W. 624–626.
[7] *Smith* v. *St. Michael, Cambridge, Overseers* (1860) 3 E. & E. 383.
[8] (1875) L.R. 10 C.P. 402.

graving dock was let by a corporation subject to certain rights of control, *e.g.*, as to opening and shutting the dock gates and seeing that the dock was cleaned out each day; it was held that no lease had been created. The same applies if no defined premises are in question; thus if there is a contractual obligation to store goods but the rooms in which they are stored may be changed from time to time at the convenience of the owner of the premises, there is no lease.[9] In such cases a mere licence is created, even if the language used clearly indicates that the parties intended to create a lease. But if the premises are clearly defined, the mere imposition of severe restrictions on the use which can be made of them will not prevent a lease from being created.[10]

Although a right to exclusive possession is an important indication that a tenancy and not a licence has been created,[11] it now seems that even a licence may confer such a right.[12] The nature of such " possessory licences " is far from clear.

B. *The Requirements as to Duration must be Satisfied*

The general nature of an estate less than freehold has already been considered,[13] and details of the requisite duration of each particular type of lease or tenancy are set out below.[14]

C. *The Lease must be Created in the Proper Way*

I. LEGAL LEASES

To create a legal estate after 1925, a lease must not only grant a term of years absolute within section 1 (1) of the Law of Property Act 1925 [15] but also be made with the proper formalities. The present position has been reached in four stages:

1. At common law, a lease could be granted in any way, even orally.

2. 1677–1845. The Statute of Frauds 1677 [16] required (*inter alia*) that every lease should be in writing (though not necessarily by

---

[9] *Interoven Stove Co. Ltd.* v. *Hibbard* [1936] 1 All E.R. 263.
[10] *Joel* v. *International Circus and Christmas Fair* (1920) 124 L.T. 459.
[11] See *Addiscombe Garden Estates Ltd.* v. *Crabbe* [1958] 1 Q.B. 513.
[12] *Errington* v. *Errington* [1952] 1 K.B. 290; *Finbow* v. *Air Ministry* [1963] 1 W.L.R. 697; for licences, see *post*, p. 378.
[13] *Ante*, p. 16.
[14] *Post*, pp. 345 *et seq.*
[15] *Ante*, p. 72.
[16] s. 1.

deed) signed by the party creating it or his agent authorised in writing; in default of this, only a tenancy at will was created. An exception was made for a lease for a period not exceeding three years from its creation at a rent of at least two-thirds of the full improved value (*i.e.*, the value taking into consideration any improvements to the property); such a lease could still be made orally.

3. 1845–1926. The Real Property Act 1845 [17] required a deed in all cases; but those leases which could be created orally were excepted.

4. Since 1925. The provisions of the Acts of 1677 and 1845 are in substance repeated by the Law of Property Act 1925, subject to certain variations. A lease cannot create a legal estate unless it is made by deed; the exception is a lease which—

    (i) takes effect in possession (*i.e.*, starts forthwith),

    (ii) for a term not exceeding three years, whether or not the lessee is given power to extend the term,

    (iii) at the best rent reasonably obtainable without taking a fine.[18]

It will be seen that (i) is new and (iii) is a modification of the previous law. If all three conditions are complied with, a legal lease can be created orally or in writing.

It should be noted that this concession applies only to the grant of an actual lease; a *contract* for a lease, for however short a period, will be unenforceable by action unless evidenced by sufficient writing or part performance.[19] Further, once a legal lease has been validly granted, a deed is required to effect a legal assignment of it, no matter how short the term; thus a legal assignment of a yearly tenancy can be effected only by deed, even if the tenancy was created orally.[20]

II. EQUITABLE LEASES

1. Informal lease void at law. A lease which did not satisfy the above requirements was void at law and passed no legal estate. However, although at law the lease was ineffective to create any tenancy, a tenancy at law might arise independently of the lease; for if the tenant took possession with the landlord's consent, a tenancy at will arose, and as soon as rent was paid and accepted, the tenancy at will was converted into a yearly or other periodic tenancy, depending on the way in which the rent was paid,[21] on such of the terms of

---

[17] s. 3.
[18] L.P.A. 1925, ss. 52 (1), 54.
[19] *Ante*, pp. 318 *et seq.*, 323 *et seq.*
[20] *Post*, p. 353.
[21] *Martin* v. *Smith* (1874) L.R. 9 Ex. 50; *post*, pp. 347–349.

the lease as were consistent with the periodic tenancy created. Thus if in 1870 a lease for 99 years was granted orally or merely in writing, the largest estate which the tenant could claim in a court of law was usually a yearly tenancy; and his claim to this depended not on the lease but upon his possession and the payment and acceptance of rent.

2. Effect as contract. Although such a lease failed to create any legal estate, it was not entirely ineffective, for it might be treated as a contract to grant the lease agreed upon. A lease is clearly distinct from a contract to grant a lease : the difference is between " I hereby grant you a lease " and " I hereby agree that I will grant you a lease." Nevertheless, both law and equity concurred in treating an imperfect lease as a contract to grant a lease, provided it was made for value and was sufficiently evidenced in writing, or, so far as equity was concerned, supported by a sufficient act of part performance.[22] The attitude of equity was particularly important, for under the doctrine of *Parker* v. *Taswell*[23] equity would first treat an imperfect lease of this kind as a contract to grant the lease, and then order specific performance of the contract.[24] Once the actual lease had been granted in pursuance of the decree of specific performance, the position of the parties was the same for the future as if the lease had been granted by deed in the first place.

3. Walsh v. Lonsdale.[25] The rights of the parties under an imperfect lease sufficiently evidenced by writing or part performance were thus clear whenever specific performance had been decreed. What was not so clear was the position if, as was far more often the case, no decree of specific performance had been granted but the parties were entitled to obtain one. In equity, the principle is " Equity looks on that as done which ought to be done," so that the parties were treated as if the lease had been granted. But there was no such principle at law, and, indeed, it would have been strange if the positive requirements of statute could have been so easily circumvented. Yet equity might intervene to restrain the parties from exercising their legal rights in opposition to their equitable obligations, and the Judicature Act 1873[26] provided that where the

[22] See *Tidey* v. *Mollett* (1864) 16 C.B.(N.S.) 298 ; but see *Harte* v. *Williams* [1934] 1 K.B. 201.
[23] (1858) 2 De G. & J. 559.
[24] *Zimbler* v. *Abrahams* [1903] 1 K.B. 577.
[25] (1882) 21 Ch.D. 9.
[26] s. 25 (11), now J.A. 1925, s. 44.

rules of law and equity conflicted, the rules of equity should prevail. Accordingly, in *Walsh* v. *Lonsdale* [27] it was held that the relationship of the parties was the same as if the lease had actually been granted. The facts in that case were as follows:

> L agreed in writing to grant by deed a lease of a mill to T for seven years, one of the terms being that T should on demand pay a year's rent in advance. No deed was executed, but T was let into possession and for a year and a half paid rent quarterly, although not in advance. L then demanded a year's rent in advance, and on T's refusal to pay, distrained for it. T then brought an action for damages for wrongful distress, and for specific performance of the agreement.

T's case was that distress was a legal, and not an equitable, remedy, and that as at law he was only a yearly tenant with no obligation to pay rent in advance, L could not distrain for the rent.[28] It was held, however, that since the distress would have been legal had the lease agreed upon been granted by deed, and since equity treated the parties as if this had been done the distress was lawful in equity; the equitable rule prevailed over the rule at law and so even at law T could not complain of the distress.

4. Differences between legal and equitable leases. The effect of *Walsh* v. *Lonsdale* is to render an enforceable agreement for a lease very nearly as good as a legal lease, and the same applies to an imperfect lease which is enforceable as an agreement for a lease. There are still, however, some points of difference.[29]

(a) *Specific performance.* The rule depends upon the willingness of equity to grant the discretionary remedy of specific performance, so that if an agreement for a lease is one of which the court will not [30] grant specific performance,[31] the position under it will be precarious. Further, if the court lacks jurisdiction to order specific performance,[32] a tenant will not be able to enforce the agreement in that court,[33] though he could defend proceedings by the landlord which ignored the agreement, as the court can give effect to an equitable defence.[34]

---

[27] *Supra.*
[28] See *Manchester Brewery Co.* v. *Coombs* [1901] 2 Ch. 608 at 617, 618.
[29] See M. & W. 632–635.
[30] *Coatsworth* v. *Johnson* (1886) 55 L.J.Q.B. 220 at 222.
[31] See *ante,* p. 63.
[32] *e.g.,* County Courts Act 1959, s. 52 (1) (*d*).
[33] *Foster* v. *Reeves* [1892] 2 Q.B. 255; contrast *Cornish* v. *Brook Green Laundry Ltd.* [1959] 1 Q.B. 394.
[34] *Kingswood Estate Co. Ltd.* v. *Anderson* [1963] 2 Q.B. 169.

(b) *Easements.* Certain easements and similar rights may be created on a grant of a legal estate which will not be created by a mere contract.[35]

(c) *Third parties.* The doctrine of *Walsh* v. *Lonsdale* does not treat an enforceable agreement for a lease as being as good as a lease as regards third parties, but only as regards the actual parties to the agreement. Thus if a tenant under a lease assigns his interest there is said to be privity of estate between the landlord and the assignee, so that the assignee becomes entitled to the benefit, and subject to the burden, of the covenants in the lease. But there is no privity of estate between the landlord and the assignee of a tenant under an agreement for a lease merely by virtue of the assignment even though it is made by deed; the original tenant's right to specific performance is not thus transferable to the assignee.[36]

Again, the rights of a tenant under an agreement for a lease, being merely equitable, are subject to the same frailty as all equitable interests, namely, they are void against a bona fide purchaser for value of a legal estate without notice of them. Thus if L makes an agreement for a lease of seven years with T and then grants a legal lease or a legal mortgage to X or conveys the legal fee simple to him, T's rights will be unenforceable against X if X took his estate in good faith and for value without notice of T's rights. Before 1926, the usual rules of actual, constructive and imputed notice applied[37]; and if T was in possession of the land, that would normally suffice to give notice of his rights to X.[38] The same rules apply after 1925, save that if T's agreement was either made or transferred after 1925, it must be registered as a land charge. Registration is deemed to be notice to the whole world; but if the agreement should have been registered and has not, it will be void against a purchaser for money or money's worth of a legal estate in the land, or (if the agreement was made before 1926 but transferred after 1925) against a purchaser for value of any interest, legal or equitable, in the property.[39] Actual knowledge does not amount to notice in these cases.[40]

---

[35] See *post,* p. 435.
[36] *Purchase* v. *Lichfield Brewery Co.* [1915] 1 K.B. 184: for privity of estate, see *post,* p. 383.
[37] *Ante,* pp. 61 *et seq.*
[38] See *Hunt* v. *Luck* [1902] 1 Ch. 428 at 432, 433.
[39] L.C.A. 1925, s. 13 (2); for land charges, see *ante,* pp. 79 *et seq.*, and more fully, *post,* pp. 541 *et seq.*
[40] L.P.A. 1925, s. 199 (1).

In practice, a written agreement for a lease is virtually as secure as an actual lease, especially if it has been registered, thus ensuring that the whole world has notice of it and so curing the principal defect to which equitable interests are subject. In the case of tenancies for a relatively short period at a rack rent it is usual to accept a mere agreement and not to register it, relying upon the tenant's evident possession of the land to put any prudent purchaser on inquiry.

Sect. 2. Types of Leases and Tenancies

A. Classification

Leases and tenancies may be classified under the five following heads.

1. Leases for a fixed period.

(a) *Certainty of term.* A lease may be granted for any certain period of certain duration, no matter how long or short. Leases for a week or for three thousand years are equally valid. Both the commencement and the duration of the term must either be certain or else be rendered certain before the lease takes effect.[41] Thus a lease for 99 years from January 1 next complies with this rule, and so does a lease from the determination of an existing tenancy for as many years as X shall name, once X has named the period; but a tenancy granted during wartime " for the duration of the war " does not.[42] An Act of 1944 [43] converted tenancies for the duration of the current war or emergency into valid tenancies for ten years determinable after the war or emergency by (usually) one month's notice; but there is nothing in the Act to rescue tenancies for other uncertain periods, such as the duration of a partnership, from the common law rule declaring them void.

(b) *Reversionary leases.* Before 1926, there was no restriction upon the length of time that might elapse before the term began; a lease could thus be granted in 1917 to commence in 1946,[44] such a lease being known as a reversionary lease. The perpetuity rule was not infringed by such a grant, for the lessee took a vested interest forthwith; only the vesting in possession was postponed.[45]

---

[41] *Harvey* v. *Pratt* [1965] 1 W.L.R. 1025.
[42] *Lace* v. *Chantler* [1944] K.B. 368.
[43] Validation of War-time Leases Act 1944.
[44] *Mann, Crossman & Paulin Ltd.* v. *Registrar of the Land Registry* [1918] 1 Ch. 202.
[45] *Ibid.*

However, the grant of a term to take effect more than 21 years from the instrument creating it is void if made after 1925 at a rent or in consideration of a fine, and the same applies to any contract made after 1925 to create such a term.[46] It will be noted that this does not affect grants or contracts made before 1926 or leases taking effect in equity under a settlement, *e.g.*, portions terms.[47]

(c) *Interesse termini.* Before 1926, there was a common law rule that a lessee acquired no actual estate in the land until he had taken possession during the term of the lease. Until he had exercised his right to take possession, he had a mere *interesse termini* (an interest in the term) which, though a right *in rem*,[48] so far fell short of an actual lease that no reversion could exist upon it; thus there could be no release of the grantor's interest to the holder of an *interesse termini*.[49]

The doctrine of *interesse termini* sometimes led to unfortunate results. Thus in one case,[50] T held land under a lease from L which had two years to run. L then granted T a new lease for 73 years, to run from the end of the two years. During the two years, T sub-leased the land to S for 21 years and S became in arrear with his rent. It was held that T had no reversion on the 21 years' sub-lease, for he had not entered upon the land during the 73 years' lease and so had only an *interesse termini*; consequently, he could not distrain for rent due under S's sub-lease, for distress is a remedy available only to reversioners or those authorised by statute. This troublesome doctrine was usually avoided by means of a grant to uses; if a grant was made to X and his heirs to the use that Y should have a lease for 21 years, the Statute of Uses 1535 conferred legal possession and thus a legal lease on the tenant without entry. The doctrine has now been abolished in respect of all leases, whether made before or after 1925.[51]

(d) *Determination.* The general rule is that a lease for a fixed period automatically determines when the fixed period expires; but there are statutory exceptions to this rule.[52]

---

[46] L.P.A. 1925, s. 149 (3); see (1947) 63 L.Q.R. 20; *Re Strand and Savoy Properties Ltd.* [1960] Ch. 582.
[47] *Ante,* pp. 205, 206.
[48] *Gillard* v. *Cheshire Lines Committee* (1884) 32 W.R. 943.
[49] Co.Litt. 270a.
[50] *Lewis* v. *Baker* [1905] 1 Ch. 46.
[51] L.P.A. 1925, s. 149 (1), (2).
[52] See *post,* pp. 589 *et seq.*

2. Yearly tenancies.

(a) *Creation.* A yearly tenancy is one which continues from year to year indefinitely until determined by proper notice, notwithstanding the death of either party or the assignment of his interest. Such a tenancy may be created either expressly or by implication. Thus an express grant to A " from year to year " or " as a yearly tenant " will create a yearly tenancy. It should be noted, however, that a grant " to X for one year and thereafter from year to year " will give X a tenancy for at least two years; for he has been given a definite term of one year followed by a yearly tenancy which can be determined only at the end of the first year thereof.[53]

A yearly tenancy arises by implication whenever a person occupies land with the owner's consent and rent measured with reference to a year is paid and accepted, unless there is sufficient evidence to show that some other kind of tenancy was intended.[54] A yearly tenancy also arises when a tenant under a lease for a fixed term holds over (*i.e.*, remains in possession at the end of his term) and rent is paid and accepted on a yearly basis. In this case, the tenant will hold under such of the terms of the expired lease as are not inconsistent with a yearly holding.[55] Thus covenants to repair,[56] or to carry on some specified trade on the premises,[57] and provisos for re-entry by the landlord on non-payment of rent,[58] may all be implied in a yearly tenancy. But a covenant to paint every three years [59] or a provision for two years' notice to quit [60] are inconsistent with the yearly tenancy and cannot be implied in this way.

The payment of rent at more frequent intervals than a year will not prevent a yearly tenancy from arising by implication. The test is the period by reference to which the parties calculated the rent. Thus an agreement for " £104 per annum payable weekly " prima facie creates a yearly tenancy; had the agreement been for " £2 per week," a weekly tenancy would be presumed, despite the fact that in each case the tenant would in fact have made the same payments, namely, £2 every week.[61]

---

[53] *Re Searle* [1912] 1 Ch. 610.
[54] *Kemp* v. *Derrett* (1814) 3 Camp. 510.
[55] *Dougal* v. *McCarthy* [1893] 1 Q.B. 736.
[56] *Wyatt* v. *Cole* (1877) 36 L.T. 613.
[57] *Sanders* v. *Karnell* (1858) 1 F. & F. 356.
[58] *Thomas* v. *Packer* (1857) 1 H. & N. 669.
[59] *Pinero* v. *Judson* (1829) 6 Bing. 206.
[60] *Tooker* v. *Smith* (1857) 1 H. & N. 732.
[61] See *Adler* v. *Blackman* [1953] 1 Q.B. 146.

(b) *Determination.* A yearly tenancy may be determined by such notice and at such time as the parties agree.[62] In default of such agreement, it can be determined by at least half a year's notice expiring at the end of a completed year of the tenancy. The meaning of "half a year" depends on the day upon which the tenancy began. If the tenancy began on one of the usual quarter-days (Lady Day (March 25), Midsummer Day (June 24), Michaelmas (September 29) or Christmas (December 25)), "half a year" means "two quarters"; otherwise, "half a year" means 182 days.[63] Thus if a yearly tenancy began on March 25, notice to quit given on or before September 29 is good, although it is less than 182 days [64]; and if a yearly tenancy began on September 29, notice must be given on or before March 25, even though it is more than 182 days. In each of these cases, the tenancy began on a quarter-day [65]; had it started on some other day, *e.g.*, March 26, at least 182 days' notice would have been required.[66] It will be noted that in neither case is the period of the notice necessarily six months, although of course the parties may agree that such shall be the notice required.

3. Weekly, monthly and other periodic tenancies. A tenancy from week to week, month to month, quarter to quarter, and the like (including a tenancy for some artificial period, such as for successive periods of 364 days [67]) can be created in a similar way to a yearly tenancy, namely, either by express agreement, or by inference, such as that arising from the payment and acceptance of rent measured with reference to a week, month or quarter, as the case may be.[68] In general, the position of the parties under such a tenancy is similar to that under a yearly tenancy, save that notice of termination is not half a period, but a full period, expiring at the end of a completed period, subject to any contrary agreement between the parties.[69] Thus in the absence of any contrary agreement, a weekly tenancy commencing on a Monday can be determined either by notice given on or before one Monday to expire on the following Monday,[70] or, since a week starting on a Monday is complete at midnight on the following Sunday, by

---

[62] *Re Threlfall* (1880) 16 Ch.D. 274 at 281, 282.
[63] *Anon.* (1575) 3 Dy. 345a.
[64] *Roe* d. *Durant* v. *Doe* (1830) 6 Bing. 574.
[65] *Morgan* v. *Davies* (1878) 3 C.P.D. 260.
[66] Co.Litt. 135b.
[67] *Land Settlement Association Ltd.* v. *Carr* [1944] K.B. 657.
[68] *Cole* v. *Kelly* [1920] 2 K.B. 106 at 132.
[69] *Queen's Club Gardens Estates Ltd.* v. *Bignell* [1924] 1 K.B. 117; *Lemon* v. *Lardeur* [1946] K.B. 613.
[70] *Newman* v. *Slade* [1926] 2 K.B. 328.

notice given on or before one Sunday to expire on the following Sunday.[71] But at least four weeks' notice is now required for premises genuinely let as a dwelling.[72]

4. Tenancies at will. A tenancy at will arises whenever a tenant, with the consent of the landlord, occupies land *qua* tenant (and not merely as a servant or agent) on the terms that either party may determine the tenancy at any time. In some cases the tenant holds rent free, as where the vendor of a fee simple, owing to some delay in completion, lets the purchaser into possession of the property before the conveyance has been executed.[73] But unless the parties agree that the tenancy shall be rent free, the landlord is entitled to compensation for the use and occupation of the land[74]; and if a rent is fixed, the landlord may distrain for it in the usual way.

A tenancy at will comes to an end when either party does any act incompatible with the continuance of the tenancy, as where the tenant commits voluntary waste,[75] or the landlord enters the land and cuts trees or carries away stone,[76] or either party gives notice to the other determining the tenancy. The tenancy is also determined if either party dies or assigns his interest in the land.[77]

If a tenancy at will is created without any agreement as to payment of rent, and rent is subsequently paid and accepted upon some regular periodical basis, a yearly, monthly or other periodical tenancy will be created in accordance with the rules set out under heads 2 and 3 above.

5. Tenancies at sufferance. A tenancy at sufferance arises where a tenant, having entered upon land under a valid tenancy, holds over without the landlord's assent or dissent.[78] Such a tenant differs from a trespasser in that his original entry was lawful, and from a tenant at will in that his tenancy exists without the landlord's assent. No rent, as such, is payable, but the tenant is liable to pay compensation for his use and occupation of the land.[79] The tenancy may be determined at any time, and may be converted into a yearly or other periodic tenancy in the usual way, *e.g.*, if rent is paid and accepted with reference to a year.

---

71 *Bathavon R.D.C.* v. *Carlile* [1958] 1 Q.B. 461.
72 Rent Act 1957, s. 16; *Schnabel* v. *Allard* [1967] 1 Q.B. 627.
73 *Howard* v. *Shaw* (1841) 8 M. & W. 118.
74 Distress for Rent Act 1737, s. 11; *Howard* v. *Shaw, supra.*
75 *Countess of Shrewsbury's Case* (1600) 5 Co.Rep. 13b.
76 *Turner* v. *Doe* d. *Bennett* (1842) 9 M. & W. 643.
77 See *Pinhorn* v. *Souster* (1853) 8 Exch. 763 at 772.
78 See *Remon* v. *City of London Real Property Co. Ltd.* [1921] 1 K.B. 49 at 58.
79 *Leigh* v. *Dickeson* (1884) 15 Q.B.D. 60.

There are statutory penalties for tenants who hold over after giving or receiving notice to quit:

(a) *Double annual value.* If the landlord gives the tenant written notice to quit and the tenant is a tenant for life or for years, the tenant is liable to pay the landlord a sum calculated at double the annual value of the land in respect of the period for which he holds over after the notice expired; this can be enforced by action but not otherwise, *e.g.,* not by distress.[80] This provision applies to tenancies from year to year as well as to tenancies for fixed terms of years or for a year certain, but not to weekly tenancies.[81]

(b) *Double rent.* If the tenant gives the landlord written or oral notice to quit, then, whatever the type of tenancy, the tenant is liable to pay double rent in respect of the period for which he holds over after the notice expired; payment can be enforced by action or distress.[82]

The curiously differing terms of these aged provisions will be noticed. The rent and the annual value may be the same, but they often differ, as where premises have been let at a reduced rent in consideration of a fine.

B. Statutory Modifications

Although the parties to a lease can in general create a lease for such periods as they think fit, statute has made some modifications to this position.

1. Leases for lives. By the Law of Property Act 1925,[83] a lease at a rent or a fine for life or lives, or for a term of years determinable with a life or lives or on the marriage of the lessee, is converted into a term of 90 years, whether it was granted before or after 1925; a contract for such a lease is treated in a similar way. The lease continues even after the death or marriage, as the case may be, although either party may determine it thereafter (but not before) by serving on the other one month's written notice to expire on one of the quarter-days applicable to the tenancy, or, if no special quarter-days are applicable, on one of the usual quarter-days. Thus leases at a rent or fine granted—

> " to A for life,"
> " to B for 10 years if he so long lives," and—
> " to C for 99 years if he so long remains a bachelor "

---

[80] Landlord and Tenant Act 1730, s. 1.
[81] *Lloyd* v. *Rosbee* (1810) 2 Camp. 453.
[82] Distress for Rent Act 1737, s. 18.

[83] s. 149 (6).

re all converted into terms which will continue for 90 years unless
y the proper notice they are determined on any quarter-day (not
ecessarily the first) after the event has occurred.

2. Perpetually renewable leases. A perpetually renewable lease
vas a lease which gave the tenant the right to renew it for another
eriod as often as it expired [84]; usually the tenant had to make some
ayment on exercising this right. By the Law of Property Act 1922,[85]
ll such leases existing at the end of 1925 were converted into terms of
wo thousand years, calculated from the beginning of the existing
erms; and perpetually renewable leases granted after 1925 take effect
s terms of two thousand years from the date fixed for the commence-
nent of the term. Any perpetually renewable sub-lease created out of
a perpetually renewable lease is converted into a term of two thousand
years less one day. The two thousand years lease is subject to the
ame terms as the original lease, with the following modifications.

(a) *Termination.* The tenant for the time being (but not the
andlord) may terminate the lease on any date upon which, but for
he conversion by the Act, the lease would have expired if it had not
een renewed, provided he gives at least ten days' written notice to
he landlord.

(b) *Assignment.* Every assignment or devolution of the lease must
be registered with the landlord or his solicitor or agent within six
nonths, and a fee of one guinea paid.

(c) *Breach of covenant.* A tenant who assigns the lease is not
liable for breaches of covenant committed after the assignment. The
general rule is that the original lessee is liable for all breaches
occurring during the term, even if they occur after he has assigned
the lease [86]; perpetually renewable leases are a statutory exception to
this rule.

(d) *Fine.* Any fine or other payment for renewal for which the
lease provides is converted into additional rent and spread over the
period between the renewal dates, except where the lease is granted
after 1925, when the obligation for payment is void.

It should be noted that the landlord has no right to determine
the lease at the renewal dates. Before 1926, if L granted T a lease
for 21 years with a perpetual right of renewal, it was T alone who
had the right to decide each 21 years whether or not to renew the

[84] See, *e.g.*, *Parkus* v. *Greenwood* [1950] Ch. 644.
[85] s. 145 and 15th Sched.
[86] See *post*, p. 384.

lease. This position is preserved, save that now the lease continue unless determined, instead of requiring renewal.

3. Over-lengthy renewals. A contract made after 1925 to renew a lease for over 60 years from its termination is void.[87] This is aimed at single renewals, not perpetual renewals, and does not affect contracts made before 1926.

4. Reversionary leases. A lease at a rent or a fine cannot be granted after 1925 to commence at too distant a future date. This has already been dealt with.[88]

C. Estoppel

1. Estoppel. On the grant of a lease or tenancy, both landlord and tenant and their successors in title are in general mutually estopped from denying the validity of the transaction. Neither landlord nor tenant will be permitted to deny that the tenancy which they have purported to create is invalid, and this is so even if the tenancy is merely oral.[89] But this does not prevent a corporation from setting up that it had no power to grant or receive the tenancy; estoppel cannot validate an *ultra vires* act.[90]

2. Tenancy by estoppel. One consequence of this rule is that if the landlord in fact has no estate in the land, then although the lease or tenancy can confer no actual estate on the tenant, and cannot be effective against third parties,[91] it is good between the parties to it and their successors in title.[92] Both landlord and tenant will be estopped from denying the validity of the lease or tenancy; they cannot " blow hot and cold " by claiming that the transaction was valid when entered into, and yet asserting subsequently that it was a nullity.

No tenancy by estoppel arises, however, if the lessor had any interest in the land when he granted the lease. If the lessor's interest was greater than the tenancy, the lease takes effect in the ordinary way; if it was equal to or smaller than the tenancy, the grant of the lease operates as an assignment of the lessor's interest.[93] Thus if L grants T a lease for 99 years and subsequently acquires the

---

[87] L.P.A. 1922, 15th Sched.
[88] *Ante*, p. 345.
[89] *E. H. Lewis & Son Ltd.* v. *Morelli* [1948] 2 All E.R. 1021.
[90] *Rhyl U.D.C.* v. *Rhyl Amusements Ltd.* [1959] 1 W.L.R. 465.
[91] *Tadman* v. *Henman* [1893] 2 Q.B. 168.
[92] See *E. H. Lewis & Son Ltd.* v. *Morelli, supra.*
[93] *Beardman* v. *Wilson* (1868) L.R. 4 C.P. 57; *Wollaston* v. *Hakewill* (1841) 3 Man. & G. 297 at 323.

fee simple (*e.g.*, under his father's will), T will take a lease for 99 years by estoppel if L had no interest in the land when the lease was granted. But if L had a lease for ten years at that time, the lease for 99 years will operate only as an assignment to T of L's lease for ten years.

3. Feeding the estoppel. If there is a tenancy by estoppel, and subsequently the landlord acquires some interest in the land, this is said to " feed the estoppel." From that moment the lease becomes fully effective, giving the tenant an actual estate in the land.[94]

Part 3

ASSIGNMENT OF LEASES

In order to effect a legal assignment of a lease, a deed must be employed,[95] even if the lease has been created by word of mouth, *e.g.*, a yearly tenancy in possession at a rack rent.[96] However, on principles similar to those applicable to the creation of leases, an oral or written assignment which is sufficiently evidenced by writing or part performance [97] will be effective in equity, though only as between assignor and assignee. Thus unless estopped from so doing the assignee may deny liability to the landlord on the covenants of the lease.[98] Other matters concerning assignments are dealt with below.[99]

The grant of sub-leases is governed by the rules relating to the grant of leases.[1]

Part 4

DETERMINATION OF TENANCIES

A lease or tenancy may come to an end in the following ways.

   (1) By expiry.
   (2) By notice.
   (3) By forfeiture.
   (4) By surrender.
   (5) By merger.

---

[94] *Macley* v. *Nutting* [1949] 2 K.B. 55.
[95] L.P.A. 1925, s. 52 (1), replacing R.P.A. 1845, s. 3.
[96] *Botting* v. *Martin* (1808) 1 Camp. 317.
[97] *Ante*, pp. 318 *et seq.*, 323 *et seq.*, 341 *et seq.*
[98] *Rodenhurst Estates Ltd.* v. *W. H. Barnes Ltd.* [1936] 2 All E.R. 3.
[99] *Post*, pp. 359, 371, 384, 387, 389.
[1] *Ante*, pp. 340 *et seq.*

    (6) By becoming a satisfied term.
    (7) By enlargement.
    (8) By disclaimer.

Sect. 1. By Expiry

As has been seen,[2] a lease or tenancy for a fixed period automatically determines when the fixed period expires, with certain exceptions. In some cases the tenant may be entitled to be granted a new lease or to remain in possession as a statutory tenant.[3]

Sect. 2. By Notice

A lease or tenancy for a fixed period cannot be determined by notice unless this is expressly agreed upon. Thus a lease for a substantial term such as 21 years often contains provisions enabling the tenant to determine it at the end of the seventh or fourteenth year, in which case the length of the notice required, the time when it is to be given, and other matters of this kind, depend on the terms of the lease. In the absence of any such provision the lease will continue for the full period.

    Yearly, weekly, monthly and other periodical tenancies can be determined by notice. These provisions, and the determination of tenancies at will and at sufferance, have already been considered.[4]

    Many periodic tenants have statutory protection against eviction.[5]

Sect. 3. By Forfeiture

A. *Right to Forfeit*

A landlord's right to forfeit a lease (*i.e.*, enforce a forfeiture of it) may arise under three heads.

    1. Forfeiture clause. Nearly every lease contains a list of things which the tenant shall and shall not do, and these may be framed as conditions or as covenants. If, as is normally the case, they are framed as covenants (*e.g.*, "The tenant hereby covenants with the landlord as follows . . ."), the landlord has no right to forfeit the lease if they are broken unless the lease contains an express provision

---

[2] *Ante*, p. 346.
[3] *Post*, pp. 589 *et seq.*
[4] *Ante*, pp. 347–350.
[5] See *post*, pp. 589 *et seq.*

for forfeiture on breach of a covenant.[6] There is no necessary connection between the tenant failing to perform a covenant made by him and the determination of the lease; every well-drawn lease consequently contains a forfeiture clause.

2. Breach of condition. If the tenant's obligations are worded as conditions, however (*e.g.*, if the lease is granted " upon condition that " or " provided always that " certain things are done or not done), the lease may be forfeited on breach of condition even if there is no forfeiture clause.[7] In such a case, the continuance of the lease has been made conditional upon the tenant performing his obligations, and upon breach of one of them the lease becomes void forthwith without the need for entry by the landlord,[8] although the tenant will not be allowed to set this up to avoid his liability under the lease if the landlord does not treat it as forfeited.[9]

3. Denial of title. If a tenant denies his landlord's title, as by asserting (even orally) that he or some third party is the true owner, the landlord is forthwith entitled to forfeit the tenancy.[10] But a mere denial of title in a pleading in an action merely puts the other party to proof of his case, and so works no forfeiture, especially if it is withdrawn before the landlord elects to take advantage of it.[11]

B. Waiver of Breach

Even if the landlord has shown that he is treating the lease as forfeited, he may subsequently prevent himself from proceeding with the forfeiture if he waives the breach of covenant; and *a fortiori* a waiver of the breach may take place before the landlord has shown that he is treating the lease as forfeited. Waiver may be express or implied. It will be implied if—

    (i) the landlord is aware of the acts or omissions of the tenant giving rise to the right of forfeiture, and

    (ii) the landlord does some unequivocal act recognising the continued existence of the lease.[12]

Both elements must be present to constitute a waiver. A waiver will be implied where a landlord, with knowledge of the breach, demands

---

[6] *Doe* d. *Willson* v. *Phillips* (1824) 2 Bing. 13.
[7] See *Doe* d. *Lockwood* v. *Clarke* (1807) 8 East 185.
[8] *Pennant's Case* (1596) 3 Co.Rep. 64a at 64b, 65a.
[9] See *Doe* d. *Bryan* v. *Bancks* (1821) 4 B. & Ald. 401.
[10] *Wisbech St. Mary Parish Council* v. *Lilley* [1956] 1 W.L.R. 121.
[11] *Warner* v. *Sampson* [1959] 1 Q.B. 297.
[12] *Matthews* v. *Smallwood* [1910] 1 Ch. 777 at 786.

or sues for or accepts rent falling due after the breach,[13] or distrains for rent, whether due before or after the breach.[14] These acts, however, will not amount to a waiver if done after the landlord has shown his final decision to treat the lease as forfeited, as by commencing an action for possession.[15]

As would be expected, the waiver of a covenant or condition extends only to the particular breach in question and does not operate as a general waiver of all future breaches, although the law was once different; the same applies to a licence granted to the tenant to do any act.[16] And waiver of the forfeiture is no bar to an action for damages.[17]

C. Mode of Forfeiture

The normal method of enforcing a forfeiture is by issuing a writ for possession; such a writ usually contains an unequivocal demand for possession, so that the mere service of the writ operates to determine the lease.[18] Alternatively, unless the premises are let as a dwelling-house on a lease and some person is lawfully residing in it or in any part of it,[19] the landlord can enforce his right of forfeiture by making peaceable entry on the land. It is usually inadvisable for a landlord to adopt this method, for if any force is used, he may be criminally (but not civilly [20]) liable under the Forcible Entry Acts 1381, 1391 and 1429.[21]

D. Conditions for Forfeiture

The conditions under which a right of forfeiture can be enforced depend upon whether the right arises from breach of the covenant or condition to pay rent or from breach of any other provision.

I. FORFEITURE FOR NON-PAYMENT OF RENT

Where a landlord has the right to forfeit a lease for non-payment of rent, two important points to be considered are the landlord's formal demand for the rent and the tenant's right to relief.

---

[13] *Goodright* d. *Charter* v. *Cordwent* (1795) 6 T.R. 219; *Segal Securities Ltd.* v. *Thoseby* [1963] 1 Q.B. 887.
[14] *Ward* v. *Day* (1863) 4 B. & S. 337 at 353; 5 B. & S. 364.
[15] *Grimwood* v. *Moss* (1872) L.R. 7 C.P. 360.
[16] L.P.A. 1925, ss. 143, 148, replacing earlier provisions which altered the law laid down in *Dumpor's Case* (1603) 4 Co.Rep. 119b.
[17] *Stephens* v. *Junior Army and Navy Stores Ltd.* [1914] 2 Ch. 516.
[18] *Elliott* v. *Boynton* [1924] 1 Ch. 236.
[19] Rent Act 1965, s. 31.
[20] *Hemmings* v. *Stoke Poges Golf Club* [1920] 1 K.B. 720.
[21] For another disadvantage, see *R.* v. *Hussey* (1924) 18 Cr.App.R. 160.

1. Landlord's formal demand: the landlord must either have made a formal demand for the rent, or else be exempted from making such a demand.

(a) *Formal demand.* To make a formal demand, the landlord or his authorised agent must demand the exact sum due on the day when it falls due at such convenient hour before sunset as will give time to count out the money, the demand being made upon the demised premises and continuing until sunset.[22]

(b) *Exemption from formal demand.* To avoid the technicalities of a formal demand, every well-drawn lease provides that the lease may be forfeited if the rent is a specified number of days in arrear, " whether formally demanded or not." The words quoted exempt the landlord from making a formal demand. However, even if a lease contains no such clause, the Common Law Procedure Act 1852 [23] dispenses with a formal demand in any action for forfeiture if—

(i) half a year's rent is in arrear, and
(ii) no sufficient distress (*i.e.,* goods available for distraint) can be found [24] upon the premises to satisfy all the arrears due.[25]

2. Tenant's right to relief: the tenant may be able to claim relief against the forfeiture. Equity considered that a right of forfeiture was merely security for payment of the rent, so that if—

(i) the tenant paid the rent due; and
(ii) the tenant paid any expenses to which the landlord had been put; and
(iii) it was just and equitable to grant relief,

equity would restore the tenant to his position despite the forfeiture of the lease.[26] Originally, there was no limit to the time within which application for relief had to be made, apart from the general principle that equity would give no assistance to stale claims.[27] But the Common Law Procedure Act 1852, ss. 210–212 [28] (replacing earlier legislation), while recognising the court's discretion to grant relief, provided that every application for relief must be made within six months of the actual re-entry, whether effected under an order of

---

[2] See 1 Wms.Saund. (1871) 434 *et seq.*
[3] s. 210, re-enacting the Landlord and Tenant Act 1730, s. 2; County Courts Act 1959, s. 191 (2).
[4] See *Hammond* v. *Mather* (1862) 3 F. & F. 151 (no distress can be " found " if the outer doors are locked).
[5] See *Cross* v. *Jordan* (1853) 8 Exch. 149.
[6] See *Howard* v. *Fanshawe* [1895] 2 Ch. 581.
[7] See *Hill* v. *Barclay* (1811) 18 Ves. 56 at 59, 60.
[8] And see County Courts Act 1959, s. 191 (3).

the court or, probably, by the landlord without such an order.[29] I
relief is granted, the tenant holds under the old lease [30] and the
execution of a new document is not required.

Where a lease is forfeited, any underleases created out of i
automatically come to an end.[31] However, an underlessee has the
same right of applying for relief against forfeiture of the head lease
as the tenant under the head lease has.[32]

II. FORFEITURE FOR BREACH OF OTHER COVENANTS OR CONDITIONS

The general rule is that forfeiture for breach of a covenant or condition
other than for payment of rent is subject to the landlord's obligation
to serve a notice in the statutory form and the tenant's right to relief
There are some exceptions to this rule, however, and there are special
provisions for sub-tenants.

1. General rule.

(a) *Service of notice.* Before proceeding to enforce forfeiture either
by action or re-entry, the landlord must serve on the tenant the
statutory notice in writing under the Law of Property Act 1925
s. 146.[33] The notice must—

   (i) specify the breach complained of; and
   (ii) require it to be remedied, if this is possible; and
   (iii) require the tenant to make compensation in money for the
         breach if the landlord requires such compensation.[34]

Thus a notice in respect of immoral use of the premises need only
specify the breach, for mere discontinuance of this use would no
remedy the breach, and the landlord need not soil his hands by
claiming compensation out of the tenant's ill-gotten gains.[35]

(b) *Time for compliance.* The landlord must then allow a
reasonable time to elapse in which the tenant may comply with
the notice. The Act does not define what is a reasonable time, but
three months is usually considered to be enough in normal circum
stances. Even if the breach cannot be remedied (as where the

---

[29] See *Howard* v. *Fanshawe, supra,* at pp. 588, 589.
[30] Common Law Procedure Act 1852, s. 212; J.A. 1925, s. 46; and see Count
Courts Act 1959, s. 191.
[31] *Great Western Ry.* v. *Smith* (1876) 2 Ch.D. 235 at 253.
[32] Common Law Procedure Act 1852, s. 210.
[33] Replacing C.A. 1881, s. 14, and C.A. 1892, ss. 2, 4.
[34] L.P.A. 1925, s. 146 (1); and see *post,* p. 373 (repairs).
[35] *Rugby School (Governors)* v. *Tannahill* [1935] 1 K.B. 87; but see *Glass* v
Kencakes Ltd. [1966] 1 Q.B. 611 (immoral user by sub-tenant unknown to tenant

provision is for forfeiture on the bankruptcy of the tenant), reasonable notice must be given so as to enable the tenant to consider his position; in such cases, two days' notice has been held to be insufficient although fourteen days may be enough.[36]

(c) *Relief.* If within a reasonable time the notice has not been complied with, the landlord may proceed to enforce the forfeiture. This he may do in person or by action, the same considerations applying as before.[37] However, while the landlord " is proceeding " to enforce the forfeiture (*i.e.,* at any time before he has actually entered [38]), the tenant may apply to the court for relief, either in any action by the landlord enforcing the forfeiture or by a separate application.[39] The court may grant relief on such terms as it thinks fit, and if relief is granted the effect is as if the lease had never been forfeited.[40] It will be noticed that there is no provision enabling the court to grant relief after forfeiture, even within six months. The right to relief is statutory; equity refused relief in all cases save those of non-payment of rent.

2. Exceptional cases. The above provisions concerning the necessity for serving a notice and the tenant's right to apply for relief do not affect forfeiture for denial of title,[41] but they govern all covenants and conditions (other than those for payment of rent) with three exceptions. These three exceptions are as follows:

(a) *Pre-1926 assignment*: when there was a breach before 1926 of a covenant against assigning, underletting or parting with the possession of the property.[42] This exception is now obsolete, for all such breaches will have been dealt with or waived long ago. The general rule applies to breaches of such a covenant committed after 1925.

(b) *Mining lease*: when there has been a breach of a covenant in a mining lease providing for inspection of the books, accounts, weighing machines or other things, or of the mine itself.[43] Since the rent reserved on such a lease usually varies with the quantity of minerals got, such a covenant is most important to the landlord;

---

6 *Horsey Estate Ltd.* v. *Steiger* [1899] 2 Q.B. 79; *Civil Service Co-operative Society Ltd.* v. *McGrigor's Trustee* [1923] 2 Ch. 347.
7 *Ante,* p. 356.
8 *Rogers* v. *Rice* [1892] 2 Ch. 170.
9 L.P.A. 1925, s. 146 (2).
0 *Dendy* v. *Evans* [1909] 2 K.B. 894.
1 *Warner* v. *Sampson* [1958] 1 Q.B. 404; revsd. on other grounds [1959] 1 Q.B. 297.
2 L.P.A. 1925, s. 146 (8).
3 *Ibid.*

there is consequently no restriction upon the landlord forfeiting the lease without serving a notice, and no provision enabling the tenant to obtain relief.

(c) *Bankruptcy or execution*: when there has been a breach of a condition against the bankruptcy of the tenant or the taking of the lease in execution.[44] This must be divided into two heads.

(1) NO PROTECTION. In five specified cases, on breach of such a condition, section 146 has no application at all; the lease can thus be forfeited at once without service of notice and without possibility of relief. These cases are those where the lease is of—

    (i) agricultural or pastoral land, or
    (ii) mines or minerals, or
    (iii) a public house or beershop, or
    (iv) a furnished house, or
    (v) property with respect to which the personal qualifications of the tenant are of importance for the preservation of the value or character of the property, or on the ground of neighbourhood to the landlord or to any person holding under him.

(2) PROTECTION FOR ONE YEAR. In all other cases, on breach of such a condition, the protection of section 146 applies for one year from the bankruptcy or taking in execution; if during that year the landlord wishes to forfeit the lease, he must serve the notice and the tenant can apply for relief. But once the year has elapsed, the tenant is no longer protected; the landlord can forfeit the lease without serving notice and the court has no power to grant relief.

In one case under this head, however, the provisions as to notice and relief apply without limit of time: if the tenant's lease is sold during the year, the protection of section 146 continues indefinitely. This allows the trustee in bankruptcy or sheriff to dispose of the lease to a purchaser at a reasonable price, for if the lease were liable to be forfeited after the year, without the service of notice or the chance of relief, it would be hard to find a purchaser.

3. Sub-tenants. Under section 146 as amended by the Law of Property (Amendment) Act 1929,[45] a sub-tenant may apply for relief against the forfeiture of his landlord's lease on whatever ground that forfeiture is being enforced; and a mere mortgagee or chargee is a " sub-tenant " for these purposes.[46] A sub-tenant has this right

---

[44] *Ibid.* s. 146 (9), (10).   [45] s. 1
[46] *Grand Junction Co. Ltd.* v. *Bates* [1954] 2 Q.B. 160; and see *post*, pp. 466 et seq.

whether the head lease is being forfeited for non-payment of rent, for one of the exceptional cases mentioned above or for any other reason, irrespective of whether the tenant himself can claim relief. If relief is granted, the court will grant the sub-tenant a term not longer than the term he held under his sub-lease.[47] The sub-tenant usually enters into a new lease direct with the reversioner of the forfeited lease on terms similar to (though not necessarily the same as) those of the old sub-lease.

Sect. 4. By Surrender

If a tenant surrenders his lease to his immediate landlord, who accepts the surrender, the lease merges in the landlord's reversion and is extinguished. The surrender must be to the immediate landlord; and transfer of the lease to a superior landlord does not work a surrender but operates merely as an assignment of the lease. Thus if A leases land to B for 99 years and B sub-leases to C for 21 years, C's lease will be extinguished by surrender if he transfers it to B but not if he transfers it to A.

Surrender may be either express or by operation of law. For an express surrender, a deed is required,[48] although probably an oral surrender made for value and supported by sufficient evidence in writing or part performance would suffice in equity. There will be surrender by operation of law if the parties do some act showing an intention to terminate the lease, and the circumstances are such that it would be inequitable for them to rely on the fact that there has been no surrender by deed.[49] Surrender by operation of law will take place if the tenant accepts a fresh lease from his immediate reversioner, even though the new lease is for a shorter term than the old one or starts at a future date[50]; and if a lease is varied by extending the term, this operates by way of surrender and regrant.[51] Similarly there will be a surrender if the tenant gives up possession of the premises and the landlord accepts it,[52] but not if there is a mere uncompleted contract by the tenant to purchase the reversion.[53]

---

[47] L.P.A. 1925, s. 146 (4); and see *Ewart* v. *Fryer* [1901] 1 Ch. 499 at 515.
[48] L.P.A. 1925, s. 52, replacing R.P.A. 1845, s. 3.
[49] See *Glynn* v. *Coghlan* [1918] 1 I.R. 482 at 485.
[50] *Ive's Case* (1597) 5 Co. Rep. 11a.
[51] *Baker* v. *Merckel* [1960] 1 Q.B. 657.
[52] See *Oastler* v. *Henderson* (1877) 2 Q.B.D. 575.
[53] *Nightingale* v. *Courtney* [1954] 1 Q.B. 399.

Sect. 5. By Merger

Merger is the counterpart of surrender. Under a surrender, the landlord acquires the lease, whereas merger is the consequence of the tenant retaining the lease and acquiring the reversion, or of a third party acquiring both lease and reversion. The principle is the same in both surrender and merger: the lease is absorbed by the reversion and destroyed.[54]

For merger to be effective, the lease and the reversion must be vested in the same person in the same right with no vested estate intervening.[55] Merger may take place even if the immediate reversion consists of a lease shorter than the lease merged.[56] Thus if A a tenant in fee simple, leases land to B for a thousand years and a few years later leases the same land to C for five hundred years the result is to give C for five hundred years the reversion on B's lease. If X then acquires both C's reversion and B's lease, the thousand years' lease will merge in the five hundred years' reversion and leave X with but five hundred years.[57] But there is now no merger if the person in whom the two interests vest intends that there shall be none.[58]

Sect. 6. By Becoming a Satisfied Term

This has already been dealt with.[59]

Sect. 7. By Enlargement

Under certain conditions, not frequently encountered in practice a lease may be enlarged into a fee simple by the tenant executing a deed of enlargement. Under the Law of Property Act 1925,[60] this can be done only if—

> (i) there is not less than two hundred years of the lease unexpired; and
>
> (ii) the lease was originally granted for at least three hundred years; and
>
> (iii) no trust or right of redemption [61] exists in favour of the reversioner; and

---

[54] See also *ante*, p. 98.
[55] See *Chambers* v. *Kingham* (1878) 10 Ch.D. 743.
[56] *Hughes* v. *Robotham* (1593) Cro.Eliz. 302.
[57] *Stephens* v. *Bridges* (1821) 6 Madd. 66.
[58] See *post*, p. 413.
[59] *Ante*, pp. 205, 206.
[60] s. 153, replacing C.A. 1881, s. 65, and C.A. 1882, s. 11.
[61] *e.g.*, a right of redemption under a mortgage; see *post*, p. 463.

(iv) the lease is not liable to be determined by re-entry for condition broken; and

(v) no rent of any money value is payable. A rent of " one silver penny if lawfully demanded " is a rent of no money value, but a rent of three shillings is not.[62] A rent under such a lease which does not exceed one pound per annum and which has not been paid for a continuous period of twenty years (five having elapsed since 1925) is deemed to have ceased to be payable and can no longer be recovered.

For a sub-lease to be capable of enlargement under the section, it must be derived out of a lease which is itself capable of enlargement. A fee simple acquired by enlargement is subject to all the provisions which affected the term of years out of which it arose.[63]

Sect. 8. By Disclaimer

In general, the doctrine of frustration has no application to leases, which are not mere contracts but create an estate in land. Thus a lease continues in being even though war or some other calamity prevents the tenant from enjoying it.[64] Further, though the performance of covenants may become impossible, as where restrictions on building prevent the tenant from repairing, there is no impossibility in his paying damages for his failure to repair.[65]

However, the legislation has intervened to a limited extent. Thus tenants whose premises were rendered unfit by war damage were given a statutory power to disclaim their tenancies; the effect of a valid disclaimer is the same as if there had been a surrender.[66] Similar rights were given to certain tenants of premises which were requisitioned under emergency powers.[67] But not all statutory provisions for disclaimer take effect as if there had been a surrender; thus a trustee in bankruptcy may disclaim an onerous lease, but by so doing he only terminates any liability of himself or the bankrupt and does not destroy the lease.[68]

---

[62] *Re Chapman and Hobbs* (1885) 29 Ch.D. 1007; *Re Smith and Stott* (1883) 29 Ch.D. 1009n.

[63] See generally T. P. D. Taylor (1958) 22 Conv.(N.S.) 101.

[64] *Cricklewood Property and Investment Trust Ltd.* v. *Leighton's Investment Trust Ltd.* [1945] A.C. 221; and see M. & W. 678–680.

[65] *Eyre* v. *Johnson* [1946] K.B. 481.

[66] Landlord and Tenant (War Damage) Acts 1939 and 1941.

[67] Landlord and Tenant (Requisitioned Land) Acts 1942 and 1944.

[68] Bankruptcy Act 1914, s. 54; *Re Thompson and Cottrell's Contract* [1943] Ch. 97 at 99.

Part 5

RIGHTS AND DUTIES OF THE PARTIES UNDER A LEASE OR TENANCY

The rights and duties of the landlord and tenant under a lease o tenancy fall under five heads. First, the lease may be silent as t everything except the essential terms as to parties, premises, rent an duration. This is not infrequently the case with weekly and othe periodic tenancies. Secondly, the parties may have agreed to b bound by the " usual covenants." Thirdly, the lease may provid in the orthodox way not only for the matters dealt with by th " usual covenants " but also for a number of other matters. Fourthly there are a number of statutory provisions relating to the right and duties of the parties to a lease. Lastly, there is the subject o fixtures.

The question how far covenants in a lease can be enforced betweer persons other than the original lessor and original lessee is considered separately.[69]

Sect. 1. Position of the Parties in the Absence of Express Provision

Except so far as the lease or tenancy agreement otherwise provides the position of the parties is as set out below.

A. Position of the Landlord

1. Implied covenant for quiet enjoyment. If the word " demise " is used (" the landlord hereby demises the premises to the tenant "). it is settled that a covenant for quiet enjoyment is deemed to have been given by the lessor.[70] The covenant extends to *all* acts of the lessor and the *lawful* acts of those claiming under him, but probably not to the acts of someone claiming by title paramount, such as a superior landlord.[71] The covenant gives the tenant the right to recover damages from the landlord if the persons to whom the covenant extends physically and substantially interfere with the tenant's enjoy- ment of the land demised.[72] The covenant is not one for " quiet "

[69] *Post*, pp. 384 *et seq.*
[70] *Hart* v. *Windsor* (1844) 12 M. & W. 68 at 85; *Baynes & Co.* v. *Lloyd & Sons* [1895] 2 Q.B. 610.
[71] See *Baynes & Co.* v. *Lloyd & Sons, supra*; *Budd-Scott* v. *Daniel* [1902] 2 K.B. 351; *Miller* v. *Emcer Products Ltd.* [1956] Ch. 304.
[72] *Owen* v. *Gadd* [1956] 2 Q.B. 99.

enjoyment in the acoustic sense; the lessor undertakes not that the tenant will be free from the nuisance of noise, but that he will be free from disturbance by adverse claimants to the property.[73] And the covenant will be broken if a lessor who has reserved the right to work the minerals under the land demised causes a subsidence of the land by his mining activities.[74]

Even if the word " demise " is not used in the lease, the mere relationship of landlord and tenant will import a covenant for quiet enjoyment.[75] However, in this case it is clear that the covenant is limited to the acts of the lessor and those claiming under him, and will not extend to the acts of others,[76] nor, indeed, to acts of the lessor under statutory authority.[77] Further, where the lease is not granted by deed, there cannot be any covenant in the technical sense, for the essence of a covenant is that it should be entered into by deed; but there will be corresponding contractual obligations.[78]

A landlord does not use the words " as beneficial owner " when granting a lease, and even if he did, these words would not import the covenants for title applicable to a conveyance.[79]

2. Obligation not to derogate from his grant. It is a principle of general application that a grantor must not derogate from his grant [80]; he must not seek to take away with one hand what he has given with the other. In the case of leases, the covenant for quiet enjoyment will extend to many of the acts which might be construed as a derogation from the lessor's grant; but acts not amounting to a breach of the covenant may nevertheless be restrained as being in derogation of the grant. Thus, if land is leased for the express purpose of storing explosives, the lessor and those claiming under him will be restrained from using adjoining land so as to endanger the statutory licence necessary for storing explosives.[81]

There must, however, be some act making the premises substantially less fit for the purposes for which they were let. No action will lie if the landlord, having let the premises for some particular trade, *e.g.*, for use as a wool shop only, lets adjoining

---

[73] *Hudson* v. *Cripps* [1896] 1 Ch. 265 at 268.
[74] *Markham* v. *Paget* [1908] 1 Ch. 697.
[75] *Markham* v. *Paget, supra.*
[76] *Jones* v. *Lavington* [1903] 1 K.B. 253.
[77] *Commissioners of Crown Lands* v. *Page* [1960] 2 Q.B. 274 (requisitioning).
[78] See *Budd-Scott* v. *Daniel* [1902] 2 K.B. 351.
[79] See *ante*, p. 334.
[80] *Palmer* v. *Fletcher* (1663) 1 Lev. 122.
[81] *Harmer* v. *Jumbil (Nigeria) Tin Areas Ltd.* [1921] 1 Ch. 200.

premises for purposes which offer trade competition; for the original premises are still fit for use as a wool shop even if the profits will be diminished.[82] Nor will mere invasion of privacy, as by erecting an external staircase passing the windows of the flat demised, amount to a breach of the obligation,[83] although interference with the stability of the house by vibrations caused by powerful engines on adjoining land may suffice, and so may excessive noise, such as that caused in altering another flat in the same building.[84]

3. In certain cases, obligations as to fitness and repair. In general, the landlord gives no implied undertaking that the premises are or will be fit for habitation,[85] nor is he liable to repair them. This rule is subject to three qualifications, which to some extent overlap.

(a) *Furnished lettings.* Where a house is let furnished, the landlord impliedly undertakes that it is fit for human habitation when let.[86] If this is not the case, the tenant may repudiate the tenancy and recover damages for any loss he has suffered.[87] But if the premises are fit for human habitation when let, the landlord need do no more; he is under no obligation to keep them in this condition.[88] And the tenant is not deemed to warrant his fitness to occupy the premises, *e.g.*, that he is free from contagious diseases.[89]

(b) *Houses let at a low rent.* Under the Housing Act 1957[90] if a house is let for human habitation at a total rent within certain limits, then, notwithstanding any stipulation to the contrary, there is—

(i) an implied condition that it is fit for human habitation at the beginning of the tenancy, and
(ii) an implied undertaking by the landlord that he will keep it in this condition throughout the tenancy.

The limits of rent are £80 a year in London and £52 elsewhere, or half these amounts if the contract of letting was made before July 6, 1957; and these provisions do not apply to leases not determinable for three years or more under which the lessee is to make the premises reasonably fit for human habitation.

---

[82] *Port* v. *Griffith* [1938] 1 All E.R. 295.
[83] *Browne* v. *Flower* [1911] 1 Ch. 219.
[84] *Newman* v. *Real Estate Debenture Corporation Ltd.* [1940] 1 All E.R. 131.
[85] *Hart* v. *Windsor* (1844) 12 M. & W. 68.
[86] *Smith* v. *Marrable* (1843) 11 M. & W. 5 (bugs).
[87] *Wilson* v. *Finch-Hatton* (1877) 2 Ex.D. 336; *Charsley* v. *Jones* (1889) 53 J.P. 280.
[88] *Sarson* v. *Roberts* [1895] 2 Q.B. 395.
[89] *Humphreys* v. *Miller* [1917] 2 K.B. 122.
[90] s. 6, extending earlier legislation.

The undertaking extends only to defects of which the landlord has notice,[91] and there is now a statutory list of matters to be considered, *e.g.*, repair, freedom from damp, natural lighting, ventilation and drainage.[92] A small defect such as a broken sash-cord may constitute a breach of the statute, for the test is not how difficult it is to repair the defect but whether the state of repair of the house " is such that by ordinary user damage may naturally be caused to the occupier, either in respect of personal injury to life or limb or injury to health." [93]

Local authorities have extensive powers of compelling the person who has control of a house (usually the owner or his agent) to make it fit for human habitation [94]; and many tenants avoid the burdens of directly enforcing their rights by setting the local authority in motion.

(c) *Short leases of houses.* In any lease or other tenancy of a dwelling-house granted after October 24, 1961, whatever the rent or rateable value, a covenant by the landlord to do certain repairs is implied if the term is less than seven years (unless the tenant can extend it to seven years or more) or if the landlord can determine it within seven years.[95] The covenant cannot be excluded or limited by any agreement to the contrary unless the county court authorises this as being reasonable; and any covenant by the tenant to repair or pay money in lieu thereof is of no effect so far as it is covered by the implied covenant.

The implied covenant is—

(1) to keep the structure and exterior in repair, and
(2) to keep in repair and proper working order the installations in the house—
    (i) for the supply of water, gas and electricity and for sanitation (including basins, sinks, baths and sanitary conveniences, but not other appliances for making use of water, gas and electricity), and
    (ii) for space heating or heating water.

In such cases there is also an implied covenant by the tenant to permit the landlord to enter and view the premises at reasonable times of the day on twenty-four hours' prior notice in writing to the occupier.

[91] *McCarrick* v. *Liverpool Corporation* [1947] A.C. 219.
[92] Housing Act 1957, s. 4; and see ss. 5, 189 (1).
[93] *Summers* v. *Salford Corporation* [1943] A.C. 283 at 289, *per* Lord Atkin.
[94] Housing Act 1957, ss. 9–15, 39.
[95] Housing Act 1961, ss. 32, 33.

B. Position of the Tenant

1. Obligation to pay rent. This is discussed below.[96]

2. Obligation to pay rates and taxes. The tenant is under an obligation to pay all rates and taxes except those for which the landlord is liable. The outgoings which must be borne by the landlord are—

(a) *Landlord's income tax.* The landlord is liable to income tax under Schedule D on the rent. If he fails to pay it, the tenant may be required to pay it up to the amount of his rent, and he may deduct any such payment from any subsequent rent due from him.[97]

(b) *Tithe redemption annuity*, unless the tenant agrees to bear it or the lease in question is for over fourteen years and the rent less than two-thirds of the annual value.[98]

3. Obligation not to commit waste. A tenant's liability for waste depends upon the nature of his tenancy. A tenant for a fixed term of years is liable for both voluntary and permissive waste, and must therefore keep the premises in proper repair.[99] A yearly tenant is similarly liable save that his liability for permissive waste is limited to keeping the premises wind- and water-tight.[1] A weekly tenant, on the other hand, is not liable for permissive waste as such, though he must take proper care of the premises, *e.g.*, by keeping the chimneys swept and the drain-pipes unblocked[2]; it is not clear whether the same rule applies to monthly and quarterly tenants. A tenant at will is not liable for permissive waste,[3] although if he commits voluntary waste his tenancy is thereby terminated and he is liable to an action for damages.[4] A tenant at sufferance is liable for voluntary waste,[5] though probably not for permissive waste.

4. Landlord's right to view. A landlord may by statute or by the terms of the tenancy be expressly authorised to enter the premises; and if he is liable to repair the premises has an implied right to

---

[96] *Post*, p. 371.

[97] Finance Act 1963, s. 16 (4). The former landlord's property tax (Schedule A income tax) and land tax were both abolished by this Act: *ibid*. s. 14 (1).

[98] Tithe Act 1936, s. 17: see *post*, p. 416.

[99] *Yellowly* v. *Gower* (1855) 11 Exch. 274: for waste, see *ante*, p. 49.

[1] *Wedd* v. *Porter* [1916] 2 K.B. 91.

[2] *Warren* v. *Keen* [1954] 1 Q.B. 15.

[3] *Harnett* v. *Maitland* (1847) 16 M. & W. 257.

[4] *Countess of Shrewsbury's Case* (1600) 5 Co.Rep. 13b.

[5] *Burchell* v. *Hornsby* (1808) 1 Camp. 360.

enter them for this purpose.[6] But otherwise he has no right to enter the premises so long as the tenancy endures.[7]

5. Right to take emblements. The nature of emblements has already been considered.[8] A tenant at sufferance has no right to emblements, but at common law a tenant at will, a yearly tenant or a tenant for years determinable with lives was entitled to them provided the determination of the tenancy was not caused by his own act.[9] A tenant for a fixed term of years could also claim emblements if his lease came to a premature end without his fault, *e.g.*, if the landlord had only a life estate and his death brought the lease to an end. However, the importance of these rules has been greatly diminished by statute. By the Landlord and Tenant Act 1851,[10] a tenant at a rack rent whose tenancy determined by the death of the landlord or cesser of his interest was given the right to continue his tenancy on the existing terms until the expiration of the current year of the tenancy, in lieu of any right to emblements. In the case of agricultural holdings, the Agricultural Holdings Act 1948[11] provides that in such a case the tenancy continues until determined at the end of a year of the tenancy by twelve months' notice to quit. These provisions coupled with the conversion of most leases for lives into terms of ninety years,[12] have made this subject of little consequence.

6. Right to estovers. A tenant for years has the same right to estovers and botes as a tenant for life.[13]

Sect. 2. Position of the Parties under a Lease Containing the Usual Covenants

1. Effect of agreement. If a lease has actually been granted, the obligations of the parties in the absence of any contrary provision in the lease are as set out above. If, on the other hand, the parties have merely agreed that a lease containing the " usual covenants " shall be granted, or if there is an agreement that a lease shall be granted, no reference being made to the covenants it should contain, then, subject to any contrary agreements by the parties, the lease must contain what-

---

[6] *Saner* v. *Bilton* (1878) 7 Ch.D. 815.
[7] *Stocker* v. *Planet Building Society* (1879) 27 W.R. 877.
[8] *Ante*, p. 53.
[9] See, *e.g.*, *Haines* v. *Welch* (1868) L.R. 4 C.P. 91.
[10] s. 1.
[11] s. 4: for agricultural holdings generally, see *post*, p. 593.
[12] *Ante*, p. 350.
[13] Co.Litt. 41b; and see *ante*, p. 50.

ever covenants and conditions may be " usual " in the circumstances, and if it does not, it may be rectified to accord with the agreement. Except in so far that they cover the same ground, the obligations imposed by the " usual " covenants and conditions are additional to those set out under Sect. 1 above.

2. The usual covenants. The following covenants and conditions are always " usual." [14]

    1. On the part of the landlord—

        a covenant for quiet enjoyment in the usual qualified form, *i.e.*, extending only to the acts of the lessor or the rightful acts of any person claiming from or under him.

    2. On the part of the tenant—

        (a) a covenant to pay rent;

        (b) a covenant to pay tenant's rates and taxes, *i.e.*, all rates and taxes except those which statute requires the landlord to bear;

        (c) a covenant to keep the premises in repair and deliver them up at the end of the term in this condition;

        (d) a covenant to permit the landlord to enter and view the state of repair, if he is liable to repair; and

        (e) a condition of re-entry for non-payment of rent, but not for breach of any other covenant.

3. Usual by custom or usage. In addition to the above provisions, which are always " usual," other covenants may be " usual " in the circumstances of the case, by virtue, for example, of the custom of the neighbourhood or trade usage; in each case, this is a question of fact for the court.[15] In the absence of such special circumstances, however, many covenants which in practice are usually inserted in leases and are therefore literally " usual " are nevertheless not deemed to be " usual " in the technical sense of the word. Examples are covenants against assignment, covenants against carrying on specified trades, and provisos for forfeiture for breaches of any covenant, whether for payment of rent or otherwise. Such provisions are frequently inserted when (as is usually the case) no contract to take a lease has been made and the terms of the lease are a matter for negotiation between the parties. But if a contract for a lease has been made, no covenant can be inserted in the lease without the concurrence of both parties unless

---

[14] See *Hampshire* v. *Wickens* (1878) 7 Ch.D. 555.
[15] See *Flexman* v. *Corbett* [1930] 1 Ch. 672.

either the contract provides for it or the covenant is technically a " usual " covenant.

Sect. 3. Position under Certain Covenants Usually Found in Leases

A number of covenants have already been considered, but certain other covenants must be mentioned.

1. Covenant to pay rent. Unless the lease provides for payment in advance, rent is normally payable in arrear.[16] It continues to be payable even if the premises cannot be used, *e.g.*, owing to destruction by fire [17] or other calamity, or seizure by military authorities for the occupation of troops.[18] However, this stern common law rule is frequently mitigated by an express provision in the lease, and in the case of war damage and requisitioning (but not other events) the tenant has been given a statutory right to disclaim his tenancy.[19]

The landlord may enforce payment of the rent—

  (a) directly, by—
      (i) an action for the money, or
      (ii) distress;
  (b) indirectly, by the threat of forfeiture if the lease contains a forfeiture clause.

Forfeiture has already been dealt with [20] and there is no need to discuss an action for the money. The subject of distress is extremely intricate,[21] and all that need be said here is that in essence it consists of the right of the landlord, exercisable without application to the court, to enforce payment by seizing and selling enough of any goods he finds on the premises.

2. Covenant against assigning, underletting or parting with possession.

(a) *The tenant's rights.* If the lease is silent on the matter the tenant is entitled to assign, underlet or part with possession of the premises without the landlord's consent; for during the term the property is the tenant's. However, a covenant against assignment, underletting or parting with possession of all or any part of the

---

[16] *Coomber* v. *Howard* (1845) 1 C.B. 440.
[17] *Belfour* v. *Weston* (1786) 1 T.R. 310.
[18] *Whitehall Court Ltd.* v. *Ettlinger* [1920] 1 K.B. 680.
[19] *Ante*, p. 363.
[20] *Ante*, pp. 356 *et seq.*
[21] See M. & W. 695–698.

premises is often inserted in leases; and although an assignment or sub-lease made in breach of covenant is valid, the breach will usually give rise to forfeiture or a claim for damages.

(b) *Unreasonable withholding of consent.* If the covenant is absolute, the landlord is entitled to waive it in any particular instance, although he cannot be compelled to do so even if his attitude is entirely unreasonable. But if the covenant is one against assigning or sub-letting " without licence or consent," the Landlord and Tenant Act 1927 [22] lays it down that notwithstanding any contrary provision the covenant shall be deemed to be subject to a proviso that the licence or consent is not to be unreasonably withheld. This does not permit the tenant to assign or sub-let without seeking the landlord's consent; if he does so, he has committed a breach of covenant even if the landlord could not properly refuse his consent.[23] But if he seeks consent and it is unreasonably withheld, he may forthwith assign or sub-let without the consent,[24] or else pursue the safer but slower course of seeking a declaration from the court of his right to do so.[25] The onus is on the tenant to show that the withholding of consent was unreasonable.[26] But in most cases no objection will be reasonable unless based on the person of the assignee or sub-tenant or the proposed use of the premises.[27] Moreover, statute provides that it is unreasonable to withhold consent " on the ground of colour, race or ethnic or national origins," though this does not apply to a tenancy of part of a dwelling-house in which some of the accommodation is shared with the landlord.[28] Unless the lease provides for it, in most cases the landlord may not require the payment of a fine or other valuable consideration for giving his consent.[29]

(c) *Breach.* To amount to a breach of a covenant against assignment or underletting, there must in general be some voluntary dealing with the property *inter vivos.* Thus a bequest of the lease is no breach,[30] nor is the involuntary vesting of the lease in the trustee in bankruptcy upon the tenant's bankruptcy,[31] or the compulsory sale of the lease under statutory provisions,[32] as distinct from a voluntary

---

[22] s. 19 (1).
[23] *Eastern Telegraph Co. Ltd.* v. *Dent* [1899] 1 Q.B. 835.
[24] *Treloar* v. *Bigge* (1874) L.R. 9 Ex. 151.
[25] *Young* v. *Ashley Gardens Properties Ltd.* [1903] 2 Ch. 112.
[26] *Shanly* v. *Ward* (1913) 29 T.L.R. 714.
[27] See *Viscount Tredegar* v. *Harwood* [1929] A.C. 72.
[28] Race Relations Act 1965, s. 5 (1).
[29] L.P.A. 1925, s. 144, replacing C.A. 1892, s. 3.
[30] *Fox* v. *Swann* (1655) Sty. 482.   [31] *Re Riggs* [1901] 2 K.B. 16.
[32] *Slipper* v. *Tottenham & Hampstead Junction Ry.* (1867) L.R. 4 Eq. 112.

sale by the tenant's trustee in bankruptcy.[33] A mortgage made by the grant of a sub-lease is a breach, but one made by a mere deposit of the title deeds is not, nor is a declaration of trust made by the tenant for the benefit of his creditors.[34] A covenant merely against under-letting is perhaps not broken by an assignment or by letting lodgings.

3. Covenant to repair.

(a) *Construction of covenant.* In long leases, the tenant usually covenants to do all repairs; in short leases, the landlord frequently assumes liability for external and structural repairs, and in some cases is compelled by statute to do so.[35] Subject to this, in every case, the matter is one for negotiation. If no provision is made for repairs, neither party is liable for them apart from statute and the general law relating to waste.[36]

The extent of the liability of any party under a repairing covenant depends of course upon the wording of the covenant, but expressions such as " tenantable repair," " sufficient repair," " good and substantial repair " seem to add little to the meaning of the word " repair." [37] " Repair " normally includes any necessary replacement of subsidiary parts (*e.g.*, the provision of new drainpipes for old), but not the re-building of the whole of the premises if through inherent defects they have become beyond repair.[38] If the covenant is qualified by words such as " fair wear and tear excepted," they exclude liability for defects due to reasonable use of the premises or the action of the elements, but not for consequential damage, *e.g.*, caused by rain entering through an unrepaired skylight.[39]

(b) *Measure of damages.* The measure of damages recoverable by a landlord for the breach of a repairing covenant formerly varied according to the time of the breach. If the breach occurred during the term, the damages were calculated on the decrease in the value of the reversion caused by the breach,[40] *i.e.*, on the difference between the value of the landlord's interest with the repairs done and its value without. Thus the longer the lease had to run, the less would be the damages. But if the breach occurred at the end of the term, the cost of repairing the premises was recoverable by the landlord [41] even if he

33 *Re Wright* [1949] Ch. 729.   34 *Gentle* v. *Faulkner* [1900] 2 Q.B. 267.
35 See *ante*, pp. 366, 367.   36 *Ante*, pp. 366–368.
37 *Anstruther-Gough-Calthorpe* v. *McOscar* [1924] 1 K.B. 716 at 722, 723.
38 *Lurcott* v. *Wakely* [1911] 1 K.B. 905; *Lister* v. *Lane* [1893] 2 Q.B. 212.
39 *Regis Property Co. Ltd.* v. *Dudley* [1959] A.C. 370.
40 *Ebbetts* v. *Conquest* [1895] 2 Ch. 377 (affd. [1896] A.C. 490).
41 *Joyner* v. *Weeks* [1891] 2 Q.B. 31.

did not propose to spend the money in making the repairs but intended
to demolish the premises instead. Now, however, by the Landlord and
Tenant Act 1927,[42] damages for breach of a repairing covenant are
not to exceed the diminution in the value of the reversion, though
if the repairs are going to be done, that diminution will usually be
measured by the cost of the repairs.[43] Further, no damages are
recoverable if the premises are to be demolished, or structurally
altered in such a way as to make the repairs valueless, at or soon after
the end of the term. There are special provisions enabling the court in
certain cases to relieve the tenant from liability for internal decorative
repairs.[44]

(c) *Leave to sue.* There are also provisions which protect the
tenant of any property (except agricultural holdings) let for a term of
years certain of not less than seven years which has at least three years
unexpired.[45] The lack of any provision for relief against claims for
damages for non-repair often enabled landlords to force tenants to
surrender their leases prematurely, and so the Leasehold Property
(Repairs) Act 1938 [46] provides that no action for damages for breach
of a covenant to repair the property can be brought unless the landlord has first served on the tenant a notice in the form required by the
Law of Property Act 1925, s. 146,[47] and one month has elapsed thereafter. Further, whether the landlord is claiming damages or forfeiture,
he cannot proceed without the leave of the court in such cases if within
twenty-eight days the tenant serves on the landlord a counter-notice
claiming the protection of the Act; and the notice served by the landlord must inform the tenant of his right to serve a counter-notice. The
court can grant leave only on certain specified ground, *e.g.*, that the
cost of immediate repair would be small compared with the cost of
repair in the future.

4. Covenant to insure. A covenant to insure against fire is broken
if the premises are uninsured for any period, however short, even if
no fire occurs.[48]

Sect. 4. Statutory Protection for Tenants

Three important classes of property are subject to special statutory
codes designed to protect the tenant, particularly by giving him

[42] s. 18 (1).   [43] *Smiley* v. *Townshend* [1950] 2 K.B. 311.
[44] L.P.A. 1925, s. 147.
[45] Leasehold Property (Repairs) Act 1938, as extended by Landlord and Tenant Act
1954, s. 51.   [46] s. 1.
[47] See *ante*, p. 358.   [48] *Penniall* v. *Harborne* (1848) 11 Q.B. 368.

security of tenure and restricting the rent. These classes are most agricultural holdings and business premises and many dwelling-houses; and they are dealt with later in the book.[49]

Sect. 5. Fixtures

In law, the word " land " extends to a great deal more than " land " in everyday speech. The general rule is " *quicquid plantatur solo, solo cedit* " (whatever is attached to the soil becomes part of it). Thus if a building is erected on land and objects are attached to the building, the word " land " prima facie includes the soil, the building and the objects affixed to it; and the owner of the land becomes owner of the building, even if it is built with bricks stolen by the builder.[50] The word " fixtures " is the name applied to anything which has become so attached to land as to form in law part of the land.

The subject of fixtures is of general application and is not confined to the relationship of landlord and tenant. However, questions arise most frequently under that head, and accordingly the subject as a whole is considered in this chapter, with suitable references to it in the other chapters.

A. Definition of Fixtures

In deciding whether or not an object has become a fixture, there are two main elements to be considered, namely—

(1) the degree of annexation, and

(2) the purpose of annexation.

1. Degree of annexation. In general, for an article to be considered a fixture, some substantial connection with the land or a building on it must be shown. An article which merely rests on the ground by its own weight, such as a cistern or a " Dutch barn," which rests upon timber laid on the ground, is prima facie not a fixture.[51] On the other hand, a chattel attached to the land or a building on it will prima facie be a fixture even if it would not be very difficult to remove it.[52]

2. Purpose of annexation. The degree of annexation is useful as showing upon whom the onus of proof lies[53]; thus if the article is securely fixed, the burden of proof lies on the party contending that it

---

49 *Post*, pp. 589 *et seq.*
50 *Gough* v. *Wood & Co.* (1894) 10 T.L.R. 318.
51 See *Wiltshear* v. *Cottrell* (1853) 1 E. & B. 674.
52 See *Buckland* v. *Butterfield* (1820) 2 Brod. & B. 54.
53 *Holland* v. *Hodgson* (1872) L.R. 7 C.P. 328 at 335.

is not a fixture. The purpose of the annexation, however, is the main factor; the modern tendency is to regard the degree of annexation as being chiefly of importance as evidence of the purpose of annexation.[54] The more securely an object is affixed and the more damage that would be caused by its removal, the more likely is it that the object was intended to form a permanent part of the land.[55]

In determining the purpose of annexation, the question to be asked is: " Was the intention to effect a permanent improvement of the land or building as such; or was it merely to effect a temporary improvement or to enjoy the chattel as a chattel? "[56] In the first case, the chattel is a fixture, in the second it is not. Thus, a wall composed of blocks of stone, or statues forming part of a general architectural design,[57] or movable dog-grates substituted for fixed grates,[58] have all been held to be fixtures, even though attached only by their own weight. In each case, the evident intention was to effect a permanent improvement to the land. But tapestry attached by tacks to wooden strips fastened to the wall by two-inch nails,[59] panelling screwed into wooden plugs let into the wall, and a collection of stuffed birds attached to movable wooden trays in glass cases attached to the walls of a bird gallery,[60] have been held not to form part of the premises and thus to be removable by the tenant who placed them there. Although in these cases there was a substantial degree of annexation, the only way in which the chattels could be properly enjoyed was to attach them to the house in some way, and thus it was easy to infer an intent to affix them for the better enjoyment of them as chattels and not for the permanent improvement of the building. Similar articles may in individual cases remain chattels or become fixtures, depending on the circumstances of their annexation, *e.g.*, tip-up seats fastened to the floor of a cinema or theatre.[61]

B. *Right to Remove Fixtures*

If according to the above rules an article is not a fixture, it can be removed by the person bringing it on to the land or by his successors in title; but if it is a fixture, prima facie it cannot be removed from the

---

[54] *Leigh* v. *Taylor* [1902] A.C. 157 at 162.
[55] *Spyer* v. *Phillipson* [1931] 2 Ch. 183 at 209, 210.
[56] See *Hellawell* v. *Eastwood* (1851) 6 Exch. 295 at 312.
[57] *D'Eyncourt* v. *Gregory* (1866) L.R. 3 Eq. 382.
[58] *Monti* v. *Barnes* [1901] 1 Q.B. 205.
[59] *Leigh* v. *Taylor* [1902] A.C. 157.
[60] *Viscount Hill* v. *Bullock* [1897] 2 Ch. 482.
[61] Contrast *Lyon & Co.* v. *London City & Midland Bank* [1903] 2 K.B. 135 with *Vaudeville Electric Cinema Ltd.* v. *Munset* [1923] 2 Ch. 74.

land and must be left for the fee simple owner, although there are some important exceptions to this. Questions of the right to remove fixtures arise between the following parties.

1. Landlord and tenant. Prima facie, all fixtures attached by the tenant are " landlord's fixtures," *i.e.*, must be left for the landlord. But the exceptions which have arisen nearly swallow up the rule; and fixtures which can be removed under these exceptions are known as " tenant's fixtures." The following are tenant's fixtures.

(a) *Trade fixtures.* Fixtures attached by the tenant for the purpose of his trade or business have long been removable by the tenant at any time during the term, but not after he has ceased to be tenant [62] and has failed to take a reasonable opportunity of removing them.[63] Vats, fixed steam engines and boilers, a shed for making varnish, shrubs planted by a market gardener and the fittings of a public house have all been held to come within this category.

(b) *Ornamental and domestic fixtures.* This exception appears to be rather more limited than the previous one, and seems to extend only to chattels perfect in themselves which can be removed without substantial injury to the building.[64] An article which can be moved entire is more likely to fall within this exception than one which cannot.[65] Thus while a conservatory on brick foundations has been held not to be removable, looking glasses, ornamental chimney pieces, window blinds, stoves, grates and kitchen ranges have all been held to be removable during the tenancy.

(c) *Agricultural fixtures.* At common law, agricultural fixtures were not regarded as falling within the exception of trade fixtures,[66] for agriculture was regarded as a normal use of land and not as a trade. But by statute [67] a tenant of an agricultural holding who has attached fixtures to the land may remove them before, or within two months after, the determination of the term, provided the following conditions are observed:

     (i) one month's written notice is given to the landlord;

     (ii) all rent due is paid and all the tenant's obligations under the tenancy are satisfied by him;

[62] *Poole's Case* (1703) 1 Salk. 368.
[63] *Smith* v. *City Petroleum Co. Ltd.* [1940] 1 All E.R. 260.
[64] See *Martin* v. *Roe* (1857) 7 E. & B. 237 at 244.
[65] *Grymes* v. *Boweren* (1830) 6 Bing. 437.
[66] *Elwes* v. *Maw* (1802) 3 East 38.
[67] Agricultural Holdings Act 1948, s. 13, replacing provisions in statutes from the Landlord and Tenant Act 1851, s. 3, onwards.

     (iii) no avoidable damage is done in the removal, and any
           damage done is made good; and

     (iv) the landlord is allowed to retain the fixtures if he pays a
           fair price for them.

2. Tenant for life and remainderman. If land is settled on A for
life with remainder to B, on the death of A the question arises whether
fixtures which A has attached to the land can now be removed and
treated as part of A's estate or whether they must be left for B. The
position here is similar to that between landlord and tenant. Prima
facie, all the fixtures must be left for B, with the common law exception of trade, and ornamental and domestic fixtures [68]; but the
statutory exception of agricultural fixtures does not apply.

3. Devisee and personal representative. If land is given by will,
the rule is that all fixtures pass under the devise; the testator's
personal representatives are not entitled to remove them for the benefit
of the testator's estate, whether they are ornamental, trade or any
other kind of fixture.[69]

4. Vendor and purchaser. Without exception, all fixtures attached
to the land at the time of a contract of sale must be left for the
purchaser [70] unless otherwise agreed. The conveyance will be effective
to pass the fixtures to the purchaser without express mention.[71]

5. Mortgagor and mortgagee. If land is mortgaged, all fixtures on
it are included in the mortgage without special mention; the exceptions as between landlord and tenant do not apply. The mortgagor is
not even entitled to remove fixtures which he has attached after the
date of the mortgage.[72]

Part 6

LICENCES

1. Nature of licences. A type of transaction which is sometimes
used instead of a lease or tenancy, but which is quite distinct from
it, is the licence. Traditionally, a licence is a permission given by
the occupier of land which, without creating any interest in land,

---

[68] See *Re Hulse* [1905] 1 Ch. 406 at 410.
[69] See *Re Lord Chesterfield's S.E.* [1911] 1 Ch. 237.
[70] *Colegrave* v. *Dias Santos* (1823) 2 B. & C. 76; *Phillips* v. *Lamdin* [1949] 2 K.B. 33.
[71] L.P.A. 1925, s. 62 (1).
[72] *Monti* v. *Barnes* [1901] 1 Q.B. 205; L.P.A. 1925, s. 62 (1).

allows the licensee to do some act which would otherwise be a trespass,[73] *e.g.*, to go on to the licensor's land to play cricket, or become a lodger in his house. Unlike a lease or tenancy, a licence normally confers no right to the exclusive possession of the land concerned.[74] Further examples of licences are—

the hire of a concert hall for several days without the hirer being entitled to exclusive possession [75];

permission to erect and use an advertisement hoarding or electric sign [76];

the grant of the " front of the house rights " in a theatre, *i.e.*, the exclusive right to supply refreshments coupled with other rights such as the use of refreshment rooms [77]; permission to view a race or cinema performance.[78]

2. Classification. Licences fall into three categories.

(a) *Bare licence.* A bare licence is a licence granted otherwise than for valuable consideration, such as a gratuitous permission to enter a field to see the view. Even if it is granted by deed, the licensor can revoke it at any time without being liable in damages,[79] but revocation does not affect acts already done under it.[80]

(b) *Licence coupled with an interest.* A licence may be coupled with some interest in the land or chattels thereon. Thus the right to enter another man's land to hunt and take away the deer killed, or to enter and cut down a tree and take it away, involves two things, namely, a licence to enter the land and the grant of an interest in the deer or tree.[81] At common law, such a licence was both irrevocable and assignable.[82] But the interest had to be a legal interest, such as a legal *profit à prendre* (which could be created only by deed or prescription (*i.e.*, long enjoyment [83])), or the ownership of timber lying on the land or to be cut forthwith (which could be transferred by word of mouth).[84] In equity, however, effect will be given to an

---

[73] See *Thomas* v. *Sorrell* (1673) Vaugh. 330 at 351.
[74] See *ante*, p. 340.
[75] See *Taylor* v. *Caldwell* (1863) 3 B. & S. 826.
[76] *Walton Harvey Ltd.* v. *Walker & Homfrays Ltd.* [1931] 1 Ch. 274.
[77] *Frank Warr & Co. Ltd.* v. *L.C.C.* [1904] 1 K.B. 713.
[78] *Hurst* v. *Picture Theatres Ltd.* [1915] 1 K.B. 1.
[79] *Wood* v. *Leadbitter* (1845) 13 M. & W. 838 at 845.
[80] *Armstrong* v. *Sheppard & Short Ltd.* [1959] 2 Q.B. 384.
[81] See *Thomas* v. *Sorrell* (1673) Vaugh. 330 at 351.
[82] *James Jones & Sons Ltd.* v. *Earl of Tankerville* [1909] 2 Ch. 440 at 442; *Muskett* v. *Hill* (1839) 5 Bing.N.C. 694 at 707, 708.
[83] See *post*, pp. 436 *et seq.*
[84] See *Marshall* v. *Green* (1875) 1 C.P.D. 35

enforceable agreement to grant an interest, so that an injunction may be granted to protect a licence coupled with a *profit à prendre* granted merely in writing.[85]

(c) *Licence for value.* Midway between a bare licence and a licence coupled with an interest is a licence for value. At common law, a licence for value resembled a bare licence in that it was not assignable; further, at common law it could be revoked at any time, even if it had been granted for a fixed period which had not expired.[86] Thus although the licensee could recover damages for breach of contract for any premature revocation,[87] he became a trespasser if he entered or remained on the land after the licence had been revoked and a reasonable time to remove himself and his belongings had elapsed.[88] However, if there was a specifically enforceable contract, express or implied, not to revoke the licence, equity regarded the matter differently. Since the Judicature Act 1873, this rule of equity prevails in all courts, and if a licensee for value, such as a member of a cinema audience, is prematurely and forcibly ejected from the land, he can now obtain not merely the return of the price of his ticket but damages for assault.[89] A licence is now regarded not as a separate entity but merely as part of the contract creating it, so that even if the contract is not specifically enforceable the licensee is probably protected.[90]

3. Status. In recent years, there has been much activity in the sphere of licences. First, a number of landlords have sought to escape the restrictions of the Rent Acts and other modern statutes which protect tenancies by instead granting licences which amounted to tenancy agreements in all but name and form; but in most cases this attempt has been frustrated by the courts construing the transaction as in fact creating a tenancy.[91] Secondly, until a few years ago, it could be said with some confidence that, in general, a licence was a mere personal arrangement between the parties, and that it created no estate or interest in the land which could bind third parties. Thus where a licence to use refreshment rooms had been granted for value, it was held by the Court of Appeal in 1936 that a purchaser

---

[85] *Frogley* v. *Earl of Lovelace* (1859) Johns. 333.
[86] *Wood* v. *Leadbitter* (1845) 13 M. & W. 838.
[87] *Kerrison* v. *Smith* [1897] 2 Q.B. 445.
[88] See *Cornish* v. *Stubbs* (1870) L.R. 5 C.P. 334.
[89] *Hurst* v. *Picture Theatres Ltd.* [1915] 1 K.B. 1.
[90] See *Winter Garden Theatre (London) Ltd.* v. *Millennium Productions Ltd.* [1948] A.C. 173 ; but see *Thompson* v. *Park* [1944] K.B. 408.
[91] See, *e.g.*, *Facchini* v. *Bryson* [1952] 1 T.L.R. 1386.

of the theatre was not bound by the licence, even though he bought with notice of it.[92] Recent decisions of the same court have sought to erode this principle. In 1952, it was held that a contractual licence to occupy a dwelling-house was binding on a devisee of the house,[93] and that a wife who had been deserted by her husband had a right, akin to a contractual licence, to continue to occupy the matrimonial home, which was binding on the husband's trustee in bankruptcy.[94] The right of the deserted wife to remain in the house was later held to be an " equity " binding on purchasers and mortgagees of the house with notice of it.[95]

This so-called " deserted wife's equity " has now been firmly repudiated by the House of Lords.[96] Any right which the wife has is exercisable against her husband alone, and not against successors in title and other third parties. The House of Lords did not have before it the question of the status of contractual licences, but it is probable that they too will be held not to be binding on third parties.[97]

4. Matrimonial home. The decision of the House of Lords repudiating the " deserted wife's equity " has been substantially reversed by the Matrimonial Homes Act 1967.[98] This Act gives one spouse the right to remain in occupation of a house vested in the other.[99] The right operates as a charge on the estate or interest of the other spouse having priority from the date of acquisition, or of the marriage or of the Act, whichever is the latest.[1] It lasts so long as the marriage lasts though the court can extend or restrict it in the event of a matrimonial dispute or estrangement.[2] It will not be binding on purchasers or mortgagees of the house unless it is registered as a land charge, or protected by an entry in the land registry if the title is registered.[3] It is wider than the " deserted wife's equity " in that it extends to husbands, but it is narrower in that it is not binding on the trustee in bankruptcy of the owner spouse.[4]

---

[92] *Clore* v. *Theatrical Properties Ltd.* [1936] 3 All E.R. 483.
[93] *Errington* v. *Errington* [1952] 1 K.B. 290.
[94] *Bendall* v. *McWhirter* [1952] 2 Q.B. 466.
[95] See *e.g., Jess B. Woodcock & Sons Ltd.* v. *Hobbs* [1955] 1 W.L.R. 152.
[96] *National Provincial Bank Ltd.* v. *Ainsworth* [1965] A.C. 1175, overruling the cases mentioned in the preceding two notes.
[97] See *National Provincial Bank Ltd.* v. *Ainsworth, supra,* at pp. 1239, 1251.
[98] In force from January 1, 1968: Matrimonial Homes Act (Commencement) Order 1967 (S.I. 1967 No. 1790).
[99] s. 1.
[1] s. 2 (1).
[2] s. 2 (2).
[3] See s. 2 (6), (7), and *post*, pp. 546, 562.
[4] s. 2 (5).

5. Revocation. The extent to which each of the different types o[f] licence is revocable has been considered above. If the licence i[s] revocable, in general no period of notice need be given before revoking it, though the licensee must be given a reasonable time in which to leave the premises.[5]

[5] *Minister of Health* v. *Bellotti* [1944] K.B. 298; but see the *Winter Garden* case *supra*.

CHAPTER 11

COVENANTS AFFECTING LAND

Part 1

GENERAL PRINCIPLES

A COVENANT is a promise under seal, *i.e.*, contained in a deed. The basic principles concerning the enforceability of covenants relating to land are as follows.

1. If there is privity of contract, all covenants are enforceable. There is said to be privity of contract when the parties concerned have made a legally enforceable agreement. Clearly, if two people have agreed to do or not to do certain things, their obligations bind them whether their contract has anything to do with land or not. The covenants can be enforced both at law, by an action for damages, and in equity, by an injunction or specific performance.

2. If there is merely privity of estate, only covenants which touch and concern the land are enforceable. There is said to be privity of estate between the parties when the relationship of landlord and tenant exists between them under the lease which contains the covenant in question. In this case, any covenants in the lease which touch and concern the land, such as repairing covenants, are enforceable both at law and in equity. But covenants which do not relate to the land are not enforceable under this head.

3. If there is privity neither of contract nor of estate, then with two exceptions, no covenants are enforceable. There is privity neither of contract nor of estate between a lessor and a sub-lessee, or between the vendor of freehold land and a person who buys it from the purchaser. In such cases, the general rule is that covenants concerning the land are not enforceable. To this rule there are two exceptions, the second of which is of great importance.

(a) *Benefit.* First, even the common law allowed the *benefit* of certain covenants (*i.e.*, the right to sue on the covenant) to be assigned with land; and equity followed the law. One example already mentioned [1] is that of covenants for title, the benefit of which runs

[1] *Ante*, p. 335.

with the land so that whoever is entitled to the land is entitled to the benefit of the covenants. But the *burden* of a covenant (*i.e.*, the liability to be sued on it) cannot be assigned; at law, if there is no privity of estate the covenantor alone can be sued on a covenant.

(b) *Restrictive covenants in equity.* Secondly, equity allows the transmission of the burden (as well as the benefit) of restrictive covenants affecting land, *i.e.*, covenants which are negative in nature, restraining the doing of some act such as building on the land. As usual, however, a purchaser of a legal estate without notice [2] takes free from such burdens.

These three principles should be borne in mind whenever considering questions of the enforceability of covenants. They should be applied in the given order: if there is privity of contract, there is no need to look further, and if there is privity of estate, there is no need to consider the third head.

Little more need be said about privity of contract, but the other two heads must be considered in some detail.

Part 2

PRIVITY OF ESTATE: COVENANTS IN LEASES

Sect. 1. Rights and Liabilities of the Original Parties

If a lease is granted by L to T, there is privity of contract between them. The effect of this is not only that L may enforce all the covenants in the lease against T while he retains it, but also that T remains liable on the covenants for the whole term, notwithstanding any assignment of the lease.[3] Thus if T takes a lease for 99 years, he makes himself liable for 99 years, even if he assigns the lease after only one year has run; L may accordingly sue T for unpaid rent or for damages if the covenant to repair is not observed by the assignee. Similarly L remains liable on his covenants for the whole term, notwithstanding any assignment of the reversion by him.[4]

Sect. 2. Rights and Liabilities of Assignees

A. Covenants Touching and Concerning Land

The rights and liabilities of assignees, either of the lease or of the

---

[2] *Ante*, p. 59.
[3] *Thursby* v. *Plant* (1670) 1 Wms.Saund. 230; for an exception in the case of perpetually renewable leases, see *ante*, p. 351.
[4] *Stuart* v. *Joy* [1904] 1 K.B. 368; L.P.A. 1925, s. 142 (2); and see *post*, p. 536.

reversion, depend on whether or not the covenant in question " touches and concerns the land " or, to use more modern phraseology, " has reference to the subject-matter of the lease." [5] Any covenant which affects the landlord *qua* landlord or the tenant *qua* tenant may be said to touch and concern the land.[6] If the covenant of its very nature and not merely through extraneous circumstances affects the nature, quality or value of the land demised, or the mode of enjoying it, it falls within the definition.[7] Some examples may be helpful; the covenants in the left-hand column have been held to touch and concern the land, while those in the right-hand column have been held not to do so.

Touch

Don't Touch

1. Covenants by a lessee

To pay rent.	To pay an annual sum to some third party.[8]
To repair.	To repair and renew the tools of a smithy standing on the land.[10]
To pay the landlord £40 towards redecoration.[9]	
To use as a private dwelling-house only.	Not to employ persons living in other parishes to work in the demised mill.[11]
Not to assign the lease without the landlord's consent.	

2. Covenants by a lessor

To renew the lease [12] (the inclusion of this is somewhat anomalous [14]).	To give the lessee the first refusal if adjoining land is sold.[13]
To supply the demised premises with water.	To sell the reversion at a stated price.[15]
Not to build on a certain part of the adjoining land.	To pay at the end of the lease for chattels not amounting to fixtures.
	To pay the tenant £500 at the end of the lease unless a new lease is granted.[16]

[5] L.P.A. 1925, ss. 141 (1), 142 (1).
[6] *Breams Property Investment Co. Ltd.* v. *Stroulger* [1948] 2 K.B. 1.
[7] *Horsey Estate Ltd.* v. *Steiger* [1899] 2 Q.B. 79 at 89.
[8] *Mayho* v. *Buckhurst* (1617) Cro.Jac. 438.
[9] *Boyer* v. *Warbey* [1953] 1 Q.B. 234.
[10] *Williams* v. *Earle* (1868) L.R. 3 Q.B. 739.
[11] *Congleton Corporation* v. *Pattison* (1808) 10 East 130.
[12] *Richardson* v. *Sydenham* (1703) 2 Vern. 447.
[13] *Collison* v. *Lettsom* (1815) 6 Taunt. 224.
[14] *Woodall* v. *Clifton* [1905] 2 Ch. 257 at 279.
[15] *Re Leeds and Batley Breweries Ltd. and Bradbury's Lease* [1920] 2 Ch. 548.
[16] *Re Hunter's Lease* [1942] Ch. 124.

B. *Principles of Transmission*

After considering which covenants touch and concern the land, the rights and liabilities of assignees must next be examined. As in every case when the question of enforcing legal liabilities arises, two separate points must be considered:

(i) Is the defendant liable? and
(ii) Is the plaintiff entitled to sue?

In the case of the rights and liabilities of assignees under covenants concerning land, this may be expressed in the form of—

(i) Has the burden of the covenant passed? and
(ii) Has the benefit of the covenant passed?

I. WHERE THE LESSEE ASSIGNS HIS LEASE

If L leases land to T, and T assigns the lease to A, the common law rule laid down in *Spencer's Case* [17] is that A is entitled to the benefit, and subject to the burden, of all covenants and conditions touching and concerning the land, for there is privity of estate. In short, both the benefit and the burden of the covenants run with the land.

In applying this rule, the following points should be noted.

1. The lease must be in due form. The benefit and burden of covenants run only with a lease by deed or a specifically enforceable agreement for a lease.[18] A mere oral tenancy has been held not to suffice,[19] but this rule may no longer be law.[20]

2. There must be a legal assignment of the whole term. The benefit and burden of covenants run with the lease only in the case of a legal assignment of the whole of the remainder of the term.[21] Where instead of an assignment there has been a sub-lease, the sub-lessee takes neither the benefit nor the burden of the covenants in the lease, even if his sub-lease is only one day shorter than the head lease. Thus if L leases land to X for 99 years, X assigns the lease to T, and T sub-leases the land to S for the residue of the term of 99 years less one day, S is not an assignee and there is privity neither of contract nor of estate between L and S. T

---

[17] (1583) 5 Co.Rep. 16a.
[18] See *Boyer* v. *Warbey* [1953] 1 Q.B. 234.
[19] *Elliott* v. *Johnson* (1866) L.R. 2 Q.B. 120.
[20] See *Boyer* v. *Warbey, supra,* at p. 246; and see *ante,* p. 341, for the tenancies which can be created orally; see also *post,* p. 391.
[21] *West* v. *Dobb* (1869) L.R. 4 Q.B. 634; *ante,* p. 353.

is still the tenant under the lease for 99 years and until he assigns it, he remains liable upon it. Consequently if S does some act which is contrary to a covenant in the 99 years' lease, L cannot sue S but can sue T. In practice, the covenants inserted in a sub-lease are always at least as stringent as those in the head lease, so that if a sub-tenant does some act forbidden by the head lease, this will constitute a breach of the covenants in the sub-lease and thus make the sub-tenant liable to the tenant.

Since only a legal assignee is liable on the covenants, a mere equitable assignee (*e.g.*, a person entitled under a contract to assign) is not liable on them,[22] and the same applies to a squatter who has become entitled to the lease by long possession under the Limitation Act 1939.[23]

3. Covenants relating to things in posse. If a covenant made before 1926 imposed an obligation upon the tenant to do some entirely new thing, such as to erect a building, the burden of the covenant ran with the land only if the lessee expressly covenanted for himself *and for his assigns* that the covenant would be performed.[24] This rule did not apply to covenants relating to things *in esse* (in existence) nor even to covenants relating only conditionally to something *in posse* (not in existence), such as a covenant to repair a new building if it is erected[25]; in such cases it was immaterial whether or not the covenant mentioned assigns. This not very creditable distinction between covenants relating to things *in posse* and those relating to things *in esse* is still in force as regards all leases granted before 1926, but it does not apply to leases made after 1925.[26]

4. Liability of assignees. Although the original lessee is liable for all breaches of covenant throughout the term of the lease, an assignee is liable only for breaches committed while the lease is vested in him. He is under no liability for breaches committed either before the lease was assigned to him[27] or after he has assigned it[28]; but if a covenant is broken while the lease is vested in him, his liability for this breach continues despite any assignment.[29] Thus while the original

---

[22] *Cox* v. *Bishop* (1857) 8 De G.M. & G. 815 ; *ante*, p. 353.
[23] See *post*, p. 536.
[24] *Spencer's Case, supra.*
[25] *Minshull* v. *Oakes* (1858) 2 H. & N. 793.
[26] L.P.A. 1925, s. 79.
[27] *Granada Theatres Ltd.* v. *Freehold Investment (Leytonstone) Ltd.* [1959] Ch. 592.
[28] *Paul* v. *Nurse* (1828) 8 B. & C. 486.
[29] *Harley* v. *King* (1835) 2 Cr.M. & R. 18.

lessee of an onerous lease cannot divest himself of liability for future breaches, an assignee can do so by assigning the lease, *e.g.*, to a pauper.[30]

5. Liability of personal representatives.

(a) *Liability*. Personal representatives may incur personal as well as representative liability.

(1) PERSONAL LIABILITY. If a lessee or assignee dies and his personal representatives take possession of the demised premises, the personal representatives occupy the position of assignees of the lease and so become personally liable on the covenants.[31] However, as regards the payment of rent (but not as regards other covenants) a personal representative may by proper pleading limit his liability to the yearly value of the premises.[32] Further, a personal representative who does not take possession of the premises incurs no personal liability upon any covenant.[33]

(2) REPRESENTATIVE LIABILITY. Upon the death of the original lessee, his personal representatives become liable upon the covenants of the lease for the rest of the term, but only to the extent of the assets of the deceased in their hands.[34] Similarly, if the deceased was an assignee, his personal representatives succeed to his liabilities (*e.g.*, for breaches of covenant committed while the lease was vested in him), but only to the extent of his assets.[35] It is irrelevant to this head whether or not the personal representatives take possession of the premises.

(b) *Protection*. If the deceased was the original lessee, the personal representatives are in a difficult position since they cannot tell what breaches of covenant may occur in the future. Although it was settled that they need not put aside part of the estate as an indemnity fund for future breaches,[36] and that it was usually a defence to plead that all the assets of the estate had been used in paying debts of equal priority,[37] their position was precarious in other respects. Thus the defence that the assets had been applied in paying debts apparently provided no protection from liability on the covenant for rent in

---

[30] *Hopkinson* v. *Lovering* (1883) 11 Q.B.D. 92.
[31] *Tilney* v. *Norris* (1700) 1 Ld.Raym. 553.
[32] *Rendall* v. *Andreae* (1892) 61 L.J.Q.B. 630.
[33] *Wollaston* v. *Hakewill* (1841) 3 Man. & G. 297 at 320.
[34] *Helier* v. *Casebert* (1665) 1 Lev. 127.
[35] See *Re Lewis* [1939] Ch. 232.
[36] *King* v. *Malcott* (1852) 9 Hare 692.
[37] See *Lyddall* v. *Dunlapp* (1743) 1 Wils.K.B. 4.

o far as they received any rent from the land [38]; further, which was more important, if the assets exceeded the liabilities, the personal representatives were liable on the covenants to the extent of any surplus and so could not safely distribute it to the beneficiaries.[39] In order to make it unnecessary for personal representatives to seek the protection of the court in all such cases, the Trustee Act 1925 [40] provides that if personal representatives in whom a lease is vested—

(i) satisfy any existing liabilities which have been claimed,
(ii) set aside any *fixed* sum agreed to be laid out on the premises, and
(iii) assign the lease to the person entitled under the will or intestacy, or to a purchaser,

they cease to be liable in respect of the assets which came to their hands. This does not render the assets immune from liability, for they may be followed into the hands of the beneficiaries; but the personal representatives need not concern themselves with this. These provisions apply equally whether the deceased was a lessee or an assignee.

6. Indemnities by assignees.

(a) *Implied indemnity.* If a covenant has been broken, the lessee and the assignee entitled to the lease at the time of the breach are each liable to be sued by the lessor. But although the lessor may sue either or both, he can only have one satisfaction: he has no right to recover twice.[41] The primary liability is that of the assignee, and if the lessee is sued, he may claim indemnity from the assignee in whom the lease was vested at the time of the breach, whether that assignee obtained the lease from the lessee or from some other assignee.[42]

(b) *Express indemnity.* In addition to this implied obligation to indemnify the lessee, it is usual for each assignee to enter into an express covenant to indemnify his assignor against future breaches of covenant, and by the Law of Property Act 1925,[43] in any assignment for value made after 1925 such a covenant is implied.

---

[38] *Hargrave's Case* (1601) 5 Co.Rep. 31a.
[39] *Davis* v. *Blackwell* (1832) 9 Bing. 6.
[40] s. 26, replacing L.P.Am.A. 1859, s. 27.
[41] *Brett* v. *Cumberland* (1619) Cro.Jac. 521.
[42] *Wolveridge* v. *Steward* (1833) 1 Cr. & M. 644; *Moule* v. *Garrett* (1872) L.R. 7 Ex. 101.
[43] s. 77 (1) (*c*); 2nd Sched., Pt. IX.

(c) *Effect.* The effect of these rights of indemnity may be
illustrated thus:

```
A
|  99 years
B——C——D——E
           |  21 years.
           F
```

A has leased land to B for 99 years; by successive assignments E has become entitled to the lease and has granted a
sub-lease to F for 21 years. If F does some act which is
contrary to a covenant in the head lease, A can sue either
B (privity of contract) or E (privity of estate). If A sues
B, B has an implied right of indemnity against E. Alternatively, if on the assignment to C a covenant of indemnity
was given to B, he may claim indemnity from C. C in turn
may claim indemnity from D, and D from E, provided in each
case that the covenant for indemnity was given on the assignment. The importance of these various rights is emphasised
if one of the parties is insolvent. Apart from the rules relating
to restrictive covenants,[44] F incurs no liability to anyone except
so far as his act was a breach of a covenant in the sub-lease
and so makes him liable to E.

II. WHERE THE LESSOR ASSIGNS HIS REVERSION

If L, a tenant in fee simple, leased his land to T, and then L sold
his fee simple, subject to the lease, to R, the common law rule was
that with the exception of " implied covenants," *i.e.*, certain covenants
which the law implied (*e.g.*, to pay rent),[45] neither the benefit nor
the burden of the covenants in the lease ran with the reversion: R
was neither able to sue nor liable to be sued. But by the Grantees
of Reversions Act 1540, ss. 1 and 2, the benefit and burden of all
covenants and provisions contained in a lease which touched and
concerned the land (or had reference to the subject-matter of the lease,
to use the modern phrase) passed with the reversion. These provisions
were subsequently replaced and extended by statute, and are now
contained in the Law of Property Act 1925, ss. 141 and 142.

The following points should be noted.

[44] *Post*, pp. 392 *et seq.*
[45] See *Vyvyan* v. *Arthur* (1823) 1 B. & C. 410.

1. The lease must be in due form. The Act of 1540 applied only
to leases under seal,[46] but under the doctrine of *Walsh* v. *Lonsdale* [47]
a specifically enforceable agreement is now treated as a lease by deed
for this purpose,[48] and it suffices if the provisions are contained or
implied in some document in writing.[49] After 1925, probably even
a mere oral tenancy is sufficient, for by section 154 of the Law of
Property Act 1925, ss. 141 and 142 extend to an underlease " or
other tenancy." [50]

2. The reversion may have been assigned in whole or in part. The
assignee of the entire reversion takes the benefit and burden of the
provisions in the lease. Where the reversion is not assigned in its
entirety, the position is not so simple. Two separate cases must be
considered :

(a) *Severance as regards the estate.* Where the assignee has part
of the reversion, *e.g.*, where a fee simple reversioner grants a lease
of his reversion to X, the reversion is severed as regards the estate.
In this case, the persons entitled to the part of the reversion fall
within the statutory provisions, so that the benefit and burden of both
covenants and conditions pass to them.[51]

(b) *Severance as regards the land.* Where the assignee has the
reversion of part, *e.g.*, where a fee simple reversioner grants the fee
simple of half the land to X, the reversion is severed as regards
the land. In this case, under the Act of 1540 the covenants ran
with the reversion.[52] But conditions [53] (*e.g.*, a condition for forfeiture
on non-payment of rent) did not, unless the severance took place by
operation of law, *e.g.*, on a compulsory acquisition.[54] However, this
position has been altered by statute; by the Law of Property Act
1925,[55] all conditions and rights of re-entry became severable on the
severance of the reversion. The old law continues to apply, however,
if the lease was made before 1882 and the reversion was severed
before 1926.

**3. Rights of an assignee of the reversion to sue and forfeit for
previous breaches.** At common law, a right to sue for damages or to

---

[46] *Smith* v. *Eggington* (1874) L.R. 9 C.P. 145.
[47] *Ante*, p. 342.   [48] *Rickett* v. *Green* [1910] 1 K.B. 253.
[49] *Rye* v. *Purcell* [1926] 1 K.B. 446 ; *Weg Motors Ltd.* v. *Hales* [1962] Ch. 49.
[50] Contrast *ante*, p. 386.
[51] *Wright* v. *Burroughes* (1846) 3 C.B. 685.
[52] *Twynam* v. *Pickard* (1818) 2 B. & Ald. 105.
[53] See *ante*, p. 355.
[54] *Piggott* v. *Middlesex County Council* [1909] 1 Ch. 134.
[55] s. 140 (1), replacing L.P.Am.A. 1859, s. 3, as extended by C.A. 1881, s. 12.

forfeit the lease for breach of covenant could not be assigned, so that if a reversion was assigned after a covenant had been broken the new reversioner could not sue [56] or forfeit [57] the lease. Now, after an assignment of the reversion, the assignee is alone entitled to sue the tenant for rent or for breaches of covenant, whether such rent accrued or such breaches occurred before or after the assignment.[58] This is brought about by the Law of Property Act 1925,[59] which also provides that rights of re-entry are enforceable by the new reversioner provided they have not been waived. Waiver may be express or implied. The conveyance of a reversion " subject to the lease ' operates as an implied waiver of any right of forfeiture for all breaches of which the assignee knew at the time of the assignment, for the words quoted clearly recognise that the lease is still subsisting [60]; but this reasoning does not apply to breaches unknown to the assignee at the time of the assignment.[61]

Part 3

PRIVITY NEITHER OF CONTRACT NOR OF ESTATE

1. Classification. Privity of estate may be regarded as an extension of privity of contract; the parties are connected by the relationship of landlord and tenant, and the covenants which are enforceable under the doctrine of privity of estate are contained in the contractual document which forms the link between the parties. Where there is privity neither of contract nor of estate, however, the enforceability of covenants no longer depends on any extension of a contractual relationship. Covenants in leases properly fall within the first division of this book, for they form part of the terms upon which the tenant holds his land, and so resemble the incidents of feudal tenure. Covenants enforceable where there is no privity, on the other hand, properly fall within the second division of this book; like easements, they are rights over the land of another. Nevertheless, it is convenient to deal with both types of covenant in the same chapter, if only to emphasise their close connection; thus a covenant in a lease may be enforceable against the tenant by privity of estate and against the sub-tenant as a restrictive covenant.

[56] *Flight* v. *Bentley* (1835) 7 Sim. 149.
[57] *Hunt* v. *Remnant* (1854) 9 Exch. 635.
[58] *Re King* [1963] Ch. 459.
[59] s. 141, replacing C.A. 1911, s. 2.
[60] *Davenport* v. *Smith* [1921] 2 Ch. 270.
[61] *Atkin* v. *Rose* [1923] 1 Ch. 522.

2. Divergence of law and equity. Law and equity have taken different views of the rights and liabilities of parties affected by covenants where there is privity neither of estate nor of contract between the parties. At law, the rule is that provided certain conditions are satisfied, the benefit of a covenant may be assigned, but not the burden. Thus if P, on buying land from V, enters into certain covenants with V, the benefit of those covenants may at law be assigned by V to X, thus enabling X to enforce the covenants against P. But this does not apply to the burden of the covenants; if Y buys P's land, he will not be bound by the covenants.

As regards the benefit of covenants, equity followed the rule at law, with some relaxation of the conditions to be satisfied. The important contribution of equity in this sphere, however, was the rule that subject to certain conditions, the *burden* of covenants could be transferred. This transformed the law of covenants in cases where there was privity neither of contract nor of estate. The effectiveness of a covenant concerning land was no longer confined to the period for which the original covenantor retained the land, but might continue indefinitely. Once it could be shown that the necessary conditions had been satisfied, a covenant might continue to burden one plot of land for the benefit of another, irrespective of the number of times each plot changed hands. This intervention of equity came soon after the outburst of building and increase of population associated with the Industrial Revolution; it became plain that the law lacked any other effective means of securing privacy and maintaining the general character of a district.

This position must now be examined in some detail; for completeness, the position of the original parties to the covenant will be considered here, although privity of contract is involved.

Sect. 1. At Law

A. The Benefit of the Covenant

I. THE ORIGINAL COVENANTEE

An original covenantee who has not assigned the benefit of the covenant can always enforce it against the original covenantor, even if the covenantee has parted with the dominant tenement.[62] Normally the original covenantee will be a party to the deed creating the

---

[62] See *L.C.C.* v. *Allen* [1914] 3 K.B. 642 at 664, and *post*, pp. 402, 403.

covenant, but by statute this is not now essential.[63] A person may now take a benefit under a deed even if he is not named as a party to it provided that the deed purports to confer that benefit upon him.[64] Thus if V sells land to P, and P binds his land by a covenant expressed to be for the benefit of V and the owners for the time being of certain adjoining plots of land, these adjoining owners can sue on the covenant as original covenantees, even though they were not parties to the conveyance creating the covenant.[65] In such a case the adjoining owners are clearly identifiable persons in existence at the time of the conveyance; but those who subsequently acquire the adjoining plots cannot claim to be original covenantees under the statutory provisions.[66] Similarly, if a covenant is made expressly for the benefit of the present owner of a plot of land and his successors in title, the owner at the time of the conveyance is an original covenantee but future owners are not; they can enforce the covenant only under the rules relating to assignees.

II. ASSIGNEES

If V sells part of his land to P in fee simple and P enters into covenants binding the land he buys, the benefit of P's covenant may run at law with V's fee simple estate in the land he retains, so that a subsequent purchaser of V's land can enforce the covenant against P. It is immaterial whether the covenant is negative (not to do something) or positive (to do something). Thus the common law doctrine applies equally to a covenant not to build on the land purchased by P or a covenant to supply pure water to the land retained by V.[67] For a covenant to be enforceable in this way, the following conditions must be satisfied.

1. The covenant must touch and concern land of the covenantee.[68] It is essential that the covenant should be made for the benefit of land owned by the covenantee (*i.e.,* V in the above examples) at the time of the covenant. In general, the test for determining whether a covenant touches and concerns the land is similar to that applicable to covenants in a lease.[69]

---

[63] L.P.A. 1925, s. 56, replacing R.P.A. 1845, s. 5; see *Beswick* v. *Beswick* [1968] A.C. 58 at 102–107.
[64] See *White* v. *Bijou Mansions Ltd.* [1937] Ch. 610 at 625; [1938] Ch. 351 at 365.
[65] See *Re Ecclesiastical Commissioners for England's Conveyance* [1936] Ch. 430 (where the liability was equitable and so fell under Sect. 2, *post*, p. 396).
[66] *Westhoughton U.D.C.* v. *Wigan Coal and Iron Co. Ltd.* [1919] 1 Ch. 159 at 169, 170.
[67] See *Shayler* v. *Woolf* [1946] 1 All E.R. 464 at 467 (affd. [1946] 2 All E.R. 320).
[68] *Rogers* v. *Hosegood* [1900] 2 Ch. 388.   [69] *Ante*, p. 384.

2. Annexation of covenant: the benefit of the covenant must be annexed to a legal estate in the land of the covenantee. At law, it is not enough to show that the covenantee has an equitable interest in the land retained. It must be shown that the covenant was made for the benefit of some legal estate into whomsoever's hands it might come, and not for the mere personal advantage of the covenantee.[70]

3. Ownership of the land: an assignee who seeks to enforce a covenant made before 1926 must show that he has the legal estate to which the benefit of the covenant was attached.[71] But a covenant made after 1925 is enforceable by those claiming under the covenantee,[72] so that whether a mere tenant under a lease can enforce a covenant annexed to the legal fee simple depends on the date of the covenant. It is immaterial whether the person enforcing the covenant knew of its existence when he obtained the land.[73]

B. *The Burden of the Covenant*

As stated above, the rule at law is that the burden of a covenant will not pass with the land concerned.[74] Yet what cannot be accomplished directly may be secured indirectly. There are three heads.

1. Chain of covenants. If V sells land to P, and P covenants, for example, to erect and maintain a fence, P will remain liable to V on the covenant by virtue of privity of contract even if P sells the land to Q. P will accordingly protect himself by extracting from Q a covenant of indemnity against future breaches of the covenant to fence. If Q then fails to maintain the fence, V cannot sue Q, but he can sue P, and P can then sue Q on the covenant for indemnity. However, although in theory liability can be maintained indefinitely in this way, with each sale of the land the chain of covenants for indemnity becomes longer, and more liable to be broken by the insolvency or disappearance of one of the parties to it. This indirect enforcement of covenants by means of indemnities is thus an imperfect substitute for the direct enforceability which the common law refuses to allow.

2. Enlarged long lease. A more effective but more artificial method

---

[70] *Rogers* v. *Hosegood* [1900] 2 Ch. 388.
[71] *Westhoughton U.D.C.* v. *Wigan Coal and Iron Co. Ltd.* [1919] 1 Ch. 159.
[72] L.P.A. 1925, s. 78; *Smith* v. *River Douglas Catchment Board* [1949] 2 K.B. 500.
[73] *Rogers* v. *Hosegood, supra.*
[74] *Austerberry* v. *Corporation of Oldham* (1885) 29 Ch.D. 750 at 781–785; *E. & G.C. Ltd.* v. *Bate* (1935) 79 L.J.News. 203; *Cator* v. *Newton* [1940] 1 K.B. 415.

is to insert the covenant in a lease which can be enlarged into a fee simple, and then to enlarge the lease.[75]

3. Conditional benefit. A man who claims the benefit of a conveyance or other deed must submit to its burdens. Thus if a conveyance of land on a housing estate gives the purchaser the right to use the estate roads but imposes on him the liability to contribute to the cost of upkeep, a successor in title cannot use the roads without paying the contributions.[76] The liability is thus not absolute but conditional: he who does not enjoy need not submit. Yet often there will be little real choice.

C. Summary of the Position at Law

It will be observed that only within narrow limits does the common law enforce covenants outside the confines of privity of contract or privity of estate. As will be seen shortly, equity became far more flexible and would enforce covenants in many cases where the common law would not. This does not, however, render the rules at law obsolete, for if a covenant is enforceable at law, the plaintiff, on proving his case, is entitled as of right to a judgment for damages (even though they may be nominal), whereas if a covenant is enforceable only in equity the court has a discretion in deciding whether to give any remedy. However, since the equitable remedy of an injunction is the one usually desired, this point is not of great practical importance. Yet it should be remembered that at law it is quite immaterial whether the covenant is negative or positive, and that in the case of a positive covenant, damages will usually be the most suitable remedy.

Sect. 2. In Equity: Restrictive Covenants

A. The Benefit of the Covenant

As mentioned above,[77] the rules in equity were similar to those at law, although rather less strict.[78]

I. THE ORIGINAL COVENANTEE

The position in equity is similar to that at law. In particular, section 56 of the Law of Property Act 1925 applies.[79] It should be

---

[75] See *ante*, p. 362; *Re M'Naul's Estate* [1902] 1 I.R. 114.
[76] *Halsall* v. *Brizell* [1957] Ch. 169.
[77] *Ante*, p. 393.
[78] For a general survey, see S. J. Bailey (1938) 6 Camb.L.J. 339.
[79] *Ante*, p. 393.

noted, however, that if the original covenantee parts with the land for the benefit of which the covenant was taken, he ceases to be able to enforce it in equity.[80]

II. ASSIGNEES

For anyone except the original covenantee to be entitled to enforce a covenant in equity, he must show that the following conditions have been satisfied.

1. The covenant must touch and concern land of the covenantee. Equity follows the law here, and the legal rules apply.[81]

2. The plaintiff must be entitled to the benefit of the covenant. He can satisfy this condition by showing either—

    (a) that the benefit of the covenant has been assigned to him and that he owns some interest in land for the benefit of which the covenant was made; or

    (b) that the benefit of the covenant has been attached to land and that he owns some interest in that land; or

    (c) that there is a building scheme or other scheme of development.

These provisions will be considered in turn.

    (a) *Assignment of benefit of covenant*: the benefit of the covenant has been assigned to the plaintiff and he owns some interest in the land for the benefit of which the covenant was made.[82]

There are two elements to consider.

    (1) ASSIGNMENT OF THE BENEFIT. The plaintiff must show that he has had the benefit of the covenant assigned to him. Where the benefit of a covenant has not been annexed to land, it will not pass automatically to the subsequent owners of the land.[83] But the covenantee may, if he wishes, expressly assign the benefit of the covenant to someone who takes all or some of the land intended to be protected by it.[84] Although at law the benefit of the covenant cannot be assigned in pieces, yet in equity this can be done if the proper conditions are observed.[85]

---

[80] *Chambers* v. *Randall* [1923] 1 Ch. 149 at 157, 158.
[81] *Re Union of London and Smith's Bank Ltd.'s Conveyance* [1933] Ch. 611.
[82] *Ibid.*
[83] *Renals* v. *Cowlishaw* (1878) 9 Ch.D. 125.
[84] *Re Union of London and Smith's Bank Ltd.'s Conveyance, supra.*
[85] *Ibid.* at p. 630.

The assignment must, it seems, be made at the time of the conveyance of the land which is to be protected.[86] An express assignment is not required if the circumstances show that the benefit of the covenant was intended to be included in the sale.[87] But once the land has been sold, the benefit of the covenant cannot be assigned: one purpose of the covenant is to make the covenantee's land more readily saleable, and if he has succeeded in disposing of the whole of his land without assigning the benefit of the covenant, it ceases to be assignable.[88] If only part of his land has been disposed of, he can assign the benefit of the covenant when he sells any of the parts still retained, but he cannot assign it to those who have already purchased part of the land.[89]

Although it is essential that the covenant should have been taken for the benefit of some or all of the land concerned, it has been held that this need not appear from the wording of the deed imposing the covenant, provided the surrounding circumstances clearly establish it.[90] And once the benefit of a restrictive covenant has been expressly assigned on the sale of land, it seems that it attaches to the land so as to pass to future owners without express assignment.[91]

(2) OWNERSHIP OF THE LAND. The plaintiff must establish that he has some interest in the land for the benefit of which the covenant was made. He need not show that he has succeeded to the covenantee's estate in the land, nor that he has the whole of the land.[92]

(b) *Covenant attached to land*: the benefit of the covenant has been attached to land, and the plaintiff now owns some interest in that land. Equity follows the law, and these provisions correspond closely to the rules at law,[93] the main difference being that the equitable rules are rather less strict. There are two separate elements to consider.

(1) THE ATTACHING OF THE COVENANT. A landowner who extracts a covenant from another landowner may do so merely for his direct personal advantage. Alternatively, he may take the covenant for the benefit of his land, deriving an advantage for as long as the land is his. Covenants of the first kind will not automatically run with the

---

[86] *Chambers* v. *Randall* [1923] 1 Ch. 149.
[87] *Renals* v. *Cowlishaw* (1878) 9 Ch.D. 125 at 129.
[88] *Re Rutherford's Conveyance* [1938] Ch. 396.
[89] *Re Union of London and Smith's Bank Ltd.'s Conveyance* [1933] Ch. 611 at 632.
[90] *Newton Abbot Co-operative Society Ltd.* v. *Williamson & Treadgold Ltd.* [1952] Ch. 286.
[91] See *Rogers* v. *Hosegood* [1900] 2 Ch. 388 at 408, not cited in *Re Pinewood Estate, Farnborough* [1958] Ch. 280.
[92] *Formby* v. *Barker* [1903] 2 Ch. 539.
[93] *Ante*, p. 386.

covenantee's land, but those of the second type will. The benefit of a covenant will be effectively attached to the land so as to run with it if in the instrument the covenant is stated either to be for the benefit of the land, or else to be made with the covenantee in his capacity of owner of the land.[94]

Even if a clear intention is shown to annex the benefit of a covenant to land, there will be no effective annexation if the area of the land is greater than can reasonably be benefited. Thus, where on a sale of land, restrictive covenants were stated to be made for the benefit of the " owners for the time being of the Childwickbury estate " (which was about 1,700 acres in extent), it was held that the benefit of a covenant could not run with the estate even in favour of someone acquiring the whole of the estate; the covenant could not benefit the whole of the estate, and the court could not sever the covenant.[95] Had the covenant been expressed to be for the benefit of the whole *or any part* of the estate, it could have been enforced by the successor in title to any part of the land which the covenant in fact benefits.[96]

(2) OWNERSHIP OF THE LAND. The rule at law (relaxed by statute for covenants made after 1925 [97]) is that the plaintiff must show that he is entitled to the same estate in the land as that to which the covenantee was entitled. But in equity, the plaintiff need only show that he has *some* interest in the land to which the benefit of the covenant has been attached; if the covenant was made before 1926 with a fee simple owner of land for the benefit of the land, a tenant for years can enforce the covenant in equity,[98] though not at law.

If the plaintiff has only part of the land to which the benefit of the covenant was attached, he can nevertheless enforce it, provided he can show from the wording of the covenant that it was made either expressly or by implication for the benefit of the whole or any part of the land.[99] Alternatively, he will succeed if the benefit of a covenant annexed to the whole only has been expressly assigned to him.[1]

If the above conditions are satisfied, the benefit of the covenant attaches to the land and passes to each successive owner for the time being, even if he was ignorant of it when he took the land.[2] As soon as the covenantee or other owner has parted with all of the land to

---

[94] See *Drake* v. *Gray* [1936] Ch. 451 at 466.
[95] *Re Ballard's Conveyance* [1937] Ch. 473.
[96] *Marquess of Zetland* v. *Driver* [1939] Ch. 1.
[97] See *ante*, p. 395.
[98] *Taite* v. *Gosling* (1879) 11 Ch.D. 273.
[99] See *Drake* v. *Gray* [1936] Ch. 451; *Russell* v. *Archdale* [1964] Ch. 38.
[1] *Stilwell* v. *Blackman* [1968] Ch. 508; *sed quaere*: 84 L.Q.R. 22.
[2] *Rogers* v. *Hosegood* [1900] 2 Ch. 388.

which the benefit of the covenant was attached, he loses his equitable right to take advantage of subsequent breaches of the covenant.[3]

(c) *Scheme of development*

(1) MUTUAL ENFORCEABILITY. Where land has been laid out in lots which are to be sold to purchasers and built upon, restrictions are often imposed on the purchasers of each lot for the benefit of the estate generally, such as covenants restraining trading on the estate, prohibiting the erection of cheap buildings and the like. In the ordinary way, these covenants would be enforceable only by the vendor. But much of the purpose of the covenants given by a purchaser of one lot would be lost if they could not be enforced—

(i) by those who have previously bought lots, and
(ii) by those who subsequently buy the unsold lots.

Each of these results could be achieved without any special rules for building schemes. The first would be achieved if the purchaser's covenants were expressly made with those who had previously bought lots as well as with the vendor.[4] The second could be achieved by the covenant being expressed to be for the benefit of the whole or any part of the land retained by the vendor, and so attaching the benefit of them to each lot sold in the future, or by the vendor expressly assigning the benefit of the covenants with each lot sold.

However, there are special rules governing building schemes which make it unnecessary for these arrangements to be made. If the requisite conditions are satisfied, the covenants given on the sale of each plot are enforceable by the owner for the time being of any plot on the estate whose land is affected. In short, the covenants form a sort of local law for the estate.

(2) CONDITIONS. The conditions which must be satisfied were for the most part laid down in *Elliston* v. *Reacher*.[5] These are as follows:

(i) The plaintiff and defendant must both have derived title from a common vendor.
(ii) Previously to the sale of the plaintiff's and defendant's plot, the common vendor must have laid out or intended to lay out [6] the estate in lots subject to restrictions which were intended

---

[3] *Chambers* v. *Randall* [1923] 1 Ch. 149 at 157, 158.
[4] See *ante*, pp. 393, 394.
[5] [1908] 2 Ch. 374 at 384; affd. [1908] 2 Ch. 665. The first real hint of the doctrine was in *Western* v. *MacDermott* (1866) L.R. 1 Eq. 499; but see *Re Pinewood Estate, Farnborough* [1958] Ch. 280 at 286, 287.
[6] See *Baxter* v. *Four Oaks Properties Ltd.* [1965] Ch. 816.

to be imposed on all of them and were consistent only with some general scheme of development.

(iii) The common vendor must have intended the restrictions to be for the benefit not merely of himself but of all lots sold.[7]

(iv) The plaintiff's and defendant's plots must both have been bought from the common vendor on the footing that the restrictions were for the benefit of the other lots.

(v) The area to which the scheme extends must be clearly defined.[8]

The whole essence of a building scheme is that each purchaser should know when he buys his plot from the common vendor that the covenants given by him are to be enforceable by the owners of all the other lots. It is not necessary to prove an express undertaking by him that this should be so, provided the circumstances show that he must have realised it. If before his purchase he saw some plan of the estate with the restrictions endorsed thereon, as in *Elliston* v. *Reacher*, this suffices; but the absence of a proper plan is often fatal.[9] The reservation by the common vendor of a power to release all or part of the land from the restrictions does not negative a building scheme, nor is it essential that the restrictions imposed on each plot should be identical; it suffices that there is some general scheme of development.[10]

(3) BUILDINGS ALREADY ERECTED. Principles similar to those applied in building schemes may operate in cases where there is no building scheme in the ordinary sense. Thus if an estate already fully built upon is disposed of in sections, and conditions analogous to those laid down for building schemes are satisfied, the covenants will be enforceable as in building schemes.[11] Again, the principle of a building scheme has been applied to a block of residential flats and the landlord restrained from letting or using any of them otherwise than for residential purposes [12]; but the court will be slow to infer a letting scheme from the mere similarity of the covenants when each floor of a large house is sub-let separately.[13]

---

[7] Which may be hard to prove: see, *e.g.*, *Tucker* v. *Vowles* [1893] 1 Ch. 195.

[8] This last condition was added by *Reid* v. *Bickerstaff* [1909] 2 Ch. 305: see *Kelly* v. *Barrett* [1924] 2 Ch. 379 at 401.

[9] *e.g.*, *Osborne* v. *Bradley* [1903] 2 Ch. 446.

[10] *Pearce* v. *Maryon-Wilson* [1935] Ch. 188; *Reid* v. *Bickerstaff* [1909] 2 Ch. 305 at 319.

[11] *Torbay Hotel Ltd.* v. *Jenkins* [1927] 2 Ch. 225 at 241.

[12] See *Hudson* v. *Cripps* [1896] 1 Ch. 265.

[13] *Kelly* v. *Battershell* [1949] 2 All E.R. 830.

B. *The Burden of the Covenant*

It will be observed that the rules in equity as to the benefit of a covenant were in the main merely a more relaxed and detailed version of the rules at law. As to the burden of the covenant, however, the rules in equity were completely different. Until *Tulk* v. *Moxhay* [14] was decided in 1848 (a time when the full effects of the vast expansion in industrial and building activities were being felt), equity had gone no further than the common law. [15] In that case it was decided that a covenant to maintain Leicester Square uncovered with any buildings would be enforced by injunction against a purchaser of the land who bought with notice of the covenant. For some while the question was thought to be one of notice; a person who took land with notice that it had been bound by some restriction could not disregard that restriction. On this footing, it was immaterial whether the restriction had been imposed to benefit other land or merely the covenantee personally; it sufficed that there was some contractual restriction on the use of the land and that the land had been acquired with notice of it. [16] But since 1882 [17] it has been accepted that equity will enforce a restrictive covenant against a purchaser only if it was made for the protection of other land. Restrictive covenants came to resemble easements as being rights over one plot of land (" the servient tenement ") existing for the benefit of another plot of land (" the dominant tenement "). In short, at a leap, the law of restrictive covenants passed from the sphere of contract to the sphere of property.

This change of attitude may be illustrated by considering a case where V sells a public-house to P, and P covenants not to employ servants of a particular type, and not to erect any further buildings. If the question were simply one of notice, when Q buys the public-house from P with notice of the covenants, Q would be bound by both covenants. But since the question is one of the benefit to other land, Q will be bound by neither covenant if V owns no neighbouring land, and only by the covenant against building if V does own such land.

I. THE ORIGINAL COVENANTOR

The original covenantor usually remains liable on the covenant, even if he has parted with the servient tenement, for the common form of

---

[14] (1848) 2 Ph. 774.

[15] Despite *Whatman* v. *Gibson* (1838) 9 Sim. 196, the question was regarded as still being open in *Bristow* v. *Wood* (1844) 1 Coll.C.C. 480.

[16] See *Luker* v. *Dennis* (1877) 7 Ch.D. 227.

[17] See *London & South Western Ry.* v. *Gomm* (1882) 20 Ch.D. 562 at 583.

covenant extends to the acts of persons claiming under him [18]; but today, words limiting its ambit are often inserted.

II. ASSIGNEES

An assignee of land of the original covenantor is bound by the covenant only if three conditions are fulfilled.

1. The covenant must be negative in nature. After a few cases in which the court was prepared to enforce positive covenants, the rule was settled in 1881 that none except negative covenants would be enforced by equity.[19] The question is whether the covenant is negative in nature: it is immaterial whether the wording is positive or negative. Thus the covenant in *Tulk* v. *Moxhay* [20] itself was positive in wording, but part of it was negative in nature (to keep land in Leicester Square " in an open state, uncovered with any buildings "), so that this part merely bound the covenantor to refrain from building, without requiring him to do any positive act.

The test is whether the covenant requires expenditure of money for its proper performance; if the covenant requires the covenantee to put his hand in his pocket, it is not negative in nature.[21] A covenant to give the first refusal of a plot of land is negative in nature, for in effect it is a covenant not to sell to anyone else until the covenantee has had an opportunity of buying; but a covenant " not to let the premises get into disrepair," despite its apparently negative form, is in substance positive, for it can be performed only by the expenditure of money on repairs. Among the restrictive covenants most frequently met with in practice are covenants against building on land, and against carrying on any trade or business (or certain specified trades or businesses [22]) on the premises concerned.

2. The covenantee must, at the date of the covenant, own land which will benefit therefrom. Here again, as mentioned above,[23] the rule was not settled at first. It is now accepted, however, that with statutory exceptions in favour of local authorities,[24] a restrictive

---

[18] *L.C.C.* v. *Allen* [1914] 3 K.B. 642 at 660, 673 ; and see L.P.A. 1925, s. 79 (1).

[19] *Haywood* v. *Brunswick Permanent Benefit Building Society* (1881) 8 Q.B.D. 403.

[20] *Ante*, p. 402.

[21] *Haywood* v. *Brunswick Permanent Benefit Building Society, supra*, at pp. 409, 410.

[22] Such covenants are not apparently subject to the doctrine of restraint of trade : *Esso Petroleum Co. Ltd.* v. *Harper's Garage (Stourport) Ltd.* [1968] A.C. 269 at 298, 309, 316, 325, 334 ; and see *Cleveland Petroleum Co. Ltd.* v. *Dartstone Ltd.* [1969] 1 W.L.R. 116 (covenant in lease).

[23] *Ante*, p. 402.

[24] See, *e.g.*, Town and Country Planning Act 1962, s. 37 (2); Housing Act 1957, s. 151.

covenant is similar to an equitable easement, and that the burden of the covenant will run with land only if the covenant was made for the protection of land belonging to the covenantee; as with easements,[25] there must be a dominant tenement.[26] Thus covenants binding land in Hampstead will be too remote to benefit land in Clapham,[27] and if the covenantee retains no other land, a purchaser of the Hampstead land will take free from the covenant. Yet a landlord's reversion on a lease is a sufficient interest to entitle him to enforce the covenant against a sub-tenant, even though he has no other adjoining land.[28]

3. The burden of the covenant must have been attached to the covenantor's land. A covenant may be confined, either expressly or by implication, so as to bind the covenantor alone.[29] In this case, assignees of the covenantor's land are not bound by the covenant. But if the covenant was made by the covenantor for himself, his heirs and assigns, the burden will normally be attached to his land. Covenants relating to the covenantor's land which are made after 1925 are deemed to have been made by the covenantor on behalf of himself, his successors in title, and the persons deriving title under him or them, unless a contrary intention appears.[30]

Burden of covenant runs in equity. If these conditions are satisfied, the burden of the covenant runs *in equity*. There are two main consequences.

(a) *Equitable remedies.* Only equitable remedies are available, and these are discretionary remedies. However, since the Chancery Amendment Act 1858,[31] equity has been entitled to award damages in any case where an injunction or specific performance could have been awarded, although the plaintiff is not, as in an action at law, entitled to insist upon some damages being awarded if he makes out his case.[32]

(b) *Purchaser without notice.* The covenant suffers from the infirmity of all equitable interests, namely, that it will not be enforced against a bona fide purchaser for value of a legal estate without notice of the covenant, or someone claiming through such a person.[33] In

---

[25] *Post*, p. 418.
[26] See *Formby* v. *Barker* [1903] 2 Ch. 539.
[27] *Kelly* v. *Barrett* [1924] 2 Ch. 379 at 404.
[28] *Regent Oil Co. Ltd.* v. *J. A. Gregory (Hatch End) Ltd.* [1966] Ch. 402 at 433.
[29] See *Re Fawcett and Holmes' Contract* (1889) 42 Ch.D. 150.
[30] L.P.A. 1925, s. 79 (1).
[31] s. 2.
[32] See *ante*, p. 63.
[33] *Wilkes* v. *Spooner* [1911] 2 K.B. 473 ; *ante*, p. 59.

this connection it will be noted that an under-lessee is always deemed to have notice of the covenants in the lease out of which his sub-lease is created, and so he will be bound in equity by restrictive covenants in the lease.[34a]

The doctrine of notice has been to some extent affected by the Land Charges Act 1925. Covenants made before 1926, and covenants in leases, whenever made, are still subject to the old rules as to notice; but a restrictive covenant made after 1925 otherwise than between lessor and lessee must be registered as a land charge.[35] If not registered, it will be void against a subsequent purchaser for money or money's worth of a legal estate in the land. One difference between the statutory and the equitable rule lies in the words " money or money's worth "; the consideration of marriage is value but not money or money's worth.[36]

Law and equity. The principal differences between law and equity in the treatment accorded to covenants when there is no privity of estate may be summarised as follows :

   (i) In equity the rules governing the transmission of the benefit of covenants are similar to, but less stringent than, those at law.

  (ii) The burden of covenants may run with land in equity but not at law.

 (iii) At law, a successful plaintiff has a right to damages, whereas in equity the normal remedy (an injunction) is discretionary.

Sect. 3. Enforceability of Restrictive Covenants

The enforceability of a restrictive covenant may come into question in any of three ways.

  1. In an action to enforce the covenant.
  2. On application to the court for a declaration.
  3. On application to the Lands Tribunal for a discharge or modification.

1. Action to enforce the covenant. Prima facie, a restrictive covenant remains enforceable indefinitely.[37] In certain cases, however, the court may refuse to enforce an action brought by the person entitled to the benefit of a covenant. Thus if the person entitled to

---

[34] *John Brothers Abergarw Brewery Co.* v. *Holmes* [1900] 1 Ch. 188.
[35] *Post,* p. 546.
[36] *Ante,* p. 59.
[37] See *Mackenzie* v. *Childers* (1889) 43 Ch.D. 265 at 279.

enforce the covenant has remained inactive in the face of open breaches for so long and in such circumstances that a reasonable person would believe that the covenant no longer applies, the court will not enforce it [38]; and the same applies if the neighbourhood is so completely changed (as from a residential to a shopping area) that an action to enforce the covenant would be unmeritorious, not bona fide and brought with some ulterior motive.[39]

2. Declaration by the court. Sometimes a landowner will be content to break a covenant and rely upon being able to establish one of the above defences if an action is brought. This, however, will not always be satisfactory, as where it is desired to sell or lease the land and the purchaser or lessee wishes to be assured that he is in no danger from the covenant. Consequently, provision has now been made permitting an application to the court for a declaration whether any freehold land is affected by any restriction, and if so, the nature, extent and enforceability of it.[40] This provision is often used in respect of the many nineteenth-century covenants which are today unenforceable through non-compliance with the rules governing the transfer of the benefit of the covenants. There is no power under this head to modify or discharge a valid covenant.

3. Discharge or modification by the Lands Tribunal. In some cases a covenant may be still enforceable, but it may be undesirable for this state of affairs to continue. Consequently, a discretionary [41] power has been given to the Lands Tribunal [42] to modify or discharge the restrictive covenant with or without the payment of compensation.[43] The applicant must bring his case within one of three heads.

(a) *Obsolete.* By reason of changes in the character of the property or neighbourhood or other material circumstances the restriction is obsolete, or the continued existence of it would impede the reasonable use of the land without giving practical benefits to anyone.

(b) *Agreement.* The persons of full age and capacity entitled to the benefit of the restrictions have agreed, either expressly or by implication by their acts and omissions, to the discharge or modification sought.

[38] *Chatsworth Estates Co.* v. *Fewell* [1931] 1 Ch. 224.
[39] *Ibid.*; *Westripp* v. *Baldock* [1939] 1 All E.R. 279.
[40] L.P.A. 1925, s. 84 (2).
[41] *Driscoll* v. *Church Commissioners for England* [1957] 1 Q.B. 330.
[42] Lands Tribunal Act 1949, s. 1 (4).
[43] L.P.A. 1925, s. 84 (1).

(c) *No injury*. The discharge or modification would not injure the persons entitled to the benefit of the covenant.

The provisions under this and the previous head apply to restrictions whenever made, but do not apply to restrictions imposed on a disposition made either gratuitously or for a nominal consideration for public purposes. They apply to restrictions on freehold land, and to restrictions on leasehold land if the lease was made for more than forty years and at least twenty-five have expired; but they do not apply to mining leases.[44]

There is also provision for the county court to authorise the conversion of a house into two or more tenements in contravention of a restrictive covenant or a provision in a lease if owing to changes in the neighbourhood the house cannot be readily let as a whole, or if planning permission for the conversion has been granted.[45]

Sect. 4. Restrictive Covenants and Town Planning

In recent years, the extension of town and country planning control [46] has to some extent reduced the importance of restrictive covenants. If planning control imposes restrictions which will preserve the amenities of a neighbourhood, landowners have little incentive to impose restrictive covenants with the same object. Nevertheless, restrictive covenants have not been superseded by planning control. A landowner must see that what he proposes to do will contravene neither the private system of restrictive covenants nor the public system of planning control; and restrictive covenants sometimes extend to matters not usually dealt with by planning law. Further, a covenantee has the enforcement of the covenant under his control, whereas a landowner may be disappointed in the way in which the local planning authority imposes or enforces planning control against his neighbours. Nevertheless, the practical advice to give a landowner whose neighbour's activities are objectionable is often not to launch proceedings to enforce any apposite restrictive covenant, with consequent delay, expense and uncertainty, but to encourage the local planning authority to exercise its powers of enforcing planning control.[47]

---

[44] *Ibid.* s. 84 (12), as amended by Landlord and Tenant Act 1954, s. 52.
[45] Housing Act 1957, s. 165. See *Josephine Trust Ltd.* v. *Champagne* [1963] 2 Q.B. 160.
[46] *Post*, pp. 573 *et seq.*
[47] For these powers, see *post*, p. 578.

CHAPTER 12

INCORPOREAL HEREDITAMENTS

IT has already been seen that incorporeal hereditaments are rights in land which do not give the owner present physical possession of the land.[1] There are two quite distinct classes of incorporeal hereditaments:

1. Those which may ripen into corporeal hereditaments. Thus a grant to A for life with remainder to B in fee simple gave B an incorporeal hereditament which becomes corporeal after A's death.
2. Those which can never become corporeal hereditaments but are merely rights over the land of another, *e.g.*, rentcharges.

The first class has already been dealt with.[2] It is with incorporeal hereditaments in the latter class that this chapter is concerned. They do not form a homogeneous class. Some, such as easements, can exist only for the benefit of other land, while others, such as rentcharges, lead an independent existence. In one sense, those in the former category are not hereditaments at all, for they cannot be inherited or dealt with except as appendages to the land which they benefit.

Part 1

RENTCHARGES

Sect. 1. Nature of Rentcharges

1. Rentcharges and rent services. Periodical payments in respect of land fall under the two main heads of rentcharges and rent services. Where the relationship of lord and tenant exists between the parties, any rent payable by virtue of that relationship by the tenant to the lord is a rent service. If there is no relationship of lord and tenant, the rent is a rentcharge. Thus if L grants a lease to T at £100 per annum and X charges his fee simple estate with the payment of £200 per annum to Y, L has a rent service and Y a rentcharge. Since the Statute *Quia Emptores* 1290, it has been impossible for a grantor to reserve any

---

[1] *Ante*, p. 68; and see generally M. & W. 784–789.
[2] *Ante*, Chap. 4, p. 84.

services on a conveyance of freehold land in fee simple, for the grantee holds of the grantor's lord, and not of the grantor.[3] Consequently, no rent reserved on a conveyance of freehold land in fee simple after 1290 can be a rent service. Although at law services could be reserved on the grant by a fee simple owner of a life estate or a fee tail, it was most unusual to do so. Thus the only rent service met with in practice is the rent reserved upon the grant of a lease for a term of years. A rent service is annexed to a reversion, while a rentcharge stands on its own. The majority of rent services reserved on the grant of a fee simple in freehold land before *Quia Emptores* 1290 have remained uncollected for so long (the fall in the value of money made them hardly worth collecting) that they have become barred by lapse of time. Such rents were usually known as chief rents in the case of freehold land, and any still existing at the end of 1925 were classed with those manorial incidents in copyhold land which were extinguished at the end of 1935 at the latest.[4]

2. Rent seck. At common law, the relationship of lord and tenant carried with it an automatic right of distress for any rent. If no such relationship existed, there was no common law right of distress, and consequently an express clause of distress was frequently inserted when reserving the rent. A rent supported by no right of distress was known as a rent seck (from the Latin *siccus*, dry, barren), and the name " rentcharge " was reserved for a rent supported by a power of distress given by the instrument creating the rent or by statute. Rent seck ceased to exist many years ago,[5] for by the Landlord and Tenant Act 1730,[6] the owners of rents seck were given the same rights of distress as a landlord has against his tenant under a lease, namely, a right to distrain as soon as the rent is in arrear.

3. Legal and equitable rentcharges. A rentcharge is real property, so that both at law and in equity it could be held for any of the usual estates or interests.[7] However, since 1925 an interest in a rentcharge can be legal only if it is—

  (a) in possession, and
  (b) either perpetual or for a term of years absolute.[8]

---

[3] *Ante*, p. 12. The Crown was excepted.
[4] *Ante*, p. 13.
[5] *Re Lord Gerard & Beecham's Contract* [1894] 3 Ch. 295.
[6] s. 5.
[7] See, *e.g.*, *Chaplin* v. *Chaplin* (1733) 3 P.Wms. 229 (entail); *Re Fraser* [1904] 1 Ch. 726 (term of years).
[8] *Ante*, p. 77.

Further, a rentcharge cannot exist at law unless the proper formalities have been employed for its creation.[9]

4. Rentcharge on a rentcharge. At common law, a rentcharge could be charged only upon a corporeal hereditament. There could be no rentcharge charged upon another rentcharge or other incorporeal hereditament[10]; a right of distress would clearly be inappropriate in such cases. However, since 1925 a rentcharge charged upon another rentcharge is valid, even if created before 1926; and special provisions have been made for enforcing payment.[11]

Sect. 2. Creation and Transfer of Rentcharges

A rentcharge may be created by statute, by an instrument *inter vivos*, or by will.

1. By statute. A rentcharge may be created either by statute, or by virtue of powers conferred thereby.[12]

2. By instrument inter vivos. Apart from statute, a legal rentcharge can be created *inter vivos* only by a deed[13]; but a document merely in writing may create an equitable rentcharge.[14]

3. By will. A will now operates only in equity,[15] so that if a rentcharge is created or devised by will, the beneficiary gets no legal interest until the personal representatives have assented to the gift.[16]

If an existing rentcharge is being transferred by deed or will, the normal rule for corporeal hereditaments applies and the whole interest in the rentcharge passes without words of limitation unless a contrary intention is shown.[17] But if a rentcharge is being created by will or (probably) by deed, only a life interest will be created unless an intention is shown to create some larger interest.[18]

Sect. 3. Means of Enforcing Payment of Rentcharges

A. Rentcharge Charged on Land

There are four remedies available to the owner of a rentcharge if it is

---

[9] *Infra.* [10] *Re The Alms Corn Charity* [1901] 2 Ch. 750 at 759.
[11] L.P.A. 1925, s. 122: *post*, p. 412.
[12] See, *e.g.*, Improvement of Land Act 1864.
[13] See *Hewlins* v. *Shippam* (1826) 5 B. & C. 221 at 229.
[14] *Jackson* v. *Lever* (1792) 3 Bro.C.C. 605; L.P.A. 1925, s. 53.
[15] See L.P.(Am.)A. 1924, Sched. IX.
[16] For assents, see *ante*, p. 314. [17] *Ante*, pp. 23, 24.
[18] See *Nichols* v. *Hawkes* (1853) 10 Hare 342; *Grant* v. *Edmondson* [1930] 2 Ch. 245 at 254; [1931] 1 Ch. 1; *ante*, p. 24; M. & W. 792.

not paid. The first remedy, namely, an action for the money, is given by the common law; the other three are created by statute,[19] and replace remedies formerly expressly conferred by most instruments creating rentcharges.

1. Action for the money. A personal action for the rent will lie against the " terre tenant " (the freehold tenant in possession of the land upon which the rent is charged) even if the rent was not created by him [20] and exceeds the value of the land.[21] If the land has been divided, the terre tenant of any part is liable for the full amount [22]; but a mere lessee for a term of years is not liable,[23] for the action lies only against the freeholder.

Although the right to sue and the liability to be sued run with the rentcharge and the land respectively, the benefit of an express covenant for payment does not run with the rentcharge without express assignment.[24] Thus if a rentcharge created by A in favour of X is conveyed to Y and the land to B, Y cannot sue A on his covenant for payment if B fails to pay.

2. Distress. If an express power of distress is given by the instrument creating the rentcharge, the extent of the right is a question of construction. If there is no such express power, and the rentcharge was created before 1882, the rentcharge owner can distrain upon the land as soon as the rent or any part of it is in arrear.[25] If the rentcharge was created after 1881, then, subject to any contrary intention, the rentcharge owner can distrain as soon as the rent or any part of it is 21 days in arrear.[26]

3. Entry into possession. If a rentcharge was created after 1881 and shows no contrary intention, the rentcharge owner may, when the rent or any part of it is 40 days in arrear, enter and take possession of the land without impeachment of waste and take the income until he has paid himself all rent due with costs.[27]

4. Demise to a trustee. If the rentcharge was created after 1881 and shows no contrary intention, the rentcharge owner may, if the rent or any part of it is 40 days in arrear, demise the land to a

---

[19] L.P.A. 1925, s. 121, replacing C.A. 1881, s. 44.
[20] *Thomas* v. *Sylvester* (1873) L.R. 8 Q.B. 368.
[21] *Pertwee* v. *Townsend* [1896] 2 Q.B. 129.
[22] *Christie* v. *Barker* (1884) 53 L.J.Q.B. 537.
[23] *Re Herbage Rents* [1896] 2 Ch. 811.
[24] See *Grant* v. *Edmondson* [1931] 1 Ch. 1, criticised (1931) 47 L.Q.R. 380.
[25] Landlord and Tenant Act 1730, s. 5.
[26] L.P.A. 1925, s. 121 (2).
[27] *Ibid.* s. 121 (3).

trustee for a term of years, with or without impeachment of waste, on trust to raise the money due, with all costs and expenses, by creating a mortgage, receiving the income or any other reasonable means.[28] If a rentcharge owner has only an equitable interest, he can grant only an equitable lease to the trustees, but the estate owner can be compelled to clothe the equitable lease with the legal estate.[29]

If the rentcharge is created after July 15, 1964, the rule against perpetuities does not apply to any powers or remedies for enforcing it.[30] If the rentcharge was created on or before that date only the last three statutory remedies were excepted from the rule, together with similar express powers conferred by any instrument.[31] Other, wider, provisions were not considered to be excepted from the rule, *e.g.,* a clause which is sometimes inserted entitling the rentcharge owner to effect a permanent forfeiture of the land if the rent is unpaid for a specified period.[32]

B. Rentcharge Charged on Another Rentcharge

Instead of the statutory remedies of distress, entry into possession and demise to a trustee, the owner of a rentcharge charged upon another rentcharge may appoint a receiver if the rent or any part of it is 21 days in arrear.[33] The receiver has all the powers of a receiver appointed by a mortgagee.[34] Thus if Blackacre is charged with a rent of £100 per annum and that rentcharge is charged with a rent of £25 per annum in favour of X, a receiver of the £100 can be appointed by X if the £25 is unpaid for 21 days.

Sect. 4. Extinguishment of Rentcharges

A rentcharge may be extinguished by release, merger, lapse of time or statutory discharge.

1. Release. The owner of a rentcharge may by deed release the land from the rent, either wholly or in part. A partial release may take the form of releasing all of the land from part of the rent,[35]

---

[28] *Ibid.* s. 121 (4).
[29] *Ibid.* ss. 3 (1), 8 (2).
[30] Perpetuities and Accumulations Act 1964, s. 11, amending L.P.A., s. 121 (6); *ante,* pp. 130, 131.
[31] L.P.A., s. 121 (6).
[32] See *Re Trustees of Hollis' Hospital and Hague's Contract* [1899] 2 Ch. 540, criticised in Challis R.P. 190.
[33] L.P.A. 1925, s. 122 (2), (3).
[34] *Ibid.* s. 122 (2); *post,* p. 478.
[35] Co.Litt. 148a.

or releasing part of the land from the whole of the rent.[36] An informal release may be valid in equity.

2. Merger. At common law, if a rentcharge became vested in the same person as the land upon which it was charged, the rentcharge became extinguished by merger, even if this was not the intention.[37] For this to occur, both the rent and the land must have been vested in the same person at the same time and in the same right.[38] This automatic rule of the common law no longer applies for, by the Law of Property Act 1925,[39] there is to be no merger at law except in cases where there would have been a merger in equity, and the equitable rule is that merger depends upon the intention of the parties.[40] Even if an intention that there should be no merger cannot be shown, there will be a presumption against merger if it is to the interest of the person concerned to prevent it.[41]

3. Lapse of time. If a rentcharge is not paid for 12 years and no sufficient acknowledgment of the owner's title is made, it is extinguished.[42]

4. Statutory discharge. By the Law of Property Act 1925,[43] provision is made for landowners to obtain the discharge of their land from rentcharges on paying to the rentcharge owner the sum representing the capital value certified by the Minister of Agriculture, Fisheries and Food.

Sect. 5. Note on the Types of Rent

A summary of the various kinds of rent may be useful.

1. Rent service: this is rent due from a tenant to his lord by reason of tenure, and is now met with only in the case of rent due under a lease or tenancy.

2. Rentcharge: this is a periodical sum charged on land independently of any relationship of lord and tenant, supported by a power of distress.

[6] L.P.A. 1925, s. 70.
[7] *Capital and Counties Bank Ltd.* v. *Rhodes* [1903] 1 Ch. 631 at 652.
[8] *Re Radcliffe* [1892] 1 Ch. 227.
[9] s. 185, replacing J.A. 1873, s. 25 (4).
[10] *Ingle* v. *Vaughan Jenkins* [1900] 2 Ch. 368.
[1] *Re Fletcher* [1917] 1 Ch. 339.
[2] See *post*, pp. 531, 538.
[3] s. 191.

3. Rent seck: this was a rentcharge with no power of distress. It is now obsolete.

4. Chief rent: this was a rent service reserved on the subinfeudation of freehold land in fee simple. The Statute *Quia Emptores* 1290 for the most part prevented such rents being created.[44] Any chief rents existing in 1925 were extinguished by the end of 1935.[45] In some parts of the country, *e.g.,* Manchester, rentcharges are sometimes called chief rents.

5. Fee farm rent: this was the name originally used for chief rents; latterly, it has been applied to rentcharges reserved on a conveyance in fee simple.

6. Quit rent: this was a rent service payable by a copyholder to his lord, whereby he went quit of his obligation to perform agricultural services; and chief rents were sometimes called quit rents. Quit rents existing in 1925 were extinguished by the end of 1935.[46]

7. Rents of assize: this term is rarely encountered today; it was applied both to chief rents and quit rents.

Part 2

ADVOWSONS

An advowson is the perpetual right of presentation to an ecclesiastical living. The owner of an advowson is known as the patron. When a living becomes vacant, as when a rector or vicar dies or retires, the patron of the living has a right to nominate the clergyman who shall next hold the living. Subject to a right of veto on certain specified grounds, the Bishop is bound to institute (formally appoint) any duly qualified person presented. This is a relic of the days when it was common for the lord of a manor to build and endow a church and in return have the right of patronage.

It is one of the curiosities of English law that an advowson is real property. In the physical sense, there is no land of which the patron is owner, yet the advowson is an incorporeal hereditament and the patron has an estate in what in law is real property; his estate in an advowson will accordingly pass under a devise of

---

[44] *Ante*, p. 409.
[45] See *ante*, p. 13.
[46] See *ante*, p. 13.

' all my real property." Legal estates and equitable interests may exist in an advowson as in other real property; thus a life interest in an advowson is necessarily equitable, while a fee simple absolute in possession may exist as a legal estate.[47]

Advowsons are subject to a number of important restrictions, both at common law and by statute,[48] which prevent serious abuses of this incursion of property into religion. In particular, no advowson may be sold after two vacancies of the benefice have occurred after July 14, 1924. These restrictions are more appropriate to books on ecclesiastical law than to a short textbook on real property.

Part 3

TITHES

A tithe was the right of a rector to a tenth part of the produce of all the land in his parish. In some cases a rector was an individual, while in others the rectory was vested in a monastery, which appointed a vicar to perform the necessary ecclesiastical duties " vicariously " for the monastery. On the dissolution of the monasteries in the reign of Henry VIII many rectories passed into the royal hands and were granted to laymen; the result was that the right to tithes in many cases passed into lay hands. Like advowsons, tithes were deemed to be land in which the various estates could exist. The history of tithes falls into four periods.

1. Before the Tithe Act 1836. Originally, tithe was payable in kind, a tenth of the corn, wood, milk, eggs and so on being handed to the tithe owner and often stored (where this was appropriate) in tithe barns, some of which remain today. To avoid the inconvenience of each landowner paying his tithe in a variety of products, in many cases an agreement was made for the satisfaction of tithe by, say, the delivery of one-quarter of the hay instead of one-tenth of all the produce of the land, or the payment of a sum of money. This was often [49] known as a " modus " (" *modus decimandi*," a method of taking one-tenth).

2. Between the Tithe Act 1836, and the Tithe Act 1925. The Tithe Act 1836 abolished the payment of tithe in kind and substituted therefor a tithe rentcharge on the land. Commissioners fixed

[47] *Ante*, p. 73.
[48] See Benefices Act 1898 and Benefices Act 1898 (Amendment) Measure 1923.
[49] Though not quite accurately : see *e.g.*, *Roberts* v. *Williams* (1810) 12 East 33.

a yearly amount which each plot of land was to bear, and this was known as the "commuted value." The actual sum payable each year, however, was not necessarily the commuted value, but varied according to the amount by which the average prices of wheat, barley and oats for the previous seven years exceeded or were less than the standard prices fixed by the Act. The sum payable thus varied directly according to the prosperity of agriculture. Tithe rentcharge was not recoverable in the same way as an ordinary rentcharge, but only under an order of the county court; the landowner was not, as in the case of ordinary rentcharges, personally liable for the money payable.

3. Between the Tithe Act 1925 and the Tithe Act 1936. The Tithe Act 1925 stabilised the amount payable for tithes. For each £100 commuted value of tithe rentcharge, £105 became payable irrespective of fluctuations in the price of corn. In the case of ecclesiastical tithe rentcharge (*i.e.*, rentcharge still payable to some church authority) a further £4 10s. was payable, making £109 10s. 0d. per £100 commuted value; this additional sum went to a sinking fund which in the course of time would have produced approximately enough income to replace the rentcharge and so allow its extinguishment. There was no similar provision for lay tithe rentcharge, but the landowner could insist on discharging his land from it by paying a lump sum ascertained by a prescribed method.

4. After the Tithe Act 1936. The Tithe Act 1936 abolished all tithe rentcharge, whether ecclesiastical or lay, as from October 2, 1936. The Act put an end to the collection of the money by the tithe owner direct from the landowner, for this had too often been made only with the assistance of the county court aided by the police and had given rise to much friction in agricultural districts, especially where farmers who were not supporters of the Church of England were compelled to provide that Church with substantial financial assistance in years when their profits from farming were small.

The main provisions of the Act are as follows.

(a) *Tithe redemption annuities.* Land formerly charged with a tithe rentcharge payable to the tithe owner now stands charged with a "tithe redemption annuity" payable to the Crown, for which the landowner is personally liable. These annuities are collected by the Commissioners of Inland Revenue, in place of the former Tithe Redemption Commission.[50]

[50] S.I. 1959 No. 1971.

(b) *Amount of annuities.* The amount of the annuity is—

> (i) £91 11s. 2d. per £100 commuted value of rentcharge if any of the land was agricultural land on April 1, 1936;
>
> (ii) £105 per £100 commuted value of rentcharge in other cases.

Thus for agricultural land the Act has reduced the annual sum payable per £100 commuted value from £109 10s. 0d. to £91 11s. 2d. in the case of ecclesiastical tithe rentcharge, and from £105 to £91 11s. 2d. in the case of lay tithe rentcharge. In the case of non-agricultural land, ecclesiastical tithe rentcharge has been reduced by £4 10s. 0d.; otherwise it is unchanged.

(c) *Period of annuities.* The annuities are payable for sixty years and then cease. From the money paid during this period a fund is being built up out of which the tithe redemption stock (see (e) below) will be redeemed. From the tithe payer's point of view the period of sixty years compares favourably with the former provision for redemption of ecclesiastical tithe rentcharge. Moreover, the tithe redemption annuities must be redeemed by a capital payment on any change of ownership of the land after October 1, 1962.[51]

(d) *Status of annuities.* The annuities are legal interests within section 1 (2) of the Law of Property Act 1925[52]; they are not registrable under the Land Charges Act 1925.

(e) *Tithe redemption stock.* Tithe owners were compensated by the issue to them of " tithe redemption stock " upon which interest of 3 per cent. per annum is paid. The payment, being charged on the Consolidated Fund, is guaranteed by the Government and is redeemable within sixty years. The stock can be bought and sold in the same way as other stock and is not, of course, an interest in real property. The interest produced by the stock is rather less than the amount of tithe formerly payable, but the tithe owner now has the certainty of receiving his income in full and without trouble, independently of the financial position of any landowner.

Part 4

EASEMENTS AND PROFITS

Sect. 1. Nature of an Easement

An easement may be defined as a right to use, or restrict the use

---

[51] Finance Act 1962, s. 32.   [52] See *ante*, p. 78.

of, the land of another person in some way. This definition is neither exact nor particularly helpful, for it includes certain rights which are not easements, such as restrictive covenants, and it fails to illustrate what sort of a right an easement is. Examples of easements are rights of way, rights of light and rights of water. The best way in which to amplify this imperfect definition is to examine—

(a) the essentials of an easement, and
(b) the distinction between easements and certain analogous rights.

A. Essentials of an Easement

1. There must be a dominant and a servient tenement.[53] If X owns Blackacre and grants a right to use a path across Blackacre to the owner for the time being of the neighbouring plot of White-acre, Blackacre is the servient tenement and Whiteacre the dominant tenement. Had X granted the right to A who owned no land at all, A would have acquired a licence to walk over Blackacre, but his right could not exist as an easement, for a dominant tenement is lacking. Put technically, an easement cannot exist in gross [54] (independently of the ownership of land) but only as appurtenant (attached) to a dominant tenement [55]; on any transfer of the dominant tenement, the easement will pass with the land, so that the tenant for the time being can enjoy it,[56] even if he is a mere lessee.[57]

2. The easement must accommodate the dominant tenement. A right cannot exist as an easement unless it confers a benefit on the dominant tenement as a tenement. It is not sufficient that the right should give the owner for the time being some personal advantage unconnected with his land, such as a right to use a wall on the servient tenement for advertising generally and not merely in connection with a business carried on upon the dominant tenement [58] : the test is whether the right makes the dominant tenement a better and more convenient tenement, *e.g.,* a right to affix to adjoining premises a signboard for a public house.[59]

---

[53] *Hawkins* v. *Rutter* [1892] 1 Q.B. 668.
[54] *Rangeley* v. *Midland Ry.* (1868) 3 Ch.App. 306 at 310.
[55] See *Re Salvin's Indenture* [1938] 2 All E.R. 498 (dominant tenement partly incorporeal).
[56] L.P.A. 1925, s. 187 (1) ; *Leech* v. *Schweder* (1874) 9 Ch.App. 463 at 474, 475.
[57] *Thorpe* v. *Brumfitt* (1873) 8 Ch.App. 650.
[58] *Clapman* v. *Edwards* [1938] 2 All E.R. 507.
[59] *Moody* v. *Steggles* (1879) 12 Ch.D. 261.

Thus if X owns land in Northumberland, he cannot burden it with an easement of way in favour of land in Kent, for although it may be very convenient for the owner of the Kentish land to walk across X's Northumberland estate when he goes north, the right of way does not improve the Kentish land as a tenement.[60] This does not mean that a right cannot exist as an easement unless the dominant and servient tenements are contiguous; even if they are separated by other land, an easement can still exist, provided it in fact confers some benefit upon the dominant tenement as such,[61] as does a right for the dominant owner to enjoy adjacent pleasure grounds.[62] Nor will a right be any the less an easement merely because it benefits other land as well as the dominant tenement.[63]

In *Ackroyd* v. *Smith* [64] it was held that a right of way granted " for all purposes " to the tenant of Blackacre and his successors in title was not an easement, for the grant permitted the way to be used for purposes not connected with Blackacre. Had the grant been worded " for all purposes connected with Blackacre " it could have created an easement; probably the words used would be construed in this sense if the case arose today. In *Hill* v. *Tupper* [65] the owner of a canal leased land on the bank of the canal to Hill and granted him the sole and exclusive right of putting pleasure boats on the canal. Tupper, without any authority, put rival pleasure boats on the canal. The question was whether Hill could successfully sue Tupper. If Hill's right amounted to an easement, he could sue anyone who interfered with it, for it was a right in land. If it was not an easement, then it could only be a licence,[66] *i.e.,* a mere personal arrangement between Hill and the canal owner not amounting to an interest in land, so that Hill would have no right to sue those interfering with it. It was held that since the right did not improve Hill's land *qua* land, but gave him a mere personal advantage, it was not an easement and thus he could not sue Tupper. The result would have been different if the right granted had been to cross and recross the canal to get to and from Hill's land; and the canal owner, of course, could have sued Tupper for trespassing on the canal.[67]

---

[60] See *Bailey* v. *Stephens* (1862) 12 C.B.(N.S.) 91 at 115.
[61] *Todrick* v. *Western National Omnibus Co. Ltd.* [1934] Ch. 561.
[62] *Re Ellenborough Park* [1956] Ch. 131.
[63] *Simpson* v. *Mayor of Godmanchester* [1897] A.C. 696.
[64] (1850) 10 C.B. 164.
[65] (1863) 2 H. & C. 121.
[66] See *ante*, pp. 378–382, and *post*, p. 425.
[67] See *Lord Chesterfield* v. *Harris* [1908] 2 Ch. 397 at 412 (affd.: [1911] A.C. 623).

3. The dominant and servient tenements must not be both owned and occupied by the same person. An easement is essentially a right in *alieno solo* (in the soil of another): a man cannot have an easement over his own land. " When the owner of Whiteacre and Blackacre passes over the former to Blackacre, he is not exercising a right of way in respect of Blackacre; he is merely making use of his own land to get from one part of it to another." [68]

It should be noted, however, that the same person must not only own both tenements but also occupy both of them before the existence of an easement is rendered impossible. Thus if an easement over Blackacre is appurtenant to Whiteacre, it will not be affected by the fee simple in each plot becoming vested in one person if the plots are occupied by different lessees [69]; unity of ownership without unity of possession is not fatal to an easement. Similarly, if the fee simple in each plot is owned by different persons, the easement will not be destroyed if the plots are leased to the same tenant, *i.e.*, by unity of possession without unity of ownership; during the currency of the lease the easement is suspended but it will revive when the lease ends. [70]

The name " quasi-easements " is often used to describe rights habitually exercised by a man over part of his own land which, if the part in question were owned and occupied by another, would be easements. These are of some importance, for in certain circumstances they may become true easements. [71]

4. The easement must be capable of forming the subject-matter of a grant. No right can exist as an easement unless it could have been granted by deed. This involves the following points.

(a) *There must be a capable grantor.* There can be no claim to an easement if at the relevant times the servient tenement was owned by someone incapable of granting an easement, *e.g.*, a statutory corporation with no power to grant easements. [72]

(b) *There must be a capable grantee.* An easement can be claimed only by a legal person capable of receiving a grant. [73] Thus a claim by a company with no power to acquire easements must fail [74]; similarly, a fluctuating body of persons, such as " the

[68] *Roe* v. *Siddons* (1888) 22 Q.B.D. 224 at 236, *per* Fry L.J.
[69] *Richardson* v. *Graham* [1908] 1 K.B. 39 ; and see *Buckby* v. *Coles* (1814) 5 Taunt. 311 at 315.
[70] *Thomas* v. *Thomas* (1835) 2 Cr.M. & R. 34 (see especially at p. 40).
[71] *Post*, pp. 434 *et seq.*   [72] *Mulliner* v. *Midland Ry.* (1879) 11 Ch.D. 61.
[73] See *Re Salvin's Indenture* [1938] 2 All E.R. 498.
[74] *National Guaranteed Manure Co.* v. *Donald* (1859) 4 H. & N. 8.

inhabitants for the time being of the village of X," cannot claim an easement, for no grant can be made to them. But such bodies may claim similar rights by showing that there is a custom to that effect, such as a customary right of way across land to reach the parish church,[75] or a customary right to water cattle at a pond,[76] or to dry nets on certain land.[77]

(c) *The right must be sufficiently definite.* The extent of the right claimed must be capable of reasonable definition. Thus although there can be an easement of light where a defined window receives a defined amount of light, there can be no easement of privacy,[78] nor of prospect (the right to a view), for " the law does not give an action for such things of delight." [79] Again, an easement for the passage of air through a defined channel may exist, but there can be no easement for the general flow of air over land to a windmill or chimney.[80]

(d) *The right must be within the general nature of rights capable of existing as easements.* Although most easements fall under one of the well-known heads of easements, such as way, light, support and so on, the list of easements is not closed. " The category of servitudes and easements must alter and expand with the changes that take place in the circumstances of mankind." [81] But there are limits. " It must not therefore be supposed that incidents of a novel kind can be devised and attached to property, at the fancy or caprice of any owner." [82] The right must fall within the general characteristics of an easement, which are almost incapable of definition. It can be said, however, that it is most unlikely that a right would be admitted as an easement if it involved the servient tenant in the expenditure of money, for no recognised easement does this,[83] except, perhaps, the obligation to fence land in order to keep out cattle, which has been described as " in the nature of a spurious easement." [84] But new rights not involving the servient owner in expenditure have from time to time been recognised as easements. Thus in 1896 the right to go upon

5 *Brocklebank* v. *Thompson* [1903] 2 Ch. 344.
6 *Manning* v. *Wasdale* (1836) 5 A. & E. 758.
7 *Mercer* v. *Denne* [1905] 2 Ch. 538; *post*, p. 426.
8 *Browne* v. *Flower* [1911] 1 Ch. 219.
9 *William Aldred's Case* (1610) 9 Co.Rep. 57b at 58b, *per* Wray C.J.
0 *Webb* v. *Bird* (1862) 13 C.B.(N.S.) 841; *Bryant* v. *Lefever* (1879) 4 C.P.D. 172.
1 *Dyce* v. *Hay* (1852) 1 Macq. 205 at 312, *per* Lord St. Leonards L.C.
2 *Keppell* v. *Bailey* (1833) 2 My. & K. 517 at 535, *per* Lord Brougham L.C.
3 See *Pomfret* v. *Ricroft* (1669) 1 Wms.Saund. 321; and see *Regis Property Co. Ltd.* v. *Redman* [1956] 2 Q.B. 612.
4 *Lawrence* v. *Jenkins* (1873) L.R. 8 Q.B. 274 at 279, *per* Archibald J.; see *Jones* v. *Price* [1965] 2 Q.B. 618; M. & W. 875.

the land of another to open sluice gates,[85] in 1915 a right to store
casks and trade produce on land,[86] and in 1955 the right to use a
neighbour's lavatory,[87] were recognised as easements. Yet a right
to park and repair lorries on land may be so ill-defined and extensive
(amounting to sole or joint possession of the land) as to be outside
the class of possible easements.[88] Similarly, a right to have the wall
of a house protected from the weather by an adjoining house is too
indefinite to exist as an easement.[89]

B. Distinction between Easements and Certain Analogous Rights

The nature of easements may be further indicated by contrasting
them with certain other rights.

I. QUASI-EASEMENTS

As already explained,[90] rights exercised by a landowner over his own
land which, if he did not own that land, could exist as easements,
are sometimes called quasi-easements.

II. OTHER NATURAL RIGHTS

In addition to his rights over his own land, every landowner has
a natural right to support, *i.e.*, a right that the support for his land
provided by his neighbour's land should not be removed.[91] A similar
right exists in cases where the surface of the land and the soil under-
neath are owned by different persons; the owner of the surface has a
natural right to have it supported by the subjacent soil [92] unless this
right is excluded by clear words or necessary implication in some
statute or agreement.

This natural right, however, extends only to land in its natural
state; there is no natural right to support for buildings or for the
additional burden on land which they cause.[93] But if support is withdrawn, and the land would have fallen even if it had not been built
upon, an action lies in respect of any damage to the buildings.[94]

[85] *Simpson* v. *Mayor of Godmanchester* [1896] 1 Ch. 214 ; [1897] A.C. 696.
[86] *Att.-Gen. of Southern Nigeria* v. *Holt* [1915] A.C. 599. The headnote calls the
   right an irrevocable licence, but it was clearly recognised as an easement: see
   p. 617 of the report.
[87] *Miller* v. *Emcer Products Ltd.* [1956] Ch. 304.
[88] *Copeland* v. *Greenhalf* [1952] Ch. 488.
[89] *Phipps* v. *Pears* [1965] 1 Q.B. 76.   [90] *Ante*, p. 420
[91] *Backhouse* v. *Bonomi* (1861) 9 H.L.C. 503.
[92] *London & North Western Ry.* v. *Evans* [1893] 1 Ch. 16 at 30.
[93] *Wyatt* v. *Harrison* (1832) 3 B. & Ad. 871.
[94] *Stroyan* v. *Knowles* (1861) 6 H. & N. 454.

Similarly, there is no natural right to have buildings supported by neighbouring buildings.[95] If no more damage is done than is necessary, a man may pull down his house without having to provide support for his neighbour's house. The right to have buildings supported by land or by other buildings can, however, be acquired as an easement.[96]

III. PUBLIC RIGHTS

An easement must always be appurtenant to land; it is a right exercisable by the owner for the time being by virtue of his estate in the land. A public right, on the other hand, is a right exercisable by anyone, whether he owns land or not, merely by virtue of being a member of the public.

The public rights which most closely resemble easements are public rights of way. The land over which a public right of way exists is known as a highway, and although most highways have been made up into roads, and most easements of way exist over footpaths, the presence or absence of a made road has nothing to do with the distinction. There may be a highway over a footpath, while a well-made road may be subject only to an easement of way, or may exist only for the landowner's benefit and be subject to no easement at all.

1. Creation. A public right of way may be created in the following ways.

(a) *By statute.* This needs no explanation.

(b) *By dedication and acceptance.*

(1) AT COMMON LAW. To establish a highway at common law by dedication and acceptance, it must be shown—

(i) that the owner of the land dedicated the way to the public, and also

(ii) that the public accepted that dedication, the acceptance normally being shown by user by the public.[97]

Dedication may be formal, although this is comparatively infrequent. It is usually inferred from long user by the public, the user thus being effective to prove both dedication and acceptance. But to raise a presumption of dedication, there must have been open use as of right for so long a time that it must have come to the notice of

---

[95] *Peyton* v. *Mayor of London* (1829) 9 B. & C. 725.
[96] *Post*, p. 456.
[97] See *Cubitt* v. *Lady Caroline Maxse* (1873) L.R. 8 C.P. 704 at 715.

the landowner that the public were using the way as of right, thus
justifying the inference that the landowner consented to this user.[9]
User with the landowner's licence is not user as of right,[99] for it
acknowledges that the way is being used not because the public has a
right to do so but because the landowner has agreed not to treat it as
a trespass in the particular case in question. Further, the use must
have been without interruption by the owner. A practice frequently
adopted to disprove any intention to dedicate is to close the way for
one day in each year, for this openly asserts the landowner's right to
exclude the public at will.[1]

The length of the enjoyment to be shown depends on the circumstances of the case. Where the circumstances have pointed to an
intention to dedicate, eighteen months has been held to be enough,
while where the circumstances are against dedication, a substantially
greater period may be insufficient.

(2) UNDER THE HIGHWAYS ACT 1959. The Rights of Way Act
1932, now replaced by the provisions of the Highways Act 1959,
simplified the position to some extent by laying down a definite
period of use which will suffice to show that a right of way exists.
The public can still claim a right of way based on use for a shorter
period than that laid down by the Act if an intent to dedicate can
be inferred.

The Act provides that a way is to be deemed to have been
dedicated as a highway if it " had been actually enjoyed by the
public as of right and without interruption for a full period of twenty
years," unless " there is sufficient evidence that there was no intention
during that period to dedicate it." [3] " Interruption " means interruption in fact, and not, *e.g.*, the mere closing of the way only at times
when nobody used or was likely to use it.[4] The absence of any intention to dedicate can be shown either in one of the usual ways, as by
closing the way for one day in each year, or by one of the special
ways provided by the Act, namely, by exhibiting a notice visible to
those using the way, or by depositing a map with the local council
with a statement of what ways the landowner admits to be highways
and lodging statutory declarations at intervals of not more than six

---

[98] *Greenwich District Board of Works* v. *Maudslay* (1870) L.R. 5 Q.B. 397 at 404.
[99] *R.* v. *Broke* (1859) 1 F. & F. 514.
[1] See *British Museum Trustees* v. *Finnis* (1833) 5 C. & P. 460.
[2] *North London Ry.* v. *The Vestry of St. Mary, Islington* (1872) 27 L.T. 672.
[3] Highways Act 1959, s. 34.
[4] *Lewis* v. *Thomas* [1950] 1 K.B. 438.

ears stating whether any other ways have been dedicated. A reversioner or remainderman upon an interest for life or *pur autre vie* is entitled to the same remedies against the public as if he were in possession.[5]

The twenty years' period is to be calculated as that next before the time when the right to use the way was brought into question by a notice exhibited to the public negativing the dedication or otherwise.

2. Extinguishment. When a highway has been established, it can only be stopped up or diverted by an order made under certain statutory provisions [6]; the mere obstruction of the highway or the failure by the public to use it will not destroy the rights of the public, for ' once a highway always a highway." [7] And a mere closing order for a highway leaves unaffected any easement over the route of the highway.[8]

IV. LICENCES

Licences resemble easements in that they authorise the use of the land of another in some way. But licences, which cannot exist as legal estates or interests and are at the most mere equities, are far more flexible and less restricted than easements. Thus they may be created without formality; they require no dominant tenement; and they may authorise the general occupation of land.[9]

V. RESTRICTIVE COVENANTS

Easements and restrictive covenants are similar in that an easement, like a restrictive covenant, may entitle a landowner to restrict the use that his neighbour makes of his land; thus the owner of an easement of light may prevent the servient owner from obstructing his light by erecting a building on the adjoining land. There are other resemblances, such as the need for dominant and servient tenements, and in general it is true to say that the law of restrictive covenants may be regarded as an equitable extension of the law of easements. However, certain points of difference should be mentioned.

1. Scope: restrictive covenants are wider in scope and more flexible than easements. As will be seen, the amount of light which

---

[5] Highways Act 1959, s. 36.
[6] *e.g.,* Town and Country Planning Act 1962, s. 153; Highways Act 1959, ss. 108–115.
[7] *Dawes* v. *Hawkins* (1860) 8 C.B.(N.S.) 848 at 858, *per* Byles J.
[8] *Walsh* v. *Oates* [1953] 1 Q.B. 578.
[9] For licences, see *ante,* pp. 378–382.

the owner of an easement of light may insist upon receiving is fixed
the standard in any given neighbourhood is absolute and an easemen
to an extraordinary amount of light cannot exist.[10] Further, there ca
be no easement entitling the dominant owner to a view.[11] But b
means of suitable restrictive covenants preventing his neighbour fron
building, a landowner can enjoy both the view and an extraordinar
amount of light.

2. Visibility: an inspection of the land will suggest the existenc
of many easements, but it is otherwise with restrictive covenants
Thus footpaths suggest an easement of way and pipes an easemen
of drainage, but no inspection of the land will reveal the existence o
a covenant against trading upon it.

3. Existence at law: an easement may be legal or equitable
whereas the burden of a restrictive covenant runs only in equity.

4. Prescription: an easement may be acquired by prescription; no
so a restrictive covenant.

5. Positive nature: a restrictive covenant is entirely negative; i
neither entitles the dominant tenant nor binds the servient tenant to
do any positive act. Easements similarly do not bind the servien
tenant to do any positive act,[12] but as regards the dominant tenant
certain easements (called " positive easements ") entitle the tenant to
do positive acts, *e.g.*, easements of way, while others (called " negative
easements ") do not, *e.g.*, easements of light. Certain easements thus
contain a positive element which is lacking in restrictive covenants.

VI. CUSTOMARY RIGHTS OF FLUCTUATING BODIES

These have been considered above.[13] They differ from easements in
that they are exercisable by all who are included within the custom,
independently of ownership of a dominant tenement. Thus the custom
may extend to all the inhabitants of a particular locality, whether they
own land or not.[14]

Sect. 2. Nature of a Profit à Prendre

A profit *à prendre* has been described as " a right to take something

---

[10] *Post*, p. 455.
[11] *Ante*, p. 421.
[12] But see the obligation to fence, *ante*, p. 421.
[13] *Ante*, pp. 420, 421 ; see also *post*, pp. 429, 430.
[14] *Race* v. *Ward* (1855) 4 E. & B. 702.

off another person's land." [15] This is too wide; the thing taken must be something taken out of the soil,[16] *i.e.*, it must be either the soil, the natural produce thereof, or the wild animals existing on it; and the thing taken must at the time of taking be susceptible of ownership.[17] A right to " hawk, hunt, fish and fowl " may thus exist as a profit,[18] for this gives the right to take creatures living on the soil which, when killed, are capable of being owned. But a right to take water from a spring or a pump, or the right to water cattle at a pond, may be an easement but cannot be a profit; for the water, when taken, was not owned by anyone nor was it part of the soil.[19] A right to take water stored in an artificial receptacle, *e.g.*, a cistern, is not an easement but may perhaps exist either as a profit or a mere licence, probably the latter.[20]

A. Classification of Profits à Prendre

I. AS TO OWNERSHIP

A profit *à prendre* may be enjoyed—

    (i) by one person to the exclusion of all others; this is known as a several profit *à prendre*, or a several profit; or

    (ii) by one person in common with others; this is known as a profit in common, or a common.

II. IN RELATION TO LAND

A profit is not necessarily appurtenant to land, as is the case with easements, and may exist in the following forms.

1. A profit appurtenant. This is a profit, whether several or in common, attached to land by act of parties. A profit appurtenant may be acquired either by grant or by prescription. In general, there must be compliance with the four conditions necessary for the existence of an easement, which can exist only as appurtenant to land.[21] Thus a profit of piscary appurtenant cannot be exploited for commercial purposes; the number of fish taken must be limited to the needs of the dominant tenement.[22]

5 *Duke of Sutherland* v. *Heathcote* [1892] 1 Ch. 475 at 484, *per* Lindley L.J.
6 *Manning* v. *Wasdale* (1836) 5 A. & E. 758 at 764.
7 *Race* v. *Ward, supra*, at p. 709.
8 *Wickham* v. *Hawker* (1840) 7 M. & W. 63.
9 See *Mason* v. *Hill* (1833) 5 B. & Ad. 1 at 24; *Manning* v. *Wasdale, supra*, at p. 764.
0 See J. S. Fiennes (1938) 2 Conv.(N.S.) 203.
1 *Ante*, pp. 418 *et seq.*
2 *Harris* v. *Earl of Chesterfield* [1911] A.C. 623.

2. A profit appendant. This is a profit annexed to land by operation of law; probably it exists only in the form of a common of
pasture.[23] If before the Statute *Quia Emptores* 1290 the lord of a
manor subinfeudated arable land to a freeholder, the freeholder
obtained, as appendant to the arable land, the right to pasture, on
the waste land of the manor, animals to plough and manure the land
granted to him.[24] This right was known as a common of pasture
appendant and was limited both as to the kind and number of
animals which could be depastured. It extended only to horses and
oxen (to plough the land) and cows and sheep (to manure it),[25] and
only to the number of these " levant and couchant " on the land to
which the right was appendant, *i.e.*, the number which the dominant
tenement was capable of maintaining during the winter.[26] It was
immaterial that the land was at any particular time used for purposes
temporarily rendering the maintenance of cattle impossible, for the
test was not the number actually supported but the number which the
land could be made to support.

No common appendant could be created after 1290, for a conveyance of freehold land in a manor after that date resulted in the
feoffee holding of the feoffor's lord, and the land passed out of the
manor altogether.[27]

3. A profit pur cause de vicinage. This exists only in the form of
a common of pasture. If two adjoining commons are open to each
other, there is a common *pur cause de vicinage* if the cattle put on
one common by the commoners have always been allowed to stray to
the other common and vice versa.[28] The claim fails if in the past the
cattle have been driven off one common by the commoners thereof,[29]
or if the commons have been fenced off,[30] or if the two commons are
not contiguous to each other, even if they are separated only by a
third common.[31]

4. A profit in gross. This is a profit, whether several or in common, exercisable by the owner independently of his ownership of
land; there is no dominant tenement. Thus a right to take fish from

[23] See 4 Halsbury (2nd ed. 1932) 552; but see Tudor L.C.R.P. 713–716.
[24] *Earl of Dunraven* v. *Llewellyn* (1850) 15 Q.B. 791 at 810.
[25] *Tyrringham's Case* (1584) 4 Co.Rep. 36b at 37a.
[26] *Robertson* v. *Hartopp* (1889) 43 Ch.D. 484 at 516.
[27] *Ante*, p. 12.
[28] *Pritchard* v. *Powell* (1845) 10 Q.B. 589 at 603.
[29] *Heath* v. *Elliott* (1838) 4 Bing.N.C. 388.
[30] *Tyrringham's Case* (1584) 4 Co.Rep. 36b.
[31] *Commissioners of Sewers* v. *Glasse* (1874) L.R. 19 Eq. 134.

a canal without stint (*i.e.*, without limit) can exist as a profit in gross,[32] but not, as already seen, as a profit appurtenant.[33] A profit in gross is an interest in land which will pass under a will or intestacy or can be sold or dealt with in any of the usual ways.

B. Distinctions between Profits à Prendre and Certain Analogous Rights

I. QUASI-PROFITS

Similar principles apply here as in the case of easements.[34]

II. OTHER NATURAL RIGHTS

The same applies.[35] An example is the right of a riparian owner to the unimpeded passage of fish from neighbouring portions of the stream.[36]

III. PUBLIC RIGHTS

The public right which most closely resembles a profit is the right of the public to fish in the sea and all tidal waters. However, since in theory the right is the Crown's, it was formerly possible for the Crown to grant to an individual the exclusive right to fish in a specified part of the sea or tidal waters; such a franchise was known as a free fishery.[37] In short, the public may fish in all tidal waters except a free fishery. But it has been held that the effect of *Magna Carta* 1215 was to prevent the Crown from creating any new free fisheries,[38] although any already existing remain valid and transferable to this day.

The right to fish in non-tidal waters is dealt with below.[39]

IV. RIGHTS OF FLUCTUATING BODIES

There can be no custom for a fluctuating body of persons to take a profit.[40] The reason is said to be that otherwise the subject-matter would be destroyed.[41] However, if in fact such a right has

---

[32] *Staffordshire & Worcestershire Canal Navigation* v. *Bradley* [1912] 1 Ch. 91.
[33] *Ante*, p. 427.
[34] *Ante*, pp. 420, 422.
[35] *Ante*, p. 422.
[36] See *Barker* v. *Faulkner* (1898) 79 L.T. 24.
[37] 3 Cru.Dig. 261; see, *e.g.*, *Stephens* v. *Snell* [1939] 3 All E.R. 622.
[38] *Malcolmson* v. *O'Dea* (1863) 10 H.L.C. 593 at 618; but see Theobald, *Land*, 58 *et seq.*
[39] *Post*, p. 459.
[40] *Alfred F. Beckett Ltd.* v. *Lyons* [1967] Ch. 449.
[41] *Race* v. *Ward* (1855) 4 E. & B. 702 at 705, 709.

been enjoyed for a long time, the courts will endeavour to find a legal origin for it. Two methods have been evolved.

1. Presumed incorporation by Crown grant. The reason why a fluctuating body cannot own a profit is that the body is not a legal person to which a grant could be made.[42] However, the Crown is able to incorporate any body of persons (*i.e.,* make them into a corporation), and so could, for example, grant a charter to a village making it a city or borough. Consequently there is nothing to prevent the Crown from making a grant of a profit to the inhabitants of a district and providing therein that for the purposes of the grant they should be treated as a corporation, though for other purposes they remain unincorporated. In fact, such grants have been made but rarely.[43] Their chief importance is that the court will presume that a grant of rights of this kind owned by the Crown at the time of the supposed grant has been made, provided—

(a) long enjoyment is proved, and

(b) those claiming the grant, and their predecessors, have always regarded themselves as a corporation and have acted as such as regards the right, as by holding meetings or appointing some officer to supervise the right.[44]

2. Presumed charitable trust. Even when the court cannot presume incorporation by Crown grant because the claimants have not acted as a corporation, if long enjoyment is shown the court may be able to find a legal origin for the right by presuming a grant of the profit to some corporation, subject to a trust or condition that the corporation should allow the claimants to exercise the right claimed. Thus in *Goodman* v. *Mayor of Saltash*[45] the free inhabitants of certain ancient tenements had for two hundred years enjoyed an oyster fishery from Candlemas (February 2) to Easter Eve each year. This right had been shared by the local corporation, which had enjoyed the right all the year round from time immemorial. The House of Lords refused to presume a grant incorporating the inhabitants for the purpose of the grant, but held that the corporation was entitled to a profit subject to a trust or condition in favour of the free inhabitants.

---

[42] *Fowler* v. *Dale* (1594) Cro.Eliz. 362.
[43] See, *e.g., Willingale* v. *Maitland* (1866) L.R. 3 Eq. 103.
[44] See *Re Free Fishermen of Faversham* (1887) 36 Ch.D. 329 ; *Lord Rivers* v. *Adams* (1878) 3 Ex.D. 361.
[45] (1882) 7 App.Cas. 633.

Sect. 3. Acquisition of Easements and Profits

An easement or profit can exist as a legal interest in land only if—

(i) it is held for an interest equivalent to a fee simple absolute in possession or term of years absolute [46]; and

(ii) it is created either by statute, deed or prescription.

A document not under seal cannot create a legal easement or profit,[47] although if made for value it may create a valid equitable easement or profit. Similarly, an oral agreement for value may create an equitable easement or profit if supported by a sufficient act of part performance, such as acting upon the rights granted.[48]

The various methods of acquisition must now be considered.

A. By Statute

Easements created by statute are most frequently found in the case of local Acts of Parliament, *e.g.*, an Act giving a right of support to a canal constructed under statutory powers.

B. By Express Reservation or Grant

When a landowner sells part of his land and retains the rest, he may reserve easements or profits over the part sold, and grant the purchaser rights over the land retained. Today, these transactions can be achieved quite simply, but this has not always been the case.

1. Express reservation. Before 1926, a legal easement or profit could not be created by a simple reservation in favour of the grantor. Two methods were available, however.

(a) *Execution by grantee*: the conveyance reserved the right to the grantor and the grantee executed the conveyance. Such a conveyance operated as a conveyance to the grantee followed by the re-grant of the easement or profit by the grantee to the grantor.[49] The effect of a simple reservation not executed by the grantee was merely to create an equitable easement or profit.[50]

(b) *Executed use*: the grantor conveyed the land to X and his heirs to the use that the grantor should have a legal easement or profit, and subject thereto, to the use of the grantee and his heirs. This method was effective if the conveyance was executed after 1881,

---

[46] *Ante*, p. 76.
[47] *Duke of Somerset* v. *Fogwell* (1826) 5 B. & C. 875.
[48] See, *e.g.*, *Mason* v. *Clarke* [1955] A.C. 778; *ante*, pp. 323 *et seq.*
[49] *Durham & Sunderland Ry.* v. *Walker* (1842) 2 Q.B. 940 at 967.
[50] *May* v. *Belleville* [1905] 2 Ch. 605.

for by the Conveyancing Act 1881 [51] the use relating to the easement or profit was duly executed; the use relating to the land was executed by the Statute of Uses 1535 in the usual way.[52]

After 1925 the second method is no longer available, for both the Statute of Uses 1535 and the Conveyancing Act 1881 have been repealed. It is no longer necessary to employ the first method, for the Law of Property Act 1925, s. 65, has provided that the reservation of a legal estate or interest shall be effective at law without any execution of the conveyance by the grantee.

2. Express grant. The ordinary case of an easement or profit created by the express words of a deed needs no discussion. In certain cases, however, an easement or profit will be created by express grant even though no mention of an easement or profit appears in any deed. The Law of Property Act 1925, s. 62 (1),[53] provides that any conveyance made after 1881 shall, subject to any contrary intention expressed in the conveyance,[54] operate to convey with the land all privileges, easements, rights and advantages appertaining or reputed to appertain to the land or part of it. Thus if the owner of a house and an adjoining field sells the house, the purchaser takes all rights which appertain or are reputed to appertain to it; consequently, if there is a footpath over the field used as a means of access to the house, the purchaser will take an easement of way by way of express grant as part of his conveyance.[55] Again, if a landlord grants his tenant a mere licence to use a coal shed for domestic purposes,[56] or to go through the landlord's house to reach the premises demised,[57] a subsequent conveyance to the tenant will operate to grant him the right as an easement. But the section will not elevate into easements or profits rights which cannot exist as such,[58] or create rights which the grantor had no power to create by express grant. The section is further discussed below.[59]

C. By Implied Reservation or Grant

1. Implied reservation. A grant is normally construed against the grantor and in favour of the grantee. Further, a grantor must not

---

[51] s. 62.   [52] *Ante*, p. 67.
[53] Replacing C.A. 1881, s. 6 (1): see also L.P.A. 1925, s. 62 (2).
[54] L.P.A. 1925, s. 62 (4).
[55] But consider *Long* v. *Gowlett* [1923] 2 Ch. 177.
[56] *Wright* v. *Macadam* [1949] 2 K.B. 744.
[57] *Goldberg* v. *Edwards* [1950] Ch. 247.
[58] *International Tea Stores Co.* v. *Hobbs* [1903] 2 Ch. 165 at 172.
[59] *Post*, pp. 435, 436.

derogate from his grant. Consequently, the general rule is that no easements will be implied in favour of a grantor; if he wishes to reserve any easements he must do so expressly.[60] To this rule there are two exceptions.

(a) *Easements of necessity.* If a grantor grants the whole of a plot of land except a piece in the middle which is completely surrounded by the part granted, there is implied in favour of the part retained a way of necessity over the part granted, for otherwise there would be no means of access to the land retained.[61] The former owner of both plots of land may select the particular way to be enjoyed, provided it is a convenient way[62]; once selected, the route cannot subsequently be changed.[63] A way of necessity will be implied even if some of the surrounding land belongs to third parties; but it is essential that the necessity should exist at the time of the grant and not merely arise subsequently.[64] Necessity is not confined to access, but extends to any facility, *e.g.*, a ventilation shaft, without which the premises cannot be used for the purpose for which it is the common intention they should be used.[65]

(b) *Intended easements.* Easements required to carry out the common intention of the parties will be implied in favour of the grantor even though not expressed in the conveyance. Thus on the grant of one of two houses supported by each other, the mutual grant and reservation of easements of support will be implied if (as is usual) such an intention can be inferred.[66]

2. Implied grant. If the owner of two plots conveys one of them, certain easements over the land retained are implied in favour of the land conveyed. The express grant of the land is said to be accompanied by the implied grant of the easements. Rights which will arise by implied grant are as follows:

(a) *Easements of necessity,* and

(b) *Intended easements.* The rules which apply in these two cases are similar to those in the case of implied reservation.[67]

(c) *Ancillary easements, i.e.,* easements necessary for the enjoy-

[60] *Wheeldon* v. *Burrows* (1879) 12 Ch.D. 31 at 49.
[61] *Pinnington* v. *Galland* (1853) 9 Exch. 1.
[62] See *Pearson* v. *Spencer* (1861) 1 B. & S. 571 at 585 ; affd. (1863) 3 B. & S. 761.
[63] *Deacon* v. *South Eastern Ry.* (1889) 61 L.T. 377.
[64] *Midland Ry.* v. *Miles* (1886) 33 Ch.D. 632.
[65] *Wong* v. *Beaumont Property Trust Ltd.* [1965] 1 Q.B. 173.
[66] *Richards* v. *Rose* (1853) 9 Exch. 221 ; contrast *Re Webb's Lease* [1951] Ch. 808.
[67] *Supra.*

ment of some right expressly granted. Thus if there is a grant of an easement of the right to draw water from a spring, a right of way to the spring will be implied.[68]

(d) *Easements within the Rule in Wheeldon* v. *Burrows.*[69] In *Wheeldon* v. *Burrows* it was laid down that upon the grant of part of a tenement, there would pass to the grantee as easements all quasi-easements over the land retained which—

    (i) were continuous and apparent,

    (ii) were necessary to the reasonable enjoyment of the land granted, and

    (iii) had been, and were at the time of the grant, used by the grantor for the benefit of the part granted.

A " continuous " easement is one giving the right to do some act of a continuous and constant nature. An " apparent " easement is one which is evidenced by some sign on the servient tenement discoverable on a careful inspection by a person ordinarily conversant with the subject.[70] Thus a drain into which water from the eaves of a house runs,[71] a watercourse through visible pipes,[72] and windows enjoying light,[73] all indicate the existence of continuous and apparent easements. On the other hand, a right to take water from a neighbour's pump from time to time [74] or a right to project the bowsprit of ships when in dock over the land of another [75] have been held to be outside the meaning of " continuous and apparent " easements. Rights of way do not in general fall within the definition, but a way over a made road, or one which betrays its presence by some indication such as a worn track, will pass under the rule in *Wheeldon* v. *Burrows.*[76]

These rules relating to implied grant apply also to cases where the grantor, instead of retaining any land himself, makes simultaneous grants to two or more grantees. Each grantee obtains the same easements over the land of the other as he would have obtained if the grantor had retained it [77]; and similarly for two or more gifts by the same will.[78]

---

[68] *Pwllbach Colliery Co. Ltd.* v. *Woodman* [1915] A.C. 634 at 646.
[69] (1879) 12 Ch.D. 31.
[70] *Pyer* v. *Carter* (1857) 1 H. & N. 916 at 922.
[71] *Pyer* v. *Carter* (1857) 1 H. & N. 916.
[72] *Watts* v. *Kelson* (1870) 6 Ch.App. 166.
[73] *Phillips* v. *Low* [1892] 1 Ch. 47 at 53.
[74] *Polden* v. *Bastard* (1865) L.R. 1 Q.B. 156.
[75] *Suffield* v. *Brown* (1864) 4 De G.J. & S. 185.
[76] See *Hansford* v. *Jago* [1921] 1 Ch. 322.
[77] *Swansborough* v. *Coventry* (1832) 2 M. & S. 362.
[78] *Schwann* v. *Cotton* [1916] 2 Ch. 459.

IMPLIED GRANT AND SECTION 62 OF THE LAW OF PROPERTY ACT 1925

The importance of the rules relating to implied grant has been considerably lessened by the Law of Property Act 1925, s. 62.[79] The width of section 62 (" all . . . rights . . . appertaining or reputed to appertain . . .") contrasts with the limited provisions of implied grants, so that the latter might seem to be superseded by the former. However, this is not the case for the following reasons.

(a) *Profits.* The rules relating to implied grant, from their very nature, are hardly applicable to profits *à prendre*: but section 62 applies to profits.[80] In this respect, section 62 is wider than the rules relating to implied grant, although in the next two respects it is narrower.

(b) *Conveyances.* The rules relating to implied grant apply to all conveyances: section 62 applies only to conveyances made after 1881.[81]

(c) *Other dispositions.* The rules relating to implied grant apply both to conveyances and to contracts, as well as to gifts by will [82]: section 62, however, applies only to " conveyances," a word which is defined to include (*inter alia*) mortgages, leases and assents, but which does not include a mere contract, *e.g.*, for a lease for over three years or for the sale of a fee simple.[83] Thus on the grant of a lease for seven years in writing, the tenant can claim only the easements which fall within the doctrine of implied grant; because the lease is not by deed, and so is not a " conveyance," section 62 does not apply.[84]

(d) *Contracts.* It will be seen from the preceding paragraph that a conveyance will sometimes convey more than the purchaser is entitled to under his contract. If a contract is silent on the question of easements, the purchaser is entitled to have conveyed to him with the land only those rights which fall within the rules relating to implied grant. If a conveyance which is silent as to easements is then executed, it may operate by virtue of section 62 to convey to the purchaser rights which are not within the comparatively narrow scope of implied grant but which fall within the section. Thus a non-apparent way may be outside the doctrine of implied grant but within

---

[79] *Ante*, p. 432.
[80] *White* v. *Williams* [1922] 1 K.B. 727; and see M. & W. 831–837.
[81] L.P.A. 1925, s. 62 (6).
[82] *Schwann* v. *Cotton* [1916] 2 Ch. 459.
[83] *Re Peck and the School Board for London* [1893] 2 Ch. 315.
[84] *Borman* v. *Griffith* [1930] 1 Ch. 493.

section 62.[85] In such a case, the vendor is entitled to insist upon the conveyance being so worded as to limit the rights conveyed to those to which the purchaser is entitled under the contract.[86] If the conveyance has already been executed, he may have it rectified to produce this result.[87] In short, in the absence of any other agreement, the rules relating to implied grant form the measure of what a purchaser is entitled to have conveyed to him: section 62 will sometimes convey to him more than he is entitled to, but then the vendor is entitled to have matters put right.

D. *By Presumed Grant, or Prescription*

I. GENERAL PRINCIPLES

The basis of prescription is that if long enjoyment of a lawful right is shown, the court will uphold the right by presuming that it had a lawful origin, *i.e.*, that there once was an actual grant of the right, even though it is impossible to produce any evidence of such a grant. However, it is not enough to show long user by itself; user of a particular kind is required. There are three types of prescription, namely, prescription at common law, prescription under the doctrine of lost modern grant, and prescription under the Prescription Act 1832. Except so far as the Act otherwise provides, a claim to an easement or profit under any head must be supported by user complying with the following conditions.

1. User as of right: the user must be as of right, which means that it must have been enjoyed *nec vi, nec clam, nec precario* (without force, without secrecy, without permission).[88] The claimant must show that he has used the right as if he were entitled to it. If, of course, the servient owner has given the claimant the right to use the easement or profit claimed, so that there has been an actual grant of such a right, the user is not *precario,* and the claimant can rely upon his grant without resorting to prescription. But if the claimant has been given permission to use the right claimed " until further notice " or has had to seek permission anew each year, the

---

[85] See *Ward* v. *Kirkland* [1967] Ch. 194.
[86] *Re Walmsley & Shaw's Contract* [1917] 1 Ch. 93.
[87] Consider *Clark* v. *Barnes* [1929] 2 Ch. 368.
[88] *Solomon* v. *Mystery of Vintners* (1859) 4 H. & N. 585 at 602 (common law prescription); *Sturges* v. *Bridgman* (1879) 11 Ch.D. 852 at 863 (lost modern grant); Prescription Act 1832, ss. 1, 2, and *Tickle* v. *Brown* (1836) 4 A. & E. 369 at 382 (prescription under the Act); and see M. & W. 837–840.

user is *precario* and no easement or profit can rise therefrom by prescription.

Evidence that the user was not of right may appear in a number of ways. Thus if the servient owner has taken steps to resist the user, as by issuing a summons or by making continuous and unmistakable protests,[89] there is evidence that the user was not of right. Again, if a dock has been supported by invisible rods sunk under the servient tenement,[90] or there have been intermittent and secret discharges of injurious chemicals into a sewer,[91] the user is *clam* and no easement can be claimed. Similarly, if applications for permission to use a way have been made by the claimant from time to time,[92] or he has made annual payments for his enjoyment, there is evidence that the user was *precario*, for such acts are inconsistent with the claimant having a right to the easement or profit claimed.

User during unity of possession, *i.e,* while the claimant was in possession of both dominant and servient tenements, is not user as of right,[93] and the same applies to user under the mistaken belief that the claimant was entitled to the servient tenement [94] or that he had the temporary permission of the landlord. But proof that the claimant exercised his right under the mistaken belief that a valid easement or profit had already been granted to him will not prevent the user from being as of right.[95] The principle involved is that the right must have been exercised *qua* easement or profit and not, for example, under any actual or supposed right of an occupant of both tenements.

2. User in fee simple: the user must be by or on behalf of a fee simple owner against a fee simple owner who both knows of the user and is able to resist it. In general, only easements or profits in fee simple can be acquired by prescription.[96] An easement or profit for life or for years, for example, may be expressly granted but cannot be acquired by prescription, for the basis of prescription is a presumed grant by the owner of the servient tenement, and only a grant in fee simple will be presumed. Consequently the claimant must show either that he is the fee simple owner himself or that he claims on behalf of the fee simple owner. A tenant under a lease must thus prescribe on

[89] *Dalton* v. *Angus & Co.* (1881) 6 App.Cas. 740 at 786.
[90] *Union Lighterage Co.* v. *London Graving Dock Co.* [1902] 2 Ch. 557.
[91] *Liverpool Corporation* v. *H. Coghill & Son Ltd.* [1918] 1 Ch. 307.
[92] *Monmouth Canal Co.* v. *Harford* (1834) 1 Cr.M. & R. 614.
[93] *Bright* v. *Walker* (1834) 1 Cr.M. & R. 211 at 219.
[94] *Lyell* v. *Lord Hothfield* [1914] 3 K.B. 911.
[95] *Earl de la Warr* v. *Miles* (1881) 17 Ch.D. 535.
[96] See, *e.g., Kilgour* v. *Gaddes* [1904] 1 K.B. 457 at 460.

behalf of the fee simple owner and not merely on his own behalf.[97]
Similarly, enjoyment of a right over land held under a lease or life
tenancy is in general not sufficient.[98] The whole law of prescription
rests upon acquiescence: and " I cannot imagine any case of acquiescence in which there is not shown to be in the servient owner: 1, a
knowledge of the acts done; 2, a power in him to stop the acts or to sue
in respect of them; and 3, an abstinence on his part from the exercise
of such power." [99] If A has granted a lease of his land and a neighbour starts to use a way over it, A may be ignorant of this user, and
even if he knows of it he usually has no power to prevent it during the
term of the lease. Again, if A leases two plots of his land to two
tenants, one tenant cannot prescribe for an easement against the
other, for otherwise the result would be that A would acquire an easement over his own land.[1]

There are certain modifications of this rule. First, profits in gross
may be acquired by prescription at common law,[2] or under the doctrine of lost modern grant. In this case, the right is not claimed in
respect of any estate but on behalf of the claimant personally. Such
prescription is known as prescription in gross. The claimant must
show that he and his ancestors have enjoyed the right,[3] instead of
showing that he and his predecessors in title to the dominant tenement
have enjoyed it; prescription in gross must be contrasted with prescription " in the *que* estate " where the user is by the claimant and
" *ceux que estate il ad* " [4] (those whose estate he has). But there can
be no prescription in gross for easements (which cannot exist in gross),
nor can a profit in gross be claimed under the Prescription Act 1832.[5]
Secondly, certain modifications are made in claims under the Prescription Act 1832. Thus under the Act easements of light can be acquired
by one tenant against another tenant of the same landlord.[6] This is
anomalous; it applies only to light and only to claims under the Act.
Other modifications under the Act will be noted later.

3. Continuous user: the claimant must show a continuity of
enjoyment. This is interpreted reasonably; in the case of easements of
way it is clearly not necessary to show ceaseless user by day and

---

[97] *Gateward's Case* (1607) 6 Co.Rep. 59b; *Dawnay* v. *Cashford* (1697) Carth. 432.
[98] *Roberts* v. *James* (1903) 89 L.T. 282.
[99] *Dalton* v. *Angus & Co.* (1881) 6 App.Cas. 740 at 773, 774, *per* Fry J.
[1] *Kilgour* v. *Gaddes* [1904] 1 K.B. 457.
[2] *Johnson* v. *Barnes* (1873) L.R. 8 C.P. 527.
[3] *Welcome* v. *Upton* (1840) 6 M. & W. 536.
[4] Litt. 183.
[5] *Shuttleworth* v. *Le Fleming* (1865) 19 C.B.(N.S.) 687.
[6] See *post*, p. 449.

night. User whenever circumstances require it is normally sufficient,[7] provided the intervals are not excessive.

The three types of prescription must now be considered in turn.

II. PRESCRIPTION AT COMMON LAW

1. Length of user. User of the nature discussed above must be shown to have continued since time immemorial, namely, since 1189. If this is shown, the court presumes that a grant was made prior to that date. The reason for 1189 being adopted is that from time to time limits were fixed within which actions for the recovery of land were to be brought. Instead of adopting a specified period of years, events such as the beginning of the reign of Henry I or the last voyage of Henry II to Normandy were periodically selected. The last choice to be made was the beginning of the reign of Richard I, namely, 1189. These periods originally had nothing to do with prescription, but the courts adopted the last date as the period of time immemorial upon which all claims based on custom or prescription depended. Modern legislation has altered the rule for claims to land, but 1189 remained the essential date for custom and prescription.[8]

2. Presumption. It is clearly impossible in most cases to show continuous user since 1189, and so the courts adopted the rule that if unexplained user for 20 years or more is shown, the court will presume that that user has continued since 1189; user for less than 20 years requires supporting circumstances to raise the presumption.[9] However, this presumption may be met by showing that at some time since 1189 the right could not or did not exist.[10] Thus an easement of light cannot be claimed by prescription at common law for a building which is shown to have been erected since 1189.[11] Consequently it was virtually impossible to establish a claim to light at common law, and many claims based on enjoyment lasting for centuries were liable to be defeated by evidence that there could have been no enjoyment of the light in 1189. Again, if it could be shown that at any time since 1189 the dominant and servient tenements had been in the same ownership and occupation, any easement or profit would have been extinguished and so any claim at common law would fail.[12]

---

[7] *Dare* v. *Heathcote* (1856) 25 L.J.Ex. 245.
[8] See generally *Bryant* v. *Foot* (1867) L.R. 2 Q.B. 161 at 180, 181.
[9] *Bealey* v. *Shaw* (1805) 6 East 208 at 215.
[10] *Hulbert* v. *Dale* [1909] 2 Ch. 570 at 577.
[11] *Duke of Norfolk* v. *Arbuthnot* (1880) 5 C.P.D. 390.
[12] See *post*, p. 452.

To meet this state of affairs, the courts invented what has been called the " revolting fiction " [13] of the lost modern grant.

III. LOST MODERN GRANT

1. The presumption. The weakness of common law prescription was the liability to failure if it was shown that user had begun at some date after 1189. The doctrine of lost modern grant avoided this by presuming from long user that an actual grant of the easement or profit was made at some time subsequent to 1189 but prior to the user supporting the claim, and that unfortunately this grant had been lost.[14] " Juries were first told that from user, during living memory, or even during 20 years, they might presume a lost grant or deed; next they were recommended to make such presumption; and lastly, as the final consummation of judicial legislation, it was held that a jury should be told, not only that they might, but also that they were bound to presume the existence of such a lost grant, although neither judge nor jury, nor anyone else, had the shadow of a belief that any such instrument had ever really existed." [15] In their anxiety to find a legal origin for a right of which there had been open and uninterrupted enjoyment for a long period, unexplained in any other way, the courts presumed that a grant had been made, and so made it immaterial that enjoyment had not continued since 1189. 20 years' user normally sufficed to raise the presumption.[16]

2. Evidence. Rather stronger evidence of user is required to induce the court to presume a lost modern grant than is required for prescription at common law.[17] Further, the doctrine can be invoked only if something prevents the application of common law prescription.[18] Since the doctrine is admittedly a fiction, the claimant will not be ordered to furnish particulars of the fictitious grant (*e.g.*, as to the parties) nor even whether the grant is alleged to have been made before or after a particular date.[19] Probably the presumption cannot be rebutted by evidence that no grant was in fact made. But the claim is defeated by proof that during the entire period when the grant could have been made there was nobody who could lawfully have made it.[20]

[13] *Angus & Co.* v. *Dalton* (1877) 3 Q.B.D. 85 at 94, *per* Lush J.
[14] See, *e.g.*, *Dalton* v. *Angus & Co.* (1881) 6 App.Cas. 740 at 813.
[15] *Bryant* v. *Foot* (1867) L.R. 2 Q.B. 161 at 181, *per* Cockburn C.J.
[16] *Penwarden* v. *Ching* (1829) Moo. & M. 400.
[17] *Tilbury* v. *Silva* (1890) 45 Ch.D. 98 at 123.
[18] *Bryant* v. *Lefever* (1879) 4 C.P.D. 172 at 177.
[19] *Gabriel Wade & English Ltd.* v. *Dixon & Cardus Ltd.* [1937] 3 All E.R. 900.
[20] *Neaverson* v. *Peterborough R.D.C.* [1902] 1 Ch. 557.

Thus the court has refused to presume a lost grant of a way where the land had been in strict settlement (under which there was no power to make a grant) from the time when the user began down to the time of action.[21]

IV. PRESCRIPTION ACT 1832

1. The Act. The Prescription Act 1832 was passed to meet the difficulties and uncertainties mentioned above, and in particular the difficulty of persuading juries to presume grants to have been made when they knew this was not the case. It is not well drafted, but in many cases it has substituted certainty for uncertainty. The Act makes special provisions for easements of light, so that the other rights under the Act will be dealt with first, and then easements of light.

2. Easements (other than light) and profits. The Act is perhaps best dealt with by giving a summary of the effect of each section and annotating the sections in groups.

Section 1: No claim to a profit shall be defeasible by showing that user commenced after 1189 if 30 years' uninterrupted enjoyment as of right is shown. If 60 years' uninterrupted enjoyment as of right is shown, the right is deemed to be absolute unless it has been enjoyed by written consent or agreement.

Section 2 makes exactly similar provisions for all easements except the easement of light, the periods, however, being 20 and 40 years respectively instead of 30 and 60.

Section 3 concerns the easement of light and is dealt with below.[22]

Section 4: All periods of enjoyment under the Act are those periods next before some action in which the claim is brought into question. Further, no act is to be deemed an interruption until it has been submitted to or acquiesced in for one year after the party interrupted had notice both of the interruption and of the person making it.

The chief points to note on this group of sections are as follows.

(a) "*Next before some action.*" The Act does not say that an easement or profit comes into existence after 20, 30, 40, or 60 years' user in the abstract; all periods under the Act are those next before

---

[21] *Roberts* v. *James* (1903) 89 L.T. 282.
[22] *Post*, pp. 447 *et seq.*

some action in which the right is questioned. Thus until some action is brought, there is a mere inchoate right to an easement or profit, however long the user.[23] Further, even if there has been user for longer than the statutory periods, the vital period is always that period (*e.g.*, of 20 years) next before some action. Thus if user commenced 40 years ago but ceased five years ago, a claim will fail if the action is commenced today, for during the 20 or 40 years next before the action, there has not been continuous user.[24] Similarly a claim under the Act will fail if there had been unity of possession for a substantial period immediately before the action, for there has not been user *as an easement* during the whole of the vital period.[25]

(b) "*Without interruption.*" The user must be "without interruption"; but a special meaning is given to "interruption." If D has used a way over S's land for over 20 years, and then a barrier is erected barring his way, D can still succeed in establishing an easement, provided that at the time an action is brought he has not acquiesced in the obstruction for one year after he has known both of the obstruction and of the person responsible for it.[26] "Interruption" means some hostile obstruction and not mere non-user.[27] User of a common is not interrupted if it ceases for reasons of animal health, or owing to the requisitioning of the common by a government department.[28] A protest against an interruption normally endures for some while after it has been made, so that there is no acquiescence in an interruption for a year merely because a year has elapsed since the last protest was made.[29]

User for 19 years and a day followed by 364 days' interruption is thus, for the purposes of the Act, 20 years' user upon which a claim will succeed. But this does not mean that 364 days is in fact deducted from the periods in the Act. To say that user for 19 years and a day is as good as user for 20 years is not accurate for—

(i) no action can be brought to establish an easement if only 19 years and a fraction have elapsed since the user began,[30] whereas after 20 years' user, an action can be started forthwith; and

[23] *Hyman* v. *Van den Bergh* [1908] 1 Ch. 167.
[24] *Parker* v. *Mitchell* (1840) 11 A. & E. 788.
[25] *Aynsley* v. *Glover* (1875) 10 Ch.App. 283.
[26] *Seddon* v. *Bank of Bolton* (1882) 19 Ch.D. 462.
[27] *Smith* v. *Baxter* [1900] 2 Ch. 138 at 143.
[28] Commons Registration Act 1965, s. 16.
[29] *Davies* v. *Du Paver* [1953] 1 Q.B. 184.
[30] *Lord Battersea* v. *Commissioners of Sewers for the City of London* [1895] 2 Ch. 708.

(ii) if an interruption commences after user for 19 years and a day, not until it has lasted for 364 days can the dominant owner commence an action to establish his easement, for not until then is there a period of 20 years.[31] If he waits another day, the interruption will have lasted for a year and his claim must fail. Thus he has only one day on which to issue his writ, whereas if he has enjoyed user for 20 years when an interruption commences, he may issue his writ on any of the next 364 days.

(c) *User " as of right."* Sections 1 and 2 provide that the enjoyment must be by a " person claiming right thereto," and section 5 provides that it is sufficient to plead enjoyment " as of right." The effect is that claims under the Act must be based on user which would have sufficed at common law, *i.e., nec vi, nec clam, nec precario.*[32]

At common law, any consent or agreement by the servient owner, whether oral or written, rendered the user *precario.* Under the Act, this rule applies to the shorter periods (20 years for easements, 30 years for profits), but a special meaning is given to *precario* in the case of longer periods (40 years for easements, 60 years for profits) by the provision that the right shall be absolute unless enjoyed by written consent or agreement. A mere oral consent given at the beginning of the period and not renewed will thus not defeat a claim based on one of the longer periods, although it would be fatal at common law. However, oral consents repeatedly given during a period will defeat a claim based even on the longer periods.[33]

(d) *Effect of consents.* The effect of consents may be summarised thus[34]:

(i) Any consents, whether oral or written, which have been given intermittently during the period make the user *precario* and defeat a claim based on either the shorter or longer periods.

(ii) A written consent given at the beginning of the user (and extending throughout) defeats a claim based on either the shorter or longer periods.

(iii) An oral consent given at the beginning of the user (and

---

[31] See, *e.g., Reilly* v. *Orange* [1955] 1 W.L.R. 616.
[32] *Gardner* v. *Hodgson's Kingston Brewery Co. Ltd.* [1903] A.C. 229 at 238, 239.
[33] *Gardner* v. *Hodgson's Kingston Brewery Co. Ltd.* [1903] A.C. 229.
[34] See *Tickle* v. *Brown* (1836) 4 A. & E. 369; *Healey* v. *Hawkins* [1968] 1 W.L.R. 1967.

extending throughout) defeats a claim based on the shorter periods but not a claim based on the longer periods.

If user commences by consent, the question whether it continues by consent is one of fact.[35]   In the case of a written consent or agreement, signature by the servient owner is not essential; one signed by the dominant owner or his leasehold tenant suffices.[36]

The remaining sections of the Act must now be dealt with.

Section 5 deals with pleadings.

Section 6 provides that enjoyment for less than the statutory periods shall give rise to no claim.   This does not prevent a lost grant being presumed from user for less than a statutory period if there is some evidence to support it in addition to the enjoyment.[37]

Section 7 provides that any period during which the servient tenant has been an infant, lunatic or tenant for life shall automatically be deducted from the shorter periods; further, the period during which an action is pending and actively prosecuted is also to be deducted.

Section 8 provides that if the servient tenement has been held under a " term of life, or any term of years exceeding three years from the granting thereof," the term shall be excluded in computing the period of 40 years in the case of a " way or other convenient [*sic*] watercourse or use of water," provided the claim is resisted by a reversioner upon the term within three years of its determination.

No more need be said about sections 5 and 6.   Sections 7 and 8 are complicated and can conveniently be dealt with together.   The following points should be noted.

(a) *Deduction.*   Where either section applies, the period deducted is excluded altogether when calculating the period next before action. Thus if there has been enjoyment of a profit for 45 years in all, consisting of 25 years' user against the fee simple owner, then 19 years against the life tenant, and then a further year against the fee simple owner, the claim fails, for by section 7 the period of the life tenancy is deducted when calculating the period next before action brought, and thus less than 30 years' user is left.   But if the user

---

[35] *Gaved* v. *Martyn* (1865) 19 C.B.(N.S.) 732; *Healey* v. *Hawkins* [1968] 1 W.L.R. 1967.

[36] *Hyman* v. *Van den Bergh* [1908] 1 Ch. 167.

[37] *Hanmer* v. *Chance* (1865) 4 De G.J. & Sm. 626 at 631.

continues for another four years, the claim would succeed, for there is 30 years' user consisting of 25 years before and 5 years after the life tenancy; since the period of the life tenancy is disregarded, the 30 years' period is, for the purposes of the Act, next before action within section 4.[38] The sections in effect connect the periods immediately before and after the period deducted, but they will not connect two periods separated in any other way, *e.g.*, by a period of unity of possession.[39]

(b) *Application.* Section 7 applies to the shorter periods both for easements and profits; but section 8 does not apply to profits at all, and applies to the longer period only in the case of easements of way " or other convenient watercourse or use of water." Possibly " convenient " is a misprint for " easement," and the phrase should read " or other easement, watercourse or use of water." If so, section 8 applies to all easements (except light): but the point is unsettled.[40]

(c) *Ambit.* Section 7 applies to the servient owner being an infant, lunatic or tenant for life: section 8 applies where the servient tenement has been held under a term for over three years, or for life. Thus a life tenancy can be deducted under both sections, but infancy or lunacy affect only the shorter periods. If D has enjoyed a way against S's land for 25 years, but S has been insane for the last 15 of those years, section 7 defeats D's claim. If D continues his user for another 15 years, however, his claim succeeds, even though S continues insane throughout.

Further, it should be noted that the only provision for deduction of leasehold terms is in section 8. Thus, where there had been user of a way for 20 years, the servient land being under lease for 15 of the 20 years, but free from any lease at the beginning and end of the period, an easement was established [41]: for section 7 makes no mention of leaseholds, and section 8 does not apply to the 20 years' period. It will be noted that here the user commenced against the fee simple owner who, by leasing the land, voluntarily put it out of his power to resist the user: had the lease been granted before the user commenced and continued throughout, the position would have been different, for no user as against a fee simple owner able to resist it could be shown.[42] In short, a lease may affect a claim in two ways:

[38] *Clayton* v. *Corby* (1842) 2 Q.B. 813.
[39] *Onley* v. *Gardiner* (1838) 4 M. & W. 496.
[40] See *Laird* v. *Briggs* (1881) 19 Ch.D. 22 at 33.
[41] *Palk* v. *Shinner* (1852) 18 Q.B. 568.
[42] *Bright* v. *Walker* (1834) 1 Cr.M. & R. 211.

(i) by showing that there has been no user against a fee simple owner who knows of it and can resist it; and

(ii) by falling within the provisions of section 8 allowing deduction.

The first of these is a common law rule not affected by the Act; the second is a creature of the statute and can apply only to claims under the Act based on the 40 years' period.

(d) *Right to deduct.* In section 7, the provision for deduction is absolute: in section 8, it is conditional, the condition being that the reversioner shall resist the claim within three years of the determination of the term of years or life. Thus if the reversioner fails to resist the claim within the three years, he has no right of deduction. Further section 8 extends only to a reversioner and not to a remainderman,[43] so that it will rarely apply to the usual trusts of a settlement.

It will be seen from this that section 7 is wide in its scope, giving an absolute right of deduction from the shorter periods for both easements and profits; section 8, on the other hand, is very narrow, giving only a reversioner a conditional right of deduction from the 40 years' period in the case of (possibly) only two classes of easements.

(e) *Commons.* An additional right to deduct from both longer and shorter periods is available in the case of commons. Where during any period a right to graze animals could not be exercised for reasons of animal health or because the common was requisitioned by a government department, the time of non-user is to be left out of account.[44]

(f) *Difference between longer and shorter periods.* In the case of the shorter periods, the only benefits which the Act confers upon a claimant are that the period for which he must show user is clearly laid down, and that he cannot be defeated by proof that his enjoyment began after 1189. The nature of the user required is still substantially the same, so that the claimant must show continuous, uninterrupted user as of right by or on behalf of a fee simple owner against a fee simple owner who both knew of the user and could resist it.

In the case of the longer periods, however, although uninterrupted user as of right is expressly required, and easements can be acquired only on behalf of a fee simple owner, the Act provides that the right

---

[43] *Symons* v. *Leaker* (1885) 15 Q.B.D. 629.
[44] Commons Registration Act 1965, s. 16.

ecomes absolute after the required period next before action has lapsed. User against a fee simple owner who both knows of it and is able to resist it is therefore not required [45]; the only exceptions to this are those provided by section 8. Thus user of a way for 20 years against land held under a life tenancy will give no claim under the Act,[46] but user for 40 years will suffice, subject to section 8.[47] It seems, therefore, that although all prescription is, in general, founded upon the presumption of a grant, there is no need to presume a grant in the case of claims based on the longer periods under the Act. This is clearly so in the case of claims to light under the Act,[48] and in the case of other easements " forty years' user has the same effect which (under the third section) twenty years' user has as to light." [49] But the point cannot be regarded as settled, and the fact that *actual* enjoyment confers an easement of light, whereas user *as of right* is required for other easements, is some indication that it is light alone which requires no presumption of a grant.

The differences between the longer and the shorter periods may be summarised thus:

   (i) A presumption of a grant is required in the case of the shorter periods, though possibly not in the case of the longer periods.

  (ii) An oral consent given at the beginning of the period defeats a claim based on one of the shorter periods, but not one based on one of the longer periods.

 (iii) The shorter periods are subject to the provisions of section 7 but not section 8: the 40 years' period is subject to section 8 in the case of easements of way and water alone, it seems, but otherwise the longer periods are subject to neither section.

3. Easements of light. Easements of light are in some respects on a footing different from that of other rights under the Act. Section 3 provides in effect that after the actual enjoyment of the access of light to a dwelling-house, workshop or other building has continued for 20 years without interruption, the right is deemed absolute unless enjoyed by written consent or agreement. On the effect of this, the main points to note are the following.

  (a) *Resemblances.* Light resembles other rights claimed under the Act in that—

[45] *Wright* v. *Williams* (1836) 1 M. & W. 77.
[46] *Bright* v. *Walker* (1834) 1 Cr.M. & R. 211.
[47] *Wright* v. *Williams, supra,* not cited in *Davies* v. *Du Paver* [1953] 1 Q.B. 184.
[48] *Tapling* v. *Jones* (1865) 11 H.L.C. 290 at 304.
[49] *Dalton* v. *Angus & Co.* (1881) 6 App.Cas. 740 at 800, *per* Lord Selborne L.C.

(1) SECTION 4 APPLIES, so that the period in question is that nex[t] before action,[50] and with the modification noted below " interruption " has the same meaning as in other cases [51]; and

(2) WRITTEN CONSENT: the rules relating to written consent are th[e] same as for other claims under the Act.

(b) *Differences.* Light differs from other rights claimed under th[e] Act in the following respects.

(1) ONLY ONE PERIOD. There is only one period for light, namely 20 years. But the war of 1939–45 and war damage made it difficul[t] for some servient owners to protect their rights, *e.g.,* to rebuild, and s[o] the period was extended to 27 years if an action claiming the righ[t] was begun after July 13, 1958, but before 1963, or if an action for a[n] infringement before 1963 is begun after 1962.[52]

(2) DISABILITIES. Sections 7 and 8 do not apply.

(3) OBSTRUCTION. Wartime restrictions and later planning contro[l] made it difficult to interrupt the enjoyment of inchoate rights of ligh[t] with screens or other erections. Instead, a servient owner may no[w] provide a notional obstruction. He must first obtain from the Land[s] Tribunal a certificate either of exceptional urgency or that due notic[e] has been given to those likely to be affected. He may then register a[s] a land charge a notice identifying the dominant and servient tenement and specifying the size and position of the notional obstruction; an[d] for a year this notice takes effect as an obstruction known to an[d] acquiesced in by all concerned. While the notice is in force, th[e] dominant owner may sue for a declaration as if his light actually ha[d] been obstructed, and for the cancellation or variation of the registra[-] tion. Further, for this purpose he may treat his enjoyment as havin[g] begun a year earlier than it did; this avoids the " 19 years and a day " type of problem.[53]

(4) ACTUAL USER SUFFICES. User as of right is not required [54] actual enjoyment suffices, provided there has been no written consent[.] Thus the provision that written consent defeats the claim is the onl[y] fragment of *nec vi, nec clam, nec precario* which is left in claims t[o] light under the Act; oral consent is no bar, even though evidence[d] by annual payments.[55] But there must be enjoyment of the light *qu[a]* easement: enjoyment during unity of possession is not enough.[56]

[50] *Hyman* v. *Van den Bergh* [1908] 1 Ch. 167.
[51] *Smith* v. *Baxter* [1900] 2 Ch. 138. [52] Rights of Light Act 1959, s. 1.
[53] Rights of Light Act 1959, ss. 2, 3; S.I. 1959 Nos. 1732, 1733; and see *ante*, p. 442
[54] *Colls* v. *Home & Colonial Stores Ltd.* [1904] A.C. 179 at 205.
[55] *Plasterers' Co.* v. *Parish Clerks' Co.* (1851) 6 Exch. 630.
[56] *Ladyman* v. *Grave* (1871) 6 Ch.App. 763.

(5) NO GRANT. There is no need to presume a grant, because the Act provides that 20 years' actual enjoyment confers an absolute right [57]; in other words, it is not necessary to show user by or on behalf of one tenant in fee simple against another. Thus the mere fact that the servient tenement has been under lease for the whole period does not prevent the acquisition under the Act of an easement of light valid against the reversioner.[58] This has been taken to its logical conclusion, so that under the Act one tenant can acquire an easement of light over land occupied by another tenant of the same landlord,[59] or by the landlord himself.[60] In the former case, on the expiration of the lease of the servient tenement, the easement is effective against the landlord and all subsequent owners of the land.[61]

(6) CROWN NOT BOUND. Sections 1 and 2 mention the Crown: section 3 does not. A statute does not bind the Crown unless it so provides either expressly or by necessary implication,[62] and so an easement of light cannot be acquired under the Act against the Crown,[63] although other easements and profits can.

4. Limits to the Act. The Prescription Act 1832 does not enable claimants to establish as easements or profits rights which could not be established as such at common law. Thus a claim by the freemen and citizens of a town to enter land and hold races thereon on Ascension Day cannot be established under the Act.[64] Nor has the Act abolished the other methods of prescription. Consequently, it is usual to plead all three methods of prescription, although the claimant does this at his own risk as to costs, *e.g.*, if this form of pleading needlessly increases the other party's expenses.[65] If a claim is made solely under the Act, it is liable to be defeated by showing unity of possession at any time during the period [66]; this is not so under the doctrine of lost modern grant [67] or at common law.[68] Again, if the claim is made solely at common law, it will be defeated if it is shown that the enjoyment started after 1189. But as seen already, this would

---

[57] *Tapling* v. *Jones* (1865) 11 H.L.C. 290 at 304, 318.
[58] *Simper* v. *Foley* (1862) 2 J. & H. 564.
[59] *Morgan* v. *Fear* [1907] A.C. 429.
[60] *Foster* v. *Lyons & Co. Ltd.* [1927] 1 Ch. 219 at 227.
[61] *Morgan* v. *Fear, supra.*
[62] *Perry* v. *Eames* [1891] 1 Ch. 658 at 665.
[63] *Wheaton* v. *Maple & Co.* [1893] 3 Ch. 48.
[64] *Mounsey* v. *Ismay* (1865) 3 H. & C. 486.
[65] *Harris* v. *Jenkins* (1882) 22 Ch.D. 481 at 482.
[66] *Damper* v. *Bassett* [1901] 2 Ch. 350.
[67] *Hulbert* v. *Dale* [1909] 2 Ch. 570.
[68] *Dalton* v. *Angus & Co.* (1881) 6 App.Cas. 740 at 814.

not defeat a claim by lost modern grant or under the Act. Nor should a claim be based on lost modern grant alone, for the court will not presume a modern grant if the right can be established in any other way.[69] However, a method of prescription under which it is legally impossible for a claim to succeed should never be pleaded. Thus a profit in gross should not be claimed under the Act,[70] although it may be claimed by prescription at common law.[71]

Sect. 4. Extinguishment of Easements and Profits

A. By Statute

An Act of Parliament may extinguish an easement or profit expressly or by implication. Under this head must be considered the extinguishment of commons by approvement, by inclosure, and by failure to register.

1. Approvement. The lord of a manor had a common law right to " approve " the manorial waste over which the tenants exercised rights of pasture. Approvement was effected by the lord taking part of the waste for his separate enjoyment. The Statutes of Merton 1235[72] and Westminster II 1285[73] confirmed this practice, but obliged the lord to leave sufficient land for the commoners. The onus of proving sufficiency was on the lord, and there had to be enough pasture for all the animals which the commoners were entitled to turn out, and not merely for those in fact turned out in recent years.[74] Since the Commons Act 1876, a person seeking to approve a common otherwise than in accordance with the strict procedure for inclosures under that Act must advertise his intention in the local Press on three successive occasions[75]; and the Law of Commons Amendment Act 1893 makes the consent of the Minister of Housing and Local Government,[75a] given after holding a local inquiry, essential to approvement.[76]

2. Inclosure. Inclosure involves the discharge of the whole manorial waste from all rights of common, whereas approvement applies only to commons of pasture appendant or appurtenant, and discharges only part of the land. From the middle of the eighteenth

---

[69] *Gardner* v. *Hodgson's Kingston Brewery Co. Ltd.* [1903] A.C. 229 at 240.
[70] *Shuttleworth* v. *Le Fleming* (1865) 19 C.B.(N.S.) 687.
[71] *Johnson* v. *Barnes* (1873) L.R. 8 C.P. 527.   [72] c. 4.   [73] c. 46.
[74] *Robertson* v. *Hartopp* (1889) 43 Ch.D. 484.
[75] s. 31.   [75a] Or the Secretary of State for Wales.
[76] Law of Commons Amendment Act 1893, ss. 2, 3; S.I. 1965 No. 143; S.I. 1967 No. 156.

century, a large number of private inclosure Acts were passed. The policy of Parliament was to encourage the efficient production of food, which was hardly possible under the relics of the feudal system. The Inclosure (Consolidation) Act 1801 and the Inclosure Act 1845 facilitated inclosures, but public opinion was aroused by the disappearance of open spaces, and the Inclosure Act 1852 prevented inclosures being made without the consent of Parliament. An application must first be made to the Minister of Agriculture, Fisheries and Food, and if a prima facie case is made out, regard being had to the benefit of the neighbourhood, a local inquiry is held. A provisional order is then submitted to Parliament for confirmation.[77]

3. Registration. Rights of common may be lost through failure to register under the Commons Registration Act 1965. The Act came into force on January 2, 1967, and requires the registration with the appropriate local authority of all rights of common (other than rights held for a term of years or from year to year) within a period which has been fixed to expire on March 31, 1970.[78] At the end of that period, no unregistered rights of common will be exercisable.[79]

B. By Release

1. Express release. At law, a deed is required for an express release.[80] In equity, however, an informal release will be effective provided it would be inequitable for the dominant tenant to claim that the right still exists, as where he has orally consented to his light being obstructed and the servient tenant has spent money on erecting the obstruction.[81]

2. Implied release. If the dominant owner shows an intention to release an easement or profit, it will be extinguished by implied release. Mere non-user is never enough by itself: an intention to abandon the right must be shown.[82] Nevertheless, non-user for a long period may raise a presumption of abandonment, and 20 years will usually suffice.[83]

---

[77] Commons Act 1876, ss. 10–12.
[78] Commons Registration Act 1965, ss. 1 (1), 2 (1), 22 (1); S.I. 1966 Nos. 971, 1470. Applications for registration cannot be entertained if made after January 2, 1970.
[79] Commons Registration Act 1965, s. 1 (2).
[80] Co.Litt. 264b.
[81] *Waterlow* v. *Bacon* (1866) L.R. 2 Eq. 514.
[82] *Swan* v. *Sinclair* [1924] 1 Ch. 254; affd. [1925] A.C. 227.
[83] *Moore* v. *Rawson* (1824) 3 B. & C. 332 at 339.

It is a question of fact whether an act was intended as an abandonment. Alterations to the dominant tenement which make the enjoyment of an easement or profit impossible or unnecessary may show an intent to abandon the right. Thus if a mill to which an easement of water is appurtenant is demolished without any intent to replace it, the easement is released.[84] Similarly the demolition of a house to which an easement of light is appurtenant may amount to an implied release, unless it is intended to replace the house by another building.[85] It is not essential that the new windows should occupy exactly the same positions as the old, provided they receive substantially the same light[86]; the test is identity of light, not identity of aperture. Further, if the dominant tenement is so altered that the burden of the easement is substantially increased, the right may be extinguished altogether.[87]

C. By Unity of Ownership and Possession

If the dominant and servient tenements come into the ownership and possession of the same person, any easement[88] or profit[89] is extinguished. Unity of possession without unity of ownership is not enough[90]: the right is merely suspended until the unity of possession ceases. Similarly, unity of ownership without unity of possession effects no extinguishment[91]: the right continues until there is also unity of possession. Thus if both dominant and servient tenements are under lease, the easement or profit will not be extinguished merely by both leases being assigned to X, nor will it be extinguished merely by Y purchasing both reversions; but if both leases and both reversions become vested in Z, the right is gone.

Sect. 5. Species of Easements

A. Rights of Way

1. Extent of easements of way. An easement of way may be either general or limited. A general right of way is one which may be used by the owner of the dominant tenement at any time and in any

---

[84] *Liggins* v. *Inge* (1831) 7 Bing. 682 at 693.
[85] *Ecclesiastical Commissioners for England* v. *Kino* (1880) 14 Ch.D. 213.
[86] *Scott* v. *Pape* (1886) 31 Ch.D. 554.
[87] *Ankerson* v. *Connelly* [1906] 2 Ch. 544; affd. [1907] 1 Ch. 678.
[88] *Buckby* v. *Coles* (1814) 5 Taunt. 311.
[89] *Tyrringham's Case* (1584) 4 Co.Rep. 36b at 38a.
[90] *Canham* v. *Fisk* (1831) 2 Cr. & J. 126.
[91] *Richardson* v. *Graham* [1908] 1 K.B. 39.

manner. A limited right of way is one which is subject to some restriction. The restriction may be as to time, *e.g.*, a way which can be used only in the daytime,[92] or it may be as to the mode in which the way can be used, *e.g.*, a way limited to foot passengers, or to cattle and other animals in the charge of a drover, or to wheeled traffic,[93] and the like.

A right of way can normally be used only as a means of access to the dominant tenement. A right to pass over Plot A to reach Plot B cannot be used as a means of access to Plot C lying beyond Plot B.[94]

In the absence of a contrary agreement or special circumstances, it is for the grantee of a way, not the grantor, to construct the way and to repair it when constructed[95]; the grantee may enter the servient tenement for these purposes.[96] If the way becomes impassable, there is no right to deviate from it unless the servient owner has obstructed it.[97]

2. Effect of mode of acquisition. The extent of an easement of way depends upon how it was acquired.

(a) *Express grant or reservation.* Here the question is primarily one of construction. If the intention is not made clear, a grant is construed most strongly against the person making it, in accordance with the general rule, while a reservation is construed in his favour, for it takes effect as a regrant by the other party. Thus an easement granted in general terms is not confined to the purpose for which the land is used at the time of the grant.[98] A right of way for general purposes granted as appurtenant to a house can accordingly be used for the business of an hotel if that house is subsequently converted into an hotel.[99]

If a way is granted " as at present enjoyed," prima facie these words refer to the quality of the user (*e.g.*, on foot or with vehicles) and do not limit the quantity of the user to that existing at the time of the grant.[1] In case of difficulty, the surrounding circumstances must be considered: thus both the condition of the way (*e.g.*, whether

---

[92] *Collins* v. *Slade* (1874) 23 W.R. 199.
[93] *Ballard* v. *Dyson* (1808) 1 Taunt. 279.
[94] *Harris* v. *Flower* (1904) 74 L.J.Ch. 127.
[95] See *Miller* v. *Hancock* [1893] 2 Q.B. 177 (not affected by *Fairman* v. *Perpetual Investment Building Society* [1923] A.C. 74 on the duty to the dominant owner).
[96] *Newcomen* v. *Coulson* (1877) 5 Ch.D. 133.
[97] *Selby* v. *Nettlefold* (1873) 9 Ch.App. 111.
[98] *South Eastern Ry* v. *Cooper* [1924] 1 Ch. 211.
[99] *White* v. *Grand Hotel, Eastbourne Ltd.* [1913] 1 Ch. 113 (affirmed on another point, 84 L.J.Ch. 938).
[1] *Hurt* v. *Bowmer* [1937] 1 All E.R. 797.

it is a footpath or a metalled road) and the nature of the dominant tenement (*e.g.,* whether it is a dwelling-house or a factory) may be of assistance.[2]

(b) *Implied grant or reservation.* A way of necessity is limited to the necessity existing at the time the right arose; thus if an encircled plot is used for agricultural purposes at the time of the grant, the way of necessity over the surrounding land is limited to agricultural purposes and cannot be used for the carting of building materials.[3]

In other cases of implied grant, the circumstances of the case must be considered. Thus where a testator devised adjoining plots of land to different persons and one plot was bought by a railway company for conversion into a railway station, it was held that a way which had been used in the testator's lifetime for domestic purposes and for the purposes of warehouses on the land could not be used as a public approach to the station.[4]

(c) *Prescription.* Where an easement of way is acquired by long user, the extent of the way is limited by the nature of the user. Thus a way acquired by long user for farming purposes cannot be used for mineral purposes or for the cartage of building materials.[5] It has been held that user during the prescriptive period as a carriageway does not authorise user for cattle,[6] although it covers use as a footway[7] (since prima facie the greater includes the less) and it extends to use for motor traffic even if the user proved was for horse-drawn vehicles alone.[8] Moreover, unless there is a radical change in the nature of the dominant tenement, the user is not limited to the number or frequency of vehicles using the way during the prescriptive period.[9]

B. Rights of Light

1. No natural right. There is no natural right to light; a land-owner may so build on his land as to prevent any light from reaching his neighbour's windows,[10] unless his neighbour has an easement of light or some other right such as a restrictive covenant against building. The access of light to windows is sometimes deliberately

[2] *Cannon* v. *Villars* (1878) 8 Ch.D. 415 at 420, 421.
[3] *Corporation of London* v. *Riggs* (1880) 13 Ch.D. 798.
[4] *Milner's Safe Co. Ltd.* v. *Great Northern and City Ry.* [1907] 1 Ch. 208.
[5] *Wimbledon Conservators* v. *Dixon* (1875) 1 Ch.D. 362.
[6] *Ballard* v. *Dyson* (1808) 1 Taunt. 279.
[7] *Davies* v. *Stephens* (1836) 7 C. & P. 570.
[8] *Lock* v. *Abercester Ltd.* [1939] Ch. 861.
[9] *British Railways Board* v. *Glass* [1965] Ch. 538.
[10] *Tapling* v. *Jones* (1865) 11 H.L.C. 290.

obstructed in order to prevent an easement of light being acquired by prescription.[11]

2. Quantum of light. The amount of light to which the dominant owner is entitled was finally settled in *Colls* v. *Home and Colonial Stores Ltd.*[12]; this amount is enough light according to the ordinary notions of mankind for the comfortable use of the premises as a dwelling, or, in the case of business premises, for the beneficial use of the premises for ordinary shop or other business purposes. The test is thus " ordinary user ": the dominant owner is not entitled to object even to a substantial diminution in his light, provided enough is left for ordinary purposes. The test is not " How much light has been taken away ? " but " How much light is left? "[13] An easement of a greater amount of light than that required for ordinary purposes cannot be acquired even if for 20 years the dominant owner has enjoyed that quantity of light and has used the premises for purposes requiring an extraordinary amount of light.[14] Conversely, the quantum of light to which the dominant owner is entitled is not affected by the fact that he has used the room in question for purposes requiring but little light,[15] for a right of light is a right to have the access of light for all purposes to which the room may be put.[16]

3. Alteration of apertures. An easement of light can exist only in respect of a window or other aperture in a building, such as a skylight.[17] If the dominant owner alters the size or position of the window, the burden on the servient tenement cannot be increased; an obstruction which would not have been actionable before the alteration will not be actionable even if it deprives the altered window of most of its light.[18] But if it is established that an obstruction is an infringement of an easement of light for one set of windows, and another set of windows (for which no easement exists) is also obstructed by it, the dominant owner can recover damages in respect of both sets of windows, for the obstruction is illegal and the damage to both sets of windows the direct and foreseeable consequence of it.[19]

---

[11] See *ante*, p. 448. [12] [1904] A.C. 179.
[13] *Higgins* v. *Betts* [1905] 2 Ch. 210 at 215.
[14] *Ambler* v. *Gordon* [1905] 1 K.B. 417 (architect's office).
[15] *Price* v. *Hilditch* [1930] 1 Ch. 500.
[16] *Yates* v. *Jack* (1866) 1 Ch.App. 295.
[17] *Easton* v. *Isted* [1903] 1 Ch. 405.
[18] *Ankerson* v. *Connelly* [1907] 1 Ch. 678.
[19] *Re London, etc. Ry.* (1889) 24 Q.B.D. 326.

4. Standard of light. The standard of light varies to some extent from neighbourhood to neighbourhood,[20] the test in each case being that laid down in *Colls'* case. There is no " 45 degrees " rule, *i.e.*, no rule that an interference with light is actionable only if the obstruction rises above a line drawn upwards and outwards from the centre of the window at an angle of 45 degrees; at the most the test provides a very slight presumption.[21]

5. Other sources. In considering whether an easement of light has been obstructed, other sources of light of which the dominant owner cannot be deprived must be taken into account, such as vertical light through a skylight.[22] In one case [23] a room was lit through two sets of windows, one set facing A's land and the other facing B's land. It was held that the light received by both sets of windows had to be considered, but that A could not obscure the greater part of the light passing over his land in reliance upon B supplying a large quantity of light. Neither servient owner could build to a greater extent than, assuming a building of like height on the other servient tenement, would still leave the dominant tenement with sufficient light according to the test in *Colls'* case.

C. Rights of Water

A variety of easements may exist in connection with water, such as rights—

to take water from a spring or a pump;
to water cattle at a pond;
to pollute the waters of a stream or river;
to discharge water on to the land of another;
to enter the land of another to open sluice gates;
to permit rain water to drop from a roof on to a neighbour's land (" easement of eavesdrop ").

D. Rights of Support

These have already been considered.[24]

---

[20] *Fishenden* v. *Higgs & Hill Ltd.* (1935) 153 L.T. 128.
[21] *Ibid.* For scientific tests as to " sill ratio " and " grumble points," see *Charles Semon & Co. Ltd.* v. *Bradford Corporation* [1922] 2 Ch. 737 and *Fishenden* v. *Higgs & Hill Ltd., supra.*
[22] *Smith* v. *Evangelisation Society (Incorporated) Trust* [1933] Ch. 515.
[23] *Sheffield Masonic Hall Co. Ltd.* v. *Sheffield Corporation* [1932] 2 Ch. 17.
[24] *Ante*, p. 423.

E. *Rights of Air*

These have already been considered.[25]

F. *Miscellaneous Easements*

There are a variety of miscellaneous easements, such as rights—

> to create a nuisance by the discharge of gases, fluids or smoke, or by making noises or vibrations;
>
> to hang clothes on a line passing over another's land [26];
>
> to mix manure on the servient tenement for the benefit of the adjoining farm;
>
> to use a wall for nailing trees thereto or for supporting a creeper;
>
> to extend the bowsprits of ships over a wharf [27];
>
> to use a coal shed for domestic purposes [28];
>
> to store casks and trade produce on the servient tenement;
>
> to let down the surface of land by mining operations under it;
>
> to enter the dominant tenement to repair buildings on the servient tenement [29];
>
> to enjoy a pleasure ground (a " *jus spatiandi* ").[30]

Certain rights are not easements but resemble them. A right to use a pew in a church has been described as not being an interest in land but an interest of a peculiar nature in the nature of an easement created by Act of Parliament [31]; and the right to require a neighbouring landowner to repair his fences exists as a spurious easement.[32]

Sect. 6. Species of Profits à Prendre

The following are the main types of profit *à prendre*. Some are usually met with as commons, and some as several profits.

A. *Profit of Pasture*

A profit of pasture may exist in the following forms.

1. Appendant. A profit of pasture appendant is limited to horses, oxen, cows and sheep, the numerical test being levancy and couchancy.[33]

---

[25] *Ante*, p. 421. [26] *Drewell* v. *Towler* (1832) 3 B. & Ad. 735.

[27] *Suffield* v. *Brown* (1864) 4 De G.J. & Sm. 185.

[28] *Wright* v. *Macadam* [1949] 2 K.B. 744.

[29] *Ward* v. *Kirkland* [1967] Ch. 194. [30] *Re Ellenborough Park* [1956] Ch. 131.

[31] *Brumfitt* v. *Roberts* (1870) L.R. 5 C.P. 224 at 233.

[32] *Ante*, p. 421. [33] *Ante*, p. 428.

2. Appurtenant. A profit of pasture appurtenant is not confined to any particular animals, but depends on the terms of the grant or, in the case of prescription, the animals habitually turned out to pasture. The number of animals may either be tested by levancy and couchancy, or be fixed; it cannot be unlimited.[34]

3. Pur cause de vicinage. Under a common of pasture *pur cause de vicinage*, the commoners of one common may not put more cattle upon it than it will maintain; thus if Common A is 50 acres in extent and Common B 100 acres, the commoners of A must not put more cattle on A than the 50 acres will support, in reliance on their cattle straying to B.[35]

4. In gross. A profit of pasture in gross may exist for a fixed number of animals or *sans nombre*. The last phrase means literally " without number " (an alternative form is " without stint "), but such a right is limited to not more cattle than the servient tenement will maintain in addition to any existing burdens.

5. Limitation of numbers. Rights of common registrable under the Commons Registration Act 1965[36] must be registered for a definite number of animals. After registration has become final, the right is only exercisable in relation to the number so registered.[37]

B. *Profit of Turbary*

A profit of turbary is the right to dig and take from the servient tenement peat or turf for use as fuel in a house on the dominant tenement. It may exist as appurtenant, or, where it is limited to some specified quantity, in gross.[38] Where it is appurtenant, the turves can be used only for the benefit of the dominant tenement and not, *e.g.*, for sale, even if the dominant owner is entitled to a fixed quantity.[39]

C. *Profit of Estovers*

A profit of estovers is the right to take wood from the land of another as hay-bote, house-bote or plough-bote.[40] It may exist as appurtenant, or, if limited to a specified quantity, in gross.

---

[34] *Benson* v. *Chester* (1799) 8 T.R. 396 at 401.
[35] *Corbet's Case* (1585) 7 Co.Rep. 5a.
[36] See *ante*, p. 451 for registration.
[37] Commons Registration Act 1965, s. 15.
[38] *Mellor* v. *Spateman* (1669) 1 Wms.Saund. 339 at 346.
[39] *Hayward* v. *Cunnington* (1668) 1 Lev. 231.
[40] *Ante*, pp. 50, 51.

D. *Profit of Piscary and Other Sporting Rights*

A profit of piscary is a right to catch and take away fish. It can exist in gross (when it may be unlimited) or as appurtenant (when it must be limited to the needs of the dominant tenement). Other sporting rights, such as a right of hunting, shooting, fowling and the like, may also exist as profits *à prendre*.[41] It is no infringement of such a right for the servient owner merely to cut timber in the ordinary way, even if he thereby drives away game,[42] but it is otherwise if fundamental changes in the land are made, as where the whole or a substantial part of the land is built upon or converted into racing stables.[43]

E. *Profit in the Soil*

A profit in the soil is the right to enter the servient tenement and take sand, stone, gravel and the like.[44] It may exist as appurtenant or in gross.

Sect. 7. Restrictive Covenants

In many ways a restrictive covenant resembles an equitable easement in the burden it imposes on land,[45] so that restrictive covenants might well find a place in this chapter. Nevertheless, it is important to consider restrictive covenants in relation to the rules governing other covenants, and they have accordingly been dealt with in the chapter on covenants.[46]

---

[41] *Ewart* v. *Graham* (1859) 7 H.L.C. 331 at 345.
[42] *Gearns* v. *Baker* (1875) 10 Ch.App. 355.
[43] *Peech* v. *Best* [1931] 1 K.B. 1.
[44] Co.Litt. 122a.
[45] See *ante*, p. 425.
[46] *Ante*, pp. 392 *et seq*.

CHAPTER 13

MORTGAGES

Part 1

NATURE OF A MORTGAGE

1. Security. When one person lends money to another, he may be content to make the loan without security, or he may demand some security for the payment of the money. In the former case, the lender has a right to sue for the money if it is not duly paid, but that is all; if the borrower becomes insolvent, the lender may lose part or all of his money. But if some security of adequate value is given for the loan, the lender is protected even if the borrower becomes insolvent, for the lender has a claim to the security which takes precedence over the claims of other creditors.

The most important kind of security is the mortgage. The essential nature of a mortgage is that it is a conveyance of a legal or equitable interest in property, with a provision for redemption, *i.e.*, that upon repayment of a loan or the performance of some other obligation the conveyance shall become void or the interest shall be reconveyed.[1] The borrower is known as the " mortgagor," the lender as the " mortgagee."

2. Other transactions. A mortgage must be distinguished from a lien, a pledge and a charge.

(*a*) *Lien.* A lien may arise at common law, in equity or under certain statutes. A common law lien is the right to retain possession of the property of another until a debt is paid; thus a garage proprietor has a common law lien upon a motor-car repaired by him. This lien is a mere passive right of retention, giving no right to sell or otherwise deal with the property,[2] and is extinguished if the creditor parts with possession to the debtor or his agent.[3]

An equitable lien is not dependent upon continued possession of the property [4] and in this respect resembles a mortgage. But it

---

1 See *Santley* v. *Wilde* [1899] 2 Ch. 474.
2 But see Disposal of Uncollected Goods Act 1952.
3 *Pennington* v. *Reliance Motor Works Ltd*. [1923] 1 K.B. 127.
4 *Wrout* v. *Dawes* (1858) 25 Beav. 369.

differs from a mortgage (*inter alia*) in that a mortgage is a right founded on contract whereas an equitable lien arises from general principles of equity which do not permit a man who has acquired property under a contract to keep it without payment.[5] Thus a vendor of land who has conveyed it without receiving the full purchase price has an equitable lien upon it for the balance unpaid.[6]

A statutory lien is the creature of the statute under which it arises and the rights which it confers depend on the terms of that statute. Railways, shipowners and solicitors have been given such rights.

(b) *Pledge.* A pledge or pawn consists of the loan of money in return for the delivery of possession of chattels to the lender. Although the lender has certain powers of sale, the general property in the goods remains in the borrower and the lender has possession; in a mortgage, on the other hand, the lender acquires ownership and the borrower usually retains possession.

(c) *Charge.* For most practical purposes, a charge is regarded as a species of mortgage, and is dealt with accordingly in this chapter. Nevertheless, there is an essential difference between a mortgage and a charge. A mortgage is a conveyance of property subject to a right of redemption, whereas a charge conveys nothing and merely gives the chargee certain rights over the property concerned as security for the loan.[7]

Part 2

CREATION OF MORTGAGES

Sect. 1. Methods of Creating Legal Mortgages and Charges

The methods of creating a legal mortgage differ for freeholds and leaseholds. In each case, some mention must be made of the history of the subject before considering the position before 1926 and after 1925.

A. Freeholds

I. HISTORY

1. Twelfth and thirteenth centuries. In the twelfth and thirteenth centuries, the mortgagor leased the land to the mortgagee, who

---

5 See *Mackreth* v. *Symmons* (1808) 15 Ves. 329 at 340.
6 *Chapman* v. *Tanner* (1684) 1 **Vern.** 267.
7 See *London County and Westminster Bank Ltd.* v. *Tompkins* [1918] 1 K.B. 515.

went into possession. This, as seen above, resembled a pledge. If the income from the land was used to discharge the mortgage debt, the transaction was known as *vivum vadium* (a live pledge), since it was self-redeeming. If the mortgagee kept the income, it was known as *mortuum vadium* (a dead pledge). This latter form was not unlawful, but the Church regarded it as sinful for a Christian to take the income. In either case, if the money was not repaid by the time the lease expired, the mortgagee could enlarge his lease into a fee simple.

2. Fifteenth century. By the middle of the fifteenth century, the usual form of mortgage had changed. Even in the thirteenth century, a form of mortgage by conveyance of the fee simple had been known and this form gradually ousted the others, for it gave seisin to the mortgagee. The mortgagor conveyed the land to the mortgagee in fee simple, subject to a condition that the mortgagor might re-enter and determine the mortgagee's estate if the money lent was repaid on a named date. The mortgagee still took possession forthwith. The condition was construed strictly; if the mortgagor was a single day late in offering to repay the money, he lost his land for ever and yet remained liable for the debt.

3. Seventeenth century. By the beginning of the seventeenth century two changes had taken place. First, the form of a mortgage was usually a conveyance in fee simple with a covenant to reconvey the property if the money was paid on the fixed date. This is the modern form, and it simplified proof of title; whether the fee simple was vested in the mortgagor or not no longer depended merely upon whether the money had been paid within the fixed time, but depended upon whether a reconveyance had been executed.[8]

Secondly, a far more important change had been made by the intervention of equity. Equity took the view that the property mortgaged was merely a security for the money lent, and that it was unjust that the mortgagor should lose his property merely because he was late in repaying the loan. At first, equity intervened in the cases of accident, mistake, special hardship and the like, but soon relief was given in all cases. Even if the date fixed for repayment had long passed, equity compelled the mortgagee to reconvey the property to the mortgagor on payment of the principal with interest

---

[8] See *Durham Brothers* v. *Robertson* [1898] 1 Q.B. 765 at 772.

and costs. The mortgagor was thus given an equitable right to redeem at a time when the agreement between the parties provided that the mortgagee was to be the absolute owner.[9] In short, for three hundred years a mortgagor has had two separate rights of redemption:

(a) *Legal right to redeem on the fixed day.* At law, a mortgagor has no right to redeem either before or after the date fixed by the mortgage for redemption, but on that one day alone.

(b) *Equitable right to redeem thereafter.* Equity allowed the mortgagor an equitable right to redeem on any day after the date fixed for redemption by the mortgage. This is a right which can be exercised only on equitable terms.

This equitable right to redeem revolutionised mortgages, and probably lies at the root of Lord Macnaghten's statement that " No one . . . by the light of nature ever understood an English mortgage of real estate." [10] The sum total of the mortgagor's rights in equity is known as his equity of redemption. This must be distinguished from his equitable right to redeem; the latter does not exist until the legal date for redemption is past, whereas the equity of redemption exists as soon as the mortgage is made.[11] The equity of redemption is the mortgagor's right of ownership of the property subject to the mortgage,[12] and is an interest in land which can be granted, devised, entailed and, in short, dealt with like any other interest in land.[13] The equitable right to redeem, on the other hand, is but one of the adjuncts of the equity of redemption; it is not the equity of redemption itself.

II. BEFORE 1926

As seen above, the usual method of creating a mortgage of freeholds before 1926 was by a conveyance of the fee simple subject to a proviso for redemption, namely, a covenant by the mortgagee that he would reconvey the property if the money was repaid on a fixed date. That date was usually six months after the date of the mortgage, even though there was no real expectation by either party that the money would be repaid then.

---

9 See *Salt* v. *Marquess of Northampton* [1892] A.C. 1 at 18, 19; and see M. & W. 882–886.
10 *Samuel* v. *Jarrah, etc., Corporation Ltd.* [1904] A.C. 323 at 326; and Maitland remarked that a mortgage is " one long *suppressio veri* and *suggestio falsi* " (*Equity*, p. 182).
11 *Brown* v. *Cole* (1845) 14 Sim. 427; *Kreglinger* v. *New Patagonia Meat and Cold Storage Co. Ltd.* [1914] A.C. 25 at 48.
12 *Re Wells* [1933] Ch. 29 at 52.
13 See *Casborne* v. *Scarfe* (1738) 1 Atk. 603 at 605.

Although a mortgage in this form left the mortgagor with a mere equity of redemption, this might be of considerable value (*e.g.,* if the loan was £1,000 and the property worth £15,000) and could itself be mortgaged. But since it was merely equitable, any mortgage of it would also be equitable, for there could be no legal mortgage of something which existed only in equity. Thus before 1926 there could be only one legal mortgage of this kind on any property; all other mortgages were necessarily equitable.

III. AFTER 1925

By the Law of Property Act 1925,[14] freeholds can no longer be mortgaged by conveyance of the fee simple. Two methods only are possible:

   (i) by a demise for a term of years absolute, subject to a provision for cesser on redemption; or
   (ii) by a charge by deed expressed to be by way of legal mortgage.

1. Demise for a term of years absolute.

(a) *Mortgages made after* 1925. The term of years granted to the mortgagee is usually a long term, *e.g.,* 3,000 years. The provision for cesser on redemption is a clause providing that the term of years shall cease when the loan is repaid; it is really unnecessary, for on repayment the term becomes a satisfied term and automatically ceases.[15] In other respects, the position is much as it was before 1926. A fixed redemption date is still named, and it is still usually six months after the date of the mortgage; thereafter the mortgagor has an equitable right to redeem in lieu of his legal right. The difficulty that a mortgagee by demise has no right to the title deeds is obviated by an express provision giving a first mortgagee the same right to the deeds as if he had the fee simple.[16]

The principal change brought about by the new legislation is that the mortgagor now retains the legal fee simple. This does not mean that the equity of redemption has lost its importance; a fee simple giving the right to possession of land only when a lease for 3,000 years has expired is of little value compared with the right to insist that the fee simple shall forthwith be freed from the term of 3,000 years on payment of the money due. Indeed, the term " equity of

---

[14] s. 85 (1).
[15] See *ante*, p. 206.
[16] L.P.A. 1925, s. 85 (1).

redemption " is sometimes used as including the mortgagor's legal estate. But the change means that the mortgagor has, in addition to his equity of redemption, a legal fee simple out of which further term of years may be granted. Consequently, second, third and subsequent mortgages may all be legal after 1925. Thus A, the fee simple owner of Blackacre, may create successive legal mortgages in favour of X, Y and Z. The term he grants to each mortgagee is usually at least one day longer than the previous mortgage. Thus X may be given 2,000 years, Y 2,000 years and a day, and Z 2,000 years and two days, so that each mortgagee has a reversion upon the prior mortgage term.

The rights of Y and Z, though seemingly rather nebulous, are in fact quite substantial. Thus if A defaults and the property is sold by X under his power of sale,[17] the money is paid first to X to discharge his mortgage, the balance to Y to discharge his, the balance to discharge Z's mortgage and any surplus to A; in short, the parties rank in the order X, Y, Z, A. Further, any mortgagee always has the right, upon giving proper notice, to insist upon redeeming any prior mortgage [18]; thus Y might insist upon buying up X's mortgage and so succeeding to X's position.

An attempt to create a first mortgage by conveyance of the fee simple now operates as the grant of a term of 3,000 years without impeachment of waste but subject to cesser on redemption.[19] An attempt to create a second or subsequent mortgage in the same way takes effect as the grant of a term one day longer than the preceding term.[20] The system is thus foolproof.

(b) *Transitional provisions.* Mortgages made before 1926 were automatically brought into line with the new scheme.[21] A first or only mortgage made by a conveyance of the legal or equitable fee simple was automatically converted at the end of 1925 into a term of 3,000 years without impeachment of waste but subject to cesser on redemption. The fee simple thus taken away from the mortgagee was automatically vested in the mortgagor or whoever else would have been entitled to have the fee simple conveyed to him if all the mortgages were paid off. Second and subsequent mortgages created by a conveyance of the legal or equitable fee simple were similarly

[17] *Post*, pp. 474 *et seq.*
[18] *Post*, p. 491.
[19] L.P.A. 1925, s. 85 (2).
[20] *Ibid.* s. 85.
[21] *Ibid.* 1st Sched., Pt. VII.

converted into terms at least one day longer than the previous term. Thus if before 1926 A had mortgaged his fee simple first to X and then to Y, at the beginning of 1926 the legal fee simple vested in A, while X took a term of 3,000 years and Y a term of 3,000 years and one day. The position would have been the same if A had mortgaged only an equitable fee simple, the legal fee simple being held by T on a bare trust for him; under the transitional provisions the legal fee simple would have vested in A, and T would have lost all interest in the property.

It will be seen that second mortgagees, who before 1926 perforce had only equitable interests, now get legal terms of years. However, this conversion from an equitable interest to a legal estate will not benefit a second or subsequent mortgagee who has not got possession of the title deeds unless the mortgage is registered; until then, in favour of a purchaser in good faith without notice of it, such a mortgage is deemed to be merely equitable, so that the purchaser will take free from it.

2. Charge by deed expressed to be by way of legal mortgage. This is a new creation of the Law of Property Act 1925 [22] which is sometimes for brevity called a " legal charge." To be effective, it must be—

(i) made by deed: a charge merely in writing will have no effect at law; and

(ii) expressed to be by way of legal mortgage; the deed must contain a statement that the charge is made by way of legal mortgage, though such a statement is not required where the title to the land is registered.[23]

The effect of such a charge of freeholds is that the chargee (whether first or subsequent) gets the same protection, powers and remedies as if he had a term of 3,000 years without impeachment of waste.[24] Although he gets no actual legal term of years, he is as fully protected as if he had one.[25] The name " charge " is thus a little misleading because although a legal charge is by nature a charge and not a mortgage,[26] for all practical purposes it is indistinguishable from a mortgage.

The advantages of a legal charge are considered below.[27]

[22] s. 87.
[23] *Cityland and Property* (Holdings) Ltd. v. Dabrah [1968] Ch. 166 ; *post*, p. 566.
[24] L.P.A. 1925, s. 87 (1).
[25] See *Regent Oil Co. Ltd.* v. *J. A. Gregory* (Hatch End) Ltd. [1966] Ch. 402.
[26] *Ante*, p. 461.
[27] *Post*, p. 469.

B. Leaseholds

I. HISTORY

The intervention of equity in the case of mortgages of leaseholds closely resembles that in the case of freeholds.[28]

II. BEFORE 1926

A legal mortgage of leaseholds could be made before 1926 in either of two ways:

(i) By assignment of the lease to the mortgagee with a covenant for reassignment on redemption; or

(ii) By the grant to the mortgagee of a sub-lease at least one day shorter than the lease, with a proviso for cesser on redemption.

The first method was rarely employed, for it meant that the mortgagee became liable on such of the covenants in the lease as touched and concerned the land. This was not so if the second method was employed, for then the mortgagee was only an under-lessee and there was privity neither of contract nor of estate between him and the lessor.[29] Whichever form was employed, the mortgage normally contained the usual provision for redemption on a fixed date six months ahead, and thereafter the mortgagor had an equitable right to redeem.

Where a mortgage had been made by assignment, second and subsequent mortgages were made by a mortgage of the mortgagor's equity of redemption. Where the prior mortgage had been made by sub-lease, subsequent mortgages were made by the grant of other sub-leases, each normally being longer than the previous one.

III. AFTER 1925

By the Law of Property Act 1925,[30] leaseholds can no longer be mortgaged by assignment. Two methods only are possible:

(i) By a subdemise for a term of years absolute, subject to a provision for cesser on redemption, the term being at least one day shorter than the term vested in the mortgagor; or

(ii) By a charge by deed expressed to be by way of legal mortgage.

---

[28] *Ante*, pp. 462, 463.
[29] *Ante*, p. 383.
[30] s. 86 (1).

1. Subdemise for a term of years absolute.

(a) *Mortgages made after* 1925. The term of the sub-lease must be at least one day shorter than the term of the lease which is being mortgaged, otherwise it would operate as an assignment.[31] If the lease requires the tenant to obtain the landlord's licence before a subdemise by way of mortgage is made, the licence cannot be unreasonably refused.[32] The first mortgagee has the same rights to the deeds as if his mortgage had been made by assignment.[33] It is usual to make the sub-term ten days shorter than the lease, so as to allow room for second and subsequent mortgages. Thus if T's 50 years' lease is mortgaged, the first mortgage will be secured by a lease for 50 years less ten days, the second by 50 years less nine days, and so on. But this is not essential, for the old rule[34] that a lease may take effect in reversion upon another lease of the same or greater length has been confirmed by the Law of Property Act 1925.[35] Thus if the first mortgage was made by a sub-term of 50 years less one day, the second mortgage would be secured by a sub-term of the same length and so on; each mortgage would take effect in its proper order.

An attempted mortgage by way of assignment after 1925 operates as a subdemise for a term of years absolute subject to cesser on redemption. A first or only mortgagee takes a term ten days shorter than the lease mortgaged. Second and subsequent mortgagees take terms one day longer than the previous mortgagee if this is possible; in every case, however, the sub-term must be at least one day shorter than the term mortgaged.[36]

(b) *Transitional provisions.* On January 1, 1926, mortgages made by assignment before 1926 were automatically converted into mortgages by subdemise, subject to cesser on redemption.[37] The length of the terms so created is the same as the terms arising on an attempted mortgage by assignment after 1925.[38]

2. Charge by way of legal mortgage.

(a) *Rights and remedies.* A charge by deed expressed to be by

[31] *Beardman* v. *Wilson* (1868) L.R. 4 C.P. 57.
[32] L.P.A. 1925, s. 86 (1).
[33] *Ibid.*
[34] *Re Moore & Hulme's Contract* [1912] 2 Ch. 105.
[35] s. 149 (5).
[36] L.P.A. 1925, s. 86 (2).
[37] *Ibid.* 1st Sched., Pt. VIII.
[38] See previous paragraph.

way of legal mortgage gives the mortgagee (whether first or subsequent) the same rights and remedies as if he had a sub-term one day shorter than the term vested in the mortgagor.[39] As in the case of freeholds, he gets no actual term of years but is as fully protected as if he had one.

(b) *Advantages of a legal charge.* There is nothing in the Law of Property Act 1925 which suggests any reason why a legal charge, either of freeholds or leaseholds, should be preferred to an ordinary mortgage. But there seem to be three practical advantages in using a legal charge.

    (i) It is a convenient way of mortgaging freeholds and leaseholds together; the deed is shortened by stating that all the properties specified in the schedule are charged by way of legal mortgage, instead of setting out the length of the mortgage terms in each case.

   (ii) Probably the granting of a legal charge on a lease does not amount to a breach of any covenant in that lease against sub-letting, for the charge creates no actual sub-lease in favour of the mortgagee but merely gives him the same rights as if he had a sub-lease.

  (iii) The form of a legal charge is short and simple.

Sect. 2. Methods of Creating Equitable Mortgages and Charges

A. Equitable Mortgages

1. Mortgage of an equitable interest. If the mortgagor has no legal estate but only an equitable interest, any mortgage he effects must necessarily be equitable. Thus before 1926, once a legal mortgage by conveyance had been created, the mortgagor retained only an equity of redemption, and all subsequent mortgages were equitable. Again, the beneficiaries under a trust have mere equitable interests and can create only equitable mortgages.

The 1925 legislation has not affected the form of equitable mortgages of equitable interests. Such mortgages are still made by a conveyance of the equitable interest with a proviso for reconveyance. The actual form of words employed is immaterial provided the meaning is plain.[40] Nor need the mortgage be made by deed,

---

[39] L.P.A. 1925, s. 87 (1).
[40] See *William Brandt's Sons & Co.* v. *Dunlop Rubber Co. Ltd.* [1905] A.C. 454 at 462.

as is essential for a legal mortgage; but it must either be in writing
signed by the mortgagor or his agent authorised in writing, or else
be made by will.[41]

2. Informal mortgages. Under the same principles as apply to
leaseholds,[42] equity treats an enforceable contract to create a legal
mortgage as an actual mortgage,[43] provided it is supported by
sufficient evidence in writing or a sufficient act of part performance.
Similarly, an imperfect legal mortgage satisfying these requirements
is treated as an agreement for a mortgage and thus as an equitable
mortgage.[44]

Evidence in writing and part performance have been discussed
above.[45] All that need be said here is that since 1783 [46] the rule has
been that a mere deposit of the title deeds which cannot be accounted
for in any other way is taken as part performance of a contract
to create a mortgage, even if not a word about such a contract
has been said [47]; such a deposit thus creates an equitable mortgage.
The deposit must be made for the purpose of giving a security,
however; delivery of the deeds by mistake or to enable a mortgage
to be drawn up does not suffice.[48] But it is not essential that all the
title deeds should be deposited, provided those which are delivered
are material evidence of title.[49]

In practice, mortgages by deposit of title deeds are nearly always
accompanied by a deed setting out the terms of the mortgage, or
requiring the mortgagor to execute a legal mortgage when so requested. This prevents disputes, and the execution of the deed gives
the mortgagee additional powers.[50]

B. *Equitable Charges*

An equitable charge is created where certain property is appropriated
to the discharge of some debt or other obligation without there
being any change in ownership either at law or in equity.[51] Thus

---

[41] L.P.A. 1925, s. 53 (1).
[42] *Ante*, p. 342.
[43] See *Ex p. Wright* (1812) 19 Ves. 255 at 258.
[44] *Parker* v. *Housefield* (1834) 2 My. & K. 419 at 420.
[45] *Ante*, pp. 318 *et seq.*, 323 *et seq.*
[46] *Russel* v. *Russel* (1783) 1 Bro.C.C. 269.
[47] *Bozon* v. *Williams* (1829) 3 Y. & J. 150 at 161.
[48] *Norris* v. *Wilkinson* (1806) 12 Ves. 192.
[49] *Lacon* v. *Allen* (1856) 3 Drew. 579.
[50] *Post*, pp. 474, 478.
[51] *London County and Westminster Bank Ltd.* v. *Tompkins* [1918] 1 K.B. 515
at 528.

if a man signs a written contract agreeing that he thereby charges his real estate with the payment of £500 to A, an equitable charge is created[52]; the same applies where a will or voluntary settlement charges money on land.[53] An enforceable contract to create a legal charge presumably creates an equitable charge.[54]

Part 3

RIGHTS OF THE PARTIES UNDER A MORTGAGE OR CHARGE

The rights of the parties under a mortgage or charge will be considered under three heads:

(i) The rights of the mortgagee or chargee;
(ii) Rights common to both parties; and
(iii) The rights of the mortgagor or chargor.

Sect. 1. Rights of the Mortgagee or Chargee

A. Remedies for Enforcing Payment

Unless the parties have otherwise agreed, a mortgagee or chargee has five remedies available for enforcing payment. Three of the remedies are primarily directed to recovering the capital due and putting an end to the security: these are an action for the money, foreclosure, and sale. The other two remedies are taking possession and appointing a receiver, and these primarily seek merely to recover the interest due. Sale and appointing a receiver are rights which used to be conferred by the mortgage deed but are now given by statute; the other remedies are inherent in the nature of the transaction. The remedies available differ according to whether the mortgage or charge is legal or equitable.

I. LEGAL MORTGAGEE OR LEGAL CHARGEE

A legal mortgagee or legal chargee has the following remedies for enforcing his security.

1. To sue for the money due. At any time after the date fixed for payment the mortgagee may sue for the money lent.[55] This remedy is, of course, in no way peculiar to mortgages.

---

[52] *Matthews* v. *Goodday* (1861) 31 L.J.Ch. 282 at 282, 283.
[53] *Re Owen* [1894] 3 Ch. 220.   [54] See *ante*, p. 342.
[55] See *Bolton* v. *Buckenham* [1891] 1 Q.B. 278; but see *post*, p. 497.

2. To foreclose.

(a) *The right of foreclosure.* By giving the mortgagor an equitable right to redeem after he had lost his legal right of redemption, equity interfered with the bargain made between the parties. But equity prescribed limits to the equity of redemption which it created. Thus before 1926, a legal first mortgagee of freeholds had the fee simple vested in him, and once the legal date for redemption had passed, the mortgagor's right to redeem was merely equitable. " Foreclosure " was the name given to the process whereby the mortgagor's equitable right to redeem was extinguished and the mortgagee left owner of the property, both at law and in equity. Equity had interfered to prevent the conveyance of the legal fee simple from having its full effect and on foreclosure " the court simply removes the stop it has itself put on." [56] From the first the mortgagee was absolute owner at law, and foreclosure, for which an order of the court is essential, made him an absolute owner in equity as well.

After 1925, a mortgagee does not have the whole legal estate of the mortgagor vested in him, but only a long term of years in the case of freeholds and an underlease in the case of leaseholds. Consequently it is no longer sufficient for a decree of foreclosure merely to destroy the mortgagor's equity of redemption, and so the Law of Property Act 1925 [57] provides that a foreclosure decree absolute shall vest the mortgagor's fee simple or term of years in the mortgagee.

The right to foreclose does not arise until the legal right to redeem has ceased to exist, *i.e.*, until the legal date for redemption has passed.[58] Once this has happened, the mortgagee may commence foreclosure proceedings unless he has agreed not to do so [59]; in practice, the mortgagee often contracts not to enforce the security by foreclosure or other means until he has given some specified notice or until the mortgagor has broken one of his covenants in the mortgage. If no redemption date is fixed or if the loan is repayable on demand, the right to foreclose arises when a demand for repayment has been made and a reasonable time thereafter has elapsed.[60]

(b) *Parties to a foreclosure action.* An action for foreclosure can be brought by any mortgagee of property, whether he is the original mortgagee or an assignee, and whether he is a first or subsequent

---

[56] *Carter* v. *Wake* (1877) 4 Ch.D. 605 at 606, *per* Jessel M.R.
[57] ss. 88 (2), 89 (2).   [58] *Williams* v. *Morgan* [1906] 1 Ch. 804.
[59] *Ramsbottom* v. *Wallis* (1835) 5 L.J.Ch. 92.
[60] *Toms* v. *Wilson* (1862) 4 B. & S. 442.

mortgagee. The effect of a foreclosure order absolute in an action brought by the first mortgagee is to make him the sole owner both at law and in equity, free from any subsequent mortgages; if the action is brought by a second or subsequent mortgagee, he will hold the property subject to prior incumbrances but free from all subsequent incumbrances.

As will be seen shortly,[61] a foreclosure action gives the mortgagor and all others interested in the equity of redemption an opportunity of redeeming the mortgage. Consequently, all persons interested in the equity of redemption must be made parties to the action. Thus if X has made successive mortgages of his property to A, B and C, and B starts foreclosure proceedings, A will not be affected by them and so need not be made a party to the action. But if the action is successful, C will lose his mortgage and X his equity of redemption, and so both must be made parties to the action.

(c) *Procedure.* The first step in a foreclosure is to obtain from the court a foreclosure order *nisi.* This provides that if the mortgagor repays the money lent on a fixed day (usually six months from the accounts being settled by the master), the mortgage shall be discharged, but that if this is not done, the mortgagor shall be foreclosed. If there are several mortgagees and the first mortgagee is foreclosing, each mortgagee is given the alternative of either losing his security or else redeeming (paying off) the first mortgage. Sometimes the court will give the mortgagees successive periods to effect this redemption, but usually there will be only one period between them.[62] At the request of the mortgagee or of any person interested (*e.g.,* the mortgagor) the court may order a sale of the property instead of foreclosure.[63]

(d) *Opening a foreclosure absolute.* If no order for sale is made and the property is not redeemed on the date fixed, a foreclosure order absolute is made. This destroys the mortgagor's equity of redemption and transfers his fee simple or term of years to the mortgagee,[64] who thus becomes sole owner at law and in equity, subject only to prior incumbrances. However, although the order of foreclosure absolute appears to be final, it is not necessarily so, for the court will sometimes open a foreclosure absolute. Circumstances which may influence the court to do this are an accident

---

[61] *Infra.*
[62] *Platt* v. *Mendel* (1884) 27 Ch.D. 246.
[63] L.P.A. 1925, s. 91 (2).
[64] *Ibid.* ss. 88 (2), 89 (2).

at the last moment preventing the mortgagor from raising the money any special value which the property had to the mortgagor (*e.g.*, if it was an old family estate), a marked disparity between the value of the property and the amount lent, and the promptness of the application. Even if the mortgagee has sold the property after foreclosure absolute, the court may still open the foreclosure; this is unlikely however, if the purchaser bought the property some time after foreclosure and without notice of circumstances which might induce the court to interfere.[65]

3. To sell.

(a) *History.* There is no right, either at common law or in equity for a mortgagee to sell the mortgaged property free from the equity of redemption, although of course he can freely transfer the estate which is vested in him subject to the equity of redemption. Consequently, an express power was usually inserted in mortgage deeds enabling the mortgagee to sell the property free from the equity of redemption if certain specified events occurred. Lord Cranworth's Act 1860 gave a limited power of sale in the case of mortgages made after 1860, but this was usually thought too narrow to be relied upon. The Conveyancing Act 1881, however, gave a satisfactory power of sale which is now contained in the Law of Property Act 1925.[66]

(b) *The power.* Every mortgagee whose mortgage was made after 1881 and shows no contrary intention has a power of sale, provided—

- (a) the mortgage was made by deed (and all legal mortgages must be made thus); and
- (b) the mortgage money is due, *i.e.*, the legal date for redemption has passed [67]; if the mortgage money is payable by instalments, the power of sale arises as soon as any instalment is in arrear.[68]

When these conditions have been fulfilled, the statutory power of sale *arises*; nevertheless, the power does not become *exercisable* unless one of the three following conditions has been satisfied [69]—

- (i) notice requiring payment of the mortgage money has been served on the mortgagor and default has been made in payment of part or all of it for three months thereafter; or

---

[65] *Campbell* v. *Holyland* (1877) 7 Ch.D. 166 at 172, 173.
[66] ss. 101–107.
[67] L.P.A. 1925, s. 101.
[68] *Payne* v. *Cardiff R.D.C.* [1932] 1 K.B. 241.
[69] L.P.A. 1925, s. 103.

(ii) some interest under the mortgage is two months or more in arrear; or

(iii) there has been a breach of some provision contained in the Act or in the mortgage deed (other than the covenant for payment of the mortgage money or interest) which should have been observed or performed by the mortgagor or by someone who concurred in making the mortgage.

(c) *Protection of purchaser.* The difference between the power of sale arising and becoming exercisable is as follows. If the power has not arisen, the mortgagee has no statutory power of sale at all; the most he can do is to transfer his mortgage. But if the power of sale has arisen, he can make a good title to a purchaser free from the equity of redemption even if the power has not become exercisable; the purchaser's title is not impeachable merely because none of the three specified events has occurred or the power of sale has in some way been irregularly or improperly exercised. Any person injured by an unauthorised, improper or irregular exercise of the power has a remedy in damages against the person exercising it.[70] Thus while a purchaser from a mortgagee must satisfy himself that the power of sale has arisen, he need not inquire whether it has become exercisable, although if he knows of some irregularity he should not proceed with the transaction.[71]

(d) *Mode of sale.* In general, the statutory power of sale is exercisable without any order of the court being required. The mortgagee may sell by public auction or private contract and has a wide discretion as to the terms and conditions upon which the sale is made.[72] The mortgagee is not a trustee for the mortgagor of his power of sale,[73] for the power is given to the mortgagee for his own benefit to enable him the better to realise his security. The mortgagee must, however, act in good faith in the conduct of the sale and must take reasonable care so as not, for example, to misdescribe the property. But he need not advertise the property or attempt to sell by auction before selling by private contract, nor need he delay a sale so as to obtain a better price.[74]

Once it is shown that the sale was carried out in good faith, any question of the mortgagee's motive for selling, such as spite

---

[70] L.P.A. 1925, s. 104 (2).
[71] *Bailey* v. *Barnes* [1894] 1 Ch. 25 at 30.
[72] L.P.A. 1925, s. 101 (1) (2).
[73] *Kennedy* v. *De Trafford* [1897] A.C. 180.
[74] *Davey* v. *Durrant* (1857) 1 De G. & J. 535 at 553, 560.

against the mortgagor, is immaterial.[75] Even if the sale is at a low or unusual price (*e.g.*, the exact amount of money due under the mortgage, with costs) the court will not interfere unless the price is so low as in itself to be evidence of fraud.[76] But the sale must be a true sale; a " sale " by the mortgagee to himself, either directly or through an agent, is no true sale and may be set aside.[77] And building societies are under a statutory obligation to take reasonable care to sell only at the best price reasonably obtainable.[78]

(e) *Proceeds of sale.* Although the mortgagee is not a trustee of his power of sale, he is a trustee of the proceeds of sale. After discharging any payments properly due, any balance must be paid to the next subsequent incumbrancer, or if none, to the mortgagor.[79] A mortgagee who has a surplus should therefore search in the registers of land charges [80] to discover the existence of any subsequent mortgages, for registration is equivalent to notice, and if he pays the money to the mortgagor he will be liable to any mortgagee who is thereby prejudiced.[81] But a sale by a mortgagee does not affect any prior mortgagee; the purchaser takes the property subject to any such mortgage, though free from the rights of the vendor, subsequent mortgagees, and the mortgagor.

4. To take possession.

(a) *The right.* Since a legal mortgage gives the mortgagee a term of years, he is entitled to take possession of the mortgaged property as soon as the mortgage is made even if the mortgagor is guilty of no default [82]; a legal chargee has a corresponding statutory right.[83] If the property is already lawfully let to a tenant, the mortgagee cannot take physical possession, but instead takes possession by directing the tenants to pay their rents to him instead of to the mortgagor.[84]

(b) *Strict account.* Yet unless he plans to sell the property, or it is already fully let, a mortgagee is slow to take possession, because if

---

[75] *Nash* v. *Eads* (1880) 25 S.J. 95.
[76] See *Warner* v. *Jacob* (1882) 20 Ch.D. 220.
[77] *Downes* v. *Grazebrook* (1817) 3 Mer. 200.
[78] Building Societies Act 1962, s. 36, replacing earlier legislation.
[79] L.P.A. 1925, s. 105 ; see *Thorne* v. *Heard* [1895] A.C. 495.
[80] See *post*, p. 544.
[81] *West London Commercial Bank* v. *Reliance Permanent Building Society* (1885) 29 Ch.D. 954.
[82] *Birch* v. *Wright* (1786) 1 T.R. 378 at 383.
[83] L.P.A. 1925, s. 87 (1).
[84] *Horlock* v. *Smith* (1842) 6 Jur. 478.

he does he is liable to account strictly on the footing of wilful default; this means that he must account not only for all that he receives but also for all that he ought to have received.[85] Thus where the mortgagee was a brewer and the mortgaged property a " free " house, a mortgagee who took possession and let the property as a " tied " house was held liable for the additional rent he would have obtained if he had let the property as a " free " house.[86] Again, if the mortgagee occupies the property himself instead of letting it he is liable for a fair occupation rent,[87] though he need pay no rent if through decay or otherwise the land is incapable of being beneficially occupied.[88] And where the property is already let, there is little risk in his taking possession.

(c) *Powers while in possession.* While in possession, a mortgagee whose mortgage was made by deed may cut and sell timber and other trees ripe for cutting which were not planted or left standing for shelter or ornament, or contract for this to be done within twelve months of the contract.[89] Although he is not liable for waste, he will be liable if he improperly cuts timber; and despite his right to work mines already opened, he may not open new mines. However, if the property becomes insufficient security for the money due, the court will not interfere if he cuts timber and opens mines, provided he is not guilty of wanton destruction.[90]

A mortgagee in possession must effect reasonable repair[91] and may without the mortgagor's consent effect reasonable but not excessive improvements; the cost will be charged to the mortgagor in the accounts.[92]

(d) *Procedure.* A mortgagee who seeks to obtain possession will usually have to take proceedings in the Chancery Division. If the mortgagor wants an opportunity to raise enough money to pay off the mortgagee, the court will usually give him a short adjournment; but otherwise the mortgagee is entitled to an order for possession.[93]

(e) *Attornment clause.* Many legal mortgages still contain an attornment clause, which is a clause whereby the mortgagor attorns, or acknowledges himself to be, a tenant at will or from year to year of

[85] *Chaplin* v. *Young (No. 1)* (1863) 33 Beav. 330 at 337, 338.
[86] *White* v. *City of London Brewery Co.* (1889) 42 Ch.D. 237.
[87] *Marriott* v. *Anchor Reversionary Co.* (1861) 3 De G.F. & J. 177 at 193.
[88] *Marshall* v. *Cave* (1824) 3 L.J.(o.s.)Ch. 57.
[89] L.P.A. 1925, s. 101 (1).
[90] *Millett* v. *Davey* (1863) 31 Beav. 470 at 475, 476.
[91] *Richards* v. *Morgan* (1853) 4 Y. & C.Ex. 570.
[92] *Shepard* v. *Jones* (1882) 21 Ch.D. 469.
[93] *Birmingham Citizens Permanent Building Society* v. *Caunt* [1962] Ch. 883.

the mortgagee, usually at a nominal rent such as a peppercorn or sixpence. Formerly this was inserted because a speedy procedure in the High Court was available to enable landlords to recover possession of the demised property from their tenants, and no such procedure was available for mere mortgagees; the attornment clause enabled mortgagees to sue for possession *qua* landlords. But changes in the rules of court in 1933, 1936 and 1937 made the speedy procedure available to mortgagees as such, so that this reason for its use has gone.[94] A surviving advantage of the clause is that covenants by the mortgagor in the mortgage relating to the premises will be enforceable against an assignee of the mortgage under the doctrine that covenants in a lease which touch and concern the land will run with the lease and the reversion.[95]

5. To appoint a receiver.

(a) *History.* In order to avoid the dangers of taking possession and yet achieve substantially the same result, mortgages used to provide for the appointment of a receiver with extensive powers of management of the mortgaged property. At first, the appointment was made by the mortgagor at the request of the mortgagee, but later, mortgagees began to reserve a power for themselves, acting in theory as agents for the mortgagor, to appoint a receiver. In such circumstances the receiver was deemed the agent of the mortgagor and the mortgagee was not liable to account strictly [96] in the same way as would have been the case if he had taken possession or the receiver had been his agent.

Lord Cranworth's Act 1860 gave a somewhat unsatisfactory statutory power to appoint a receiver, but the Conveyancing Act 1881, and now the Law of Property Act 1925,[97] confers a power which satisfies most mortgagees.

(b) *The power.* The statutory power to appoint a receiver arises and becomes exercisable in the same circumstances as the power of sale.[98] The mortgagee makes the appointment by writing, and may remove or replace the receiver in the same way. The receiver is deemed the agent of the mortgagor, who is solely responsible for his acts unless the mortgage otherwise provides. The receiver has power to recover the income of the property by action, distress or otherwise,

---

[94] But see *Dudley and District Benefit Building Society* v. *Gordon* [1929] 2 K.B. 105.
[95] *Regent Oil Co. Ltd.* v. *J. A. Gregory (Hatch End) Ltd.* [1966] Ch. 402. For the doctrine, see *ante,* pp. 384 *et seq.*
[96] *Ante,* p. 476.   [97] s. 101.   [98] L.P.A. 1925, ss. 101 (1), 109 (1).

and to give valid receipts for it. The money received by the receiver, after discharging outgoings, interest on prior incumbrances and payment of the receiver's commission and other expenses, is used to pay the interest due under the mortgage. If the mortgagee so directs in writing, any surplus may be applied towards discharge of the principal money lent on mortgage; otherwise, it is payable to the person who would have been entitled to it had the receiver not been appointed, normally the mortgagor.[99]

The mortgagee's remedies are cumulative. A mortgagee is not bound to select one of the above remedies and pursue that and no other: subject to his not recovering more than is due to him, he may employ any or all of the remedies to enforce payment.[1] Thus if he sells the property for less than the mortgage debt, he may then sue the mortgagor upon the personal covenant for payment[2]; and this is so even if the sale was by the court and the mortgagee, bidding by leave of the court, has purchased the property.[3]

However, if he wishes to sue after foreclosure, he can do so only on condition that he opens the foreclosure[4]; for despite the foreclosure he is treating the mortgage as being still alive. Consequently, if by disposing of the property after foreclosure the mortgagee has put it out of his power to open the foreclosure, he cannot sue upon the personal covenant.[5]

It may be noted that two of the mortgagee's remedies are derived from the common law (an action on the covenant, and the right to take possession), one is equitable (foreclosure) and two were formerly contractual and are now statutory (sale, and the appointment of a receiver).

II. EQUITABLE MORTGAGEE OR CHARGEE

The extent to which the foregoing remedies are exercisable by an equitable mortgagee or chargee is as follows.

1. To sue for the money due. The position is the same as for a legal mortgage.

2. To foreclose. An equitable mortgagee may foreclose in the same way as a legal mortgagee.[6] An equitable chargee, however, has

---

[99] *Ibid*. s. 109.   [1] *Palmer* v. *Hendrie* (1859) 27 Beav. 349 at 351.
[2] *Rudge* v. *Richens* (1873) L.R. 8 C.P. 358.
[3] *Gordon Grant & Co. Ltd*. v. *Boos* [1926] A.C. 781.
[4] *Perry* v. *Barker* (1806) 13 Ves. 198; and see *ante*, p. 473.
[5] *Palmer* v. *Hendrie* (1859) 27 Beav. 349.
[6] *James* v. *James* (1873) L.R. 16 Eq. 153.

no right of foreclosure,[7] for a charge effects no conveyance of a legal or equitable interest.

3. To sell. The statutory power of sale [8] applies wherever the mortgage or charge was made by deed; other mortgagees or chargees have no power of sale. But although an equitable mortgagee or chargee by deed has the statutory power of sale, this generally does not enable him to convey the legal estate to the purchaser.[9] To overcome this defect, either or both of two conveyancing devices are employed.

(a) *Power of attorney*: an irrevocable power of attorney is inserted in the deed empowering the mortgagee or his assigns to convey the legal estate.

(b) *Declaration of trust*: a clause is inserted in the deed whereby the mortgagor declares that he holds the legal estate on trust for the mortgagee and empowers the mortgagee to appoint himself or his nominee as trustee in place of the mortgagor. The mortgagee can thus vest the legal estate in himself or the purchaser.

4. Possible right to take possession. Although it is usually said that an equitable mortgagee, having no legal estate, has no right to possession, on principle there seems no reason why, like a tenant under an equitable lease, he should not be entitled to it.[10] But if the land is let, he cannot collect the rent from the tenant, for that is payable to the legal reversioner [11]; and an equitable chargee, who has not even the benefit of a contract to create a legal mortgage, cannot even claim possession.

5. To appoint a receiver. As in the case of the power of sale, the statutory power to appoint a receiver [12] exists only if the mortgage or charge was made by deed. In other cases, a receiver can be obtained only by application to the court.

B. Other Rights of a Mortgagee

Certain other rights of a mortgagee must now be considered. The

---

[7] *Re Lloyd* [1903] 1 Ch. 385.   [8] *Ante*, pp. 474 *et seq.*
[9] See *Re Hodson and Howes' Contract* (1887) 35 Ch.D. 668; contrast *Re White Rose Cottage* [1965] Ch. 940 at 951.
[10] See M. & W. 917–918; *ante*, p. 342.
[11] *Finck* v. *Tranter* [1905] 1 K.B. 427.
[12] *Ante*, pp. 478 *et seq.*

position of these and other matters is in general the same for both mortgages and charges, whether legal or equitable, and " mortgage " will accordingly be used hereafter to include all such incumbrances unless the contrary is indicated.

1. Right to fixtures. It is a question of construction to determine what property is included in a mortgage. However, subject to any contrary intention, a mortgage includes all fixtures attached to the land either at the date of the mortgage or thereafter; the exceptions as between landlord and tenant do not apply.[13]

2. Right to possession of the title deeds. A first mortgagee has the same right to the title deeds as if he had the fee simple or an assignment of the lease which has been mortgaged, as the case may be [14]; but under all mortgages made since 1881, the mortgagor is entitled to inspect and make copies of the deeds, despite any contrary agreement.[15] If the mortgage is redeemed by the mortgagor, the mortgagee must deliver the deeds to him, unless he has notice of some subsequent incumbrance, in which case the deeds should be delivered to the incumbrancer next in order of priority of whom the mortgagee has notice. Contrary to the general rule that registration is notice, registration under the Land Charges Act 1925 or in a local register is not deemed to be notice for this purpose,[16] although as has been seen a mortgagee is bound to search before he distributes any surplus after a sale.[17] If a mortgage becomes statute-barred by lapse of time,[18] the mortgagee must return the deeds even if no part of the mortgage debt has been or will be paid.[19]

3. Right to insure against fire at the mortgagor's expense. Under the Law of Property Act 1925,[20] replacing provisions in the Conveyancing Act 1881, a mortgagee may insure the mortgaged property against fire and charge the premiums on the property in the same way as the money lent; this power, which is given only where the mortgage was made by deed, is exercisable as soon as the mortgage is made. The amount of the insurance must not exceed the amount specified in the deed, or, if none, two-thirds of the amount required to restore the property in case of total destruction. But the mortgagee cannot exercise his power if—

---

13 *Ante*, pp. 377, 378.
15 *Ibid.* s. 96 (1).
17 *Ante*, p. 476.
19 *Lewis* v. *Plunket* [1937] Ch. 306.

14 L.P.A. 1925, ss. 85 (1), 86 (1).
16 *Ibid.* s. 96 (2), added by L.P.(Am.)A. 1926, Sched.
18 *Post*, p. 531.
20 ss. 101 (1), 108.

(i) the mortgage deed declares that no insurance is required; or

(ii) the mortgagor keeps up an insurance in accordance with the mortgage deed; or

(iii) the mortgage deed is silent as to insurance and the mortgagor keeps up an insurance to the amount authorised by the Act with the mortgagee's consent.

4. Right to consolidate.

(a) *The right.* Consolidation may be described as the right of a person in whom two or more mortgages are vested to refuse to allow one mortgage to be redeemed unless the other or others are also redeemed. In its basic form, the principle is simple. If A has mortgaged both Blackacre and Whiteacre to X, each property being worth £1,500 and each loan being £1,000, it would be unfair, if the value of Blackacre subsequently sinks to £500 and the value of White acre doubles, to allow A to redeem Whiteacre and leave Blackacre unredeemed. In such a case, equity permits X to consolidate, and so to oblige A to redeem both mortgages or neither; in seeking redemption, A is asking for the assistance of equity, and equity puts its own price upon its interference, saying that he who seeks equity must do equity.

This simple concept has been elaborated to some extent; different considerations may arise where third parties are concerned, *e.g.*, by transfer of a mortgage. The rules on the subject may be stated as follows.

(b) *Conditions.* There can be no consolidation unless the following four conditions are satisfied:

(1) RESERVATION OF RIGHT: either both the mortgages were made before 1882, or at least one of the mortgages shows an intent to allow consolidation. Before 1882, the right existed automatically provided the other conditions were satisfied; but after 1881, the Conveyancing Act 1881 made it necessary to reserve the right. The Law of Property Act 1925, s. 93, now provides that with the two exceptions stated above there is no right to consolidate. It is common practice for a mortgage to contain a clause excluding the operation of section 93, so permitting consolidation.

(2) REDEMPTION DATES PASSED: in the case of both mortgages, the legal dates for redemption have passed.[21] Consolidation is an equitable doctrine and does not come into play unless only the equitable rights to redeem are concerned.

[21] *Cummins* v. *Fletcher* (1880) 14 Ch.D. 699.

(3) SAME MORTGAGOR: both mortgages were made by the same mortgagor.[22]   Mortgages made by different mortgagors can never be consolidated, even if both properties later come into the same hands. This is so even if X makes one mortgage and Y, as trustee for X, makes the other, or if A makes one mortgage and A and B jointly make the other.[23]   But it is immaterial whether or not the mortgages were made to the same mortgagees.

(4) SIMULTANEOUS UNIONS OF MORTGAGES AND EQUITIES: there has been a time when both the mortgages have been vested in one person and simultaneously both the equities of redemption have been vested in another.[24]   If this state of affairs exists at the time when redemption is sought, the mortgagee can consolidate, subject to the other conditions being fulfilled.   Even if this state of affairs has ceased to exist when redemption is sought, and the equities of redemption are then owned by different persons, a mortgagee who holds both mortgages can consolidate.

(c) *Illustrations*.   There is no need to illustrate (1) and (2), but the following examples may be given of the operation of (3) and (4).

(i)

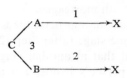

This represents the following steps:

    (1) A mortgages one estate to **X**.
    (2) B mortgages another estate to **X**.
    (3) C purchases the equities of redemption of both properties.

There can be no consolidation here, even though Condition (4) is satisfied, for the mortgages were made by different mortgagors.

(ii)

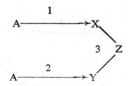

[2] *Sharp* v. *Rickards* [1909] 1 Ch. 109.
[3] *Thorneycroft* v. *Crockett* (1848) 2 H.L.C. 239.
[4] See *Pledge* v. *White* [1896] A.C. 187 at 198.

    (1) A mortgages one estate to X.
    (2) A mortgages another estate to Y.
    (3) Z purchases both mortgages.

Here Z can consolidate, provided Conditions (1) and (2) are satisfied. Condition (3) is satisfied and so is Condition (4).

    (iii)

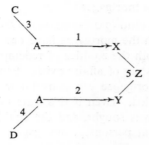

    (1) A mortgages one estate to X.
    (2) A mortgages another estate to Y.
    (3) C purchases the equity on the first estate.
    (4) D purchases the equity on the second estate.
    (5) Z purchases both mortgages.

There can be no consolidation here, for Condition (4) is not satisfied. It is true that at one stage (after Step (2)) both equities were in
one person's hands, and that at another stage (Step (5)) both mortgages were in another person's hands; but at no one moment have
both these conditions obtained. The equities separated before the
mortgages came together.

If C instead of D had purchased the equity on the second estate, Z
could have consolidated, even though at the time of C's purchase no
right to consolidate had arisen; the purchaser of two or more equities
takes subject to the risk of the mortgages coming into the same hand
and so permitting consolidation.

    (iv)

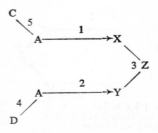

This represents the same position as the previous example, except that Steps (3) and (5) have changed places. As Z has now purchased both mortgages *before* A parted with either equity, Z may consolidate the mortgages provided Conditions (1) and (2) are satisfied. In this event, if C seeks to redeem his mortgage, Z can refuse redemption unless C purchases the mortgage on D's property as well as redeeming his own mortgage.

(d) *More than two mortgages.* These rules of consolidation apply equally when it is sought to consolidate more than two mortgages. Sometimes it will be found that while Mortgage I can be consolidated with Mortgages II and III, there is no right to consolidate Mortgages II and III with each other, *e.g.,* if only Mortgage I contains a consolidation clause. Examples containing more than two mortgages are best worked out by taking the mortgages in pairs and applying the rules to each pair in turn.

(e) *Extent of doctrine.* The nature of the mortgages or the property mortgaged is immaterial. There can be consolidation even if one mortgage is legal and one equitable, or if both are equitable, or if one mortgage is of personalty and the other of realty,[25] or if both are mortgages of personalty. The doctrine has even been applied to two mortgages on the same property.[26] Further, it is immaterial whether the equity of redemption has been conveyed *in toto* or whether it has merely been mortgaged; a mortgagee of an equity of redemption is a purchaser *pro tanto, i.e.,* to the extent of his interest. Thus if a mortgagee has a right of consolidation, it is effective against subsequent mortgagees of the property as well as the mortgagor.

(f) *Purchasers.* The doctrine of consolidation makes it dangerous to buy property subject to a mortgage without careful inquiry. If a right to consolidate has once arisen, a person who subsequently acquires one or both of the equities of redemption is liable to have the mortgages consolidated against him; and even if no right to consolidate has arisen, a person who acquires two equities of redemption is liable to have the mortgages consolidated if one person acquires both of them. But a person who acquires only one equity of redemption at a time when no right to consolidate has arisen normally suffers no risk of consolidation.[27]

[25] *Tassell* v. *Smith* (1858) 2 De G. & J. 713.
[26] *Re Salmon* [1903] 1 K.B. 147; *sed quaere.*
[27] *Harter* v. *Coleman* (1882) 19 Ch.D. 630.

5. Right to tack. This is considered below.[28]

Sect. 2. Rights Common to Both Parties

A. Power of Leasing

1. Leases not binding. The most important right common to both parties is the right of leasing the mortgaged property. Apart from any statutory or contractual provisions, the position of a mortgagor as soon as he has made a mortgage is that he has granted a long term of years to the mortgagee and retains merely the reversion on that lease together with an equity of redemption. The mortgagor consequently has no right to possession of land and so cannot grant a lease giving anyone else the right to possession. In practice, however, the mortgagor is usually left in possession of the land, and it was held before 1926, when mortgages were created by conveying the whole of the mortgagor's estate, that if the mortgagor granted a lease, he was unable subsequently to deny the validity of that lease and eject the tenant, for the lease bound both the mortgagor and the tenant under the doctrine of estoppel.[29] But the mortgagee is not bound, and in the same way that he can take possession from the mortgagor, he can take possession from a tenant of the mortgagor.[30] As to the mortgagee, although he is entitled to possession of the land at law, leases granted by him will cease to be binding on the mortgagor if he redeems the mortgage,[31] for in equity the mortgagor is entitled to redeem his property as free from incumbrances as it was when mortgaged.

It will be seen from this that once property had been mortgaged, a satisfactory lease could be made only if both mortgagor and mortgagee concurred in granting it, or if the mortgage gave either or both of the parties power to grant binding leases. However, statute has materially altered this position, and the following provisions apply to all mortgages made after 1881 if the parties have not expressed a contrary intention, either in the mortgage or otherwise in writing.[32] It is common for mortgages to preclude the mortgagor from exercising any power to grant leases or tenancies.

2. Power to lease. A power to grant leases which will be binding on both mortgagor and mortgagee is exercisable—

---

[28] *Post,* pp. 510 *et seq.*
[29] *Cuthbertson* v. *Irving* (1859) 4 H. & N. 742 at 754; *ante,* p. 352.
[30] *Rogers* v. *Humphreys* (1835) 4 A. & E. 299 at 313.
[31] See *Chapman* v. *Smith* [1907] 2 Ch. 97 at 102.
[32] L.P.A. 1925, s. 99, replacing C.A. 1881, s. 18.

(1) by the mortgagee, if he is in possession or has appointed a receiver who is still acting; otherwise,

(2) by the mortgagor, if he is in possession.

3. Term of lease. A lease may be granted for the following terms—

(1) if the mortgage was made before 1926, for not more than—
  (i) 21 years for agricultural or occupation purposes;
  (ii) 99 years for building:

(2) if the mortgage was made after 1925, for not more than—
  (i) 50 years for agricultural or occupation purposes;
  (ii) 999 years for building.

4. Conditions of lease. To fall within the statutory powers, any case granted must comply with the following conditions:

(1) It must be limited to take effect in possession not later than twelve months after its date.

(2) It must reserve the best rent reasonably obtainable, and with certain qualifications no fine may be taken.

(3) It must contain a covenant by the lessee for payment of rent and a condition of re-entry on the rent not being paid for a specified period not exceeding thirty days.

(4) A counterpart of the lease must be executed by the lessee and delivered to the lessor. A counterpart of any lease granted by the mortgagor must be delivered within one month to the mortgagee.[33]

Neither the statutory powers of leasing nor any provision in the mortgage excluding these powers (as is common in the case of the mortgagor) deprives either party of his common law right to grant a lease which will not bind the other unless adopted by him.[34] Further, the parties may extend the statutory powers by an agreement in writing, whether in the mortgage or not.[35]

B. *Power of Accepting Surrenders of Leases*

In the case of a mortgage made after 1911, if the parties have not expressed a contrary intention, either in the mortgage or otherwise in writing, statute [36] enables a surrender of any lease or tenancy to be effected, binding the parties to the mortgage, on the following terms.

---

[33] See *Public Trustee* v. *Lawrence* [1912] 1 Ch. 789.
[34] *Rust* v. *Goodale* [1957] Ch. 33 ; contrast *Taylor* v. *Ellis* [1960] Ch. 368.
[35] L.P.A. 1925, s. 99 (14).
[36] *Ibid.* s. 100, replacing C.A. 1911, s. 3.

(a) *Power to accept.* The surrender may be accepted—

    (1) by the mortgagee, if he is in possession or has appointed a receiver who is still acting; otherwise,

    (2) by the mortgagor, if he is in possession.

(b) *Conditions of surrender.* For the surrender to be valid—

    (1) an authorised lease of the property must be granted to take effect in possession within one month of the surrender;

    (2) the term of the new lease must not be shorter than the unexpired residue of the surrendered lease; and

    (3) the rent reserved by the new lease must not be less than the rent reserved by the surrendered lease.

The statutory power of accepting a surrender is thus exercisable only for the purpose of replacing one lease by another [37]; but the power may be extended by an agreement in writing, whether in the mortgage or not.

Sect. 3. Rights of the Mortgagor

A. Right of Redemption

I. PROTECTION OF THE MORTGAGOR

One aspect of equity's protection of the mortgagor's equity of redemption is to be found in the maxim " once a mortgage, always a mortgage." This is applied in two ways.

1. The test of a mortgage is substance, not form: if a transaction is in substance a mortgage, equity will treat it as such, even if it is dressed up in some other guise, as by the documents being cast in the form of an absolute conveyance.[38] Thus if a mortgage is expressed in the form of a conveyance with an option for the mortgagor to repurchase the property in a year's time, the mortgagor is entitled to redeem it even after the year has expired.[39]

2. No clogs on the equity: there must be no clog or fetter on the equity of redemption. This means not only that the mortgagor cannot be prevented from eventually redeeming his property, but also that he cannot be prevented from redeeming it free from any conditions or stipulations in the mortgage.

[37] See *Barclays Bank Ltd.* v. *Stasek* [1957] Ch. 28.
[38] *Barnhart* v. *Greenshields* (1853) 9 Moo.P.C. 18.
[39] See *Waters* v. *Mynn* (1850) 15 L.T.(o.s.) 157.

(a) *No irredeemability*: it is impossible to provide that a mortgage shall be totally irredeemable [40] or that the right of redemption shall be confined to certain persons or to a limited period.[41] A provision in a mortgage that the property shall become the mortgagee's absolutely when some specified event occurs is void.[42] In all such cases, the owner of the equity of redemption may redeem as if there had been no such restriction. But once the mortgage has been made, equity will not intervene if the mortgagor, by a separate and independent transaction, gives the mortgagee an option of purchasing the property and thus of depriving the mortgagor of his equity of redemption.[43] While the mortgagor is in the defenceless position of seeking a loan, or arranging for a transfer of the mortgage,[44] equity will protect him; but once he has obtained the loan or secured the transfer, this protection is not needed.

A provision postponing the date of redemption until some future period longer than the customary six months, *e.g.*, for forty years, is valid, provided the mortgage as a whole is not so oppressive and unconscionable that equity would not enforce it, and provided it does not make the equitable right to redeem illusory.[45] In one case, a lease for twenty years was mortgaged on conditions which prevented its redemption until six weeks before the end of the term; such a provision rendered the equitable right to redeem illusory and so was held void.[46] In another, the amount payable on redemption was so large as to render the equity of redemption valueless; the mortgage was held redeemable on repayment of principal and a reasonable rate of interest.[47] But subject to cases such as these, the court will not interfere with a bargain made between two parties on an equal footing, even if this does postpone redemption for a considerable period.

Limited companies are not protected by this rule, for by statute a debenture may be made wholly or partly irredeemable, and even an ordinary mortgage by a company is a debenture.[48]

(b) *Redemption free from conditions in the mortgage*: the mortgagor cannot be prevented from redeeming the property free

---

[40] *Re Wells* [1933] Ch. 29 at 52.
[41] *Salt* v. *Marquess of Northampton* [1892] A.C. 1.
[42] *Toomes* v. *Conset* (1745) 3 Atk. 261.   [43] *Reeve* v. *Lisle* [1902] A.C. 461.
[44] *Lewis* v. *Frank Love Ltd.* [1961] 1 W.L.R. 261.
[45] *Knightsbridge Estates Trust Ltd.* v. *Byrne* [1939] Ch. 441 (affirmed on other grounds: *infra*, n. 48).
[46] *Fairclough* v. *Swan Brewery Co. Ltd.* [1912] A.C. 565.
[47] *Cityland and Property (Holdings) Ltd.* v. *Dabrah* [1968] Ch. 166.
[48] Companies Act 1948, s. 89; *Knightsbridge Estates Trust Ltd.* v. *Byrne* [1940] A.C. 613.

from all conditions or stipulations in the mortgage. The essence of a mortgage is a loan of money in return for security. Sometimes terms are inserted in a mortgage which give the mortgagee some other advantage in addition to his security. If this advantage is obtained by fraud or oppression, it will be set aside, but otherwise there is no objection to an advantage which ceases whenever the mortgage is redeemed, such as a provision making the mortgaged property, a public-house, a " tied " house until redemption.[49] Yet such a provision may be void as being an unreasonable restraint of trade.[50] The general enforceability of advantages which end on redemption represents an advance on the attitude which the courts had at one time adopted, rendering all collateral advantages for the mortgagee void.[51] After the last of the statutes dealing with usury was repealed in 1854, the courts gradually became more liberal and it is now settled that in certain cases a collateral advantage may remain effective even after redemption.

The chief difficulty in stating the present position lies in trying to reconcile the clog held void in *Bradley* v. *Carritt* [52] with the collateral advantage held valid in *Kreglinger* v. *New Patagonia Meat, etc., Co. Ltd.*[53] In *Bradley's* case the substance of the transaction was a mortgage of shares in which the mortgagor bound himself to endeavour to induce the company to employ the mortgagee as broker, and if the company did not, to pay the mortgagee an amount equivalent to the broker's fees. In *Kreglinger's* case, the substance of the transaction was a loan of money to a meat company in return for an option for five years on any sheepskins which the company had for sale. The differing results in these cases may perhaps best be explained by saying that in *Bradley's* case the agreement fettering the mortgagor was a mere clause put in a mortgage, and so void, the basis of the agreement being a mortgage and nothing else; in *Kreglinger's* case, on the other hand, the transaction was substantially the grant of an option in return for a loan of money, with the result that the option was not merely a part of the mortgage but a separate and independent transaction and so valid. But the matter is far from clear.[54]

---

[49] *Biggs* v. *Hoddinott* [1898] 2 Ch. 307.
[50] *Esso Petroleum Co. Ltd.* v. *Harper's Garage (Stourport) Ltd.* [1968] A.C. 269.
[51] See *Jennings* v. *Ward* (1705) 2 Vern. 520 at 521.
[52] [1903] A.C. 253.
[53] [1914] A.C. 25.
[54] See generally Waldock, *Mortgages* (2nd ed., 1950), pp. 183–192.

II. WHO CAN REDEEM

Redemption is usually sought by the mortgagor; but the right to redeem is not confined to him and may be exercised by any person interested in the equity of redemption.[55] Thus the right to redeem extends to assignees of the equity of redemption, subsequent mortgagees, and even a lessee under a lease granted by the mortgagor but not binding on the mortgagee.[56]

III. EFFECT OF REDEMPTION

Where redemption is effected by the only person interested in the equity of redemption, and the mortgage redeemed is the only incumbrance on the property, the effect of redemption is to discharge the mortgage and leave the property free from incumbrances. But if there are several mortgages on the property, the effect of redemption will normally be that the person paying the money takes a transfer of the mortgage, as where a second mortgagee redeems the first mortgage. If several incumbrancers seek to redeem a mortgage, the first in order of priority has the best claim.[57] However, if the mortgagor redeems a mortgage which has priority over one or more subsequent mortgages, the redemption discharges the mortgage and the mortgagor cannot claim to have it kept alive to the prejudice of the subsequent mortgagees,[58] for his mortgage to them included all the rights he had, including those against the prior mortgagee. But no such rule binds his successors in title.[59]

An incumbrancer who is entitled to redeem a mortgage may usually, instead of redeeming, insist upon the mortgagee transferring the mortgage to a nominee of the person paying the money.[60]

IV. TERMS OF REDEMPTION

A mortgage may be redeemed either in court or out of court; the latter is the more usual. If a mortgagee unreasonably refuses to accept a proper tender of the money due and so makes an action for redemption necessary, he may be penalised in costs.[61]

The mortgagor may redeem on the legal date for redemption without giving notice of his intention to do so. After that date,

[55] *Pearce* v. *Morris* (1869) 5 Ch.App. 227 at 229.
[56] *Tarn* v. *Turner* (1888) 39 Ch.D. 456.
[57] *Teevan* v. *Smith* (1882) 20 Ch.D. 724 at 730.
[58] *Otter* v. *Lord Vaux* (1856) 6 De G.M. & G. 638.
[59] *Whiteley* v. *Delaney* [1914] A.C. 132.
[60] L.P.A. 1925, s. 95.
[61] *Graham* v. *Seal* (1918) 88 L.J.Ch. 31.

when he is forced to rely upon his equitable right to redeem, it is a rule of practice that he must either give the mortgagee reasonable notice of his intention to redeem (six months usually sufficing), or else pay him six months' interest in lieu thereof [62]; it is only fair that the mortgagee should have a reasonable opportunity of finding another investment for his money. But the mortgagee is not entitled to any notice or interest in lieu thereof—

  (i) if he has taken steps to enforce his security, as by taking possession, or commencing foreclosure proceedings, or giving the mortgagor notice to repay the loan so as to entitle the mortgagee to sell on default being made [63]; or

  (ii) if the loan is merely of a temporary nature, as is usually the case in an equitable mortgage by deposit of title deeds.[64]

If the mortgagor gives six months' notice and fails to pay on the proper day, he must usually give a further six months' notice or pay six months' interest in lieu thereof,[65] unless he can give a reasonable explanation of his failure to pay, in which case it suffices to give reasonable notice, *e.g.*, three months.[66]

V. " REDEEM UP, FORECLOSE DOWN "

The maxim " Redeem up, foreclose down " applies where there are several incumbrancers and one of them seeks by action to redeem a superior mortgage. The effect is best shown by an example. X has mortgaged his property successively to A, B, C, D and E, the mortgages ranking in that order; X thus ranks last, *e.g.*, in claiming any surplus if the property is sold. Suppose that D wishes to redeem B and owing to the complexity of the accounts or some other circumstance an action for redemption is commenced. Before B can be redeemed, the exact amount due to him must be settled by the court. This amount, however, does not affect only B and D, for C, E and X are all concerned with the amount which has priority to their interests; thus if the property were to be sold, C, E and X would all wish to know whether what B was entitled to was, say, £6,000 or £7,000, for upon that figure might depend their chances of receiving anything from the proceeds of sale. Consequently, the court will insist upon their being made parties to D's action for

---

[62] *Johnson* v. *Evans* (1889) 61 L.T. 18.
[63] See *Bovill* v. *Endle* [1896] 1 Ch. 648.
[64] *Fitzgerald's Trustee* v. *Mellersh* [1892] 1 Ch. 385.
[65] *Re Moss* (1885) 31 Ch.D. 90 at 94.
[66] *Cromwell Property Investment Co. Ltd.* v. *Western* [1934] Ch. 322.

redemption so that they can be represented in the taking of the accounts between B and D and thus be bound by the final result.

However, it would be unfair to give C, E and X the trouble and expense of taking part in the action merely to watch accounts being taken,[67] with the risk of a similar event taking place in the future, and so the court insists that the rights of all parties concerned in the action shall be settled once and for all. A is not concerned: it is immaterial to him what is due to B, for A's mortgage has priority to B's.[68] But all the other parties are concerned, and the order of the court will be that D shall redeem not only B, but also C, for both their mortgages have priority to D's. Further, E and X must be foreclosed: that is, each of them will have the opportunity of saving his rights by paying off the prior mortgages concerned in the action, but if he fails to do so, he will be foreclosed. Thus if E and X fail to redeem and are foreclosed, the final result will be that D, at the price of redeeming B and C, now holds the equity of redemption subject only to the first mortgage in favour of A.

The principle may be stated thus:—a mortgagee who seeks to redeem a prior mortgage by action must not only redeem any mortgages standing between him and that prior mortgage,[69] but must also foreclose all subsequent mortgagees and the mortgagor[70]; in short, " redeem up, foreclose down."

It should be noted that this rule does not apply to redemptions out of court,[71] and that there is no rule " foreclose down, redeem up "; a mortgagee who forecloses is under no obligation to redeem any prior mortgages,[72] although he must foreclose all subsequent mortgagees as well as the mortgagor.[73] In other words, for foreclosure the rule is simply " foreclose down ": a mortgagee cannot foreclose a subsequent mortgagee or the mortgagor unless he forecloses everyone beneath him.

VI. TERMINATION OF EQUITY OF REDEMPTION

An equity of redemption may be extinguished against the mortgagor's will:

    (i) by foreclosure[74];

[67] *Ramsbottom* v. *Wallis* (1835) 5 L.J.Ch. 92.
[68] *Brisco* v. *Kenrick* (1832) 1 L.J.Ch. 116.
[69] *Teevan* v. *Smith* (1882) 20 Ch.D. 724 at 729.
[70] *Farmer* v. *Curtis* (1829) 2 Sim. 466.
[71] See *Smith* v. *Green* (1844) 1 Coll.C.C. 555.
[72] *Richards* v. *Cooper* (1842) 5 Beav. 304.
[73] *Anderson* v. *Stather* (1845) 2 Coll.C.C. 209.
[74] *Ante*, pp. 472 *et seq.*

    (ii) by sale [75]; or

    (iii) by lapse of time.[76]

In addition, the mortgagor may himself extinguish it by releasing it to the mortgagee, or by redeeming.

B. *Other Rights*

The mortgagor has various other rights, including the right to have the property sold by the court, the right to inspect the title deeds, the right to compel a transfer of the mortgage and the right to bring actions. All except the last point have been dealt with already.[77] As to the right to bring actions, before 1926 the mortgagor normally had no legal estate in the land and so could bring no actions which depended on having such an estate, *e.g.*, on the covenants of a lease or tenancy which had been granted before the mortgage was made, so that the legal reversion on it had passed to the mortgagee [78]; and after 1925 the mortgagor's only interest is normally a reversion upon a long lease. But by statute,[79] provided the mortgagee has not given notice of his intention to take possession or enter into receipt of the rents and profits, the mortgagor in possession may sue in his own name for possession or for the rents and profits; he may bring an action to prevent, or recover damages for, any trespass or other wrong; and he may enforce all covenants and conditions in leases of the property.

Part 4

TRANSFER OF RIGHTS

Sect. 1. Death of Mortgagor

A mortgagor's equity of redemption has always been considered as realty, and accordingly passed to the devisee or heir in the same way as other realty. Unless the mortgagor left a will showing a contrary intention, his devisee or heir was entitled to call upon the personal representatives of the deceased to pay off the mortgage out of the deceased's estate in the same way as the other debts of the deceased

---

[75] *Ante*, pp. 474 *et seq.*
[76] *Post*, p. 531.
[77] *Ante*, pp. 473, 481, 491.
[78] See, *e.g.*, *Turner* v. *Walsh* [1909] 2 K.B. 484.
[79] L.P.A. 1925, ss. 98, 141, replacing earlier legislation.

had to be paid, and so free the property from the mortgage.[80] However, this applied only in respect of the personal covenant of the original mortgagor, and on the death of some other person in whom the equity of redemption was vested, such as a purchaser, his devisee or heir had no such right, for the mortgage debt was not a debt due from the estate of the deceased.[81]

This position was altered by the Real Estate Charges Acts 1854, 1867 and 1877 (known as Locke King's Acts), now replaced by the Administration of Estates Act 1925, s. 35. Before 1926, these provisions extended to all interests in realty and leaseholds, but not to pure personalty, such as rights under a trust for sale of land. In the case of deaths after 1925 the provisions extend to all property, whether real or personal. Their effect is that unless the deceased has shown a contrary intention[82] in any document (whether his will or some other document) the property devolves upon the person entitled under the will or intestacy subject to the mortgage or charge; but these provisions do not extend to a person who takes not as legatee or devisee but, *e.g.*, as a purchaser under an option given to him by the will.[83]

These provisions do not affect any rights the mortgagee may have against the estate of the mortgagor; they merely ensure that as between the person taking the mortgaged property and the other beneficiaries, the burden of the mortgage should fall upon the former.

Sect. 2. Death of Mortgagee

A. Death of Sole Mortgagee

1. Freeholds. Before 1926, a mortgagee of freeholds had two separate rights vested in him:

   (i) the legal estate, which was realty; and
   (ii) the right to the money lent, which was personalty.

Consequently on the death of a sole mortgagee, the right to the mortgage money passed to his personal representatives, and the legal estate passed to his devisee or heir, who held it on trust for the persons entitled to the money. Thus if the mortgagor wished to redeem, he had to pay the money to the persons entitled to it under the will or intestacy, and obtain a reconveyance of the legal estate

---

[80] *Galton* v. *Hancock* (1743) 2 Atk. 427.
[81] *Butler* v. *Butler* (1800) 5 Ves. 534.
[82] See *Re Wakefield* [1943] 2 All E.R. 29; *Re Neeld* [1962] Ch. 643.
[83] *Re Fison's W.T.* [1950] Ch. 394.

from the devisee or heir. Apart from requiring two separate transactions, this might well be inconvenient, as when the mortgagee had
devised his realty equally between his fifteen children, so making it
necessary for all of them to execute the reconveyance. Now, by
statute,[84] where a mortgagee dies after 1881 the legal estate in such
cases vests in his personal representatives notwithstanding any
disposition by the mortgagee's will.

2. Leaseholds. Leaseholds, being personalty, have always passed
to the personal representatives, so that no difficulty arose on the death
of a sole mortgagee of leaseholds.

B. Death of One of Several Mortgagees

1. At law. Where two or more persons lent money on mortgage
of freeholds or leaseholds, the legal estate was usually conveyed to
them as joint tenants. On the death of one, his interest passed to the
others by virtue of the *jus accrescendi,* and the survivors could
reconvey the legal estate to the mortgagor when he redeemed.

2. In equity. In equity, however, there is a presumption of a
tenancy in common where two or more together lend money on
mortgage.[85]   Accordingly, in the absence of any provision to the
contrary, when one of the mortgagees died his share passed to his
personal representatives, and if the mortgagor redeemed they would
have to join in the transaction. If the mortgagees were trustees lending trust money, the disclosure of this fact would be sufficient to rebut
the presumption, for trustees are always joint tenants[86]; but this
would have the disadvantage of bringing the trusts on to the title.[87]

3. Joint account clause. The practice accordingly grew up of
inserting a " joint account clause " in mortgages where two or more
persons lent money. This clause rebutted the presumption of a tenancy in common so far as the mortgagor was concerned and made it
safe for him to pay his money to the surviving mortgagees. Since
1881 such a clause is unnecessary, for statute[88] has provided that as
between the mortgagor and the mortgagees, the mortgagees are
deemed to have advanced the money on a joint account unless a

---

[84] A.E.A. 1925, ss. 1 (1), 3 (1), replacing C.A. 1881, s. 30.
[85] *Ante,* p. 214.
[86] *Ante,* p. 209.
[87] See, *e.g., Re Blaiberg and Abrahams* [1899] 2 Ch. 340.
[88] C.A. 1881, s. 61, replaced by L.P.A. 1925, s. 111.

contrary intention appears. The result is that the survivor or survivors can give a complete discharge for all moneys due notwithstanding any notice of severance which the mortgagor may have. This, however, is mere conveyancing machinery; it does not affect the position of the mortgagees *inter se*, and if they are beneficially entitled and not trustees, the survivors must account to the personal representatives of the deceased mortgagee for his share.[89] Although a joint account clause in a mortgage today is thus strictly unnecessary, it is often inserted *ex abundanti cautela*.

Sect. 3. Transfer of Equity of Redemption Inter Vivos

A mortgagor may at any time without the mortgagee's consent make a conveyance of his property subject to the mortgage. However, notwithstanding any such conveyance, the mortgagor remains personally liable on the covenant to pay the money.[90] He therefore usually takes an express covenant for indemnity from the transferee, although such an obligation is implied.[91]

A mortgagor who wishes to sell free from the mortgage may do so—

   (i) if he redeems; or

  (ii) if the mortgagee consents (as he may well do if the security is adequate or if some other property is substituted for the property in question); or

 (iii) if the mortgagor takes advantage of the statutory provision enabling the court to declare property free from an incumbrance upon sufficient money being paid into court.[92]

An assignee of the equity of redemption in general steps into the shoes of the mortgagor; but he does not merely by the assignment become personally liable to the mortgagee to pay the mortgage debt.[93]

Sect. 4. Transfer of Mortgages Inter Vivos

A. In General

A mortgagee may transfer his mortgage at any time without the concurrence of the mortgagor. However, for various reasons it is advisable for the mortgagor's concurrence to be obtained, *e.g.,* in

---

[89] See *Re Jackson* (1887) 34 Ch.D. 732.
[90] *Kinnaird* v. *Trollope* (1888) 39 Ch.D. 636.
[91] *Bridgman* v. *Daw* (1891) 40 W.R. 253.
[92] L.P.A. 1925, s. 50, replacing C.A. 1881, s. 5 (1).
[93] *Re Errington* [1894] 1 Q.B. 11.

order to obtain his admission of the state of accounts showing the amount still due under the mortgage.[94]

Once the transfer has been made, the transferee should give notice of it to the mortgagor, unless the mortgagor has notice already, *e.g.*, because he was a party to the transfer. If the mortgagor has no actual or constructive notice, the transferee cannot complain if the mortgagor pays to the transferor money due under the mortgage.[95]

B. Sub-Mortgages

A sub-mortgage is a mortgage of a mortgage. A mortgagee may, instead of transferring his mortgage, borrow money upon the security of it. Thus if X has lent £20,000 upon a mortgage made by B, and X then wishes to raise a temporary loan of £2,000 himself, it would clearly be inadvisable for X to call in the whole of his loan. Consequently, X would raise the money by mortgaging his mortgage, *i.e.*, by making a sub-mortgage.

Before 1926, a sub-mortgage was effected by a transfer of the mortgage subject to a proviso for redemption. After 1925, this form is still available if the mortgage is equitable or is a legal charge; but where it has been created by the grant of a term of years, a legal sub-mortgage can be made only by the grant of a sub-term or by a legal charge.[96] In general, the sub-mortgagee takes over the mortgagee's rights of enforcing payment under the original mortgage; thus he may sell the property. Alternatively, he may exercise his remedies against the mortgage, as by selling it.[97]

Sect. 5. Discharge of Mortgage

A. Before 1926

Upon the redemption of a legal mortgage of a fee simple before 1926, the mortgagee had to execute a reconveyance of the fee simple. In the case of leaseholds, there was a reassignment or, if the mortgage had been made by subdemise, a surrender of the sub-lease. In each case, the document contained a receipt for the money paid. However, in the case of a mortgage to a building society, a mere receipt indorsed on the mortgage deed operated both as a discharge of the

---

[94] See *Turner* v. *Smith* [1901] 1 Ch. 213.
[95] *Dixon* v. *Winch* [1900] 1 Ch. 736 at 742.
[96] L.P.A. 1925, s. 86 (1), (3).
[97] See generally Fisher & Lightwood, *Mortgages* (7th ed., 1931), p. 102.

mortgage and a reconveyance of the estate [98]; and an equitable mortgage was sufficiently discharged by an indorsed receipt.

B. *After* 1925

In the case of any mortgage discharged after 1925, a receipt indorsed on or annexed to the mortgage deed, signed [99] by the mortgagee and stating the name of the person paying the money, normally operates as a surrender of the mortgage term or a reconveyance, as the case may be, and discharges the mortgage.[1] But if the receipt shows that the person paying the money was not entitled to the immediate equity of redemption and makes no provision to the contrary, it operates as a transfer of the mortgage to him.[2] Building society mortgages may still be discharged by a special form of receipt.[3]

Apart from these provisions, once a mortgage by subdemise has been redeemed, the sub-term becomes a satisfied term and ceases forthwith.[4] But although when coupled with this provision it might be thought that an ordinary receipt (*i.e.*, one not complying with the conditions relating to indorsed receipts, and bearing only a 2d. stamp) would operate as a sufficient discharge and save the stamp duty of one shilling per £100 required on a receipt discharging a mortgage, conveyancers do not in practice rely upon such a receipt, for it is only prima facie proof of payment.

Part 5

PRIORITY OF MORTGAGES

Where there is more than one mortgage on the same property, it is sometimes necessary to determine the priority of the mortgages, *e.g.*, if the property is sold by one mortgagee and there is not enough money to satisfy all. The general rules for determining priority will be discussed first, followed by the rules relating to tacking, which is a mode of altering the priorities settled by the general rules. In each case the 1925 legislation has made important changes, so that separate consideration must be given to the positions before 1926 and after 1925.[5]

---

[98] Building Societies Acts 1836, s. 5; 1874, s. 42.
[99] See *Simpson* v. *Geoghegan* [1934] W.N. 232.
[1] L.P.A. 1925, s. 115 (1). [2] *Ibid*. s. 115 (2).
[3] See now Building Societies Act 1962, s. 37, which has equated the two forms of receipt. [4] *Ibid*. ss. 5, 116; *ante*, p. 464.
[5] The best modern survey of this difficult subject is in Waldock's *Mortgages* (2nd ed., 1950), Chap. 14.

Sect. 1. General Rules

A. Priority Before 1926

Before 1926, there was one set of rules for determining priorities where the property mortgaged was an interest in land, and a separate set of rules for cases where the property mortgaged was an equitable interest in pure personalty. These will be considered in turn.

I. MORTGAGES OF AN INTEREST IN LAND

If an interest in land had been mortgaged, the two following basic rules applied, whether the interest was legal or equitable and whether the land was freehold or leasehold:

(i) *" Qui prior est tempore, potior est jure "* (he who is first in time is stronger in law); mortgages primarily ranked in the order of their creation, or " First made, first paid ": but

(ii) *" Where the equities are equal, the law prevails "*; if, apart from the order of their creation, a legal and an equitable mortgage had equal claims to be preferred, the legal mortgage would have priority.

A conflict between two mortgages might fall under any of four heads:

(i) Where both mortgages were legal.
(ii) Where the first was legal and the second equitable.
(iii) Where the first was equitable and the second legal.
(iv) Where both were equitable.

These will be considered in turn.

1. Both mortgages legal. Conflicts where both mortgages were legal rarely came before the courts, since most mortgages were mortgages of freeholds effected by a conveyance of the fee simple, which made the creation of subsequent legal mortgages impossible. However, successive legal mortgages could be created by the grant of successive terms of years, and a lease might be mortgaged by the grant of two successive sub-leases.[6] In such cases, priority normally depended on the order of creation, for after the grant of one lease, the second lease must take effect in reversion upon the first, and a legal estate in reversion was postponed to one in possession.

2. Legal mortgage followed by equitable mortgage. Where a legal mortgage was followed by an equitable mortgage, the legal

[6] *Jones* v. *Rhind* (1869) 17 W.R. 1091.

mortgage had a double claim to priority, both as being prior in point of time and as being a legal mortgage in competition with a mere equitable mortgage.

However, this natural priority might be displaced in a number of ways.

(a) *By fraud.* If the legal mortgagee was guilty of some fraud whereby the equitable mortgagee was deceived into believing that there was no legal mortgage on the property, the legal mortgagee was postponed to the equitable mortgagee.[7]

(b) *By estoppel.* If the legal mortgagee either expressly or by implication made some misrepresentation by which the equitable mortgagee was deceived, the legal mortgagee might be estopped from asserting his priority.[8] Thus if the legal mortgagee indorsed a receipt for his money on the mortgage and somebody was thereby induced to lend money on an equitable mortgage of the property, the legal mortgagee could not afterwards claim priority for his loan if in fact it had not been discharged.[9] Again, if the legal mortgagee parted with the deeds to the mortgagor to enable him to raise money, he was postponed to any subsequent mortgagee who lent money without notice of the first mortgage, even if the mortgagor had agreed to inform the second mortgagee of the first mortgage, or had agreed to borrow only a limited amount which in fact he exceeded.[10] Once the mortgagee had clothed the mortgagor with apparent authority to deal with the property freely, he could not afterwards claim the protection of any undisclosed limits set to this authority.

(c) *By gross negligence in relation to the title deeds.* If the legal mortgagee was grossly negligent in failing to obtain the title deeds, he was postponed to a subsequent equitable mortgagee who had exercised due diligence. Failure to ask for the deeds at all would postpone a legal mortgagee [11]; it was otherwise if he inquired for them and was given a reasonable excuse.[12]

If the legal mortgagee obtained the deeds, it appears that no amount of carelessness in failing to keep them in safe custody would postpone him, *e.g.,* if through his carelessness the mortgagor obtained the deeds and deceived a second mortgagee [13]; but this has been questioned.

---

[7] *Peter* v. *Russel* (1716) 1 Eq.Ca.Abr. 321.
[8] *Dixon* v. *Muckleston* (1872) 8 Ch.App. 155 at 160.
[9] *Rimmer* v. *Webster* [1902] 2 Ch. 163.
[10] *Perry Herrick* v. *Attwood* (1857) 2 De G. & J. 21.
[11] *Walker* v. *Linom* [1907] 2 Ch. 104.   [12] *Manners* v. *Mew* (1885) 29 Ch.D. 725.
[13] *Northern Counties, etc., Insurance Co.* v. *Whipp* (1884) 26 Ch.D. 482.

3. Equitable mortgage followed by legal mortgage. Where an equitable mortgage was followed by a legal mortgage, the primary rule that the mortgages rank in the order of creation might be displaced by the superiority of a legal estate. For this to occur, the legal mortgagee had to show that he was a bona fide purchaser for value of a legal estate without notice of the prior equitable mortgage.[14] Usually the inability of the mortgagor to produce the title deeds would amount to notice to the legal mortgagee that some prior mortgage already existed [15]; but if the legal mortgagee's inquiries for the deeds were met by a reasonable excuse (*e.g.,* that the deeds were in Ireland, where the property was [16]), he would succeed in his claim to be a purchaser without notice and so to have priority over the equitable mortgagee.

4. Both mortgages equitable. Where both mortgages were equitable, the primary rule was that priority depended upon the order in which the mortgages were created; this, however, was subject to the equities being in other respects equal,[17] so that the order might be altered by the inequitable behaviour of the prior mortgagee.[18] Accordingly, a first mortgagee who failed to ask for the title deeds, or who, having obtained them, redelivered them to the mortgagor without pressing for their early return, might be postponed to a second mortgagee who took all proper precautions but who was nevertheless deceived.[19]

II. MORTGAGES OF AN EQUITABLE INTEREST IN PURE PERSONALTY

Legal mortgages of chattels fall under the head of bills of sale and are outside the scope of this book. Equitable interests in pure personalty, on the other hand, include the rights of those interested under a trust for sale [20] and so must be dealt with here. To mortgages of such interests, the rule in *Dearle* v. *Hall* [21] applied. This laid down that priority depended upon the order in which notice of the mortgages was received by the owner of the legal estate or interest (the trustees, in the case of a trust for sale). This, however, was subject to the important qualification that a mortgagee who,

---

[14] *Pilcher* v. *Rawlins* (1872) 7 Ch.App. 259; *Att.-Gen.* v. *Biphosphated Guano Co.* (1879) 11 Ch.D. 327.
[15] *Oliver* v. *Hinton* [1899] 2 Ch. 264.
[16] *Agra Bank Ltd.* v. *Barry* (1874) L.R. 7 H.L. 135.
[17] *Rice* v. *Rice* (1853) 2 Drew. 73.
[18] See *Taylor* v. *Russell* [1891] 1 Ch. 8.
[19] *Farrand* v. *Yorkshire Banking Co.* (1888) 40 Ch.D. 182.
[20] *Lee* v. *Howlett* (1856) 2 K. & J. 531.
[21] (1828) 3 Russ. 1.

when he lent his money, had actual or constructive notice of a prior mortgage could not gain priority over it by giving notice first.

Various explanations have been given of the reason for this rule, perhaps the least unsatisfactory of which is that as between two equally innocent incumbrancers, priority should be given to the one who, by giving notice, had prevented the mortgagor from representing that he was still the unincumbered owner of the interest and so defrauding third parties.[22] It will be noticed that for a second mortgagee to claim priority over a first mortgagee by giving notice first, he must be able to show that at the time of lending his money he had no notice of the first mortgage.[23] If at that time he had notice, and yet he lent his money, it would be inequitable for him subsequently to claim priority merely because he gave notice first, for the failure of the first mortgagee to give notice had in no way prejudiced him; he lent his money knowing of the first mortgage. But if he lent his money without notice of the first mortgage, it was immaterial that he had notice of the first mortgage at the time when he gave notice to the trustees.[24] Indeed, such knowledge is just what would impel him to give notice.[25]

The following points on the rule should be noted.

1. Priority depended upon notice being received, not given. Although it was both usual and advisable for a mortgagee to give express notice, the test was not whether the mortgagee had taken active steps to give notice but whether the trustees had received knowledge of the mortgage from any reliable source. Clear and distinct oral notice sufficed,[26] but not a statement made in a casual conversation with a trustee.[27] Knowledge received through reading a notice in a paper,[28] and knowledge acquired by a trustee before his appointment which continued to operate on his mind after his appointment,[29] have both been held sufficient to protect a mortgagee against a later mortgagee who gave express notice, although neither would suffice to gain priority for a later mortgagee over a prior mortgagee[30]; stronger measures are needed to upset the natural order of the mortgages than are needed to maintain it.

[22] See *Ward* v. *Duncombe* [1893] A.C. 369 at 392.
[23] *Re Holmes* (1885) 29 Ch.D. 786.
[24] *Mutual Life Assurance Society* v. *Langley* (1886) 32 Ch.D. 460.
[25] See also *post*, p. 511.
[26] *Re Worcester* (1868) 3 Ch.App. 555.
[27] *Re Tichener* (1865) 35 Beav. 317.
[28] *Lloyd* v. *Banks* (1868) 3 Ch.App. 488.
[29] *Ipswich Permanent Money Club Ltd.* v. *Arthy* [1920] 2 Ch. 257.
[30] *Arden* v. *Arden* (1885) 29 Ch.D. 702.

2. It was advisable to give notice to all of the trustees. This may be amplified as follows:

(i) Notice given to all the existing trustees remained effective even though they all retired or died without communicating the notice to their successors.[31]

(ii) Notice given to one of several trustees was effective against all incumbrances created during his trusteeship, and remained effective despite his death or retirement.[32]

(iii) On the other hand, notice given to one of several trustees was not effective against incumbrancers who advanced money after the death or retirement of that trustee without having communicated the notice to one or more of the continuing trustees.[33]

(iv) If the mortgagor was a trustee, the mere fact that he knew of the transaction would not affect priorities, for such notice afforded no protection to subsequent mortgagees.[34] But if the mortgagee was a trustee his knowledge of the transaction did affect priorities; for to protect his mortgage he would readily disclose its existence to any prospective incumbrancers.[35]

3. A mortgagee who lent his money with notice of a prior mortgage could not gain priority over it by giving notice first. This has been discussed above.[36]

In addition to securing priority, notice to the trustees safeguarded the mortgagee by ensuring that his claims should not be disregarded when the funds were distributed. Trustees were not liable if they distributed the trust funds to the prejudice of a mortgagee of whom they were unaware.[37] Nor were they bound to answer inquiries either by the beneficiary or a prospective mortgagee as to the extent to which the beneficiary's share was incumbered: " it is no part of the duty of a trustee to assist his *cestui que trust* in selling or mortgaging his beneficial interest and in squandering or anticipating his fortune." [38]

---

[31] *Re Wasdale* [1899] 1 Ch. 163.
[32] *Ward* v. *Duncombe* [1893] A.C. 369.
[33] *Re Phillips' Trusts* [1903] 1 Ch. 183.
[34] *Lloyds Bank* v. *Pearson* [1901] 1 Ch. 865.
[35] *Browne* v. *Savage* (1859) 4 Drew. 635.
[36] *Ante*, pp. 502, 503.
[37] *Phipps* v. *Lovegrove* (1873) L.R. 16 Eq. 80.
[38] *Low* v. *Bouverie* [1891] 3 Ch. 82 at 99, *per* Lindley L.J.

B. *Priority After* 1925

The general scheme of the 1925 legislation called for some amendment of the rules relating to priority. In particular, the old rule of the superiority of the legal estate was clearly inappropriate to a system which encouraged the creation of more than one legal mortgage of the same property. Further, since the interests of beneficiaries under strict settlements can no longer be legal, for the purposes of priority they could conveniently be classed with interests under a trust for sale. But subject to the statutory changes, the old rules still apply, so that, *e.g.*, competing equitable mortgages still prima facie rank according to the order of creation.[39]

Before 1926, the line of cleavage was whether the interest mortgaged was an interest in land or an interest in pure personalty: if the former, the case was governed by the rules relating to the order of creation and the superiority of the legal estate; if the latter, the rule in *Dearle* v. *Hall* applied. After 1925, the question is whether the interest mortgaged is legal or equitable. A mortgage of a legal estate in land now depends for its priority upon possession of the title deeds, or, in default, upon registration: a mortgage of an equitable interest in realty or personalty depends upon the rule in *Dearle* v. *Hall*. Thus if an equitable interest in settled land was mortgaged before 1926, priority depended on the order in which the mortgages were created: if it is mortgaged after 1925, the rule in *Dearle* v. *Hall* applies.

Priorities acquired before 1926 are not affected by the new rules, which apply only to mortgages created after 1925.[40]

I. MORTGAGES OF A LEGAL ESTATE [41]

1. Mortgages included. It should be noted that this head includes all mortgages of a legal estate, whether the mortgage itself is legal or equitable. The question is " Has a legal estate been mortgaged? ", not " Is the mortgage legal or equitable? "

2. Principles. The two main principles are these:

(a) *Mortgages protected by deeds*: a mortgage " protected by a deposit of documents relating to the legal estate affected " is expressly excepted from the provision of the 1925 legislation requiring registration of land charges.[42] Such mortgages appear to rank for priority according to the dates upon which they were created.

[39] *Beddoes* v. *Shaw* [1937] Ch. 81.
[40] L.P.A. 1925, ss. 97, 137 (7); L.C.A. 1925, s. 13 (2).
[41] See the discussion in (1940) 7 Camb.L.J. 243.   [42] L.C.A. 1925, s. 10

(b) *Mortgages not protected by deeds*: a mortgage made after 1925 and not protected by a deposit of documents relating to the legal estate affected should be registered as a land charge. If the mortgage is legal, it should be registered as a puisne mortgage (Class C (i)); if the mortgage is equitable, it should be registered as a general equitable charge (Class C (iii)).[43]

3. Reasons for registration. The reasons for registering such a mortgage are as follows:

(a) *Priority*. Section 97 of the Law of Property Act 1925 provides that every such mortgage " shall rank according to its date of registration as a land charge pursuant to the Land Charges Act, 1925."

(b) *Void for want of registration*. Section 13 (2) of the Land Charges Act 1925 provides that a Class C land charge created after 1925 shall " be void as against a purchaser of the land charged therewith, or of any interest in such land, unless the land charge is registered in the appropriate register before the completion of the purchase." In the Act, unless the context otherwise requires, " purchaser " means " any person (including a mortgagee or lessee) who, for valuable consideration, takes any interest in land or in a charge of land." [44] Thus an unregistered puisne mortgage is void against a purchaser of the fee simple, even if he had actual knowledge of it, for where an interest is void for non-registration as against a purchaser, he is not prejudicially affected by notice of it.[45]

4. Effect. The effect of these provisions upon two successive mortgages must be considered under the four possible heads.

(a) *Each mortgage protected by a deposit of deeds*. There is nothing to require the deposit of all the deeds, so that it may be possible for two or more mortgages of the same property to be exempted from registration and fall under this head. In such a case, the mortgages would probably rank in the order of their creation, subject to the old law as to loss of priority, *e.g.*, by fraud, or the plea of purchaser without notice.[46]

(b) *Neither mortgage protected by a deposit of deeds*.

(i) CONCORD. If neither mortgage is protected by a deposit of deeds, no difficulty arises if the first mortgage is duly registered

[43] See *post*, p. 544.
[44] L.C.A. 1925, s. 20.
[45] L.P.A. 1925, s. 199.
[46] *Ante*, p. 501.

before the second is made. Even if the first is equitable and the second legal, the first prevails, for section 97 expressly provides that they shall rank in the order of registration, and the provision that registration amounts to notice prevents the legal mortgagee from claiming to be a purchaser without notice. Nor is there any difficulty if neither mortgage is registered. Even if the first mortgage is legal and the second equitable, under section 13 (2) the first is void against the second for want of registration and so the second has priority. Indeed, if there are several successive registrable mortgages, none of which has been registered, the maxim *"qui prior est tempore, potior est jure"* seems to have been reversed, for the last will rank first and so on.

(ii) DISCORD. The difficult case is where the first mortgage was registered after the creation of the second mortgage. For example:

January 1	A grants a mortgage to X
February 2	A grants a mortgage to Y
March 3	X registers
March 4	Y registers

In such a case, the order according to section 97 is X, Y; according to section 13 (2) it is Y, X, for X's mortgage is void against Y. It is hard to say which section prevails. In favour of section 97, the chief point is that it is expressly dealing with the priority of mortgages, whereas section 13 (2) makes unregistered mortgages void against subsequent mortgages only by virtue of the provision that " purchaser " includes a mortgagee. On the other hand, the provision in section 13 (2) that an unregistered land charge is void against a subsequent purchaser makes it hard to see how the registration of X's mortgage can give priority to something which, as regards Y, has no existence. Further, the Land Charges Act 1925 is technically a later statute than the Law of Property Act 1925 and so to the extent of any conflict should prevail. The problem still awaits solution; possibly section 13 (2) will prevail. Even more complicated problems can be constructed, *e.g.,* where X has priority over Y who has priority over Z who has priority over X; but these need not be discussed here.[47]

(iii) PRIORITY NOTICES AND OFFICIAL SEARCHES. At the beginning of 1926, there was the difficulty that it was physically impossible to register a land charge the instant after it had been created; thus

[47] See M. & W. 965–968.

there was a dangerous gap between the creation of a mortgage and its registration. Further, even if a search for prior incumbrances was made, the mortgagee could not be sure that no incumbrance had been registered between the time of his search and the completion of the mortgage. These difficulties have been met by the devices of the priority notice and the official search which are dealt with below.[48]

(c) *First but not second mortgage protected by a deposit of deeds.* In this case, the first mortgage, by taking its priority from the date of its creation, will normally have priority over the second mortgage.

(d) *Second but not first mortgage protected by a deposit of deeds.* Here, sections 13 (2) and 97 work in harmony. If the first mortgage is registered before the second is made, the first ranks for priority " according to its date of registration " (s. 97), *i.e.,* prior to the second mortgage, and section 13 (2) has no application. If the first mortgage is not registered when the second mortgage is made, the first mortgage is void against the second for want of registration, and even if it is subsequently registered, it takes priority from the date of registration.

5. Summary.

(a) *Deposit of deeds.* A mortgage protected by a deposit of deeds ranks according to the date on which it was created. The mortgagee may lose priority—

(i) by conduct which before 1926 would have had this effect; or
(ii) if his mortgage is equitable, by a legal mortgage being made to a mortgagee for value without notice.

(b) *No deposit of deeds.* A mortgage not protected by deposit of deeds should be protected by registration. If the mortgagee fails to do this, he will not, it seems, be protected against a subsequent mortgagee (s. 13 (2)), unless, perhaps, he registers before him (s. 97). If he does register he will be protected against all mortgages made thereafter.

II. MORTGAGES OF AN EQUITABLE INTEREST

Where the subject-matter of a mortgage is an equitable interest in any property, whether land or pure personalty, the rule in *Dearle* v. *Hall,*[49] as amended by the Law of Property Act 1925,[50] now applies.

---

[48] *Post,* p. 550.
[49] *Ante,* pp. 502 *et seq.*
[50] ss. 137, 138.

The amendments made by the Law of Property Act 1925 are as follows:

1. Notice in writing. No notice given or received after 1925 can affect priority unless it is in writing.[51] Apart from this, no alteration has been made in the rule relating to notice.

2. Persons to be served. The persons to be served with notice are [52]:

(i) in the case of settled land, the trustees of the settlement;

(ii) in the case of a trust for sale, the trustees for sale;

(iii) in the case of any other land, the estate owner of the land affected.

Thus the person to be served is normally the owner of the legal estate, except in the case of settled land, where notice to the tenant for life might well be no protection, *e.g.,* if it was his life interest which had been mortgaged. In cases other than the three mentioned above, no special provision has been made, so that notice must be given to the legal owner as before 1926. Nor has any alteration been made to the law relating to notice received by one of several trustees.

3. Indorsement of notice. If for any reason a valid notice cannot be served (*e.g.,* where there are no trustees), or can be served only at unreasonable cost or delay, a purchaser may require that a memorandum be indorsed on or permanently annexed to the instrument creating the trust, and this has the same effect as notice to the trustees. In the case of settled land, the trust instrument, and in the case of a trust for sale, the instrument creating the equitable interest, is the document to be used for this purpose.[53]

4. Notice to trust corporation. The instrument creating the trust, the trustees or the court, may nominate a trust corporation to receive notices instead of the trustees. In such cases, only notice to the trust corporation affects priority; notice to the trustees has no effect until they deliver it to the trust corporation, which they are bound to do forthwith. Provision is made for the indorsement of notice of the appointment on the instrument upon which notices may be indorsed, for the keeping of a register of notices, for the inspection of the register, for the answering of inquiries and for payments of fees therefor.[54] In practice, little use is made of these provisions.

[51] L.P.A. 1925, s. 137 (3).   [52] *Ibid.* s. 137 (2).

[53] *Ibid.* s. 137 (4), (5).   [54] *Ibid.* s. 138.

5. Production of notices. On the application of any person interested in the equitable interest, the trustees or estate owner must now produce any notices served on them or their predecessors.[55] This emasculates *Low* v. *Bouverie*.[56]

C. *Summary*

A summary of the principal divisions of the rules relating to the priority of mortgages may be useful.

1. Before 1926.

(a) *Mortgages of a legal or equitable interest in land*: priority was governed by the order of creation, subject to the doctrine of purchaser without notice, and to fraud, estoppel and gross negligence.

(b) *Mortgages of an equitable interest in pure personalty*: *Dearle* v. *Hall* applied.

2. After 1925.

(a) *Mortgages of a legal estate in land*: priority is governed by the order of creation, subject to the registration provisions and the doctrine of purchaser without notice.

(b) *Mortgages of an equitable interest in any property*: *Dearle* v. *Hall* applies.

It may be added that although the rules governing priorities are complicated, and at least in theory have been made no simpler by the 1925 legislation, difficulties rarely arise in practice; for mortgagees normally act with great prudence and caution.

Sect. 2. Tacking

A. *Before* 1926

Tacking is a method by which the rules relating to priorities may be modified, both for realty and for personalty. Before 1926, there were two forms of tacking:

    (i) The *tabula in naufragio* (" the plank in the shipwreck ").

    (ii) The tacking of further advances.

---

[55] *Ibid.* s. 137 (8), (9).
[56] *Ante*, p. 504.

I. THE TABULA IN NAUFRAGIO

1. The doctrine. If an equitable mortgagee lent money without notice of a prior equitable mortgage, he could gain priority over it if he subsequently acquired a legal estate in the land with priority over it.[57] This was so because, apart from the order of creation, between the mortgagees the equities were equal and so the holder of a legal estate prevailed[58]; the subsequent mortgagee could tack, or attach, his mortgage to the legal estate. Thus if A mortgaged his property to X by a legal mortgage and then to Y and Z by successive equitable mortgages, Z's mortgage would take priority over Y's if Z bought X's mortgage, provided Z had no notice of Y's mortgage when he advanced his money.[59] X's legal mortgage was the plank in the shipwreck, and whichever of Y and Z acquired it had the better chance of being saved if there was not enough money to pay both.

2. No notice. For the doctrine to apply, it was essential that the mortgagee seeking to tack should have had no notice of the prior equitable mortgage when he advanced his money; if he had notice, he could not tack.[60] But if he had no notice at that time, it was immaterial that he obtained notice later, *e.g.*, when he acquired the legal estate[61]; indeed, on principles similar to those applied under the rule in *Dearle* v. *Hall*,[62] notice of the prior equitable mortgage at the time when the later mortgagee acquired the legal estate is " the very occasion, that shows the necessity of it." [63]

3. Legal estate. Normally the mortgagee seeking to tack actually took a transfer of the legal estate; but this was not essential, for he could tack if he had the best right to call for the legal estate,[64] as where the legal estate was held on trust for him. Further, if the mortgagee acquired a legal estate, it was not necessary that it should be the estate mortgaged; a mere term of years sufficed.[65] And even a legal estate created subsequently to the mortgage against which tacking was to be effected might suffice.[66] But a legal estate could

---

[57] *Marsh* v. *Lee* (1671) 2 Ventr. 337.
[58] *Wortley* v. *Birkhead* (1754) 2 Ves.Sen. 571 at 574.
[59] *Brace* v. *Duchess of Marlborough* (1728) 2 P.Wms. 491.
[60] *Lacey* v. *Ingle* (1847) 2 Ph. 413.
[61] *Taylor* v. *Russell* [1892] A.C. 244 at 259.
[62] *Ante*, p. 502.
[63] *Wortley* v. *Birkhead* (1754) 2 Ves.Sen. 571 at 574, *per* Lord Hardwicke L.C.
[64] *Wilkes* v. *Bodington* (1707) 2 Vern. 599 at 600.
[65] *Willoughby* v. *Willoughby* (1756) 1 T.R. 763.
[66] *Cooke* v. *Wilton* (1860) 29 Beav. 100.

not be used to alter priorities if it was acquired with notice that the conveyance was a breach of trust, for this made the mortgagee a trustee himself.[67]

4. Later mortgage. Although tacking under this head usually took place when a later mortgagee acquired a legal estate, the doctrine applied equally to a legal mortgagee who acquired a later mortgage without notice of an intervening incumbrancer.[68]

II. TACKING OF FURTHER ADVANCES

A mortgagee might lend the money and later make a further advance to the mortgagor. Before 1926, there were two cases in which the mortgagee could tack his further advance to his original mortgage and claim priority over an intervening incumbrancer for both loans.

1. Agreement of intervening incumbrancers. The mortgagee could tack if the intervening incumbrancer agreed; it was immaterial whether the first mortgage was legal or equitable. Building estates sometimes provided examples of this: the owner required more money to build on his estate and thus make it a better security. The second mortgagee, not wishing to lend any more money, might agree to the first mortgagee making a further advance to be expended on further building and to rank in priority to the second mortgage.

2. No notice of intervening incumbrance. If a further advance was made without notice of the intervening mortgage, it could be tacked in either of two cases:

(a) *Legal estate*: if the further advance was made by a legal mortgagee,[69] or by an equitable mortgagee with the best right to the legal estate.[70]

(b) *Term of mortgage*: if the prior mortgage expressly provided that it should extend to any further advances, whether or not it was obligatory for the mortgagee to make them. This second case was independent of any legal estate, and was tacking by virtue of the contract in the prior mortgage that it should be security for any further advances.[71]

---

[67] *Saunders* v. *Dehew* (1692) 2 Vern. 271.
[68] *Morret* v. *Paske* (1740) 2 Atk. 52 at 53.
[69] *Wyllie* v. *Pollen* (1863) 3 De G.J. & S. 596.
[70] See *Wilmot* v. *Pike* (1845) 5 Hare 14.
[71] See *Calisher* v. *Forbes* (1871) 7 Ch.App. 109; *Re O'Byrne's Estate* (1885) 15 L.R.Ir. 373 at 375.

It will be noticed that there could be no tacking under either branch of this head if the mortgagee seeking to tack had notice of the intervening incumbrance when he made his further advance,[72] even if the prior mortgage made such an advance obligatory.[73]

B. *After* 1925

The Law of Property Act 1925, s. 94, has considerably altered the law of tacking.

I. THE TABULA IN NAUFRAGIO

Without prejudice to any priority gained before 1926, tacking by means of the *tabula in naufragio* was abolished at the end of 1925.[74]

II. TACKING OF FURTHER ADVANCES

The tacking of further advances has been modified so as to make it immaterial whether any of the mortgages concerned are legal or equitable. After 1925, a prior mortgagee may tack further advances in the following cases[75]:

1. Agreement of intervening incumbrancer. The position is unchanged.

2. No notice of intervening incumbrance. Any mortgagee, whether legal or equitable, may tack a further advance if it was made without notice of the intervening mortgage. Where the intervening mortgage is protected by a deposit of deeds and is thus not registrable, the normal rules as to notice operate. If the mortgage is not protected in this way and is accordingly registrable, the rule that registration amounts to notice will apply and so protect it if it is registered. In one case, however, registration is not deemed to be notice: if the prior mortgage was made expressly for securing further advances, such as a current account (*e.g.*, an overdraft at a bank, where the debt is increased and decreased as sums are drawn out or paid in), registration alone is not deemed to be notice, unless the intervening mortgage was registered when the last search was made by the mortgagee.[76]

---

[72] *Hopkinson* v. *Rolt* (1861) 9 H.L.C. 514.
[73] *West* v. *Williams* [1899] 1 Ch. 132.
[74] L.P.A. 1925, s. 94 (3).
[75] *Ibid*. s. 94 (1).
[76] *Ibid*. s. 94 (2).

An example may make this clearer. Mortgages have been made to A (who took the deeds) and B, in that order, and A has made further advances. If when A made his further advances he had actual, constructive or imputed notice of B's mortgage, he cannot tack under this head even if his mortgage, without obliging him to make further advances, was stated to be security for any further advances he might choose to make. If he had no such notice of B's mortgage when he made his further advances, but B's mortgage was registered at that time, then if A's mortgage is silent as to further advances, the registration amounts to notice and prevents A from tacking. But if A's mortgage was expressed to be security for any further advances that he might make, the registration will not prevent him from tacking, and thus he need not search before making each further advance.

This points a practical moral. Even if a second mortgage has been duly registered, the mortgagee should give express notice of his mortgage to the first mortgagee, for this—

(i) prevents tacking under this head; and

(ii) compels the first mortgagee to hand over the deeds to him when the first mortgage is discharged.[77]

3. Obligation to make further advances. A further advance may be tacked if the prior mortgage imposes an obligation on the mortgagee to make it. In this case, not even express notice will prevent tacking.[78] If in return for a mortgage a bank binds itself to honour a customer's cheques up to an overdraft of £1,000 there is no question of the bank having to search before honouring each cheque, for not even express notice will prevent the bank from tacking each further advance.

---

[77] *Ante,* p. 481.
[78] *West* v. *Williams* (*ante,* pp. 512, 513) has thus been reversed by statute.

CHAPTER 14

DISABILITIES

CERTAIN persons are subject to disabilities as to the interests in land which they can hold, create or alienate.

Sect. 1. Infants

An infant is a person who has not attained his majority. A person attains his majority at the first moment of the day preceding the twenty-first anniversary of his birth.[1] The following are the main points to note concerning an infant's rights in land.

1. Ownership of land. Before 1926, an infant was capable of holding both legal estates and equitable interests in land. After 1925, an infant cannot hold a legal estate in land,[2] although he may still hold an equitable interest.

2. Attempted conveyance to an infant. An attempt after 1925 to convey a legal estate to an infant alone or jointly with other infants operates as a contract for value to make a proper settlement by means of a vesting deed and trust instrument, and in the meantime to hold the land in trust for the infant or infants.[3] An attempted conveyance of a legal estate to an infant jointly with a person of full age vests the legal estate in the person of full age on the statutory trusts (*i.e.*, the trust for sale implied in the case of a tenancy in common [4]) for himself and the infant.[5] These provisions do not apply to a conveyance to an infant as mortgagee or trustee, for which special provisions are made.[6]

3. Mortgages. An infant cannot be a legal mortgagee after 1925. An attempt to grant a legal mortgage to one or more persons who are all infants operates as an agreement for value to execute a

---

[1] See, *e.g.*, *Re Shurey* [1918] 1 Ch. 263.
[2] L.P.A. 1925, s. 1 (6).
[3] S.L.A. 1925, s. 27 (1) (a statutory exception to the equitable rule that an imperfect voluntary conveyance will not be treated as a declaration of trust; *ante*, p. 239).
[4] *Ante*, p. 216.
[5] L.P.A. 1925, s. 19 (2).
[6] See *infra*.

proper mortgage when the infant or infants are of full age, and in the meantime to hold the beneficial interest in trust for those intended to benefit.[7]   A mortgage to an infant and other persons of full age operates, so far as the legal estate is concerned, as if the infant were not named, although his beneficial interest is not affected.[8]

4. Personal representatives. An infant can be neither an executor [9] nor an administrator [10]; this was so before 1926.[11]   If an infant would, but for his infancy, be entitled to be an administrator, or is appointed sole executor, he cannot take a grant until he is of full age; in the meantime a grant may be taken by someone on his behalf, *e.g.*, his guardian.   In the case of administration, the grant must be made to at least two persons or a trust corporation on the infant's behalf, since an infant is interested in the estate.[12]   If an infant is appointed one of several executors, the rest of whom are of full age, he must wait until he attains his majority, when he can join in the grant of probate previously made to the others.

5. Trustees. No infant can be appointed a trustee after 1925.[13] This applies to trusts of any property, real or personal.   If there is a purported conveyance of a legal estate in land to an infant as trustee, the effect is as follows:

(i) If the infant is a sole trustee, the conveyance operates as a declaration of trust by the grantor; the effect is the same if the conveyance is to two or more trustees, all of whom are infants.[14]

(ii) If the infant is one of two or more trustees, at least one of whom is of full age, the conveyance operates as if the infant were not named, although this does not prejudice any beneficial interest thereby given to him.[15]

These provisions do not prevent an infant from becoming a trustee in other ways, *e.g.*, under a constructive trust.[16]

6. Settled land. As was the case before 1926, land to which an infant is entitled in possession is deemed to be settled land.[17]   This is

---

[7] L.P.A. 1925, s. 19 (6).
[8] *Ibid*.
[9] J.A. 1925, s. 165.
[10] *In b. Manuel* (1849) 13 Jur. 664.
[11] J.A. 1925, s. 165, replaces A.E.A. 1798, s. 6, with amendments.
[12] See *ante*, p. 316.
[13] L.P.A. 1925, s. 20.
[14] *Ibid*. s. 19 (4).
[15] *Ibid*. s. 19 (5).
[16] *Ante*, p. 241.
[17] *Ante*, p. 161.

so even if the infant is absolutely entitled. In such a case, the statutory powers before 1926 were exercisable by the trustees of the settlement,[18] although the legal estate might still be vested in the infant. After 1925, both the legal estate and the statutory powers are vested in the statutory owner.[19]

7. Transitional provisions. Legal estates which were vested in infants before 1926, whether beneficially, as mortgagee, trustee or otherwise, were automatically vested in persons of full age at the first moment of 1926.[20] In general, if an infant was entitled jointly with other persons of full age, they took the legal estate. If an infant was solely entitled, in the case of settled land the legal estate vested in the trustees of the settlement, or, if none, in the Public Trustee; in other cases, it vested in the Public Trustee. However, he will normally not deal with the land, for he is here mainly intended as a temporary home for ownerless legal estates, and unless requested to act by the infant's parents or guardian, he has no powers over the land. Further, the parents or guardian may divest the Public Trustee of the legal estate by appointing new trustees in his place, and the legal estate will vest in them.

8. Voidable dispositions. Any disposition by an infant of any interest in land is voidable at the option of the infant (but not of the grantee[21]) on the infant attaining his majority,[22] or within a reasonable time thereafter[23]; if the infant dies under age, his personal representatives may avoid the disposition within a reasonable time.[24] The same rule applied before 1926. As the disposition is voidable and not void, it is binding if the infant fails to repudiate it within a reasonable time after attaining his majority.[25]

In one case an infant is authorised to make a binding disposition. By the Infant Settlements Act 1855, a male infant of twenty years or more or a female infant of seventeen years or more can make a binding marriage settlement of property owned by him or her, or over which he or she has a power of appointment, provided the consent of the Chancery Division of the High Court is obtained. The

---

[18] S.L.A. 1882, ss. 59, 60.
[19] *Ante*, pp. 147, 153.
[20] L.P.A. 1925, 1st Sched., Pt. III; S.L.A. 1925, 2nd Sched., para. 3.
[21] *Zouch* d. *Abbot* v. *Parsons* (1765) 3 Burr. 1794.
[22] *Ashfeild* v. *Ashfeild* (1628) W.Jo. 157.
[23] *Carnell* v. *Harrison* [1916] 1 Ch. 328.
[24] 4 Cru.Dig. 69.
[25] *Edwards* v. *Carter* [1893] A.C. 360.

only case in which such a disposition is not fully binding is where the court has permitted the infant to bar an entail or exercise a power of appointment held by him as tenant in tail, and he dies under age; in this case, the effect is as if the disposition has not been made.

9. Transfer on death. Although normally any equitable interest vested in an infant will pass on his death under his will or intestacy, there is one exception. By the Administration of Estates Act 1925, s. 51 (3), if an infant who dies after 1925 without ever having married was entitled at his death under a settlement to a vested equitable interest in land in fee simple, or an absolute interest in property settled to devolve with such land or as freehold land, he is deemed to have had an entailed interest.

The objects of this somewhat strange subsection appear to be—

   (i) to make it unnecessary always to take out a grant of administration to the infant's estate; and

   (ii) to make the land revert to the donor.

For example, if D settled land on A for life with remainder to B (an infant) in fee simple, and B died an infant without having married, he is deemed to have had an entail. Since he can have had no legitimate children, his notional entail comes to an end and D is entitled to the fee simple, subject to A's life interest. This is probably closer to D's intentions than that the land should pass under B's intestacy to, perhaps, his father or uncle. Further, no grant of probate or administration to B's estate is needed in respect of the land. But if B had married, then whether or not he had issue, the subsection would not apply and the land would pass under his will or intestacy.

It is not clear to what extent this provision restricts the power of disposition over realty given by the Wills (Soldiers and Sailors) Act 1918 to infant soldiers and members of the Air Force in actual military service, and mariners at sea [26]; read literally, it deprives them of any testamentary power over realty until they marry.

10. Leases. Although a legal estate cannot be vested in an infant, a beneficial interest in a lease granted to an infant can only be enjoyed by him subject to the obligations attached to the lease. Further, unless he repudiates the lease within a reasonable time after attaining his majority, he is bound by it [27]. Even if he repudiates the lease, he cannot recover the rent he has paid [28].

---

[26] *Ante*, p. 274.   [27] *Davies* v. *Benyon-Harris* (1931) 47 T.L.R. 424.
[28] *Valentini* v. *Canali* (1889) 24 Q.B.D. 166.

Sect. 2. Married Women

In general, a married woman is today subject to no disability. She can acquire, hold and dispose of property as if she were a feme sole (pronounced fem soul) *i.e.*, an unmarried woman. Formerly there were two exceptions to this.

1. Non-separate property. It is hardly possible for any non-separate property of a married woman to exist today. In order to understand the position, it is necessary to consider the changes that have taken place in the law.

(a) *At common law.* At common law, a married woman was incapable of disposing by herself of any property which she owned; the concurrence of her husband was necessary for an effective disposition to be made.

(i) REAL PROPERTY could be disposed of in fee simple only by a fine levied by the wife in which the husband concurred; this was the same action as was used for barring an entail.[29] The wife had to be separately examined (*e.g.*, by a " Perpetual Commissioner ") so that it could be ascertained in the absence of her husband that she agreed to the transaction. After the Fines and Recoveries Act 1833 had abolished fines, the form of conveyance was a deed in which the husband concurred. Separate examination was still necessary until abolished at the end of 1925.[30] Apart from a disposition made thus, the wife had no power to dispose of her property *inter vivos*; and except with the husband's concurrence, she had no general power of disposition by will.[31] The husband, acting by himself, could dispose of an estate for his own lifetime but no longer.

(ii) LEASEHOLDS remained vested in the wife, but her husband could dispose of them in his lifetime without the concurrence of his wife. He could not, however, dispose of them by his will, and on his death the wife's rights revived.

(iii) PURE PERSONALTY vested in the husband absolutely and passed under any disposition by him whether *inter vivos* or by will, or on his intestacy.

(b) *In equity.* In view of the stringency of the common law rules, equity held that any property conveyed either to trustees or to the

---

[29] *Ante*, pp. 37, 38.   [30] L.P.A. 1925, s. 167.
[31] See *Willock* v. *Noble* (1875) L.R. 7 H.L. 580 at 590.

husband " for the separate use " of the wife could be dealt with by her in equity as if she were unmarried.   The Married Women's Property Act 1882 extended this principle considerably by providing that all legal estates and equitable interests which either—

(i) were acquired after 1882, or

(ii) belonged to a woman who married after 1882,

should be the separate property of the married woman and could be disposed of by her as if she were a feme sole.

(c) *Today.* Consequently, property of a married woman could only be non-separate property today, and so subject to the severe restrictions set out above, if—

(i) it was acquired before 1883, and

(ii) the marriage took place before 1883 and still exists, and

(iii) the property was not conveyed to the separate use of the married woman.

There can hardly be any such property left today, though Parliament still legislates for it.[32]

The Law Reform (Married Women and Tortfeasors) Act 1935 renders obsolete the expression " her separate property " and refers to " her property "; but if any non-separate property still exists, it remains subject to the old law.

2. Property subject to a restraint on anticipation.

(a) *The restraint.* Although the restraint upon anticipation has now been abolished, it was until recently of considerably greater importance than non-separate property, and for some while to come some knowledge of it will be important in conveyancing. The invention by equity of " the separate use " made it possible for a married woman to deal by herself with property subject to such a use, but it did not protect her from yielding to the asperities or blandishments of her husband and conveying the property to him, nor did it protect her against her creditors if she were improvident. Consequently, equity made it possible on the grant of property to a married woman for the grantor not only to give it for her separate use but also to subject it to a restraint on anticipation. If imposed in a grant to a feme sole, the restraint was effective only during coverture (marriage); during spinsterhood or widowhood it was inoperative, but it attached as soon as the woman became a feme covert (married woman). Thus

---

[32] See, *e.g.*, Agricultural Holdings Act 1948, s. 85.

property given to a spinster subject to a restraint on anticipation would be free from the restraint until she married, when it would attach; on the death or divorce of her husband, it would disattach, and on re-marriage would revive again. If a feme sole wished to prevent the restraint from attaching on her marriage, she could execute a deed poll declaring that the trustees of the property should hold it for such purposes as she should appoint, and provided this deed was communicated to the trustees before her marriage, the property would remain free from the restraint.[33] An attempt to impose such a restraint in a limitation to any person other than a female was void as being repugnant to the nature of property.[34]

(b) *Property subject to the restraint.* Both legal estates and equitable interests could be subjected to restraints upon anticipation. Care was necessary in framing such restraints, for if property was given to an unborn female subject to a restraint on anticipation, then even though the interest was bound to vest within the perpetuity period, if at all, the restraint might well fail to attach until after the expiration of the period; the consequence of this possibility was that the restraint infringed the rule against inalienability and the property would be taken free from the restraint.[35]

(c) *Effect of restraint.* An effective restraint on anticipation prevented the married woman from disposing of or charging the capital or future income in any way. Each instalment of income could be disposed of as soon as it was paid, but neither the married woman nor her creditors could attack the capital or future income. However, the court had power to authorise a disposition of property subject to a restraint, provided the disposition was for the benefit of the married woman, and she consented.[36] Further, whenever a married woman was entitled in possession to land subject to a restraint on anticipation, the land was settled land and could be disposed of by the married woman as tenant for life, subject to compliance with the usual Settled Land Act procedure.[37] Thus if a feme covert was entitled in possession to the fee simple in Blackacre subject to a restraint on anticipation, she could sell as tenant for life and the purchaser would take a good title, provided he paid the purchase-money to the trustees (being two or more in number or a trust corporation) or into court. The restraint on anticipation was transferred to the purchase-money.

---

[33] *Re Chrimes* [1917] 1 Ch. 30.
[34] See *Brandon* v. *Robinson* (1811) 18 Ves. 429; *ante*, p. 33.
[35] *Ante*, p. 132. [36] L.P.A. 1925, s. 169.
[37] *Ante*, p. 161.

(d) *Abolition of restraint.* There were two stages.

(i) By the Law Reform (Married Women and Tortfeasors) Act 1935, no restraint on anticipation could be imposed by any document (including a settlement or will) executed after 1935, except in pursuance of an obligation imposed before 1936 otherwise than by a special power of appointment. Further, no will of a testator who died after 1945 could impose a restraint on anticipation, even if the will was made before 1936. Thus those who before 1936 made wills imposing a restraint on anticipation were given ten years after 1935 in which to amend their wills; if the testator failed to do so and died after the ten years had expired, any direction imposing a restraint on anticipation was ineffective. The Act did not affect existing restraints but only prevented the imposition of new restraints.

(ii) On December 16, 1949, the Married Women (Restraint upon Anticipation) Act 1949 abolished all existing restraints upon anticipation and prevented the creation of any more of such restraints. No restriction on anticipation or alienation is valid if it could not have been attached to the enjoyment of the property by a man.

Sect. 3. Lunatics

If a person is of unsound mind, there are two points to consider: first, some control must be exercised over his person, and secondly, someone must be appointed to manage his property. Only the second of these points is relevant here.

1. Control over property. Under the fourteenth-century statute *De Prerogativa Regis* and later under the Lunacy Act 1890 and other statutes, the Crown had a jurisdiction over the property of a lunatic which was exercised by the Lord Chancellor and certain of the judges. Until the Mental Health Act 1959 came into force on November 1, 1960, there were two methods of exercising control over the property.

(a) *Committee.* There could be a formal inquisition under the Master in Lunacy, assisted sometimes by a jury, to decide the question of insanity. A person found insane by this method was called a lunatic so found, and some fit person was appointed as his committee (pronounced with the accent on the last syllable) to control both his person and his property.

(b) *Receiver.* Without holding an inquisition, application could be made to the court under the Lunacy Act 1890, s. 116, for the appointment of a receiver to exercise control over the property, but not the person, of the lunatic. Those in respect of whom these proceedings had been taken, in common with lunatics in respect of whom no proceedings had been taken, were called lunatics not so found. In practice, inquisitions became very rare and the simpler procedure under section 116 was usually employed.

2. Dispositions of property. The power of disposing of a lunatic's property depended on whether or not a committee or receiver had been appointed.

(a) *Committee or receiver appointed.* If a lunatic was so found, or a receiver had been appointed, the lunatic ceased to have control over his property. He remained the owner, both at law and in equity, but control passed to his committee or receiver. Thus even in a lucid interval, any disposition by him was void, although a will made during a lucid interval was valid. The committee or receiver could dispose of the lunatic's property only under an order in lunacy; the disposition was made in the name of the lunatic. The lunacy jurisdiction of the court was exercised by the Lord Chancellor and the Lords Justices of Appeal (later replaced by the judges of the Chancery Division), one or more of whom constituted the Judge in Lunacy; in practice, most of the work was done by the officials of the Court of Protection under the Master in Lunacy.

(b) *No committee or receiver.* If the lunatic was not so found and no receiver had been appointed, any voluntary disposition of his property was absolutely void, unless made during a lucid interval. A disposition for value was normally not void, but voidable, *i.e.*, it remained valid until set aside; however, if the disposition was made during a lucid interval, or took effect in favour of a person not aware of the insanity, it was valid.[38]

3. Mental Health Act 1959. The Mental Health Act 1959 repealed the former statutory provisions and established a complete statutory code for " patients," the name now given to those formerly known as " persons of unsound mind," and, before that, as " lunatics." Inquisitions and committees have been abolished, and control of a patient's property is now exercised through receivers,[39] under the Court of Protection and certain nominated juges of the Chancery Division. Subject to this, the position is substantially as it was before the Act.

[38] *Imperial Loan Co.* v. *Stone* [1892] 1 Q.B. 599.
[39] Mental Health Act 1959, s. 105.

4. Settlement to avoid injustice. The nominated judge has a wide power to order the making of a settlement of the property of a lunatic.[40] This power can be exercised, for example, where a change in the laws of intestacy might work an injustice, although in the case of realty the retention of the old rules of descent in certain cases [41] will often exclude this contingency. Any person who has or has had a chance of succeeding to the property may apply for such a settlement to be made.

Sect. 4. Traitors and Felons

1. Attainder. Before the Forfeiture Act 1870, attainder of treason or felony deprived the criminal of his property, both real and personal. In the case of treason, the property was forfeit to the Crown, while in the case of a felony, land escheated to the feudal lord (subject to the Crown's right to enjoy it for a year and a day) and goods were forfeited to the Crown.[42] The escheat or forfeiture of land related back to the commission of the offence, so that dealings between the commission of the crime and conviction were void; in the case of goods, there was no relation back and intermediate dealings were valid.

2. Forfeiture Act 1870. The Forfeiture Act 1870 abolished all forfeiture and escheat for attainder of treason or felony. The Act further provided that a convict (as defined in the Act) could not make any disposition of his property during the period of his sentence, either by way of conveyance or contract. There was provision for the appointment by the Home Office of an administrator in whom vested all property which belonged to the convict beneficially. The administrator had full power to dispose of the property but he could not bar an entail vested in the convict; if, however, the convict barred the entail, the resulting fee vested in the administrator, who could dispose of it.[43] Until the appointment of an administrator, the justices might appoint an interim curator who could, with the leave of the justices or the court, sell the convict's personal (but not real) property.

3. Criminal Justice Act 1948. All these provisions for the vesting and administration of a convict's property ceased to have effect on April 18, 1949.[44] Convicts now deal with their property in the normal way, acting through agents where necessary.

---

[40] *Ibid.* s. 103 (1). See, *e.g.*, *Re D.M.L.* [1965] Ch. 1133 ; *Re L. (W.J.G.)* [1966] Ch. 135.   [41] *Ante*, p. 309.
[42] See M. & W. 18.   [43] *Re Gaskell and Walters' Contract* [1906] 2 Ch. 1.
[44] Criminal Justice Act 1948, s. 70 (1) ; S.I. 1949 No. 139.

Sect. 5. Aliens

An alien is a person who is not a British subject. At common law, an alien could not hold land, and any conveyance to an alien made the land liable to forfeiture to the Crown. There were certain minor exceptions to this rule, *e.g.*, permitting friendly aliens to hold certain short leases. By statute [45] an alien can now in general hold and acquire real and personal property in the same way as a British subject.

Sect. 6. Corporations

1. Mortmain. By the Mortmain and Charitable Uses Act 1888, an assurance to a corporation which had no authority to hold land, either by statute or by licence from the Crown (called a licence in mortmain), made the land, whether freehold or leasehold, liable to forfeiture to the Crown,[46] though any mesne lords were entitled to enter within a limited time, and so secure the forfeiture instead.

2. Origin. This rule had its origin in Magna Carta 1215. Its purpose was to restrict conveyances to monasteries, for inasmuch as corporations never died or married and were never infants or convicted of felony, many valuable feudal incidents would have been lost by such a conveyance. With changing conditions, many statutory exceptions were made, but although in modern times few corporations were caught by the rule, it could not be disregarded; in all cases it was essential to ascertain that the corporation concerned had authority to hold land.

3. Exceptions. Examples of corporations with authority to hold land were—

    (i) Companies incorporated under the Companies Acts [47]; but a company not incorporated for the purpose of gain, such as a company to promote science or art, could not hold more than two acres of land without the consent of the Board of Trade.

    (ii) The Universities and colleges of Oxford and Cambridge.

    (iii) Corporations created by a special statute providing for the holding of land, such as railway companies.

---

[45] Status of Aliens Act 1914, s. 17, replacing Naturalization Act 1870, s. 2.

[46] *Att.-Gen.* v. *Parsons* [1956] A.C. 421.

[47] See, *e.g.*, Companies Act 1948, ss. 14, 408, replacing earlier provisions.

4. Abolition. The law of mortmain was out of accord with modern ideas and, on July 29, 1960, it was abolished.[48] Today, no disposition to a corporation makes the land liable to forfeiture for mortmain.

5. Dispositions. In general, a corporation which has power to hold land has also the power to dispose of it. This rule is subject to certain exceptions; thus dispositions by the Universities and colleges of Oxford, Cambridge and Durham are restricted by provisions somewhat similar to those which regulate dispositions by tenants for life.[49]

Sect. 7. Charities

Formerly there were complex and far-reaching restrictions on dispositions to a charity and by a charity. These have been drastically curtailed by the Charities Act 1960. The present position is as follows.

1. Dispositions to a charity. Formerly assurances *inter vivos* to a charity were subject to one set of conditions and gifts by will to another. These have all been repealed, and there are now no special restrictions on such dispositions.[50]

2. Dispositions by a charity. Land held on charitable trusts is settled land, and the trustees have all the powers given by the Settled Land Act 1925 to a tenant for life and trustees of the settlement.[51] This provision does not make the land settled land for all purposes. Thus it does not require a conveyance to a charity to be made by a vesting deed and a trust instrument, nor does it disable a sole trustee from giving a good receipt for capital money if the scheme governing the charity authorises this.[52] But the powers that it gives are exercisably only subject to important restrictions. No land which forms part of the permanent endowment of the charity, or is or has been occupied by the charity, may be disposed of in any way without an order of the court, the Charity Commissioners or the Minister of Education. Other land (*e.g.*, land held for investment purposes) is free from these restrictions; and even where they apply, leases granted for not more than 22 years without a fine, and any dispositions of an advowson, are excepted. Further, certain charities (*e.g.*, the Universities of Oxford and Cambridge and their colleges) are exempt from the restrictions.[53]

---

[48] Charities Act 1960, s. 38.
[49] Universities and College Estates Acts 1925 and 1964.
[50] Charities Act 1960, s. 38 (2), (3), 7th Sched.   [51] S.L.A. 1925, s. 29.
[52] *Re Booth and Southend-on-Sea Estates Company's Contract* [1927] 1 Ch. 579.
[53] Charities Act 1960, s. 29, 2nd Sched.

CHAPTER 15

LIMITATION

THE fundamental principle of the Limitation Act 1939, which consolidates and amends earlier legislation, is that unless claims are enforced within a limited time, they become barred. It is more important that long and undisturbed possession of land should be protected, even if initially it was wrongful, than that the law should lend its aid to the enforcement of stale claims.

1. Limitation and prescription. Limitation must be distinguished from prescription.[1] Two differences may be mentioned.

(a) *Subject-matter.* Limitation often concerns the ownership of the land itself, whereas prescription is directed to the acquisition of easements and profits over the land of another.

(b) *Limitation negative.* Prescription operates positively so as to presume the grant of an easement or profit by the owner of the land; title is thus derived from him. Limitation, on the other hand, operates negatively so as to bar a claim to the land, thus leaving some other claimant to the land free from the competing claim. Limitation may operate comparatively, barring one person but not another. Thus it may bar a tenant under a lease but not his landlord.

2. Possession as the basis of title. In English law, the basis of title to land is possession. Possession of land by itself gives a title to the land good against the whole world except a person with a better right to possession.[2] If X takes possession of A's land, X has a title which will avail against all save A; a title acquired by wrong is still a title. X has a fee simple, and so has A; but all titles are relative, and so although X's fee is good, A's is better.[3] If, however, A fails to take steps to recover the land in due time, his claim will be barred by limitation, and X's fee, freed from the superior claims of A's fee, will be good against all the world.

3. Elements of limitation. In every case of limitation, three points must be considered, namely—

[1] *Ante,* p. 436.
[2] *Asher* v. *Whitlock* (1865) L.R. 1 Q.B. 1.
[3] See *Leach* v. *Jay* (1878) 9 Ch.D. 42 at 44, 45.

(1) The length of the period;

(2) When time starts to run; and

(3) The effect of the lapse of time.

These will be taken in turn.

Part 1

THE LENGTH OF THE PERIOD

1. The main periods. There are two main periods of limitation:

(a) *Six years*: a period of six years for actions on simple contracts (*e.g.*, for money lent without security) or claims for rent, and actions in tort.[4]

(b) *Twelve years*: a period of twelve years for the recovery of land or of money charged on land, as by a mortgage.[5]   Under the Real Property Limitation Act 1833 the period was twenty years, but the Real Property Limitation Act 1874 reduced it to twelve.   Twelve years is also now the period for actions for money due upon a covenant, in place of the former period of twenty years.

2. Special provisions. There are also certain special provisions.

(a) *Crown land*.   In the case of Crown lands the period is now thirty years.[6]   Formerly it was sixty years, a period which has been retained in the one case of foreshore owned by the Crown.

(b) *Charitable corporation sole*.   A spiritual or eleemosynary (*i.e.*, charitable) corporation sole, such as a bishop or the master of a hospital, is barred after thirty years.[7]   Formerly the period was two successive incumbencies plus six years after the appointment of the third incumbent, or sixty years, whichever was the longer.

(c) *Advowson*.   A claim to an advowson is barred after the period during which three successive incumbencies have been held adversely to the owner of the advowson, or sixty years of adverse possession, whichever is the longer, with an overriding maximum of one hundred years.[8]   This represents no change in the law.

---

[4] Limitation Act 1939, ss. 2, 17.

[5] *Ibid*. ss. 4, 18.

[6] *Ibid*. s. 4.

[7] *Ibid*. s. 4.

[8] *Ibid*. s. 14.

Part 2

THE RUNNING OF TIME

The running of time falls into four sections: first, when time begins to run; second, what will postpone this date; third, what will start time running afresh; and fourth, what will suspend the running of time.

Sect. 1. When Time Begins to Run

In the case of actions for the recovery of land or capital sums charged on land, time begins to run in accordance with the following rules.

1. Owner in possession. Where the owner of land is entitled in possession, time runs against him from the moment " adverse possession " is taken by another.[9]   Before 1833 the word " adverse " was used in a highly technical sense; but today it merely means that there must be possession inconsistent with the title of the true owner [10] and not for example, possession by a trustee on his behalf. Time does not begin to run merely because the owner abandons possession, for until some other person has taken possession of the land there is nobody against whom the owner is failing to assert his rights.   If the owner has little present use for the land, much may be done on it by others without demonstrating a possession inconsistent with the owner's title; thus cultivating the land and later using it for training greyhounds may fail to be " adverse possession." [11]

2. Future interests. A person entitled in reversion or in remainder at the time when adverse possession is taken has alternative periods: he has 12 years from adverse possession being taken or six years from the falling of his interest into possession, whichever is the longer.[12]   Thus if land is settled on A for life with remainder to B, and X dispossesses A ten years before A dies, B has six years from A's death in which to sue; but if X had dispossessed A three years before A's death, B would have 12 years from the dispossession of A. If X had not taken adverse possession until after A's death, B's interest would no longer have been a future interest, and he would have the normal period of 12 years from the taking of adverse possession.   Further, if A's interest had been an entail, then even if he

---

[9] Limitation Act 1939, s. 10.
[10] See *Moses* v. *Lovegrove* [1952] 2 Q.B. 533 ; *Hughes* v. *Griffin* [1969] 1 W.L.R. 23.
[11] *Williams Brothers Direct Supply Ltd.* v. *Raftery* [1958] 1 Q.B. 159.
[12] Limitation Act 1939, s. 6.

had been dispossessed by X, B would have been barred 12 years later; the alternative six years' period does not extend to a reversioner or remainderman whose interest was liable to be barred by the barring of a prior interest in tail.[13]

3. Leaseholds. The above provisions do not apply to a reversioner on a lease for a term of years when the tenant has been ousted. Irrespective of when the dispossession occurred, time does not run against the reversioner until the lease expires, because, until then, he has no right to possession.[14]   Thus if L grants T a lease for ninety-nine years and T is dispossessed by X, the twelve year period runs against T from the dispossession but against L only from the determination of the lease.

A tenant cannot acquire a title to the land demised against his landlord during the currency of the lease, even by prolonged failure to pay rent.   There is one exception to this in the case of a lease capable of enlargement into a fee simple.   If a rent not exceeding £1 per annum reserved by such a lease has not been paid for a continuous period of twenty years, five of which have elapsed since 1925, the rent ceases to be payable; neither the arrears nor any future payment can be recovered and the lease may be enlarged into a fee simple.[15] Further, where the tenant takes possession of adjoining land of the landlord, time will run in his favour if (and only if) his possession is solely for his own benefit and is not a mere extension of the land demised to him.[16]   But a tenant's adverse possession of adjoining land of a third party is prima facie for the benefit of the landlord as well as the tenant.[17]

A landlord may be barred if adverse possession is taken not of the land but of the rent from it; for if for twelve years the tenant pays a rent of at least £1 per annum to some person who wrongfully claims the reversion, this bars the landlord's right to the reversion.[18]

4. Tenants at will and at sufferance. A tenant at will is in a better position than a tenant under a lease for a fixed term of years, for time runs against the landlord from the expiration of one year after the commencement of the tenancy, or after its determination, whichever is the earlier.[19]   Time begins to run anew, however, whenever rent is paid or a written acknowledgment is given,[20] though,

---

[13] *Ibid.* ss. 6, 31.   [14] *Ibid.* s. 6.
[15] L.P.A. 1925, s. 153; *ante*, p. 362.
[16] *J. F. Perrott & Co. Ltd.* v. *Cohen* [1951] 1 K.B. 705.
[17] *King* v. *Smith* [1950] 1 All E.R. 554.   [18] Limitation Act 1939, ss. 9, 10.
[19] *Ibid.* s. 9.   [20] See *post*, p. 535.

subject to this, the landlord will be barred when thirteen years have elapsed since the tenancy began.

In the case of a tenancy at sufferance, time runs from the commencement of the tenancy.

5. Yearly or periodic tenants. A tenant under a yearly or other periodic tenancy who does not hold under a written lease is in a similar position to a tenant at will; time runs from the end of the first year or other period of the tenancy, subject to extension by payment of rent or written acknowledgment.[21] If there is a lease in writing, time runs from the determination of the tenancy.

6. Rentcharges. In the case of a rentcharge in possession, time runs from the last payment of rent to the owner of the rentcharge.[22] Thus the owner's rights are barred—

(i) if no rent is paid for twelve years, in which case the rentcharge is extinguished; or

(ii) if the rent is paid to a stranger for twelve years, in which case the rentcharge remains enforceable against the land but the former owner's claim to it is extinguished in favour of the stranger.

Similar rules apply to other rents not due under a lease.

7. Mortgages. As soon as a mortgagee goes into possession, time begins to run against subsequent mortgagees and the mortgagor so as to bar their rights to redeem.[23] As regards the mortgagee's right to recover the money charged on the land, or to foreclose, time runs against him from the date upon which the money was due[24]; and when he is barred, his mortgage ceases to exist.[25] In each case, any written acknowledgment or any payment on account of principal or interest starts time running afresh.[26]

8. Claims through Crown or corporation sole. It has been seen that the Crown is entitled to a thirty years' period instead of the usual twelve.[27] If a person against whom time has started to run conveys his land to the Crown, the only change is that the limitation period

[21] Limitation Act 1939, s. 9; see, *e.g.*, *Moses* v. *Lovegrove* [1952] 2 Q.B. 533; *Hayward* v. *Chaloner* [1968] 1 Q.B. 107.
[22] Limitation Act 1939, s. 31.
[23] *Ibid.* s. 12; see, *e.g.*, *Young* v. *Clarey* [1948] Ch. 191.
[24] Limitation Act 1939, s. 18.
[25] *Cotterell* v. *Price* [1960] 1 W.L.R. 1097.
[26] Limitation Act 1939, s. 23.

[27] *Ante*, p. 528.

becomes thirty years from the dispossession instead of twelve. But in the converse case where time has started to run against the Crown and the Crown then conveys the land to X, the rule is that X is barred at the expiration of thirty years from the original dispossession or twelve years from the conveyance to him, whichever is the shorter.[28] Thus X is entitled to twelve years from the date of the conveyance unless at that time there were less than twelve years of the Crown period unexpired, in which case X merely has the residue of that period.

Similar rules apply[29] to the longer periods for a spiritual or eleemosynary corporation sole.[30]

9. Trusts.

(a) *Adverse possession by stranger.* Equitable interests in land or under trusts for sale of land are in general treated as " land," and so as subject to the twelve years' period.[31] But adverse possession of trust property by a stranger does not bar the trustee's title to the property until all the beneficiaries have been barred.[32] Thus if land is held on trust for A for life with remainder to B, twelve years' adverse possession of the land by X bars A's equitable interest and, but for the provision just mentioned, would bar the trustee's legal estate. But time will not start to run against B's equitable interest until A's death,[33] and the same accordingly applies to the trustee's legal estate. Consequently, after the twelve years have run, the trustee will hold the legal estate on trust for X for the life of A, and subject thereto on trust for B. This is so even if A is the trustee, as will normally be the case with settled land.

(b) *Adverse possession by trustee.* Trustees cannot obtain a title against their beneficiaries by adverse possession of the trust property; for there is no period of limitation for an action by a beneficiary to recover from his trustees the trust property or its proceeds in their possession or converted to their use, or in respect of any fraud by the trustees.[34] Thus if land is conveyed to X and Y as tenants in common, X cannot obtain a title to the land as against Y, no matter how long he excludes Y from the land or its rents and profits; for X and Y hold the legal estate on the statutory trusts for themselves as tenants

[28] Limitation Act 1939, s. 4.   [29] *Ibid.*
[30] *Ante*, p. 528.
[31] Limitation Act 1939, ss. 7, 18.
[32] *Ibid.* s. 7.
[33] *Ante*, p. 529.
[34] Limitation Act 1939, s. 19.

in common,[35] and X is thus a trustee for Y.[36]   But subject to this, the period in respect of a breach of trust (*e.g.*, for paying income to the wrong person) is six years.

(c) *Adverse possession by beneficiary.*   Time does not begin to run against the trustees or beneficiaries if settled land or land held on trust for sale is in the possession of a beneficiary who is not solely and absolutely entitled.[37]

Sect. 2. Postponement of the Period

The date from which time begins to run may be postponed for disability, fraudulent concealment, or mistake.

A. Disability

If the owner of an interest in land is under disability when the right of action accrues, then even if the normal period of limitation expires, the period is extended to six years from the time when he ceases to be under a disability or dies, whichever happens first, with a maximum period in the case of land of thirty years from the date when the right of action first accrued.[38]   Thus if X takes possession of A's land at a time when A is a lunatic,[39] A will have twelve years from the dispossession or six years from his recovery from lunacy in which to bring his action, whichever period is the longer.   The following points should be noted:

(a) *Disability.*   A person is under a disability for this purpose if he is an infant or a lunatic.[40]   Coverture and absence beyond the seas were once disabilities, but this is no longer the case, and similarly for convicts who, prior to April 18, 1949, were under disability if no administrator or curator had been appointed.[41]

(b) *Supervening disability.*   A disability is immaterial unless it existed at the time when the cause of action accrued.   Thus if A becomes insane the day before he is dispossessed, the provisions for disability apply, whereas if he becomes insane the day after he has been dispossessed, they do not.

---

[35] *Ante*, p. 216.
[36] See *Re Landi* [1939] Ch. 828.
[37] Limitation Act 1939, s. 7.
[38] *Ibid.* s. 22.
[39] For brevity: " person of unsound mind " is the term in the Act.
[40] Limitation Act 1939, s. 31 ; Mental Health Act 1959, 7th Sched.
[41] See *ante*, p. 524.

(c) *Successive disabilities.* In the case of successive disabilities, if a person is under one disability and before that ceases another disability begins, the period is extended until both disabilities cease, subject to the maximum of 30 years. But if one disability comes to an end before another disability starts, or if the person under disability is succeeded by another person under disability, time runs from the ceasing of the first disability. For example, A is an infant when the cause of action accrues. If later, during his infancy, he becomes insane, the six years does not start to run until he is both sane and of full age. But if he reaches full age before he becomes insane, or if he dies an infant and B, a lunatic, becomes entitled to the land, the six years run from A's majority in the first case and his death in the second.

B. *Fraud, Fraudulent Concealment and Mistake*

Where—

(i) an action is based on the fraud of the defendant or his agent, or of any person through whom he claims or his agent, or

(ii) a right of action is concealed by the fraud of any such person, or

(iii) the action is for relief from the consequences of a mistake,

then time does not begin to run against the landowner until he discovers the fraud or mistake or could with reasonable diligence have discovered it.[42] To amount to fraudulent concealment, there must be some designed concealment, although it is not necessary that active steps should have been taken to ensure concealment. Thus the open occupation of land is not fraudulent concealment, even though it is subterranean, and the owner has no knowledge of it.[43] On the other hand, it was held that there had been fraudulent concealment where an illegitimate eldest son, who had been brought up as legitimate but who learned of his status on attaining majority, joined with his father in barring an entail and resettling the land without disclosing the facts to his younger brother, who was legitimate and thus entitled to the entail.[44]

The rule as to mistake applies only where mistake is the basis of the action, as where the action is to recover money paid under a mistake of fact. There is no general doctrine that making a mistake (*e.g.,* as to the true position of a boundary) stops time running.[45]

---

[42] Limitation Act 1939, s. 26.   [43] *Rains* v. *Buxton* (1880) 14 Ch.D. 537.
[44] *Vane* v. *Vane* (1872) 8 Ch.App. 383.
[45] See *Phillips-Higgins* v. *Harper* [1954] 1 Q.B. 411.

Neither fraud nor mistake will postpone the running of time as against a subsequent purchaser for value without knowledge or reason to believe that there was fraud or mistake.[46]

Sect. 3. Starting Time Running Afresh

Time may be started running afresh—

   (i) by a signed acknowledgment in writing of the plaintiff's title; or

   (ii) by part payment of principal or interest.[47]

The acknowledgment or payment must be signed or made by the person in whose favour time is running, or by his agent, and must be made to the person whose title is being barred, or to his agent.[48] Once, however, the full period has run, no payment or acknowledgment can revive any right to recover land, for the lapse of time will have extinguished not only the owner's remedies for recovering the land but also his right to it.[49] It is otherwise in the case of other actions, where lapse of time bars only the remedy and not the right.

Sect. 4. Suspension of the Period

In general, once time has begun to run, it runs continuously.[50] Disability or fraud may postpone the date when time begins to run, and an acknowledgment or part payment may start time running afresh, but until recently there was no provision whereby the running of time might be suspended for a time and then resumed. The Limitation (Enemies and War Prisoners) Act 1945 retroactively provided that as from September 3, 1939, the running of time was to be suspended while any necessary party to an action was an enemy or was detained in enemy territory: " enemy " and " enemy territory " were widely defined. Two or more periods of suspension were to be treated as a single period beginning with the first period and ending with the last. There was an overriding provision that where the period had been suspended under the Act, it should not expire until a year after the person concerned had ceased to be an enemy or be detained in enemy territory, or a year after March 28, 1945 (when the Act was passed), whichever was the later.

---

[46] Limitation Act 1939, s. 26.
[47] *Ibid.* s. 23.
[48] *Ibid.* s. 24.
[49] *Ibid.* s. 16; *Nicholson* v. *England* [1926] 2 K.B. 93.
[50] *Bowring-Hanbury's Trustee* v. *Bowring-Hanbury* [1943] Ch. 104.

Part 3

THE EFFECT OF THE LAPSE OF TIME

Sect. 1. Title to Land

1. The squatter's title.

(a) *No " Parliamentary conveyance."* Although the effect of the Limitation Act 1939 is to extinguish the title of the former owner, it is not correct to say that the former owner's title is transferred to the " squatter," *i.e.,* the person who has occupied the land and in whose favour time has run. There is no " Parliamentary conveyance " of the former owner's title. The effect of the Act is not positive but negative; it transfers nothing and merely extinguishes the former owner's claim. A squatter may thus see his title improved as lapse of time successively bars different persons with claims to the land, until ultimately his fee simple is free from rival claims.

(b) *Burdens binding the squatter.* Even if a squatter can show that the fee simple owner has been barred, however, he may not be able to take a clean title, for burdens which bound the land will continue to bind it in the hands of the squatter. For example, a squatter will be bound by a restrictive covenant attached to the land unless he can show that it is no longer enforceable, *e.g.,* by lapse of time since a breach of it, for until a breach occurs the covenantee has no right of action and time does not run against him; a squatter without notice is not a purchaser without notice.[51] Again, a squatter on leasehold land who obtains a title against the tenant but not against the landlord is not in the position of an assignee of the lease. An assignee is liable to be sued for a breach of covenant committed while he held the lease, even if at the time of the action the lease has expired[52]; but a squatter cannot be sued after the expiration of a lease for breaches of covenant committed while he was in possession.[53] Yet during the term of the lease, he can be forced to pay the rent and perform the covenants by the threat of forfeiture, if the lease contains a forfeiture clause; yet he has no right to apply for relief against forfeiture[54] and he is of course bound by any restrictive covenants. Moreover, if the squatter takes advantage of some clause in the lease, such as a proviso that the rent should be halved if the covenants are observed, he cannot " blow

[51] *Re Nisbet & Potts' Contract* [1906] 1 Ch. 386.
[52] *Ante,* p. 387.
[53] *Tichborne* v. *Weir* (1892) 67 L.T. 735.
[54] *Tickner* v. *Buzzacott* [1965] Ch. 426.

hot and cold "; if he accepts the benefits of the lease, he cannot refuse the burdens. Consequently, he will be estopped from denying that he is bound by the lease.[55] But the mere payment of rent in a lease with no such clause will not operate as an estoppel.[56]

(c) *Barred leaseholds.* If a squatter bars a tenant but not the freeholder, and then the tenant acquires the freehold, time begins to run against the freehold; but until it has run, the tenant, by virtue of owning the freehold, may evict the squatter: for the freehold is not barred, and the former tenancy has merged in the freehold.[57] Further, if instead the tenant surrenders his tenancy to the freeholder, this enables the freeholder to evict the squatter forthwith, for the surrender removes the only interest which prevented the freeholder from claiming possession of the land that he owns.[58]

2. Proof of title. It should be noted that a good title cannot be shown merely by proving adverse possession of land, for however long a period. If A and his predecessors in title have been in possession of land for twenty, fifty, or a hundred years, that does not prove A is entitled to it, for the true owner—

(a) might have been under disability at the time of dispossession; or
(b) might have been the Crown; or
(c) might have been the reversioner or remainderman under a settlement; or
(d) might be the reversioner on a long lease.

Consequently, to establish a good title by the operation of the Act, it must be shown—

(i) who was the true owner of the interest in land in question; and
(ii) that he has been barred by lapse of time.

A vendor who can do this can establish a title which the courts will force even an unwilling purchaser to accept.[59] However, in practice, it is comparatively unusual for a title to land to be acquired by limitation, except in the case of encroachments upon neighbouring land.

---

[55] *Ashe* v. *Hogan* [1920] 1 I.R. 159.
[56] *Tichborne* v. *Weir, supra.*
[57] *Taylor* v. *Twinberrow* [1930] 2 K.B. 16.
[58] *Fairweather* v. *St. Marylebone Property Co. Ltd.* [1963] A.C. 510; but see 78 L.Q.R. 33.
[59] *Re Atkinson & Horsell's Contract* [1912] 2 Ch. 1; contrast *George Wimpey & Co. Ltd.* v. *Sohn* [1967] Ch. 487.

3. Successive squatters. Even before the statutory period has expired, a squatter has a title good against everyone except the true owner.[60] To hold otherwise would mean that a squatter who had not barred the true owner would have no remedy against somebody who dispossessed him; this might lead to breaches of the peace by competing squatters. Consequently, if a squatter who has not barred the true owner sells the land he can give the purchaser a right to the land which is valid against all except the true owner. The same applies to devises, gifts or other dispositions by the squatter; in each case the person taking the squatter's interest can add the squatter's period of possession to his own.[61] Thus if X, who has occupied A's land for eight years, sells the land to Y, A will be barred after Y has held the land for a further four years. Again, if a squatter is himself dispossessed, the second squatter can add the former period of occupation to his own. For example, if land owned by A has been occupied by X for eight years and Y dispossesses X, A will be barred when twelve years have elapsed from X first taking possession. But although at the end of that time A is barred, X will not be barred until twelve years from Y's first taking possession, for Y cannot claim to be absolutely entitled until he can show that everybody with any claim to the land has been barred by the lapse of the full period.

There is no right to add together two periods of adverse possession if a squatter abandons possession before the full period has run and some time elapses before another person takes possession of the land. During the interval, there was no person in adverse possession whom the true owner could sue; thus time started to run afresh when the second squatter took possession of the land.[62]

Sect. 2. Arrears of Income

The question of the recovery of arrears of income is distinct from that of the recovery of the land or capital money which produces it. The arrears of rent which the landlord or the owner of a rentcharge can recover by action or distress are limited to the arrears accrued due during the previous six years.[63] In the case of agricultural holdings,

---

[60] *Perry* v. *Clissold* [1907] A.C. 73 ; *ante*, p. 527.
[61] *Asher* v. *Whitlock* (1865) L.R. 1 Q.B. 1.
[62] *Trustees, Executors and Agency Co. Ltd.* v. *Short* (1888) 13 App.Cas. 793 ; Limitation Act 1939, s. 10.
[63] Limitation Act 1939, ss. 17, 31.

the landlord's right of distress is further restricted to the year preceding the distress [64]; and special provisions exist for bankruptcy.[65]

There is also a six years' period for arrears of mortgage interest.[66] But a mortgagee who exercises his power of sale may retain all arrears of interest out of the proceeds of sale, for this is not recovery by action [67]; and a mortgagor who seeks to redeem can do so only on the equitable terms of paying all arrears, however old.[68]

---

[64] Agricultural Holdings Act 1948, s. 18.
[65] Bankruptcy Act 1914, s. 35.
[66] Limitation Act 1939, s. 18.
[67] *Re Marshfield* (1887) 34 Ch.D. 721.
[68] *Dingle* v. *Coppen* [1899] 1 Ch. 726.

CHAPTER 16

REGISTRATION

Part 1

TYPES OF REGISTRATION

THERE are three types of registration in force in England. These are:
- (i) Registration of incumbrances.
- (ii) Registration of deeds.
- (iii) Registration of title.

1. Registration of incumbrances. Various registers are provided in which any person claiming to be entitled to certain incumbrances on any land in England should register his claim. There is no investigation or guarantee by the registrar; all that the applicant need do is to fill in a form containing the necessary particulars and file it in the appropriate registry.

The object of this system is to enable a purchaser of land to discover easily what incumbrances exist. Despite the general rule that a purchaser is bound by equitable rights of which he has notice, he is not bound by equitable rights which ought to have been registered but have not, so that as far as registrable rights are concerned, a search will reveal every right which will bind him.

2. Registration of deeds. This is very limited in extent. It applies only to land in Yorkshire, although before 1937 (when registration of title became compulsory in Middlesex [1]) it applied also to land in Middlesex. Registration of deeds is similar to registration of incumbrances in that the registrar neither investigates nor guarantees the document registered, but differs in that a full copy of the deed must be filed with the original, the latter being duly returned indorsed with a statement that it has been registered. Further, the documents registered frequently form links in the title and do not merely create incumbrances on the land. The object of such registration is to assist a purchaser in verifying the title and to prevent the alteration or suppression of documents.

[1] Land Registration Act 1936, s. 2; *post*, p. 553.

3. Registration of title. The title to any land in England may be registered, but only in certain parts of the country, known as the compulsory areas, is registration compulsory.[1a] Registration of title differs from both the previous types of registration in several ways:

(i) The system deals with registration of the whole title to the land and not merely each individual transaction.

(ii) The registrar not only investigates the title but also, when satisfied, guarantees it.

(iii) Registration of title normally puts an end to the usual investigation of title; for instead of having to examine all the deeds for the last thirty years or more, as is the case with ordinary land, a purchaser of registered land merely inspects the register to see that the vendor is certified to be the owner of the land. The register also discloses many, but not all, of the incumbrances affecting the land.

Part 2

REGISTRATION OF INCUMBRANCES

Three classes of registers must be considered, namely, the Land Charges Register, the Yorkshire Deeds Register, and the various Local Land Charges Registers.

Sect. 1. Land Charges Register in London

A. *Registrable Interests*

The Land Charges Act 1925 is the present statute governing the registration of incumbrances, which has so largely superseded the equitable doctrine of purchaser without notice.[2] Although the Act to some extent repeats earlier statutes which need not be considered here, it also considerably extends the system by making many interests registrable after 1925 for the first time.

Five separate registers are kept in the Land Charges Department of the Land Registry in London. The last of these is of considerably greater importance than the others.

1. Pending actions.[3] A pending action (sometimes called a *lis pendens*) is any action, information or proceeding pending in court

---

[1a] See *post*, p. 558, for the present limits on voluntary registration.
[2] See *ante*, p. 79.   [3] L.C.A. 1925, Pt. I.

relating to any interest in land. It includes a petition in bankruptcy filed after 1925. Thus anyone who claims to be entitled to land and who brings an action to enforce his rights should register it as a pending action so as to ensure that if the present owner tries to sell the land before the case has been decided, the purchaser will be bound by the claim. Registration lasts for five years; if the case has not then been decided, registration may be renewed for successive periods of five years.

2. Annuities.[4] For the purposes of Part II of the Land Charges Act 1925, an annuity is a rentcharge or an annuity for a life or lives, or for an estate determinable on a life or lives (*e.g.*, " to X for ninety-nine years if he so long lives ") created after April 5, 1855, but before 1926, and not created by a marriage settlement or will. No annuity can be entered in this register after 1925, though certain annuities are registrable in other registers.

The registration of annuities may be summarised as follows. There are three classes:

(i) Annuities which were both created and registered before 1926. These are the only annuities in the register now under consideration.

(ii) Annuities created before 1926 but not registered until after 1925. These are registrable as Class E land charges.[5]

(iii) Annuities created and registered after 1925. These are registrable as Class C (iii) land charges (" general equitable charges "),[6] provided they do not arise under a settlement or trust for sale.

It should be noted that annuities created by a marriage settlement or will are not registrable. Thus the majority of annuities are exempt from the effects of registration and are subject to the normal rules; if legal they bind everyone, if equitable they bind everyone except a purchaser without notice, and if they arise under a settlement they are liable to be overreached.

It will be seen that the register of annuities and the register of Class E land charges will both die out in the course of time.

3. Writs and orders affecting land.[7] This head does not include writs employed to commence an action relating to land; these come

---

[4] *Ibid.* Pt. II.
[5] *Post*, p. 546.
[6] *Post*, p. 544.
[7] L.C.A. 1925, Pt. III.

under the head of pending actions. The register of writs and orders is directed towards writs and orders *enforcing* judgments and orders of the court. The chief writs and orders included in this register are—

(i) writs or orders affecting land made for the purpose of enforcing a judgment, statute or recognisance or any obligation to the Crown; this head includes an order of the court charging a judgment debtor's land with payment of the money due (in place of the old writ of elegit) [8];

(ii) an order appointing a receiver or sequestrator of land;

(iii) a receiving order in bankruptcy made after 1925.

Registration remains effective for five years, but may be renewed for successive periods of five years.

4. Deeds of arrangement.[9] The Deeds of Arrangement Act 1914 elaborately defines deeds of arrangement. For the present purpose, a deed of arrangement may be taken as any document whereby control over a debtor's property is given for the benefit of his creditors generally, or, if he is insolvent, for the benefit of three or more of his creditors. A common example is an assignment by a debtor of all his property to a trustee for all his creditors.

Registration is effective for five years and may be renewed for successive periods of five years. The registration may be effected by the trustee of the deed or by any creditor assenting to or taking the benefit of the deed.

5. Land charges.[10] These are divided into five classes, A, B, C, D and E.[11] The most important classes, C and D, are subdivided.

Class A consists of charges imposed on land by some statute, but which come into existence only when some person makes an application. Thus where a landlord who is not entitled to land for his own benefit has to pay compensation to an agricultural tenant, the landlord may apply to the Minister of Agriculture, Fisheries and Food for a charge on the land for the amount of compensation.[12] A Class A charge is registrable whenever created. If it was created after 1888, it should be registered forthwith; if it was created before 1888, it must be registered within a year of the first transfer of it made after 1888.[13]

---

[8] Administration of Justice Act 1956, ss. 34, 35.
[9] L.C.A. 1925, Pt. IV.
[10] *Ibid.* Pt. V.
[11] *Ibid.* s. 10.
[12] Agricultural Holdings Act 1948, s. 82.
[13] L.C.A. 1925, ss. 13, 14.

Class B consists of charges which are similar to those in Class A except that they are not created on the application of any person, but are imposed automatically by statute. Most charges thus imposed are local land charges, and as these are registrable in a separate register, few charges are registrable in Class B, *e.g.*, a charge for money paid to redeem land tax.[14] Such a charge should have been registered forthwith if created after 1925, or, if created before 1926, within one year of the first transfer after 1925.[15]

Class C land charges are divided into four categories:

C (i): A PUISNE MORTGAGE. This is a legal mortgage not protected by a deposit of documents relating to the legal estate affected.

C (ii): A LIMITED OWNER'S CHARGE. This is an equitable charge which a tenant for life or statutory owner acquires under any statute by discharging death duties or other liabilities, and to which the statute gives special priority. Thus on the death of a tenant for life of settled land, estate duty must be paid; if the next tenant for life finds the money out of his own pocket instead of throwing the burden on the settled property itself, he is entitled to a charge on the land in the same way as if he had lent money to the estate on mortgage. Such a charge is registrable under this head.

C (iii): A GENERAL EQUITABLE CHARGE. This is any equitable charge which—

    (i) is not included in any other class of land charge;
    (ii) is not protected by a deposit of documents relating to the legal estate affected; and
    (iii) does not arise, or affect an interest arising, under a trust for sale or settlement.

This is a residuary class which catches equitable charges not registrable elsewhere. It includes equitable mortgages of a legal estate but not equitable mortgages of an equitable interest under a settlement or trust for sale or other charges on the proceeds of sale of land.[16]

C (iv): AN ESTATE CONTRACT. This is a contract (whether oral [17] or in writing) to convey or create a legal estate, made by a person who either owns a legal estate or is entitled at the date of the contract to have a legal estate conveyed to him. Options of purchase, rights

---

[14] Finance Act 1949, s. 40. For land tax, see *ante*, p. 78.
[15] L.C.A. 1925, ss. 13, 14.
[16] *Georgiades* v. *Edward Wolfe & Co. Ltd.* [1965] Ch. 487 (estate agents' commission).
[17] *Universal Permanent Building Society* v. *Cooke* [1952] Ch. 95 at 104.

of pre-emption and other like rights are expressly included, even if contained in a lease.[18] A contract made with X to convey land to Y falls under this head [19]; and it suffices if the person who makes the contract owns any legal estate in the land, even if it is less substantial than the estate which he has agreed to convey or create, as where a yearly tenant agrees that if he acquires the reversion he will grant his sub-tenant a lease for ten years.[20] Also included is the notice given by the tenant of a long lease of his desire to purchase the freehold, or take a long lease [21]; but a notice to treat given in connection with a compulsory purchase is not registrable.[22]

Class D land charges are divided into three categories:

D (i): DEATH DUTIES. This class consists of any charge for death duties arising on a death after 1925. Prior to the Finance Act 1949, which abolished both legacy duty and succession duty, death duties were of three kinds:

(i) Estate duty, which is borne by all property and varies according to the total value of the property passing or deemed to pass on the death.

(ii) Succession duty, which was borne by all property settled before the death of the deceased, and all land, whether settled or not. This varied according to the relationship of the successor to the deceased, being 2 per cent. for spouses, ancestors or descendants, 10 per cent. for brothers and sisters or their descendants, and 20 per cent. for others.

(iii) Legacy duty, which was borne only by pure, unsettled personalty, at the same rates as for succession duty.

Estate duty is not a charge on leaseholds and is thus not registrable; a purchaser is not concerned with it. But in the case of freeholds, estate duty is a charge on the property and consequently must be registered; in practice, however, this is rarely done.

Succession duty is a charge on the beneficial interests in property to which a successor succeeds. Thus if land is sold by the personal representatives (*e.g.*, to pay debts) a purchaser is not concerned with succession duty, for there has been no beneficial succession to the land. A purchaser from a devisee, however, is concerned with it.

---

18 *Beesly* v. *Hallwood Estates Ltd.* [1960] 1 W.L.R. 549; in C.A. [1961] Ch. 105. Contrast restrictive covenants: *post*, p. 546.
19 *Turley* v. *Mackay* [1944] Ch. 37.
20 *Sharp* v. *Coates* [1949] 1 K.B. 285; *sed quaere*.
21 Leasehold Reform Act 1967, s. 5 (5).
22 *Capital Investments Ltd.* v. *Wednesfield U.D.C.* [1965] Ch. 774.

As a claim for estate or succession duties is barred by the lapse of twelve years from the death, a purchaser is today never concerned with these duties in respect of a death before 1926. In the case of deaths after 1925, a purchaser is not concerned with them unless they are registered.

D (ii): RESTRICTIVE COVENANTS. Under this head, any covenant or agreement restrictive of the user of land may be registered provided it was—

(i) entered into after 1925, and

(ii) not made between a lessor and lessee.

Thus restrictive covenants in leases are never registrable; the normal rules as to privity of contract and privity of estate apply, and when there is neither, the question, as usual, is one of notice. Similarly, restrictive covenants made before 1926 still depend upon notice, being enforceable against everyone except a purchaser of a legal estate without notice.[23]

D (iii): EQUITABLE EASEMENTS. Any "easement, right or privilege over or affecting land" is registrable under this head, provided—

(i) it is merely equitable, and

(ii) it was created after 1925.

Thus a perpetual easement created by a document not under seal, or an easement for life, even if created by deed, is registrable under this head if made after 1925. Each is necessarily equitable, the first for lack of a deed and the second as not falling within section 1 of the Law of Property Act 1925.[24] Presumably equitable profits *à prendre* are included under this head.[25] But the apparent width of "right or privilege" is restricted by the context, and thus a requisition of land under Defence Regulations was held not registrable under this head.[26]

Class E: Annuities created before 1926. These have already been dealt with.[27]

Class F: A spouse's right to occupy a house owned by the other spouse.[28]

---

[23] *Ante*, p. 404.

[24] *Ante*, pp. 68, 71, 72.

[25] *E.R. Ives Investment Ltd.* v. *High* [1967] 2 Q.B. 379 at 395.

[26] *Lewisham Borough Council* v. *Maloney* [1948] 1 K.B. 50; and see *E.R. Ives Investment Ltd.* v. *High* [1967] 2 Q.B. 379.

[27] *Ante*, p. 542.

[28] Added by Matrimonial Homes Act 1967, s. 2 (6). For this right, see *ante*, p. 381.

Companies. Most charges created by a company for securing money require registration within 21 days in the Companies Register maintained under the Companies Act 1948. This suffices in place of registration in the Land Charges Register, and has the same effect.[29]

B. *Effects of Registration and Non-Registration*

1. Effect of registration.

(a) *Notice.* By the Law of Property Act 1925,[30] registration under the Land Charges Act 1925 constitutes actual notice of the interest registered to all persons and for all purposes connected with the land affected.[31] There are exceptions to this rule,[32] but in general it prevents any person claiming to be a purchaser without notice of a registered interest.

(b) *Names register.* The most serious defect of the system from the point of view of a purchaser is that the registers are registers of the names of persons; an incumbrance is registered against the name of the estate owner at the time and not against the land. Thus on a purchase of 14 Newcastle Street it is not possible to search against 14 Newcastle Street, and a search must be made against the names of all previous owners of the land. The rights most likely to concern a purchaser, namely, Classes C and D, only became registrable after 1925, but in course of time the cost of searches may become considerable. The remedy is the preservation by each purchaser in turn of the certificate of the search he made when purchasing the land, and his handing the certificates on with the title deeds so that subsequent owners can rely upon them.

(c) *Lessees.* The doctrine that registration constitutes notice *per se* may work especial hardship in the case of lessees. Where a lease is granted by a tenant in fee simple at a low rent in consideration of a fine, the lessee usually stipulates that he shall be entitled to investigate the lessor's title, whereas if the lease is granted at a rack rent, the lessee usually takes it for granted that the lessor is able to grant it and so does not investigate his title. Further, by statute,[33] under an open contract[34] to grant a lease the lessee is not entitled to investigate the freeholder's title. In *Patman* v. *Harland*[35] it was held that

[29] Companies Act 1948, s. 95; L.C.A. 1925, s. 10 (5); contrast *post*, p. 556.
[30] s. 198.   [31] See, generally, S. J. Bailey (1949) 10 Camb.L.J. 241.
[32] *Ante*, pp. 481, 513.
[33] L.P.A. 1925, s. 44, replacing Vendor and Purchaser Act 1874, s. 2.
[34] *Ante*, p. 328.   [35] (1881) 17 Ch.D. 353.

since a lessee under an open contract might have made a special contract entitling him to investigate the lessor's title, he was fixed with notice of all that he would have discovered had he made a proper investigation.

The rule in *Patman* v. *Harland*, which caused some hardship and was much criticised, has been abolished for all leases made after 1925. However, the provisions for the registration of land charges such as restrictive covenants made after 1925 have created a new difficulty due to registration being effected against the name of the person making the covenant and not against the land. A prospective lessee will be able to search against the name of the lessor, but if he is not entitled to investigate the lessor's title he will not know the names of the previous owners of the land and so will not be able to discover restrictive covenants registered against their names. Nevertheless, registration is notice to all persons and for all purposes connected with the land,[36] and so the lessee is deemed to have notice of the covenants. The position may be summarised thus:

(i) Lease and restrictive covenant both made before 1926: the lessee is caught by *Patman* v. *Harland*.

(ii) Lease and restrictive covenant both made after 1925: the lessee is caught by the provisions for registration.

(iii) Restrictive covenant made before 1926, lease made after 1925: here alone is the lessee's position improved. The lessee is safe unless he has notice in some other way, for *Patman* v. *Harland* does not apply and the restrictive covenant, being made before 1926, is not registrable.[37]

2. Effect of non-registration. The effect of non-registration varies according to the interest. There are two main categories:

(a) The incumbrance may be void against a purchaser for value of any interest in the land; or

(b) The incumbrance may be void against a purchaser for money or money's worth of a legal estate in the land.

One difference between (a) and (b) is that a purchaser of an equitable interest is protected by (a) but not by (b). Another is that marriage is " value " but is not " money or money's worth," and consequently in the case of land settled on an ante-nuptial marriage settlement, the spouses and issue will be protected by (a) but not by (b). In each

[36] L.P.A. 1925, s. 198.
[37] See, *e.g.*, *Shears* v. *Wells* [1936] 1 All E.R. 832.

case " purchaser " has an extended meaning and includes a lessee, mortgagee or other person taking an interest in land for value. The effect of non-registration may be expressed as follows.[38]

(i) In general, whichever register is concerned, non-registration of any registrable matter in the appropriate register makes it void against a purchaser for value of any interest in the land.

(ii) If, however, a land charge falls within Class C (iv) (estate contracts) or Class D, and was created after 1925, non-registration makes it void only against a purchaser of a legal estate for money or money's worth. It will be noticed that an estate contract created before 1926 falls under the previous head.

(iii) Bankruptcy petitions (registrable as pending actions) and receiving orders (registrable as writs and orders) are void only against a bona fide purchaser of a legal estate for money or money's worth without notice of an available act of bankruptcy, *i.e.,* an act of bankruptcy not more than three months old.

(iv) Any other pending action is void against a purchaser for value of any interest in the land, provided he had no express notice of it.

It will thus be seen that with the comparatively unimportant exceptions of (iii) and (iv) above, actual knowledge is immaterial. The Law of Property Act 1925 [39] provides that where an interest is void against a purchaser under the Land Charges Act 1925, he shall not be affected by notice thereof. Thus it is immaterial that the purchaser bought with the actual knowledge of the unregistered interest and that the land was conveyed to him expressly subject to it [40]: the effect of registration and non-registration is automatic. It should be noted that the crucial time in each case is the completion of the transaction, *i.e.,* the purchase of the legal estate or the equitable interest, as the case may be; subsequent registration cannot impose any burden on the purchaser.

3. Companies. If a charge registrable in the Companies Register is not duly registered, it is in addition void as a security as against the liquidator and all creditors of the company, and the money becomes immediately payable.[41]

---

[38] L.C.A. 1925, ss. 3, 5, 7, 9, 13. [39] s. 199.
[40] See *Hollington Bros. Ltd.* v. *Rhodes* [1951] 2 T.L.R. 691.
[41] Companies Act 1948, s. 95; *ante,* p. 547.

C. Differences Between Class C and Class D Land Charges

The main difference between Class C and Class D land charges is that a Class C land charge can be registered if it is either created or transferred after 1925, whereas a Class D land charge can be registered only if it is created after 1925.[42] Thus a Class D land charge arising before 1926 can never be registered, but a Class C land charge created before 1926 becomes registrable as soon as the benefit of the charge (as distinct from the land on which it is charged) is transferred after 1925. Failure to register a Class C land charge within a year of the first transfer of it after 1925 renders it void against a purchaser.[43]

There is, however, one Class C land charge, namely, a puisne mortgage created before 1926, which can be registered even before it is transferred.[44] The reason for this is that many puisne mortgages were equitable before 1926 but became legal by the operation of the transitional provisions of the Law of Property Act 1925.[45] These provisions laid down that until such mortgages were registered they would gain no advantage by their conversion. Thus registration is essential if such mortgages are to be freed from their vulnerability to a bona fide purchaser for value of a legal estate and translated to a status of validity against the whole world.

A further difference between Class C and Class D land charges is the effect of non-registration considered above[46]; this, however, is not a true class distinction, since Class C (iv) charges created after 1925 fall into the same category for this purpose as Class D.

Classes C and D resemble each other in that there was no provision before 1926 for the registration of either.

D. Searches and Priority Notices

1. Searches. The means by which an intending purchaser of land can discover registrable incumbrances is by a search. This may be made in person, but it is advisable to obtain an official certificate of search, for—

    (i) it is conclusive in favour of a purchaser, and so frees him from liability for registered rights which it fails to disclose[47];

---

[42] L.C.A. 1925, s. 10.
[43] *Ibid.* s. 14.
[44] *Ibid.* s. 10.
[45] 1st Sched., Pts. VII, VIII; *ante*, p. 465.
[46] *Ante*, pp. 548, 549.
[47] See, *e.g., Stock* v. *Wanstead and Woodford Borough Council* [1962] 2 Q.B. 479; *Oak Co-operative Building Society* v. *Blackburn* [1968] Ch. 730 at 743.

(ii) it protects a solicitor or trustee who makes it from liability for any error; and

(iii) it provides protection against incumbrances registered in the interval between search and completion. For if a purchaser completes his transaction before the expiration of the fourteenth day after the date of the certificate (excluding days on which the registry is not open to the public), he is not affected by any entry made after the date of the certificate and before completion, unless it is made pursuant to a priority notice [48] entered on the register before the certificate was issued.[49]

There is no need to search each register separately; a single search is effective for all divisions of all registers.

2. Priority notices. Special provision has been made to provide for a rapid sequence of transactions, such as the creation of a restrictive covenant followed immediately by the creation of a mortgage before there has been time to register the covenant. Thus if V is selling land to P, who is raising the purchase-money by means of a loan on mortgage from M, and is to enter into a restrictive covenant with V, the sequence of events will be—

(i) conveyance from V to P, reserving the restrictive covenant, followed a few minutes later by

(ii) mortgage by P to M.

In such a case, V's restrictive covenant could not be registered in the few minutes between its creation and the making of the mortgage, and so it will be void against M, a purchaser for money or money's worth of a legal estate, unless V has availed himself of the machinery of the priority notice. To do this, he must give a priority notice to the registrar at least fourteen days before the creation of the restrictive covenant, and then, if he registers his charge within twenty-eight days of the entry of the priority notice in the register, the registration dates back to the moment of the creation of the restrictive covenant, *i.e.,* to the execution of the conveyance from V to P ; once again, days on which the registry is not open to the public are excluded.[50] It will be noted that the notice must be given fourteen days before completion; this is to allow the expiry of the fourteen

---

[48] See *infra.*
[49] L.C.A. 1925, s. 17 ; L.P. (Am.) A. 1926, s. 4 ; S.R. & O. 1940 Nos. 1998, 2195.
[50] L.P. (Am.) A. 1926, s. 4 ; S.R. & O. 1940 Nos. 1998, 2195.

days' period of protection given to those who made official searches before the priority notice was lodged.[51]

Priority notices are not, of course, confined to restrictive covenants, but apply to all land charges.[52]

Sect. 2. Yorkshire Deeds Register

As will be seen,[53] certain land charges affecting land in Yorkshire are registrable in the Yorkshire Deeds Register instead of the Land Charges Register.

Sect. 3. Local Land Charges Registers

In addition to the registers kept by the Land Charges Department of the Land Registry, registers of local land charges are kept by each district or borough council and each county council.[54] These registers differ from those kept at the Land Registry in that the charges are registered against the land itself and not against the owner of it. Thus a series of searches against successive owners is unnecessary.

The interests registrable are any charges acquired by any local authority by statute. Many widely differing matters are registrable,[55] though in general they may be classified as financial, restrictive or acquisitive; and they have the general nature of being public rights, whereas the land charges registers are essentially registers of private rights. A few examples of local land charges are: charges for making up a road imposed in respect of land fronting the road, and charges for sanitary works; prohibitions or restrictions on the use of land, whether under planning law[56] or otherwise (*e.g.*, " building lines," preventing any building nearer a road than the prescribed line); and certain proceedings for compulsory acquisition under the Town and Country Planning Act 1962.

Failure to register a local land charge, whether created before or after 1925, renders it void against a purchaser for money or money's worth of a legal estate in the land affected who completes before the charge is registered.[57]

An official search can be obtained for local land charges also.

---

[51] *Supra.*
[52] See, *e.g.*, *ante*, p. 507.
[53] *Post*, p. 553.
[54] L.C.A. 1925, s. 15.
[55] See, generally, Garner's *Local Land Charges* (5th ed., 1966).
[56] See *post*, pp. 573 *et seq.*
[57] L.C.A. 1925, s. 15.

Part 3

REGISTRATION OF DEEDS

Sect. 1. Middlesex

The Middlesex Deeds Register was set up by the Middlesex Registry Act 1708. By the Land Registration Act 1936, s. 2, no memorial of a document executed after 1936 is registrable in the deeds register for Middlesex. Deeds, conveyances and wills affecting land in Middlesex and coming into operation before 1937 were registrable in the register until 1939. In 1940, the register was finally closed.[58] Middlesex became a compulsory registration area after 1936, and thus any dealing with the land will normally lead to registration of the title to the land.

Sect. 2. Yorkshire

Any document dealing with land in Yorkshire (except the City of York) must still be registered under the Yorkshire Registries Act 1884 by filing either a copy or a memorial which gives full details of the document. Any mortgage, lease for over twenty-one years, will or similar document is registrable, provided (if made after 1925) that it creates or transfers a legal estate.[59] Mere licences and contracts are not registrable. Puisne mortgages affecting land wholly in Yorkshire and registered there are not registrable in the Land Charges Register ; before 1937 a similar rule applied to Middlesex.[60]

General equitable charges, restrictive covenants, equitable easements and estate contracts which affect land in Yorkshire must be registered in a land charges register in the Yorkshire Registry instead of in the Land Charges Register.[61] This rule applies also to any other land charge (not being a local land charge) provided it shows on the face of it that it affects land in Yorkshire. In neither of these cases is there any requirement that the whole of the land affected should be in Yorkshire.

The general effect of non-registration is that the document concerned is void against a subsequent purchaser or mortgagee for value. In Yorkshire this is so even if the subsequent purchaser or

---

[58] Middlesex Deeds Act 1940.
[59] L.P.A. 1925, s. 11.
[60] *Ibid.*
[61] L.C.A. 1925, s. 10 (6) ; L.P. (Am.) A. 1926, Sched.

mortgagee had actual or constructive notice of the unregistered document, unless he was guilty of fraud [62]; in Middlesex it was otherwise.[63] Documents take priority from the date of their registration, except that if probate is registered within six months of the death, it has priority according to the date of the testator's death.

Part 4

REGISTRATION OF TITLE

Sect. 1. Introductory

1. History. Today, registration of title is of great and increasing importance ; but it is by no means new. Acts were passed in 1862 and 1875,[64] providing for voluntary registration of title, but not until the Land Transfer Act 1897 made registration of title compulsory on dealings with land in the County of London were any substantial number of titles registered. The present Act is the Land Registration Act 1925 (as amended by the Land Registration Act 1936 and the Land Registration Act 1966), supplemented by the Land Registration Rules 1925, as amended by the Land Registration Rules 1930, 1936, 1956 and 1967. Over a third of the work of conveyancing is estimated to concern registered land so that this has become an important branch of the law.

2. Basis of the system. The basic idea is to replace the separate investigation of title that takes place on every purchase by a title guaranteed by the State. In the case of unregistered land, a purchaser must satisfy himself from the abstract of title, the deeds, his requisitions on title, his searches and his inspection of the land that the vendor has power to sell the land and that it is subject to no undisclosed incumbrances. In the case of registered land, on the other hand, the purchaser can discover from the mere inspection of the register whether the vendor has power to sell the land and what the more important incumbrances are; the other incumbrances must be investigated in much the same way as in the case of unregistered land. The complexity of rights in land is such as to render it impossible to make the transfer of registered land as simple as the

---

[62] Yorkshire Registries Act 1884, s. 14.
[63] *Le Neve* v. *Le Neve* (1747) Amb. 436.
[64] Land Registry Act 1862 ; Land Transfer Act 1875.

transfer of shares registered in the books of a company, but the present system of registration of title may be said to go almost as far on that road as is practicable.

3. Classification of rights. The system of registration of title in no way amounts to a separate code of land law. In the main it is concerned with actual or potential transfers of rights existing under the general law, and it leaves the main basis of this unaffected. In this connection, the differing classes of rights in land must be distinguished.

(a) *Unregistered land.* In the case of unregistered land, there is first the estate which the purchaser is buying. Secondly, there are a number of claims adverse to the land which the abstract may not disclose, but which, being legal, will bind a purchaser, such as the rights of squatters in the process of acquiring title under the Limitation Act 1939. The purchaser must therefore satisfy himself as to these rights by making proper inquiries and inspecting the land. There are other claims adverse to the land which the abstract may not disclose but from which, being equitable, a purchaser will take free if either they are overreached (*e.g.,* interests under a trust for sale) or they are interests of which he has no notice, *e.g.,* restrictive covenants. In short, subject to the provisions relating to the registration of land charges, there are the following three classes of rights:

    (i) The estate which is to be dealt with.

    (ii) Legal rights in the land which will bind a purchaser, whether or not disclosed by the abstract or otherwise.

    (iii) Equitable rights in the land which require protection against a purchaser either by the machinery of overreaching, or by fixing him with notice.

(b) *Registered land.* In registered land, there is a similar but not exactly corresponding division, namely:

    (i) Registered interest, *i.e.,* rights in respect of which a title has been granted by the registrar.

    (ii) Overriding interests, *i.e.,* rights which will bind a purchaser whether or not disclosed by the register or otherwise.

    (iii) Minor interests, *i.e.,* rights which need to be protected by some entry on the register.

4. Other registrations. If the title to land is registered, there is no question of registration in the Land Charges Department or in a deeds registry, for entries on the Land Register take the place of these. But entries must still be made on the local land charges registers. Further, most charges created by a company for securing money require registration in the Companies Register in addition to protection by an entry on the Land Register.[65]

5. Privacy. Unlike deeds registers and the registers of land charges, the Land Register is not open to inspection by the public. In general, nobody can inspect it without the authority of the registered proprietor.[66] But an Index Map and a Parcels Index are open to public inspection, as also is a list of pending applications, and from these it can be discovered whether or not any particular property has been or is about to be registered.

Sect. 2. Interests in Registered Land

The three types of interest in registered land (namely, registered interests, overriding interests and minor interests) will now be considered in turn.

A. Registered Interests

1. Estates which can be registered. After 1925, the only estates in respect of which a proprietor can be registered are estates capable of subsisting as legal estates.[67] Thus a fee simple absolute in possession and (with certain exceptions [68]) a term of years absolute are registrable interests.

2. The register. The register itself is divided into three parts

(a) *The property register.* This describes the land and the estate for which it is held, refers to a map or plan showing the land, and contains notes of interests held for the benefit of the land, such as easements and other legal rights of which the registered land is the dominant tenement. The boundaries shown on the map are general and are not so exact as to show which side of a hedge or fence they run unless stated by the register to be " fixed." [69]

---

[65] Companies Act 1948, s. 95; contrast *ante*, p. 547, and see *ante*, p. 549.
[66] L.R.A. 1925, s. 112.
[67] *Ibid.* s. 2.
[68] See *post*, pp. 557, 558.
[69] L.R.A. 1925, s. 76; L.R. Rules 1925, r. 278; *Lee* v. *Barrey* [1957] Ch. 251.

(b) *The proprietorship register.* This states the nature of the title (*i.e.,* whether it is absolute, good leasehold, qualified or possessory [70]), states the name, address and description of the registered proprietor, and sets out any cautions, inhibitions and restrictions [71] affecting his right to deal with the land.

(c) *The charges register.* This contains entries relating to rights adverse to the land, such as mortgages or restrictive covenants, and in general all notices [72] protecting rights over the land.

The register is kept at the appropriate District Land Registry. The Land Registry has its headquarters in London but has been decentralised. The three parts of the register in respect of each property are kept together. A copy of these entries is included in the " Land Certificate," and is given to each registered proprietor as his document of title which he retains until he sells or charges the land.[73] The title deeds, stamped with a notice of registration, are also usually returned when the title is first registered. But the registered proprietor's proof of title is the register itself and not the Land Certificate, which may well be out of date owing to entries having been made in the register since the certificate was last in the registry.

3. Compulsory and voluntary registration.

(a) *The areas.* The compulsory areas at present consist [74] of Greater London, Kent, Surrey and Berkshire and nearly eighty other boroughs and urban districts throughout the country. The rapid extension has for the time being been halted. The location of land in a compulsory area does not mean that every title to land there must be registered in any event; registration is compulsory only on a conveyance on sale of the fee simple, or the creation or assignment on sale of certain leases.

(b) *Leases.* The position as to leaseholds, which is a little complicated, may be summarised as follows.[75]

(1) REGISTRATION PROHIBITED. The registration of a lease is prohibited, even if the land is in a compulsory area, if the lease—

---

[70] See *post*, pp. 558, 559.
[71] *Post*, p. 564.
[72] See *post*, p. 563.
[73] See *post*, pp. 564, 566.
[74] (1965) 62 *Law Society's Gazette* 585; (1966) *ibid.* 515.
[75] L.R.A. 1925, ss. 8, 18, 19, 123; 3 K. & E. 115.

    (i) was granted for a term of 21 years or less; or

    (ii) contains an absolute prohibition against assignment; or

    (iii) is a mortgage term still subject to a right of redemption.

(2) REGISTRATION COMPULSORY. The registration of a lease not falling under any of the above heads is compulsory—

    (i) if the land is in a compulsory area and the transaction consists of the grant of a lease for 40 years or more, or the assignment on sale of a lease with 40 or more years unexpired; or

    (ii) if the title to the freehold or leasehold out of which the lease is granted has been registered, and the transaction consists of the grant of a lease for more than 21 years, whether or not the land is in a compulsory area. This rule springs from the requirement that dispositions by a registered proprietor must themselves be registered; for the grant of a lease is a " disposition."

(3) REGISTRATION OPTIONAL. The registration of any other lease of land in a compulsory area is optional, *e.g.*, a lease for 30 years granted by a freeholder whose title is not registered.

(c) *Non-registration.* Where registration is compulsory because the land is in a compulsory area, the transaction is void as to the legal estate unless application for registration is made within two months, or such extended period as the registrar or the court allows.[76] Where registration is compulsory because the lessor's title is registered, no legal estate passes until registration, but the time limit of two months is not applied.[77]

(d) *Voluntary registration.* Applications to register titles to land outside the compulsory areas will not be entertained except in such classes of cases as the registrar has specified.[78] Building estates consisting of 20 or more plots form the principal class of case of which voluntary registration will be accepted.

4. Titles. There are four classes of title with which an applicant for registration may be registered.

(a) *Absolute.* In the case of freeholds, this vests in the first registered proprietor the fee simple in possession together with all

---

[76] L.R.A. 1925, s. 123.
[77] *Ibid.* ss. 19, 22.
[78] L.R.A. 1966, s. 1 (2).

rights and privileges (*e.g.,* easements) belonging thereto subject only to—

    (i) entries on the register;

    (ii) overriding interests, except so far as the register states that the land is free from them; and

    (iii) minor interests of which he has notice, if he is not entitled to the land for his own benefit ; thus trustees for sale who are registered as proprietors will still hold subject to the claims of the beneficiaries.[79]

In the case of leaseholds, an absolute title vests the leasehold in the first registered proprietor subject to the rights set out above and in addition to—

    (iv) all the liabilities of the lease and any defects in the lessor's title.[80]

An absolute title in the case of leaseholds guarantees not only that the registered proprietor is the owner of the lease but also that the lease was validly granted.

(b) *Qualified.* In the case of freeholds, this has the same effect as an absolute title except that the property is held subject to some defect or right specified in the register. This title is granted when an absolute title has been applied for but the registrar has been unable to grant it owing to some defect in the title. A qualified title to leaseholds has the same effect as an absolute or good leasehold title, as the case may be, except for the specified defect.[81]

(c) *Possessory.* In the case of either freeholds or leaseholds, first registration with possessory title has the same effect as registration with an absolute title, save that the title is subject to all rights existing or capable of arising at the time of first registration.[82] In short, the title is guaranteed as far as all dealings after the date of registration are concerned, but no guarantee is given as to the title prior to first registration, which must accordingly be investigated by a purchaser in the same way as if the land were not registered.

(d) *Good leasehold.* This is applicable only to leaseholds. It is the same as an absolute title, save that the lessor's right to grant the lease is not guaranteed.[83] Thus should it appear that the lessor was never entitled to grant the lease, the lessee is protected if he has an absolute title, but unprotected if he has a good leasehold title.

[79] L.R.A. 1925, s. 5.
[80] *Ibid.* s. 9.
[81] *Ibid.* ss. 7, 12.
[82] *Ibid.* ss. 6, 11.
[83] *Ibid.* s. 10.

Since a lessee cannot investigate the freehold title unless he stipulates for this in his contract,[84] he usually cannot give the registrar evidence of the freehold title and so can apply only for a good leasehold title. The registrar may nevertheless be able to grant an absolute title if the title to the freehold is registered, and, though unknown to the lessee, his landlord is the registered proprietor.

Application may be made in the first instance for any of the above titles except a qualified title which can only be applied for if an absolute title is refused.

5. Conversion of titles. When registration has taken place with any of the above titles other than absolute, conversion of the title may take place subsequently.[85] There are two classes of case.

(a) *Conversion as of right.* Provided he is satisfied that the proprietor is in possession of the land in question, the registrar is *bound* to convert the title—

(i) to absolute, in the case of a freehold registered with possessory title for fifteen years;
(ii) to good leasehold in the case of a leasehold registered with possessory title for ten years.

(b) *Discretionary conversion.* The registrar *may* convert the title—

(i) to absolute or good leasehold, if the land was registered with possessory title before 1926;
(ii) to absolute or good leasehold, if the land is registered with qualified, possessory or good leasehold title and is transferred for value;
(iii) to absolute, if the land has been registered with good leasehold title for ten years and the registrar is satisfied that the owners of the lease have been in possession for that period.

6. Application for first registration. With the exceptions set out above,[86] an application for registration may be made by any estate owner, including those holding the estate as a trustee. Further, anyone entitled to call for a legal estate to be vested in him (except a mere purchaser under a contract, or a mortgagee) can apply for registration.[87] Thus if A holds land on a bare trust for B, B can apply for registration without first requiring a conveyance to be

---

[84] See *ante*, p. 547.
[85] L.R.A. 1925, s. 77.
[86] *Ante*, pp. 557, 558.
[87] L.R.A. 1925, ss. 4, 8.

executed in his favour though normally A will have to join or concur in the application.

The registrar examines the title and enquires into any objections that may be made to the proposed registration. He has power to accept a defective title if in his opinion it is " a title the holding under which will not be disturbed." [88] There is no appeal to the court from a refusal to register.[89]

7. Cautions. Any person interested in land who thinks that he may be prejudiced by an application to register any title to it may lodge a caution with the registrar.[90] This entitles him to be informed by the registrar of any application to register the title. Thus a person who claims that the execution by him of a conveyance of his unregistered land was obtained by fraud might lodge a caution against first registration to prevent the grantee registering the title without his knowledge.

A caution may also be lodged to prevent a conversion of the title.

The notice given to the cautioner requires him to make his objections to the registration or conversion within a fixed time, usually 14 days. Abuse of this procedure is discouraged by a provision that any person who causes damage to another by unreasonably lodging a caution is liable to pay him compensation.[91]

B. Overriding Interests

1. Nature. Overriding interests bind the proprietor of registered land, even though he has no knowledge of them and no reference is made to them in the register. In general, they are the kind of rights which a purchaser of unregistered land would not expect to discover from a mere examination of the abstract and title deeds, but for which he would make inquiries and inspect the land. Most, though by no means all of them, are legal rights; but it must be emphasised that as far as incumbrances on registered land are concerned, the issue in deciding whether a purchaser is bound where there is no entry on the register is not whether the rights are legal or equitable but whether they are overriding interests or minor interests.

[88] L.R.A. 1925, s. 13.
[89] *Dennis* v. *Malcolm* [1934] Ch. 244.
[90] L.R.A. 1925, s. 53.
[91] *Ibid.* s. 56.

2. The interests. The list of chief overriding interests is set out in the Land Registration Act 1925, s. 70. The most important are:

(1) Rights of common, public rights, profits *à prendre*, rights of way, watercourses, rights of water, and other easements not being equitable easements required to be protected by notice on the register. Thus all easements, except apparently equitable easements, are capable of taking effect as overriding interests.

(2) Tithe redemption annuity.

(3) Rights acquired or being acquired under the Limitation Act 1939.

(4) Rights of every person in actual occupation of the land or in receipt of the rents and profits, unless inquiry made of such person fails to disclose the right. Such rights include an option to purchase the reversion contained in a lease.[92] A tenant is not in actual occupation of land which he allows a licensee to occupy for his own benefit. Similarly a house occupied by the wife of the owner is not in actual occupation by the owner.[93] This important head produces for registered land much the same effect as the doctrine of notice produces for unregistered land.[94]

(5) Rights excepted from the effect of registration, such as rights existing at the time of first registration where only a possessory title is granted.

(6) Local land charges, until protected by entry on the register.

(7) Leases for not more than 21 years at a rent without a fine ; nearly all leases, however, unless entered on the register, will take effect as overriding interests under head 4 above, even if they are for more than 21 years.[95]

3. Entries on register. The registrar *may* make entries on the register stating that the land is free from or subject to certain overriding interests. The only *obligation* upon him is to enter a notice of the existence of any easement, right, privilege or benefit created by an instrument (and not, for example, an easement acquired by prescription) which appears on the title at the time of first registration.

C. *Minor Interests*

1. Definition. The Act elaborately defines minor interests,[96] but

---

[92] *Webb* v. *Pollmount Ltd.* [1966] Ch. 584.
[93] *Strand Securities Ltd.* v. *Caswell* [1965] Ch. 958. See *ante*, p. 381, and *post*, p. 563, for the rights of occupation of spouses.
[94] See *Grace Rymer Investments Ltd.* v. *Waite* [1958] Ch. 831 at 849; *ante*, p. 61.
[95] See *Strand Securities Ltd.* v. *Caswell* [1965] Ch. 958.   [96] L.R.A. 1925, s. 3.

for present purposes it may suffice to say that minor interests are those which require protection by some entry on the register. Registered interests are protected by the grant of the registered title, overriding interests need no protection, but all other interests fall into the class of minor interests and so need to be protected by an entry on the register. There are two classes of minor interests:

(i) those which will not bind a purchaser even when protected by an entry on the register, but which will be overreached, such as the equitable interests of beneficiaries under a settlement or trust for sale ; and

(ii) those which will bind a purchaser provided they are protected in the appropriate way, *e.g.*, restrictive covenants.

2. Protection of minor interests. A minor interest may be protected by a notice, caution, inhibition or restriction.

(a) *Notices.*

(1) EFFECT OF NOTICE. In general, the effect of the entry of a notice is to ensure that any subsequent dealing with the land will take effect subject to the right protected by the notice [97]; the mere entry of a notice will not, of course, give validity to an invalid claim. A notice also serves to fix the registered proprietor with notice of the claim as from the moment of entry.

(2) RIGHTS PROTECTED. The rights which can be protected by notice include all land charges under the Land Charges Act 1925, legal rentcharges, a spouse's right to occupy a house owned by the other spouse,[98] the right conferred on a tenant of a long leasehold to serve a notice of his desire to acquire the freehold or an extended lease,[99] and the rights of creditors when a bankruptcy petition has been presented against the registered proprietor. In this last case, the notice is called a " creditor's notice." [1]

(3) MODE OF ENTRY. Normally before the notice can be entered, the land certificate must be produced to the registrar. Thus unless the land is already charged so that the certificate has been deposited at the Land Registry,[2] a notice cannot be entered without the co-operation of the registered proprietor. Exceptionally, a creditor's notice can be entered without production of the land certificate.[3]

---

[97] *Ibid.* s. 52. See *Re White Rose Cottage* [1964] Ch. 940.
[98] Matrimonial Homes Act 1967, s. 2 (7); see *ante*, p. 381.
[99] Leasehold Reform Act 1967, s. 5 (5).
[1] L.R.A. 1925, s. 61. [2] See *post*, p. 566.
[3] L.R.A. 1925, s. 64.

(b) *Cautions.* If the registered proprietor refuses to co-operate, the remedy of the owner of the minor interest is to lodge a caution against dealings.[4] The effect of a caution has already been discussed.[5]

(c) *Inhibitions.* An inhibition is an order of the court or entry by the registrar which forbids any dealing with the land, either absolutely or until a certain time or event.[6] It may be made on the application of any person, and is in general intended for use only where there is no other way of protecting the claim. Nevertheless, it is used as a matter of routine in a few cases; thus where a receiving order in bankruptcy is made, a " bankruptcy inhibition " is entered preventing the registered proprietor from disposing of the land.[7]

(d) *Restrictions.* A restriction is similar to an inhibition in that it prevents any dealing with the land until some condition has been complied with; it differs in that it is an entry made by or with the consent of the registered proprietor himself.[8] Thus a restriction is a friendly entry, while inhibitions and cautions are hostile. Cases in which restrictions are appropriate include those where the registered proprietor is the tenant for life of settled land and restrictions are entered prohibiting the registration of a disposition not authorised by the Settled Land Act 1925, or one in which capital money arises unless it is paid to the trustees, being at least two in number or a trust corporation, or into court. Similar restrictions are imposed in the case of trusts for sale. In practice, the registrar sees that suitable restrictions are framed and entered; if the registered proprietor fails to apply for their entry, any person interested may do so with his consent.[9]

Sect. 3. Certain Dealings with Registered Land

In general, the registered proprietor can deal with or dispose of his land to the same extent as an owner with an unregistered title. The Act expressly authorises a wide range of dealings of which the most important are outlined below.[10]

A. Transfer Inter Vivos

1. Transfer. The transfer of registered land *inter vivos* is effected by a simple form of transfer which must be lodged at the Land

---

[4] L.R.A. 1925, ss. 54, 55. [5] *Ante*, p. 561.
[6] L.R.A. 1925, s. 57. [7] *Ibid.* s. 61. [8] *Ibid.* s. 58.
[9] L.R. Rules 1925, r. 236. [10] See L.R.A. 1925, ss. 18, 21, 25, 40, 66.

Registry together with the land certificate. The registrar makes the necessary entries on the register and the land certificate, and returns the latter to the new proprietor if the whole of the land has been sold. If part only has been sold, the original certificate is amended and returned to the vendor, and a new certificate for the part sold is issued to the purchaser. No legal estate passes until the transfer is registered.[11]

The transferee takes the land with all the benefits, *e.g.,* implied easements,[12] but subject to all the interests which bound the transferor, save that if he is a purchaser for value he takes free from minor interests other than those which bind him through being protected by an entry on the register.[13]

2. Search. As the register is private, an intending purchaser cannot have it searched without the vendor's authority.[14] He is bound to give this authority, however, which is normally required to enable the purchaser to confirm the accuracy of the copy of the entries on the register with which the vendor will have supplied him in lieu of an abstract of title.[15] Alternatively, and more commonly, the vendor obtains an office copy of the entries from the Registry which he hands to the purchaser. The latter can rely on this and need only search for entries after the date of the office copy. If the purchaser obtains an official search, he is not affected by entries on the register made between the date of the certificate of search and his application for registration, provided this application is delivered at the Registry in the proper form before it opens or is deemed to open on the fifteenth day (excluding days on which the Registry is not open to the public for registration) after the date of the certificate.[16]

B. Transfer on Death

On the death of a sole registered proprietor, his personal representatives may either [17]—

    (i) apply for registration themselves, on producing to the registrar the grant of probate or letters of administration ; or

---

[11] L.R.A. 1925, ss. 19–23.
[12] See *ante*, pp. 433 *et seq.*
[13] *Ibid.* ss. 20, 23.
[14] *Ante*, p. 556.
[15] L.R.A. 1925, s. 110.
[16] L.R. Rules 1925, r. 323 ; 1930, rr. 1, 6 ; 1936, r. 1 ; 1956, r. 2.
[17] L.R.A. 1925, ss. 37, 41 ; L.R. Rules 1925, rr. 168, 170.

> (ii) without being themselves registered, transfer the land direct either to a purchaser or to the person entitled under the will or intestacy; in this case, both the transfer or assent and the probate or letters of administration must be lodged with the application for registration.

The name of a joint proprietor will be removed from the register on proof of death.[18]

C. *Transfer on Bankruptcy*

The steps taken on bankruptcy, so far as they affect registered land, are briefly as follows.

(1) A bankruptcy petition is presented; this is protected by the entry of a creditor's notice, which prevents the debtor from selling the land free from the claims of the creditors.

(2) A receiving order is made; this is protected by a bankruptcy inhibition, which prevents the registered proprietor from dealing with the land at all.

(3) The registered proprietor is adjudicated bankrupt. His trustee in bankruptcy (or, until a trustee is appointed, the official receiver) may be registered as proprietor in place of the bankrupt on production of an office copy of the adjudication, a certificate of his appointment as trustee and a declaration that the land is part of the bankrupt's property divisible among his creditors.[19]

D. *Mortgages*

Subject to any restriction on the power of mortgaging which may be entered on the register, a mortgage of registered land may be effected in three ways.

1. By registered charge. A registered charge may be effected by any deed charging the land by reference to its registration number or in any other identifiable way,[20] though no legal estate arises until it has been registered.[21] The expression " by way of legal mortgage " is not essential to the creation of a valid legal charge of registered land.[22] On registration, an entry is made in the charges register giving details of the charge. The land certificate must be deposited

---

[18] L.R. Rules 1925, r. 172.
[19] L.R.A. 1925, s. 42; L.R. Rules 1925, rr. 174–177.
[20] L.R.A. 1925, s. 25.
[21] *Grace Rymer Investments Ltd.* v. *Waite* [1958] Ch. 831.
[22] *Cityland and Property (Holdings) Ltd.* v. *Dabrah* [1968] Ch. 166; *ante*, p. 466.

at the Registry for as long as a registered charge exists, and a charge certificate is issued to the chargee as his document of title.[23]

A registered chargee has all the powers of a legal mortgagee, unless the register otherwise provides.[24] The priority of registered charges is governed by the order of entry in the register, unless it otherwise provides.[25] As regards tacking, section 94 of the Law of Property Act 1925 does not apply to registered land; but further advances may be tacked only if made by a chargee under an obligation to do so which has been entered on the register, or if made before notice of the intervening incumbrance sent by the registrar ought, in due course of post, to have reached the chargee making the advance.[26]

2. By unregistered mortgage. Registered land may be mortgaged in the same way as if it were unregistered. Such mortgages take effect only as minor interests until they are protected by being registered. Alternatively they may be protected by the entry of a " mortgage caution " in the proprietorship register. A mortgage by deed so protected may subsequently be registered with the same priority as the caution, whereupon the mortgagee will have the same powers as a registered chargee.[27] Such cautions are rare in practice.

3. By deposit of the land certificate. Since the land certificate takes the place of the title deeds, a lien may be created by deposit of the land certificate. A chargee can similarly create a lien on his charge by deposit of his charge certificate.[28] In such cases, the lender may have a notice of the deposit entered on the charges register of the interest affected ; this operates as a caution.[29]

A lien may also be created by giving the registrar a notice of intention to deposit the land certificate.[30] This procedure is useful where a loan is made in connection with the purchase of the land. Naturally the certificate is not available until the transfer has been registered following the completion of the purchase. The certificate is delivered to the person named in the notice by the registrar.

[23] L.R.A. 1925, ss. 25, 26, 65 ; L.R. Rules 1925, r. 262.
[24] L.R.A. 1925, ss. 27, 34.
[25] *Ibid.* s. 29.
[26] *Ibid.* s. 30; L.P.(Am.)A. 1926; for tacking, see *ante*, pp. 510 *et seq.*
[27] L.R.A. 1925, s. 106.
[28] *Ibid.* s. 66.
[29] L.R. Rules 1925, r. 239.
[30] L.R. Rules 1925, rr. 240–242.

E. Limitation and Prescription

A title to registered land may be acquired under the Limitation Act 1939 by adverse possession in the same way as in the case of unregistered land. However, in the case of registered land, no legal title is acquired by the adverse possessor until he has been registered as proprietor ; until then, the registered proprietor holds the land on trust for him.[31] Registration of the squatter's title may be made with absolute, qualified, good leasehold or possessory title as the case may be, but interests not extinguished by the adverse possession are not affected.

" Easements, rights and privileges adversely affecting registered land " are capable of being acquired by prescription in the same way as if the land were not registered.[32]

F. Dealings with Minor Interests

When beneficial interests under a settlement or trust for sale of unregistered land are assigned or mortgaged, the assignees or mortgagees preserve priority by giving written notice of their interests to the trustees under the rule in *Dearle* v. *Hall*.[33] In the case of registered land, priority is governed instead by the order in which the assignments or mortgages are protected by " Priority Inhibitions " or " Priority Cautions " entered in the " Index of Minor Interests "[34]; the inhibition is used for an absolute assignment, the caution for other cases. The rule that the order of entry governs priority appears to be absolute, so that a mortgagee may be postponed to a subsequent mortgagee who registers first, even though the subsequent mortgagee had notice of the prior mortgage when he advanced his money.[35]

" Index of Minor Interests " is a misleading title for what is in no way an index of minor interests. No entry is made on it until there has been some dealing with a minor interest: the sole function of entries made on the index is to take the place of *Dearle* v. *Hall* notices. The index is no part of the register, and a purchaser of registered land is not concerned with it, for the rights of the beneficiaries will be overreached.

Sect. 4. Rectification and Indemnity [36]

(a) *Rectification.* Wide powers are given to the court or the

[31] L.R.A. 1925, s. 75.
[32] L.R. Rules 1925, r. 250.
[33] *Ante*, p. 502.
[34] L.R.A. 1925, s. 102.
[35] Contrast *ante*, pp. 502, 503.
[36] For a critical review of the operation of the provisions for rectification and indemnity, see Cretney & Dworkin (1968) 84 L.Q.R. 528.

registrar to rectify the register when there is any error or omission, as when a person with no title to the land has been registered in place of the true owner. However, if the registered proprietor is in possession, the register cannot be rectified so as to affect his title save in a limited class of cases, *viz.*:

    (i) to give effect to an overriding interest;

    (ii) where the proprietor " has caused or substantially contributed by his act, neglect or default, to the fraud, mistake or omission " which has led to the claim to rectify;

    (iii) where the immediate disposition to the proprietor is void;

    (iv) where it would be unjust not to rectify.[37]

(b) *Indemnity.* Any person suffering loss by reason of such rectification is entitled to be indemnified out of an insurance fund.[38] The loss, however, must be caused by the rectification. Thus where the registered proprietor bought the land with a squatter in possession of part of it, the subsequent rectification of the register by excluding that part from the title merely gave effect to the squatter's overriding interest, and this formal recognition of the existing position gave no right to compensation.[39] Similarly, if the applicant has himself caused or substantially contributed to the loss, by his fraud, act, neglect or default, indemnity will be withheld.[40]

---

[37] L.R.A. 1925, s. 82. See *Chowood Ltd.* v. *Lyall* [1930] 1 Ch. 426, affd. [1930] 2 Ch. 156; *Re 139 Deptford High Street* [1951] Ch. 884; *Claridge* v. *Tingey* [1967] 1 W.L.R. 134.

[38] *Ibid.* s. 83.

[39] *Re Chowood's Registered Land* [1933] Ch. 574; contrast *Re Boyle's Claim* [1961] 1 W.L.R. 339.

[40] L.R.A. 1925, s. 83 (5), as amended by L.R.A. 1966, s. 1 (4).

CHAPTER 17

OWNERSHIP AND ITS LIMITS

Part 1

GENERAL RIGHTS OF OWNERS

THE owner of the largest estate known to the law, the fee simple absolute in possession, has long enjoyed wide powers of control, disposition and use of the land in which his estate subsists.

1. Ownership. The maxim is *cujus est solum, ejus est usque ad coelum et ad inferos*; he who owns the soil is presumed to own everything " up to the sky and down to the centre of the earth." [1] This prima facie includes all mines and minerals,[2] and any chattel not the property of any known person [3] which is found under or attached to the land, *e.g.*, in the bed of a canal,[4] but probably does not include a chattel merely resting on the surface.[5]

2. Disposition. The owner can dispose of his land or part of it as he wishes.[6] Thus he may sever it horizontally as by disposing separately of the minerals under the surface, or even by disposing separately of an upper floor of a building.

3. Use. The owner may in general use the land in the natural course of user in any way he thinks fit. He may waste or despoil it as he pleases and is not liable merely because he neglects it.[7]

4. Qualifications. The absolute rights of the owner outlined above are qualified in a number of ways. He is naturally subject to the rights which others have over his land, such as rights of way, the rights of tenants under leases and the rights of mortgagees. Further,

---

[1] *Corbett* v. *Hill* (1870) L.R. 9 Eq. 671 at 673.
[2] *Mitchell* v. *Mosley* [1914] 1 Ch. 438 at 450; for exceptions, see *post*, pp. 571, 588.   [3] See *Moffatt* v. *Kazana* [1968] 1 All E.R. 271.
[4] *Elwes* v. *Brigg Gas Co.* (1886) 33 Ch.D. 562.
[5] *Hannah* v. *Peel* [1945] K.B. 509; contrast *Re Cohen* [1953] Ch. 88.
[6] For the origin of the right of the tenant in fee simple to dispose of his estate, see *ante*, p. 29.
[7] *Giles* v. *Walker* (1890) 24 Q.B.D. 656.

he has always been subject to some restrictions in the interests of the Crown, the public and his neighbours, and in the last century his rights have been successively eroded by legislation. Indeed, it has been said that "the fundamental assumption of modern statute law is that the landowner holds his land for the public good." [8] The remainder of this chapter discusses in outline these increasing restrictions.

Part 2

COMMON LAW RESTRICTIONS ON OWNERSHIP

1. Liability in tort. A landowner may be liable in tort for injuries caused to third parties by his acts and omissions in respect of things brought or artificially stored on the land, *e.g.*, if water in a reservoir escapes, or if a lamp projecting over a highway gets into a dangerous state of repair and injures a passer-by. He may similarly be liable for nuisance, *e.g.*, if he makes an unusual and excessive collection of manure which attracts flies and causes a smell. [9]

2. Gold and silver. The Crown is entitled to all gold and silver occurring in any mine, [10] and is also entitled to all "treasure trove." Objects amount to treasure trove only if—

(i) they consist of gold or silver, whether in bullion, coin or some manufactured object;

(ii) they have been hidden in or on the land deliberately, and not merely lost; and

(iii) the true owner is unknown. [11]

3. Wild animals. Wild animals are not the subject of ownership. [12] But a landowner has what is sometimes called a "qualified property" in them, consisting of the exclusive right to catch, kill and appropriate the animals on his land; and as soon as the animals are killed they fall into the ownership of the landowner, even if killed by a trespasser. [13]

4. Water. A landowner has no property in water which either percolates through his land or flows through it in a defined channel.

---

[8] W. I. Jennings (1936) 49 Harv.L.R. 426 at 436.
[9] *Bland* v. *Yates* (1914) 58 S.J. 612.
[10] See *Att.-Gen.* v. *Morgan* [1891] 1 Ch. 432.
[11] See *Att.-Gen.* v. *Trustees of the British Museum* [1903] 2 Ch. 598 at 608–611.
[12] *The Case of Swans* (1592) 7 Co.Rep. 15b at 17b.
[13] *Blade* v. *Higgs* (1865) 11 H.L.C. 621.

In the case of percolating water, the landowner may draw off any or all of it without regard to the claims of neighbouring owners.[14] In the case of water flowing through a defined channel, the riparian owner (the owner of the land through which the water flows) cannot always take all the water but has certain valuable rights. The owner of only one bank of a stream prima facie may exercise riparian rights up to the middle of the stream.

(a) *Fishing.* As part of his natural right of ownership, he has the sole right to fish in the water. Except in tidal waters, the public has no right of fishing even if there is a public right of navigation.[15]

(b) *Flow.* He is entitled to the flow of water through the land unaltered in volume or quality, subject to ordinary and reasonable use by the upper riparian owners; and he is bound by a corresponding obligation to the lower riparian owners.

(c) *Abstraction.* The ordinary and reasonable use which a riparian owner was formerly entitled to make of the water flowing through his land was [16]—

(i) the right to take and use all water necessary for ordinary purposes connected with his riparian tenement (such as for watering his cattle or for domestic purposes, or, possibly, in some manufacturing districts, for manufacturing purposes), even though this completely exhausted the stream; and

(ii) the right to use the water for extraordinary purposes connected with his riparian tenement, provided the use was reasonable and the water was restored substantially undiminished in volume and unaltered in character. Such purposes include irrigation and, in all districts, manufacturing purposes, such as for cooling apparatus. The amount by which the flow might be diminished was a question of degree in each case.[17]

These rights have now been curtailed by statute. An owner of land cannot take any water without the licence of a river authority. Exceptions are water taken for—

(i) the domestic purposes of the occupier's household, or

(ii) agricultural purposes other than spray irrigation.[18]

[14] *Chasemore* v. *Richards* (1859) 7 H.L.C. 349.
[15] See *Blount* v. *Layard* [1891] 2 Ch. 681.
[16] *McCartney* v. *Londonderry and Lough Swilly Ry.* [1904] A.C. 301 at 306, 307.
[17] See *Rugby Joint Water Board* v. *Walters* [1967] Ch. 397.
[18] Water Resources Act 1963, ss. 23, 24 (2), 135 (1).

Part 3

STATUTORY RESTRICTIONS ON USE AND ENJOYMENT

Sect. 1. Planning Control

A. Growth of Control

1. Control by schemes. At common law, any landowner was free to develop his land as he wished, provided he did not infringe the rights of others. He could erect whatever buildings he wished, however unsuitable they might be, and however injurious to the amenities of the district. Not until the Housing, Town Planning, &c., Act 1909 was enacted was there any general power for local authorities to control the development of land. Successive statutes strengthened and extended this control, culminating in the Town and Country Planning Act 1932, which for the first time conferred planning powers over land in the country, as distinct from towns. The essence of this and the earlier Acts was the preparation of a scheme. Each local authority was empowered to prepare a scheme showing what development would be permitted on each part of the land: and there were powers of enforcement against those who carried out development contravening the scheme.

2. Interim development control.

(a) *Defects.* The system suffered from a number of defects. First, it was optional: there was no obligation for any local authority to prepare a scheme, and many did not. Secondly, there was the long period which usually elapsed between the decision of the local authority to prepare a scheme and the final approval of the scheme. During this period, the land was subject to " interim development control." Under this, any landowner could develop his land at his own risk: if when at last the scheme was made the development accorded with the scheme, it was safe, whereas if it did not accord with it, the local authority could take enforcement action under the scheme and, for example, secure the removal of any offending buildings.

(b) *Permission.* To guard against this risk, an application for interim development permission could be made before carrying out the work. If this was given, the development was immune from enforcement action even if ultimately it was found to contravene the scheme.

But if development was carried out without interim development permission, there was no power to take enforcement action against it during the interim development period; and some speculative developers relied successfully on the probability that no scheme would come into force until they had been able to reap the profits of their development.

(c) *Ribbon development.* Only in one special respect was there a direct control of land irrespective of any scheme. After the 1914–1918 war, it became increasingly common for houses to be built on each side of any new road constructed for traffic purposes; in this way, the builders saved the cost of making their own roads to the detriment of traffic flow and the safety of the occupants of the houses. The Restriction of Ribbon Development Act 1935 dealt with this by prohibiting the making of any means of access to certain roads, or the erection of any building within a specified distance of the centre of those roads, unless the consent of the highway authority was obtained. The Act applied automatically to classified roads (the more important highways), and could be applied to other roads if the highway authority so resolved and the Minister of Transport approved; the specified distance was 220 feet in the former case, and not more than 80 feet in the latter.

3. The Act of 1943. This system continued until the Town and Country Planning (Interim Development) Act 1943 was passed. At that time, a mere 4 per cent. of England and Wales was subject to operative schemes; another 70 per cent. was subject to interim development control; and the remaining 26 per cent. was subject to no control. The Act imposed interim development control on all land in this last category, so that thenceforward the whole of the land in the country was under interim development control save for the 4 per cent. governed by schemes.[19] Secondly, the Act enabled local authorities to take enforcement proceedings against those who subsequently developed their land without obtaining interim development permission : unauthorised buildings could be demolished, and unauthorised uses penalised.[20]

These provisions transformed planning control. Formerly, over a quarter of the country was free from control, and all save some 4 per cent. of the rest was free from any control save the indefinite risk of a scheme ultimately being made which would be inconsistent with the

[19] s. 1.   [20] s. 5.

development. After the Act of 1943, the whole of the country was subject to a system under which effective action could forthwith be taken against any future development carried out without permission.

B. *Town and Country Planning Acts*

1. Acts of 1947 to 1960. The Town and Country Planning Act 1947 was passed on August 6, 1947, and came into operation on the " appointed day," July 1, 1948.[21] It was subsequently amended extensively, notably by the Town and Country Planning Acts 1953, 1954 and 1959, and the Caravan Sites and Control of Development Act 1960. The Act of 1947, which was complex and far-reaching and repealed all the previous law, had two main objects : first, a general revision and strengthening of the existing system of planning control; and secondly, the imposition of a new system of " development charges." The main object of development charges was to prevent landowners profiting from the great increases in value of their land which accrued without effort on their part when, for example, the spread of a town transformed into valuable building land some meadows which had previously had only a low value for agricultural purposes. The system of development charges proved unworkable and was abolished by the Act of 1953, but the planning provisions of the Act of 1947 remained.

2. Acts of 1962 to 1968. In 1962 the previous legislation from the Act of 1947 onwards was repealed and re-enacted in the consolidating Town and Country Planning Act 1962. This in turn has been subsequently amended by the Town and Country Planning Acts 1963 and 1968, the Control of Office and Industrial Development Act 1965, and Part 3 of the Industrial Development Act 1966. All these Acts are together known as the Town and Country Planning Acts 1962 to 1968.

3. Land Commission Act 1967. As mentioned above, the development charges introduced by the Act of 1947 were later abolished as unworkable. In 1967 a new attempt was made to secure for the state, part of the increased value which accrues to land as a result of surrounding development. The new charge is known as " betterment levy " and was introduced by the Land Commission Act 1967.

4. Division of subject. In the following pages the control of development will be discussed first, followed by an outline of the

[21] S.I. 1948 No. 213.

betterment levy provisions, and finally a note on the effect of planning law on the law of property.

C. Control of Development

1. Development. The fundamental concept underlying the planning legislation is " development," which is defined as meaning—

(i) " the carrying out of building, engineering, mining or other operations in, on, over or under land," or

(ii) " the making of any material change [22] in the use of any buildings or other land." [23]

Many of the expressions in the definition are themselves defined by the Act, though the only phrase which need be mentioned here is that " engineering operations " includes " the formation or laying out of means of access to highways " [24]; this, coupled with the other provisions controlling development, has made it possible to repeal the Restriction of Ribbon Development Act 1935 and treat the control of ribbon development as an integral part of planning law instead of as a separate system. The Act makes it clear that it is development to begin using one dwelling-house as two or more separate dwelling-houses,[25] or to extend dumps of refuse or waste materials; on the other hand, " development " does not include improvements or alterations to a building which do not materially affect its external appearance, the use of any buildings or other land within the curtilage of a dwelling-house for any purpose incidental to the enjoyment of the dwelling-house as such, the use of any land for agricultural purposes, and any change from one use to another use within the same class in the nineteen classes of use set out in the Town and Country Planning (Use Classes) Order 1963.[26] The Act further provides in effect that the definition does not include certain cases of reverting to a former use, including resuming the normal use where the land was subject to a temporary use on the appointed day, and reverting to the last use of the land before the appointed day in cases where the land was unoccupied on the appointed day.[27]

2. Planning permission.

(a) *Permission.* The general rule is that any person who proposes

[22] See *Guildford R.D.C.* v. *Fortescue* [1959] 2 Q.B. 112 (intensification of use not a change).
[23] Act of 1962, s. 12 (1).　　　　　　　　　　　　　　　　[24] *Ibid.* s. 221 (1).
[25] See *Ealing Corporation* v. *Ryan* [1965] 2 Q.B. 486.
[26] Act of 1962, s. 12 (2), (3).
[27] *Ibid.* s. 13 (2)–(4).

to develop land must first obtain planning permission from the local planning authority (*i.e.*, the appropriate county council or county borough council) or from the Minister of Housing and Local Government on appeal; and such permission may be granted either unconditionally or subject to such conditions as are thought fit.[28] Although the refusal of permission may be a very serious matter for the landowner, no compensation is payable except in a very limited class of cases.[29]

An applicant must give prior notice of his application to certain other persons owning interests in the property; and in a few cases of development likely to offend neighbours, he must first advertise his application, so that they may be able to object before permission is given.[30] Every local planning authority is bound to maintain a register of applications for permission and the results of such applications[31]; this is quite distinct from the local land charges register.

(b) *Development and structure plans.* Each local planning authority was also bound to prepare a development plan by July 1, 1951, showing the proposed development of its area.[32] These plans, which had to be reconsidered every five years, form a prophecy of the permissions likely to be granted and those likely to be refused; but unlike planning schemes under the old system, the plan itself authorises no development, and it is as necessary to obtain planning permission after the plan has come into force as before. Planning schemes under the old law have ceased to be effective, and the whole country is now covered by a uniform system of control resembling the former interim development control. All development plans were subject to amendment and approval by the Minister after holding a public inquiry. Under the most recent Act, there is to be a gradual replacement of development plans by less detailed " structure plans " which will sketch in general lines of development.[33] Structure plans, which will require the approval of the Minister, will be supplemented by local plans which will not normally be under the Minister's control.[34]

(c) *Permitted development.* By the Town and Country Planning General Development Order 1963 (as amended) planning permission is given[35] for 23 classes of development, subject to certain conditions

28 *Ibid.* ss. 13 (1), 17, 18, 23 ; and see *Fawcett Properties Ltd.* v. *Buckingham C.C.* [1961] A.C. 636.
29 Act of 1962, ss. 108–117, 123, 3rd Sched., Pt. II; Act of 1963.
30 *Ibid.* ss. 15, 16.   31 *Ibid.* s. 19.
32 Act of 1947, s. 5.   33 Act of 1968, Part I.
34 *Ibid.* s. 6.   35 See *Cater* v. *Essex C.C.* [1960] 1 Q.B. 424.

and so in these cases there is no need for an application to the local planning authority for permission. The Order includes such matters as minor alterations to dwellings, temporary uses, and much development by gas, water, electricity and other undertakings.

3. Enforcement notices.

(a) *The notice.* If development is carried out without the requisite permission, or if any conditions to which a permission was subject have not been complied with, the local planning authority may serve an enforcement notice on the owner and occupier of the land, specifying the unauthorised development or breach of condition. The notice takes effect at the end of the period specified in it, being at least 28 days after service; and it may require appropriate steps to restore the land or comply with the conditions to be taken within a further specified period, *e.g.,* the discontinuance of a use, or the removal of offending structures.[36] An enforcement notice which does not fairly comply with the statutory requirements (*e.g.,* by not stating correctly what is complained of) is void.[37]

(b) *Time limit.* The notice may be served at any time to enforce the discontinuance of an unauthorised use, other than a use which began before 1964, or which consists in changing the use of a building to use as a single dwelling-house.[38] Notices to enforce all other breaches of planning control (including a change to use as a single dwelling-house) must be served within four years of the breach.[39]

(c) *Stop notice.* A local planning authority may, on or after serving an enforcement notice, serve a stop notice. Its effect is to prohibit the continuance of the operations which are alleged to be a breach of planning control. It does not apply to changes of use. Its purpose is to stay operations until the validity or otherwise of the enforcement notice has been established and so nullify the effects of delaying tactics by developers.[40]

(d) *Appeal.* An appeal to the Minister against an enforcement notice may be made before it has taken effect. The Minister has wide powers to grant permission for the development, or vary or quash the enforcement notice; and a further appeal lies to the High Court, but only on a point of law.[41]

---

[36] Act of 1962, s. 45; *Burgess* v. *Jarvis* [1952] 2 Q.B. 41.
[37] *East Riding C.C.* v. *Park Estate (Bridlington) Ltd.* [1957] A.C. 223; *Francis* v. *Yiewsley and West Drayton U.D.C.* [1958] 1 Q.B. 478.
[38] Act of 1968, s. 15.
[39] Act of 1968, s. 15, replacing Act of 1962, s. 45.
[40] Act of 1968, s. 19.   [41] Act of 1962, ss. 46, 180.

(e) *Penalties.* If an enforcement notice is not obeyed, the penalty is a fine not exceeding £100. In addition, there may be a daily penalty not exceeding £20 if after conviction a use required to be discontinued is carried on; and if any other steps required by the notice have not been taken (*e.g.*, the demolition of an offending structure), the local planning authority may enter the land, take the steps, and sue the owner for the cost of so doing.[42] Further, if these powers prove an insufficient deterrent, the Attorney-General may permit the local planning authority to sue in his name for an injunction.[43] If a stop notice is not obeyed, the penalty is a fine not exceeding £400 on summary conviction, or an unrestricted fine on conviction on indictment. If the offence is continued there may be a daily fine of up to £50 on summary conviction, unrestricted on conviction on indictment.[44]

4. Additional controls. In addition to regulating development the Act provides for certain additional controls. Local planning authorities can make Tree Preservation Orders prohibiting in the interests of amenity the cutting of trees.[45] The demolition or alteration of buildings of special architectural or historic interest may be prevented by Building Preservation Orders or " listing." [46] Further, a local planning authority may serve on the owner and occupier of any garden, vacant site or other open land which seriously interferes with the local amenities a notice to abate the injury [47]; and there is a new and elaborate system for the control of advertisements on land.[48]

D. Betterment Levy

1. General nature. Betterment levy represents a further attempt to secure for the state some of the increase in the value of land which has accrued to it without effort on the part of the owner.[49] It is a charge or tax on development value which is realised after April 6, 1967.[50] When a landowner obtains planning permission to develop his land and thus put it to more profitable use, its value is thereby enhanced even before the building or other development which is

---

[42] Act of 1962, ss. 47, 48.
[43] See, *e.g.*, *Att.-Gen.* v. *Smith* [1958] 2 Q.B. 173.
[44] Act of 1968, s. 19 (5).
[45] Act of 1962, s. 29.
[46] Act of 1962, ss. 30–32, to be replaced by Act of 1968, Part V.
[47] Act of 1962, s. 36. See *Britt* v. *Buckinghamshire C.C.* [1964] 1 Q.B. 77.
[48] Act of 1962, ss. 34, 35; S.I. 1960 No. 695; S.I. 1965 No. 555.
[49] For the former " development charge," see *ante*, p. 575.
[50] Land Commission Act 1967, s. 27 (1). References in the following pages are to sections in that Act. April 6, 1967, is the first appointed day under the Act.

authorised by the permission has been carried out. It is this enhanced value which is taxable, that is, the difference between the " existing use " value of the land and its market value with the benefit of the planning permission.

2. Rate. Unlike the old development charge which sought to absorb the whole of the development value, betterment levy only takes a proportion of the development value as prescribed by the Minister of Housing and Local Government with the consent of the Treasury.[51] It has been fixed initially at 40 per cent., but it is expected to be raised to 45 per cent. and later to 50 per cent.

3. Material development. Betterment levy is not charged on the realisation of all increase in the value of land attributable to potential development, but only to potential development which is " material." Material development is development as defined in the Town and Country Planning Act 1962,[52] with three exceptions.[53] These are—

(a) development authorised by a General Development Order,[54]
(b) development falling within the Third Schedule (other than paragraph 4) to the Act of 1962 (minor development connected with the existing use of land), and
(c) development of a class excluded by regulations.

A good deal of development has already been excluded under the last head, including the conversion of houses into separate dwellinghouses.[55]

4. Chargeable events. Levy is not chargeable when the land acquires an added value, *e.g.*, from the grant of a planning permission, but when such value is realised. It is deemed to be realised in six cases.[56] They are as follows.[57]

A: Sale. The conveyance on sale of the freehold or the assignment on sale of a tenancy.

B: Lease. The grant of a tenancy.

C: Development. The commencement of a project of material development.

---

[51] s. 28.
[52] See *ante*, p. 576.
[53] s. 99 (2).
[54] See *ante*, pp. 577, 578.
[55] Material Development Regulations 1967 (S.I. Nos. 494, 1074).
[56] s. 27 (2).
[57] ss. 29–35.

D: Compensation. The receipt of compensation for the revocation or modification of a planning permission or as the result of an order under the Act of 1962 requiring a use of land to be discontinued or buildings removed.

E: Easements. The grant of an easement or the release or modification of an easement or restrictive right which is a separate transaction and not part of a Case A or Case B transaction.

F: Miscellaneous. Any other events which are designated as chargeable by regulations.

5. Notification. Levy is payable by the owner realising the development value, *e.g.*, the vendor, lessor, or grantor,[58] and therefore the Act lays on the other party, the purchaser, lessee or grantee, the obligation of notifying the Land Commission of the transaction and thereby setting in motion the procedure for assessing the amount of the levy.[59] Notification is obligatory in cases A, B, C and D (other than for transactions involving the grant or assignment of a tenancy of less than seven years). In all other cases notification is optional. It is normally in the interest of the purchaser, lessee or grantee to notify, as once development value has been realised and the levy paid, that value cannot be assessed again. In Case C it is the developing owner who has to notify the Commission.[60] If he fails to do so, he may be liable to a penalty of £500 or twice the levy, whichever is the greater.[61]

6. Calculation of levy. Levy is charged at the prescribed rate [62] on the net development value, the calculation of which depends upon the Case which is applicable. The detailed provisions are of immense complexity,[63] but the basic process is relatively simple. The net development value is the difference between the open market value of the land on the one hand, and the sum of two other values on the other. These two values are the value of any improvements which the owner himself has effected, and on which he thus ought not to be taxed, and the base value. The base value is either eleven-tenths of the current use value of the land, or, in some cases the price which the owner himself paid for the land. The current use value is assessed

---

[58] s. 36.
[59] ss. 37, 40–43.
[60] ss. 38, 39.
[61] s. 80.
[62] See *ante*, p. 580.
[63] 4th, 5th, 6th Scheds.

on the basis that permission would be granted for any development which is not material development. The increase of one-tenth is an allowance to encourage the release of land for redevelopment.

7. Exemptions. A number of local and public authorities are exempt from the levy [64] as also to a limited extent are charities.[65] In addition, certain transactions are exempt. One such case is where a project of material development is begun by a transferee of land within two years of obtaining the land.[66] This exemption is only available if the project was begun pursuant to a planning permission in force at the time of the transfer, and if the Land Commission approves. Another case of exemption is where an owner builds a dwelling-house for himself or a member of his family on land which he owned on September 22, 1965.[67] This exemption is not available to any owner for more than one house.

E. Effect on the Law of Property

When the Act of 1947 was enacted, some strange suggestions were made as to its fundamental effect on English land law. It was even contended that the fee simple in land no longer existed, but instead each landowner had merely a fee simple in the existing or permitted use of his land. This view appears to have been based on the need to obtain permission for any development, and on the obligation to pay a development charge. The substance of the first of these changes, however, had already been made by the Act of 1943 (which none had regarded as being epoch-making), and the second of the changes more resembled a tax on development than anything else. Further, on this view, no purchaser of land in, say, 1950, received more than a fee simple in an existing use, and so today, despite the abolition of development charges, he still has no fee simple in the land. Yet again, it ignored " existing or permitted buildings," in which the landowner had the same kind of rights as in the " existing or permitted use."

In truth, the theory would not bear examination, and it has gained no foothold in the courts or among practitioners. Planning control affects the use and enjoyment of land, but not the estates or interests in it; and development charges, while they existed, were a purely fiscal burden as is the present betterment levy. Planning matters must be

[64] ss. 56, 58, 59.
[65] s. 57.   [66] s. 60.
[67] s. 61. The date is that of the Government White Paper announcing the proposed levy.

duly investigated for the protection of purchasers, but they are not technically matters of title. The right to use property in a particular way is not in itself property.[68] The fee simple in land remains the same fee simple as before. " All that has happened is that the fruits of ownership have become less sweet; but, that is nothing new in land law." [69]

Sect. 2. Miscellaneous Control

A number of other statutes control the use and enjoyment of land and the buildings on it, of which the following are the most important:

1. The Housing Acts 1957–1965. Under these Acts the appropriate local authority, subject in some cases to the consent of the Minister of Housing and Local Government, has power to require a landowner to repair certain houses, to demolish insanitary or obstructive houses, or to clear his land of buildings or, in default, to convey it to the local authority for clearance and redevelopment.

2. The Public Health Acts 1936–1961. These Acts formerly empowered local authorities to make bye-laws regulating such matters as the construction, materials, height, lighting, ventilation, sanitation and size of rooms of new buildings, and now empower the Minister of Housing and Local Government to make building regulations for the same matters.[70]

3. Offices, Shops and Railway Premises Act 1963. The purpose of this Act is to secure the health, safety and welfare of persons employed to work in the various kinds of premises named in the title by ensuring that the premises are sufficiently spacious and airy, and have proper amenities and safety precautions.

4. Agricultural control. The Agriculture Act 1947 gave the Minister of Agriculture, Fisheries and Food (acting through County Agricultural Executive Committees) wide powers of controlling farming operations and of securing a proper standard of good estate management, especially in the provision and maintenance of fixed equipment. It was repealed by the Agriculture Act 1958. All that

---

[68] *Belfast Corporation* v. *O. D. Cars Ltd.* [1960] A.C. 490.
[69] Megarry, *Lectures on the Town and Country Planning Act 1947* (1949), p. 104: see generally at pp. 102–109.
[70] See Act of 1936, ss. 61, 62; Act of 1961, ss. 4–11.

remains is a limited power in the Agricultural Land Tribunal (the successor to some of the functions of the County Agricultural Executive Committee) to direct a landlord to provide fixed equipment required to enable the tenant to comply with statutory provisions (*e.g.*, for producing clean milk); but failure to comply is treated merely as a breach of the terms of the tenancy, giving the tenant the right to do the work himself and to recover the cost from the landlord.[71]

5. Air-space. Even at common law, probably no action lay for trespass in respect of passage through the air-space above land in such circumstances as to involve no interference with the reasonable use of it. This has now been reinforced by the Civil Aviation Act 1949,[72] which provides that no action shall lie in respect of trespass or nuisance merely by reason of the flight of aircraft over property at a height which is reasonable under the circumstances, provided the proper regulations are observed. But an action for nuisance lies for the passage of dangerous projectiles 75 feet over land [73]; and the permanent occupation of the air-space over the land of another without his consent, *e.g.*, by telephone wires or a cornice or branches of a tree, is both a nuisance [74] and a trespass.[75]

Part 4

STATUTORY RESTRICTIONS ON OWNERSHIP AND DISPOSITION

Sect. 1. Compulsory Purchase

1. Powers. A landowner is subject to what is sometimes called " eminent domain," namely, the right of Parliament, as part of its legislative omnipotence, to authorise the compulsory acquisition of land by some government department, public authority or public utility company. There are many Acts authorising such acquisition.

(a) *General.* Ever since the building of the railways in the first half of the last century there has been an increasing spate of legisla-

---

[71] Agriculture Act 1958, s. 4.
[72] s. 40, replacing Air Navigation Act 1920, s. 9.
[73] *Clifton* v. *Viscount Bury* (1887) 4 T.L.R. 8.
[74] See McNair, *Law of the Air* (3rd ed., 1964), Chap. 3.
[75] *Kelsen* v. *Imperial Tobacco Co.* (*of Great Britain and Ireland*) *Ltd.* [1957] 2 Q.B. 334.

tion authorising all kinds of public bodies to acquire land compulsorily for the purpose of carrying out their various functions.[76]

(b) *Planning.* A new departure was made by the Town and Country Planning Act 1947.[77] Under that Act a development plan might designate land as subject to compulsory acquisition not only when it was required for the specific functions of some public body, but also when it was necessary to secure its development in accordance with the plan.[78]

(c) *Land Commission.* The Land Commission has extensive powers to acquire land compulsorily which it thinks is suitable for material development.[79] It may also acquire land if

   (i) some development has been authorised but not carried out;
   (ii) the land is designated in the development plan for compulsory acquisition;
   (iii) the land is wanted for the site of a new town;
   (iv) the land is a clearance area under the Housing Acts.

(d) *Useless land.* A form of compulsory purchase in reverse was introduced by the Town and Country Planning Act 1947.[80] Where planning permission is refused or conditions are imposed, a landowner may sometimes serve on the local authority a notice requiring the authority to purchase the land compulsorily. He can do this only if " the land has become incapable of reasonably beneficial use in its existing state," [81] and cannot be rendered capable by carrying out any development that is permitted.

2. Procedure. It is, of course, possible that the Act which confers the *power* to acquire land compulsorily should also lay down the *procedure* to be followed. But for the most part the procedure has become standardised, and is to be found in enabling Acts which are incorporated by reference into the Act which confers the power of compulsory acquisition.[82] The main steps are as follows

---

[76] Stewart-Brown's *Guide to Compulsory Purchase and Compensation* (5th ed., 1962) has a list of over seventy " main Acts " in its appendices.
[77] It had been foreshadowed by the more limited Town and Country Planning Act 1944.
[78] Act of 1947, s. 38; now replaced by Act of 1962, s. 68.
[79] For the meaning of "material development," see *ante*, p. 580.
[80] Act of 1947, s. 19, now replaced by Act of 1962, ss. 129–137.
[81] See *R.* v. *Minister of Housing and Local Government, ex p. Chichester R.D.C.* [1960] 1 W.L.R. 587.
[82] Acquisition of Land (Authorisation Procedure) Act 1946; Compulsory Purchase Act 1965.

(a) *Order*. When an authority wishes to make a specific purchase, it makes a provisional compulsory purchase order. The order is not effective unless and until it is confirmed by the appropriate Minister, who has to hear any objections, usually at a public inquiry conducted by an inspector.

(b) *Notice to treat*. After the order has become operative, the next step is for the acquiring authority to serve a notice on the owner known as a notice to treat.[83] The notice does not by itself create a contract for sale, but it gives either party the right to have the compensation assessed. When the price has been ascertained, by the Lands Tribunal in default of agreement, there is then an enforceable contract of which specific performance will be granted.

(c) *Entry*. After the compensation has been assessed, the acquiring authority naturally can obtain possession by completing the contract. Yet at any time after the notice to treat and before completion the acquiring authority can enter on fourteen days' notice. In such a case the authority will pay interest running from the date of entry on the compensation money after it has been assessed.[84]

3. Compensation. The Town and Country Planning Act 1947 laid down a new basis for compensation payable on a compulsory purchase which gave the owner only the value of the land in its " existing use." No payment was made for its potential development value.[85] This basis was abandoned in 1959 following the abolition of development charges, and compensation is now based on " open market " value. The change was effected by the Town and Country Planning Act 1959; and its provisions on this point have now been consolidated and replaced by corresponding provisions in the Land Compensation Act 1961.

(a) *Open market value*. The most important result of the Act of 1959 was the restoration of the open market value of the land as the measure of compensation to be paid on a compulsory acquisition. This value depends not only on any actual planning permissions that have been granted but also on what planning permissions were likely to be granted. It is accordingly provided that for this purpose it is to be assumed that various forms of development would be permitted, including the development for which the compulsory acquisition is

---

[83] Compulsory Purchase Act 1965, s. 5.
[84] *Ibid*. s. 11 (1).
[85] Act of 1947, ss. 51, 52.

being made, any development foreshadowed by the development plan, and any development certified by the local planning authority as being appropriate.[86]

(b) *Variations.* If the landowner has become entitled to any compensation for the refusal of planning permission, this must be deducted; and any enhancement in the value of the land due to the acquiring authority's proposals for other land must be excluded.[87] On the other hand, if within five years after the completion of the sale planning permission is given for other development on the land that would make it more valuable, the vendor is entitled to correspondingly additional compensation.[88]

(c) *No market.* If the land is devoted, and but for the acquisition would continue to be devoted, to a purpose for which there is no general demand or market (*e.g.*, a church), compensation may be assessed on the basis of equivalent reinstatement, provided that reinstatement in some other place is intended.[89]

Sect. 2. Crownholds

It will be recalled that the Land Commission has wide powers to acquire land which is suitable for development.[90] The Commission is not required to manage or develop such land itself but may make such dispositions of it " as appear to them to be expedient in the public interest." [91] A disposition will normally take the form of a sale of a freehold or grant of a leasehold interest at the full market price or rent.[92] The Commission may, however, grant a special form of interest known as a " crownhold." [93]

1. General. The object of a crownhold disposition is to secure that any future development value goes to the Commission. It is thus a sale by the Commission of an estate in fee simple or the grant of a tenancy which

---

[86] Act of 1959, s. 1, and ss. 2–5, replaced by Act of 1961, ss. 14–17.
[87] Act of 1959, ss. 9, 17, replaced by Act of 1961, ss. 6–9, 12, 1st Sched.
[88] Act of 1959, ss. 18–21, replaced by Act of 1961, ss. 23–26.
[89] Act of 1961, s. 5 (5). See *West Midland Baptist (Trust) Association (Inc.)* v. *Birmingham Corporation* [1968] 2 Q.B. 188.
[90] *Ante,* p. 585.
[91] Land Commission Act 1967, s. 16 (1).
[92] *Ibid.* s. 16 (2).
[93] *Ibid.* ss. 17–21. The Chairman of the Commission has stated that the Commission does not intend to use crownhold dispositions to any great extent: Encyclopedia of Betterment Levy (1967), para. 5–105.

(a) states that the interest is to be held by way of crownhold, and
(b) contains such covenants by the purchaser or the tenant restricting the carrying out of development or clearing of the land as are necessary to retain for the Commission the development value.[94]

The covenants, known as crownhold covenants, are registrable as restrictive covenants.[95] They bind subsequent purchasers and others interested in the land and cannot be released or modified by the Lands Tribunal. If they are broken the Commission may forfeit the land by executing a vesting declaration.[96]

2. Concessionary crownholds. The Commission may dispose of the land for less than the best price obtainable if it is to be used for the provision of housing accommodation. Such a disposition is known as a concessionary crownhold disposition. It has to specify the amount by which the price falls short of the best price obtainable, and it has to contain suitable crownhold covenants to ensure

(a) that no tenancy of the land shall be granted without the consent of the Commission; and
(b) that the Commission have a right of pre-emption at the market value less the value of the concession if the crownholder proposes to sell the land.[97]

Sect. 3. Minerals

As has been seen, the Crown is entitled at common law to all gold and silver occurring in any mine. Statute has deprived landowners of certain other minerals occurring in or under their land.

1. Petroleum and natural gas. Under the Petroleum (Production) Act 1934 there was vested in the Crown petroleum existing in its natural condition in strata, including any mineral oil or relative hydrocarbon and natural gas.[98]

2. Coal. Under the Coal Act 1938, all interests in coal (except interests arising under a coal-mining lease) were vested in the Coal Commission in return for compensation; and these interests (including coal-mining leases) have now vested in the National Coal Board.[99]

---

[94] Land Commission Act 1967, s. 17.
[95] *Ibid.* s. 19. For registration see *ante*, p. 546 (unregistered land) and *ante*, p. 563 (registered land).
[96] Land Commission Act 1967, s. 20.   [97] *Ibid.* s. 18.
[98] s. 1.   [99] Coal Industry Nationalisation Act 1946.

Sect. 4. Protection of Tenants

The modern tendency is to enact legislation designed to protect tenants against their landlords. At common law, the matter was in general one of contract: provided a landlord did not contravene the terms of his bargain, he might at will evict his tenant, or under the threat of eviction secure his agreement to pay an increased rent of whatever amount he could exact. Although a number of matters such as fixtures, emblements and the like are of importance, the two crucial matters in any scheme for protecting tenants are protection against eviction, and control of rent: and these subjects will be dealt with here.

Legislation has been piecemeal. Apart from some relatively mild provisions concerning agricultural land, beginning with the Agricultural Holdings (England) Act 1875, no real system of control existed until the first of the Rent Acts was enacted in 1915. There is little common design to be found in the various statutes: as will be seen, protection against eviction is provided by a wide variety of devices, and so is control of rent. The general basis of the various systems will be considered in turn.

A. Business Premises

1. The Act of 1927. Business premises were first protected [1] by Part I of the Landlord and Tenant Act 1927. This gave the tenant the right to a new lease (or compensation in lieu thereof) provided he could establish that by reason of the carrying on by him or his predecessors in title at the premises of a trade or business for not less than five years, goodwill had become attached to the premises by reason whereof they could be let at a higher rent than they otherwise would have realised.[2] The mere building up of goodwill was thus not enough, for often the tenant, on leaving, would carry much of it with him. What had to be shown was goodwill which remained adherent to the premises after the tenant had gone. This was usually difficult to prove and, indeed, normally impossible except in the case of shops; and tenancies of professional premises were outside these provisions. The procedural requirements for making a valid claim under the Act were complicated, too, and many claims failed on purely technical grounds. These relatively ineffectual provisions were replaced by the far-reaching terms of the Landlord and Tenant Act 1954, Part II. The closely restricted right for business tenants to claim compensation for

---

[1] Apart from nearly a year's protection under the Rent Acts: Act of 1920, s. 13.
[2] Landlord and Tenant Act 1927, ss. 4, 5.

improvements, subject to certain conditions, continues in an amended form.[3]

2. The Act of 1954.

(a) *Tenancies within the Act.* Part II of the Landlord and Tenant Act 1954 applies to any tenancy where the property comprised in it is or includes premises occupied by the tenant for the purposes of any trade, profession or employment[4]; there is no requirement of adherent goodwill. The principal exceptions from the Act are the following: agricultural holdings; controlled tenancies under the Rent Act 1968[4a]; mining leases; most licensed premises other than bona fide hotels and restaurants; and certain tenancies granted to a servant during his employment, or granted for not more than three months.[5] Tenancies at will or at sufferance are also outside the Act.[6]

(b) *Security of tenure.* Security of tenure is secured by the simple provision that a tenancy within Part II " shall not come to an end unless terminated in accordance with the provisions of this Part of this Act." [7] Thus a tenancy for a fixed term may continue indefinitely despite the expiration of the fixed term, and an ordinary notice to quit given by the landlord will be inoperative; but the tenancy may still determine by notice to quit given by the tenant or by surrender or forfeiture. In order to determine the tenancy the landlord must give not less than six nor more than 12 months' notice in the statutory form, to expire not earlier than the date when, apart from the Act, the tenancy could have been determined by notice to quit, or would have expired.[8] If within two months of receiving this notice the tenant gives the landlord notice that he is not willing to give up possession of the premises, he may, not less than two nor more than four months after the landlord's notice was given, apply to the court for a new tenancy.[9] Alternatively, a tenant holding for a fixed term (and not merely under a periodical tenancy) may serve on the landlord a statutory form of request for a new tenancy in place of the old, to begin not less than six nor more than 12 months later; and not less than two nor more than four months after serving this request he must apply to the court.[10]

---

[3] *Post*, pp. 592, 593.
[4a] See *post*, p. 603.
[6] *Wheeler* v. *Mercer* [1957] A.C. 416.
[7] Act of 1954, s. 24.
[8] *Ibid.* s. 25.
[9] *Ibid.* s. 29.
[10] *Ibid.* ss. 26, 29.

[4] Landlord and Tenant Act 1954, s. 23.
[5] *Ibid.* s. 43.

(c) *Opposition to new tenancy.* The court is bound to grant the tenant a new tenancy unless the landlord establishes one of the seven statutory grounds of opposition. The landlord can rely only on the grounds stated in his statutory notice or in a notice served on the tenant within two months of receiving his request for a new tenancy. Some of the grounds are based on default by the tenant and others on the landlord's needs; and only the first three and the fifth, by using the word "ought," give the court any discretion. The seven grounds are as follows.[11]

(1) REPAIR: that the tenant ought not to be granted a new tenancy in view of the state of the "holding" (*i.e.,* the premises let, excluding any part not occupied by the tenant or a service tenant of his) due to the tenant's failure to comply with his repairing obligations.

(2) RENT: that the tenant ought not to be granted a new tenancy in view of his persistent delay in paying rent.

(3) OTHER BREACHES: that the tenant ought not to be granted a new tenancy in view of other substantial breaches by him of his obligations under the tenancy, or for any other reason connected with his use or management of the holding.

(4) ALTERNATIVE ACCOMMODATION: that the landlord has offered and is willing to provide or secure the provision of suitable alternative accommodation on reasonable terms.

(5) PART OF WHOLE: that the premises are part of larger premises held by the landlord and the tenant ought not to be granted a new tenancy because the landlord could obtain a substantially greater rent for the property as a whole than for the parts separately.

(6) DEMOLITION OR RECONSTRUCTION: "that on the termination of the current tenancy the landlord intends to demolish or reconstruct the premises comprised in the holding or a substantial part of those premises or to carry out substantial work of construction on the holding or part thereof and that he could not reasonably do so without obtaining possession of the holding."

(7) OWN OCCUPATION: "that on the termination of the current tenancy the landlord intends to occupy the holding for the purposes, or partly for the purposes, of a business to be carried on by him therein, or as his residence." But this head is not open to a landlord whose interest was purchased or created less than five years before the termination of the current tenancy.

[11] *Ibid.* ss. 29, 30.

The landlord cannot have the intention required by the last two heads unless at the date of the hearing he has not a mere hope but a firm, settled intention, not likely to be changed, to do something that he has a reasonable prospect of bringing about.[12] Normally an undertaking to the court given by a responsible person or body conclusively shows an intention to do what is undertaken, *e.g.,* to demolish the premises.[13] A landlord who genuinely intends to reconstruct the premises and then occupy them himself is not affected by the five years rule, for the existence of Ground 7 does not prevent him from relying on Ground 6.[14]

(d) *Terms of new tenancy.* When premises are first let to a business tenant, there is no restriction on the amount of rent he may be charged, and no power to secure its revision while the initial tenancy continues. But if the tenant obtains a new tenancy under the Act, the rent is to be the open market rent, and this and the other terms of the tenancy are to be determined by the court in default of agreement.[15] The rent may thus be raised or lowered, but the tenant is protected against unreasonable demands by the landlord. The duration of any new tenancy is whatever the court considers reasonable, not exceeding 14 years [16]; but there is no limit to the number of renewals. The basic idea of the Act is thus that a business tenant has a prima facie right to continue his business indefinitely in the premises, and although there is no restriction on the terms of the tenancy under which he first occupies the premises, any renewals are controlled by the court.

(e) *Compensation for eviction.* A tenant who fails to obtain a new tenancy is entitled to no compensation unless he fails only because the court is precluded from granting a new tenancy solely by reason of one or more of the last three grounds set out above, all of which are for the landlord's benefit. In these cases, the landlord must pay the tenant compensation equal to the rateable value of the premises, or twice that sum if the tenant and his predecessors in the business have occupied the premises for business purposes for the previous 14 years.[17]

(f) *Compensation for improvements.* Under the Landlord and Tenant Act 1927,[18] if a tenant of premises used for a trade, business

---

[12] *Betty's Cafés Ltd.* v. *Phillips Furnishing Stores Ltd.* [1959] A.C. 20.
[13] *Espresso Coffee Machine Co. Ltd.* v. *Guardian Assurance Co. Ltd.* [1959] 1 W.L.R. 250.
[14] *Fisher* v. *Taylors Furnishing Stores Ltd.* [1956] 2 Q.B. 78; (1956) 72 L.Q.R. 21.
[15] Landlord and Tenant Act 1954, ss. 32, 34, 35.
[16] *Ibid.* s. 33.
[17] *Ibid.* s. 37.
[18] ss. 1–3, as amended by the Landlord and Tenant Act 1954, Part III.

or profession carries out improvements to the premises which add to their letting value, the tenant may recover compensation from the landlord on leaving. But the tenant must satisfy a number of conditions; in addition to making his claim at the right time and in due form, he must give the landlord three months' notice of his intention to make the improvement. The landlord may then exclude the tenant's right to compensation if he successfully objects to the improvement, or carries it out himself in return for a reasonable increase of rent.

B. *Agricultural Holdings*

1. Introduction. The Agricultural Holdings (England) Act 1875 was the first of a long series of Acts regulating agricultural holdings. At first, the Acts were mainly directed towards securing proper compensation for the tenant, initially for improvements and, latterly, also if his tenancy was determined without good cause.[19] The Agriculture Act 1947 first gave security of tenure and protection as to rent, in place of the limited security of tenure provided during the war by Defence Regulations. The principal Act today is the Agricultural Holdings Act 1948, which consolidated the Act of 1947 with the Agricultural Holdings Act 1923, and was itself amended by the Agriculture Act 1958.

2. Jurisdiction. The Acts confer many powers on the Minister of Agriculture, Fisheries and Food, on County Agricultural Executive Committees, on Agricultural Land Tribunals, and on arbitrators. In general, the Act of 1958 transferred powers of determining disputes from the Minister and the Committees to the Tribunals, which previously had mainly appellate functions. Each of the nine areas into which England and Wales are divided has a Tribunal presided over by a lawyer appointed by the Lord Chancellor; and the Council on Tribunals supervises both the Tribunals and any arbitrators (unless appointed by agreement).[20]

3. " Agricultural holding." The Acts apply to any " agricultural holding." This means the aggregate of land used for the trade or business of agriculture which is comprised in a contract of tenancy for years, or from year to year; but, oddly enough, tenancies for more than

---

[19] A.H.A. 1923, s. 12.
[20] Agriculture Act 1947, s. 73, 9th Sched.; Agriculture Act 1958, ss. 8, 10, 1st and 2nd Scheds.; Tribunals and Inquiries Act 1958, s. 1, 1st Sched.; S.I. 1959 Nos. 81, 83.

one but less than two years are not included.[21] The definition also extends to agreements for value made after February 1948 for a tenancy or licence for an interest less than a tenancy from year to year in circumstances which would otherwise make the land an agricultural holding. But this does not apply to agreements approved by the Minister, nor to those made in contemplation of the land being used only for grazing or mowing during some specified period of the year, even if the " period " is 364 days.[22] " Agriculture " is widely defined, and includes horticulture, fruit growing, seed growing and market gardening.[23] On mixed lettings (*e.g.*, of pasture, an orchard and an inn), the Acts apply to all or none; the test is whether as a whole the tenancy is in substance a tenancy of agricultural land.[24]

4. Notices to quit. As under earlier legislation, a notice to quit an agricultural holding (including a notice exercising an option of termination in the tenancy agreement [25]) is invalid if it purports to determine the tenancy in any way save by twelve months' notice to expire at the end of a year of the tenancy [26]; and this is so even if the notice was given by the tenant.[27] Further, a tenancy for a fixed term of two years or more granted since 1920 will determine at the end of the fixed period only if written notice to quit has been given by one party to the other not more than two years nor less than one year before the end of the term; if this is not done, the tenancy continues as a tenancy from year to year, notwithstanding any contrary agreement.[28]

5. Security of tenure. The landlord's right to serve a notice to quit, as modified in this way, remains unaffected. However, if within one month of receiving a notice to quit the tenant gives the landlord a counter-notice,[29] then with seven exceptions the notice to quit becomes ineffective unless the Agricultural Land Tribunal consents to it taking effect: and only in five cases can the Tribunal give that consent.[30] There are thus three categories.

---

[21] *Gladstone* v. *Bower* [1960] 2 Q.B. 384.
[22] A.H.A. 1948, ss. 1, 2; *Goldsack* v. *Shore* [1950] 1 K.B. 708; *Scene Estate Ltd.* v. *Amos* [1957] 2 Q.B. 205; contrast *Rutherford* v. *Maurer* [1962] 1 Q.B. 16.
[23] A.H.A. 1948, s. 94.
[24] *Dunn* v. *Fidoe* [1950] 2 All E.R. 685; *Howkins* v. *Jardine* [1951] 1 K.B. 614; *Monson* v. *Bound* [1954] 1 W.L.R. 1321.
[25] See *Edell* v. *Dulieu* [1924] A.C. 38.   [26] A.H.A. 1948, s. 23.
[27] *Flather* v. *Hood* (1928) 44 T.L.R. 698.   [28] A.H.A. 1948, s. 3.
[29] See *Mountford* v. *Hodkinson* [1956] 1 W.L.R. 422 (abusive letter), and contrast *Frankland* v. *Capstick* [1959] 1 W.L.R. 204.
[30] A.H.A. 1948, ss. 24, 25, as amended by Agriculture (Miscellaneous Provisions) Act 1954, s. 7, and Agriculture Act 1958.

(a) *No security.* The notice to quit will be effective if either the tenant fails to serve a counter-notice or else the case falls within one of the following seven heads. In the latter case the notice to quit must make it plain on which of the seven heads the landlord will rely.[31]

(1) PRIOR CONSENT: the Tribunal has previously consented to the notice being given.

(2) PLANNING PERMISSION: the land is required for some non-agricultural use for which planning permission has been given or (in certain cases) is not required.

(3) BAD HUSBANDRY: on an application made within the previous six months the Tribunal has certified that the tenant was not farming in accordance with the rules of good husbandry.

(4) UNREMEDIED BREACH: the tenant has failed within a reasonable time (two months in the case of rent) to comply fully [32] with a notice by the landlord requiring him to remedy a breach of a term of his tenancy.[33]

(5) IRREPARABLE BREACH: the landlord's interest in the holding has been materially prejudiced by an irreparable breach of a term of the tenancy.

(6) BANKRUPTCY: the tenant is bankrupt or has compounded with his creditors.

(7) DEATH: the notice is given within three months after the death of the tenant with whom the original contract of tenancy was made, or the death of the last survivor of original joint tenants; for the personal abilities of a farm tenant are usually important to the landlord.

(b) *Security dependent on reasonableness.* If the landlord satisfies the Agricultural Land Tribunal that the case falls within any of five heads, the Tribunal must consent to the notice to quit taking effect unless it appears that a fair and reasonable landlord would not insist on possession, in which case the Tribunal must withhold consent.[34] Any consent may be made subject to conditions (which may later be varied or revoked) to ensure that the land is used for the purposes stated by the landlord. The five heads are as follows.

(1) GOOD HUSBANDRY: the landlord proposes to terminate the tenancy in order to carry out a purpose desirable in the interests of good husbandry of the holding.

[31] A.H.A. 1948, s. 24, as amended; *Cowan* v. *Wrayford* [1953] 1 W.L.R. 1340.
[32] *Price* v. *Romilly* [1960] 1 W.L.R. 1360.
[33] See *Lloyds Bank Ltd.* v. *Jones* [1955] 2 Q.B. 298 (personal residence).
[34] A.H.A. 1948, s. 25, as amended.

(2) SOUND MANAGEMENT: that purpose is desirable in the interests of the estate of which the holding constitutes all or part.[35]

(3) RESEARCH: that purpose is desirable for the purposes of agricultural research, education, experiment or demonstration, or for the purposes of statutes relating to smallholdings or allotments.

(4) GREATER HARDSHIP: withholding consent would cause greater hardship than granting it.

(5) NON-AGRICULTURAL USE: the land is required for some non-agricultural use not within paragraph (2) of the foregoing list of seven cases.

(c) *Full security.* In all cases not falling within the foregoing heads, the notice to quit is ineffective [36] and the tenancy continues unaffected.

6. Protection as to rent. When an agricultural tenancy is first granted, the parties are free to agree whatever rent they please. However, not more frequently than once in every three years, either party may require the amount of the rent to be submitted to arbitration. Any increase or decrease awarded by the arbitrator takes effect as from the next day on which the tenancy could have been determined by a notice to quit given when the reference to arbitration was demanded.[37] Accordingly, no revision of rent is possible during a tenancy for a fixed term which is not determinable by notice to quit. In addition, the landlord may increase the rent in respect of certain improvements carried out by him.[38]

7. Compensation for disturbance. If a tenant quits the holding in consequence of a notice to quit given by the landlord (even if the notice is in fact invalid [39]), he is entitled to compensation for disturbance of not more than two years' rent nor less than one.[40] No agreement can exclude this or any other provision in the Act as to compensation,[41] and a provision which by implication does this (*e.g.,* by providing for determination of the tenancy at such short notice as to leave no time to claim compensation) is void.[42]

[35] See *Evans* v. *Roper* [1960] 1 W.L.R. 814.
[36] A.H.A. 1948, s. 24, as amended.
[37] *Ibid.* s. 8; see *Sclater* v. *Horton* [1954] 2 Q.B. 1.
[38] A.H.A. 1948, s. 9.
[39] *Kestell* v. *Langmaid* [1950] 1 K.B. 233.
[40] A.H.A. 1948, s. 34, replacing earlier provisions.
[41] *Ibid.* s. 65.
[42] *Coates* v. *Diment* [1951] 1 All E.R. 890.

8. Compensation for improvements. When an agricultural tenant quits his holding at the end of his tenancy, he is entitled to compensation for certain improvements carried out by him, provided he has observed the necessary conditions. Such improvements fall into three main categories. First, there are certain long-term improvements (*e.g.*, planting orchards) for which the landlord's consent is required. Secondly, there are other long-term improvements (*e.g.*, the erection of buildings) for which either the landlord's consent or the Tribunal's approval is necessary. Thirdly, there are some short-term improvements (*e.g.*, the chalking or liming of land) for which neither consent nor approval is needed. The measure of compensation is the increase in value of the holding, or, in the case of a short-term improvement, the value of the improvement to an incoming tenant.[43]

C. Furnished Dwellings

1. Contracts within the Act. Until the Furnished Houses (Rent Control) Act 1946 was passed, there was no effective provision to protect residential tenants of premises let with furniture or services. The Act established a system of control by setting up a number of rent tribunals, which are now under the control of the Council on Tribunals.[44] The Act was amended by the Landlord and Tenant (Rent Control) Act 1949, and the statutory provisions regulating furnished lettings have been consolidated and replaced by Part VI of the Rent Act 1968. The Act of 1946 formerly applied however great the rateable value of the premises, but since July 6, 1957,[45] only those premises within the general limits of rateable value for the purposes of the Rent Act 1968 are protected though the Minister of Housing and Local Government may raise the limits by order.[46] Subject to this, the Act applies whenever a person has by contract been granted the right to occupy as a residence a house or part of a house at a rent which includes payment for the use of furniture or for services, or on terms that he shares living accommodation with his landlord; the inclusion of any substantial payment for board, however, excludes the Act.[47]

2. Rent. Any such tenant may refer his contract to the tribunal, which, after hearing the parties, may approve or reduce the rent, but

---

[43] A.H.A. 1948, ss. 46–51, 3rd and 4th Scheds., as amended by Agriculture Act 1958.
[44] Tribunals and Inquiries Act 1958, s. 1, 1st Sched.
[45] See Rent Act 1957, s. 12, now repealed. The date is that on which the Act came into force. [46] Rent Act 1968, s. 71. For the limits, see *post*, p. 602.
[47] *Ibid*. s. 70.

cannot increase it except for increased cost of services since September 3, 1939.[48] The rent determined by the tribunal is then registered with the local authority, and thereafter it becomes an offence to require or receive more than the registered rent, or to charge any premium, in respect of the premises.[49] If circumstances subsequently change, the tribunal may reconsider the rent, and either approve, reduce or increase the rent.[50] The tribunal is still bound to consider the reference even if the tenant quits before the hearing.[51]

3. Security of tenure. If these provisions stood alone, a landlord could usually deter tenants from referring cases to the tribunal by the threat of serving a notice to quit. Accordingly, there are two methods of providing security.

(a) *Automatic.* Where the tenant has referred a contract to the tribunal, no notice to quit subsequently served on him is to take effect before the expiration of a period of six months after the decision of the tribunal; the tribunal may, however, substitute a shorter period for the statutory six months.[52]

(b) *On application.* Except where such a reduction has been made, the Act of 1949 provides for successive extensions of security of tenure. Where any contract has been referred to a tribunal and a notice to quit has been served, then at any time before the expiration of the period at the end of which the notice to quit will take effect, the tenant may apply to the tribunal for the extension of that period; and the tribunal may extend that period by not more than six months.[53] Thus, if a weekly tenant refers a contract to the tribunal, and the landlord promptly serves a notice to quit, the tenant should apply for further security of tenure within six months of the decision of the tribunal; and provided he makes successive (and successful) applications every six months, the operation of the notice to quit will be repeatedly postponed. If the landlord had served no notice to quit until, say, a year after the first reference to the tribunal, the tenant can apply for security of tenure at any time before the notice to quit expires.[54]

(c) *Exceptions.*

(1) PRIOR OR NO NOTICE. If the landlord serves a notice to quit

[48] *Ibid.* ss. 72, 73.   [49] *Ibid.* ss. 74, 76.
[50] *Ibid.* s. 75.
[51] *R.* v. *West London Rent Tribunal, ex p. Napper* [1967] 1 Q.B. 169.
[52] Rent Act 1968, s. 77.   [53] *Ibid.* s. 78.
[54] See *Preston and Area Rent Tribunal* v. *Pickavance* [1953] A.C. 562.

before the first reference to the tribunal, or if the tenancy, being for a fixed period, requires no notice to quit to determine it, the provisions as to security of tenure do not apply at all.

(2) OWNER-OCCUPIER. The security of tenure provisions do not apply to a temporary furnished letting of his house by an owner-occupier who wishes to recover it for the occupation of himself or a member of his family.[55]

D. Unfurnished Dwellings.

1. Application of the Act. The complex and important body of legislation which protects tenants of unfurnished dwellings began with the Increase of Rent and Mortgage Interest (War Restrictions) Act 1915. However, that Act, as amended, was later repealed, and there followed a series of statutes together known as the Rent Acts which consisted of the Rent and Mortgage Interest Restrictions Acts 1920 to 1939, the Landlord and Tenant (Rent Control) Act 1949, the Housing Repairs and Rents Act 1954, the Rent Act 1957, and the Rent Act 1965. These in turn were repealed and replaced by the consolidating Rent Act 1968. The Act applies to every " dwelling-house " of an appropriate rateable value [56] which satisfies certain conditions. " Dwelling-house " means any house (or part of a house) which is " let as a separate dwelling." [57] Thus the existence of a tenancy is essential; this requirement excludes a mere licensee from the Act, but not a tenant at will or at sufferance. Whether the premises are let " as " a dwelling depends on the use provided for or contemplated by the tenancy agreement, or, in default, by the *de facto* user at the time in question.[58] And the letting must be as " a " (*i.e.,* one) dwelling and not as two or more dwellings.[59]

The word " separate " formerly excluded lettings where the tenant was required to share living accommodation such as a kitchen.[60] However, statute has modified the rule, so that where the sharing is with the landlord the tenant is protected in the same way as if the letting was furnished,[61] and where the sharing is with other tenants, the tenant is protected as for an unfurnished letting, subject to certain

---

[55] Rent Act 1968, s. 79.
[56] See *post*, p. 602.
[57] Act of 1968, s. 1 (1).
[58] *Wolfe* v. *Hogan* [1949] 2 K.B. 194.
[59] See *Whitty* v. *Scott-Russell* [1950] 2 K.B. 32.
[60] *Neale* v. *Del Soto* [1945] K.B. 144.
[61] Act of 1968, s. 101, replacing Act of 1949, s. 7; *ante*, p. 597.

modifications.[62] Lastly, despite the requirement that the letting must be as a " dwelling," the use of some (or even the major part) of the premises for business purposes does not prevent the tenancy from being a controlled tenancy under the Act,[63] provided the premises are let as a dwelling, as where the tenant uses most of the house for taking in paying guests but lives in the remainder.[64] Often what is structurally a single dwelling-house contains many " dwelling-houses " for the purposes of the Rent Acts, even if it has not been physically divided into self-contained flats; for one or two rooms, with a right to share the bathroom and lavatory, may for this purpose constitute a " dwelling-house."

2. Exceptions. Certain tenancies which would otherwise fall within the Acts are nevertheless excepted from them. In some cases, the exception is personal to the landlord. Thus, the Crown is not bound by the Acts,[65] nor are local authorities, new town development corporations or certain housing associations or housing trusts.[66] In such cases, the exemption does not operate in favour of other persons concerned with the property, such as sub-tenants or purchasers. Other exceptions depend on the nature of the tenancies. Thus the Acts do not apply where the letting is rent free or the rent is less than two-thirds of the rateable value.[67] Again, the Acts are excluded where the rent includes payments in respect of board, attendance or the use of furniture, and (except in the case of board) the amount of rent fairly attributable thereto (regard being had to the value of the same to the tenant) forms a substantial portion of the whole rent.[68]

Most of the exceptions, however, depend on the nature or status of the premises themselves. Thus for diverse reasons, public houses,[69] and parsonage houses of the Church of England [70] (*e.g.,* the ordinary rectory or vicarage), are outside the Acts. Agricultural holdings occupied by the farmer are also outside the Acts (but, of course, within the Agricultural Holdings Act 1948).[71] Lastly, although in general any land or premises let together with a dwelling-house are treated as being part of the dwelling-house, if the dwelling-house is

---

[62] Act of 1968, s. 102, replacing Act of 1949, s. 8.
[63] Act of 1968, s. 9. But it is otherwise for regulated tenancies: see *ante*, p. 590, and *post*, p. 603.   [64] *Vickery* v. *Martin* [1944] K.B. 679.
[65] Act of 1968, s. 4.
[66] Act of 1968, s. 5.
[67] Act of 1968, ss. 2 (1) (*a*), 7 (3).
[68] Act of 1968, s. 2; *Palser* v. *Grinling* [1948] A.C. 291.
[69] Act of 1968, s. 9 (2).
[70] *Bishop of Gloucester* v. *Cunnington* [1943] K.B. 101.
[71] A.H.A. 1948, 7th Sched.

let together with more than two acres of agricultural land, both house and land are excluded from the Acts [72] ; in the case of property subject to " old control " (dealt with below) the criterion is not two acres of agricultural land, but whether the land or premises, if let separately, would have at least one quarter the rateable value of the house.[73]

3. Old control and new control.

(a) *Act of 1920.* The Act of 1920 applied if either the rateable value or the recoverable rent of the dwelling-house did not exceed £105 in London or £78 elsewhere. Under the Act of 1923, a dwelling-house was decontrolled (*i.e.,* excluded from the Acts) as soon as the landlord obtained actual possession of it, or granted the tenant a lease of a specified length. Thus on a change of tenants, the position of the new tenant would depend on whether or not the landlord had decontrolled the house.

(b) *Act of 1933.* The Act of 1933 drastically modified this system of gradual decontrol. All houses not then within the Acts (*e.g.,* because they were not let) were forthwith excluded from the Acts. Those still within the Acts were divided into three classes. Class A houses, with a rateable value (or recoverable rent) in April 1931 exceeding £45 in London and £35 elsewhere, were forthwith decontrolled. At the other extreme, Class C houses, with a rateable value in April 1931 not exceeding £20 in London and £13 elsewhere, were made undecontrollable: even if the landlord obtained actual possession, future tenants would still be protected. The intermediate group of houses, Class B, continued within the Acts, and remained subject to decontrol, *e.g.,* by the landlord obtaining actual possession.

(c) *Act of 1938.* The Act of 1938 carried this process further. It decontrolled all houses not then within the Acts, and also all Upper Class B houses, *i.e.,* those with a rateable value in April 1931 exceeding £35 in London and £20 elsewhere. The remaining Class B houses (" Lower Class B ") were rendered undecontrollable, like Class C houses. Any landlord of a Lower Class B or a Class C house who claimed to have decontrolled the house before it became undecontrollable was obliged to preserve his claim to decontrol by registering it with the local authority.

(d) *Act of 1939.* The Act of 1939 left undisturbed those houses which were still subject to the Acts; they continued to be governed by

---

[72] Act of 1968, s. 1 (2).
[73] Act of 1968, 14th Sched., para. 1 (1).

the existing law, which is usually called "old control." The Act introduced a modified system of control, usually called "new control," and applied it to all dwelling-houses which were free from old control but had a rateable value in April 1939 not exceeding £100 in London and £75 elsewhere.[74] Thus new control might apply not only to a large house in London with a rateable value of £95 which had never before been controlled, but also to a small house with a rateable value of £10 which, having formerly been controlled, had been decontrolled under the Act of 1923. In most respects old control and new control are similar or identical. Formerly there were some important differences, especially in relation to the standard rent; but the differences now surviving are small and unimportant.[75]

4. Rent Act 1957. Subject to certain temporary provisions,[76] the Act of 1957 decontrolled many houses forthwith, and provided for the gradual decontrol of many others.[77]

(a) *Rateable value over £40 or £30.* All houses with a rateable value which on November 7, 1956, exceeded £40 in London and £30 elsewhere were decontrolled forthwith.

(b) *New tenancies.* Whatever the rateable value, the Rent Acts did not apply to any tenancy created by a lease or agreement coming into operation after July 5, 1957. This provision did not, however, apply where the new tenancy was granted to the sitting tenant and the premises comprised in the old tenancy and the new were the same, or had at least a part in common.

5. Rent Act 1965. The Rent Act 1965 abruptly reversed the process of decontrol which had been set in motion by the Act of 1957. It applies to all houses of which the rateable value on March 23, 1965, did not exceed £400 in Greater London and £200 elsewhere. It protects those tenancies which were previously unprotected either because the rateable value was too high or because they were created after July 5, 1957.[78] It also protects tenancies of houses which have been built or converted after August 1954 and which were not subject to the former system of control.[79]

---

[74] Act of 1939, s. 3.
[75] See *ante*, p. 601, for one such difference.
[76] See Act of 1957, ss. 13–15, 4th Sched.; Landlord and Tenant (Temporary Provisions) Act 1958 (now expired).
[77] Act of 1957, s. 11.
[78] Act of 1965, ss. 1, 43.
[79] See Housing Repairs and Rents Act 1954, s. 35; Act of 1965, s. 1 (2).

6. Systems of control. The upshot is that there are now two systems of control

(a) *Controlled tenancies.* These are tenancies existing before July 6, 1957, of houses with a rateable value which on November 7, 1956, did not exceed £40 in London and £30 elsewhere.

(b) *Regulated tenancies.* These are all other tenancies of houses with a rateable value which on March 23, 1965, did not exceed £400 in Greater London and £200 elsewhere.[80]

7. Statutory tenancy. The Rent Act protects a tenant from eviction by prohibiting the courts from making any order for possession except on specified grounds, and giving him the right to continue in possession of the premises despite the termination of his tenancy by notice to quit or otherwise. The Acts thus bring into being what is usually called a " statutory tenancy "; this is the right of the tenant to remain in possession, despite the determination of his contractual tenancy, on all the terms of the contractual tenancy which are not inconsistent with the Acts, until the court makes an order for possession against him.[81] A statutory tenancy is not really a " tenancy " at all, in the common law sense of the word; the tenant has no estate or interest in the land, but a mere personal right of occupation. He cannot dispose of his statutory tenancy by assignment [82] or by will, and it will not vest in his trustee in bankruptcy.

Further, a statutory tenancy will cease to exist if the tenant ceases to occupy the premises as his home [83] or one of his homes.[84] Mere temporary absences are immaterial; but once an absent tenant has lost either his *animus revertendi* (intention of returning) or his *corpus possessionis* (visible indication of his *animus*, such as the presence on the premises of some caretaker on his behalf), his statutory tenancy is at an end.[85] If a house is totally destroyed, any statutory tenancy perishes with the house, whereas a contractual tenancy would continue to exist in the ruins.[86] A statutory tenancy is thus an anomaly which fits into no recognised category of property law. If the tenant dies, his widow, if residing with him at his death, or otherwise any member of his family who has resided with him for at least the previous six

---

[80] Act of 1968, ss. 1, 6, 7, 2nd Sched., Part I.
[81] See Act of 1968, s. 12.
[82] But see Act of 1968, s. 14.
[83] *Skinner* v. *Geary* [1931] 2 K.B. 546.
[84] *Hallwood Estates Ltd.* v. *Flack* (1950) 66 (2) T.L.R. 368.
[85] *Brown* v. *Brash* [1948] 2 K.B. 247; *Tickner* v. *Hearn* [1960] 1 W.L.R. 1406.
[86] *Ellis & Sons Amalgamated Properties Ltd.* v. *Sisman* [1948] 1 K.B. 653.

months, becomes statutory tenant in his place.[87] Formerly no second
transmission could take place,[88] but this is now permitted. If it
occurs when the tenancy is controlled, it will become regulated on the
second transmission.[89]

8. Order for possession. If a landlord seeks an order for possession, he must satisfy the conditions in either the first two or the
third of the following heads.

(a) *Reasonablesness.* The landlord must satisfy the court that in
all the circumstances of the case it is reasonable to make an order
for possession.[90]

(b) *Grounds for possession.* The landlord must further establish
that one of the nine grounds for possession exists. Some of these are
based on misconduct by the tenant, others on the landlord's needs, or
the existence of alternative accommodation. The grounds are as
follows.[91]

(1) BREACH: rent lawfully due has not been paid, or some other
obligation of the tenancy that is consistent with the Acts has been
broken.

(2) NUISANCE: the tenant, his lodger or sub-tenant has been guilty
of conduct which is a nuisance or annoyance to adjoining occupiers,
or has been convicted of illegal or immoral user of the premises.

(3) WASTE: the tenant, his lodger or sub-tenant has permitted the
condition of the premises to deteriorate.

(4) TENANT'S NOTICE TO QUIT: the tenant has given notice to quit
and the landlord has acted upon it so as to be seriously prejudiced if he
could not obtain possession.

(5) ASSIGNING OR SUB-LETTING WITHOUT CONSENT: the tenant,
without the landlord's consent, has assigned or sub-let the whole of
the premises, or has sub-let part, the remainder being already sub-let.

(6) OFF-LICENCE IN JEOPARDY: the tenant has done certain acts
putting in jeopardy an off-licence attached to the premises.

(7) NEEDED FOR LANDLORD'S SERVANT: the premises are reasonably required as a residence for a whole-time servant of the landlord,

---

[87] Act of 1968, s. 3, 1st Sched., paras. 1–3.
[88] *Summers* v. *Donohue* [1945] K.B. 376.
[89] Act of 1968, s. 28, 1st Sched., paras. 4–7, 9.
[90] Act of 1968, s. 10 (1).
[91] Act of 1968, s. 10 (1), 3rd Sched., Part I.

and they were let to the tenant in consequence of his former employment by the landlord or a previous landlord.

(8) NEEDED FOR LANDLORD OR HIS FAMILY: the landlord reasonably requires the premises for occupation as a residence for himself, a child of his over 18 years old, or one of his parents. There are two exceptions. First, this head is not available to a landlord who became landlord by purchasing [92] any interest in the premises after March 23, 1965 (or after November 7, 1956, in the case of a controlled tenancy). This prevents a landlord who buys the premises subject to a sitting tenancy from evicting the tenant under this head.[93] Secondly, this head does not apply if the tenant satisfies the court that in all the circumstances " greater hardship " would be caused to all persons likely to be affected [94] by making the order for possession than by refusing it.

(9) EXCESSIVE RENT ON SUB-LETTING: the tenant has sub-let part of the premises at an excessive rent.

(10) ALTERNATIVE ACCOMMODATION: Suitable alternative accommodation is available for the tenant, or will be available when the order for possession takes effect. This accommodation need not be as suitable as the existing accommodation, and may even be part of it.[95]

(c) *Unrestricted grounds.* There are four exceptional cases where the landlord can obtain an order for possession as of right without proof of reasonableness. They are available only where the tenancy is regulated.[96] They are as follows.[97]

(1) OWNER-OCCUPIER: an owner-occupier who lets his house can recover it for his own occupation or for some member of his family who resided with him when he last lived there.

(2) MINISTER OF RELIGION: the house is held in order to be available for occupation by a minister of religion as a residence from which to perform his duties, and is required for this purpose.

(3) AGRICULTURAL WORKER: the house is required for an agricultural worker.

(4) REDUNDANT FARMHOUSE: a farmhouse made redundant by an amalgamation of farms is required for an agricultural worker.

---

92 See *Powell* v. *Cleland* [1948] 1 K.B. 262.
93 See, *e.g.*, *Wright* v. *Walford* [1955] 1 Q.B. 363.
94 See *Harte* v. *Frampton* [1948] 1 K.B. 73.
95 *Parmee* v. *Mitchell* [1950] 2 K.B. 199.
96 Act of 1968, s. 10 (2).　　　　97 *Ibid.* 3rd Sched., Part II.

9. Rent limit: controlled tenancies.

(a) *Standard rent.* Before the Act of 1957, the system of control-ling rents had been based on the " standard rent " of the premises in question. This was the rent at which the premises were let on August 3, 1914, in the case of old control, and September 1, 1939, in the case of new control, with further provisions for cases when the premises were not let on those dates. The standard rent was thus a permanent attribute of the dwelling-house, and affected all tenancies of it. In addition, certain " permitted increases " could be made, *e.g.,* for increased rates paid by the landlord, or improvements made by him. The total of the standard rent and the permitted increases was known as the " recoverable rent."

(b) *Abolition of standard rents.* This system was unsatisfactory in many respects. Sometimes it was difficult to discover exactly what rent was being paid on the relevant date, often many years earlier, and in any case two houses of equal value might well have been let at very different rents. When in 1956 rating lists prepared on a uniform national basis instead of varying local bases came into force,[98] it was for the first time possible to evolve a satisfactory system of restricting rents by reference to rateable values; and the Rent Act 1957 did this. In place of the former " recoverable rent " there is now a " rent limit " for controlled tenancies; and this, unlike the " standard rent," is an attribute not of the premises but of the particular tenancy in question.

(c) *Rent limit.*[99] Notwithstanding any contrary agreement, the landlord is not entitled to recover more than the rent limit. This is ascertained by taking the gross value of the premises for rating pur-poses on November 7, 1956, and multiplying this by the " appropriate factor." To this sum are added, when appropriate, certain sums for rates, services and furniture; and the total, converted into terms of the " rent period " (*e.g.,* a week for a weekly tenancy) is the rent limit. The appropriate factor is derived from the repairing obligations of the tenant under the tenancy. If apart from internal decorative repairs he is responsible for all repairs, the factor is four-thirds; if he is respon-sible for none, it is two; and if he is liable for some repairs, it is whatever intermediate figure the parties agree in writing or the county court determines.[1]

---

[98] Local Government Act 1948, Part III.
[99] Act of 1957, s. 1, 1st Sched., now Act of 1968, s. 52, 9th Sched.
[1] See *Regis Property Co. Ltd.* v. *Dudley* [1959] A.C. 370.

There are certain variations. If the landlord is responsible for internal decorative repairs, the factor is increased by an additional one-third. Further, the amount of any rates borne by the landlord during the " basic rental period " (*i.e.,* that which included July 7, 1957) must be added. Again, if during that period the landlord provided any services for the tenant or the tenancy gave the tenant the right to use any furniture, there must be added whatever sum the parties agree in writing or the county court determines. Finally, if the rent limit as thus ascertained is less than the recoverable rent under the old law during the basic rental period, the latter rent becomes the rent limit.

(d) *Variation of rent limit.* There are four main ways in which the rent limit may subsequently be varied.

(1) DISREPAIR. If the tenant successfully pursues a complex and lengthy process of obtaining an effective certificate of disrepair, the main consequence is that the appropriate factor becomes four-thirds.[2]

(2) RATES. If the landlord bears any rates, the rent limit rises and falls with any difference between the current rates and those for the basic rental period.[3]

(3) SERVICES OR FURNITURE. If in comparison with the basic rental period there is any relevant difference in the services or furniture, or in any circumstances relating to them, the rent limit is to be increased or decreased by an appropriate amount, as agreed in writing by the parties or determined by the county court.[4]

(4) IMPROVEMENTS. The landlord may increase the rent limit by $12\frac{1}{2}$ per cent. of his expenditure on any improvement or structural alteration [5] of the premises completed after July 6, 1957, including private street works, as in making up an unmade road outside the house.[6]

(e) *Notice of increase.* No increase of rent, whether initial or on account of changed circumstances, can be made except by serving a proper notice of increase; the only exception is an increase on account of changed circumstances relating to furniture or services, where the agreement between the parties or decision of the court suffices to effect the increase. In general, a three months' notice must be given; but increases for improvements may take effect forthwith and operate

---

[2] Act of 1968, 9th Sched.
[3] *Ibid.* s. 54.
[4] *Ibid.* s. 55.
[5] See *Morcom* v. *Campbell-Johnson* [1956] 1 Q.B. 106.
[6] Act of 1968, ss. 56–58.

retrospectively, and increases for rates may be retrospective for not more than six weeks.[7]

The Act gives the landlord no power to make an increase in breach of the terms of the tenancy; increases can be made only as against statutory tenants, or contractual tenants whose tenancies permit increases to be made. But if when a notice of increase is served a notice to quit given at the same time could have determined the contractual tenancy before the date on which the increase is to take effect, the notice of increase operates as a notice to quit, and converts the tenancy into a statutory tenancy as from that date.[8]

10. Rent limit: regulated tenancies.

(a) *Existing rent.* Unless and until a rent is registered under the provisions mentioned below, the rent recoverable under a regulated tenancy is limited to the last rent payable under the last previous regulated tenancy during the three years before the tenancy began, or, if there was none, the rent payable under the existing tenancy.[9]

(b) *Registered rent.* The rent thus frozen may be displaced by obtaining a registered rent for the house. Either the landlord or the tenant may apply to the rent officer for the area for the registration of a rent. The rent officer, after giving the parties an opportunity to make representations, registers the rent if he thinks it fair, or if not determines and registers what he thinks would be a fair rent. There is a right of appeal to a rent assessment committee. For a period of three years after registration neither party can apply for the registration of a different rent without the concurrence of the other.[10]

(c) *Fair rent.* In determining what is a fair rent, regard must be had " to all the circumstances (other than personal circumstances) and in particular to the age, character and locality of the dwelling-house and to its state of repair." There must, however, be disregarded the effect of local shortages of accommodation, and disrepair or default attributable to a failure by the tenant to comply with his obligations, and any voluntary improvement carried out by the tenant.[11]

---

[7] Act of 1968, ss. 53–56.
[8] *Ibid.* s. 60.
[9] Act of 1968, ss. 20, 22.
[10] *Ibid.* s. 44, 6th Sched., Part I.
[11] *Ibid.* s. 46.

11. Premiums. There are wide provisions prohibiting any person from requiring a premium as a condition of the grant, renewal, continuance, or assignment of any tenancy within the Acts,[12] and preventing a statutory tenant (who has no assignable interest) from asking or receiving any consideration from any person except the landlord as a condition of giving up possession.[13]

12. Mortgages. Where the Act restricts a landlord as against his tenant, it is right that the landlord should be correspondingly protected against any mortgagee of the property; and the Act so provides,[14] except in the case of a mortgage created after December 7, 1965,[15] or a mere equitable charge or mortgage.[16] There are two systems of protection, one where the property was on that date subject to a controlled tenancy, and the other where the tenancy was regulated.

(a) *Controlled mortgages.* The Act applies, with certain exceptions, to prevent the mortgagee from taking any steps to enforce his security, until interest is 21 days in arrear, or the mortgagor is guilty of breach of covenant (other than for repayment of principal) or has failed to keep the property in proper repair or to pay some interest or instalment of principal recoverable under a prior incumbrance.[17] The court has power to relax these restrictions on the ground that " greater hardship " would be caused if they remained.[18] In addition to restrictions on the right to enforce the security, no increase in the mortgage interest above the standard rate of interest can be made, save that under old control an increase of not more than 1 per cent. can be made, with a " ceiling " of $6\frac{1}{2}$ per cent.[19] The standard rate of interest is the rate of interest payable on August 3, 1914, for old control, or September 1, 1939, for new control, or, if the mortgages were created subsequently, the original rate of interest.[20]

(b) *Regulated mortgages.* There is no automatic protection of a mortgagor under a regulated mortgage, but he may apply to the court for relief if he will be caused " severe financial hardship " by an increase in mortgage interest, the enforcement of the mortgage, or the registration of a reduced rent.[21]

---

[12] See *Elmdene Estates Ltd.* v. *White* [1960] A.C. 528.
[13] Act of 1968, ss. 13, 85, 86.   [14] Act of 1968, ss. 93, 94.
[15] *Ibid.* s. 93.
[16] *London County and Westminster Bank Ltd.* v. *Tompkins* [1918] 1 K.B. 515.
[17] Act of 1968, s. 96 (1), 12th Sched., Part II.
[18] *Ibid.* s. 96 (2).   [19] *Ibid.* s. 96 (1), 12th Sched., Part I.
[20] *Ibid.*   [21] *Ibid.* s. 95.

E. Long Tenancies

A long tenancy is one granted for a term exceeding 21 years.[22] From 1957 [23] to 1967 [24] all long tenancies were outside the Rent Acts, but now the Rent Act 1968 applies regardless of the length of term. However, many long tenancies are outside the scope of the Rent Act 1968 because the rent is less than two-thirds of the rateable value.[25] This particularly applies where the original lease was a building lease so that the rent is a ground rent only. Long tenancies at low rents have two forms of protection: Part I of the Landlord and Tenant Act 1954 and Part I of the Leasehold Reform Act 1967.

I. LANDLORD AND TENANT ACT 1954

1. Tenancies protected. A tenant under a long tenancy will be protected by Part I of the Act of 1954 at the end of the term if he would then have been entitled to the protection of the Rent Act 1968 but for the lowness of the rent.[26] Thus Part I protects only residential tenants in occupation of premises of a type within the Rent Act 1968.

2. The protection. When Part I applies, the tenancy is automatically continued, if the tenant so desires.[27] The landlord may terminate the tenancy in two ways. First, he may serve a " notice to resume possession " and apply to the court for possession on grounds similar to those under the Rent Acts.[28] Secondly, he may instead serve a notice proposing a statutory tenancy. In this case the parties (or in default of agreement the county court) determine the rent and other terms of the tenancy. If the rateable value of the house would have left it controlled even after the Act of 1957, the rent must not exceed the rent limit as for a controlled tenancy [29]; otherwise it is subject to the provisions for assessment and registration applicable to the rents of regulated tenancies.[30]

II. LEASEHOLD REFORM ACT 1967

1. General. The Leasehold Reform Act 1967 gives further protection to some tenants holding long leases at low rents. It is

---

[22] Landlord and Tenant Act 1954, s. 2 (5); Leasehold Reform Act 1967, s. 3 (1).
[23] Rent Act 1957, s. 21 (1).   [24] Leasehold Reform Act 1967, s. 39.
[25] See *ante*, p. 600.   [26] Landlord and Tenant Act 1954, ss. 1, 2.
[27] *Ibid*. ss. 5, 17.   [28] *Ibid*. s. 12, 3rd Sched.
[29] Act of 1957, 6th Sched., para. 8 (1) (2); see now Rent Act 1968, s. 7 (1), 2nd Sched., para. 1 (*c*).
[30] Leasehold Reform Act 1967, 5th Sched., paras. 3, 4; see now Rent Act 1968, s. 7 (2). See *ante*, pp. 603, 606, 608.

based on the "principle" that under a building lease "the land belongs in equity to the landowner and the house belongs in equity to the occupying leaseholder,"[31] thus abrogating the normal rule "*quicquid plantatur solo, solo cedit*."[32] The Act allows the tenants to whom it applies to exercise one of two rights, either to demand the conveyance of the freehold, or to demand the grant of a new lease of 50 years.

2. Tenancies protected. The tenancy must be a long tenancy at a low rent of premises having a rateable value of not more than £400 in Greater London or £200 elsewhere on March 23, 1965, in respect of which two further conditions are satisfied.[33]

(a) *Residence.* At the time of his claim the tenant must have occupied the house or part of it as his only or main residence for the last five years, or for periods totalling five years during the last ten years.

(b) *House.* The premises must be a house. This includes a semi-detached or terraced house, but not a flat. Long leases at low rents of flats are thus protected only by the Act of 1954.

3. Mode of claiming. A qualified tenant who wishes to acquire the freehold or a new lease has to serve a notice in a prescribed form upon his landlord. The service of the notice constitutes a contract to convey the freehold or grant a new lease, as the case may be, and is registrable as an estate contract and may be the subject of a notice or caution if the title to the land is registered.[34] The tenant may serve his notice at any time during the continuance of his long tenancy, including any period during which it is being continued by Part I of the Act of 1954, but if the landlord has served a notice under that Act,[35] the tenant must serve his notice within two months or he will lose his rights.[36]

4. Enfranchisement. If the tenant has elected to purchase the freehold he is entitled to have the estate in fee simple conveyed to him subject to the tenancy and incumbrances on it, but free from other incumbrances such as mortgages and rentcharges charged on the freehold interest.[37] The price is based on the market value of the

---

[31] White Paper on Leasehold Reform (1966, Cmnd. 2916), para. 4.
[32] See *ante,* p. 375.   [33] Leasehold Reform Act 1967, ss. 1, 2.
[34] *Ibid.* s. 5 ; see *ante,* pp. 545, 563.   [35] See *ante,* p. 610.
[36] Leasehold Reform Act 1967, 3rd Sched., para. 2.   [37] *Ibid.* s. 8.

land, but disregarding the value of the buildings on it.[38] In addition
the tenant has to pay the landlord's reasonable costs and expenses.

5. New lease. If the tenant is claiming a new lease, he is entitled
to a lease in substitution for his existing lease to run for a period
to end 50 years after the expiry date of the existing lease. The rent
is to be the current letting value of the site only. It may be revised
after 25 of the 50 years has run.[39] The tenant has to pay the landlord's reasonable costs and expenses.

6. Exemptions. In certain cases the landlord may defeat or
modify one or both of the claims.

(a) *Redevelopment.* A landlord may resist a claim to an extended
lease (or determine it if it has already been granted) if he proposes
to demolish or reconstruct the house.[40]

(b) *Residence.* A landlord may defeat a claim either to the
freehold or an extended lease if he reasonably requires the house as
a residence for himself or a member of his family.[41]

(c) *Management powers.* The landlord of an estate containing
many long leaseholds may be entitled to retain management powers
and control over the development and use of the houses in the area
of the estate. The landlord has to obtain a certificate from the
Minister and obtain the approval of the court to a scheme of
management.[42]

(d) *Public authorities.* Local authorities and similar public bodies
may retain land if they have a certificate from a Minister that it will
be required for development for the purposes of the authority within
the next ten years.[43]

(e) *Crown land.* A direct tenant of the Crown cannot make a
claim.[44]

F. *Other Systems of Control*

In addition to the various systems of protecting tenants which have
been outlined above, there are a number of other statutory provisions

[38] See *ibid.* s. 9.
[39] *Ibid.* ss. 14, 15.
[40] *Ibid.* s. 17.
[41] *Ibid.* s. 18.
[42] *Ibid.* s. 19.
[43] *Ibid.* s. 28, and see s. 29.
[44] *Ibid.* s. 33.

protecting various types of tenant. Thus, under the Reserve and Auxiliary Forces (Protection of Civil Interests) Act 1951, a wide variety of statutory protection is given to service men and women, other than those in the regular services. In particular, Part II extends the protection of the Rent Acts and the powers of rent tribunals to a number of cases which otherwise would be outside their ambit. It also restricts to some extent the grounds on which possession can be obtained in cases within the Rent Acts or Agricultural Holdings Act 1948. Again, if under the Housing (Rural Workers) Act 1926,[45] a grant has been made for the reconstruction or improvement of a house for agricultural workers or persons in a similar economic position, the house becomes subject to certain conditions, including a limitation of the maximum rent. The Housing (Financial Provisions) Act 1958 [46] makes similar provisions for grants for the improvement or conversion of houses generally. In these cases, the conditions remain enforceable for 20 years, and breach of them may make the landlord liable to repay part of the grant with compound interest.

G. Status

1. Protection. Today, most tenants in this country are protected by some statutory provision or other; the largest single class of unprotected tenants probably consists of residential tenants of houses owned by local authorities. Leasehold tenants, who in early law were regarded as holding mere contracts, and not until the sixteenth century became recognised as owners of estates,[47] have some claim now to have travelled from contract via estate to status: for their more important rights depend in large part not on the contracts which they have made but on the positive protection conferred on them by statute, overriding any contractual arrangements. Yet the variations between the statutory provisions are so great that it is difficult to discern much common ground between the systems.

2. Rent. Thus as regards rent, even though the premises have been let before, there may or may not be initial control as to rent: contrast business, agricultural and furnished lettings with the Rent Act. Again, control as to rent may attach only on a renewal of the tenancy (business), or at stated intervals (agriculture), or on application to a tribunal (furnished lettings). Yet again, the rent may be fixed

---

[45] See s. 3.
[46] See ss. 33, 34, 4th Sched.; House Purchase and Housing Act 1959, s. 11.
[47] *Ante*, pp. 7, 8, 19.

by the court (business), an arbitrator (agriculture), or a tribunal (furnished lettings). Finally, the rent may or may not be subject to increase as well as decrease: contrast business and agriculture with the limited provisions as to furnished lettings and the Rent Act.

3. Security of tenure. Security of tenure is equally varied. There are five main methods by which it may be provided. First, there is the drastic method of giving the tenant the right to purchase the landlord's interest (long lease). Secondly, there may be a restriction on determining the existing tenancy until the tenant has been able to apply to the court for a new tenancy (business). Thirdly, there may be a power for the tenant to paralyse a notice to quit by serving a counter-notice unless the landlord obtains permission from a tribunal for his notice to operate (agriculture). Fourthly, there is the automatic suspension of a notice to quit for a limited period, with power for the tenant to apply to a tribunal for an extension (furnished lettings). Fifthly, there is the mere passive right for the tenant to remain, despite the termination of the contractual tenancy, until ordered to go by the court (the Rent Act). There are also differences in whether or not the tenant need take any active steps to be protected, and whether or not tenants for fixed periods (as distinct from periodic tenants) are protected.

4. Status. The variations are thus great. Yet both on major issues and on many minor matters a tenant today will look more often to the rights conferred on him by the Statute-Book than to the terms of his tenancy. In that sense it is perhaps true to say that there is an ill-defined but nevertheless real status of protected tenant.

CHAPTER 18

ENVOI

In a final chapter, two matters may be singled out for attention.

Sect. 1. Effect of Increased Taxation

In 1900 the standard rate of income tax was raised from eightpence to one shilling in the pound,[1] and surtax did not exist. An income of £10,000 a year bore approximately £500 in tax; in 1969, if unearned, it bears some £6,000. The estate of a person who left property worth a million pounds was liable for estate duty of 7·5 per cent.; if he died in 1969, the estate duty would be 75 per cent. The cumulative effect of estate duty is especially apparent when it is realised that if property is settled on persons in succession, estate duty on the full capital value of the property is payable each time a tenant for life dies.

In addition to leading to the break-up of large estates, these changes have transformed the types of settlement which are employed. A settlement in the old form, with successive interests to a long list of beneficiaries, attracts a disastrous burden of taxation. Instead, the tendency is towards discretionary trusts, where the death of a mere potential beneficiary attracts no estate duty. Further, many parents now make substantial gifts of property to their children *inter vivos*, long before they die; for although most gifts made within seven years of death are liable to estate duty, those made more than seven years before death are not. Again, the high rates of income tax and surtax have made the maintenance of large estates difficult or impossible, and the strict settlements of great estates so often made in the eighteenth and nineteenth centuries are rarely created today.

Perhaps the greatest change of all lies in the domination now exercised by taxation over the great majority of wills and settlements of any substantial property, and, indeed, many other transactions. Fifty years ago, the testator or settlor was primarily concerned with the beneficial interests, and paid little heed to matters of taxation. Today, the effects of heavy taxation on the proposed dispositions are often predominant; and some transactions are entered into with little or no object other than that of mitigating the burden of taxation.

[1] Finance Act 1899, s. 15; Finance Act 1900, s. 15.

Sect. 2. Changes effected by the 1925 Legislation

The other matter that must be dealt with here is the changes in land law effected by the 1925 legislation.[2] The principal alterations may be grouped under three heads:

(a) The assimilation of the law of real property to that of personal property.
(b) The abolition of unnecessary historical survivals.
(c) The simplification of conveyancing.

A. Assimilation of the Law of Real and Personal Property

It is obviously convenient that so far as possible the same law should govern real and personal property. However, in many cases the nature of the subject-matter makes assimilation impracticable: it is as unusual to have a right of way over a pound of tea as it is to sell land in paper bags. Nevertheless, some measure of uniformity had been achieved before 1926 (*e.g.*, as to property vesting in personal representatives [3]), and the 1925 legislation carried the process a long way further. It will be noticed that in all the following cases except the last two, it is substantially the personalty rule which has prevailed over the realty rule.

1. Settlements: future interests in land can now exist only in equity under a trust, and are kept off the title.[4] This has always been the case with pure personalty.

2. Intestacy: there is now a uniform code for the devolution of property on intestacy, resembling, in the main, the old rules for personalty.[5]

3. Words of limitation: the transfer of personalty without words of limitation normally resulted in the grantor's whole interest passing; a similar rule has now been adopted for realty.[6]

4. Form of mortgages: freeholds are now mortgaged in the same way as leaseholds always have been, namely, by the grant of a long term of years.[7]

---

[2] See M. & W. 1120–1123 for the background.
[3] See *ante*, p. 313.
[4] *Ante*, p. 99.
[5] *Ante*, pp. 302 *et seq.*
[6] *Ante*, pp. 23, 24.
[7] *Ante*, p. 464.

5. Priority of mortgages: there has been some assimilation here by the extension of the rule in *Dearle* v. *Hall* [8] to mortgages of equitable interests in realty.[9]

6. Entails of personalty: it is now possible to entail personalty in the same way as realty.[10]

7. " Die without issue ": the rules for a gift over of land on death without issue have been extended to pure personalty.[11]

B. *Abolition of Unnecessary Historical Survivals*

A number of the rules governing real property had outgrown their utility; the 1925 legislation effected a long overdue spring-cleaning. The following are the principal changes.

1. Reduction of tenures : for practical purposes, all tenures except socage have been abolished.[12]

2. Abolition of the rule in *Shelley's Case*.[13]

3. Repeal of the Statute of Uses 1535.[14]

4. Future interests : legal remainders and legal executory interests have been abolished.[15]

5. Abolition of the rule in *Whitby* v. *Mitchell*.[16]

6. Abolition of special occupancy.[17]

7. Abolition of the doctrine of *interesse termini*.[18]

8. Modification of the rule in *Spencer's Case*.[19]

9. Abolition of the *tabula in naufragio* in mortgages.[20]

C. *Simplification of Conveyancing*

A balance has to be struck between making it easy for a purchaser to acquire land free from incumbrances, on the one hand, and on the

[8] (1828) 3 Russ. 1.
[9] *Ante*, p. 508.
[10] *Ante*, p. 42.
[11] *Ante*, p. 286.
[12] *Ante*, p. 13.
[13] (1581) 1 Co.Rep. 88b ; *ante*, p. 28.
[14] *Ante*, p. 67.
[15] *Ante*, p. 99.
[16] (1890) 44 Ch.D. 85 ; *ante*, p. 103.
[17] *Ante*, p. 48.
[18] *Ante*, p. 346.
[19] (1583) 5 Co.Rep. 16a ; *ante*, p. 387.
[20] *Ante*, p. 513.

other, imperilling the position of those who own incumbrances. The 1925 legislation has succeeded in lightening the purchaser's burden in a number of respects, of which the following may be mentioned here.

1. Legal estates and interests: there has been a reduction in the number of estates and interests that can exist at law and so bind a purchaser without notice.[21]

2. The " curtain ": the provisions relating to overreaching have been extended.[22]

3. Tenancies in common: legal tenancies in common can no longer exist.[23]

4. Registration of charges: a greater number of interests now have to be registered as land charges in order to bind a purchaser.[24]

5. Registration of title: the areas in which registration of title is compulsory have been extended.[25]

D. Conclusion

In general, it can be said that the 1925 legislation has been most successful. Some of the devices introduced by it have found little favour with practitioners, such as *ad hoc* settlements and trusts for sale, and some provisions are of deplorable complexity, *e.g.*, the transitional provisions relating to co-ownership [26]; nor has the Settled Land Act curtain proved to be as opaque as might have been hoped.[27] Yet on the whole there can be no doubt of the success of the legislation.[28]

---

[21] *Ante*, p. 72.
[22] *Ante*, pp. 192 *et seq.*
[23] *Ante*, p. 216.
[24] *Ante*, pp. 541 *et seq.*
[25] *Ante*, p. 557.
[26] *Ante*, p. 219.
[27] See A. H. Withers (1946) 62 L.Q.R. 167.
[28] See M. & W. 1126–1129; and *cf.* G. A. Grove (1961) 24 Mod.L.R. 123.

INDEX

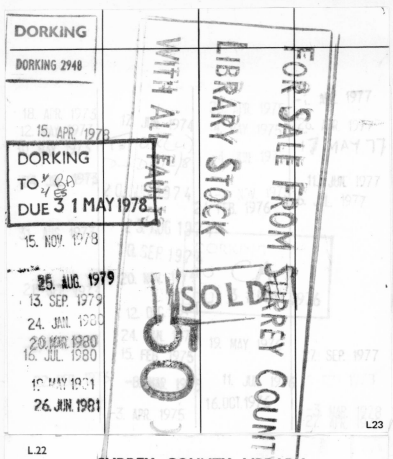
SURREY COUNTY LIBRARY
(Headquarters, 140 High Street, Esher)

3   69-153882

This book must be returned to the Branch or Travelling Library from which it was borrowed, by the latest date entered above.

Charges will be payable on books kept overdue.